How to Do *Everything* with Your

iMac

Second Edition

Todd Stauffer

Osborne/McGraw-Hill

Berkeley   New York   San Francisco
Auckland   London
Madrid   Mexico City   M   Delhi
Pan   São Paulo
Singapore   Toronto

Osborne/**McGraw-Hill**
2600 Tenth Street
Berkeley, California 94710
U.S.A.

For information on translations or book distributors outside the U.S.A., or to arrange
bulk purchase discounts for sales promotions, premiums, or fund-raisers, please contact
Osborne/**McGraw-Hill** at the above address.

How to Do Everything with Your iMac, Second Edition

1234567890 AGM AGM 019876543210

ISBN 0-07-212416-4

Publisher: Brandon A. Nordin
Associate Publisher and
Editor-in-Chief: Scott Rogers
Acquisitions Editor: Jane K. Brownlow
Project Editor: Madhu Prasher
Acquisitions Coordinator: Tara Davis
Technical Editor: John Rizzo
Copy Editors: Claire Splan and Barbara Brodnitz
Proofreader: Paul Tyler
Indexer: Claire Splan
Computer Designers: E. A. Pauw, Dick Schwartz, and Gary Corrigan
Illustrators: Beth Young and Robert Hansen
Series Design: Peter Hancik
Cover Design: Dodie Shoemaker

For Daisy T.,

because I promised not to dedicate
books to people.

About the Author...

Todd Stauffer is the author or co-author of more than 20 books on computing, including the first edition of *How to Do Everything with Your iMac* and *How to Do Everything with Your iBook.* He's a contributing editor for MacCentral.com and has written for a number of publications, including *MacTech*, *MacAddict*, and CMP Online. He's the publisher of Mac-Upgrade.com as well as the writer and co-host of the Emmy-winning television program, "Disk Doctors."

About the Reviewer...

John Rizzo is the author of several books about Macs, a computer magazine columnist, a consultant, and the founder of the MacWindows.com Web site. He was an editor at *MacUser* magazine and a columnist for *MacWeek* magazine.

Contents

Acknowledgments xix
Introduction xxi

PART I	Get Started

CHAPTER 1	Welcome to iMac **3**

How to... 4
What Makes iMac Different and Cool 6
What Is the Internet? 7
iMac Is Still a Mac 7
iMac Uses a New Type of Hardware 8
iMac: A Quick Tour 9
Different iMac Models 10
From the Front 11
From the Side 13
Before You Set Up iMac 15
Get a Surge Protector 15
Keep Glare to a Minimum 15
Don't Forget the Ergonomics 16
Set Up iMac 17
Get Online with the Assistants 18
The Mac OS Setup Assistant 19
The Internet Setup Assistant 20
iMac: On, Off, Sleep, Info 21
Which Mac OS Do You Have? 21
Turn Off iMac 22
Restart iMac 22
Reset Your iMac When Frozen 23

CHAPTER 2	Get Acquainted with iMac **27**

How to... 28
What Is the Desktop? 29
What's an Icon? 29
What's a Menu? 30
What's a Window? 31

V

Using the Mouse and Keyboard 31
    Click with the Mouse 32
    Special Keyboard Keys 34
    The Mouse and Keyboard Connectors 35
Work with Icons and Windows 36
    In Depth with Icons 36
    Rename Icons 37
    Open Up Windows 38
Hard Disks, CD-ROMs, DVDs, and Peripherals 40
    Storage vs. Memory 41
    The Hard Disk Icon 41
    The Trash Icon 42
    CDs and DVDs 42
    Removable Disks 44
    Printer Icons 44
Change Settings with the Control Strip 45
    Turn on Control Strip 45
Get a Quick Start on the Internet 47
    Sign On to Your ISP (Modem Connections) 47
    Browse the Internet 48
    Get Your Mail 50
    Sign Off of Your ISP (Modem Connections) 52

CHAPTER 3   Manage Your Files with the Finder 53
    How to... 54
Finder 101: Windows 55
    Dig Deep into Finder Windows 55
    Move Icons to Finder Windows 56
    Select Items in the Finder 58
    Get Information from Finder Windows 60
Finder 201: Create Folders, Copy Files, and Build Aliases 61
    Create a New Folder 61
    Create a Duplicate 62
    Create an Alias 63
    Find the Alias's Original 64
    Fix an Alias 64
Finder 301: Delete Icons 64
    Toss Icons 64
    Retrieve Items from the Trash 65
    Empty the Trash 65
Finder 401: Get Information on Files 66
Finder Grad School: Get Organized 66
    Organize Documents Using Aliases 68
    Use Labels to Organize 69
    Change How Folders Are Displayed in the Finder 70

CHAPTER 4	**Pull Down the Apple Menu**	**75**
	How to...	76
	What Is the Apple Menu?	77
	Items on the Apple Menu	78
	Desk Accessories	79
	Control Panels	82
	Aliases	82
	Use the Recent Menus	83
	Select a Recent Menu	83
	Customize the Recent Menus	84
	Create and Use Favorites	84
	Create a Favorite	86
	Use a Favorite	86
	Put Your Own Aliases on the Menu	86
	The Automatic Way	86
	The Manual Way	87
	Shuffle the Order of Items	87
CHAPTER 5	**Work with Applications and the Applications Menu**	**89**
	How to...	90
	What Are Applications?	91
	Start Up Applications	91
	Start-Up Trouble	92
	Create a New Document	92
	Open a Document	93
	Save Your Document	95
	Basic Application Commands	97
	Print	97
	Selecting and Select All	98
	Cut, Copy, and Paste	99
	Undo	100
	Quit the Application	101
	Preferences	102
	Other Interface Elements	102
	Buttons, Check Boxes, and Sliders	102
	Toolbars	103
	The About Box	103
	Multitasking: Use More Than One Application	104
	The Application Menu	104
	Switch Between Applications	104
	Hide and Show Applications	105
CHAPTER 6	**Search for Things**	**107**
	How to...	108
	You Can Find Anything with iMac	109
	Meet Sherlock	109
	Save Searches	111

Search for Files 111
The Basic Search 111
The Advanced Search 113
Custom Searches in Sherlock 2 116
Find by Content 118
Index Documents 118
Perform the Search 120
Search the Internet 120
Start the Search 121
Sherlock 2's Channels 122
Update Your Search Sites 123
Add New Search Sites 123

CHAPTER 7   Get Some Help 125
How to... 126
The Help Systems 127
Apple Help 128
Browse for Help 128
Search for Help 129
The Help Center 130
Apple Guide 130
Help by Topic 131
Index and Search 131
Balloon Help 132
Other Types of Help 133
The AppleWorks (QuickHelp) Help System 133
Read Me Files and PDFs 136

PART II   Get Your Work Done

CHAPTER 8   Create Printed Documents 141
How to... 142
Write with Your iMac 143
AppleWorks vs. The Other Guys 144
Begin Your Document 144
Fonts, Styles, and Sizes 146
Save Often 148
Format Your Document 149
Format Paragraphs 149
Insert Elements 154
Format the Whole Document 157
Format the Section 159
Tabs and the Ruler 161
Spell, Find, Change, and Count 162
Check Spelling 162
Find and Change 163

Standardize with the Stylesheet Window   165
Use Stationery for Automatic Documents   166
    Create a Document from Stationery   166
    Save a Document as Stationery   167

CHAPTER 9   **Work with Numbers, Build Charts** **169**
    How to...   170
The Spreadsheet Defined   171
    Why Use Spreadsheets?   171
    The Cell   172
Get the Spreadsheet Started   173
    Move in the Spreadsheet   173
    Select Cells   174
    Save the Spreadsheet   175
Enter and Format Data   175
    Format Text and Cells   175
    Enter and Format Numbers   177
Add Formulas to the Spreadsheet   180
    Anatomy of a Formula   180
    Add Functions to Your Formulas   184
    Some Cool Functions   186
Chart Your Data   188
    Create the Chart   189

CHAPTER 10   **File Information and Ideas with Databases** **193**
    How to...   194
What's a Database?   195
    When Can You Use a Database?   195
    How Databases Work   196
Create Your Database   197
    Plan Your Database   197
    Field Types   197
    Add Your Fields   198
Enter and Find Records   202
    List View   203
    Find Records   203
    Save Your Search   204
    Print Records   204
Give It a New Layout   205
    Choose a Layout or Start a New One   205
    Edit the Layout   206
Sort and Report   206
    Sort   208
    Save a Sort   208
    Build a Report   209

CHAPTER 11   **Paint, Draw, and Create Presentations** **211**
　　　　　　　　How to... 212
　　　　Painting vs. Drawing 213
　　　　Start Your Painting 213
　　　　　　　　Document Size 214
　　　　　　　　Use the Tools 214
　　　　　　　　Add Text 220
　　　　　　　　Save Your Image 221
　　　　Draw Objects and Text 221
　　　　　　　　Draw in Databases and Spreadsheets 221
　　　　　　　　Create Objects 221
　　　　　　　　Manipulate Objects 225
　　　　Creating a Slide Show 229

CHAPTER 12   **Use AppleWorks for Layout** **233**
　　　　　　　　How to... 234
　　　　How Layouts Work 235
　　　　　　　　The AppleWorks Frame 235
　　　　　　　　What Can You Lay Out? 236
　　　　　　　　Assistants 237
　　　　Layout Basics: Text Frames 238
　　　　　　　　Getting Started 239
　　　　　　　　Create Text Frames 240
　　　　　　　　Add Text 242
　　　　　　　　Link Text Frames 243
　　　　　　　　Resize Frames 244
　　　　　　　　Align Frames 246
　　　　　　　　Lock Frames 246
　　　　Graphics, Floating Text, and Shapes 247
　　　　　　　　Add Graphic Frames 247
　　　　　　　　Create Floating Text 248
　　　　　　　　Wrap Text 249
　　　　　　　　Shape and Lines 251
　　　　Build Layouts Quickly 252
　　　　　　　　The Word Processing Layout 253
　　　　　　　　Stationery 256
　　　　Mail Merge 256
　　　　　　　　Set Up the Database 256
　　　　　　　　Add Field Variables to Your Document 257
　　　　　　　　Print the Merge 258

CHAPTER 13   **Manage Your Finances with Quicken** **259**
　　　　　　　　How to... 260
　　　　What Is Quicken? 261
　　　　　　　　Install Quicken 261
　　　　　　　　The Tutorial and Quicken Help 262

Create Accounts and Enter Data 263
    Create a New Account 263
    Add and Edit Transactions 264
    Delete or Void a Transaction 266
    Create a Recurring Transaction 266
    Create and Edit Categories 267
    Reconcile Bank Accounts 268
Budget Your Money 271
    Create a Budget 271
    Monitor the Budget 273
Manage Loans and Investments 274
    Create a Loan 275
    Create a Portfolio 277
Generate Reports 280
    QuickReport: Search the Registers 280
    Edit and Print the Report 281

CHAPTER 14   **Work with Movies, Sounds, and Images** **285**
    How to... 286
QuickTime Movies 287
    What QuickTime Is to You 287
    The QuickTime Software 288
The QuickTime Player Application 289
    QuickTime Player Favorites 290
    View a Streaming Movie 292
    View a QuickTime VR Movie 293
    QuickTime Web Browser Plug-in 293
PictureViewer and Images 295
    View Images 295
    Image Format 296
    Save Images 296
QuickTime Player Pro 297
    Movie Types 298
    Sound File Formats 299
    Edit Video 299
    Saving the Movie 300
    Export Video or Sound 301
Play Audio CDs 302
    Launch AppleCD Audio Player 302
    Customize Tracks and the Playlist 303
Play a DVD Movie 305

CHAPTER 15   **Edit Your Own Movies** **307**
    How to... 308
Digital Video Explained 309

Get Video into Your iMac 310
　　Hook Up Your Camera 310
　　Import the Clips 311
　　Preview Your Clips 312
　　Toss a Clip 312
Edit Your Video 313
　　Crop Your Clips 313
　　Split Your Clips 314
　　Rename Clips 314
　　Arrange the Clips 314
Transitions, Sounds, and Titles 315
　　Transition Between Clips 315
　　Add Titles to the Video 316
　　Drop in Sound Effects 317
　　Lay in Some Music 319
View and Export Your Movie 320
　　View the Movie 320
　　Export to Your Camera 321
　　Export to QuickTime 321

CHAPTER 16　**Play Games with iMac** **323**
　　How to... 324
Play Nanosaur 325
　　Get Started 326
　　Play the Game 327
Play Bugdom 329
　　Get Started 330
　　Play the Game 331
Check Your 3-D Specifications 333
Add Game Controllers 334
　　Configure InputSprocket 335
　　Other Drivers 335
The World Book Encyclopedia 336
　　Get Started with World Book 336
　　Using the Encyclopedia 337
　　Browse the Encyclopedia 338
　　Search for Articles 338
　　Other Special Features 341
　　Consult a Wizard 342
　　Update the World Book 342

CHAPTER 17　**Tracking Your Schedule and Contacts** **343**
　　How to... 344
Get Started with Palm Desktop 345
　　The Instant Palm Desktop Menu 346
　　The Palm Desktop Interface 346

Manage Appointments, Events, and Tasks 347
    Create an Appointment 349
    Create a Banner Event 351
    Add Your Tasks 353
Manage Your Contacts 357
    Create a New Contact 357
    View the Contact List 360
    Attach Contacts to Items 361
Create and Manage Notes 363
    Create the Note 363
    View the Note List 365
    Attach Notes 366
Synchronizing with a Palm Device 366
    Set Up HotSync 366
    Set Conduit Settings 367
    Synchronizing Data 369
    Install Palm Applications 369

PART III   **Get Online**

CHAPTER 18   **Manage Your E-mail** **373**
    How to... 374
Is Your Account Set Up? 375
    How E-mail Addresses Work 375
    The Internet Control Panel 376
Get, Read, and Reply to E-mail 379
    Read Your Mail 380
    Reply to a Message 381
    Create a New Message 384
    Delete a Message 385
    Format Your Message 385
    Send and Get Attachments 386
    Use More Than One Account 390
Organize Your E-mail 391
    Create and Delete Folders 391
    Create a Subfolder 392
    Automate Using Rules 392
    Add a New User 397

CHAPTER 19   **Surf with Internet Explorer and Netscape** **399**
    How to... 400
Web Browser Basics 401
    The Web Browser 401
    The Internet Address 402
    Start Up and Open an Address 403
    Surf the Web 404
    Click a Multimedia Link 405
    Work with Frames 406

Choose a Home Page 407
    Change Your Home Page 407
    Edit the Home Page 408
Manage Bookmarks, Favorites, and History 409
    Edit Favorites 409
    Edit Bookmarks 410
    Follow Your History 411
Fill in a Form and Buy Things Online 412
    Fill in the Form 412
    Check for a Secure Connection 413
Browse Offline and Automatically 414
    Subscribe to Sites 414
Java and Plug-ins 414
    Embedded Plug-in Files 415
    Add Plug-ins 416
    Work with Java 416
    Troubleshoot Java Applets 417

CHAPTER 20   **Download, Back Up, and Transfer Online** **419**
    How to... 420
Transfer Files over the Internet 421
    The Virtual Floppy 421
    File Transfer Protocol 424
    Compress Files and Decompress Files 427
Back Up Online 429
Work with Floppy Images 430
    Types of Floppy Images 430
    Create an Image File 431
Find and Use Shareware and Freeware Programs 432
    Find Good Shareware 433

CHAPTER 21   **Get on America Online** **435**
    How to... 436
Sign Up and Dial In 437
    Dial In the First Time 437
    Create an Account 438
    Use Your Existing Account 440
    Sign On and Off 441
    Create a New Screen Name 441
    Parental Controls 442
    Delete a Screen Name 443
    Restore a Screen Name 443
Get Your E-mail 444
    Create a New Message 446
    Send Waiting Mail 448

Move Around the Service 449
    Welcome 449
    Channels 449
    People Connection 449
    Find by Keyword 449
Chat and Read Message Boards 450
    Chat: The People Connection 451
    Read and Write in Message Boards 453
Use AOL Link and Get on the Internet 455
    AOL's Internet Tools 455
    AOL Link and Internet Applications 456
    AOL's Web Storage Space 457

CHAPTER 22   **Create Your Own Web Pages** **459**
    How to... 460
The Web Page Revealed 461
Create Your Page 462
    Begin the Page 463
    Style Your Text 463
    Create a List 465
    Add Images 465
    Add Links 467

CHAPTER 23   **Customize the Internet and Go Faster** **469**
    How to... 470
Configure TCP/IP, Modem, and Remote Access 471
    The TCP/IP Control Panel 471
    The Remote Access Control Panel 473
    The Modem Control Panel 475
    DialAssist 476
    Configure a New Account 477
Get High-Speed Internet Access 478

PART IV   **Customize Your iMac**

CHAPTER 24   **Change iMac's Appearance and Attitude** **483**
    How to... 484
Adjust Your iMac's Monitor 485
    Monitor Settings 485
    Change the Geometry 488
    Calibrate the Monitor 489
Sound and Alert Settings 490
    Sound Settings in Mac OS 9 490
    Sound Settings in Monitors and Sound 491
    Alerts 492

Time and Date Settings 493
General Controls 494
Memory Settings 495
Save Energy by Automating Startup and Shutdown 497
    Sleep Timer 497
    Startup and Shutdown 497
Change the Appearance 498
Keychain Access 499
    Create Your Keychain 500
    View Your Keychain 501
Speech Technologies 503
    Text-to-Speech 503
    Speakable Items 504

CHAPTER 25   **Set Up Your iMac for Multiple Users** **507**
    How to... 508
How Multiple Users Works 509
Turn On and Create Users 510
    Turn on Multiple Users 510
    Create User Accounts 511
    Save and Edit Users 514
    Delete a User 514
Global Multiple User Options 515
    Login Settings 515
    CD/DVD-ROM Access 516
    Other Options 517
Login and Passwords 518
    Log In to Your Account 518
    Change Your Password 520

CHAPTER 26   **Print Your Documents, Manage Fonts, and Send Faxes** **523**
    How to... 524
Choose a Printer 525
    Laser vs. Inkjet 525
    Connection Technologies 526
    Printer Languages 527
    Using PC Printers 528
Set Up Your Printer and iMac 528
    Choose a USB or Serial-Adapted Printer 529
    Choose an Ethernet Printer 529
Print Stuff and Manage Print Jobs 530
    Page Setup 531
    The PrintMonitor 532
    The Desktop Printer 532
Understand and Add Fonts to Your iMac 533
    Add Fonts 534
    Delete Fonts 534

Fax with Your iMac 535
 Send a Fax 535
 Receive a Fax 536

CHAPTER 27 **Upgrade Your iMac** **539**
 How to... 540
Upgrade with USB and Firewire 541
 Why USB? 541
 Why Firewire? 542
 USB Ports and Hubs 543
 Install a USB or Firewire Device 544
Add a Mouse, Keyboard, or Controller 544
Add an External Drive 545
 Install an External Drive 547
 Back Up to the Removable 548
 CD-R and CD-RW Drives 550
Scanners and Digital Cameras 550
 Add a Scanner 551
 Add a Digital Camera 551
Special USB and Firewire Adapters 552
Add Microphones and Speakers 554
Install RAM or the AirPort Card 554
 RAM Types and Installation 554
 The AirPort Card 555

CHAPTER 28 **Network iMac and Transfer Files** **559**
 How to... 560
Get Connected to a Network 561
 Ethernet Connections 561
 Choose Your Protocol 562
 The AppleTalk Control Panel 563
 The TCP/IP Control Panel 564
 The AirPort Application 566
 Browse the Network 566
 Use the Chooser 568
Set Up Your Own Network 569
 Set Up File Sharing 569
 Create Users and Groups 570
 Set Sharing Privileges 572
 Set Up Web Sharing 573
Network Two Macs Together 574

CHAPTER 29 **Work with DOS and Windows Files and Programs** **577**
 How to... 578
Mount and Use PC Disks 579
Load and Save PC Documents 580
 Translate a Document 580
 Save a File for Use on a PC 583

The File Exchange Settings   584
    PC Exchange Settings   584
    File Translation   586
The Run DOS and Windows Programs   587

CHAPTER 30   **Troubleshoot, Update, and Maintain Your iMac** **589**
    How to...   590
Find Tech Support Online   591
Troubleshoot Your iMac   592
    Hardware Symptoms   592
    What Is PRAM?   594
    Software Problems   595
    Software Symptoms   596
    Error Messages   597
    Crashes   599
Freezes and Hangs   601
    Fix Problems with Icons and Aliases   602
Troubleshoot the System Folder   603
    Is the Conflict a "Known Issue"?   603
    Extensions Manager: Test for Conflicts   604
    Resolve the Conflict   606
Reinstall, Restore, and Update   606
    Uninstall and Reinstall Applications   607
    Software Restore   607
    Update Your iMac's System Software   609
Maintain Your iMac   611
    The iMac Maintenance Schedule   611
    Check for Viruses   613
    Disk Doctors   616

APPENDIX A   **Upgrade the Mac OS** **619**
    How to...   620
Update to Mac OS 8.6   621
Upgrade to Mac OS 9   622

Index **624**

Acknowledgments

The original *How to Do Everything with Your iMac* was the result of a fairly unique idea: a big book about a little computer. With the help and support of some great people, I took a stab at putting together a book that I hoped would help many readers get the most—for business, pleasure, or education—out of their iMac.

But the iMac product line is changing swiftly; new Mac OS versions are coming out and even more exciting capabilities are being built into the iMac. Those changes, coupled with the success of the first edition, have us at it again to bring you this second edition covering all the latest additions to and possibilities of the iMac.

My thanks go first to Heidi Poulin, project editor on the first edition, who helped shape the original content and much of the structure that continues into this edition. Likewise, thanks to Bob LeVitus for his technical review and preface for the original edition.

Jane Brownlow, acquisitions editor for both editions, was largely responsible for the success of the first edition and made it possible for me to write the second. My thanks to her for flexible deadlines and creative management as we tried to get this book done as completely as possible.

Madhu Prasher, project editor, was a helpful and friendly taskmaster throughout the process. Claire Splan and Barbara Brodnitz were invaluable as copy editors on the project, making me look as if I have some sort of handle on the English language (and continuing my somewhat lengthy education in its proper usage).

Tara Davis, acquisitions coordinator, kept the whole thing running smoothly, including covering up for hectic submissions gaffes and keeping us all on our toes, except when she took a sprawling and luxurious (though no doubt deserved) vacation. It's a testament to her that we almost completely fell apart while she was out.

Very heartfelt thanks go to John Rizzo for his technical edits. The new technical information on AirPort, Mac OS 9, and the iMac DV (the surprise announcement of which fell right in the middle of our original writing schedule) was enough to keep my head swimming. With John watching my back, I feel confident that you're getting great, accurate information in this book.

Thanks also to Rich Voelker and Voelker Research in Colorado for helping me get key Apple products when most people were still wondering if their backorders would ever ship. I'd also like to thank Leo Jakobson for keeping the Mac-Upgrade.com Letter going strong while he also provided a temporary roof over all of my test Macs and equipment.

Finally, my thanks to Donna Ladd, who put up with plenty of my late nights working on the project and who didn't object too strenuously on numerous occasions when I opted to order in takeout food when I finally got home to collapse.

Introduction

The original idea of *How to Do Everything with Your iMac* was a simple one. The iMac is a complete computer with a wonderful bundle of applications that enable you to do just about anything you need a computer to do. So, I wanted my book on the iMac to be as comprehensive as possible, teaching the reader how to be productive while enjoying this exciting little tool.

It was a risk, though, because the prevailing winds suggested that iMac owners might want thin books with only the basics to get up and running with their easy-to-use iMac. A 600-page book on the iMac? To some, it didn't make sense. Would readers buy this book?

The results speak for themselves, with the original book selling tens of thousands of copies over the course of just a few months. Reprints were issued much more quickly than expected, with each order growing larger. The folks at Osborne/McGraw-Hill were tickled enough to create an entire series of *How to Do Everything* books, including this second edition you're reading now.

I've received wonderful mail from readers, most of whom have found the first edition useful. A few have even managed to use the book to help them work with Windows-based PCs, although how, exactly, still escapes me. Others tell me that they're glad to know their investment in the iMac was a smart one, since they found out through the book that there is so much you can do with it.

In *How to Do Everything with Your iMac, Second Edition,* I've extended the original book's coverage to include Mac OS 9 features, the iMac DV series, Palm Desktop, Outlook Express 5.0, Sherlock 2, Quicken 2000, QuickTime, and AirPort technology. Not that original iMac owners are left out—the earlier versions of the Mac OS and applications that shipped with all iMacs are covered as well.

In this edition, I'm able to discuss, in detail, how to accomplish important computing tasks with your iMac, from the first time you press the power button. Since the iMac comes bundled with powerful applications, I show you how to create documents, reports, memos, newsletters, spreadsheets, databases, and charts. And I mean how to *use* them in real-world situations to oversee projects, turn in to teachers, present to your clients, or manage your hobbies.

You'll see how to create slide-show presentations. How to create a mail-merge form letter. How to use templates and assistants for all sorts of things. How to manage your calendar, task list, and contacts with aplomb. How to create databases to track just about anything—sports teams, weddings, recipes, projects, or classroom assignments.

The iMac is about creativity and fun, too. You can draw, paint, and even create a newsletter or high-end report. You'll learn about QuickTime, digital audio, digital video, and even a little about creating your own movies. Plus, there's an entire chapter on games and multimedia: how to play the iMac's games, how to add new games, and how to get the best gaming experience. And if you happen to have a new iMac DV model, its great new capabilities are covered, including digital video editing with iMovie and expansion via the built-in Firewire ports.

Beyond that I'll talk about printing documents, adding fonts, scanning photos, backing up data, adding a removable drive, and customizing your settings. You can even work with Microsoft Windows computers and network your iMac to a group of other Macs. Plus, you'll read about the exciting new AirPort technology that allows you to create a connection between your iMac and other Macs or the Internet without any cables at all.

Of course, we spend six whole chapters on the Internet, including e-mail, Web browsing, downloading files, reading the news, chatting in message groups, and exploring America Online.

And whatever iMac model you have, if you're running Mac OS 9 there's a slew of new features to explore, including Sherlock 2, support for multiple users on one iMac, and exciting new voice technologies.

The book communicates all this information very simply in four major parts: Get Started, Get Your Work Done, Get Online, and Customize Your iMac. The book is both a reference and a tutorial. It's arranged so you can move quickly to an interesting topic you look up in the index, or you can just read straight through to get a complete understanding of a given topic. Plus, special elements help you along the way, including notes, tips, shortcuts, and warnings. And every chapter includes a special "How To…" sidebar that explores one special feature to show you how to make the most of your iMac.

Want to reach me? You can, through my Web site for this book. It's **http://www.mac-upgrade.com/imac_book/**. Or send e-mail directly to me at **questions@mac-upgrade.com**.

Part I

Get Started

Chapter 1

Welcome to iMac

How to...

- Prepare yourself for using your iMac
- Figure out all the parts of the iMac
- Set up and move your iMac
- Start, restart, and put iMac to sleep

In 1998, Apple Computer set out to create a slightly different sort of computer from those that had been seen in the past—one designed specifically for consumer users who wanted to get on the Internet. They called it the iMac to suggest that it was the first "Internet" Macintosh marketed. It uses a lot of the parts and software that a regular Macintosh computer uses, but it offers enough differences to make it a whole new idea. And it's a very exciting idea—a friendly, easy-to-use computer that can still do just about anything at all.

In the fall of 1999, Apple refreshed the iMac line with a new iMac called the iMac DV. This iMac may look only slightly different from the original iMac, but it piles on the features, including more RAM, a faster processor, and better video. The major difference, though, is the addition of digital video capabilities, both the ability to watch DVD movies and the ability to edit your own movies created with a digital camcorder. Along with that comes support for Firewire, the connection standard used both for digital camcorders and for high-speed peripherals like external hard disks and removable disk drives.

Of course, one of the main differences between the iMac and most other computers is its looks. Designed as an all-in-one computer, the iMac is also attractive—something that not many other computer manufacturers have accomplished. The idea that an iMac could more easily be integrated into the decor of your home or office was apparently a big hit, and iMac has been a huge hit.

Actually, there are tons of cool things about the iMac, including:

- A radical new design that conserves space and offers a tapered back end so it fits better on many tables and desks.

- A side-mounted door for cables and wiring that helps control wires and keeps the back of the iMac from looking like the Frankenstein monster. On the newer slot-loading iMac and iMac DV models, the door is gone, but the ports are still easily accessible on the side of the iMac's enclosure.

- An integrated monitor that's much higher quality than that of most any competitor, with a higher *scan rate* than most monitors, resulting in a rock-solid display.

- Special keyboard and mouse, both designed to be compact and stylish, and which work for adults and kids.

- Improved and simplified upgrading through the *Universal Serial Bus* (USB).

- Lots of ways to get sound into and out of the machine, including built-in speakers and dual headphone jacks for sharing the iMac, playing games, listening to music, or working with educational software.

- Networking connections and a modem (for a telephone connection to the Internet or other online services) built-in.

- A handle! It's a 40-pound machine, but the iMac is still somewhat portable, which is quite a feat for a full-sized computer.

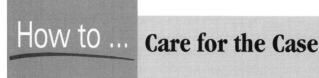

Care for the Case

Wondering how to clean your iMac's case? The plastics are durable, but they can still be scratched by abrasives or hard-edged objects. Of course, any computer case can be scratched, but the iMac will look a little worse for the wear since it's designed to be more attractive than most computers.

To clean the case, Apple recommends you shut down the iMac, pull its plug (from the wall socket or surge protector), and wipe the case with a dry, lint-free cloth. Avoid using water or liquid cleaners, since the iMac's case has seams where liquid could conceivably penetrate the case and damage the electronics.

To clean the screen, use a slightly damp, clean, lint-free cloth or a cloth from packets designed specifically to clean computer monitors (you can get them at computer and office-supply stores). Don't spray liquids directly on the iMac (spray water lightly on the cloth itself) and don't use any harsh cleaners.

- Special to the iMac DV models is support for digital video, including a DVD-ROM drive for watching DVD movies and Firewire ports for connecting a digital camcorder (and other high-speed peripherals) to the iMac.

On top of all this, the iMac is great-looking. (The translucent, polycarbonate shell is actually the same plastic used to make bullet-proof shielding.) But don't let the fashionable looks fool you. The iMac is a full computer, based on the Macintosh operating system (called *Mac OS*).

Your iMac can run just about any Macintosh program, read and edit just about any computer document, and can certainly take full advantage of the Internet. In fact, it's designed to be just as functional in a school or small business as it is at home.

As the title of this book suggests, if you have an iMac, you can do just about anything you can do with any other sort of computer. You're ready to go.

What Makes iMac Different and Cool

iMac offers a number of distinguishing features beyond looks. The iMac is a powerful computer, based on Apple's PowerPC G3 processors. It has at least 32 megabytes of computer memory (which allows you to run more than one computer program at once) and at least a 4-gigabyte hard disk for storing programs and documents.

Ease of use was important when Apple created iMac. The iMac is designed to help you get on the Internet, connect peripherals, and even attach to a network easily. It has all the important stuff built in—a modem, Ethernet port, graphics—plus the easy, modern way to add extras, the Universal Serial Bus. Moreover, it comes with applications already installed that you can use for a variety of home or home-office tasks.

The iMac is also designed to work collaboratively with other computers over the Internet or a local area network of Macs or PCs. It offers some special ways to transmit, share, and translate files that other computers use so you can share and edit them with others.

What Is the Internet?

It's obvious just from the iMac's name that the Internet will be a huge focus of this book and your experience with the computer, so you'll need to know what it is. The Internet is the name given to a global system for connecting computers to one another using various sorts of cable and wire. Once connected, these computers can share documents and transfer files among one another. The result is electronic mail, message areas, and the World Wide Web.

The Internet began as a government project to move data over long distances, with redundancies to survive some sort of wartime or natural disaster. Eventually, it became an important way to connect university computing centers and, later on, individuals. In the early 1990s the corporate world caught on and electronic mail and messaging became one of the most popular ways to use a personal computer.

So what makes it the Internet? Any computer using a particular language called the Transmission Control Protocol/Internet Protocol (TCP/IP) can connect to the Internet. All you need is a modem or a network connection and an Internet connection through an Internet Service Provider (ISP). The ISP gives you an address on the Internet, called an IP address, which gives your Mac a unique identity on this global network. Once you have an address, you're ready to send and receive Internet documents.

NOTE   *To learn more about using the iMac with the Internet, see the section "The Internet Setup Assistant" in this chapter, as well as Chapters 18 through 23, in which I discuss the Internet in detail.*

iMac Is Still a Mac

The iMac, ultimately, is a Macintosh computer. It's been simplified, designed in very clever ways, and made to work well on the Internet. At the heart of the iMac, though, is a standard PowerPC G3 processor and the Mac OS.

Any of those Macintosh programs (designed for your iMac's version of the Mac OS) available in the store or through mail order will work with your iMac. Even new versions of the Mac OS available from stores support the iMac automatically—you don't have to buy special software that's only for iMac. There are really only three things you need to look for when shopping for software:

- ■ **Does it run on CD-ROM?**   Remember, the iMac doesn't have a floppy drive. iMac DV and DV Special Edition models can also support software that runs on a DVD-ROM.

- ■ **Is it designed for PowerPC?**   Some older Macintosh programs aren't specifically designed for PowerPC processors like the powerful processor in an iMac. Those old programs should still run, but they might slow down the system.

- ■ **Is it designed for your iMac's version of the Mac OS?**   Make sure the program is designed to be compatible with the version of the Mac OS that your iMac is running. That means, specifically, that it is compatible with Mac OS 8.1-9 (or later, if you've updated to a version of Mac OS 9 or later). It's possible that you'll encounter software designed to run on Mac OS X, Apple's next-generation Mac OS. If your iMac isn't running Mac OS X, then those programs will not work with your iMac.

The iMac does not run software specifically written for DOS, Windows, Windows 95/98, or Windows NT/2000, although many programs are written in both PC and Macintosh versions. Sometimes you'll even find both versions on the same CD-ROM.

And that's not to say the iMac can't run PC software at all—it just can't run PC software right out of the box. Special software programs, such as Connectix Virtual PC and FWB Software's SoftWindows, allow you to run those programs on your iMac. That software, called *emulation* software, can trick Windows programs into believing that they're being run on a Windows-based machine, even as they're being run on your iMac. It's a neat trick and it can be done pretty inexpensively.

NOTE   *Computers that use Intel-compatible processors and DOS, Windows, or Windows NT are often called "PCs" for the sake of convenience and to differentiate them from Macs and iMacs. I'll follow that convention despite the fact that your iMac is a "personal computer." Also, Windows and DOS compatibility for your iMac is discussed in greater detail in Chapter 29.*

iMac Uses a New Type of Hardware

Get your iMac home and there's a decent chance that you'll soon want external peripherals for it—you may want a printer, a document scanner, and a digital camera, or you may want to connect your iMac to other computers and copy files between them. Part of the excitement of the iMac stems from its Universal Serial Bus (USB) and Ethernet ports for upgrading. iMac DV models also include Firewire ports that can be used to connect high-speed peripherals.

USB is incredibly easy to use—you pretty much just plug things in and they work. Plus, it's a standard that the latest Mac and PC computers can both use. That means your iMac is compatible with most of the USB peripherals that are being made for computers these days.

When you shop for USB peripherals, have these two things in mind:

- **USB**   Make sure the peripheral offers a USB connector or adapter designed specifically for that item.

- **Mac Driver Software**   Some USB peripherals require special driver software for compatibility with the iMac. Some peripherals don't require driver software, including most keyboards, mice, trackballs, and USB *hubs* (devices that give you more USB ports). More sophisticated devices require the software, so read the box carefully, ask a salesperson, or just focus on USB devices that show up in the Mac section of the store. If it has a Mac or iMac logo on the box, then it likely includes the software drivers you need.

You can also upgrade using the Ethernet port, which is a special port designed for high-speed networking connections for transferring files between computers. The port doesn't *have* to be used for networking—there are actually some very clever peripherals and adapters that use the Ethernet port to make it easy to upgrade your iMac. Most of the time, though, you'll find the Ethernet port is used to connect your iMac to other computers. Devices like high-speed modems, cable-Internet access boxes, and high-speed printers use the Ethernet port.

If you have an iMac DV model, your iMac includes additional ports, called Firewire ports. These high-speed ports are included on the iMac DV for copying data between your iMac DV and a digital camcorder so you can edit video. But that's not all Firewire is good for. It is also popular for connecting other devices, including high-speed external hard disks and removable disks. You'll find that many external devices are available with Firewire connections. As an added bonus, Firewire is easy to set up, with the same "hot-pluggability" that USB offers.

You need to watch out for peripherals made for older Mac computers. These days, all of Apple's new products use USB ports, but older Mac printers and scanners may use either *serial* ports or *SCSI* ports for their connections. That's not the end of the world—actually, many of those other peripherals made for older Macintosh computers can still be used, but you'll need an adapter and some know-how. We'll discuss various peripherals in Chapter 27.

iMac: A Quick Tour

Before you get into the heart of setting up your iMac, let's take a quick look at it to get an idea what everything is and how things connect. You'll find that the iMac has some interesting and surprising nooks and crannies.

Different iMac Models

Among the things you'll need to know throughout this book are the different iMac models. This is important for two different reasons. First, some iMac models offer particular software bundles and computer programs that other iMacs don't. If I discuss a program that you don't have, you'll want to be sure it's because you have a different iMac model, not because you've lost the CD. (I'll point out which models have what software throughout this text.) Second, some iMac models differ significantly in how you deal with them, including, for instance, how you plug in devices or how you insert CD-ROMs.

Original iMacs

There are four distinct versions of the original iMac series, if you don't count each color as a different version. Each of these iMac versions has a tray-loading CD-ROM drive:

- **iMac, Rev A.** This was the original iMac, which came only in Bondi blue and had a 233MHz PowerPC G3 processor, 4GB hard disk, and 2MB of video RAM.

- **iMac Rev B.** This iMac was also Bondi blue and had a 233MHz processor. The major difference was its 6MB of video RAM, making it more capable for gaming.

- **iMac 266.** These were the first iMac models available in five different colors (blueberry, tangerine, strawberry, grape, and lime). These iMacs had a 266MHz processor, 32MB of RAM, a 6GB hard disk, and 6MB of video RAM.

- **iMac 333.** These were the second iteration of colorful iMacs, with a 333MHz processor, 32MB of RAM, a 6GB hard disk, and 6MB of video RAM.

Slot-loading iMacs

In the fall of 1999, Apple introduced a new line of iMacs that all feature slot-loading CD-ROM or DVD-ROM drives. These currently (at the time of writing) come in three different models:

- **iMac (slot-loading).** This is the base model, which features a 350MHz processor, 64MB of RAM, a 6GB hard disk, and 8MB of video RAM. It has a CD-ROM drive and does not feature Firewire or a video-out port, although it does have a slot to accept an AirPort wireless networking card. It is only available in blueberry.

- **iMac DV.** This is the first model to support digital video viewing and editing. It features a 400MHz processor, 64MB of RAM, a 10GB hard disk, and 8MB of video RAM. It has a DVD-ROM drive, Firewire ports, a slot for an AirPort card, and a video-out port. It's available in all five iMac colors.

- **iMac DV Special Edition.** This model is similar to the iMac DV but includes 128MB of RAM and a 13GB hard disk. It's available in graphite only.

All slot-loading iMacs also feature improved, higher-fidelity sound thanks to improved integrated speakers. These iMacs have also been designed to avoid using an internal fan, so they run quieter than most other computers.

1

From the Front

Here you can get acquainted quickly with the all the different ways you'll interact with your iMac on a daily basis. Figure 1-1 shows an original iMac form factor from the front. Figure 1-2 shows a slot-loading iMac from the front.

Here are some basic notes about the front of your iMac:

■ Note that the mouse is close to the keyboard and that it is on a mouse pad, which is recommended for smooth movement and to help keep the inside of the mouse clean.

■ Both the keyboard and the iMac's front have a POWER key. The two keys are functionally equivalent except that the iMac's front POWER key can be used to restart some iMacs when frozen (see the section later in this chapter on resetting your iMac).

NOTE *On the slot-loading iMac, the power button on the front of the iMac pulses while the iMac is in Sleep mode.*

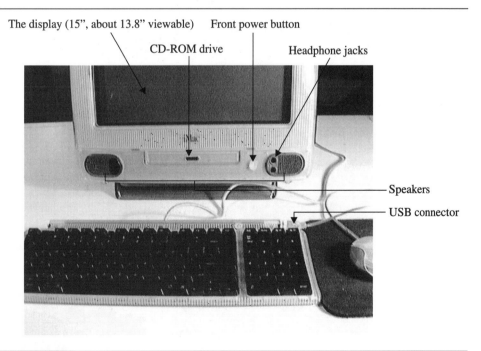

The display (15", about 13.8" viewable)   Front power button

CD-ROM drive   Headphone jacks

Speakers

USB connector

FIGURE 1-1   The original iMac form factor from the front

■ You may also notice that the iMac has, in fact, a full-featured keyboard—it even includes PAGE UP and PAGE DOWN keys and ARROW keys. The keyboard is meant to save space but still offer nearly all the special keys of a typical Macintosh keyboard.

■ Feel free to switch the mouse from one side to the other. USB devices can be unplugged and plugged back in even while the iMac is turned on and active.

■ On the original iMac, the CD-ROM drive needs to be worked with carefully. If you don't have a CD in the drive already, you can open it by pressing the colored button on the front. The drive pops open. (If you do have a CD in the drive, drag the CD icon on the iMac's desktop to the Trash icon. This is explained more in Chapter 2.) You'll need to pull the CD-ROM drive tray out with a finger. Then, place CDs as you would in any CD player and lightly push the tray back until it clicks shut. You'll hear the drive whir up to speed and the CD's icon will appear on the Mac's desktop.

Speakers (improved in this version)

Power button

slot-loading CD-ROM or DVD-ROM drive

FIGURE 1-2   The slot-loading iMac from the front

■ On the slot-loading iMac, CDs and DVDs are a little easier to deal with. Just slide the disc lightly into the drive until the drive catches and pulls it in the rest of the way. (If you don't feel the drive catch, don't force it—make sure you don't already have a disc in the drive first.) When is a CD is ejected, be careful not to grab it too quickly; make sure it's completely ejected by the iMac first, then grab it.

From the Side

The ports for your iMac's peripherals and Internet or network connections are on the side of the iMac. On the original iMac, you open the port door by putting your finger in the hole and lightly pulling down and away. Now you'll see the ports for connecting your iMac to devices, to the phone line, and to the Internet. Figure 1-3 shows those ports.

The slot-loading iMac doesn't have a port door. Instead, the ports are simply recessed in the side of the iMac. Figure 1-4 shows the slot-loading iMac's ports.

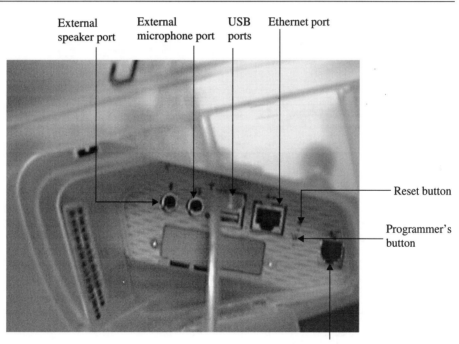

FIGURE 1-3   The original iMac's ports

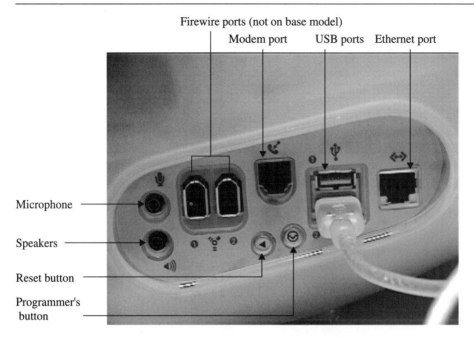

Firewire ports (not on base model)

Modem port   USB ports Ethernet port

Microphone

Speakers

Reset button

Programmer's
 button

Video out (behind door, not on base model)

FIGURE 1-4   The slot-loading iMac's ports

Here are some things to keep in mind about the side of your iMac:

- The modem and Ethernet ports look similar, but they accept different types of cable.
  The phone cable accepts a typical RJ-11 "modular" telephone cable connector. The
  Ethernet port accepts an RJ-45 10BaseT cable (also "twisted-pair") connector. If
  your connector isn't fitting properly, examine the cable and the ports carefully.

- On the original iMac, the reset and programmer's buttons are best selected with
  a straightened paperclip. On the slot-loading iMac, the reset button is an actual
  button. Be careful though—selecting either while your iMac is running will cause
  you to lose data!

- USB ports accept USB cables in one direction only, so if the USB connector
  doesn't fit easily, turn it over. Firewire ports are the same way.

- The ports for the external speaker and microphone are stereo miniplug ports. The
  microphone port will accept a PlainTalk microphone (from Apple), a miniplug-
  compatible microphone, or a line-in connection from an audio source, like a stereo
  receiver. The speaker port is a line-out source; it isn't amplified, so it will only

work with powered speakers or a stereo receiver, not with headphones or inexpensive, nonpowered PC speakers.

■ iMac DV models include a video-out port, which you can use for video mirroring. This allows you to connect an external monitor that can display the same image as the iMac's screen at the exact same time.

Before You Set Up iMac

If you've just gotten your iMac and you're waiting for me to tell you how to get started, this is your section. I'll also talk about some relevant issues for users who have their iMac running—stuff not necessarily covered by the iMac manual from Apple. Let's take a quick look.

Get a Surge Protector

Not enough people get surge protectors for their computers, and I suggest you run out and buy one right now (or at least later today) if you plan to start or continue using your iMac. A surge protector is usually a power strip that plugs into the wall outlet, then allows you a number of sockets into which you can plug computer components. (This will be really important if you need to plug in a printer, scanner, camera, and so on, as well as an iMac!)

The surge protector is designed to stop power surges from reaching your valuable equipment. It keeps your iMac from getting fried, basically, when a power surge occurs thanks to a lightning strike, power outage, or problem with your (or your power company's) wiring.

You need to get the kind of surge protector that includes protection for the phone line, too. In my experience, extreme surges occur more frequently over phone lines than over power lines. Since your phone line will probably almost always be plugged into your Mac's modem port, it's possible for such a surge to go straight into the modem, causing it to cease functioning. In fact, this could affect your entire iMac.

A good surge protector costs at least $25, probably more depending on the features. Don't get an $8 protector and think you're done—often, those are just power strips (giving you more plug outlets), not protectors. Check the box to see if the manufacturer offers a guarantee or equipment replacement insurance. If so, there's a decent chance the protector actually works well.

Keep Glare to a Minimum

Another important consideration before you set up your iMac is where the windows are. I mean actual windows—those things in the wall that let sunlight in.

In general, avoid having a window directly in front of the iMac (that is, when you sit at the iMac, the window is at your back) or directly behind the iMac (when you look at the iMac's screen, you can see the window behind it). The reason for this is simple—glare and eyestrain. If the window is directly behind you, then sunlight will glare off the screen and make it harder to see text and images on your iMac. If the window is directly behind the iMac, your eyes will have trouble adjusting to the varying levels of light, causing strain and fatigue.

Along those same lines, it's always a good idea to look away from your monitor for a minute or more every 15 minutes. That means looking out the window (which should be directly to your right or left if possible), reading a bit, performing eye exercises, raising a dumbbell, getting up for some water, or simply doing whatever else you do to relax.

Don't Forget the Ergonomics

It's also important—especially if you plan to use your iMac for an extended period of time—to consider the ergonomic implications of your setup. While I'm not a doctor or chiropractor, I can pass on some general advice. You might want to consult an expert regarding your setup, especially if you're experiencing any pain or strain from repetitive movements.

First, your hands and legs should generally approach the table and chair that support your iMac at a 90-degree angle. That means elbows at 90 degrees and knees at 90 degrees with your feet flat on the floor, if possible. Adjust your table and/or chair if neither of these angles is correct.

Next, you shouldn't look far down or far up at your monitor—don't crane your neck, in other words. If you're looking down on your monitor, make a trip to the computer store to purchase a stand to raise the iMac. (You can also lower your adjustable chair, if you have one, as long as that doesn't adversely affect your sitting position.) The top of the iMac's screen should be level with your eyes when you're looking straight ahead.

In fact, looking straight ahead is exactly what you want to do. Do you have a desk that positions the monitor off to the side at an angle? They should be illegal. You should look *directly* at a monitor that is in front of you, not to one side. Otherwise you'll have your neck and/or back cocked sideways for minutes or hours at a time—not a good thing. It's like driving cross-country while looking out the driver-side window. That would start to hurt after a while, wouldn't it?

Need to make some adjustments to your iMac? Here's how:

1. The iMac screen position is adjustable. You can choose to set the iMac straight down on its little feet, or lift the iMac and swing out the optional tilt bar on the bottom of the iMac. This will raise the screen slightly.

2. The keyboard is similarly adjustable. Pick up the keyboard and you'll see there's a bottom bar you can swing out to tilt the keyboard up in back a little, which is probably the more comfortable position.

3. Some folks don't like the iMac's mouse, but its compact size actually has ergonomic advantages. Try loosely cupping the mouse in the palm of your hand instead of gripping it with your fingers—I find that more comfortable. You end up clicking the

mouse with the inside of your knuckles (if you have average adult-sized hands) and you may find it's more comfortable. In any case, always try to have a relaxed grip on the mouse.

> **TIP** *Still don't like the mouse? A number of companies make snap-on plastics for the iMac mouse that turn it into something a little larger and easier to handle for some folks. Look for them in Mac catalogs or stores. Of course, you can also opt for a new USB mouse, which should connect just as easily as the iMac's mouse does.*

4. Some physical therapists also recommend that your mouse and keyboard be as close together as possible (and always on the same level) so you're not reaching far for the mouse. With the iMac's compact keyboard, that's not a problem at all. Put your mouse right next to the keyboard on a clean mouse pad.

Do you have lots of mouse pads and wrist accessories? Don't let them allow you to get lazy. The ideal wrist position is actually over the keys slightly, not resting on the wrist pad—at least, according to most things I've heard and read. If you took piano lessons as a kid, then you know how you're supposed to hold your hands. Keep them aloft for a while. When you're tired, don't rest your wrists on little gel things—quit typing.

Finally, the second you start to feel pain or strain, get ahold of your doctor. You may be able to get add-on keyboards, mice, or some other solution for working with your iMac. Or your doctor may prescribe a vacation to the Bahamas for two weeks, especially if you slip her five bucks or so.

Set Up iMac

Now for the moment of truth. When you've accounted for surges, glare, and ergonomics, the setup instructions that come with your iMac are perfectly acceptable.

1. Pull the iMac out of the box, place it on the table, and use the little bar to tilt it up slightly, if desired.

> **NOTE** *Even though, technically, it's portable, the iMac is heavy, at 40 pounds (35 for the slot-loading model). Apple recommends grasping both the handle and the area under the front of the iMac's screen, right under the CD-ROM drive, and you should lift or carry the iMac with both hands.*

2. Plug the power cord into the power socket on the back of the iMac, then plug it into your surge protector.

3. Put your finger in the hole in the door on the lower-right side of your iMac and pull the door open. (On the slot-loading iMac, you don't need to do this. The ports are in recessed holes on the side of the iMac.)

4. Using the phone wire that came with the surge protector (or another that you have around the house), connect the phone wire from your wall socket to the Phone In socket on your surge protector. Use the phone cord that came with your iMac to stretch from the Phone Out on the surge protector to the modem socket on the iMac. (Note: you can use a small phone splitter from Radio Shack or a similar store if you want to place a telephone next to your iMac.)

5. Plug the iMac's keyboard cord into one of the two USB ports.

6. Place the keyboard cord in one of the lower corners of the iMac's port door and close the door. It should snap shut with room for the cable to snake out without being pinched.

7. Plug your iMac's mouse into the appropriate USB port on the keyboard (depending on whether you work the mouse with your left hand or right hand).

8. Press the POWER key on the iMac's keyboard. The little light on the POWER key built into the iMac (not on the keyboard) will light up.

That's it. If all goes well, your iMac should fire up and be ready to go. You'll see the famous Happy Mac, followed by the "Welcome to Macintosh" message. Soon, if this is the first time you've turned on your iMac, you'll be greeted by the Setup and Internet Assistants.

If you don't see anything on the screen, if you see something blinking, or if it's been, say, 20 minutes and nothing is happening and the power light is either amber or off, turn to Chapter 30 to troubleshoot your iMac.

Get Online with the Assistants

Once the iMac has started up and loaded (all the little icons have traveled across the bottom of the screen and the desktop appears), you'll be greeted by an Assistant. The Mac OS's Assistants are designed to walk you through some of the basic settings that your iMac needs to operate without making you dig too deep into all the configuration controls. The Assistant, instead, asks you plain questions and helps you enter the answers (see Figure 1-5).

NOTE
On some newer iMacs, you'll be greeted by a different Assistant that helps you register your iMac with Apple and set up Internet access. Oddly, these iMacs (in my experience) don't go on to launch the Mac OS Setup Assistant. I'd still recommend you launch this Assistant, however, since it helps you make some important settings. To launch the Mac OS Setup Assistant, double-click your Macintosh HD icon, then double-click the Assistants folder icon. Now, double-click the icon called Mac OS Setup Assistant. Now you can follow along with the rest of this section.

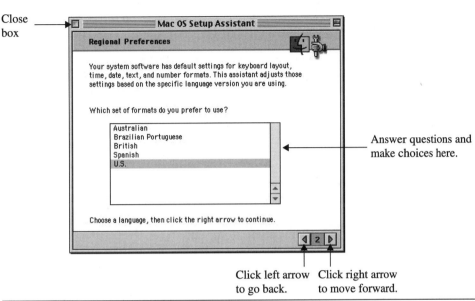

Close box

Answer questions and make choices here.

Click left arrow to go back.   Click right arrow to move forward.

FIGURE 1-5   Most of the Mac OS's Assistants work this way.

The Mac OS Setup Assistant

The first Assistant you'll encounter is the Mac OS Setup Assistant. This little guy's job is to learn what it can about you and your iMac so it can make some basic settings. Run through the Setup Assistant and answer the questions. When you've answered a question, click the right arrow to continue. If you need to go back to a previous question, click the left arrow.

A few notes about the Setup Assistant's questions:

1. The name, organization, date, and other questions should be fairly self-explanatory. Enter all this information, clicking the right arrow to move to the next screen.

2. When you're asked if you want to use the Simple Finder, the answer is No. Simple Finder just hides some of the basic commands for dealing with files. I'll discuss all that stuff thoroughly, so you'll want all those options available in the Finder.

3. On the next screen, the computer's name can be anything: "Todd's Computer," "Sleepy," "iMac 2079-34," "Fourth Graders' iMac," and so on. If you connect the iMac to a network, this is the name that will be used to represent your iMac to any

other computers on the network. (This doesn't include the Internet—just networks in offices, schools, on university campuses, or in your house if you have two or more computers hooked up to one another.)

4. The password can be anything up to eight characters long, but it needs to be something you can remember and keep private. You won't need it to get into your iMac and use its files—it's only for when you want to access your iMac from another computer, over a network connection.

5. On the next screen, you probably won't want a shared folder unless you're setting up a network in your office or organization. (See Chapter 28 for more on networking.)

6. If your printer is connected via a USB port, it's a Direct Connection. If it's connected via the Ethernet port (or if you print to a printer somewhere else on the network), it's a Network Connection. If you don't have a printer yet, choose Direct Connection.

7. Finally, choose the type of printer you have—if it's an Apple-brand printer. (Other printers need to be set up separately, as shown in Chapter 26.)

That's it. With all those decisions made, you can click the Go Ahead button and the settings are entered. Next up, it's the Internet Setup Assistant.

> **TIP** *You can quit the Assistant at any time without causing undue harm to your iMac— just choose File | Quit or click the close box. If necessary, you can start up the Assistant again. It's located in the Assistants folder on your iMac's hard drive.*

The Internet Setup Assistant

The first major decision you need to make regarding the Internet is how you plan to connect. There are four basic ways to do it. The first way is through a special deal that Apple has made with the Earthlink service. It's also the easiest one. The second way is through any different Internet Service Provider (or ISP). You'll find these both nationally and locally; check your local newspaper if you'd prefer to go with a local service. The third way is using the America Online service, which can also act as an ISP. The fourth way is to hook up to the Internet over a network instead of using your modem. Depending on which option you choose, you'll answer the Internet Setup Assistant differently.

■ **Earthlink or Other Apple-Recommended ISP** If you choose to create a new Earthlink account, click Yes when asked if you want to set up Internet access. Then click No when you're asked if you already have an account. Follow the onscreen instructions for finding and creating a new Internet account.

■ **Your Own ISP** Choose Yes, you want to set up Internet access and Yes, you already have an account. You'll need to enter information about your ISP, which the service provider should be able to give you easily. (See Chapter 23 to learn more about the information required for an Internet account.)

- **America Online**   Tell the Assistant No, you don't want to set up Internet access. Do it through the AOL service. (See Chapter 19 for more on America Online.)

- **Over a Network**   If you have a LAN, cable modem, DSL, or similar connection that uses Ethernet, tell the Assistant Yes, you want to set up Internet access and Yes, you already have an account. Then choose to connect via Network. This is discussed more in Chapter 23.

If all goes well, you'll end up with an Internet account. I briefly discuss how to connect to the Internet in Chapter 2; then you'll see all sorts of things you can do on the Internet in Chapters 17 through 21.

iMac: On, Off, Sleep, Info

Once you get past the Assistants, you're greeted with the desktop—the space that shows your hard drive icon, a few words across the top of the screen, and even a little Trash can. I'll discuss this area in more depth in Chapters 2 through 5. For now, we need to talk about a few important commands.

Which Mac OS Do You Have?

The first one is the About This Computer command. Throughout this book, I'll be referring to different versions of the Mac OS. In order to know if a particular feature is available to you, you'll need to know if you have Mac OS 8.1, Mac OS 8.5, Mac OS 8.6, Mac OS 9, or a later version loaded on your iMac. To find out, move your mouse pointer to the top of the screen and point it at the little multicolored Apple picture. Click the mouse button once. A menu appears.

Now, move the mouse down the menu until it points at About This Computer. Click the mouse button again. The About This Computer window appears.

This window tells you some other things about your iMac, including how much system RAM (random access memory) it has and how that RAM is being used.

Turn Off iMac

You've already turned on your iMac successfully using the POWER key on the iMac's keyboard. Actually, the POWER key on the front of the iMac will work pretty much the exact same way—just tap it to turn on the iMac. The light glows amber to show you that it's powering up, then it turns green when it successfully lights up the screen.

But what about turning off the iMac? There are a couple of different ways to do that, and it's important to turn it off correctly.

Let's start with the one way *not* to turn off your iMac. Don't just cut power to the machine. That means don't just pull the cord out of the wall or surge protector, and it means don't just throw the power switch on the surge protector. If your iMac ever crashes you may have to resort to this sort of thing, but not yet.

Instead, shut down your iMac gracefully by choosing the aptly named Shut Down command. In the Finder, move the mouse up to the Special menu. (If you don't see the Special menu, click once anywhere on the desktop background.) Click once on the Special menu item and the full menu appears. Now point to the Shut Down command and click the mouse again. Your iMac shuts down.

Another way to do this is to tap the POWER key on the keyboard or on the iMac's chassis once. A dialog box appears, allowing you to do a number of power-related things. To shut down, just click the Shut Down button with your mouse.

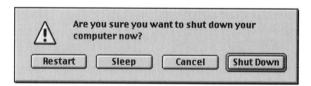

You may notice that, after choosing Shut Down, your iMac goes through a few hoops. It will ask all open application programs if they need to save anything, then it tells them to quit. During that process, the application may ask *you* if you want to save something. Once all that business has been taken care of, the iMac quits all those programs, writes some last-minute things to the hard disk, and shuts itself down. To start up again, tap the POWER key.

Restart iMac

Sometimes you don't really want iMac to shut all the way down. Instead, you want it to simply restart—maybe you've just installed a new program or you're experiencing odd behavior because of an errant program or similar issue. In that case, you'll choose Restart from the Special menu. You can also tap the POWER key and choose Restart. Your iMac goes through the same procedure as when you issue the Shut Down command, except that the power is never turned off to the iMac, and the Mac OS starts right back up again after the contents of system memory are cleared.

Reset Your iMac When Frozen

Unfortunately, your iMac will sometimes "freeze" while you're working with it—things on the screen stop moving around and you can't move the mouse pointer and/or click on

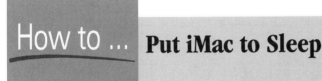

How to ...   **Put iMac to Sleep**

Here's the cool option. You know how it takes a minute or so for your iMac to start up when it's completely off? Well, you can choose to put the iMac to sleep instead, so that it wakes up more quickly and is ready to work. The best part is that the iMac is still using very little power, even though it's turned on and working. That means two things. First, you don't have to shut down your applications before iMac can go to sleep. You can open things up and get right back to work. (You will, however, have to quit your Internet or America Online session if you're using the modem.)

Second, it means the iMac can still receive a fax, even though it's in low-power mode. That's great for when you want to leave your office or home office for the day but are expecting an incoming fax. Just put your iMac to sleep and it will save power but still be ready when the calls comes in. Same thing goes for automated backup and even getting your e-mail messages. All of that can be automated so the iMac wakes up and goes back to sleep on its own.

A lot of this is covered in Chapter 24. For now, you just need to know the Sleep command. Click once on the Special menu, then click the Sleep command. Your iMac's screen blanks after a few seconds and the POWER key turns amber. (On a slot-loading iMac, the Power Button actually strobes, almost as if the iMac were snoring.) This tells you that iMac is in Sleep mode. You can also tap the POWER key while iMac is still awake to get that same windowful of options. Click the Sleep button to put iMac into Sleep mode.

To wake up your iMac, just tap the POWER key or any other key. The screen will light back up (it may also shimmer a bit) and iMac will beep to acknowledge your command. You're ready to compute.

things. This can be the sign of a software or hardware problem—the sort of thing discussed in Chapter 30. But it also just sometimes happens when a minor error occurs. In that case, you should know how to quickly get your iMac working again.

First of all, make sure your iMac is really frozen. There are a few steps you can take to figure out if it's really time to restart your iMac:

- **Is iMac waiting for you to do something?** Sometimes you need to insert a particular CD-ROM, click a certain option, or otherwise follow the instructions before iMac can continue.

- **Can you move the mouse pointer around?** If you can but nothing happens when you click and there's no waiting message, iMac might just be thinking things through. Wait a few minutes to see if anything happens.

- **Can you interrupt the current application?** If you can move the mouse pointer but nothing else is happening, try to interrupt the current program. Press the ESC key or simultaneously press the ⌘-. (period) keys. You should also try pressing ⌘-Q to quit the application.

- **Can you force the current application to quit?** Sometimes an application encounters an error, but it doesn't give control back to the iMac. In that case, you'll need to force-quit the application. Press ⌘-OPTION-ESC. Then, click the Force Quit button. This should quit the application and return you to the Finder. Save work in your other applications and restart your iMac.

- **Can you emergency recover?** If nothing else is working, try pressing ⌘-POWER (that's the actual POWER key on the keyboard). If a text box appears on the window, type **G F** and press RETURN. That might return you to the Finder. Save your data and restart the iMac.

- **Can you reset with the power button?** If all else fails, hold down the POWER key *on the iMac's front* until you hear the startup chime. (This can be five seconds or more.) That will reset your iMac.

The POWER key only works on Revision B and newer iMacs (those built in late 1998 and on, including the "flavored" iMacs and the slot-loading iMacs). If you have an original Revision A iMac, you'll need to straighten a paperclip and insert it in the reset button hole to restart your iMac. (You may need to do this for other iMacs that don't respond when you press the POWER key on the front.) Figure 1-6 shows you how.

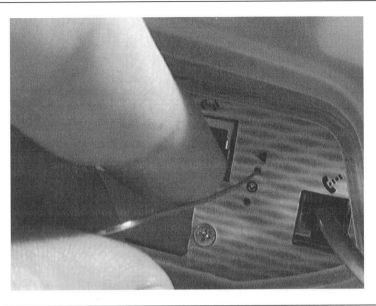

FIGURE 1-6   Resetting an original iMac form factor using its reset button

 If you have a slot-loading iMac, the reset button is a raised button on the right side of the iMac near the ports. The button has a small triangle on it.

 This procedure may cause you to lose data—it's only recommended as a last resort.

Finally, did none of that work? Then unplug the iMac, wait 30 seconds, and plug it back in. Press the POWER key on the keyboard (or on the front of the iMac) to see if it starts up.

Chapter 2

Get Acquainted with iMac

How to...

■ Figure out what the desktop is for

■ Use the mouse

■ Click and drag on the screen

■ Get to know icons and windows

■ Change settings with the Control Strip

■ Get a quick start on the Internet

The iMac really is pretty easy to get set up and powered on, since everything is clearly labeled and there are only a few different cords to deal with. If you've worked your way through Chapter 1, then, hopefully, you've gotten past the Assistants, you have an Internet account, and all your settings are in order.

Now let's take a look at what you see once you've powered up your iMac. Your iMac is a combination of hardware—things on the outside that you touch and push like the CD-ROM or DVD-ROM drive, the mouse, and the keyboard—and software—pictures and words on the screen like icons, menu items, and windows.

In this chapter you'll see how those things come together. You'll learn how to move around on the screen, work with the mouse and keyboard, even how to insert CD-ROMs and DVD-ROMs, work with the internal hard disk, and change things like the sound settings.

What Is the Desktop?

Let's begin at the beginning. After you've pressed the POWER key and your iMac has started up, you'll see the desktop (assuming you've gotten past all that Assistant stuff discussed in Chapter 1). The *desktop*, for all practical purposes, is the background pattern or color you see on the main screen of your iMac when it first starts up. Think of it in terms of 3-D: The little hard disk picture, the Trash picture, and everything else is sitting *on top of* the desktop, as shown in Figure 2-1.

If it's called the desktop, then clearly this is supposed to have some relationship to a typical desk, right? Sort of. The desktop represents the top of a desk, but there's stuff on it that you wouldn't normally put on the top of your desk, like a trash can and a hard disk. But, for the most part, the metaphor holds up.

So what are you looking at? The desktop is comprised of three major components: icons, menus, and windows. Each represents a real-world idea you'd find near, or on, a desk.

What's an Icon?

Icons are the small pictures that represent parts of your iMac or files on your computer. The Macintosh HD icon, for instance, represents the hard disk that's inside your iMac's case. A hard disk is used for storage—it's sort of a virtual filing cabinet. The icon, then, allows you to open that filing cabinet and root around in the file folders.

The Trash icon is similar—it's where you toss files that you no longer need in your filing cabinet. You put files in the Trash, then you empty it using a special command that deletes files from your iMac's hard disk.

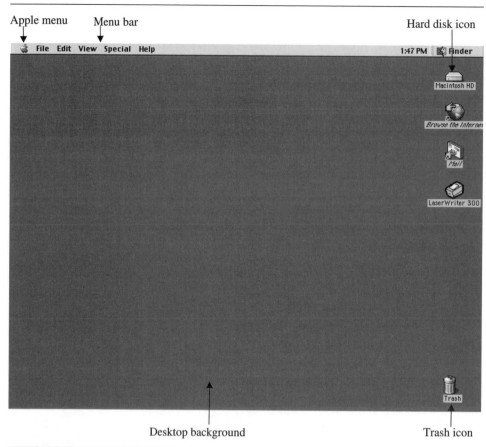

FIGURE 2-1   The desktop is the pattern or color behind everything else on your iMac's screen.

 If you've used Microsoft Windows 95 or Windows 98, you'll find that the Trash is very similar to the Recycle Bin in Windows. The major difference is that entire folders are stored, intact, in the iMac's Trash, while the Windows Recycle Bin will usually do away with folders.

What's a Menu?

The little words at the top of the iMac screen are called *menus*—they're situated in the long, white menu bar. Each of these menus holds related commands that allow you to accomplish things on your iMac, almost as if they were the drawers full of pencils, staplers, and scissors you'd find in a real desk. The menus that appear when you first start your iMac are part of an application called the Finder, which is started automatically whenever you turn on your iMac. The Finder is specially designed to help you manage your documents and file folders.

Note that the menu bar offers two other distinct menus, shown in the following illustration. Both of these menus will appear no matter what application you're using on your iMac. One is the Apple menu; the other is the application menu. Pull down the application menu (the icon in the top-right corner marked "Finder" in the illustration) and you can switch between programs that are currently open. Pull down the Apple menu and you can access a whole bunch of different applications and accessories to help make your computing tasks simpler. In a sense, the Apple menu is the "junk drawer" of your iMac desktop.

Apple menu   Application menu

| TIP | *If you're used to Windows 95 or 98, you'll notice that menus on the iMac work slightly differently. In Windows, each individual window has its own menu bar within that window. On the iMac, the menu bar is always at the top of the screen. Other than that, there really isn't much difference. It may seem like the iMac menus are always the same, but the menu bar actually changes every time you load or switch to a different application.* |

What's a Window?

Our final element, the window, is sort of like a piece of paper you might find on your real-world desktop. It's in windows that you'll type things, read things, draw things, and so on. In fact, on the iMac, just about anything you do will take place in a window, like the ones shown in Figure 2-2. If you'd like to see a window, point your mouse at the Macintosh HD icon and click the mouse button twice quickly. (That's called a "double-click" and it almost always *opens* the item you double-clicked.) We'll talk about windows in greater depth later in this chapter.

Using the Mouse and Keyboard

The most basic skill requirement for using a modern computer is knowing how to use a mouse and keyboard. The mouse, perhaps, is primary on the Macintosh, since Macs were designed from the outset to use the little guy. On your iMac, the mouse is the little round disk attached to the keyboard by a thin cord.

If you've used a mouse in the past on other computers, you'll notice immediately that the iMac's little round design is somewhat different. It looks like a compelling device, but it can take some getting used to. The biggest problem is keeping it oriented correctly. "Up" means you have the mouse button and the mouse cord pointed in the general direction of

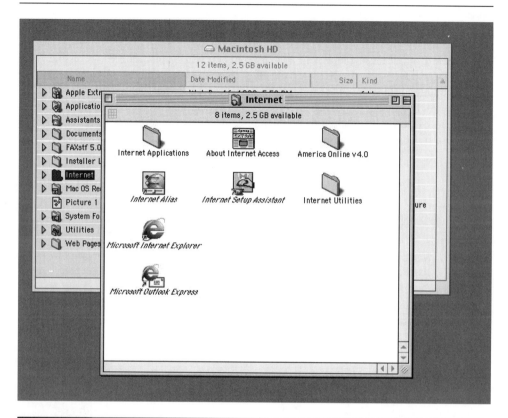

FIGURE 2-2 Windows can be stacked on one another like pieces of paper.

the iMac. (If you have your mouse off to one side, you don't need to point the mouse directly at the iMac, just toward the iMac and away from you.)

One way to keep the mouse oriented is to place it in the palm of your hand and rest the tip of your finger on the mouse's cable. That way you won't accidentally grab the mouse sideways, which can result in very odd reactions on your screen. (For instance, you're expecting to go up the screen and you end up heading left!)

If you have an iMac bought new in the Fall of 1999 or later, you have another clue to help you keep the mouse oriented—a small indentation on the mouse button will help you remember which way is up.

Click with the Mouse

The mouse is used to point at, grab, carry, and activate items on the desktop. It'd be more convenient if you could just reach into your iMac screen to grab things, but that gets expensive really fast since you'd have to buy all those new iMacs. (Plus, you'd end up cutting yourself a lot on the screen's glass.) Instead, you use the mouse to point and grab for you.

When you move the mouse, a little arrow on the screen moves around with you to indicate where the mouse is currently pointing. That arrow is called the "mouse pointer," and it's something you'll get to know very well. (It's also sometimes called a "cursor," but mouse pointer is the correct name.) No matter what you want to do with your iMac, you'll likely do it by rolling the mouse pointer over to an icon (or menu item or window) on your screen and clicking the mouse button.

NOTE *Mouse movements are relative, not absolute. That means if you pick up the mouse and put it down in a different place, the location of the mouse pointer on the screen won't change. Only rolling the mouse in a particular direction will move the mouse in that direction.*

There are three basic actions that the mouse allows you to perform: select, open, and drag-and-drop. Each of these is a combination of pointing the mouse and clicking the mouse button:

- ■ **Select**   To select an item, move the mouse pointer until it's touching that item, then press and release the mouse button once. A selected icon becomes highlighted, a selected window comes to the *foreground* (it appears "on top" of other windows), and a selected menu drops down to show you its contents. In the case of a menu, you move your mouse down to the menu item and click again to select that menu item. You'll also find buttons and menus within applications that need to be selected.

- ■ **Open**   Icons like the Macintosh HD and the Trash are opened (to reveal their contents) by pointing the mouse at the item and double-clicking the mouse button. Other icons can be opened, too, like document and application icons.

NOTE *You can also open icons and folders in the Finder by selecting them (pointing at the icon and clicking once), pointing at the File menu and clicking once, then pointing at the Open command and clicking once.*

- ■ **Drag-and-Drop**   On the desktop and in the Finder, you can drag icons around to move them from one place to another. Place the mouse pointer on an item, click and hold down the mouse button, and move the mouse. Now you're dragging. To drop the icon in its new location, let go of the mouse button.

You'll also find that the mouse pointer changes sometimes to reflect different things that are happening. It'll turn into a little rotating beach ball, for instance, when the iMac is busy doing something that can't be interrupted. It'll turn into an *insertion point* (also called an I-beam)—a capital "I"—when the mouse is hovering over a window (or sometimes a portion of a window, such as a part of an electronic form) where you can type. Click the mouse once in that window and the insertion point is placed in the document, as shown in Figure 2-3. Type with the keyboard and your words appear.

Special Keyboard Keys

So you use the mouse for selecting, opening, and moving things around on the screen. You use the keyboard, then, for getting text into your iMac. Most of the time, you'll find that typing on the iMac keyboard is like typing on any computer terminal, typewriter, or word processor. But there are special keys on the iMac's keyboard and special key combinations you'll use for various things.

The special keys are the CONTROL (Control), OPTION (Option), and ⌘ (Command) keys. These keys, along with the more familiar SHIFT key, can be used in various combinations to perform special commands in your application or in the Finder.

You'll see these special keyboard commands throughout the text. In order to use them, you'll need to hold down all of the keys at once, then release them all together. For instance, ⌘-S can be used to save a document; press ⌘ first and then the S key, release them together, and the command will execute.

Some of the most common keyboard commands are discussed in Chapter 8; others are discussed throughout the book.

| FIGURE 2-3 | The insertion point shows you where typed text will appear. |

This brings up a fourth instance where you can use the mouse to perform some interesting tasks. Hold down the CONTROL key, click the mouse, and then release them both. Do this in the right place (usually when pointing at an object in the Finder or in an application) and you'll get a *contextual menu*—a special "pop-up" menu of options regarding that object, as shown in the accompanying illustration. In essence, iMac is offering a special set of menu commands that are relevant to the object you've chosen.

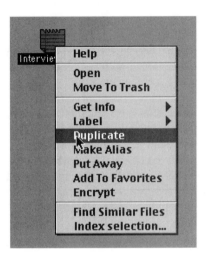

If you're used to Microsoft Windows, you'll notice that the iMac mouse only has one button. This CONTROL-click scheme is sort of like "right-clicking" in Windows.

The Mouse and Keyboard Connectors

You've just seen how to use the keyboard and mouse. Let's talk for a moment about the devices themselves. Your iMac's mouse and keyboard both connect to the iMac using one of the two USB (Universal Serial Bus) ports on the side of the iMac. The keyboard is plugged into the iMac, then the mouse is plugged into one side or the other of the keyboard. (You can also plug your mouse into the USB port on the iMac's side, but I can't really think of a good reason for doing so.)

If one or both of these plugs work loose, don't worry about it too much. USB is called a *hot-pluggable* technology, which basically means that it's OK to connect and disconnect devices while your iMac is running. Bottom line: If one of the devices comes unplugged, plug it back in. It should work right away.

You'll see more about this in Chapter 27, but your iMac's keyboard is actually a USB hub. That means its second USB port can be used for connecting another USB device, such as a joystick, trackball, or even an image scanner.

Work with Icons and Windows

I mentioned that icons are the small pictures on your iMac screen which represent parts of your iMac's internal filing system. And while icons represent different parts, windows are the way you view those parts—when you open a file folder or a document, you'll view its contents using a window. Let's look at icons and windows each in turn.

In Depth with Icons

You can often tell right away what a given item is based on the way its icon looks. There are about six different types of icons you'll encounter on your iMac, and each gives you an idea of what it does based on its general appearance.

- **Hardware Icons**   These icons appear automatically on the desktop to help you interact with some of the hardware in or attached to your iMac. Whenever you start up your iMac, for instance, the internal hard disk is recognized and the Macintosh HD icon is placed on the desktop. Similarly, if you pop a CD-ROM into your iMac's CD-ROM or DVD-ROM drive, that CD's icon appears on the desktop. Another major type of hardware icon are printer icons, which allow you to manage any printers you have attached (or networked) to the iMac. *Hardware icons generally look like the devices they're representing—the disk icons look like little disks and the printer icons look like little printers.*

- **Folders**   Open your Macintosh HD and a window appears that shows you more icons—most of them will be folders. Folder icons are used by the Finder to help you manage your documents and applications. You can create a storage system by creating new folders that organize your documents and applications. *Folder icons look like file folders.*

- **Programs**   Application programs like AppleWorks or Internet Explorer have their own icons, too. When you "open" an application (by pointing to its icon and double-clicking the mouse) you start up that application, loading all of its menu commands and, probably, a document window. You can then start creating. *Program icons are often the most creative—they tend to be unique icons designed by the application programmers.*

- **Documents**   Document icons are created whenever you save a document from an application. If you create a report in AppleWorks, for instance, a new document is created when you invoke the Save command, and a new icon appears in the Finder. Just as with a document in a physical filing system, you can move that document icon to a folder where you want it stored. *Documents often, although not always, look like pieces of paper or some variation on that theme— a piece of paper with a special logo, for instance.*

2

- **System Icons**   This is a catchall category that we won't discuss too much right now. The Mac OS features many special little icons that perform certain tasks behind the scenes on your iMac. For instance, there are system icons that represent the fonts you use in your documents and the control panels you use to change settings on your iMac. You'll read a lot more about system icons in Parts IV and V of this book.

- **Aliases**   An alias is a special "empty" icon that doesn't really represent a file or a device—instead, it *points* to that file. For instance, an alias allows you to have a pointer to a document or application on your desktop while the actual document or application is stored deep in your hard disk's file folders. Instead of being an entire *copy* of a file, an alias is simply an icon that represents the file. *An alias looks like the document or application it points to, but it has a special arrow as part of the icon and its text is always italic.*

Icons will respond to the mouse commands described early in this chapter. They can be selected, opened, and moved around the screen using drag-and-drop. In fact, you'll find that there's often reason to drag an icon over another icon and drop the first icon on the second icon. For instance, you can drop a document icon on top of a folder icon to store that document in that folder. Similarly, you can drop a document icon onto an application icon to start that application and view the document.

Rename Icons

Want to give an icon a new name? It's easy enough, as long as the icon isn't stored on a locked disk or on a CD-ROM or DVD-ROM. (You'll learn about read-only disks later in this chapter.) Here's what you do:

1. Find the icon you want to rename.

2. Click the mouse once on the name of the icon.

3. Press RETURN. The name portion of the icon changes and an insertion point appears.

4. Type the new name (or press DELETE to edit the current one).

5. Click elsewhere—on the desktop, away from the icon—when you're done editing.

Open Up Windows

So what do you do with these icons? In most cases, you open them. When you open them, a window appears. Double-click the Macintosh HD icon, for instance, and a window appears that reveals that disk's folders and other icons, as shown in Figure 2-4.

Any window has standard parts that make it easy to deal with. All of these parts allow you to move things around, resize them, stack windows—do different things while you're working with the windows. Here's what the different parts do:

- **Close Box** Click this to close the window. Note that you're dealing with an application's window, so closing the window doesn't necessarily quit the application. You'll often have a different command to Quit (usually in the File menu).

- **Title Bar** This part of the window tells you what the window represents. It's also used to drag the window around the screen: Click and drag on the title bar, then release the mouse button to drop the window.

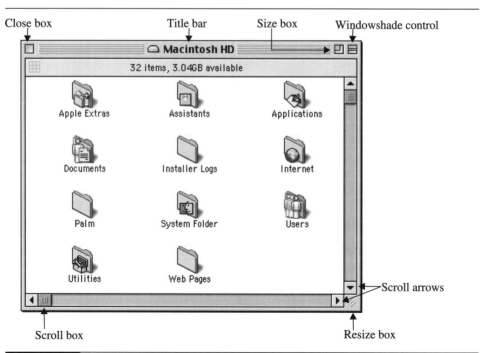

FIGURE 2-4 The parts of a window

2

- **Size Box**   Click this box to resize the window to optimum (in many cases). Click it again to revert to the original size.

- **Windowshade Control**   Click this control to "roll up" the window so that only the title bar appears.

- **Scroll Bar**   This bar shows you that the window can be scrolled. If more information is in the window than can be shown at once, you'll be able to scroll to see it.

- **Scroll Box**   Click and drag the scroll box to scroll the window's contents up and down (or side to side, if you use the bottom scroll bar).

- **Scroll Arrows**   Click the arrows to scroll up and down or side to side within the window.

- **Resize Box**   Click and drag the resize box to make the window larger or smaller.

You'll also encounter some different sorts of windows, called dialog boxes. These windows are designed so that the Mac OS can ask you questions or get you to provide information. Usually, dialog boxes require you to click Cancel or OK after you've finished entering information (these tend to look like alerts). They don't always, though. As shown in this illustration, some dialog boxes (called *modeless* dialog boxes) require you to click the close box once you're done with them.

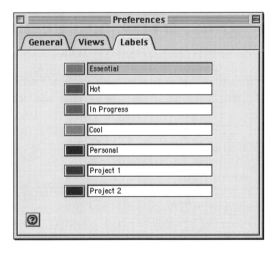

NOTE *If you have experience with Microsoft Windows 95 or 98, you'll notice some minor differences in the way Mac OS works with windows. In Microsoft Windows, the close box is on the far right side; in Mac OS, the close box is far left. It works the same way in both, except that the close box in Mac OS doesn't usually quit the application (sometimes it does quit the application in Microsoft Windows). Also, Microsoft Windows doesn't offer a Windowshade control, whereas Mac OS doesn't have a Minimize button.*

Another type of dialog box is called an *alert*. These messages appear when the Mac OS or an application needs to get your attention because something immediate is happening. This can range from something wrong with a printer or peripheral to a problem with a crashed or misbehaving application. Alerts are like regular dialog boxes, except they're outlined in red. You can usually dismiss an alert by clicking the OK button.

NOTE *If your iMac has Mac OS 8.5 or higher installed, it may be set to read alert text out loud using a technology called PlainTalk. This can be helpful if you're not sitting in front of your iMac's screen. Also, if you have Mac OS 9 or higher installed, you may see a special kind of alert pop up every once in a while, called a floating alert. These are smaller alert windows that don't have an OK button—instead, you click their close boxes to get rid of them.*

Hard Disks, CD-ROMs, DVDs, and Peripherals

You've already seen that one of the major types of icon is the hardware icon—the type that allows you to deal with hardware items found inside or attached to your iMac. Your hard disk is where you'll store most of your documents and any new applications that you install on your iMac. The hard disk is a small box inside your iMac that uses magnetic technology to write down the ones and zeros that make up "digital data." Visually, this digital data is represented by folder, application, document, and system icons that are displayed when you double-click the disk icon in the Finder.

CD-ROM and DVD-ROM discs are slightly different. CD-ROM and DVD-ROM are *read-only* technologies because you can't actually save any files to the discs, delete files stored on the discs, or move things to different folders on the discs. Instead, you can only copy from the CD-ROM or DVD-ROM to another disk, start up an application, or open a document directly from the CD-ROM or DVD-ROM. (CD-ROM stands for Compact Disc–Read-Only Memory; DVD-ROM stands for Digital Versatile Disc–Read-Only Memory.)

Of course, not every disc you deal with is a data disc. You can also listen to music stored on audio CDs on your iMac, and you can watch DVD movies on iMacs equipped with DVD players.

 *You can create CDs and DVDs using special hardware and software that allows you to "burn" your own discs by copying data from your iMac. For more on that, see Chapter 27.*

Storage vs. Memory

Storage disks are different from main memory in any computer. Main memory is called *Random Access Memory (RAM)* and is actually comprised of little computer chips—usually arranged on a special plug-in module—that hold digital information. RAM is sort of the short-term memory of your iMac. Anything currently on the screen, anything being printed, and some behind-the-scenes work goes on in RAM. (In Chapter 1 you saw how to get the About This Computer information, which tells you the current status of RAM.)

But your iMac can easily forget what's in RAM, since RAM is wiped clean whenever you power down your iMac. In fact, if a power surge, a kicked power cord, or some other uncontrollable circumstance cut power to your iMac, you'd also lose whatever was in RAM at that time. RAM needs power in order to remember things.

That's why you have storage disks. Hard disks and removable disks (like Iomega's Zip disks) are used for writing things down and saving them long term. Whenever you create a document using your iMac, you'll want to save it to a disk—that lets you keep the document over the long term. The same goes for applications. If you bought and wanted to use Microsoft Office, you'd need to "install" the application by copying it to your hard disk. That way it's easily accessible to your iMac—your iMac will remember, long term, how to run Microsoft Office.

The Hard Disk Icon

The hard disk icon is always there on the desktop. As the iMac starts up, it looks for the hard disk and other storage disks that are attached to the machine. Any disks found are "mounted" on the desktop. That is, the icon is made to appear on the desktop, available for you to use. The Mac OS automatically places these icons in the top-right corner of the desktop as the iMac is starting up. If you insert a disk (like a CD) after startup, the Mac OS places the CD's icon as close to the top-right corner as it can get without covering up another icon.

To peer into the hard disk's contents, you can point the mouse at the icon and double-click. This opens the main-level window that shows all of the folders used to store things on your iMac. The hard disk icon can be renamed—you can even change the look of the icon—but you can't throw the icon away or store it inside a folder or on another storage device.

 *If you're having trouble renaming your hard disk or another disk (aside from a CD, which can't be renamed), you may have File Sharing turned on. See Chapter 28 for more information on the File Sharing feature.*

The Trash Icon

We'll talk about the Trash in more depth in Chapter 3. Basically, it's the one way you delete things from your hard disks, removable disks, or desktop. You simply drag-and-drop icons onto the Trash. When you've dropped something on the Trash icon, that icon changes to reflect the fact that the Trash is now "full."

That doesn't mean that items have been deleted yet, though. You can still double-click the Trash to open its window, and then drag files or folders out of the Trash and back onto the desktop or your hard disk.

You can't throw the Trash icon away (well, you could try, but good luck) and you can't easily change the name, appearance, or location of the Trash icon. (You can move it around the screen but you can't store it in a folder.) In that respect, it's probably the most stubborn of the desktop icons.

The Trash icon is also used for something else—ejecting CDs and other removable disks. It takes some getting used to, but after you've dragged a CD or removable disk icon to the Trash, it will pop out of its drive (or the CD-ROM drive will open up). Disks are not deleted or erased when dragged to the Trash. There's a special command that erases entire disks when it's necessary to do so.

    Erasing disks is discussed in Chapter 30.

CDs and DVDs

CD and DVD icons appear when you insert a CD or DVD into the CD-ROM or DVD-ROM drive of your iMac. How you insert the disc depends on what type of iMac you have. Earlier iMacs have a tray-loading CD drive that has a button on its front. Press the colored button on the front of your iMac right below the "iMac" label. The CD-ROM tray pops out slightly—you can use a finger to pull it out the rest of the way. Now, place a CD in the tray, label-up, just as you would with an audio CD player. Gently push the tray back into the iMac. Once it snaps shut, the iMac will go to work spinning the CD and taking a look at it.

Newer iMac models offer a "slot-loading" CD or DVD drive. In this case, you insert a CD or DVD the same way you slide them into the slot on a car-stereo CD player. If there's no CD or DVD currently in the iMac, just slide your disc into the open slot. After you've placed it part of the way in, it will be pulled the rest of the way in by its mechanism.

When iMac has recognized the disc, it puts a new icon on the desktop to represent that disc. If the disc is a CD-ROM or DVD-ROM (that is, if they're *data discs* designed to store data files that your iMac can access in the form of icons), then you can double-click the icon to open it and view the files, as shown in Figure 2-5.

FIGURE 2-5   The contents of a data CD

NOTE   *While DVD drives are generally more useful for playing DVD movies, the computer industry is slowly moving toward storing software on DVD-ROM discs, which offer much greater capacity than CD-ROM discs. Eventually, you'll start finding more and more software—especially games, education, and reference titles—available in DVD-ROM format.*

If the disc is an audio CD, you'll see a generic CD icon, probably named "Audio CD 1." In that case, double-clicking the CD icon will open up a window that shows you the different music tracks on the CD. Double-clicking one of the music tracks will open the Apple CD Player and play that track. Also, in most cases audio CDs just start right up when you insert them.

If the disc is a DVD video, then opening it reveals its contents—movie data—in a window. Double-clicking certain items may launch the Apple DVD Player, or you can launch the Apple DVD Player yourself (it's in the Applications folder on your hard disk) and it will automatically detect the presence of a DVD in the drive.

Since a CD-ROM or DVD-ROM is *read-only*, you can't drag an icon from the desktop or your hard disk to the disc icon or window. You can drag icons the other way, though, causing the items on the disc to be copied to your hard disk or desktop. (Actually, stuff copied to your desktop is also stored on your hard disk. You just see it on the desktop.)

To eject the CD or DVD, you can do one of three things. You can select the disc icon with your mouse, then choose File | Put Away in the Finder. That ejects the disc. You can also select the disc and choose Special | Eject. Or, as mentioned before, you can drag the disc icon to the Trash. That ejects the disc; it doesn't erase it.

You can invoke the Put Away and Eject commands using keyboard shortcuts. Put Away is ⌘-Y and Eject is ⌘-E. Just select the icon, then press ⌘ and the appropriate letter key at the same time.

After you eject the disc, if you have a tray-loading iMac, the tray pops out of the front of the iMac (again, you'll pull it the rest of the way out with a finger). If you have a slot-loading iMac, the disc slides gently out of the slot in the front of the iMac. Now you can remove the disc and close the tray (if appropriate) or replace the disc with another one and start again.

Removable Disks

If you have an Iomega Zip drive, a SuperDrive, or some other sort of external storage drive, those disks will appear on your desktop as well. Usually you just pop the disk into the drive and, after a short delay, its icon appears on the desktop. It'll work just like a CD, with the exception that you'll be able to save files to removable storage disks.

You eject removable disks the same way you eject a CD: Select the disk and choose File | Put Away, select the disk and choose Special | Eject, or drag the disk's icon to the Trash.

Printer Icons

Once you've attached your printer and properly set it up in the Chooser (as discussed in Chapter 26), you'll have a new icon on the desktop—a printer icon. The printer icon works a little like the Trash icon, although you can rename the printer icon or store it in a folder if you want.

You can also drag documents onto the printer icon. When you drop them, the document's application is automatically opened and told to print the document; then the document is in the printer queue. The printer icon can be double-clicked to show the items that are in the printer queue to be printed, as shown in Figure 2-6.

In fact, every time you choose the Print command from within an application you create a *print job*. Each job appears in the print queue, which shows you which jobs are planned and their order. You can drag jobs around in the print queue to change their order, or you can select a job and use the buttons in the print queue to pause, start, schedule, and delete jobs.

2

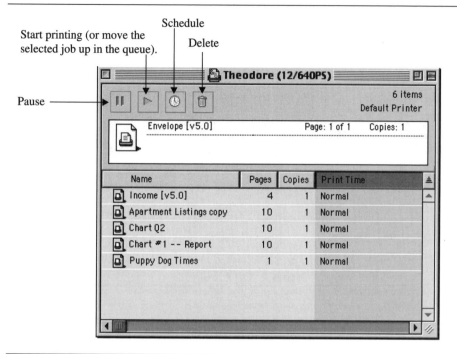

Start printing (or move the
selected job up in the queue).

Schedule

Delete

Pause

FIGURE 2-6   The printer icon opens to reveal the print queue and a few
printer-management commands.

NOTE   *For more on printing and desktop printer icons, see Chapter 26.*

Change Settings with the Control Strip

The easiest way to change settings is through the Control Strip. The Control Strip can be
used to change many things about your iMac's behavior, but we'll focus on a simple task
in this section—changing the sound volume.

Turn on Control Strip

First, if you don't see the Control Strip, you need to do the following:

1. Move your mouse up to the Apple menu and click once to open the menu.

2. Move down to the Control Panels entry. Another menu opens to the side.

3. Slide the mouse over and highlight Control Strip, then click the mouse button.
This opens the Control Strip control panel.

4. Choose Show Control Strip. This is a radio button—just click the button next to the option you want to make active.

5. Click the control panel's close box.

Now the Control Strip should appear on your iMac screen. One of the first things you may need to do is adjust the sound on your iMac. To open the Control Strip, click once on the little tab that appears at the edge of the screen. When you click the tab, the Control Strip pops out, as shown in the following illustration. To close it back up, click the tab again.

Click the tab.

 Want to move the Control Strip around? Point the mouse to the tab and hold down the OPTION key. The mouse pointer turns into a little hand. Now you can drag the Control Strip up and down the side of the screen. If you want to switch sides of the screen, just drag the Control Strip over to the other side.

How to ... Change the Volume

Now, with the Control Strip open, you can adjust the sound volume on your iMac. Here's how:

1. Move the mouse to the small icon that looks like a speaker and click the mouse button.

2. Now, move the mouse up and down the slider bar to choose the volume level.

3. When you've chosen an acceptable level, click the mouse button.

Your iMac reacts by beeping to show you how loud the sound is set. If you're happy with the level, you can click the tab again to close the Control Strip. We'll discuss all the other features of the Control Strip throughout the book.

Get a Quick Start on the Internet

This may seem like an odd place to discuss your first foray onto the Internet, but it so happens that this chapter (and Chapter 1) has covered all the tools necessary for you to get online. Plus, the Internet is just plain important when it comes to working with your iMac (remember, Internet is what the "i" in "iMac" stands for). I'll be discussing the Internet throughout this book (even before we get to a specific discussion of the Internet in Part III). Let's get you online quickly so you can go exploring.

The tools we'll use are the Control Strip, the Browse the Internet icon, and the Mail icon. These last two should appear on your desktop by default.

Sign On to Your ISP (Modem Connections)

If you used the Internet Setup Assistant to create a new Internet account or to enter information about an existing account, everything should be set up for you to dial your iMac's modem and connect to the Internet. Probably the easiest way to do so is through the Control Strip.

> **NOTE** *If you have a different type of connection to the Internet, such as a DSL, cable modem, or Ethernet connection, then you don't need to initiate the connection. Instead, you can generally just begin using your Internet applications, since most of these networking methods are "always-on" connections.*

Open the Control Strip and you should see the Remote Access control—it looks like a little Mac and a telephone pole. This is the control you'll use to sign onto the Internet.

> **NOTE** *This works the same in Mac OS 8.1 if you have an early iMac, but the control is called PPP, not Remote Access.*

Here's how to connect to the Internet:

1. Click once on the control and the Remote Access Control Strip's menu will appear.

2. Make sure your iMac's modem is connected to the phone line and make sure the phone line isn't currently in use. Click Connect.

3. You should hear your iMac pick up the phone and start dialing. (If you don't hear dialing, adjust the iMac's volume as discussed earlier in the "Change Settings with the Control Strip" section.)

4. Now iMac goes through the Internet sign-on phase. If all goes well, the Remote Access control will change and start to show a counting clock that shows the amount of time you've been connected. If things don't work out, you'll see an error message telling you why Remote Access can't sign on.

Once you're connected, you'll also see a blinking icon where the Apple menu's icon appears. The blinking continues for the entire time that you're connected to the Internet. You're ready to run Internet programs.

 *If you want a little more feedback while you're trying to get connected, choose the Remote Access control, then choose Open Remote Access from the menu. This opens the entire Remote Access control panel, where you can watch the connection and change settings according to instructions in Chapter 23.*

Browse the Internet

Once you're connected to the Internet, you can double-click the Browse the Internet icon in order to start up your Web browser and begin to explore the Internet. By default, this launches Internet Explorer (see Figure 2-7).

What you'll most often do on the Internet is read documents and click links to new documents. Sometimes you'll do other things, such as filling in forms and downloading files, which we'll discuss in depth in Chapter 19.

If you want to get a quick start, though, here are the basics:

- A *hyperlink* is text that appears underlined and in blue. (Images and buttons on the page can also be hyperlinks.) Click a hyperlink once with the mouse to open a new Web page. Hyperlinks are the basic method for "browsing" on the Web—click a link you think is interesting to see the associated document.

- The *Back* and *Forward* buttons are used to move to a previous page, then forward again (if desired). If you click a hyperlink, for instance, read the page, and then decide to go back to the previous page, click the Back button.

Back   Forward   Go to Home page   Address box

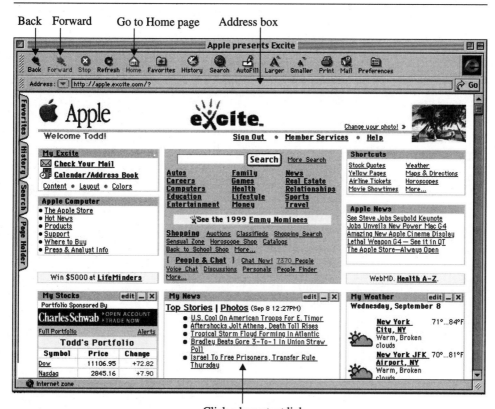

Click a hypertext link.

FIGURE 2-7	Internet Explorer is a Web browser—an application that allows you to browse the World Wide Web and other parts of the Internet.

■ The *address box* is used to enter direct Web page addresses and other sorts of addresses, as discussed in Part III. It's in the address box that you'll type addresses (like **http://www.apple.com/**), then press RETURN to visit that address. You should enter addresses as precisely as possible including all the dots (.) and slashes (/).

Other than that, just experiment with the other buttons and settings. You'll notice that there are already some preprogrammed Favorites that allow you to visit interesting spots on the Internet, and there are buttons for changing preferences, changing the text size, or going directly to a "search" page where you can enter keywords and find new Web pages to visit.

To quit Internet Explorer, choose File | Quit from the menu. Once you've quit the browser, you might also want to sign off of the Internet so you don't keep the phone line tied up. That's discussed later in the section "Sign Off of Your ISP."

 *If you don't see the Browse the Internet icon on the desktop, it may have been thrown away. In Mac OS 8.6 and earlier, you can invoke the same command by clicking on the Apple menu, then clicking the Internet Access item. Now, click Browse the Internet.*

Get Your Mail

We'll discuss this one *really* briefly. Double-click the Mail icon on the desktop and (by default) Outlook Express appears. If this is the first time you've run Outlook Express, you may see a dialog box with a bunch of settings. If you've already used the Internet Setup Assistant, you can just click OK in this settings dialog box.

Now, in the main Outlook Express window, you'll see the mail interface, as shown in Figure 2-8.

If your Internet connection is up and active, click the Send and Receive button. This causes Outlook Express to sign onto your e-mail server computer (which is at your Internet Service Provider's location) and get any e-mail you have waiting.

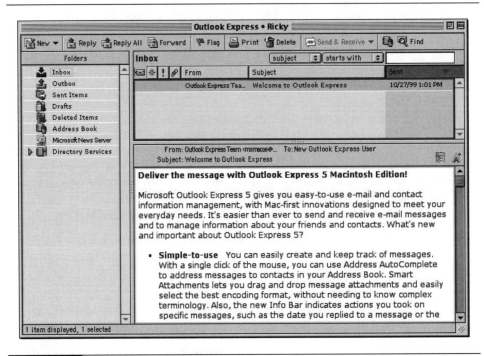

FIGURE 2-8   The Outlook Express 5.0 interface

Once retrieved, new e-mail appears in the top-right window pane. All you'll see is the subject line and information about who sent the message and when. New mail is boldfaced. To read a message, click once on the name of the message. Its contents appear in the bottom-right pane of the window.

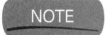

If you don't see your new messages, make sure you have the Inbox selected in the left pane of the Outlook Express window. If you have it selected and you still don't see any messages, it probably means you haven't received any new messages.

While you're reading the message you can elect to reply to or forward the message by clicking the appropriate button in the toolbar. If you forward or create a new message, you'll need make sure you've entered the recipient's e-mail address in the To: line of the message (it's automatically placed there if you're replying), then enter your message in the body of the message window. When you're finished, click Send Now (see Figure 2-9).

Of course, there's a heck of a lot more you can do. If any of this is confusing or you need more information, Chapter 18 discusses e-mail in depth. To quit Outlook Express,

FIGURE 2-9 Composing an e-mail message in Outlook Express 5.0

choose File | Quit from the menu. Once you've quit the e-mail program, you might also want to sign off of the Internet so you don't keep the phone line tied up.

Sign Off of Your ISP (Modem Connections)

When you're done with the Internet connection over a modem, you can select the Remote Access control in the Control Strip again. You'll have the option to Disconnect—click it. After a few seconds, you're disconnected and your phone line is ready to be used again.

Chapter 3

Manage Your Files with the Finder

How to...

- Dig through and organize Finder windows
- Select and move icons in the Finder
- Create folders, duplicate files, and deal with aliases
- Delete files and toss out the Trash
- Get information on your disks, folders, and files
- Organize your iMac with folders, aliases, and labels
- Change the way you view your folders

W hen you first start up your iMac, in addition to seeing the desktop, you're also seeing the application that creates the desktop—the Finder.

The Finder is a special application that's always active and can't easily be "quit." It's the Mac OS's built-in application for dealing with the files on your hard drive, CD-ROM or DVD-ROM drive, and removable media. It does some other important things, too.

Finder 101: Windows

The Finder offers you the tools for a basic filing system on your iMac. It allows you to create and name folders, move documents around, store application programs where you want them, and delete icons of all sorts when necessary. In a way, it's convenient to think of the Finder as an icon management utility.

You've already seen that the Finder is also responsible for helping you manage the iMac itself. For instance, it offers you the commands to shut down, restart, or put your iMac to sleep. The Finder also provides the About this Computer command in the Apple menu, which allows you to view how system RAM is being used by applications.

Most of all, though, the Finder is about managing files.

In fact, the Finder works a little like a filing cabinet. Open the cabinet (that is, open a disk), root through folders, and create new ones when you need to file away documents for a new project. The only difference is that you have to do all this on your computer screen. (Oh, and you never have to run out for any of those smelly markers from the office supply store.)

NOTE   *If you're used to Microsoft Windows, you may be happy or unhappy to learn that the iMac really doesn't have an equivalent to the File Manager or Windows Explorer. Instead, you just use the Finder method of opening and closing folders to organize your files. Windows 95/98 has a similar capability, allowing you to open folders from the My Computer icon to view their contents. Since this is the only way to manage files on your iMac, though, the Finder's use of drag-and-drop is much more sophisticated.*

Dig Deep into Finder Windows

The Finder doesn't really help you *search* for things in an automated way—that's for Sherlock to do, as discussed in Chapter 6. Instead, the Finder helps you organize and look for things manually.

In a way, it's like comparing a library card catalog system to a computerized library search system. With the Finder, you'll be opening a lot of drawers and flipping through a lot of cards.

The most basic way to find something in the Finder is to dig for it. To do that, start out at the desktop and double-click the icon for your hard disk, CD-ROM, or removable disk. This opens the window for that device so you can see its folders. Then, find the folder you want to look in next and double-click it. That folder's window opens. Keep double-clicking folders until you find the item you're looking for, as shown in Figure 3-1.

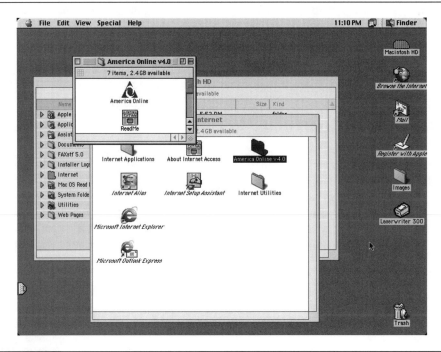

FIGURE 3-1 Dig into your iMac's folders using the Finder.

After a while, this can get tedious. Still, it's easier to find the icon you're looking for when your folders are subdivided.

 There's a special trick to getting through many windows while keeping Finder clutter to a minimum: Hold down the OPTION key as you open new windows. Every time you open a new window, the previous one will close behind you if you're holding down OPTION as you double-click.

Move Icons to Finder Windows

A big part of using the Finder is mastering drag-and-drop. You'll move files and folders around a lot in the Finder—from one folder to another, for instance. You do that by dragging the icon in question from one part of the Finder and dropping it on another part.

TIP *Here's a neat trick. Say you have a window open but you want to view the window of the folder or drive that contains the folder you're looking at. (In computing parlance, we'd call that the "parent folder.") Hold down the ⌘ key and click the name of the folder in the title bar. A little menu appears allowing you to open parent folders to view their contents.*

Spring-Loaded Folders

The Finder offers some interesting ways to accomplish your dragging and dropping. Consider this: What if you have a file on the desktop that needs to go into a subfolder—say, a folder named Memos inside the folder named Documents? If the file you're moving is on the desktop, you have two choices. First, you can open the Macintosh HD by double-clicking; then you open the Documents folder by double-clicking; then you open the Memos folder. With the Memos window open on the screen, you could drag your file into that window. But that's messy.

The better way to get that file into a particular folder is to use the spring-loaded folders feature in the Finder. Pick up the icon you want to move (point the mouse pointer at it and hold down the mouse button) and drag it over to the Macintosh HD icon.

Now, leave it on top of the icon (so that the Macintosh HD icon is highlighted) for a few seconds. Keep holding down the mouse button—don't drop the file yet. Suddenly, the Macintosh HD window springs open! Now, locate the Documents folder icon and do the same thing—keep holding down the mouse button while hovering over the Documents icon. It'll spring open, too. You can keep doing that until you reach the folder you want to drop the icon in. When you get there, release the mouse button and you've successfully moved the icon. In fact, this feature is so cool that the other windows will close as you open the next window, just to keep things neat and tidy.

Pop-Up Windows

Here's another cool feature of Finder windows. If you have a window open that you use a lot—like the Documents window—you can keep it open all the time, but out of the way. Just grab the window by its title bar and drag it to the bottom of the screen. Get far enough down and suddenly the window becomes anchored to the bottom and the title bar becomes a little tab, as shown in Figure 3-2.

You can also select any open window in the Finder and choose View | As Pop-up Window from the Finder's menu to change it into a pop-up window.

To open the window and see its contents, just click the tab once. The window pops up. If you want to drag an item to a pop-up window, just hover over the tab itself (with the dragged item in tow) and the window pops up to reveal its contents.

You can also resize the window using the little resize tools (the diagonal lines) on the side of each pop-up window.

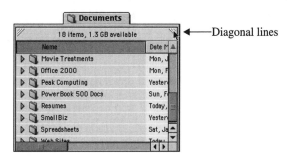

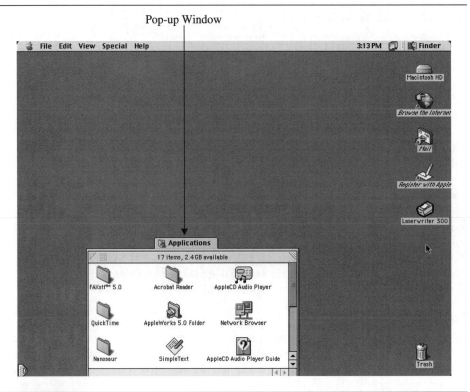

Pop-up Window

FIGURE 3-2   Tabbed windows are a great way to store often-used windows accessibly, yet out of the way.

To turn a pop-up window back into a regular window, just drag the tab up until the outline turns into a normal window. Release the mouse button and the window is back to normal. You can also select the pop-up window and choose View | As Window to change it into a regular window.

Select Items in the Finder

You already know how to select items and how to drag-and-drop. But what if you want to gather more than one icon at a time? There are two ways to do it.

First, you can select more than one icon at a time by dragging a box around the items. Here's how:

1. Place the mouse pointer just above and to the left of the first icon you want to select.

2. Hold down the mouse button and drag the mouse pointer toward the icon you want to select.

3. Once the first icon is highlighted, keep dragging diagonally to expand the box you're creating. As you expand the box, every item inside the box becomes highlighted.

4. When you've highlighted everything you wanted to highlight, release the mouse button (see Figure 3-3).

Now you have multiple items highlighted. Click and drag one of the items and they all come along—you can treat them all as if they were a single icon, moving them *en masse* to a different folder, to the printer icon, to the Trash, opening them all using the File | Open command, and so on. To deselect them, just click anything else on the screen (such as part of the desktop or a different icon).

If you want to add icons that aren't grouped together on the screen, you can add them individually by holding down the SHIFT key as you select each icon. Now, each time you click another icon with the SHIFT key held down, it gets added to all the others that are highlighted, as shown in Figure 3-4.

SHORTCUT *Want to find a particular file in a folder? You can just begin typing its name. Type an **S**, for instance, and "Sales Presentations" might be selected; type **SI** and "Simple Plan" might be selected; type **SIZ** and "Sizing Reports" might be highlighted. Keep typing letters in the name of the file or folder you want to select until it's highlighted.*

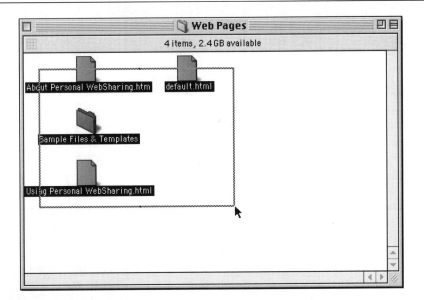

FIGURE 3-3 Drag a square around multiple icons that you want to highlight.

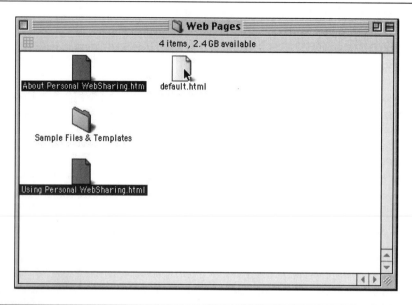

FIGURE 3-4 The SHIFT key lets you select icons that aren't physically close to one another.

Remember that these selections don't just work in Icon view windows—you can drag a rectangle around List view windows as well, and you can select additional items in List view windows using the SHIFT key. (List view and other views are discussed toward the end of this chapter in the section "Change How Folders Are Displayed in the Finder.")

Get Information from Finder Windows

You can actually learn quite a bit about your iMac's hard disk and any other disks you have attached to your iMac from their Finder windows. That's because the Finder windows are usually doing a little math in the background for you.

One of the main concerns you may have as a computer owner is maintaining your hard disk and making sure you have enough space to store new files. It's a constant struggle that may keep you up nights. Often, the only answer is to delete older files that you don't use anymore—at least once your disk gets a little closer to full. But how can you tell if your drive is getting full?

Look at a Finder window. If you open the Macintosh HD window (or any folder window) and take a look at the top of it, you'll see some information about the Macintosh HD, as shown in Figure 3-5. Specifically, you'll see how many items are in that folder and how much storage space is left on that particular disk. This works just as well with a CD-ROM or removable disk, too.

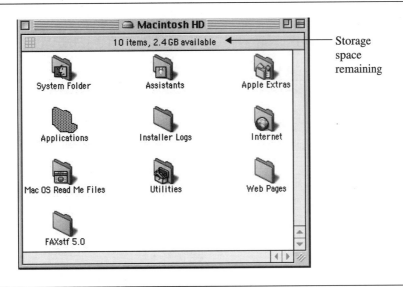

Storage space remaining

FIGURE 3-5   Finder windows show you how much storage space is remaining on that disk.

Finder 201: Create Folders, Copy Files, and Build Aliases

Before you get too busy moving things around, you'll need to create some folders you can move things into. You'll also find that it's often important to duplicate items or create aliases to those items. The Finder is designed to help you do just that.

Create a New Folder

You'll probably learn pretty quickly that it's a good idea to create folders of your own and store them on your hard disk or within other folders. For instance, I think it's a good idea to create a folder called Documents almost right away. We'll discuss a method for storing documents later in this chapter, but it's generally good to have a single Documents folder on your hard drive that contains subfolders where you organize all of your documents. That way, you always know where your documents are. It also makes it easier to back up your documents—copy them to a removable disk—for safekeeping.

To create a new folder, open and select the window where you'd like the folder to appear. (If you want it to appear on the desktop, you don't need to select a window.) Then, choose File | New Folder. (You can also just press ⌘-N.)

When the folder appears, its name is already highlighted. Just type to give the folder a new name. When you're done naming it, press RETURN. Now you have a new folder, as shown in Figure 3-6.

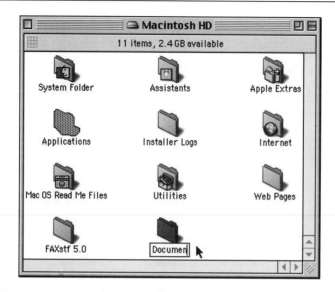

FIGURE 3-6   A new folder, created and named in the Finder

You'd think the next logical step would be creating a document, right? Well, you can't really create a document in the Finder—that's what applications like AppleWorks do. You'll be creating documents soon enough (in Chapter 5, to be precise). In the meantime, you can *duplicate* existing documents using the Finder.

Create a Duplicate

The Finder makes it easy to move files around, and it makes it simple to create a duplicate of an existing document, application, or folder. All you have to do is select the item and choose File | Duplicate. You could also select the item and press ⌘-D.

Duplicating creates an exact copy of the file, except that no two items can have the same name and be stored in the same folder, so the duplicate gets the appendage "copy" added to its name. Now, if you like, you can move that duplicate to another folder and rename it.

Remember, this is a duplicate of the original and it no longer has a relationship to the original file. For instance, if you had a memo document called *Memo to Bob* and you created a duplicate, you'd now have two memos. If you subsequently opened the duplicate memo in AppleWorks and edited it to say "Dear Sue," the original *Memo to Bob* would not be altered. Only the copy is affected.

Another note about duplicating—it takes up space. Every file you create takes up space on the hard disk in your iMac. If you create many duplicates, then you'll be filling up your hard disk. Instead, you might want to consider creating aliases.

SHORTCUT *Instead of duplicating the file, moving it, and then renaming it, how about duplicating the file "on the fly"? It's easy. Pick up the original icon you want to duplicate and drag it to the location where you want the duplicate to appear (you can use spring-loaded folders and all that jazz). Now, when you're in the final spot for the duplicate, hold down the OPTION key. Did you see the pointer turn into a plus sign? That means when you let go of the mouse button, a duplicate will be created. Keep holding down the OPTION key and release the mouse button. Your duplicate is made.*

Create an Alias

In Mac parlance, an *alias* is simply an icon that represents another file. For instance, when the desktop first appears on a brand-new iMac, some aliases to Mail and Browse the Internet appear. These alias icons point toward real files buried deep in the Internet folder. The aliases are on the desktop for convenience.

There are a couple of advantages to creating aliases for your important files:

- ■ **Convenience** Say you have the real AppleWorks icon buried three folders deep on your hard disk. If you like, you can create an alias icon for AppleWorks right on your desktop.

- ■ **Size** Aliases are very small files—unlike a duplicate, an alias isn't a complete copy of the file. It's basically just an icon. So you can have many aliases in different folders on your iMac and still not be taking up too much storage space.

- ■ **Safety** Why is it safer to create aliases? Because if you (or a co-worker, partner, or kid) throw away an alias, the original item doesn't get destroyed. If I take that AppleWorks alias I created and trash it, for instance, then AppleWorks itself is unharmed back in the Internet Applications subfolder. However, if I had dragged the actual program out to the desktop and trashed it, I'd be in trouble. The actual program would have been deleted.

Convinced? If so, get started creating aliases. In the Finder, select the file for which you'd like an alias. Then, choose File | Make Alias or press ⌘-M.

An alias appears, complete with italicized text and the word "alias" appended to the name. Now you can move the alias anywhere you want to and rename it, if desired.

SHORTCUT *Want to create an alias that immediately appears in its final resting place? Here's how: Drag the original icon to the place where you want the alias to appear—you can use the spring-loaded folders or just drag it to the desktop. Now, instead of letting go, hold down the OPTION and ⌘ keys. See the pointer turn into a little curved arrow? That means when you drop the icon, it'll create an alias instead of moving the original. Keep holding down OPTION and ⌘, then let go of the mouse button. Voilà! Your alias is ready.*

Find the Alias's Original

Sometimes an alias just isn't good enough—you need to deal with the real file. If that's the case, you can select the alias's icon and choose File | Show Original (or press ⌘-R). This will cause the folder containing the alias's original file to appear in the Finder.

Fix an Alias

Aliases can break sometimes—suddenly, the alias will no longer point to its original file. This happens for a variety of reasons, but mostly it happens because you move, delete, or otherwise mangle the original file. Perhaps you have an alias to Internet Explorer on your desktop, then you install a new version of Internet Explorer. The alias on your desktop points to the older version (which you've since deleted, let's say) and not the new one.

If an alias can't find its original, this dialog box appears:

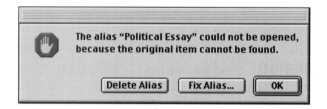

If you don't need the alias anymore, you can click Delete Alias and the alias will trouble you no longer. (Actually, it's simply been moved to the Trash, not permanently deleted.) If you want to continue to use the alias, click Fix Alias and the Fix Alias dialog box appears. Find the file you want the alias to point to, select it in the dialog box, and click Choose. Now the alias is pointing to the chosen file. (The Fix Alias dialog box works just like the Open dialog box, which is discussed in Chapter 5.)

Finder 301: Delete Icons

The Mac OS really only offers one way to delete Finder icons—by moving them to the Trash can. Actually, this is a good thing, because it makes you think carefully about what you're doing before you make a mistake and accidentally delete something. (Ask one of your Unix- or DOS-using friends if they've ever accidentally deleted something.) Plus, the Trash offers a way to recover files before they're permanently deleted, even if they've already been thrown away.

Toss Icons

If you're pretty sure you don't need a particular item anymore, you can drag it straight from its current location in the Finder to the Trash. Just drag the icon over the Trash until the Trash icon becomes highlighted, then release the mouse button. The item is dropped and the Trash can becomes "full." (The Trash's icon changes so that the lid is off and you can see bits of "trash" inside.) You can throw out multiple files just as easily—select them all by dragging a box around them or holding down the SHIFT key, then drag the group to the Trash icon.

If this is all too much mousing for you, there are three other ways to move files to the Trash:

- With the file(s) selected in the Finder, choose ⌘-DELETE to move items to the Trash.

- Select the file(s) in the Finder and choose File | Move to Trash from the menu.

- CTRL-click on a file, then choose Move to Trash from the contextual menu.

Retrieve Items from the Trash

Just because an item has been thrown in the Trash doesn't mean it's been deleted. If you have something in the Trash that you need to get back, just double-click the Trash icon. This opens the Trash window, allowing you to see everything that's been thrown away. When you find what you need, you can drag it back out of the Trash onto the desktop or into another window.

Documents and applications can't be launched from the Trash—they must be dragged out to a folder or the desktop before they can be used.

Empty the Trash

The step that really gets rid of the items in the Trash is emptying the Trash. Once it's been emptied, you can't get those items back. (Unfortunately, there's no "iMac Dumpster" to go rooting through.)

Think carefully before emptying the Trash. If you delete something accidentally, you'll have to buy a special utility program, like Norton Utilities, to get the item back.

If you're sure you want to get rid of the items in the Trash can and reclaim the storage space that they're taking up, then choose Special | Empty Trash. The Finder will count up the items in the Trash and tell you how many items will be deleted and how much space you'll recover. If that all sounds good, click OK. Once you click OK, the files are gone forever (at least, without a special recovery utility program). Say "Bye, bye!"

Want to skip the alert box that tells you how much stuff will be thrown away? Hold down the OPTION key as you choose Special | Empty Trash. The Trash is emptied immediately.

What do you do if you really, really didn't want to delete a file and you've emptied the Trash? Well, it may require a special purchase. There's a chance it can be recovered, especially if you haven't used the disk much after emptying the trash, but you'll need a special program like Norton Utilities. See Chapter 30 for tips on getting yourself out of trouble spots like an accidentally tossed file.

If you do want to undelete files, the best plan is to stop using the iMac until you get your undelete utility program. That way, the iMac won't overwrite the area where the thrown-out files used to be on the disk. If the files are overwritten (usually by new, saved files you create) then they're almost impossible to recover.

Finder 401: Get Information on Files

Another unique Finder responsibility is the Get Info command, which allows you to learn more about files in the Finder. The Get Info command can be used to tell you how much storage space an item takes up, who created the item, and any comments that have been stored about that item.

To get info, select the item in the Finder and choose File | Get Info. The Get Info dialog box appears, offering you information about the selected file, as shown in Figure 3-7. (Note that the Get Info dialog box's title bar name changes for the individual item you're getting info on.)

In the Get Info dialog box you'll see information based on the type of file selected— that is, an alias offers different information from a folder, which is different from an application. You may also see a special pull-down menu, which you can use to switch between General Information and information on Sharing (networking) and Memory, depending on the type of item you're getting information on.

To close the Get Info box, click its Close box.

Want to learn more about your hard disk or other storage device? Get info on it. There you'll see how much storage space the drive initially offered, how much is being used, and how much is left.

Finder Grad School: Get Organized

With all these Finder concepts under your belt, you're ready for the next step—getting your files organized. I realize you may not yet have a ton of documents and applications since you haven't gotten around to working with them much. Actually, that's a good thing. The earlier you implement a good organizational scheme, the better your entire experience with your iMac will be.

One of the main reasons to get organized is to make it easier to back up your data. *Backing up* is the process—automated or not—of systematically copying your documents and important files from your iMac's hard disk to some other storage facility—either to removable media like SuperDisks or Zip disks, or to a network drive or an Internet backup

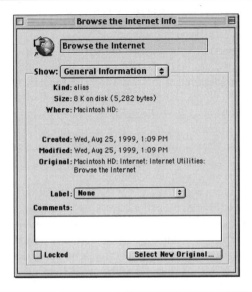

FIGURE 3-7   The Get Info box tells you basic information about your files.

area. You do that in case catastrophe strikes; for example, if your hard disk fails or an errant program (or virus) destroys data on your iMac. In most cases your data can be worth a lot to you, so you'll definitely want to back it up.

The best way to be ready for backing up is to store things in an organized fashion. You've already seen that it's a good idea to create a Documents folder and save all of your creative work in that folder—that way, you can easily back up all of the documents you create by dragging the folder to a removable media disk icon. (Your applications and the Mac OS don't necessarily have to be backed up, since you can always restore them from the CD-ROMs included with your iMac and subsequent application purchases. It's not a bad idea to back up your application *preferences*, though, as discussed in Chapter 27.)

Of course, organization goes beyond backup. Once you get a couple hundred files on your hard disk, you'll begin to find that you don't know immediately where everything is. In that case, you'll want a little help through organization.

TIP   *If you don't already have one, create a folder called Documents on your hard disk. Then, open the General Controls control panel (choose Apple | Control Panels | General Controls). In that control panel you can select the Documents Folder option down in the bottom-right corner of the control panel under the heading "When opening or saving a document, take me to..." Now, when you're working in an application, your Open or Save dialog box should open right to the Documents folder.*

Organize Documents Using Aliases

Should you save documents by type or by the project they relate to? If you want, you can use aliases to help you track your projects in their own folder. For example, as a freelance writer, I often send out invoices on projects I'm working on. I like to have all my invoices in the same folder (called Invoices) so I can see how many have gone out, what I numbered them, and so on. But what if I've created a folder called "Ergo County Consulting Project" and I want to store the invoices related to that project in that folder as well? Easy enough—I just create an alias to the invoice and put it in the project folder.

The best part about the alias is that I can double-click it to launch the document, but it's not a duplicate of the original—since it's an alias, I'm always changing the actual copy. And, I can delete the alias without harming the original.

See how useful aliases can be? You can put them on the desktop, you can put them in project folders. One of my favorite uses of aliases is to create folders that are specifically for a given project. You can put any alias you want in the folder—even an alias to the applications you want to use or documents that are normally buried deep on your iMac's hard disk. Then, you can store the entire project folder on the desktop until you're done with the project (see Figure 3-8). At the end of the project you can either file away the project folder or delete all the aliases and leave the originals intact.

SHORTCUT *Create your project folder in the Documents folder itself—or wherever you eventually want the folder stored—then drag it out to the desktop. Now, when you're done with the project folder, you can choose File | Put Away in the Finder to automatically send the folder to its storage space in the Documents folder. Cool, huh?*

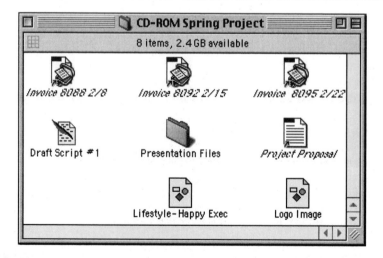

FIGURE 3-8   Aliases allow you to create project folders that can be used to temporarily store aliases to documents and applications you plan to use frequently.

3

Use Labels to Organize

The Finder is capable of giving individual folders or items a special label that marks the folder with a particular priority and changes the color of the folder or icon. That may not seem immediately important, but it has some sophisticated implications.

To change the label on an item, choose the item in the Finder, then choose File | Label. A number of label options pop up in the Label menu. Choose one of those color labels and it's assigned to the selected icon, as shown in Figure 3-9.

Why do this? First, a folder with a certain color may come to mean important things to you—that it needs immediate attention, that it's a project folder holding a bunch of aliases, or something along those lines. Perhaps more importantly, though, you'll often encounter applications and utilities that can read the label and do something accordingly— for instance, you might label a particular folder as "Hot" and have an automatic backup program choose to back up all Hot folders. You can even search your hard drive using Sherlock (discussed in Chapter 6) to find all the Hot folders or a similar label.

Fortunately, you can change the label names. Choose Edit | Preferences in the Finder and click the Labels tab. Now, click in the box where you see the name of each label and edit it to suit your needs. You could label things according to backup priority, according to the names of everyone who uses your iMac (Little Billy's file folders are all in Purple), or for whatever other reasons strike your fancy.

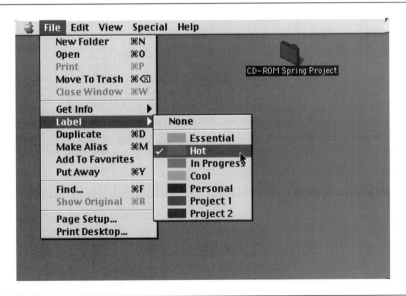

FIGURE 3-9   Assign a label to icons you want specifically flagged.

Change How Folders Are Displayed in the Finder

While we're on the topic of changing the way things look, managing the way your Finder windows appear can go a long way toward helping you find files. To change the way you view a Finder window, open that window and select it in the Finder, then choose the appropriate view from the View menu. The Finder offers three basic options when it comes to how the Finder window displays its files:

■ **As Icons** In this view, the window is filled with icons that can be arranged any way you like. This is the default view in most cases.

■ **As Buttons** Buttons are like icons except they only require a single click to activate them. (To select, rename, and drag-and-drop a button, select its name instead of its icon, since a single click activates them.) Buttons are an odd way to arrange most windows, although not a bad idea for a quick pop-up window at the bottom of the Finder screen that could be filled with application aliases. That makes a quick mini-launcher that can be very convenient.

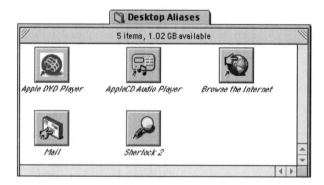

■ **As List** If you have a lot of items in a particular folder window, this is the way to go. Viewing as a list allows you to do two things. First, you get a whole lot of files on the screen at once in a very orderly manner, as shown in Figure 3-10. Second, you can use the little triangles to look inside subfolders without doing a lot of double-clicking.

Customize the List View

Once you have a folder in List view, you can do some other things to make that folder work better for you. At the top of the window, you'll find column listings for the different information that's offered about each file. Place the mouse pointer between two columns and it'll change to a little cursor with an arrow coming out of each side. That's your cue that you can drag the column divider to change the width of the column.

Want to change the order of List view columns? Go up to the column head name and click and hold the mouse button. Now drag the mouse pointer to the left or right—the

3

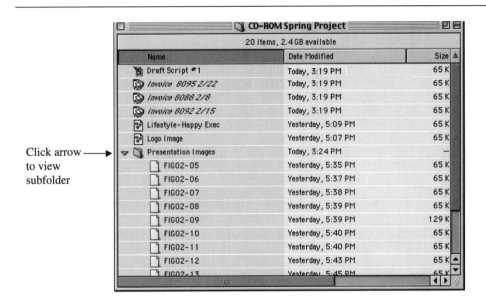

Click arrow →
to view
subfolder

FIGURE 3-10   The List view makes it easy to see a lot of items quickly.

pointer changes to a hand and you're able to move the column to wherever you'd like it in the window. Let go of the mouse button to drop the column in place.

To order the window according to a particular column, just click that column's heading name. To view your files organized by date created, for instance, just click the Date Created column head. You can also change the order of that listing by clicking the direction control—now the listing switches from ascending to descending or vice versa (see Figure 3-11).

Don't like what you've done? You can choose View | Reset Column Positions to put the columns back the way you found them.

Arrange Other Views

If you're not in List view, there's still some arranging you can do. In Icon and Button views, you can select the Finder window, then choose View | Arrange. That brings up a menu that lets you choose how you'd like your icons arranged.

If you want your Icon and Button views to appear a bit more uniform, you can select the window in the Finder, then choose View | Clean Up. This will move the icons or buttons around so that they're equally spaced and as many as possible fit in the open window.

TIP   *With any Finder window you can click the resize box to automatically reshape the window to display all or as many files as possible. Hold down the OPTION key and click the resize box to maximize the window onscreen.*

Click the column name to sort by its contents

Drag the column to change its location

Point here to change column widths

Click the direction button to change the sorted order

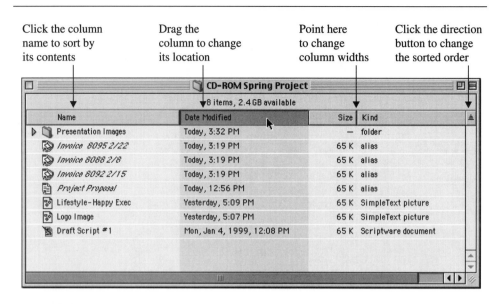

Name	Date Modified	Size	Kind
▷ 📁 Presentation Images	Today, 3:32 PM	—	folder
📄 *Invoice 8095 2/22*	Today, 3:19 PM	65 K	alias
📄 *Invoice 8088 2/8*	Today, 3:19 PM	65 K	alias
📄 *Invoice 8092 2/15*	Today, 3:19 PM	65 K	alias
📄 *Project Proposal*	Today, 12:56 PM	65 K	alias
📄 Lifestyle-Happy Exec	Yesterday, 5:09 PM	65 K	SimpleText picture
📄 Logo Image	Yesterday, 5:07 PM	65 K	SimpleText picture
📄 Draft Script #1	Mon, Jan 4, 1999, 12:08 PM	65 K	Scriptware document

CD-ROM Spring Project — 8 items, 2.4 GB available

FIGURE 3-11   Click a column head to sort by that column.

Auto-Arrange the View

Choosing View | Arrange rearranges your Finder windows just that one time. Would you like it to be arranged all the time? That's easy enough. Select the window in the Finder, then

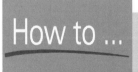 **Drop Items in the List View**

One peril of using the List view (and this occasionally happens in some other views as well) is that it can be tough to drop items in the open folder window, especially if you have a lot of subfolders in that window (or if you're trying to drag something *from* a subfolder in that same window). Here's the trick—if you want to drop something in the current folder, drag it to the little information bar at the top of the window, just below the title bar. Release the mouse button to drop the item. This drops it in the main folder instead of in one of the subfolders.

choose View | View Options. In the View Options dialog box, you can choose to have the window automatically arrange icons. The choices are

- **None**   The icons will not be auto-arranged.

- **Snap to Grid**   The icons won't be put in any particular order, but they will always appear in uniform rows and columns, no matter where you drag-and-drop them within the window.

- **Keep Arranged**   This option allows you to force the window to automatically keep icons in order at all times, even when new icons are dropped into the folder. Choose the radio button next to this option to activate it, then choose *how* to arrange the icons from the pull-down menu.

- **Set to Standard View**   This button at the bottom of the View Options window allows you to set the window to whatever has been set as the "standard" for this sort of view (Icon, Button, or List). It just looks up the setting in the Finder Preferences settings and applies it to the selected Finder window.

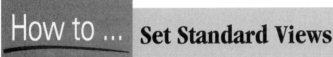

How to ... Set Standard Views

Choose Edit | Preferences in the Finder. In the Finder Preferences dialog box, choose the Views tab. Now, choose the standard view you'd like to edit from the menu (Icon, Button, or List), then use the check box options to change the standard view. Click the Close box to close Finder Preferences—your changes are automatically applied to all Finder windows that are set to Standard view.

Chapter 4

Pull Down the Apple Menu

How to...

- Learn about the Apple menu and its special qualities
- Explore the desktop accessories and other items on the Apple menu
- Quickly relaunch items, applications, and servers using the Recent folders
- Add Favorites to the Apple menu
- Add and arrange items on the Apple menu

As I've mentioned, the Apple menu is a sort of junk drawer of the Mac OS. It's where all those little things that might come in handy one day are stored. It's in the Apple menu where you'll find the virtual equivalents of solar-powered calculators, battery-tester packages, and fingernail clippers.

Actually, some of that is true. The Apple menu is a repository for a number of small programs, called *desk accessories*, which allow you to quickly manage small tasks and deal with printers, networks, and other devices that are connected to your iMac. Plus, it's a great place to find shortcuts and other tools to help you use your iMac more efficiently.

What Is the Apple Menu?

The Apple menu is the menu on the far left of the iMac's menu bar that, instead of bearing a name, is represented by the six-color Apple logo. Pull down that menu and you'll gain access to all sorts of settings, small programs, and shortcut menus.

Here's an important tidbit about the Apple menu: It's always there. The Apple menu is always on the menu bar regardless of whether or not you're in the Finder. It's part of the overall Mac OS, a permanent fixture no matter what application you're currently using. That means you can access the Apple menu at any time, regardless of what you're doing. Plus, everything on the Apple menu stays the same when you move from menu to menu. So, you'll always be able to access everything that's on the Apple menu, even if you're working in different applications.

But the Apple menu is even more interesting than that. Unlike most menus, the Apple menu is completely customizable. In fact, all of its contents are stored in a regular folder that's in the System Folder on your iMac's hard disk. That means you can very easily add to or remove from the menu anything you want.

And the Apple menu is hierarchical. That means you can have menu items within the Apple menu that spawn submenus—they just keep traveling across the screen until you run out of menus or run out of room (or you reach five levels, whichever comes first).

By using a feature like Favorites, discussed later in this chapter, it's actually possible to gain access to every file on your hard disk through the Apple menu. This is one seriously high-tech junk drawer (see Figure 4-1).

Overall, the Apple menu works like any other menu—you move the mouse pointer up to the Apple icon, click the mouse button, and the menu appears. Then, move the mouse pointer down the menu until you're pointing at the item you want to select. If it's a menu, it'll have a little arrowhead pointing to the right—another menu will appear directly to the right once the mouse reaches the arrowhead. You can then move to the right and choose something from the new menu. If there's anything that's remarkably different about the Apple menu, it's the simple fact that you're usually launching something—a desk accessory, a control panel, an alias—instead of choosing a command. Most commands in the Finder and in other applications are for performing a task; the Apple menu, on the other hand, is pretty much a quick-launcher.

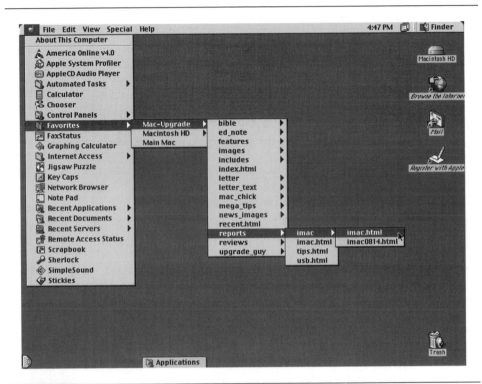

FIGURE 4-1 The Apple menu is sort of a junk drawer for your iMac.

You'll notice that, even visually, the Apple menu differs from most menus since it shows icons in the menu itself.

Items on the Apple Menu

So what's on this menu? Lots of things. Let's cover the different *types* of things you'll find on the menu, then we'll talk more specifically about what you can accomplish with the Apple menu.

Here are the basic types of things that have the right stuff to make it on the Apple menu:

■ **Desk Accessories** Desk accessories are little programs that usually have only one task, like allowing you to take notes or offering some basic calculator functions. They're sort of like the sticky notes and steno pads you might have hanging out on a regular desk.

■ **Control Panels** The Mac OS has special programs called *control panels* that allow you to control various settings on your iMac. These are stored in the System

Folder, but the easiest way to get to them is here, through the Apple menu. Just point at the Control Panels menu item to see a menu of all the control panels.

■ **Aliases**   You can actually put any sort of alias you want on the Apple menu. The Mac OS programmers have gotten you started by dropping aliases to popular utilities on the Apple menu. You may find that some other programs will drop aliases on there, too. America Online, for instance, put an alias to itself on my Apple menu when I installed it.

■ **Menus**   On the Apple menu you'll find a number of submenus that offer you a convenient path to applications, scripts, or aliases on your hard drive. For instance, the Mac OS includes a number of "recent" menus where documents and applications you've recently worked on will appear. (If you don't see any submenus, refer to the section "Customize the Recent Menus," later in this chapter.)

Let's look at each category in turn and see what you can do with all these items.

Desk Accessories

Originally, desk accessories were the only types of program that could multitask on the Macintosh. Very early Macs could only run one application—like a word processor—at a time. So, Apple had to create desk accessories to help out with important tasks that you need to perform while still using the application. That's why they're small, single-function programs like the Calculator or the Note Pad.

These days the line between full-fledged utility program and desk accessory is blurred somewhat. For the most part, desk accessories are stored in the Apple Menu Items folder (instead of being aliases) and they usually don't allow you to create and save documents; they either automatically save your work or are designed to do something quickly on screen. Most of the desk accessories are basic and useful—just choose the Calculator, Graphing Calculator, or Jigsaw Puzzle for some pretty self-explanatory fun. Here are the rest of the desk accessories and what they do:

NOTE   *If you have Mac OS 9 on your iMac (or if you've upgraded to it), you might not find some of these accessory programs on your Apple menu. Instead, they are in the Apple Extras folder or in the Applications folder. That's OK—you can drag them to the Apple Menu Items folder inside your iMac's System Folder and they'll appear on the Apple menu.*

■ **Apple System Profiler**   This utility is designed to tell you quite a bit about the hardware and software installed in and connected to your iMac. (This tool is also good for telling tech support representatives about your iMac when you're talking to them on the phone.)

■ **Apple CD Audio Player**   This accessory allows you to play audio CDs using your iMac's CD-ROM or DVD drive. You'll notice that the controls are just like a

CD player in the real world, as shown in Figure 4-2—play, stop, pause, eject, move forward and backward between tracks, fast forward, and reverse. There's a volume slider control on the right-hand side. Click the Normal, Shuffle, and Prog buttons to choose how you listen to the CD. Click the small triangle and you can see each track individually—you can even click in the CD's title and the track titles and edit them to show the title of each song. The CD Audio Player will recognize the audio CD the next time you insert it and display the names again.

■ **Chooser** The Chooser is a special desk accessory that helps you select printers and connect to networked computers. You can read more about the Chooser in Chapters 23 and 25.

■ **Key Caps** This little program helps you figure out what key combinations you need to press in order to type certain characters. Launch it, then choose the font you want to use from the Font menu. Now, try different modifier keys—⌘, OPTION, CONTROL, SHIFT—in various configurations. The letter keys will change to show you the character that will appear when you press that same combination of modifier keys and that letter key.

FIGURE 4-2   The Apple CD Audio Player lets you groove to CD tunes while you work.

■ **Network Browser**   If your iMac is attached to a network, especially a large one, the Network Browser makes it easy to see all the different machines and hard drives to which you have access. This accessory is discussed in detail in Chapter 28.

■ **Note Pad**   The Note Pad is surprisingly handy. Select it and you're presented with a little window where you can type (or drag-and-drop) plain text on the pad. At the bottom-left corner of the page you'll see a little turned-up corner—click it to move to the next page or click the page below the turned-up corner to move back a page. By default, the Note Pad only has eight pages, but you can easily add pages at the end of the pad by selecting File | New Note. Another cool thing: You don't have to save your notes. Just click the Note Pad's Close box when you're done with it and the notes will be there the next time you access the Note Pad from the Apple menu. Very handy. (I like to use the Note Pad for quickly pasting text I've found while surfing the World Wide Web, as shown in Figure 4-3).

■ **Scrapbook**   The Scrapbook is designed for cutting and pasting multimedia elements that you'd like to save for the future—stuff like pictures, drawings, audio clips, even QuickTime videos. All you have to do is highlight the desired item in an application, then choose Edit | Copy or Edit | Cut. Switch to the Scrapbook and choose Edit | Paste and your clipping is added at the end of the Scrapbook's pages.

4

Click to see the next page ───

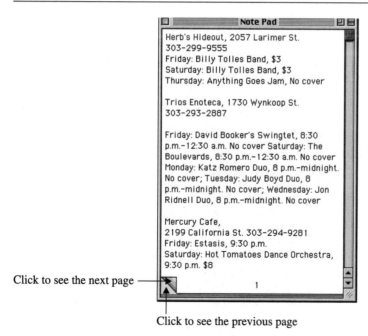

Click to see the previous page

FIGURE 4-3   You can use Note Pad for quick notes or cut-and-paste text from other applications, like your Web browser.

Now, when necessary, you can copy the multimedia clipping out of the Scrapbook and into some other applications. (Note: The Scrapbook is fully drag-and-drop aware, so you can drag-and-drop from applications to the Scrapbook, and vice versa, if you prefer.) To close the Scrapbook, click its Close box. Anything you've pasted into the Scrapbook will be there the next time you launch it—it's saved automatically. To remove something from the Scrapbook, view it, then choose Edit | Clear from the menu.

- **Sherlock** Sherlock (or Sherlock 2, in Mac OS 9) is the high-end search utility, discussed in Chapter 6.

- **Stickies** These ought to look familiar. Launch Stickies from the Apple menu and you've got little sticky notes you can add to your screen, sort of. Just type your message on a note, then position it on the screen; you can choose File | New Note if you need more little colorful opportunities to express yourself. (Choose the colors by selecting a note and then choosing the color from the Color menu.) Stickies don't need to be saved unless you want the note to no longer appear on the screen. In that case, click the note's Close box and you'll be asked if you want to save the note as a text file. I personally leave Stickies open all the time. They can run in the background, then you can switch to them when you need to jot something down or read the notes. You can quit Stickies by choosing File | Quit in the Stickies menu.

Control Panels

Control panels are used to customize and make choices about your iMac. They can range from the droll, like setting the clock or deciding what sort of text the OS should use, to the fun, like the Appearance Manager, which allows you to change the colors and appearance of your iMac's interface.

Throughout this book I'll touch on most of these control panels; a lot of the appearance and customization panels are covered in Chapter 24. All you need to know now is that they're there on the Apple menu, they'll pop right open when you select them in the Control Panels menu, and you can close them all by clicking the Close box.

You might also be interested to know that control panels are stored in the System Folder on your iMac's hard drive in the folder called Control Panels. Any control panels in that folder will appear in the Control Panels menu on the Apple menu.

Aliases

In the Apple menu, you'll also find aliases to applications or utilities that are actually stored elsewhere on the hard disk. Most of these are added by non-Apple installation programs or by you. All you need to do is create the alias and put it in the Apple Menu Items folder in the System Folder. We'll get deeper into that later in this chapter.

Other aliases are added by installers—America Online and FaxSTF, for instance, both add aliases to the Apple menu to make it easier for you to start up an application conveniently or look into things like the status of your fax receiving.

Use the Recent Menus

If they're set up and working, the Recent menus make it easy for you to reload or relaunch a document, application, or network connection that you've used recently. You can set the number of recent items that are tracked and those that you're most interested in.

Select a Recent Menu

To use the Recent menus, just click the Apple menu, then point the mouse at Recent Applications, Recent Documents, or Recent Servers (see Figure 4-4). Then, select the item you'd like to relaunch. Your iMac will switch back to the Finder (if necessary) and launch the application and/or open the document you've chosen.

If you choose a server (actually, a server's disk), you may need to log back into the server to access it. If you're not familiar with the process, consult Chapter 28.

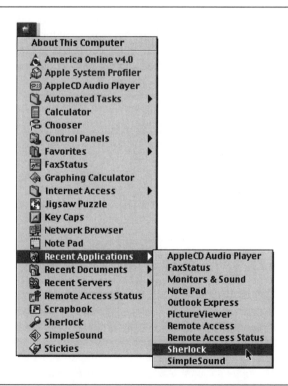

FIGURE 4-4   The Recent menus let you pick documents, applications, or servers that you've worked with recently.

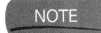 *A "server," in this context, is a computer that your iMac is connected to by networking cables or by wireless AirPort technology, if your iMac is so equipped. The server computer stores documents that are shared by everyone on your network. It may also allow you to print documents and store personal documents in a central location so they can be accessed from other computers.*

Customize the Recent Menus

If you'd like to change the behavior of the Recent menus, you can do so through the Apple Menu Options control panel. Select the Apple menu, then point to the Control Panels. Select the Apple Menu Options control panel. In the control panel you can decide whether or not the Apple menu should have hierarchical menus by clicking the On or Off radio button. (It's probably a good idea to leave them on so that you have access to recent items, but they can slow things down a bit.)

Then you can decide if you want to use the Recent menus; if not, click to make sure there's no check mark in the check box next to the Remember Recently Used Items option. If you are using Recent menus, you can select how many items your iMac remembers—the default is 10. If you want to change that number, just click in the entry box and edit the number. (A reasonable number is probably 25-40. If the number is too large, it may slow down your iMac when you choose the Apple menu. A large number of entries may also be tough to wade through.) When you're done, click the Close box in the Apple Menu Options control panel. Your changes are noted and put into action.

Create and Use Favorites

Favorites are really pretty cool. They allow you to choose parts of the Mac OS and sort of *bookmark* them for future use. If you've used a Web browser much, you might be familiar with this concept of electronic bookmarking. If you've used books much, you're probably also familiar with the concept of bookmarking. Haven't heard of either? Just read on...

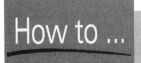 **Delete Entries from Recent Menus**

Open the Apple Menu Items folder that's stored in your System Folder. Now, open the folder that corresponds to the Recent menu you want to clean out. In that folder, each alias corresponds to an entry on that Recent menu; drag any of the aliases to the Trash. Check the Recent menu in the Apple menu; those trashed items should be gone from the menu.

The idea is this: Say you use a folder called Reports in your Documents folder all the time. To open that folder in the Finder, you usually have to double-click the Macintosh HD, then double-click your Documents folder, then double-click the Reports folder. What if, instead, you could just open directly to the folder using a menu in the Apple menu? That's one advantage to using Favorites.

But Favorites do even more than that. First, Favorites actually allow you to create a menu. You do that by choosing a *folder* as a Favorite. The items in that folder become menu items in the associated menu! If you turn your Internet folder into a Favorite, for instance, you'll create an Internet menu under the Favorites menu on the Apple menu. What will show up on that Internet menu? The items that are in the Internet folder (see Figure 4-5).

Second, Favorites show up in the new, advanced Open and Save dialog boxes used by applications written (or rewritten and upgraded) to recognize Mac OS 8.5 and higher. That means, in many cases, you'll be able to access your Favorites as you're trying to open or save documents. That's a nice time-saver, as you'll see in Chapter 5.

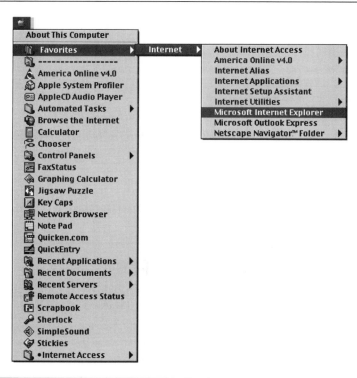

FIGURE 4-5   Creating a Favorite makes that item appear in the Favorites menu on the Apple menu for easy access.

Create a Favorite

Before all this magic can happen for you personally, though, you're going to need to create a Favorite. Follow these steps:

1. Select an item in the Finder—it can be a file, a folder, or even a disk. It's probably best that it's a folder, though. (Select the folder icon, not an open folder window.)

 You can select a disk icon and make it a Favorite, but that will likely slow down your iMac when you access the Apple menu. The iMac is forced to check all of those subfolders (at least, four levels deep) so that it knows what to put on the menus. That can cause a little delay while the Apple menu is opening up.

2. Then choose File | Add to Favorites.

This creates an alias to that item and places it in the Favorites folder that's stored in the Apple Menu Items folder, which, in turn, is in the System Folder on your iMac's hard drive.

Use a Favorite

Once you've got a Favorite created, you can use it immediately:

1. Select the Apple menu and point to the Favorites item. If you have any Favorites created, they'll appear in a menu to the right.

2. Now, point to the Favorite you want to work with. If it's a folder, that folder's contents will appear in yet another menu. In fact, all of the subfolders become menus, too, allowing you to keep moving down the menu items and dig deeper into the subfolders on your iMac's hard disk.

3. Once you find the item you want, you can select it. If you select a folder, it will appear in the Finder. If you select a file, it will be launched. If it's a document, its associated application will also be launched.

Put Your Own Aliases on the Menu

If you'd like to add items directly to the Apple menu instead of going through Favorites, you can do that easily. It works a lot like the Favorites discussed above, except it uses an AppleScript (assuming you want to do this the automatic way).

The Automatic Way

In this case, you'll use an AppleScript to place the item on the Apple menu. All this AppleScript does is make an alias of the selected item and place it in the Apple Menu Items folder, which is in the System Folder. Here's what you do to add an item to the Apple menu:

NOTE *You may not have an Automated Tasks menu in Mac OS 9 or higher.*

4

1. Select the item in the Finder. It can be a drive icon, a folder, or a file.

2. Select the Apple menu and point to the Automated Tasks menu.

3. Select Add Alias to Apple Menu. This is an AppleScript—a small program written in Mac OS's special automating language—that automatically creates an alias of the item and adds it to the Apple Menu Items folder. When it's done you'll see a message that says the alias has been added:

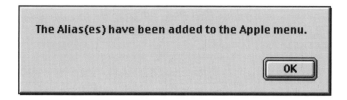

The Alias(es) have been added to the Apple menu.

[OK]

4. Check the Apple menu—you should see your item in the main level of the menu.

The Manual Way

You may have already caught on—if the AppleScript simply adds an alias of the selected icon to the Apple Menu Items folder in the System Folder, then you can do that on your own to the same effect, right? Select an item in the Finder, make an alias of it, and drag that alias to the Apple Menu Items folder in the System Folder. Rename the item if desired. Close the Apple Menu Items folder and check the Apple menu—the new item has been added.

You can also make an alias to a folder or a disk and put it in the Apple Menu Items folder. This creates a new menu on the Apple menu that allows you to access the contents of that folder. Don't forget that folders with many files and subfolders can slow down the Apple menu quite a bit.

TIP *Want to remove items from the Apple menu? Just remove them from the Apple Menu Items folder (drag them to the Trash or to a different folder). Once they've been removed from the Apple Menu Items folder, they'll no longer appear on the Apple menu.*

Shuffle the Order of Items

While you're in the Apple Menu Items folder, you might want to take advantage of the moment and reshuffle items in the Apple menu. As a rule, items are listed alphabetically. Changing the order of items is as simple as renaming them so that they show up in the alphabet where you want them on the menu.

In general, you'll probably want to move certain items to either the top of the menu or the bottom. If you don't feel like giving them new names, you can use this trick: Putting a blank space at the beginning of a menu item's name will put it at the top of the menu. Similarly, putting a bullet point (⌘-8) at the beginning of an item's name will put it at the bottom of the menu. So, rename the items and aliases in the Apple Menu Items folder using these codes and you can force items to the top or bottom easily (see Figure 4-6).

> **TIP** *Want divider lines in your Apple menu? This is a little advanced, but forge ahead if you're brave about your iMac's System Folder. (You probably won't mess anything up.) Go into the System Folder and make an alias of the Apple Menu Items folder. Rename that alias "--------------------------" or something similar to create a dividing line. Now, drag the alias into the Apple Menu Items folder. Next, check the Apple menu—any file that has a space as the first character in its name will appear over the dividing line. Plus, selecting the line opens the Apple Menu Items folder in the Finder for you to edit easily!*

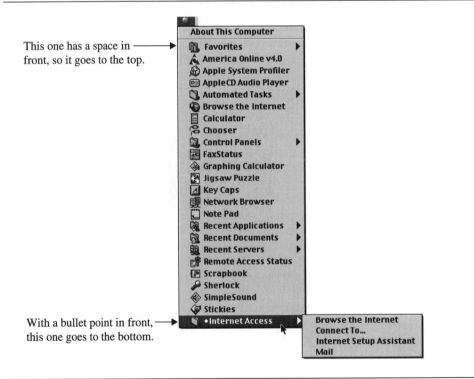

FIGURE 4-6   Apple menu items can be rearranged on the menu using special characters.

Chapter 5

Work with Applications and the Applications Menu

How to...

- Launch and work with applications
- Create, open, and save documents
- Use commands to perform basic tasks like printing, selecting text, cutting, copying, and pasting
- Undo mistakes, close documents, and quit applications
- Dig into the preferences settings of your applications
- Multitask: switch between active applications

In Chapter 3, I outlined a good deal of the organizational tasks you can accomplish with the Finder. One thing I didn't mention much, though, is one of the Finder's primary functions—launching programs. While the Finder itself is designed to help you manage documents you create in applications, you've got to get those applications started before you can create documents to work with.

That's what this chapter is about—getting started with any application and most other types of Macintosh programs. If you haven't used Macintosh applications in the past, get ready to learn a little bit about all of them.

5

What Are Applications?

A lot of times you'll hear the words "program" and "application" used interchangeably. That's usually OK, although I'm more inclined to say a *program* is any computer file that stores a series of instructions you run on a computer; an *application* is a large program that usually allows you to create a document of some sort. Its tools are *applied* toward some end goal.

One thing I can say about Macintosh applications—they all have a number of things in common. One of the reasons that the Macintosh has been considered an easier-to-use computer for all these years is because Macintosh application developers are required to follow some pretty strict rules. The result: Every single Macintosh application will likely have things in common with other Macintosh applications. And all those elements make it easier for you to learn new tasks since they share common methods.

NOTE   *In this chapter I don't talk about any specific application, but if you'd like to follow along, most of the examples use SimpleText—a basic text editor that comes with the iMac. You should find its icon in the Applications folder.*

Start Up Applications

The first method common to most applications is how you start them up. Applications need to be opened or "launched" before you can start working with them.

You can start up applications in a few different ways:

- **Double-click the application icon.**   This launches right into the application and, in most cases, a default or blank document is loaded. (If the icon for the application is in the form of a button, you'll only click it once.)

- **Select the application from the Recent Applications menu in the Apple menu.** Pull down the Apple menu and you'll see an item called Recent Applications; highlight it and you'll see the last ten (or more) applications that were used. Your iMac keeps track of that for you, so you can get to often-used applications quickly.

NOTE   *The Recent folders are discussed at length in Chapter 4.*

■ **Double-click one of the application's document icons.**   When you do this, it launches the application and causes it to load the document you double-clicked. This works great when you're loading a document that has been saved by that same application previously (like when you double-click an AppleWorks document and you have AppleWorks installed on your iMac).

■ **Drag-and-drop a document onto the application's icon.**   This works well if you're trying to launch a document that was not originally saved by the application. In many cases, the application will launch and attempt to translate the document if necessary, so that you can work with it.

After you tell an application you want to use it, it starts up, asks the Macintosh for a certain amount of RAM memory, and warns the iMac's processor that it's going to have some tasks to assign it. Then the application loads computer code from the hard disk into RAM memory so that it's ready to be used. Next, it draws the screen, puts its menus on the menu bar, and may or may not open a document for you to edit. Once it's done with the preliminaries, it waits for you to do something.

Start-Up Trouble

If you double-click a document that your iMac hasn't properly associated with an application (maybe you copied the document over the Internet or over a network connection), then you'll see a special alert box. This tells you that the iMac doesn't know which application to use to load the document, so you'll need to tell it (see Figure 5-1).

In the list, select an application that can successfully load or translate the file. If it's a graphics file, you'll probably have success loading it into a program that includes QuickTime translation; a text document may be successfully translated by AppleWorks or, if you have it, Microsoft Word.

TIP
If you don't see an application that you know could open the document, try clicking the check box that says Show Only Recommended Choices so that it's unchecked. Then you'll see nearly every application on your iMac—hopefully, the one you want will show up now.

Once you've found the right application, select it in the window and click the Open button. Nothing really bad happens if you select the wrong application, by the way, so feel free to make a guess. If it doesn't work out, you'll just have to try again.

Create a New Document

Sometimes an application will create a blank document for you as it opens. Other times, it just launches and sits there. If that's the case (or if you're already working in the application and you want a new document), you can create a new document by choosing File I New. This works in *any* application that creates documents.

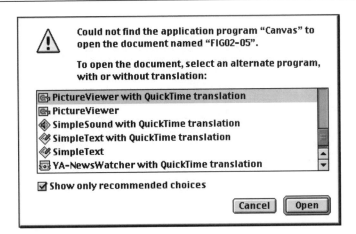

FIGURE 5-1   This alert allows you to choose the application you'll use to edit the document.

What happens next can vary. In some cases, a document just pops up. (That's what happens in a program like SimpleText.) In other cases, you may be greeted by a dialog box that requires you to make choices as to what sort of document you want to create, whether or not you want special help creating the document, and so on. We'll get more into those options as we create different documents in Part II of this book. You can also use ⌘-N to create a new document, by the way. For now, just remember File | New.

Open a Document

If you've already created a document you want to work on, the first thing you'll do after the application has started up is head to the File menu and choose Open. That brings up the Open dialog box, which may look something like Figure 5-2. If it doesn't look like Figure 5-2, it'll likely look more like Figure 5-3. If it still doesn't look like either of these, then you're probably working with a Microsoft application. They like to be different.

The Open dialog box offers a lot of different options to help you get to the document you're looking for, and its basic functions are easy to work with. In the file window, you can choose a document to open (if you see the one you want) or select a folder or storage disk to dig into. Click Open to open the highlighted item. If you're digging deeper, you can repeat the process—keep opening folders until you find the document you're looking for. Once it's in the window, select it and click Open. That opens the document for editing in the application.

 *You can double-click folders and storage devices in the file window to open them more quickly.*

Open a recent file ┐ ┌ Open a Favorite

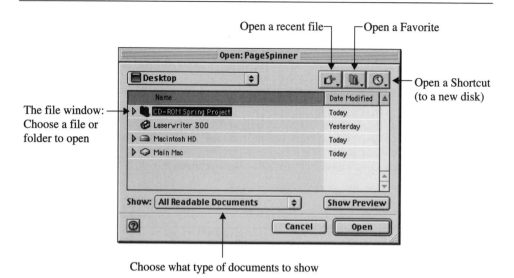

The file window: Choose a file or folder to open

Open a Shortcut (to a new disk)

Choose what type of documents to show

FIGURE 5-2 The new, improved Open dialog box appears in applications that have been updated to use it.

Use the menu to return to a parent folder

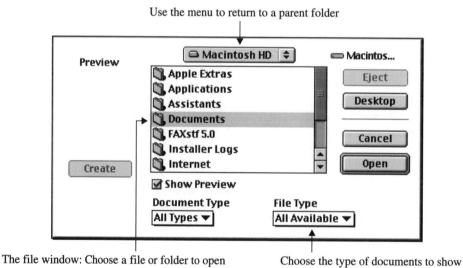

The file window: Choose a file or folder to open

Choose the type of documents to show

FIGURE 5-3 The older Open dialog box still shows up in applications that haven't been updated.

Not all programs' dialog boxes have a Show or Document Type menu, but when they do, you can use it to narrow down the number of files you'll see in the dialog box. The application itself will offer suggestions like "AppleWorks Document" or "PageSpinner HTML" that you can choose if that's the sort of file you're looking for. If you choose something other than "All Documents" or "All Readable Documents," then be aware that you're not seeing every file in the folder. You're seeing a subset that matches the Document Type menu criteria.

In the newer dialog box, shown in Figure 5-2, you can use the Shortcuts, Favorites, and Recent buttons to move quickly to different parts of your iMac's storage system. Shortcuts point to the different disks and removable media currently mounted on your iMac's desktop, while the Recent button allows you to open a document or folder you've opened in the recent past.

The Favorites button lets you choose from Favorites that you set yourself through the Finder (see Chapter 4) or in the Open dialog box. If you're currently looking at a folder or item you want to make a Favorite, select it in the file window and choose Add To Favorites from the Favorites button. (These buttons work just like menus.) You can also select Remove From Favorites to edit the Favorites you've created in the past.

NOTE *These dialog boxes were brand new when Mac OS 8.5 was released and, at the time of writing, only some applications have been updated to use them. It usually takes a while for applications to get updated, after all. Don't be surprised if you don't see many of these dialog boxes for a while. Eventually, updated applications will begin to use them more.*

In the more traditional Open dialog box, you have the same basic tools for opening folders and finding files. This Open dialog box is a little more simple in its offerings—and is especially lax in its extras (like the Favorites and Recent buttons) for helping you move around quickly. Still, it gets the job done.

Save Your Document

Save quickly and save often. This is some of the best advice I can give you. When I'm writing a typical book chapter, I save that document just about every three sentences or so. That's right—every three *sentences.* Why? Because I don't want to type them again.

Whenever you're working in an application there's always a chance that the application could run into an error, something could go wrong in the Mac OS, or something could go wrong with your iMac. Whatever happens, losing a lot of data because you forgot to save regularly is no fun. So, learn to save.

The first time you save a document, you'll need to find a place to put it and you'll need to name it. To do that, become acquainted with another dialog box. Choose File | Save to bring up the Save dialog box and start the saving process. Figure 5-4 shows something that should look pretty familiar—this is the new Save dialog box that's very similar to the newer Open dialog box described earlier in this chapter.

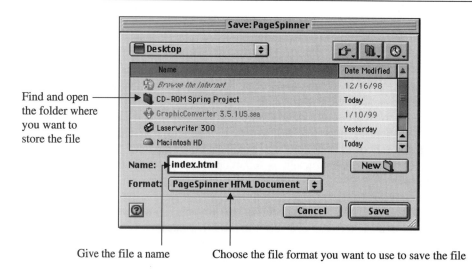

Find and open
the folder where
you want to
store the file

Give the file a name   Choose the file format you want to use to save the file

FIGURE 5-4   The newer Save dialog box is similar to the new Open dialog box.

This dialog box is fairly straightforward if you're used to the Open dialog box.

1. Select and open the folder you want to use to save the file. You can create a new folder for the file by clicking the New Folder button if you need to. Once that folder is open, you can enter a name for the file in the Name entry box.

2. With the name typed, you can choose the file format from the Format menu (if necessary) and then click Save.

3. The document is saved and you're returned to the document to continue working.

The older Save dialog box (see Figure 5-5) works the same way. The only difference is the absence of those Favorites, Shortcuts, and Recent buttons to play with.

Once you have the document saved, you can choose File | Save to save any changes to that same document—you won't see the Save dialog box, since the application already knows where to save the file and what to call it. In fact, for even faster saving you can just press ⌘-S to instantly save what you're working on. (That's what I do every three sentences.)

What if you want to save this file in a new place and/or with a new name? In that case, you use the Save As command in the File menu. That brings the Save dialog box back up, allowing you to save the document (and any unsaved changes) to a new document located

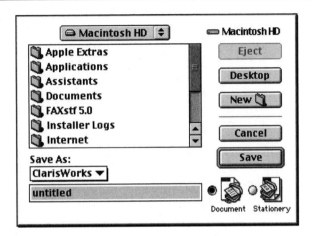

FIGURE 5-5   The older Save dialog box. Boring.

in a new folder. This is sort of like duplicating the file in the Finder—you create an entirely new copy of the document, which you can give a different name and put in a different folder, if you like.

Plus, after you've invoked the Save As command, the document file on your screen is the new document you just created. This can be useful if you want to keep the original file as it was, but you want to alter a copy of it to use for some other reason. Perhaps you're creating an invoice—you open last month's invoice, choose File | Save As to create a new copy with a new name, then edit the new copy for this month's invoice.

Basic Application Commands

Now that you've seen how to create, open, or save documents, you're ready to actually do something within those documents. Obviously, what you do depends somewhat on the application in question (I wouldn't try writing a novel in the Quicken financial management software, for instance), but there are some common commands that you'll find in nearly every application you encounter. Let's look at some of them.

Print

Open the File menu, choose the Print command, and the Print dialog box appears. This dialog box varies depending on the printer you use—in the examples here I'm using a

LaserWriter 300. Your printer will likely offer some of the same options and some different options that reflect the printer's capabilities (see the following illustration).

Number of copies to print   Which pages to print

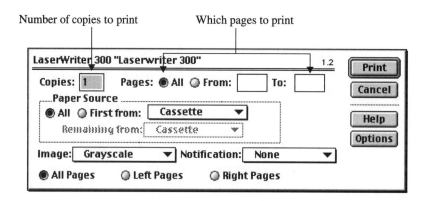

Common to all printers is the ability to print more than one copy when you enter a number in the Copy entry box. You can also select which pages are to be printed. By default, the All radio button is selected. If you want to print a range of pages within the document (say, pages 6-12), you can click once to select the From radio button, then enter the page numbers for your range in the entry boxes. (If you want to print just one page, put its page number in both boxes, such as From: **6** To: **6**.)

Now you can make other choices in the dialog box. You may have the option to change the Quality setting, especially if you have an inkjet printer. In most cases, the lower the quality, the less ink the printer uses. You can choose to print in a lower-quality mode if you want to conserve ink and/or don't expect to distribute the document to friends or colleagues. You may also have options for managing color printing, choosing how images should be printed, and setting which paper tray the paper should come from for this printing. Make all those choices, then click the Print button to send the job to your printer.

After the application has finished sending the job to the printer, your printer icon (on the desktop) takes over. You can double-click the printer icon to watch or manage the print job as it happens. Or, you can return to your application and continue working while the document is printed in the *background*, that is, while you're using the computer for another task.

 *If you have trouble, see Chapter 26 for help on setting up your printer. Also note that the Print dialog box can be different for different printers, but they all usually have these basic functions.*

Selecting and Select All

You're familiar with selecting icons in the Finder with the mouse. Selecting text (or objects like spreadsheet numbers or graphical images) in a document is similar, although it can vary a bit. For instance, if you're typing text in a text editor or word processor, you can't just point and click the mouse once to select a word in that document. You can, however, point and *double-click* to select a word.

To select more than one word, hold down the mouse button and drag the mouse pointer across the words you want to select. The words (or parts of words) become highlighted, just as if you were selecting multiple icons in the Finder (see Figure 5-6). You can drag the mouse pointer from left to right and/or up/down the page to select multiple words or lines of text.

There are a couple of tricks, too. In most text programs, triple-clicking will select an entire paragraph or a continuous line of text. In applications where triple-clicking doesn't select the entire paragraph, try clicking four times rapidly.

If you'd like to select everything in a given document, there's a command for that, too. Select the Edit menu and choose Select All. All the text (or objects) in the document will be highlighted. You can also invoke this command from the keyboard by pressing ⌘-A in nearly any application, including the Finder.

Cut, Copy, and Paste

These three are present in nearly every application ever written. The Cut, Copy, and Paste commands allow you to move text and objects around within documents or from one document to another. In fact, you can cut and paste between applications in most cases.

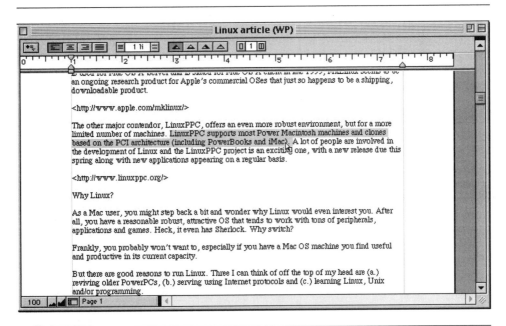

FIGURE 5-6   Highlighting text with the mouse pointer

The Cut and Copy commands are similar. Highlight text or objects in your document and select the Edit menu. Choose Cut if you'd like to delete the text or objects from the current document or current spot in the document; if you just want to copy the selection to use elsewhere, choose Copy. You can also use the keyboard: ⌘-C invokes Copy and ⌘-X invokes Cut.

Your selection is moved to something called the Clipboard—it's a file that's stored in the System Folder on your iMac's hard disk. Now, the contents of the Clipboard can be pasted into another section of the document or another document all together.

To paste, place the insertion point in the document where you'd like the text or objects to appear. (In some documents you don't place the insertion point; you just click the document window to make sure it's active.) Then, pull down the Edit menu and choose Paste. (Or, press ⌘-V on the keyboard.) The text or objects will appear in the document.

Want to do it another way? In many applications you can drag-and-drop text to different parts of the document, to a new document, or even to the Finder. Try this:

1. Using the mouse pointer, highlight some text you've typed into a SimpleText document.

2. Now, point the mouse pointer at the highlighted text, click the mouse button, and hold it.

3. Drag the text to another part of the document, another document entirely, or to the desktop.

4. Release the mouse button.

When you're finished you've effectively cut and pasted the text, even though you didn't use the commands. Plus, if you dragged the text to the Finder, you've got a cool little text clipping that you can save, rename, or use to drop the text back into another document at some later date, as shown in Figure 5-7.

NOTE *In the case of a desktop text clipping, the original highlighted text is left in the document, so that the process is more like a copy-and-paste operation.*

You can copy and paste much more than just text and objects like drawings and images. If you can select it in an application, there's a good chance you'll be able to copy and paste it. When in doubt, try the commands and see if they work.

Undo

Here's another perennial favorite of application programmers—the Undo command. This command is designed to immediately countermand the most recent action or command you've performed. For instance, if you just deleted an entire paragraph in AppleWorks,

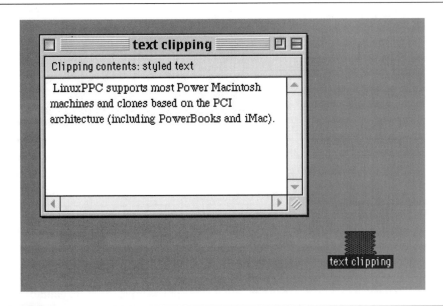

FIGURE 5-7   Create a text clipping by dragging text to the Finder.

choose Edit | Undo to get that paragraph back. It usually works for formatting text or objects, pasting, deleting, typing, and so on. Most any activity can be taken back. You can usually undo immediately by pressing ⌘-Z on the keyboard.

Many programs will also have a Redo or similar command that is designed to undo an Undo command. If you undo something you didn't actually want to undo, head back to the Edit menu and look for the Redo command.

NOTE   *Some applications have multiple undo capabilities. Basically, that means you can undo more than one command—keep choosing the Undo command and the program will keep working backward through your most recent actions. It's a convenient feature to have, but it's usually only implemented in higher-end, more expensive applications.*

Quit the Application

About done with that application? All applications have a Quit command that closes the application, hands the RAM memory space back to the Mac OS, and cleans up any open files. Usually that command is in the File menu under Quit. You can also press ⌘-Q in almost any Mac application to quit.

When you quit a program, it should ask you to save any unsaved documents and may ask you to make other decisions—like hanging up the modem or waiting until a particular activity is finished. Of course, it depends on the program.

 Most of the time, closing a window in a program does not actually quit the program. Many beginning Mac users make the mistake of closing a document window and believing the application is also closed. You can close a window by clicking its Close box, choosing File | Close, or pressing ⌘-W. But that rarely quits the program—it just closes the current window or document. You need to invoke the Quit command in applications; otherwise, they remain open, take up RAM, and make it more difficult for you to run other programs.

Preferences

Most applications offer a dialog box that allows you to set your preferences for how the program behaves, what values it defaults to, and so on. The preferences are completely up to the individual application—there really isn't too much in the way of standardization, except for the location of the Preferences command. I discussed the Finder Preferences in Chapter 3; I'll talk about the preferences settings in AppleWorks, Quicken, Outlook Express, Internet Explorer, and your other iMac applications throughout the book.

To open the Preferences dialog box you'll usually invoke the Preferences command. In most applications it's under the Edit menu, since you're trying to "edit" the preferences. If you don't find it there, look under the File menu. If you don't see it in either of those two menus, then chances are good that you're using a Microsoft application. Look in the Tools menu for a command called Options or Preferences.

Other Interface Elements

You already know a lot about what to expect from applications. You'll see windows, menus, icons, pointers, and other little tidbits. But let's focus for a few moments on some elements you're likely to see pop up in various parts of the different applications you'll be working with. You'll want to be familiar with these parts of the interface so you can get your work done.

Buttons, Check Boxes, and Sliders

You'll find that many preferences settings, dialog boxes, and other components that make up applications—and even parts of the Mac OS—rely on some typical controls to help you make decisions. You've already seen some of these, but let me go ahead and define them formally. Here's what they do:

 ■ **Radio Buttons**   This type of control allows you to make one selection among two or more different choices. Click the button next to the item you want to choose.

- **Check Boxes**   A check box allows you to choose each item individually—if you want the item active, you'll click in the box next to the item and a check mark (sometimes it's an "x") will appear in the box.

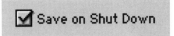

- **Sliders**   A slider bar allows you to choose a range of values from low to high just as you might for a volume control on a home stereo system. In fact, slider bars are used most often for changing the volume level, brightness level, and so on. The volume control in the Control Strip (discussed in Chapter 2) is a slider control. You just drag the slider back and forth on the control to change the value.

Toolbars

While not required of Macintosh applications, toolbars are a popular addition. Toolbars put small *iconic* buttons in a special bar below the menu bar in an application, giving you quick access to the most popular commands in that program. An example is the following illustration, which shows the toolbar from AppleWorks.

It allows you to quickly access fonts, font styling, and many other commands that you might use frequently in the program.

Often, at least for me, the little icon buttons on toolbars make no sense whatsoever. In that case, the solution is usually to point at an icon with the mouse pointer and wait a few seconds. Most applications have a little pop-up window or other way of showing you what a particular icon is for. If you're still not getting any help, open the Help menu and choose Balloon Help, then go back and point at the icon in question. That may solve the problem and tell you what the icon is for. (Balloon Help is discussed in Chapter 7.)

The About Box

Want to know more about an application? All applications are required to have an About box, which you can access while the application is active. If you're currently working with the application, pull down the Apple menu. You'll see that the first menu item is About… followed by the name of the application. Choose that item and you'll see a little something about the application. Some applications will place help, tips, and other buttons in the About window that will, occasionally, give you help when using the application.

Multitasking: Use More Than One Application

Even though the iMac is cute, it is a very powerful computer. So powerful that you'll probably find very quickly that you want, need, and enjoy the idea of using more than one program or application at once. You may be downloading your e-mail messages while surfing the Web. When you find the article you're looking for, you might want to switch back to AppleWorks to type more into your report document. And so on.

There are good reasons to run more than one program at a time—so many good reasons that the process has a name: *multitasking*. Your iMac is able to do a perfectly good job of multitasking if you know the secrets.

The first secret is this: You'll need to start up more than one application if you want to use more than one application. You can do that by switching back to the Finder.

 *Once you have more than one application running, you can use the Cut, Copy, and Paste commands to move text and images between the applications. You can often drag-and-drop from one application's window to another's, just like you can often drag-and-drop text and images from applications to the Finder and back again.*

The Application Menu

Up in the top-right corner of your iMac's screen you'll always find the Application menu, a menu dedicated to switching between your open applications. Which menu is it? It's the one with the name and icon of whatever applications you're currently running. Point to that icon and name, then click the mouse button to open the menu.

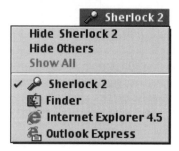

Switch Between Applications

If you have an application other than the Finder open, you can head up there right now, pull down the Application menu, and see all of your open applications. Choose one of those applications and it'll move to the *foreground*—you'll suddenly see that new application's menus and windows in front of you, ready to be worked on.

If you don't have any applications open, use the Application menu to switch to the Finder. (You can also just click the desktop to switch to the Finder.) Now, from the Finder, you can launch more applications. You could also, if you prefer, launch an application from the Apple menu if you've set things up correctly (see Chapter 4).

Once you have a couple of applications open, you can begin to see the power of the Application menu. Just pull it down and choose another application. It instantly comes to the front. Plus, your iMac is still multitasking—most of the time, programs in the background will continue working even if you switch away from them.

You can switch between applications with a keystroke, too. Press ⌘-TAB to switch from application to application. You can press ⌘-SHIFT-TAB to switch back in the opposite order.

Hide and Show Applications

The Application menu has some other useful commands that help you when you switch between applications. If you've switched applications, and windows from another application are getting in your way or cluttering up the screen, you can pull down the Application menu and choose Hide Others, which hides all applications except the one you're currently working in. Now, the other applications' windows disappear. The applications are still running and you can still switch to them using the Application menu—only their windows are currently hidden.

You can also hide the application that you're working in—perhaps so you can see an open window in a background application. To do that, pull down the Application menu and choose Hide ... (the ellipse represents the name of the current application).

You'll probably use the Hide command the most when you switch to the Finder, since switching to the Finder doesn't automatically cause the windows of other applications to disappear. If you switch to the Finder and can't see parts of the desktop you need revealed, choose Hide Others from the Application menu; then you can work in the Finder.

The Show All command does exactly what you think it would—it reveals the windows of all hidden applications. You can also reveal individual applications by switching to them using the Application menu.

TIP *Want to hide an application as you switch away from it? If you're in AppleWorks and you want to switch to the Finder and hide AppleWorks at the same time, it can be done. Just hold down the OPTION key as you switch between applications. The application you're switching from gets hidden as you switch to the new application.*

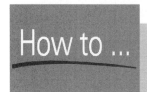 **Float the Application Menu**

If you select the Application menu and hold down the mouse button, then drag straight down the menu right off the bottom edge, you'll "tear away" the menu. Suddenly it becomes a floating window that includes the icons and names of the currently running applications.

The window will always float *on top* of all your other applications, so you'll always be able to see it. To switch to a different application, all you have to do is click once on that application's icon.

You can also customize the window somewhat. Do you want just icons and no words? Click the zoom box and the menu shrinks down to small icons. If you'd like the icons bigger, hold down OPTION and click the zoom box. If you'd like to change from vertical to horizontal, hold down SHIFT-OPTION and click the zoom box.

If you'd like to customize the look further, you can use some prewritten AppleScripts to change the menu more. From the Finder, choose Help | Mac OS Help (or Help | Mac Help). Search for the Help topic "Switching between open applications." In that topic you'll find links to AppleScripts that will help you customize the menu even further.

Need to get rid of the floating menu window? Click its Close box and it's gone. You can still, as always, use the Application menu the next time you need to switch applications.

Chapter 6

Search for Things

How to...

- Find anything with your iMac
- Search for files by filename
- Use a customized search to find a file
- Search within the contents of files
- Search the Internet
- Understand Sherlock 2's Channels
- Add search sites and channels to Sherlock

With the large hard disk that's included with an iMac—and the infinitely larger Internet that your iMac is most likely attached to—you'll soon discover that mousing around and double-clicking isn't always the most efficient way to find something. Instead, you'll probably discover yourself wishing you could figure out how to find things more directly and quickly. Fortunately, it's really easy to do.

Plus, you'll find that the Mac OS offers some really advanced searching options that you might not have thought of—things like searching the Internet from your iMac's desktop. This can be a great timesaver for finding things on the Internet, with the added bonus that you don't have to learn special commands for using a Web browser. With the Mac OS, the searches happen right on your screen using familiar menus and commands.

You Can Find Anything with iMac

Although the iMac's basic interface—all those icons and windows—is called the Finder, it's really not that good at automatically seeking out files and folders on your iMac. That sort of task is left to a program called Sherlock.

Sherlock is a very powerful program, capable of doing these three basic types of searches: Find File, Find by Content, and Search Internet.

Sherlock's Find File tool can search your iMac's own hard disk and any additional disk you have attached to it. It can even search hard disk on other computers if your iMac is attached to a network.

Sherlock's second tool, Find by Content, may be slower but it's very cool—it allows you to search *inside* documents for phrases or keywords. You could search, for instance, for something like "Dear Grandma" to find documents on your hard disk that included those words.

Third, Sherlock can search the Internet. If you have any experience with the Internet, you know that a big part of the process is searching for pages, usually at popular search sites like Yahoo (**http://www.yahoo.com**), Excite (**http://www.excite.com**), or Infoseek (**http://www.infoseek.com/**). Well, Sherlock's Search Internet tool allows you to access the same sort of searches, but from within the Mac OS, inside Sherlock itself. This results in search listings from many of the most popular Internet search sites, including those just mentioned and others like Hotbot (**http://www.hotbot.com/**) and Lycos (**http://www.lycos.com**).

Meet Sherlock

The easiest way to launch Sherlock is from the Finder itself—click once on the desktop to make sure you've switched to the Finder. Now, choose File I Find or press ⌘-F on your keyboard.

If you're not currently in the Finder and you don't feel like switching to it, you can also launch Sherlock from the Apple menu. Just pull down the Apple menu and select the entry for Sherlock.

When Sherlock launches, its searching dialog box appears (see the following illustration). Notice that the Sherlock interface includes tabs at the top of the dialog box that allow you to switch between the different types of searches. Each of these tabs represents one of the three types of search you can do: Find File, Find by Content, and Search Internet.

If your version of Sherlock doesn't look like the above image, then you've probably got Sherlock 2, which comes with Mac OS 9. (Some earlier iMacs shipped with Mac OS 8.5 or 8.6, which includes the original Sherlock.) If that's the case, your version of Sherlock probably looks more like the following.

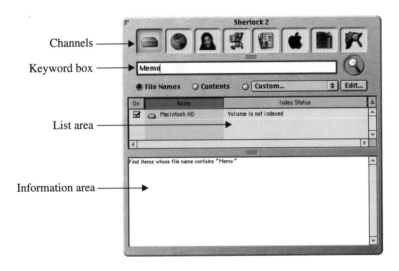

NOTE: In this chapter I'll primarily be covering the original Sherlock, but whenever something is different in Sherlock 2, I'll try to point that out. If you don't have either version, then you probably have an original iMac running Mac OS 8.1. In that case, you'll have the Find File program instead of Sherlock; the only section in this chapter that will apply to you is the "Search for Files" section.

Sherlock is pretty much its own small program; in Mac parlance, it's a desk accessory, which means it loads with its own menu bar and window, but the entire program quits if you close its window. (This is different from most applications, which continue to run even when you close a document window.) Try it—close the Sherlock window by clicking its Close box and Sherlock itself will quit. You can also choose File | Quit to close Sherlock.

Are you a keyboard speed demon? You can switch between Sherlock's tabs using keyboard commands, if you like. With Sherlock open, use ⌘-F for Find File, ⌘-G for Find by Content, and ⌘-H for Search Internet. With Sherlock 2 and Mac OS 9, you can also use ⌘-G in the Finder.

Save Searches

No matter which sort of search you perform, remember that you can always save what you've done and return to it at a later time. That goes for file, content, and Internet searches. To save your search criteria (after you've crafted a doozie of a search), choose File | Save Search Criteria. This will open a standard Save dialog box, allowing you to name the search and save it to your iMac's hard disk. If you want to load the search again, choose File | Load Search Criteria.

Search for Files

The first tab in Sherlock's window is the Find File tab. With this selected, you're able to search for files on your iMac's hard disk, on disks attached to your iMac, or on disks attached over a network connection. You can also search the disk(s) in many different ways, including by the name (or part of the name) of the file, by the file's size, by the type of file it is, and many other criteria. In fact, you can put a number of different criteria together in order to find a file with pinpoint accuracy.

NOTE
In Sherlock 2, you accomplish this by clicking the File Names button in the Files channel. If you don't see a File Names button, first click the hard disk icon at the top of the Sherlock 2 window.

The Basic Search

Much of the time that you search for a file, you'll probably do so using part of the file's name. After all, you may have a reasonably logical system for naming your files (at least, it might seem logical to you) that you can use as the basis for naming your files. (If you don't, you might consider how this tactic might help you with file management.) Using even a few letters you think are in the name of the file, you can begin a search:

1. Make sure the Find File tab is selected. (In Sherlock 2, select the File Names button.)

2. In the Find Items menu, choose On Local Disks. This means only on disk connected directly to your iMac. (In Sherlock 2, you place a check mark next to each disk you want to search.)

6

Sherlock 2 will allow you to search only in a particular folder. To add a folder you'd like to search to the list, find it in the Finder and drag it to the list of disks. That folder will now appear as a search volume—you can click to place a check mark next to it (or remove the check mark) just as you can with other disks. And, you can always add and select more than one folder at once, if you like.

3. You can leave the other menus the same—you're searching for files whose names contain certain letters.

4. Enter the letters or part of the filename in the text box. Examples might be "letter" if you're searching for business correspondence, "memo" or "invoice," or maybe "1999" or "March" if you tend to include dates in the names of your files.

5. Click Find.

That's it. After a few seconds, Sherlock will pop up an Items Found window (see Figure 6-1) that tells you all of the files it found that met your criteria. (In Sherlock 2, it doesn't open a new window; instead, you'll see the found files in the list area right below the box you typed the filename into.) You can then scroll through the list and click once on each result to see exactly where the file is located (the path to the file will appear in the bottom pane of the Items Found window).

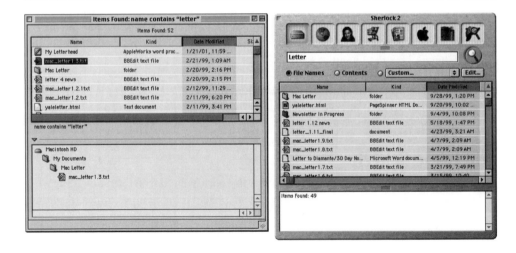

FIGURE 6-1   In Sherlock (left), you'll see a new results window. In Sherlock 2 (right), you'll see results listed in the list area.

So what can you do in the Items Found window or the list area? Quite a lot, actually. You can double-click the resulting document to open it in its associated application (or, if the result is an application, double-clicking will launch it). In the bottom pane (the *information area* in Sherlock 2) you can double-click the icon for the same result. Or, you can double-click any folder that appears in the bottom pane or information area and that folder will open in Finder.

You can also select an item in the Items Found window or list area and choose File | Get Info (⌘-I) to get more information about the item. Or select an item and choose File | Open Enclosing Folder (⌘-E). As the name implies, this will open the entire folder in which the selected file is stored.

Want to move the icon out to the desktop? You can do that, too. Just click and drag the icon from Sherlock out to the desktop, then release the mouse button. You can also drag these icons to folders on the desktop, icons in the Application Switcher window, or even to the Trash, if you like. Likewise, you can drag items from a Sherlock window to a removable disk or network drive and the items will be copied to that disk.

> **TIP**
> *In Sherlock, you can watch the Items Found window in action by choosing Edit | Preferences and putting a check next to Show Current Search Status For Find File. It slows things down a bit, but can be useful if you want to watch the search as it happens. There's no such preference in Sherlock 2.*

The Advanced Search

I promise you'll use basic search a lot—but it may not be the only type of search you conduct. The more hidden a file (especially if you've forgotten that *really clever* place you put the file or the *really clever* name you gave the file so that you'd *definitely remember* where or what it was), the more advanced your search will need to be. And even if the file isn't particularly well hidden, an advanced search can be used for other reasons, too, like finding files created after a certain date or finding files that take up a certain amount of space. Both instances are helpful when you plan to back up your hard drive or conduct a little spring cleaning and delete files.

> **NOTE**
> *Sherlock 2 offers advanced searches, but not quite in this way. Instead, see the section "Custom Searches in Sherlock 2," later in this chapter.*

You may have already noticed that building a search in Sherlock is a whole lot like playing that old car-travel game, Mad Libs. You choose from the different menu choices and enter keywords that completely change the search sentence. (The search sentence always says "Find items … whose …" but the rest can be changed.) The first item you can change is where you want Sherlock to look for the file(s) in question.

Search Locations

The first thing you're going to tell Sherlock is where you want it to search. That's the menu right after Find Items that generally defaults to On Local Disks. Pull down that menu and you'll see other options.

If you search On All Disks, then Sherlock will look at every single disk—hard disk, CD-ROM, DVD-ROM, Zip, SuperDisk, network disk—that the iMac has access to. Local Disks means only disks physically attached to the iMac and On Local Disks, Except CD-ROMs means Sherlock will skip the iMac's CD-ROM or DVD-ROM drive, even if it has a disc in it. (Since you can't save files to a CD-ROM or DVD-ROM drive, this choice can be a timesaver when you're looking for a document file that you created and saved yourself.) Choose On Mounted Servers and Sherlock will only look for files on network disks that you've signed onto through the Chooser or the Network Browser. (If the network drive's icon appears on your desktop, then it's been mounted.)

The other two search locations are interesting: On The Desktop means what it says—it searches the desktop; In The Finder Selection will search in any windows or folders that are currently selected and frontmost in the Finder. And, at the bottom of the menu, you can choose individual disks themselves—if you don't have any attached disks, you'll just see "Macintosh HD" (or whatever you've named your iMac's hard disk).

 *Want to quickly search a particular folder? Open the folder (or just highlight the folder icon) in the Finder, then switch to Sherlock and choose to find items In The Finder Selection. This will quickly search the open folder and its subfolders instead of searching the entire hard disk.*

The Search Criteria

So you know how to customize where Sherlock searches. But what about *what* it searches? A basic search for a filename won't always cut it. Instead, it's often clever to search by some of the other criteria—things like the size of the file, the label, or the date modified. Think of this: You could search for all files modified after a particular date—say, a week ago. Now you suddenly have a listing of documents that have recently been changed. What could you do with that? You could copy them onto a Zip, SuperDisk, or out onto the network to create a safe, backup copy!

The search criteria should be self-explanatory, although some of them get into slightly more advanced concepts. As a general rule, all of these criteria are things found in the Get Info dialog box that appears when you select an icon in the Finder and choose File | Get Info. These are mostly file attributes to help you narrow down your search.

You will also notice something interesting when you change from one criteria to the next—the menu after it may also change. That's because Sherlock tries to help you find relevant information depending on the criteria you choose. If you choose to search by modified date, for instance, you probably don't want to enter an exact date—instead, you'll want to search by a range of dates. Sherlock helps you with that.

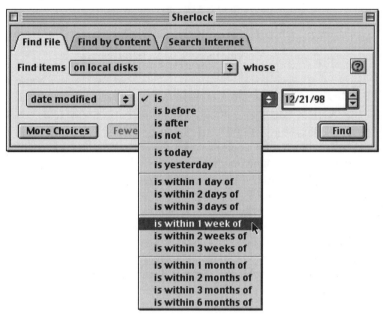

> **TIP**   *There are also some hidden criteria, if you know how to find them. Hold down the OPTION key as you select the criteria menu. You'll see a few additional Mac file attributes down at the bottom of that menu.*

Add More Choices

So you've got all these ways to search for files. But what if that isn't helping much? You can narrow things down even further by mixing and matching your search criteria. Here's where the real power kicks in. Down at the bottom of the Sherlock window you'll see a More Choices button. Click it and your Mad Libs search sentence changes a little (see the following illustration).

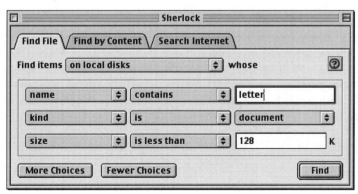

Using More Choices, you can add as many criterion lines as you need to in order to pinpoint the file you're looking for. If you hit the More Choices button too many times, just click the Fewer Choices button to return to fewer criterion lines.

Got a completely cool search? Don't forget you can save the criteria and use them again, if you like. Choose File | Save Search Criteria.

Custom Searches in Sherlock 2

Like the original Sherlock, Sherlock 2 allows you to customize file searches beyond simply typing the filename (or part of it) and clicking the magnifying glass. You can actually build pretty sophisticated searches with a ton of search criteria at your disposal. But, first, let's start with something a little easier.

Apple has saved some custom searches that you can experiment with. Select the Custom pop-up menu in Sherlock 2 (you need to have selected the File channel by clicking the hard disk icon at the top of the Sherlock window), and you'll see some interesting entries. You can select from: Applications, Larger Than 1MB, Modified Today, and Modified Yesterday. If you select one of those, you can click the magnifying glass and any file that meets the chosen criterion will appear in the list menu.

Of course, it's probably not too often that you'll want to simply know every file on your hard disk that is larger than 1MB. More often, you want to know about files with certain filenames that meet other criteria as well. So, you can select a custom search criterion, then enter a filename (or partial filename) in the keyword box. Now your results will include files that meet both criteria—for instance, files with "letter" in their name that are over 1MB in size.

Neat-o, eh? You can do still more. Select the Edit button and you can create your own custom searches, complete with tons of different criteria. After you've selected the Edit button, you'll see the More Search Options window, shown in Figure 6-2.

If you read the previous section on adding criteria in the original Sherlock, you remember that I mentioned how it can be a little like playing that game called Mad Libs. It is in the More Search Options dialog box where you build each criterion for your custom search by choosing options from pop-up menus, entry boxes, and so on.

If you'd like to use a particular criterion, first click its check box. Next, select items from the pop-up menu that determine how the criterion will be limited. (They don't all have menus, but most do.) Finally, you'll often enter some text, date, or number or choose another value from a menu that will finish out the criterion statement.

It's actually pretty simple. If you want to search files that are new since 10/15/1999, click the check box next to "date created" and choose "is after" from its pop-up menu. Now, in the date entry box, enter **10/15/1999** or use the little arrows to select that date. Other criteria work similarly; you can create custom searches that check the date modified, the size of the file, the kind of file it is, the label on the file, and so on.

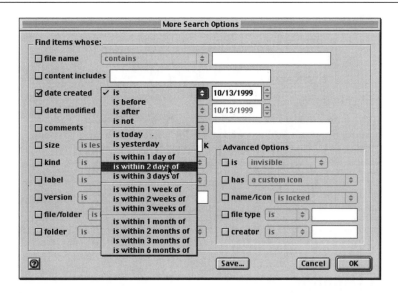

FIGURE 6-2   The More Search Options window is the world's most intimidating Mad Libs game.

If you'll only be using this search once, click OK in the More Search Options window, then return to the Sherlock 2 window, enter a filename if you want, and click the magnifying glass. Your search is conducted.

If you've created a search you really like in the More Search Options window, click the Save button. Enter a name and click Save again. Now you've got a new custom search on that custom menu back in Sherlock 2's main window. You can use it like all the other custom searches on that menu—select it, enter a filename in the keyword entry box if desired, then click the magnifying glass to seek out files!

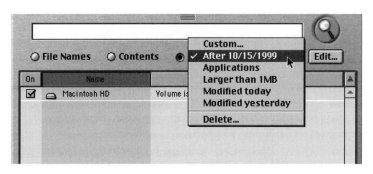

Find by Content

This is an example of how computers *should* work. For years we've been too focused on how we name our files, the little codes we use, the folders, and so on. It's too much work. What if you could just search the insides of files to find what you're looking for?

Find by Content in Sherlock and Sherlock 2 helps you with just that. It's a fairly new technology, so it's not ready to completely take over for Find File yet. But maybe one day. In the meantime, you can use Find by Content to help out when you just can't seem to give Find File enough information to locate a particular document.

Notice the use of the word "document" throughout this section. Find by Content is only useful for searching document files—files you've created in applications like AppleWorks, PageMill, Microsoft Word, or SimpleText— since those are the files that contain text. (With Sherlock 2, you can also search Adobe PDF files.) If you're searching for images, applications, utilities, or other files, you need to use Find File.

Index Documents

Find by Content requires a little work on your part. Specifically, you're going to have to index your hard disk so that Find by Content can look through your files in a speedy manner. If you don't have your hard disk indexed, then Sherlock can't search its contents. I'll explain how to index your hard disk after the next paragraph.

Click the Find by Content tab in Sherlock and the first thing you'll see is everything to get you started—there's a box for entering the text to be sought and there's a Find button. There's also a place to choose the hard disk you want Sherlock to search. If you haven't yet indexed a hard disk or other volume, you can't choose one to search in Sherlock. In Sherlock 2, you can choose the unindexed disk, but it won't do you any good (see Figure 6-3).

To index a drive, follow these steps:

1. Click the Index Volumes button (in Sherlock) or choose Index Volumes from the Find menu (in both). That brings up the Index Volumes dialog box.

2. Here you select the disk you want to index—probably your iMac's main hard disk. Then click the Create Index button.

3. You'll see an alert box that tells you it'll take a while to index the disk. If you're ready, go ahead and click Create.

Now, the index begins to be created. At this point, you might want to switch over and read your e-mail, write a letter in AppleWorks, or head out to the local theater and take in a movie. Seriously, depending on the size of your disk and the number of files on it, indexing can easily take 30 minutes, an hour, or longer—especially the first time you do it.

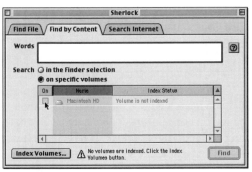

FIGURE 6-3   Attempting to choose an unindexed disk in Sherlock (left) and
Sherlock 2 (right)

> **TIP**   *Are you really going to keep working while the index is created? If so, choose Edit |*
> *Preferences. Now, use the slider bar under System Responsiveness to determine if*
> *your iMac will focus more on its indexing tasks (Faster Indexing) or whether*
> *Sherlock will be a good citizen and allow the iMac to be more responsive when*
> *you're working on other things (More Responsive).*

If you like, you can schedule the indexing. In fact, this is a good idea for keeping the index
current, even if you've already created it once. As you add new documents, you have to index
again to make them searchable. Getting Sherlock or Sherlock 2 to index automatically is the
easiest way to accomplish that.

To schedule indexing:

1. Click the Schedule button in the Index Volumes window.

2. Now, in the Schedule dialog box, choose what days of the week you want the
index updated and at what time during the day. (It's best to schedule this for
sometime when you're not using the computer—Sherlock is able to index local
disks even while your iMac is asleep.)

3. Close the Schedule dialog box once you've made your selections and Sherlock
will now be regularly updated for searches.

> **TIP**   *Indexing a server disk? Make sure you have permission, then go ahead. Once a*
> *server is indexed, anyone with access to it (who also happens to have a Mac and*
> *is running Sherlock) can search that disk by content. (In Sherlock 2, you can't*
> *index a server volume unless you run Sherlock 2 from that server computer.)*

Perform the Search

Once you have the indexes created for your hard disks and other disk volumes, searching by content is really very easy. All you need to do is have the Find by Content tab selected in Sherlock, then enter the text you want Sherlock to search for. (In Sherlock 2, make sure the Files channel is active—click the disk icon at the top of Sherlock 2's window—then click the Contents button to search by contents.) Now, put a check mark next to the volumes you want Sherlock to include in its search. Click the Search button and you're off to the races. When Sherlock is done, the Items Found dialog box appears and you can manipulate the found documents just as you would anything else found in Sherlock. (In Sherlock 2, results appear in the list area.)

Actually, there's something special you can do with these found documents. Since they're indexed, Sherlock has a good idea of what's in the document. As such, Sherlock is able to create an actual summary of the document. Want to see it? CTRL-click a document in the Items Found dialog box. You'll see the contextual menu appear with a Summarize to Clipboard command. Choose that command.

Now, switch to the Finder. There, in the clipboard viewer (Edit | Show Clipboard), you'll see a summary of the document. (If you like, you can use the Edit | Paste command in any application to paste that summary text into a document.)

This only works with certain types of documents, including plain text and HTML documents. (Sherlock 2 can also summarize PDF documents.) Sherlock can't summarize Microsoft Word, AppleWorks, and other similar documents.

Search the Internet

Finding files and searching by content are both very cool—I don't mean to take away from either of those glorious features. But the real excitement over Sherlock is its ability to search the Internet from within the Mac OS—you don't have to open up Internet Explorer or another Web browser. It can also search more than one Internet search engine at once, meaning you don't have to jump around from search engine to search engine on the Web—Sherlock does all of this for you.

The best part is that it's very easy to search the Internet using Sherlock, and it's highly customizable—many Web sites and search engines are creating their own Sherlock plug-ins that make it possible to customize Sherlock and search for all sorts of different things using the same basic tools.

Confused by the Internet and Web jargon? You might want to flip over to Chapter 19 quickly to read about the Web and Internet Explorer, then come back here when you're ready to do some searching.

Start the Search

Using Sherlock to search the Internet is really very easy. Click the Search Internet tab, then enter words you want Sherlock to search for on the Internet. (In Sherlock 2, click the earth icon at the top of the Sherlock window.) You can simply separate the words with spaces; if you want to search for a phrase, put the phrase in quotation marks.

NOTE *If you use your iMac's modem to connect to the Internet, you need to have established the Internet connection before searching the Internet with Sherlock. You can also set the dialer to connect automatically whenever an Internet application is launched—see Chapter 23.*

Now, put a check mark next to the Internet search sites you want to use—they appear in the Search pane at the bottom of the Sherlock window. (In Sherlock 2 they appear in the list area.) With your Internet search sites selected, click Search (or the magnifying glass in Sherlock 2).

Sherlock returns an Items Found list after it has searched using all of the different search engines (see Figure 6-4). (In Sherlock 2 this list appears in the list area.) Each listing is a different Web page. Notice that you see three things about each page—the name, the site, and the relevance of that result. Relevance just tells you how likely of a match Sherlock believes that page is for your criteria. It's based on how many of your keywords appear in the Web page and how often they appear.

Name	Relevance	Site
GAMECENTER.COM - Reviews - Monday...		www.gamecenter.com
Monday Night Football Trivia Contest		www.atscom.net
ABC Monday Night Football brought to y...		excite.mplayer.com
ABC Monday Night Online		www.abcmnf.com
Current Picks Record- We play Mon...		www.dragup.com
ABC NFL Monday Night Football on WCH...		www.wchstv.com
Welcome to Master Mind - Monday Nigh...		www.mondaynitefootball.com
GAMECENTER.COM - Reviews - Monday...		www.gamecenter.com
ABC Monday Night Football 98 - Games ...		www.gamesdomain.com
ABC 28 Sports: Monday Night Football S...		www.kamc28.com
Monday Night Football		www.kpug.com
ABC Sports		www.abcsports.com
Games Domain: ABC Monday Night Footb...		www.gamesdomain.com

FIGURE 6-4 After an Internet search, Sherlock and Sherlock 2 return a list of Web pages ranked by relevance.

To see a summary of the Web page that's been found, click the Web page's entry once. The summary appears in the bottom pane (or the information area in Sherlock 2). You can now double-click the item to launch it in your Web browser. If you'd prefer to simply save a Web link on the desktop, you can drag the item from the top of the Items Found window to the desktop. It will become an Internet location file.

Sherlock 2's Channels

In Sherlock 2, there's a little more to searching the Internet than there was back in the original Sherlock. Specifically, Sherlock 2 has been updated with its new Channels technology.

Channels technology does two things. First, it places those little icons at the top of the Sherlock window, which you can click to select different groupings of Internet search sites. Click the shopping cart icon, for instance, and you'll see a different list than when you click the earth icon.

You can drag the little bar between the channels icons and the keyword box. Drag it downward and you'll see more spaces for channels; drag it upward to cover all but the first row again.

Second, the Channels technology actually offers different *types* of channels, which allow you to search for different types of information and see results listed in different ways. Depending on the type of channel you're using for a search, the results will be formatted differently. In a regular Internet search (like the one you implement when you click the earth icon) you'll see the relevance-ranked results list that we've already discussed. But if you clicked the shopping cart icon and did a search, you'd see something different. You'd see results ranked by price and availability.

The reason for this is simple—they're different types of channels. In fact, there are four different types of channels in Sherlock 2:

- **Searching**   These channels return relevance-ranked results.

- **People**   People channels return information about the person, like e-mail address and phone number.

- **Shopping**   Shopping channels return information that includes a description, price, and availability date.

- **News**   News channels don't actually offer different results from Internet channels, which sort of throws off my whole theory. But they're a great place to find news-oriented Internet search sites.

Try it. Select a channel and you'll see the different Internet search sites for each channel. Try a search in each one and you'll see different types of results in the different channels.

Update Your Search Sites

Sherlock will notify you when you attempt a search and one of your search sites has been updated. Click the Update button to update that particular search site. If you haven't used Sherlock in a while, you can manually have it search for updated sites by choosing Find | Update Search Sites. If any updates are found, Sherlock will let you know.

NOTE   *There's no Find | Update Search Sites command in Sherlock 2.*

Add New Search Sites

The other thing you might like to do is add third-party search sites to your Sherlock window. That means you can use Sherlock to search all kinds of sites, including Amazon.com, CD-Now, Encyclopedia.com, and many others. The more you use your iMac, the more you'll see what an exciting tool Sherlock is. Apple keeps track of the plug-ins being offered by other companies. Visit **http://www.apple.com/sherlock/** on the Web for a listing and instructions for downloading those Internet search site plug-ins.

When you find a Sherlock plug-in you want, download it to your iMac using Internet Explorer or an FTP program (see Part III of this book for much more on Internet tools).

To install the new plug-in:

1. Drag the plug-in file (it'll be called "*something*.src") to the System Folder icon on your iMac's startup disk (probably the main hard disk).

2. Drop the plug-in on the System Folder.

3. The Finder will respond by telling you the plug-in needs to be put in the Internet Search Sites folder. Click OK.

Now the new search site is available as one of the options on the Search Internet tab in Sherlock.

In Sherlock 2, new Internet search sites appear under the Custom channel (click the icon that looks like Sherlock Holmes' hat). Then if you want to, you can drag the new Internet search site from the list area to another channel in the channel area. (More on that in the next section, " How to Create a New Channel in Sherlock 2.")

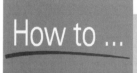 **Create a New Channel in Sherlock 2**

If you have Sherlock 2 on your iMac, then you can go even a little further than simply adding Internet search sites. You can actually create a whole different channel at the top there. Then, you can drag Internet search sites from other channels to your new channel, if you'd like to. Here's how to create a channel:

1. Choose Channel | New Channel.

2. In the New Channel dialog box, enter a name for the channel in the Name The Channel entry box.

3. In the Channel Type menu, choose the type of channel you want to create. (The types are discussed earlier in the section, "Sherlock 2's Channels.")

4. Now, click the up and down arrows next to the icon to choose an icon for this channel.

5. Enter a description if you want to, then click OK.

Now you've got a new channel. You can drag Internet search sites from other channels to your channel, or, if you'd dragged new Internet search sites to the System Folder to install them, you can drag those from the Custom channel (the one with Sherlock Holmes' hat) to your new channel.

Chapter 7

Get Some Help

How to...

- Decide which component of Apple's Help system to use
- Use Apple Help to link to help documents
- Follow along as Apple Guide teaches you topics interactively
- Use the QuickHelp system specific to AppleWorks and Palm Desktop
- Get other kinds of help and information about your applications

Over the years, the Mac's reputation for being easy to use has encouraged Apple's engineers to work on innovative Help systems to assist you in understanding how things work and how to get things done. In fact, they've worked so much on the Help system that they've ended up with what might be a few too many ways to get help. It can get a little confusing.

The Help Systems

These days, the main Help system is the Apple Help system. The best thing about the Apple Help system is that it's based on the same technology that World Wide Web pages on the Internet use.

This makes it easier for application developers to build the Help system for their applications, since most of them already know how to create Web pages. It also makes it a little easier for us as users; if you understand how Web pages work, you'll understand how Apple Help works. Even if you don't, it's an easy system to use.

There are other kinds of help, too, including Apple Guide, Balloon Help, application help, Read Me files, and online sites. We'll take a look at all of them in this chapter.

Every application that runs in the Mac OS has a Help menu, since Apple engineers think it's important that Mac applications all have a similar look. Select that Help menu and you'll be able to see what that particular application offers in the way of help—it might be using the Apple Help system, Apple Guide technology, or another Help system, and you'll always have Balloon Help (although it won't necessarily be implemented).

NOTE   *Apple Help isn't a particular command, it's a system. So each application that uses the Apple Help system will have its own name. In the Finder, you'll find "Mac OS Help" or "Mac Help" in the Help menu—it's using the Apple Help system.*

You can also press keys to bring up the default Help system. You've got two choices. First, you can press the Help key on the iMac keyboard (it's on the top-left corner of the number pad) to bring up help. Second, you can press ⌘-? (the question mark key) to get some help.

It's rare, but if you're not finding help through the Help menu, you should also try the Apple menu. Sometimes you'll find help (or some sort of documentation) when you select About this Program (it'll actually say the program name like "About Internet Explorer"). You should also look in the application's folder on your hard disk—you may find a document of some sort in the folder that offers instructions or help.

Apple Help

The Apple Help system, as mentioned, is based on the Web technology using *hyperlinks*, which allow you to move from topic to topic in the Help system by clicking the blue, underlined text. This makes it easy to learn about a topic, then click to see a related topic.

In order to see this help, open the Help menu and choose the *Application Name* Help command. An example might be "Mac OS Help" or "Mac Help" (in Mac OS 9). This loads the Help Viewer—the browser application that you'll use to find the help you need (see Figure 7-1).

> **NOTE**   *Actually this won't always load the Apple Help system—sometimes it will load Apple Guide or the application's own internal Help system.*

Browse for Help

With the Help Viewer open, you have a couple of choices. You can begin by clicking on the hyperlinks on the page. The hyperlinks are the blue, underlined words. Clicking a hyperlink causes the Help Viewer to show you that topic. This method is a little like using the Table of Contents in a book. Click the topic that seems most appropriate. When the document for that topic appears in the Help Viewer, you can click the subtopic that seems most appropriate for your situation.

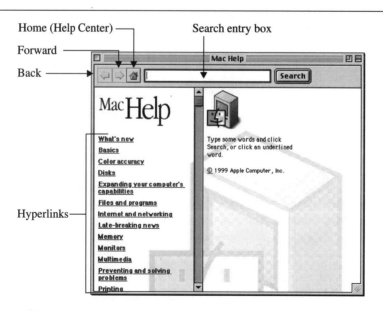

FIGURE 7-1   The Help Viewer is the main online Help system for your iMac.

After you've clicked the subtopic, you'll most likely see an instructional document that walks you through that topic. While you're reading the instructions you'll see three different types of hyperlinks. If the hyperlink doesn't have a special icon next to it, it's designed to move you to another, related topic. If the link *does* have an icon next to it, that means the link is designed to help you do something—it'll open a control panel or document or change a setting for you.

The third type of link points to a Web site on the Internet. If your Internet connection is running, you can click one of these links to load your Web browser and view the help that's online.

To leave a particular page, you can either click the Back button in the Help Viewer (which returns you to the list of topics) or click a link that takes you to another, related topic.

Search for Help

If the Table of Contents approach doesn't work for you, you can search directly for a topic using keywords. In the Search entry box at the top of the screen, enter a few words that suggest the issue you want to learn about. You don't need to enter complete sentences—something like "application menu" or "mail merge" should be good enough. (You can narrow things down by including more keywords.) Then click Search. After your iMac thinks things over, the Help Viewer will display a Search Results page, as shown in Figure 7-2.

7

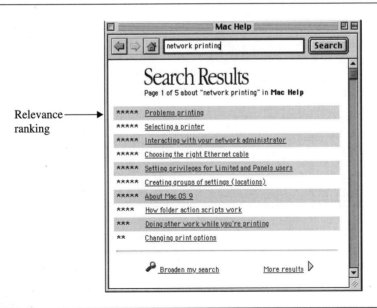

FIGURE 7-2   The Search Results page shows you the Help documents that might relate to your search keywords.

Results from a Help search are ranked by relevance—the Help Viewer decides if a Help topic is relevant based on the number of times your keywords show up in the document. Then, it shows the Help topics in descending order, along with up to five asterisks to represent relevance. (The more asterisks, the more relevant.)

When you see a topic that looks good, click its hyperlink to see the associated Help document. If you don't see the topic you want, you can click the More Results link at the bottom of the page if the Help Viewer has identified other relevant topics. If there are no more results to examine, you can click the Broaden Search hyperlink. This forces the Help Viewer to relax the search criteria and even check other applications' Help documents.

The Help Center

In some Help menus you'll see an additional choice: the Help Center. (You can also get to the Help Center by clicking the Home button—it looks like a little house—in the Help Viewer.) The Help Center works within the Help Viewer, allowing you to search and browse across all of your applications' Help systems, including those designed for the Mac OS itself and for AppleScript. If you'd like to see help for all Help Viewer–compatible applications, fire up the Help Center.

Apple Guide

In some ways, Apple Guide is similar to the Apple Help system—it offers both topic listings and a search approach to finding what you need to know. (It also offers an index of terms that is more extensive than what's found in Apple Help.) Once you find the Help topic you're looking for, Apple Guide walks you through the process in small steps, often telling you and showing you exactly what to do on the screen. You may notice, for instance, that some Apple Guide lessons will circle menus or highlight menu commands in red to help you find the correct command. More than just Help documents, Apple Guide offers something akin to electronic lessons on different topics:

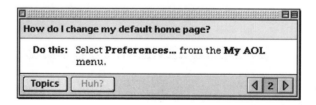

To start up Apple Guide, pull down the Help menu and look for an entry called *Application* Guide. An example might be "AOL Guide," the Help system for America Online 4.0, the version included with most iMacs. Choose that item on the Help menu and that particular Guide system appears.

 *Another way that Apple Guide is invoked is through Apple Help documents. If you see a link in an Apple Help document that starts with "Help me...," then there's a chance it will use Apple Guide technology to walk you through the steps of a lesson.*

Help by Topic

With the Apple Guide open onscreen, click the Topics button to see the various topics for which Help articles have been written. On the left side of the screen you'll see general topic areas. Click one that seems appropriate and specific Help questions appear in the Guide window. To open a Help lesson, select it and click the OK button.

After you've chosen a topic, just sit back and be taught by the Guide. Read each screen carefully, then do what's recommended on the screen. Once you've finished everything the screen says to do (or if it only provides information and doesn't offer any specific instructions), click the right arrow.

If something on the screen doesn't make sense to you, click the Huh? button, which will help by defining the technical terms onscreen. Otherwise, continue to follow the instructions on each screen of the Guide until you've solved the problem or answered your question. When you're done, you can click the Guide's Close box to end the Help session or click the Topics button to return to the Topics window.

Index and Search

One of the best ways to get to a particular Guide topic is to look it up in the index. Here's how:

1. In the main Guide window choose the Index button to look at an index of keywords that are covered in the Guide's lessons.

2. Drag the slider along the letters to change to a different letter or just click directly on one of the letters to see an alphabetical listing of keywords.

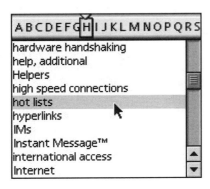

3. When you find the keyword that seems to relate to your problem, select it. A list of topic phrases appears in the right side of the window.

4. Select one of the topic phrases, then click OK. The lesson begins.

You can also search for lessons using your own keywords:

1. Click the Look For button in the main Guide window and you'll see the search box.

2. Enter keywords in the entry box, then click the Search button. (Notice that in order to type in the Guide window you'll need to click the arrow button to the left of the entry box.)

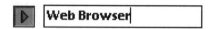

3. After clicking Search, related topic phrases appear on the right side of the window.

4. Choose one of the topic phrases and click OK to begin the lesson.

Balloon Help

Balloon Help's simple role is to tell you what something is when you point to it. Unfortunately, Balloon Help isn't universally implemented by applications. It's useful when it is, though, so it's always worth checking for Balloon Help when you have a question about an application's interface.

To turn on Balloon Help, choose Help I Show Balloons. Now, aim the mouse pointer at anything onscreen that you'd like to learn more about. If Balloon Help has been implemented for that application and that item, a small cartoon-like balloon appears at the mouse pointer, offering information.

To turn off Balloon Help, choose Help I Hide Balloons.

You'll find that Balloon Help always works in the Finder and works in a number of commercial applications like AppleWorks, Microsoft Office 98, and America Online, to name a few. You'll also find that Balloon Help is great for identifying files in your iMac's System Folder, such as control panels, extensions, fonts, and other system file types. Just turn on Balloon Help and point at any item—in the Finder or in another application—that confuses you.

Other Types of Help

Application programs can have their own types of help that they implement outside of the Apple-provided systems. Apple Help, Apple Guide, and Balloon Help are only suggested options (however strong those suggestions might be), not mandates.

In fact, you'll find that most alternative Help systems will likely offer something along the lines of hypertext links within explanatory documents. For instance, consider the types of help implemented by the different applications that came with the iMac and which are discussed in this book:

- AppleWorks uses a third-party Help system called QuickHelp, which is described in the next section. Palm Desktop also uses this system.

- Quicken and America Online 4.0 rely on the Apple Guide system for most of their Help topics.

- Microsoft's Outlook Express and Internet Explorer both use a system that's similar to Apple Help, but doesn't offer search capabilities—you just click from one topic to the next.

- Netscape Navigator and Communicator use a Help system based on Web pages that appear in the Netscape browser window.

When in doubt, choose the Help options on the Help menu, and start by looking for hyperlinks to click, topics to explore, or a search box that lets you enter keywords. You'll find that most alternative Help systems will likely offer something along the lines of hypertext links within explanatory documents. Most of them will be similar enough to the Apple Help system that you should be able to figure them out with relative ease.

The AppleWorks (QuickHelp) Help System

This is a special case because, as an iMac user, you're likely to be using AppleWorks Help all the time. And, if your iMac or iMac DV came with the Palm Desktop software, you'll find that its Help system uses the same QuickHelp engine. This section is specifically about AppleWorks Help, but the lessons are applicable elsewhere as well. So, let's take a closer look at the QuickHelp system.

This system actually works a lot like the Apple Help system, making using of hypertext links and a search engine to locate particular Help topics. You can also choose to open directly to an index of terms, which allows you to look up any concept that confuses you. The interface looks a little different from Apple Help, but the difference is mostly visual (see Figure 7-3).

7

Click to see the index ⌐   ⌐ Enter a search phrase

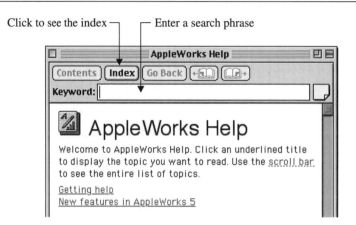

QuickHelp is similar to Apple Help, with links and a search box.

To begin, in AppleWorks choose Help | AppleWorks Help Contents. If you choose Contents, there are three basic ways you can get help from the AppleWorks Help system:

■ **Click Links** AppleWorks Help opens to an introductory document that shows you major topic areas to explore. In the AppleWorks Basics section you can click the particular type of document you're trying to create in AppleWorks to learn more about how the different tools and options work. In the Beyond the Basics section you can learn about using the different types of tools and documents together—things like getting the database module to share data with a word processing document. There's also a reference section to see terms defined or keyboard commands used in AppleWorks.

■ **Search by Keyword** At the top of the AppleWorks Help window you'll find an entry box that allows you to enter a keyword (or two) that helps you search for Help topics. Click that box to place the insertion point, then begin typing your keyword. As you type, AppleWorks Help tries to find a corresponding index entry. Press RETURN once you've finished typing your keyword. This brings up the index dialog box, with the keyword shown in the window.

■ **Search by Index** Click the Index button in the Contents window or choose Help | AppleWorks Help Index from the AppleWorks menu and you're shown the index. Now you can scroll through all of the available Help topics. (You can press a letter on the keyboard to move immediately to that part of the alphabetical listing. Typing two or more letters quickly will move you even closer to the term—typing **F** moves you to "facing pages" while typing **FI** moves you to "field.") Once you find a topic, double-click it to read the associated Help document or select the topic (see Figure 7-4), click the View Topic button to change the viewer, or click the Go To Topic button to change the viewer and dismiss the Index dialog box.

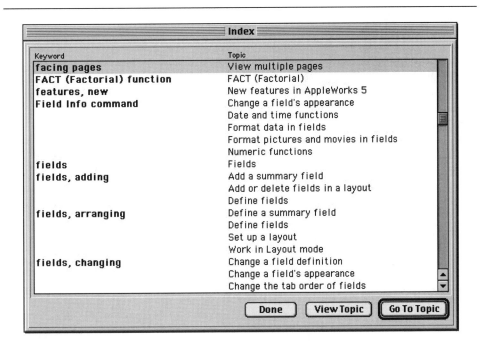

7

The Index view allows you to move quickly to a Help topic.

With the Help document windows you can do two interesting things—you can add your own notes to a topic and you can create a bookmark for a topic document. Here's how you can create a bookmark:

■ **Create a Bookmark**   This makes it easy to return quickly to a particular Help document. With the document open in the Help viewer, select Bookmark | Set Bookmark. This adds the Help document to the Bookmark menu. Now, when you're browsing Help and you want to move immediately back to this particular Help topic, just select the Bookmark menu and then select the topic. To edit (or delete) bookmarks, choose Bookmarks | Edit Bookmarks.

Notice that the AppleWorks Help menu gives you some other options, too. You can click and drag from the notepad icon in the top-right corner of the Help window to create a note. Choose Help | AppleWorks Help Index to open directly to the Index dialog box. Or, you can choose Frequently Asked Questions to see the answers to common questions from AppleWorks users—this option uses Apple Guide technology. Finally, you can choose from a list of relevant AppleWorks Assistants. (AppleWorks Assistants are discussed in Chapters 8 and 12.)

Read Me Files and PDFs

You may not have much in the way of formal help under the Help menu at all. In that case, you should check out the program's folder on your hard disk. It's possible that you'll find documentation or help there, in the form of a text or *portable* document.

Read Me files are actually a special case—they're usually designed to tell you about the installation and history of the program, not necessarily how to use it. You should read the Read Me file if it exists, though, since it can tell you a lot about troubles that the program's author realizes the program may have. If there's a known conflict, for instance, it'll be in the Read Me file. So will any special instructions for installing or using the program successfully.

Your iMac already has a number of Read Me files scattered around its hard disk, some of which you'll probably want to read:

■ **Mac OS Read Me Files**   This is actually a folder on your main hard drive that includes many different Read Me files installed by the Mac OS. Here you'll find information about known problems with your version of the Mac OS, including other applications that may cause conflicts or crashes.

■ **Apple Extras**   Check out the individual subfolders within the Apple Extras folder to see Read Me files on a variety of subjects. They'll tell you a little more about the technologies and small applications found in the Apple Extras folder.

■ **Applications**   AppleWorks, Adobe Acrobat, FaxSTF, QuickTime, and most other application folders you install should include a Read Me file that tells you what possible conflicts, bugs, or other problems have been identified by the application authors.

You may find other documents that tell you how to use the program. These may appear in different formats. The most common of these will be SimpleText documents, so that any Mac owner can read them. (SimpleText comes with all Mac, iMac, and iBook computers.)

Another popular way to include formatted documentation is using Adobe Portable Document Format (PDF) documents. These documents appear in the Adobe Acrobat Reader application, which allows them to be easily viewed, read, and printed on your iMac, even if you don't have all the original fonts or the program used to create the document. Since the Acrobat Reader is installed on your iMac, you can just double-click a PDF file to view and read it (see Figure 7-5).

The Acrobat Reader is located in the Applications folder, just in case you want to go find it and double-click to launch the Reader.

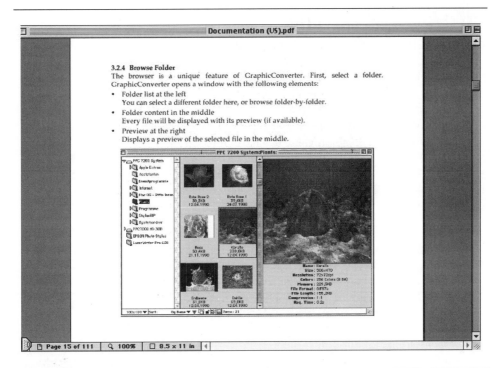

FIGURE 7-5   Acrobat PDF files are simply regular documents that maintain their formatting to make them easier to read and pleasing to the eye.

 **Get Help Online**

If you've rooted around in the Help menu and in your program's folder and you still can't find what you need to know, you should try the program author's Web site. If it's a large company, they'll likely provide plenty of help on the World Wide Web. Even if it's a smaller company or an individual, you'll probably be able to find out what you need to know by visiting the Web site and, perhaps, sending your question through e-mail.

The first thing you'll need to do is understand how to get on the World Wide Web, which is discussed in Chapter 19. Then, you'll need to find the software author's Web address—it's probably in the Read Me file or the About This Program window, or it might be elsewhere in a document in the program's folder. Enter the Web address in your Web browser to visit the site.

At the Web site you should look for two things. First, look for a customer support section—you'll likely find a link called "Support" or something similar on any reputable software company's Web page. Once there, see what you can drum up on the program you're working with. In particular, you should look for any Frequently Asked Questions (FAQ) lists that the software author has posted. Reading any FAQ document(s) is an important component in etiquette on the Internet, since it assures you that you won't be writing the author about a question that's already been published online.

If you can't find your answer, look for online message areas or some other forum for discussing the product. (You'll often find these on America Online, too, if you choose to use the service.) If you can't find a way to post your question publicly or submit it via a form, look for a customer service e-mail address and send them the question. If you've paid for the program, after all, you do deserve answers.

If you're very adventurous, you might find that other users can help you find the answer. Chapter 30 discusses some of the places where knowledgeable Mac users and professionals tend to hang out. If you join some of those groups or sign up for the electronic newsletters, you may find that they're a great way to get quick answers to problems that other folks have encountered and solved.

Apple also offers a special Web site where you can get information about your iMac, including help when something goes wrong with it or when it needs a software update. You can visit that site at **http://www.apple.com/support/** on the Web. We'll discuss these resources in more detail in Chapter 30.

Part II

Get Your Work Done

Chapter 8

Create Printed Documents

How to...

- Get acquainted with AppleWorks
- Create a word processing document
- Type your document and format the text
- Format paragraphs, align elements, and create headers and footers
- Format the entire document, including margins, sections, and tabs
- Spell-check and find and replace automatically
- Create Stylesheets and paragraph styles
- Use prebuilt Stationery and create your own document templates

As you know, a computer makes you a better writer. My ramblings, for instance, are almost instantly translated into readable, friendly, and useful text, thanks to my iMac. Otherwise, not only would my text be misspelled, grammatically unapproachable, and improperly formatted, it would also be completely unintelligible and morally reprehensible.

OK, so that's a bit of an exaggeration. A computer isn't about writing better—it's about typing a little better, formatting documents more professionally, and being able to edit, cut, paste, and shape your document without scissors and glue.

Write with Your iMac

If you need to write documents with your iMac, you'll likely turn to a word processing application—an application designed to accept typed input and allow you to manipulate it on the page. Unless you've chosen to install a different word processing application, your best bet is to launch AppleWorks, which came with your iMac, to begin word processing.

A word processing program is designed to do a number of things. It's designed to accept text and images that you type or add through menu commands, then allow you to format the text and images in many different ways. It's worth saying that word processors are designed to help you format entire documents—from memos and letters to longer documents like reports, pamphlets, and books. Word processors allow you to do many things to long and short documents:

- Change the document size, margins, and spacing
- Insert headers and footnotes
- Change the font, style, and formatting of text
- Create documents in outline form
- Format text in tabular form
- Format text with bullets, numbers, or special tabs and indents
- Check spelling
- Change formatting for paragraphs, sections, or the entire document

In most cases, however, a word processor is not designed for creating a particular *page*. That's what layout applications like QuarkXPress and Adobe PageMaker are designed for. Such applications have highly sophisticated tools that allow a page designer to drop text, images, effects, lines, and shapes onto a page and manipulate them freely to create the most stunning advertisement, pamphlet, or publication. Even within AppleWorks we'll use a different module to create newsletters and similar layouts.

So, word processing really is a little closer to the typewriter than it is to the layout table. But there is a difference between a typewriter—even most electronic, computerized typewriters—and a word processing application. Word processing applications allow you to change your mind. You can experiment with documents after the fact. That means you can create the document first, then worry about how it will be formatted.

8

AppleWorks vs. The Other Guys

AppleWorks is what's referred to as a "Works" application, because it's designed to perform more than one major function. While a program like Microsoft Word is designed solely for word processing, AppleWorks offers a number of different modules, allowing you to create word processing documents, spreadsheets, databases, images, drawings, and other types of documents. So why would you choose anything else?

In most cases you probably won't have to. AppleWorks is a very good program that allows you to do some rather unique things—including putting its parts together to create layouts that feature word processing, images, spreadsheet tables, and database data in the same documents. In that respect, it's a very powerful and very enjoyable program to work with.

But you may need more specialized capabilities or you may need to use a particular program—like Microsoft Word—because the rest of your office, school, organization, or secret-handshake society requires it. That's okay, but you'll need to spend more money and install that application yourself.

In exchange, you'll get a program that's specifically tailored to the task at hand. Microsoft Word, for instance, offers a lot of tools for collaborating on important word processing documents—you can embed comments, track changes, and even give different human editors a different color to use within the document so it's easy to see who is making what changes. We used Microsoft Word to create this book, for instance, largely because of its collaborative capabilities.

So, you'll want to use a tool that's designed for the job. The question becomes, how do you know? Let me reiterate that AppleWorks is truly an impressive application, and you'll be able to accomplish a lot with it. If your tasks are personal, educational, or even for a small business, you'll likely find it completely adequate for your needs.

But even if it doesn't fit all of your needs, in nearly all cases, documents created in AppleWorks can be translated into documents that can be read by other applications like Word, Excel, QuarkXPress, and others when the times comes. So, feel free to try things in AppleWorks first, then move on to something else if you need more power.

Begin Your Document

To begin, launch AppleWorks or choose File | New if AppleWorks is already open. The New Document window appears, allowing you to choose the type of document you'd like to begin. In this case, you're interested in creating a word processing document, so leave that selection highlighted and click OK.

NOTE   *In AppleWorks, the type of document you choose helps determine what sort of tools and menu commands you see at first—you'll see the word processing commands and a blank document window now.*

Start typing. There are actually a couple of rules you should follow when typing in a word processor, especially if you're used to a typewriter. Some of these rules are:

■ **Don't press TAB to indent the first line of a paragraph**   You can format paragraphs so that they are indented automatically, either before or after you type them.

■ **Don't press RETURN at the end of a line**   You only need to press RETURN at the end of a paragraph. Whenever you type to the right margin of the page, the next thing you type will automatically *wrap* to the next line.

■ **Don't put two spaces after a period**   Many typists get used to pressing the SPACEBAR twice after the end of a sentence, but that throws off the automatic spacing capabilities of a word processing program and it just looks bad with many standard Mac fonts.

■ **Don't worry about double-spacing while you type**   You'll be able to set line spacing for your document at 1.5, double-, or triple-space after you've typed it (or, as you'll see, before you begin).

■ **Don't press RETURN many times to get to a new page**   You can easily insert a page break if you're done on one page and want to begin on another one.

■ **Don't enter asterisks, dashes, or numbers for lists**   You can do all that automatically. If you need to create a list like the one you're reading right now, you can do that with commands—just enter each line and press RETURN. You'll be able to go back and format the bulleted or numbered list later.

■ **Don't do anything weird to change the margins**   You don't need to insert many spaces, add tabs, or press RETURN in order to create special margin spacing—for instance, if you want to have a block of quoted text that's squeezed onto the page. Again, you can do that with special document formatting commands, covered later in this chapter. For now, just type the paragraph normally.

■ **Don't uses spaces to create columns or table layouts**   At the very least, you should use tabs and the document ruler to set up the spacing in your document. That's covered later in this chapter, too.

Most of these issues are addressed in the section "Format Your Document," which appears later in this chapter. You'll find that what you need to do while typing is pretty simple:

1. Type words.

2. When you get to the end of a sentence, type a period, then press the SPACEBAR once.

3. When you get to the end of a paragraph, press RETURN.

That's pretty much it while you're typing your document. Remember, you'll be able to change just about anything once you have the words on the page. For now, getting those words on the page is the primary goal.

Fonts, Styles, and Sizes

Aside from the typing basics, there are two other precepts for the accomplished word processing typist. (That's you.) The first is to *save often,* which is covered in the next section. The second is to format your text as you're typing. It's not mandatory, but learning to format as you type makes creating your documents easier.

By text formatting I mean three things: the font, the style, and the size of the text. These things can be changed easily before or while you're typing a line of text, so I'll include them here while you're getting started with your word processor.

Fonts

The word "font" is used in most Macintosh applications to mean "typeface," which is defined as a general design for a set of characters. Popular typefaces are Courier, Times New Roman, Helvetica, and so forth.

If you'd like your typed text to appear in something other than the default font, you can head up to the Font menu, choose a new font, and begin typing. Your text appears in that new font.

Similarly, you can select existing text and change it to a new font. To select text, move the mouse pointer to the left of the first word you want to highlight, press the mouse button, and drag the mouse pointer to the right of the last word you want to choose, then release the mouse button. If you want to choose all the words in your document, choose Edit | Select All. Then select the Font menu and click the font you want to use for the highlighted text. Your text should change immediately (see Figure 8-1).

You may notice one cool thing about AppleWorks' Font menu—it shows you each font name in its actual design so you can get a quick idea of how the font will appear in your document once chosen.

Styles

The text styles represent different effects you apply to the fonts for emphasis—things like italics and boldfacing. You can change the style of your text in either of the two ways that you change the font—before you type, or by selecting text that's already been typed.

To change the style, select the Style menu in AppleWorks, then click on the style you want to use. Begin typing and your text appears in that style.

To change the style of text that already appears, select that text in the document window and then pull down the Style menu. Choose the style you want to use and the highlighted text changes immediately to that style.

Often, though, you won't want to do it this way, especially with the four major styles: Plain, Italic, Bold, and Underlined. In these special cases, you'll probably want to learn the keyboard commands for changing text styles. Except for the Plain command, these commands are the same in many applications, including AppleWorks:

⌘-B	Boldface	⌘-U	Underline
⌘-I	Italic	⌘-T	Plain, unstyled text

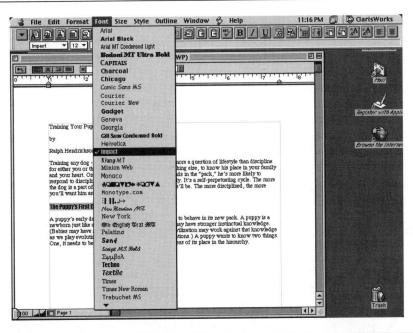

FIGURE 8-1   Choose a new font from the Font menu and you'll see it in your document.

Knowing these keyboard commands, you can quickly switch styles while typing. Press ⌘-I, type a word in italics, then press ⌘-T to return to plain text. (You can also press ⌘-I to turn italics off again—you'll find that some applications don't support ⌘-T.) Press ⌘-U and ⌘-B and you'll be typing bold, underlined text; press ⌘-T and you're back to plain text again.

Sizes

You can change the size of text in your document by highlighting the text and pulling down the Size menu to choose the point size you want. Points are a traditional way of sizing fonts in publishing terms—72 points equals about one inch, so 12 points equals about one-sixth of an inch in height. Traditionally, 72-point text was reserved for newspaper headlines that declared war or the surprise winner of a presidential election—these days the biggest headline on the front page on any given morning is probably about 72 points.

Readable body type is typically about 12 points; 14 points looks like "big" type you find in some of those movie novelizations. Try 18 points for a subhead in your report—24 or so can look good for the title of your report (see Figure 8-2).

You can also change text sizes as you type. Pull down the Size menu and choose the new size from the menu, then type in that new size. If you want to use the keyboard commands, they might take some memorizing: ⌘-SHIFT-< makes text smaller and

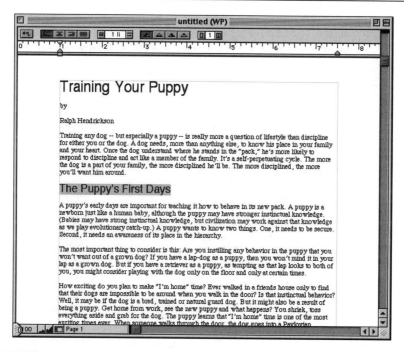

FIGURE 8-2 Different point sizes clearly define the parts of your document.

⌘-SHIFT-> makes it bigger. (Note, by the way, that these are specific AppleWorks keyboard commands and don't work in all applications.)

Save Often

If you've been following so far, you might see from the figures in this chapter something terribly wrong is going on. The document I'm working on is still untitled, which means it hasn't been saved!

My rule: Save every three sentences. It usually doesn't take long for each save (once the initial save is complete) and it'll sure make you happy if and when your iMac or your application crashes. (It does happen. That fashionable iMac encourages you to put it in high-traffic areas where you're bound to trip over the power cord.) Having saved very recently, you won't be as upset when you only have to retype a few sentences to catch up. If you have to retype an entire page or two, you won't be nearly as pleased.

To save the document the first time, choose File | Save once you've typed something. Use the Save dialog box to find the folder where you want to store the file, then give it a name and click Save.

From then on, you can just press ⌘-S to save as you're typing. Every three sentences, remember? (For more on saving, see Chapter 5.)

 *AppleWorks doesn't offer an AutoSave command, but it can be added with a $10 shareware program called SuperSave that autosaves in nearly every Mac application you have. See Chapter 20 for more on downloading shareware.*

Format Your Document

I know I've been a little forceful about the whole "just type your document" thing—I hope I didn't scare you with that. It's just that it's so much easier to set up the document to work the way you want it to before or after you type—not during. Let me show you what I mean. This sections covers a lot of stuff in a little space, including:

- Formatting paragraphs: indenting, spacing, alignment

- Inserting elements: page breaks, headers, footers

- Formatting whole documents: margins, page numbers

- Formatting sections: book-type formatting

- Using tabs and the ruler: making changes visually

See, that's quite a bit. Whether you're writing reports, documentation, thesis papers, research, legislation, contracts, or books, you'll find you're able to get pretty deep into this stuff without filling too much of the space in your head. After all, you've got important things to store in your brain, including birthdays, phone numbers, where your aunt hid her will, and how to tie a double-Windsor knot.

Format Paragraphs

There are three basic things you'll be managing when it comes to your paragraphs, and it all happens in the Paragraph dialog box. To start formatting a paragraph, click the mouse button to place the insertion point in that paragraph (you don't have to select the whole thing, but you can if you like). To format more than one paragraph at once, select them. (Remember that triple-clicking usually selects paragraphs.) With that out of the way, choose Format | Paragraph. That causes the Paragraph dialog box to appear:

	Paragraph	
Left Indent: `0 in`	Line Spacing: `1`	`li ▼`
First Line: `0 in`	Space Before: `0`	`li ▼`
Right Indent: `0 in`	Space After: `0`	`li ▼`
Label: `None ▼`	Alignment: `Left ▼`	
`?`	`Apply` `Cancel`	`OK`

8

Indenting

Now, in the Paragraph dialog box you can make some choices about how that paragraph is going to look. On the left side of the dialog box, you have three choices. All three are entered in the entry boxes in inches—a standard indent is about 0.5 inches. You can indent either or both margins (usually for block quotes, programming code listings, or lists) or you can indent just the first line of the paragraph.

Click in the entry box next to the type of indent you want, then enter the number of inches you want for the indent. You can press TAB to move to the next box or press RETURN to accept the value and close the dialog box. If you'd like to see how something looks before you close the dialog box, click the Apply button. That makes your changes but leaves the dialog box open for further changes or experimentation. By the way, you can also move this dialog box around if you need to see how your paragraph looks after the change is applied.

TIP   *You don't need to type the "in" for inches when entering your own number—just the number will suffice.*

Line Spacing

In the Line Spacing entry box enter a number, then choose the units for that number in the little pull-down menu next to it. If you want to double-space, you can just keep the units at "lines."

You can also fine-tune your spacing to give yourself more or less space between lines as necessary. For instance, you'll sometimes want a document to look like it's double-spaced, but you need it squeezed a bit. In that case, you should choose Points as the units for Line Spacing and select a point size that's just less than twice the point size of your text. If your text is 12 points, for instance, you could choose 20 points to get a slightly squeezed double-spacing effect. (Perfect for cheating on the line spacing for term papers—did I say that?)

NOTE   *You'd think you could just choose 1.75 lines for the Line Spacing, but AppleWorks rounds it up to 2 lines. It will only accept whole and half values, so 1.5 is acceptable, but 1.25 gets rounded up to 1.5.*

The other spacing options allow you to add additional space above and below a paragraph—this can often be useful if you choose a more contemporary style for your document in which you don't indent the first line of your paragraphs. In that case, a little extra space before and after a paragraph will make it clear where it ends and the next paragraph begins.

Make a List

When you build a list in AppleWorks, you press RETURN after each list item. So, technically, you're creating a number of different paragraphs, even if they're really short. In order to turn them into a list, you can select each item and give it a Label in the Paragraph dialog box. The labels vary from bullet points to numbers to roman numerals.

There's a slightly more efficient way to make a list:

1. In the document window, type each list item and press RETURN after each.

2. Drag the mouse pointer to select every item in the list.

3. Select Format | Paragraph.

4. Choose the Label menu from the Paragraph dialog box and select Bullet. (See Figure 8-3.)

5. Click Apply or OK.

That's it—the list is created. Every item you've highlighted becomes its own list item. If you're still in the Paragraph dialog box, you can change the item's left and right indent to taste—sometimes you'll want a list indented from the left margin to help it stand out.

If you want to change a bulleted paragraph back to a regular paragraph, select it and choose None from the Label menu in the Paragraph dialog box. That will return the paragraph to normal, nonbullet mode.

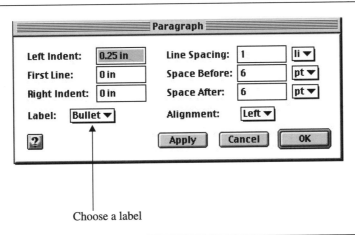

Choose a label

FIGURE 8-3   Choose the Bullet label to change your highlighted paragraphs into list items.

Alignment

The last little task for the Paragraph dialog box is aligning the paragraph. You can align the paragraph in four different ways:

- ■ **Left**   Paragraph is flush with the left margin and ragged on the right margin.
- ■ **Right**   Paragraph is ragged on the left margin and flush with the right margin.
- ■ **Center**   Both left and right margins are ragged, but the entire paragraph is balanced toward the center.
- ■ **Justify**   The paragraph is spaced so that the text is flush with both the left and right margins, like most columns of text in a newspaper.

To choose one of the alignments, just pull down the Alignment menu and make your choice. Click Apply and you'll see the paragraph's alignment change.

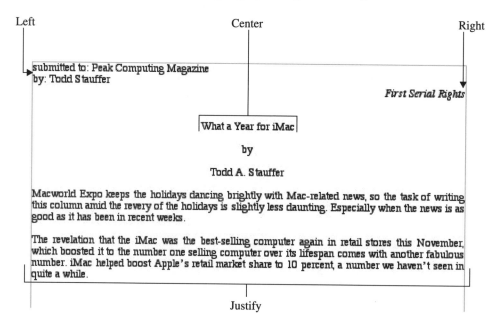

Format Multiple Paragraphs

Clearly, it could get a bit tedious to format every paragraph of a document manually like this. Fortunately, that's not mandatory. If you like, you can select as many paragraphs as you like—or even choose Edit | Select All to highlight the entire document—and perform the same Paragraph dialog box changes to them all at once.

You can also copy one paragraph's traits and apply them to another paragraph. To do that, place the insertion point in the paragraph you want to use as a model, then choose Format | Copy Ruler (⌘-SHIFT-C). This copies the paragraph settings. Now, place the cursor in the paragraph you want to change to the copied settings (or select multiple paragraphs). Choose Format | Paste Ruler (⌘-SHIFT-V). The selected paragraphs change to reflect the model paragraph's settings.

Why are these commands called Copy Ruler and Paste Ruler? Because the ruler in the document window reflects all of the settings you can make in the Paragraph dialog box. See the next section for information about using it to quickly format paragraphs.

Shortcut: Use the Ruler

Some of these formatting options—alignment, basic line spacing, and bullets—are offered right in the document window if you have the ruler visible. (To show the rulers, choose Window | Show Rulers. To hide rulers, choose Windows | Hide Rulers.)

Small, clickable icons on the ruler will allow you to do the same things you can do in the Paragraph dialog box.

For instance, if you'd like to align a paragraph, place the insertion point somewhere in that paragraph and click one of the alignment buttons in the ruler. You can tell by looking at the buttons how they align—left, center, right, and justify (see the following illustration). If you don't like how the paragraph looks, click another alignment button. The changes are made instantly.

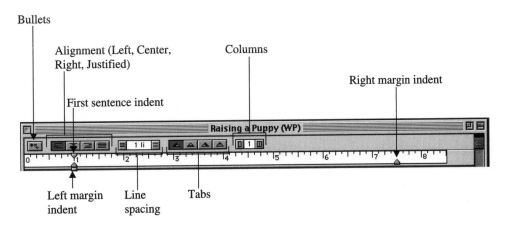

The other buttons work the same way. Select the paragraphs you want to turn into bullet items, then choose the bullet you want to use from the Label menu on the ruler. The series of paragraphs become bullet items.

For line spacing, the button on the left pushes lines together while the button on the right spreads them apart. Select the paragraph(s) for which you want to alter the line spacing, then click on the line spacing button of your choice.

Here's a cool trick—if you double-click the line-spacing number box where it says 1.5in or 2in, you'll immediately open the Paragraph dialog box.

The ruler can also be used to quickly format the indenting of paragraphs. Select the paragraph(s) you want to indent, then drag the little indent sliders. (Point at a slider with the mouse pointer, hold down the button and drag it to the right or left. Let go of the mouse button to place the slider.)

The sliders determine how things are indented—on the left side, the top slider determines the first line indent and the bottom slider determines the left side indent of the rest of the paragraph. Notice what this lets you do—if you indent *only* the bottom slider, then you'll end up with a paragraph whose first line is flush with the left margin and the rest of the lines are indented, just like in academic bibliography entries.

The right margin indent slider controls just the right-side indent of the entire paragraph. Using a combination of the three you can quickly and visually accomplish anything you can do with indents in the Paragraph dialog box. Of course, you'll have to eyeball the measurements—in the control panel you can be exact to a fraction of an inch.

Insert Elements

Once you have your paragraphs nice and neat you may start to get the feeling that there are still some things missing—elements you'll usually find at the edges of your document. Here are some of the special elements you can insert into your document:

- **Headers**   Need something at the top of every page? Add a header and it'll automatically be put at the top of all your pages.

- **Footers**   Create a footer and the same thing appears at the bottom of your pages.

- **Page Numbers**   Add page numbers that automatically count up for you.

- **Date and Time**   Choose a quick menu item to add these to your documents in the header, footer, or wherever you like.

- **Section Breaks**   Dividing your document into sections—for new chapters, for instance—makes it easier to renumber and manage things.

- **Page Breaks**   When you're ready for a new page, but not finished with the last one, you can break immediately and start a fresh page.

- **Footnotes**   Writing a scientific, academic, or commercial report that needs footnotes? You've got 'em.

Headers and Footers

These small sections appear at the top and bottom of the page and allow you to add your name, the document's name, a page number, the date and time, or just about anything else required.

To create a header, select Format | Insert Header. A small section appears at the top of the current page in your document window. Now, you can type anything you need in that section—you can even adjust what you type using the paragraph formatting tools.

Header

Footers work the same way—choose Format I Insert Footer and a small section appears at the bottom of the page. In either a header or footer you can press the RETURN key to add additional lines—it'll take away space from the document, not from the margins, which will always stay the same as their setting in the Document dialog box (discussed in the section "Format the Whole Document," later in this chapter).

Now all you need is something to put in the header and footer.

Page Number, Date, and Time

Over in the Edit menu, AppleWorks makes it easy to add the page number, current date, and current time into your document. You can add them anywhere, but the best plan is to put them in the header or footer of your document. And the best part is that the date, time, and page numbers will be updated automatically. The Date and Time commands are a great way to get an automatic record of when documents are modified.

To insert a date, time, or page number, place the insertion point in the header or footer where you want the date to appear. Then, choose the appropriate Insert command from the Edit menu. The element you're inserting appears, as shown here:

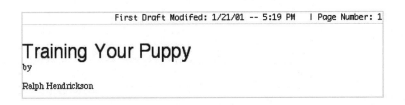

Want to enter a date, time, or page number that never changes automatically? Hold down the OPTION key as you select one of the Insert commands in the Edit menu.

When you select the Insert Page Number command, you'll get a small dialog box that allows you to choose which page-related number you want to enter. Here's the breakdown:

- **Page Number**   Inserts the current page number for that page in the document or section.

8

- **Section Number**   Inserts the current section's number. You can create different sections of a document—for instance, for chapters—and number them. We'll cover sections next in this chapter.

- **Section Page Count**   Enters the number of total pages in the current section.

- **Document Page Count**   Enters the total number of pages in the document. This would be useful for something at the top of the page that said "Page 4 of 15"—you'd get the "15" to automatically update by inserting the Document Page Count command.

Beyond these, there's a Representation menu you can use to choose how the page numbers will be shown. If you want something that says "Section C, Page 4," you can have those numbers automatically updated, too.

The point of having all of these different page numbering options is to give you the opportunity to choose different combinations of page numbering schemes and have them automatically updated. Plus, you can add your own text in the header to help explain your scheme.

Section Breaks

While we're on the topic of all this numbering, let's quickly look into section breaks. You can create a section break anywhere in your document—a section is simply an internal label for parts of your AppleWorks document. Sections allow you to divide a large document up into chapters, lessons, segments or, well, sections. You can then number the sections separately, start over with new page numbering, and so on, as discussed earlier.

To create a section break, place the insertion point where you'd like the new section to begin, then select Format I Insert Section. Now, a line appears dividing the two sections of the document. (This line will not print in the final document.) If you've used the automatic section numbers with the Insert Page Number command, then the section numbers on subsequent pages will reflect the new section.

You can do a whole lot more with sections, too. That's discussed in "Format the Section," later in this chapter.

Page Breaks

If you're typing along in your document and you decide you want a new page, you can choose Format I Insert Page Break. That automatically moves you to the top of a new page. Plus, your text will always appear at the top of a new page after a page break, even if you add text before the page break occurs. If you just press RETURN a bunch of times to get to a new page, you'd have to go back and fix the Returns every time you reformatted, added text, or otherwise messed with the text in the document.

Footnotes

If you need footnotes in your document, they're pretty easy to add. Place the insertion point at the end of the word or sentence you want to footnote. Then, choose Format I Insert

Footnote. A superscript footnote number appears next to the selected word, and you're transported to the bottom of the page (or the end of the document) where you can type the footnote text, as shown in Figure 8-4.

You can choose where footnotes are added—at the bottom of the page or the end of the document—using the Document dialog box, which is covered in the next section, "Format the Whole Document." If you're currently set up to place footnotes at the end of your document, the command will be Insert Endnote instead of Insert Footnote.

To get rid of a footnote, delete the footnote number in the body of the document. The footnote itself will automatically disappear.

Format the Whole Document

After you're done formatting individual paragraphs, you may have reason to make some more global choices—in that case, you'll want to get into the Document formatting preferences. Select Format I Document and the Document dialog box appears (see Figure 8-5).

Your first Document options focus on the margins for your document. You can select the top, left, right, and bottom margins for the entire document from this dialog box. Just enter the value for each margin, in inches. The larger the margin numbers, the more white space will appear around the text in your document.

While you're in this dialog box, you'll probably want to decide whether or not you desire to work with facing pages versus pages that come one after the other. What's the

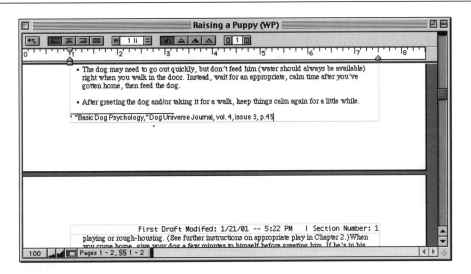

FIGURE 8-4   Adding impressive-looking footnotes is automatic and easy.

8

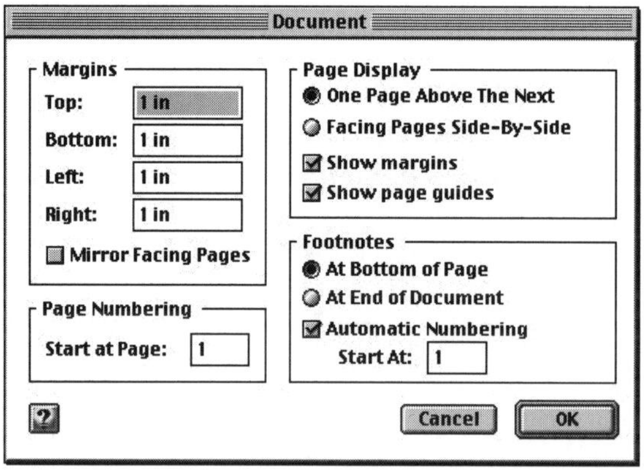

FIGURE 8-5   The Document dialog box

difference? Think about a typical letter or memo—usually, pages come right after one another and no one really expects you to print on the back side of pages. When you finish one page you move it out of the way and read the next page.

If you're writing a book, report, pamphlet, or similar document, you'll want facing pages. That is, readers expect to turn the page in a book and read the back side of that same page, then move over to the right side page and read that one. Those are facing pages, and you can set up AppleWorks to work with facing pages in the Document dialog box.

While working with the margin numbers you can select the Mirror Facing Pages check box in order to change the margin options slightly. The Left and Right margin options change to Outside and Inside margins. Why? Because once you have pages set up to face one another, you can adjust the inside margins together to provide a uniform look. This is important if you plan to distribute your documents in a booklet, pamphlet, or newsletter form—you'll want facing pages to look right when placed next to one another (see Figure 8-6).

Of course, if you'll be formatting and printing your documents as facing pages, you'll probably want to view them as facing pages, so select the radio button next to Facing Pages Side-By-Side in the Page Display section of the dialog box. Now the pages are moved so that the document window looks more like Figure 8-6. (Likewise, click the button next to One Page Above The Next to return to the default behavior.) You can also make choices as to whether or not margins and page guides, the light gray lines that show you the boundaries of the page, should be displayed.

The last little section in the Document dialog box allows you to choose how footnotes will appear—if space is left for them at the bottom of every page or if they all appear at the end of the document. You can also have footnotes automatically numbered, if you desire—just check the check box and enter the number the footnotes should start with in the entry box.

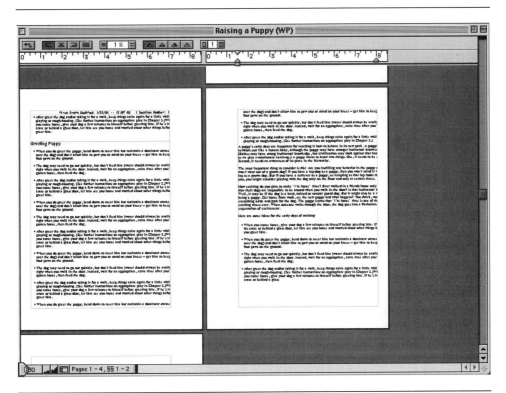

FIGURE 8-6 Facing pages need mirror-image margins to look right once they're in book or booklet form.

Format the Section

You saw earlier in the section "Insert Elements" how to create section breaks. Now, with your document broken out into sections, you can choose Format | Section to format each individual section. In fact, even if you don't break your document into different sections, you can still format it as one, big section. There are options in here you might want to check out, including the ability to make the first page of your document a "title page" (meaning it has no headers or footers) and the opportunity to choose different headers and footers for left- and right-facing pages.

To begin, place the insertion point somewhere in the section you want to format (or anywhere in the document if you haven't added any section breaks). Now select Format | Section. The Section dialog box appears, as shown in Figure 8-7.

> NOTE *You may have noticed that I'm ignoring most things that have to do with columns in this chapter. We'll discuss them in more depth in Chapter 12, which covers creating brochures, newsletters, and similar page layouts that use multiple columns.*

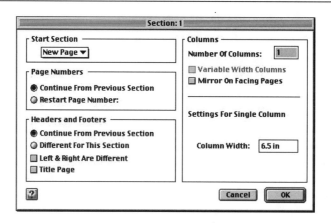

FIGURE 8-7   The Section dialog box gives you even more formatting options.

At the top of the dialog box you'll see that the title bar tells you which section you're working with—a handy feature. Your first decision, though, is how this new section should manifest itself. Choose one of the following from the Start Section menu:

- **New Line**   Choose this option and the section really is pretty much invisible—it'll be for your reference, but readers won't necessarily notice it.

- **New Page**   If the section is to be a new chapter or a major section in a pamphlet, for instance, you'd choose New Page to insert a page break along with the new section.

- **Left Page or Right Page**   If you've formatted your document with facing pages (read about it in the earlier section "Format the Whole Document"), then you can choose if this new section begins with a left or right page. If the new section represents a new chapter, for instance, you'd likely choose to start it as a right page.

In the Page Numbers portion of the dialog box, you have some housekeeping options. If you've chosen to have your new section begin on a new page, you can now choose to have it begin a new page counting scheme. You can have the page count start over at 1, for instance, so you can keep track of the count in the section or chapter instead of in the whole document. (You'll find that many pamphlets and booklets will number with a section number and a page number, like "C-3" or "3-3." You can do the same thing by inserting section and page numbers into the header or footer of your document.)

Finally, you can choose to have the headers and footers the same as they were in previous parts of the document, or choose to build all new headers and footers for this section. (Choose between Continue From Previous Section or Different For This Section by clicking the appropriate radio button.) If you will have new ones, you can click the Left & Right Are Different option to have different headers and footers on the left and right pages. Click the Title Page option to have the first page of the section appear without headers or footers.

Got it all set? Click the OK button and you're returned to the document, complete with its new section formatting. Now, if you chose to have new headers and footers in this section, you'll want to insert and edit them.

Tabs and the Ruler

The TAB key on your iMac keyboard can be a powerful tool in the fight against chaos in your documents. By default a standard document offers tab points every half-inch or so. But you might want more specialized tabs than that—tabs that help you align text, for instance.

There are four different types of tabs you can add to your document: left-aligned, right-aligned, centered, and aligned to a particular character, usually a decimal. What that does, in most cases, is give you an interesting freedom to align things for impromptu tables and arrangements of text in your documents.

Say, for instance, that you want to create a table of contents. In that case you'll need two things, a right-aligned column of chapter descriptions and a column that's aligned to the dash that separates a document's section and page number. (OK, so maybe this example is an overly regimented military-type report. Just bear with me.) It'll look something like Figure 8-8.

How does this work? Before you type any text, just drag the tab you want to the point on the ruler where you think it should go.

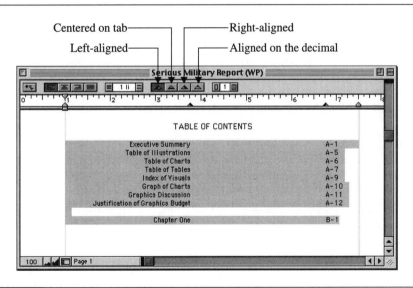

FIGURE 8-8   An orderly use of tabs

If you want a right-aligned column to end on the two-inch mark, drag it there. If you want to align a column of currency figures, put the decimal-aligned tab on the six-inch mark and that's where the dollars will line up.

Need to switch some things around? Three rules:

- If you need to change a tab that affects more than one row of text, select *every* row first, then change the tab in the ruler. Otherwise, you'll only change it for the row where the insertion point is. This will happen to you a lot by accident, so be wary.

- If you need to change a tab that you've already dragged to the ruler, double-click it. The Tab dialog box appears, allowing you to make changes. For instance, you can change the alignment of the tab, add a fill (automatically fill in behind the tab with dots or dashes), or tweak the location of the tab by entering the inch mark where it should appear.

- To get rid of a tab, select *all* rows that are affected by the tab—they all need to be highlighted—then pick up the tab and drag it back up to the top of the ruler. It'll disappear.

It's worth emphasizing that if you can't find a tab, if a tab is still there even though you moved it, or if only part of your document is lined up to tabs correctly, there's a good reason. It's because you didn't select every line in your document affected by that tab. Go back, select all the lines, and make your change once more.

Spell, Find, Change, and Count

You've finally gotten through most of your document creation. You've formatted the text, cleaned it up with tabs, and saved every three lines. Now that you've seen what a computer can do to help you format an important report or document, how about seeing what it can do to help you clean up and edit the words themselves? Here's where some of that computerized speed and savvy comes into play.

Check Spelling

By brute force your word processor can jump quickly through a document and check every word against an internal dictionary. If it finds one it's not familiar with, it'll suggest other words that seem to be similarly spelled. If you see the word you meant to type, you can choose it from the list. Otherwise, you can either add the word that AppleWorks doesn't recognize, type the correct spelling yourself, or just skip the suggestion.

Here's how it works:

1. When you're ready to check spelling, select Edit | Writing Tools | Check Document Spelling.

2. AppleWorks begins checking. When it finds a word it doesn't like, it pops up in a dialog box like the one here:

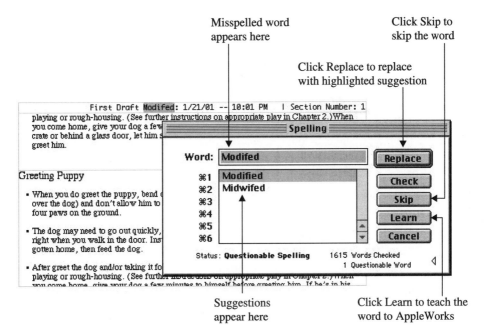

Misspelled word appears here

Click Skip to skip the word

Click Replace to replace with highlighted suggestion

Suggestions appear here

Click Learn to teach the word to AppleWorks

3. If AppleWorks offers the correct spelling, select it in the box and click Replace (or press the keyboard command ⌘-*number* where *number* is the number of the suggestion in the list). If you don't see the correct spelling, you can type it into the entry box. If you type something you want to check against AppleWorks' dictionary, click the Check button. If the word is spelled correctly, click Learn. If the word isn't worth worrying about (it's an odd abbreviation or something), then click Skip.

4. AppleWorks moves on to the next word it finds misspelled.

If you don't need to check the entire document, you can check just a selection of text—highlight the text you want to check, then select Edit I Writing Tools I Check Selection Spelling.

Find and Change

The Find and Change features use some of the same technology as spell-checking, but instead of checking the document against an internal dictionary, they check the file against whatever text you enter in the Find dialog box. They can then change the found text to whatever text you choose.

Need an example? As I wrote the original draft of this chapter, half the time I called this program ClarisWorks, since that's what it was called for nearly ten years—and I'm a slow learner. The fact is, though, that Apple renamed it "AppleWorks," so that's what I want you to see in the final product. So, when I got to the end of the draft, I told the program to perform a selective Find and Change to help me find all instances of "ClarisWorks" so I could change most of them to "AppleWorks."

Here's how to do a Find and Change:

1. Select Edit | Find/Change. In the submenu that comes up, select the Find/Change command.

2. In the Find/Change dialog box, enter a word you'd like to search for in the Find entry box. If you plan to replace that word with something else, enter it in the Change entry box.

3. Click the Find Next button. The first instance of the word is found (if there are any instances of that word).

4. If you want to change this instance of the word, click Change. You can also click Change, Find, if you want to change the word and move instantly to the next instance of the word. If you don't want to change this instance, click Find Next.

5. Rinse and repeat. If you want to stop finding, click the close box on the Find window.

If you just want AppleWorks to find and change every instance of a word, you can click the Change All button instead of going through the entire document by hand. Think carefully before doing that, though, since you could accidentally change words you don't mean to change. Consider my example, where I found and changed nearly every instance of ClarisWorks in this chapter to AppleWorks. If I'd performed a Change All on that Find search, I would have changed the sentence right before this one you're reading. The sentence would then read: "Consider my example, where I found and changed nearly every instance of AppleWorks in this chapter to AppleWorks."

In the Find/Change window you'll find two check box options:

- **Find Whole Word** Check this option to find instances where the word in the Find entry box matches only a whole word in the document. If you search for the word "pup" without this option checked, it'll find the letters "pup" within the word "puppy." If you check the Find Whole Word check box, it will only find the word "pup," not parts of words that include the letters "pup."

- **Case Sensitive** Check this option and Find will pay attention to the upper- and lowercase letters you type in the Find entry box. If you search for "Puppy" with the Case Sensitive option checked, Find will not stop on the words "puppy" or "puppY."

 *You can replace words with spaces or nothing at all. That's a great way to delete every instance of a particular word. You can also search for just about anything you can cut and paste into the Find entry box, including spaces and line returns. Get creative—use ⌘-V to paste things into the Find entry box for more advanced searches.*

Standardize with the Stylesheet Window

If you're serious about word processing, you should get to know the Stylesheet window. What does it do? When you create a paragraph style you really like, you can give it a name and save it. Then, you can invoke that style anytime by simply selecting it in the Stylesheet window. Instant high-end formatting—perfect if you do a lot of the same sort of documents and you want to stop reinventing the wheel.

To open the Stylesheet window, select Window | Show Stylesheet Window. The Stylesheet window appears.

To select a style, just click it once in the Stylesheet window. The currently selected paragraph in your document will instantly change to that style. If you select more than one paragraph and then select a style in the Stylesheet window, they'll all change to that style. If you don't like the style you've changed it to, click Body or another style. You can also choose Unapply Style from the Stylesheet window's Edit menu.

To add your own style, format a paragraph just the way you want it. Make sure the insertion point is in that paragraph. Then, in the Stylesheet window, click the New button. In the New Style dialog box, give your style a name and choose the Paragraph radio button. Click the Inherit Document Selection Format option, then click OK. The style is created. You can now select it in the Stylesheet window to format other paragraphs.

 *The Stylesheets can be used for other styles, too, including table and outline styles.*

Use Stationery for Automatic Documents

AppleWorks has built into it Assistants (little programs that walk you through a task) and Stationery (template documents) that can help you create a number of different types of documents. We'll focus on some of the Assistants—those that create business documents like newsletters, business cards, brochures, and such—in Chapter 12. For now, let's see some Stationery that can help you with memos and letters.

Stationery is a document template that's been preformatted, often by professional designers, to make you look good. When you create a new document using Stationery, you get a new document that already has some attractive elements created for you. Then, you enter your own information to finish the document. In letter Stationery, for instance, you can select the sections of the document that are currently generic looking and change them into something you can use. For example, you can change the "Company Name" section and address to your own, as shown here:

Stauffer Productions

2301 Pennings Circle
Santa Fe
New Mexico 87154
(505) 555-1541

NOTE   *Actually, Stationery is a feature of Mac OS, not just AppleWorks, and you can create Stationery documents for many applications. In the Finder, find a document you've created that you really like. Select the document's icon, then select File | Get Info. At the bottom of the Get Info window, there's a Stationery Pad check box. Select it and close the window. Now the document will act just like Stationery, exactly as described in the next sections.*

Create a Document from Stationery

To use Stationery, you'll begin by creating a new document by selecting File | New or pressing ⌘-N. (Or, if you are just starting up AppleWorks, the New dialog box will automatically appear.) In the New dialog box, click the radio button option for Use Assistant or Stationery. The list in the window changes to reflect the Stationery and Assistants you can use. In the menu, choose an appropriate topic—Letters and Letterhead, Memos, or something similar.

Word processing Stationery appears with a big "A" as the icon. Select a Stationery that looks interesting (under the Letters and Letterhead topic, try "Letterhead 1"), and click OK. Using the Stationery, AppleWorks creates a new, styled document.

You'll find that some Stationery is more involved than others. Some feature special Stylesheets, for instance, that allow you to continue to format the paragraphs according to the Stationery's theme.

At some point you'll want to save the document—just save it like any other document. You can always go back to the Stationery list in the New dialog box to create another document that looks like it. An even better solution, though, is to use the document to create your own Stationery.

Save a Document as Stationery

Actually, it doesn't matter if you've created the document from AppleWorks Stationery or not—if you have a particular document design that you like a lot, you can save it as Stationery. That way you can use it to automatically create new documents that look like it.

With the document created, choose File I Save As. Give your Stationery a name, then click the Stationery icon down in the corner. You'll be automatically transported to AppleWorks' Stationery folder. Click the Save button and your Stationery is saved. Now, the next time you want to create a document in that style, you can choose your Stationery from the New dialog box (see Figure 8-9).

> **TIP** *If you've created a document you need to save as an actual document, do that first. Then you may want to clear out parts of the document—like the salutation and the body—that are specific to that letter or memo so you have a more generic document to use as Stationery.*

8

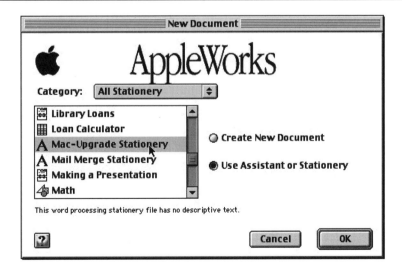

FIGURE 8-9   Choose your new Stationery just as if it were a prebuilt AppleWorks Stationery template.

Chapter 9

Work with Numbers, Build Charts

How to...

- Learn why it's a good idea to use spreadsheets
- See the basics of spreadsheets
- Enter and format text and numbers in your spreadsheet
- Cut, copy, paste, and sort your data
- Build formulas that work with your data
- Use advanced formulas for "what-if" scenarios
- Chart your data to see it visually

The computing industry likes to think in terms of something called "killer applications" (or "killer apps" in a *Wired Magazine* hip shorthand). Basically, the killer app is a reason to use a computer that's so new and so compelling that it drives millions to buy new machines and software to join the revolution. In the mid-to-late 1980s, for instance, the Mac's early ability to offer desktop publishing capabilities—allowing you to format text, add images, and arrange pages completely onscreen, then print it all to laser or color printers— was its killer application. In some ways, the Mac is still superior for that sort of work.

Before this happened, though, there was another time in Apple's history when it saw its computer sales spike—the killer app that prompted that spike was the spreadsheet. At the time (the late 1970s), the spreadsheet was called VisiCalc, the concept was completely new, and the computer that sold like gangbusters as a result was the Apple II.

We've come a long way. With the iMac, computers have become cute and with AppleWorks, spreadsheets have become easy to use. Just you wait and see.

The Spreadsheet Defined

A *spreadsheet* application is one that allows you to create what amounts to a digital ledger book. Ebenezer Scrooge, for instance, might have tracked his accounts in one of those cool-looking, lined, leather-bound ledger books. But times have changed. These days we have electronic spreadsheets instead of ledger books. And it's the iMac that looks cool.

Why Use Spreadsheets?

So, this is a like a ledger book, but better. Why? A spreadsheet allows you to do three major things well:

- ■ **Math**   You can concoct all sorts of formulas and impose them upon the numbers you've entered into your spreadsheet. Do loan calculations, find the average or standard deviation, figure the net present value—there are tons of things that no human should try without computerized help. By getting your numbers into the spreadsheet—where every cell has a name—you can perform many different mathematical functions.

- ■ **What-If**   Once you have a spreadsheet full of data and calculations, the spreadsheet allows you to change numbers quickly and see how that affects the whole. This was probably actually the *killer* part of the *app* when spreadsheets first appeared. Say you've laid out an entire budget for the next six months. What if you decide to take a job that pays less but allows you to perform that invaluable human service and boost your ego to that stratospheric level that you've had your eye on? Edit that income number in your budget and see how things shake out.

9

■ **Charts** Once you have the data entered and represented the way you like it, you can create graphics from the numbers that allow you to more clearly make your case at the next board, team, faculty, or family meeting. AppleWorks is capable of creating all sorts of charts, including exciting 3-D charts that will wow them for weeks.

So, all you have to do is enter the data, format it correctly, then get working on your calculations, what-if scenarios, and charts. Before you do that, though, you're going to have to know how to enter the data into the spreadsheet.

The Cell

The building block of any spreadsheet document is the *cell*—the conjunction of a column and a row that is given a unique name in the two dimensions of a spreadsheet. In that cell you can put text, numbers, formulas—even images, although there's less reason to do that. As shown next, those cells, because they're uniquely named (with names like "A2" and "F18"), can be added together, subtracted from one another, even cosined and tangented, if those are words. (I never did terribly well in trigonometry.)

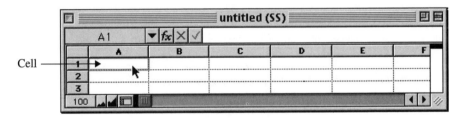

In working with spreadsheets, you'll need to get to know cell notation—the cell's name acts as a *variable* in formulas you build to work with the numbers in those cells. It's basic algebra—you'll create a formula that says "add C3 to C4" which tells the spreadsheet to sum the values it finds in cells C3 and C4. So how does it know which cells those are?

In the typical spreadsheet (AppleWorks included) the columns are lettered from left to right across the top of the document and the rows are numbered from top to bottom. So, the first cell at the top-left corner is A1. The cell C3, then, is the cell at the conjunction of column C and row 3.

Sound exciting yet? Let's run through how to create your own spreadsheets, doctor them up, and make them look nice. There are a couple of Stationery spreadsheets you can use to create different types of document as well; we'll discuss those later in the chapter.

By default, a spreadsheet in AppleWorks is 40 columns wide (reaching cell AN) and 500 rows long. You can add to them both—the limit is 256 columns and 16,384 rows.

Get the Spreadsheet Started

Spreadsheet documents start the same way any other documents begin—with the New command. In AppleWorks, choose File | New. In the New dialog box, choose Spreadsheet and click OK. A blank spreadsheet appears.

Move in the Spreadsheet

The first thing you'll want to do is learn how to get around. It's pretty basic. You'll start out in the top-left cell, but you can click anywhere on a cell and instantly be transported there. Once you have a cell selected, you can enter something in that cell by simply typing. Notice, when you start typing, that nothing actually appears in the cell.

You edit in the Entry Box at the top of the document window. You won't see the results in the cell until you move on from the cell—you do *that* by pressing TAB, RETURN, or an arrow key. Table 9-1 shows you how to move around in a spreadsheet document.

It won't take too long before these keys will become second nature to you. You just need to remember that if you want to edit something that's already in a cell, move to that cell (with the keys or the mouse) and edit it in the Entry Box, not in the cell itself (the program won't let you edit in the cell).

9

NOTE *The arrow keys don't allow you to leave a cell if you're currently editing data in that cell, because then you can't use those keys to move the insertion point around in the Entry Box. If you'd prefer that arrow keys allow you to immediately leave a cell, select Edit | Preferences. From the pull-down menu, choose Spreadsheet. Now, select Always Selects Another Cell. Notice you can also change the behavior of the RETURN key in this dialog box. Click OK to exit Preferences.*

You can enter either text or numbers in a spreadsheet, although it's best to have a plan before you jump in and start entering things randomly. In general, you'll want series of numbers—budget numbers for every month of the year, for instance—to be in a row or a column, unbroken by other text or numbers. Figure 9-1 shows an example of a nice, neat spreadsheet that will be easy to deal with when it comes to building formulas and creating "what-if" scenarios.

Press This	To Do This
RETURN or DOWN ARROW	Move down one cell
TAB or RIGHT ARROW	Move right one cell
SHIFT-RETURN or UP ARROW	Move up one cell
SHIFT-TAB or LEFT ARROW	Move left one cell
ENTER (on number pad)	Accept data in cell without moving to a new cell

TABLE 9-1   Moving Around in a Spreadsheet Document

Entry Box

	A	B	C	D	E	F	G	H	I	J
1	Annual Household Budget									
2		January	February	March	April	May	June	July	August	
3										
4	Work Income	3000	3000	3000	3000	3000	3000	3000	3000	
5	Investment Income	200	200	200	200	200	200	200	200	
6	Savings Interest	15	15	15	15	20	20	20	20	
7	Other Income	0	0	350	0	0	350	0	0	
8	**Total Income**	**3215**	**3215**	**3565**	**3215**	**3220**	**3570**	**3220**	**3220**	
9										
10	Rent	750	750	750	750	750	750	750	750	
11	Car	225	225	225	225	225	225	225	225	
12	Insurance	50	50	50	50	50	50	50	50	
13	Medical Insurance	120	120	120	120	120	120	120	120	
14	Groceries	240	240	240	240	240	240	240	240	
15	Dining	200	200	200	200	200	200	200	200	
16	Entertainment	300	300	300	300	300	300	300	300	
17	Clothing	500	100	100	500	100	100	500	100	
18	Household	150	150	150	150	150	150	150	150	
19	Misc.	75	75	75	75	75	75	75	75	
20	**Cash Expenses**	**2610**	**2210**	**2210**	**2610**	**2210**	**2210**	**2610**	**2210**	
21										
22	Mastercard	50	50	50	50	50	50	50	50	
23	Discover	25	25	25	0	0	0	0	0	
24	American Express	75	75	75	75	75	75	75	75	
25	**Credit Expenses**	**150**	**150**	**150**	**125**	**125**	**125**	**125**	**125**	
26										
27	**Over/Under**	**455**	**855**	**1205**	**480**	**885**	**1235**	**485**	**885**	
28										
29										

FIGURE 9-1 The best spreadsheets are arranged logically in a table format.

Select Cells

There are three basic ways to select cells in the spreadsheet window:

■ If you're selecting a single cell, click it once. Its frame becomes outlined.

■ To select more than one cell, click and hold the mouse button on the first cell you want to select, then drag the mouse across the other cells you'd like to select. When you've highlighted all the cells you need, release the mouse button. Now those cells are selected and are ready to have some action performed on them. (Note that the first cell in your selection will not be highlighted—the frame will be outlined. It's still selected, though.)

■ To select an entire row or column, click its letter or number once. In the F column, for instance, you can click the "F" at the top of the screen to highlight the entire column. If you want to select more than one column or row at a time, hold down the SHIFT key and click once for each column or row that you want to add. Notice that multiple columns or rows must be adjacent in order to be selected and you can't select both rows and columns at once.

Save the Spreadsheet

To save a spreadsheet, just select File | Save or File | Save As. The Save As dialog box appears, allowing you to name the document and find a folder to save it in. When you've made those choices, click Save. From there on, you can quickly save the spreadsheet every few minutes by selecting the Save command again or pressing ⌘-S on your keyboard.

Enter and Format Data

In most spreadsheets, you'll enter text to label the rows and columns that will be filled with numbers. With both the text and the numbers, it's possible to do some rather intricate formatting, including the basics like font, size, style, and alignment. You'll also find some formatting options that are different from those in word processing—options like formatting numbers as currency, dates, or times.

 *Actually, it's possible to perform calculations on text as well—you can do a number of things with text, including comparisons for word length, changing the case of text, sorting the text, adding text strings together (concatenating them), and so on.*

Format Text and Cells

Let's begin with text, since you'll likely begin with text in your spreadsheet. (You'll need to create labels for the columns and rows of numbers you plan to enter.) You might want to begin by typing a title into the first cell of the spreadsheet—cell A1. You can type text that's longer than the cell, and all of the text will actually appear just fine—as long as you haven't typed text into the adjoining cells. If you're creating the title line for your spreadsheet, that should be no problem.

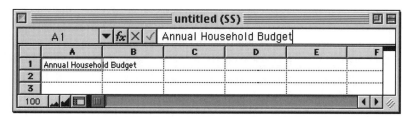

 *Want text to wrap within the cell instead of continuing off the edge? Highlight the cell and choose Format | Alignment | Wrap. Now text will wrap within the cell.*

You can also format text using pretty much the same tools that you use in a word processor—font, size, styles, and alignment. The major difference is that all of those commands appear in the Format menu. You can't format selected text differently within the same cell—formatting for text in the cell applies to all text in that cell.

Here's how to format:

1. Select the cell(s) that have text you want to format.

2. Select the Format menu and point the mouse at the type of formatting you'd like to change—Font, Size, Style, Font Color, or Alignment.

3. In the menu that appears, make your formatting selection.

All the text in the cell will be affected, although the cell itself won't be. That can be a problem if you've changed the size of the text in the cell, for instance, and can no longer read it clearly. The solution: Resize the cell.

Actually, you can't really change the size of an *individual* cell—you change the size of either its row or its column. To change the size of a row, point the mouse all the way over at the numbers that label each row. If you place the mouse pointer on the line that appears between any two rows, the mouse pointer changes to a pair of arrows. That's your cue that holding down the mouse button and dragging will change the size of the row, as shown in the following illustration. A column can be resized in the same way—just drag the line between the numbers.

Text is important in most spreadsheets, especially if you want other people to understand what the heck your spreadsheet is for. Text is also very useful for charting data, which we'll get into later in this chapter. AppleWorks likes to find text on the top and left borders of your numbers; it can use that text for labels in charts, for instance. So, think in terms of labeling your data in rows and columns—the more structured the data, the more easily it will be viewed and manipulated.

One special case is alignment—you'll probably want to format your columns and rows so that they line up together nicely. This is best done with the Alignment commands—in fact, you can select an entire range of cells or an entire column or row and use the Alignment commands in the Format menu to align every cell in the range to the left, right, centered, or justified. In a similar way, you can choose rows of your "label" cells and format them as bold, larger text, or what-have-you.

Want to delete text? Just select the cell and press DELETE. Likewise, you can highlight more than one cell and press DELETE to clear many cells of text (or numbers and formulas, for that matter) at once.

Enter and Format Numbers

Once you've got text in your cells and the rows and columns lined up the way you want them, you're ready to enter numbers in your spreadsheet. Numbers are entered the same way as text—just select a cell, type the number, then exit the cell. The number appears in the cell.

AppleWorks automatically recognizes a number as a number (not as text) when you type a number into a cell. In fact, in order to type a number as text, if you need to, you must enter a sort of mini-function that looks like this: **="5467"**. Using this formula, the number is treated as if it were text. This might be useful if you needed to label a column or row with a number—for instance, if you wanted your columns to represent years. If you enter **2001**, that's seen as two thousand and one. Enter **="2001"** and it's treated as text, so you can use it as a label.

Otherwise, numbers are numbers. If you need to enter a negative number, enter a minus sign (–) before it, such as **–5467**. And, as is true with text, you can copy and paste numbers from one cell into another if you like.

Number Formats

Numbers can be formatted in the same way as text—font, size, style, color, and alignment—by selecting the cell or cells and using the Format menu. Numbers, however, also have their own formatting schemes that can be used specifically to make them more meaningful, easier to read, or both. Those formatting options appear in the Format menu under the Number command. You can also access the Format Number, Date, and Time dialog box (shown in Figure 9-2) by double-clicking a cell.

9

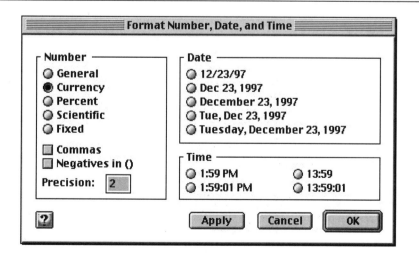

FIGURE 9-2   Format numbers using this dialog box.

In the dialog box you'll find the following option groups:

■ **Number** Here you have a few different radio button options that allow you to change the appearance of your numbers—they can be regular numbers, currency, percentages, scientific notation, or fixed decimal numbers (with a certain number of decimal places shown). Using the check boxes, you can also decide the precision of the numbers and whether or not negative values will appear in parentheses, which is common in accounting and financial notation.

■ **Date** Chose one of these radio buttons and the numbers typed into selected cell(s) will be formatted as dates following the specific form shown.

■ **Time** Choose one of these radio buttons and the selected cell(s) will accept numeric values as time values, formatted as chosen.

You'll probably often want to format an entire row or column with a certain type of number formatting—Currency, for instance. Go ahead and select an entire range of cells or even a complete column, row, or series of either to format. In fact, you can still have text in the same columns or rows and the text won't be affected by what you do with the numbering (see Figure 9-3).

Cut, Paste, Fill

In spreadsheets, you can cut and paste either text or numbers very easily. In the sample budget document I've created for this chapter's figures, a lot of numbers repeat. It's possible to select an entire range of numbers—part of a column, for instance—then copy and paste it into the next column.

Another way to quickly enter numbers is to use the Fill Right or Fill Down commands in the Calculate menu. Enter a value for one cell, then highlight that cell and a number of

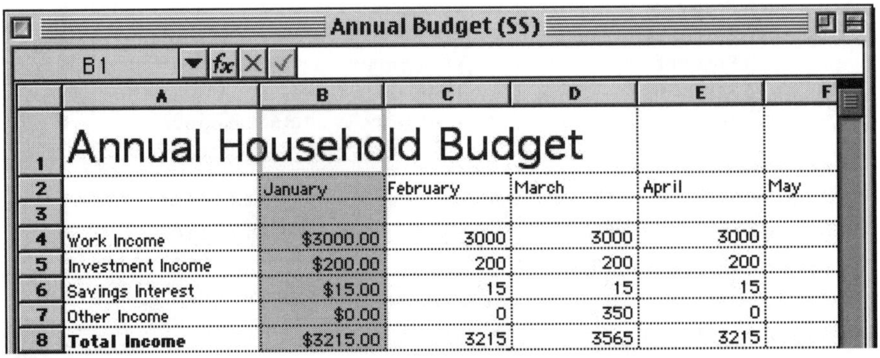

	A	B	C	D	E	F
1	Annual Household Budget					
2		January	February	March	April	May
3						
4	Work Income	$3000.00	3000	3000	3000	
5	Investment Income	$200.00	200	200	200	
6	Savings Interest	$15.00	15	15	15	
7	Other Income	$0.00	0	350	0	
8	**Total Income**	$3215.00	3215	3565	3215	

FIGURE 9-3 Select an entire column and you can format all the numbers in it at once.

cells to the right or down from that cell. Now, choose the appropriate command—Calculate | Fill Right or Calculate | Fill Down—and all those cells are filled with the first cell's value.

Sort the Spreadsheet

Once you have a ton of data entered into your spreadsheet, you might suddenly think it'd be groovy to have that data sorted in some different way. What if, let's say, all of your expenses were sorted from highest to lowest (based on the first month)? Or if they were just listed alphabetically? Easily done.

To sort a range of data, follow these steps:

1. Select a series of rows or columns of data. You'll need to make sure the data is all a single data set, so you don't accidentally sort a row or column that isn't related. (When you do that, it ain't pretty.) Figure 9-4 shows an example of a good data set to sort—each column or row should have the same kind of data.

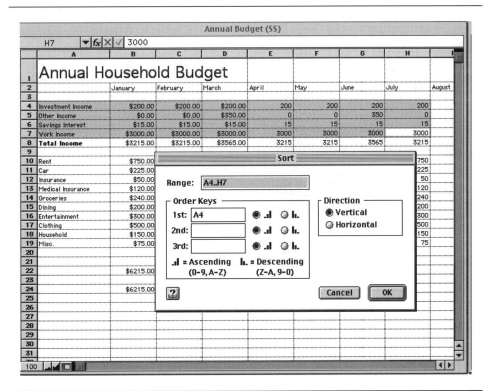

FIGURE 9-4   Select a range of "sortable" data before you perform the sort function.

NOTE
By "data set" I mean data that logically belongs together. In the sample budget, each of the rows I want to sort is a similar type of data—they're all income lines. The data you choose to sort needs to be similar, so that if each row (or column) gets moved around it won't hurt the spreadsheet overall.

2. With a series of rows or columns chosen, select Calculate | Sort. The Sort dialog box appears. At the top of the dialog box you'll see the range of cells that are to be sorted. Next, you'll see entries for the Order Keys. In order to sort, AppleWorks takes a look at one of the cells, which you specify, and sorts the data set based on that column (if you're sorting rows) or that row (if you're sorting columns).

3. In the 1st: entry box, type the cell address that holds the main *type of* value against which you're going to sort the data set. (In the example, I've entered **A4** to sort alphabetically; I'd enter **B4** if I wanted to sort according to the January values. Notice that I could enter **A5**, **A6**, or **A7** to sort alphabetically, too. The Sort dialog just needs to know, in general, which column or row of data you want to sort on.)

4. Click the radio button to select whether the data set will be sorted in Ascending or Descending order.

5. Finally, make sure the setting for which way the data will be sorted— vertically (by row) or horizontally (by column)—is correct. AppleWorks will sometimes get this wrong if you don't choose complete rows or columns for your sorting.

6. Click OK. Your data gets sorted and is placed in the spreadsheet in the order you specified.

TIP
If you don't like the new sort order, immediately choose Edit | Undo and the sort order will return to its original state.

Add Formulas to the Spreadsheet

Here's where the real power of the spreadsheet model shines through—creating formulas that allow you to manipulate the data. So far, you've entered text that labels data and you've entered numbers that represent data. Now it's time to put some of that algebraic knowledge swimming around in your head to the task of creating formulas that work with your data. In this section I'll show you the anatomy of a formula, then we'll move on to some of the formulas included in AppleWorks.

Anatomy of a Formula

You've already seen that when you simply type text and numbers into the cell, AppleWorks can differentiate between the two for formatting purposes. It can immediately tell the difference between a number and text.

It can't, however, tell the difference between the cell reference "A3" and the text "A3." In order to differentiate a formula, AppleWorks needs a little code. That code comes in the form of an equals (=) sign. If you begin your typing in a cell with an equals sign, AppleWorks will interpret what follows as a formula.

> **NOTE** *After you exit the cell, if you've typed the formula correctly you won't see it again in the cell. Instead, you'll see the result of that formula. (If you highlight the cell you'll again see the formula up in the Entry Box.)*

Formula Types

Beyond the equals sign, there are two basic types of formulas you'll create. The first is a straight mathematical formula with addition (+), subtraction (–), multiplication (*), division (/), or exponential (^) operators. A typical mathematical formula could easily be =34+45 or =34^2 although that'd be reasonably useless in a spreadsheet (you'll see why in a moment).

The other type of formula uses a built-in function from AppleWorks. These functions range from financial to trigonometric to logical. An example might be =AVERAGE (34, 45, 56), which would return the average of those three numbers.

As you might guess, it's also possible to use these two types of formulas together in the same cell, so that =34+45+(AVERAGE (34, 45, 56)) is a legal formula, too. Notice, by the way, that parentheses are used pretty liberally in these formulas to separate one operation from another. Again, it's like algebra—functions and math inside parentheses get done first, then the result gets entered into the larger equation.

Build with Cell Addresses

What's missing, of course, is the cell address. By using cell addresses as *variables*, you're suddenly able to do amazing things with formulas. For instance, while =34+45 isn't terribly useful in a spreadsheet (since you could just enter **79** and be done with it), the formula =B3+B4 could be *very* useful. Why? Because if you change the value in B3 or in B4—or in both—the result changes as well. And getting results is what spreadsheets are all about.

Now you're able to create a cell whose value is based on values in other cells. You could take this even further. How about a cell whose value is the sum of many different cells—something along the lines of =B4+B5+B6+B7? That's shown in Figure 9-5.

Notice that the cell addresses are starting to get a little out of hand, even with just four—what if you were adding together 400 cells? In your spreadsheet you can use a special notation to denote a range of cells to be acted on. The range is separated by two periods, as in =SUM(B4..B7), which gives the same result as =B4+B5+B6+B7. Notice with ranges that you're forced into using functions to perform even basic math.

> **TIP** *Once a formula is evaluated, you can use that formula's cell address in another formula. If you put **SUM(B4..B7)** in cell B10, you can type **B10** in another formula, where it will represent the result of that sum.*

9

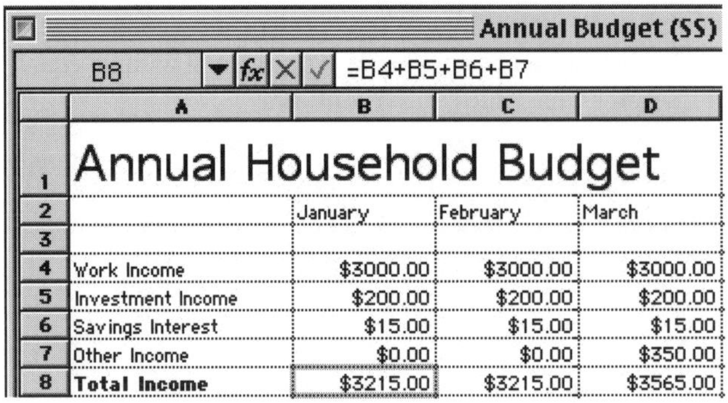

FIGURE 9-5   A basic formula for adding cell values together

Relative vs. Absolute

The cell addresses we've been talking about are called *relative* addresses. What does that mean? Say you wanted to use the Copy and Paste or Fill Right/Fill Down commands with a formula you've created. With relative addressing, the addresses within that formula will change relative to the cell you paste the formula into. For example, if cell B29 had the formula =SUM(B10..B27) in it, you could copy that formula from cell B29 and paste it into cell C29. The formula in C29 is changed slightly, though, to =SUM(C10..C27). AppleWorks is just assuming that's how you want it.

But what if you don't want that automatic translation done for you? Easy. You can create an absolute address using dollar signs ($). The address $B$10 is an absolute address that always points to cell B10. If I create a formula in cell B29 that looks like =$B$10+B11, then copy that formula to cell C29, the result will be =$B$10+C11. Since the second address was relative, it changed. But the first address is still B10.

> NOTE   *How clever are you? If you're very clever, you may come up with a good reason to use partial absolute addressing, as in $B10. Now, the "B" part of the address is absolute, but the "10" part isn't—the row number will change if this reference is cut and pasted into a lower or higher row. I'm not that clever, but, then again, my finances are always a mess. Maybe there's a relationship there?*

More Operators

Want a little more confusion? First, there are two more numeric operators designed for use with cell addresses. You can use these two operators to change the way numbers are evaluated—the percent operator (%) turns a number into a decimal percentage, while the minus sign (–) can be used in front of a cell address to make it negative.

And other operators can be used in your formulas besides the numeric ones—the relational and text operators. The relational operators offer comparisons between two values. They are:

=	Equal to
<>	Not equal to
>	Greater than
>=	Greater than or equal to
<	Less than
<=	Less than or equal to

Using a formula like =A3>A4 will return a value of either True or False, which will appear in the cell. If you don't find this useful, you'll likely want to use these operators within logical functions like the IF function. (The IF function does something *if* something else is true. For instance, *if* A3 is greater than A4, *then* do some sort of math or perform some function. IF is discussed later in this chapter, with examples.)

There's also one text operator, the ampersand (&), which allows you to concatenate text. The formula =B5&" "&B6 would create one long string of text with a space between the two cells' text entries (the quotes allow you to add text between the text in the two cells).

NOTE   *What happens when you concatenate numbers? They're turned into text. It works fine, but you won't be able to perform any math on the text-ified numbers until you turn them back into numbers with the TEXTTONUM function.*

Operator Precedence

Before you can build formulas you need to know one last little thing about them—operator precedence. We used to call this "order of operations" back in algebra class. Say you have the formula =40+10*3. What's the answer? It depends on what you do first. If you evaluate from left to right, then 40 plus 10 is 50; 50 times 3 is 150. If you evaluate the multiplication first, then 10 times 3 is 30 and 40 plus 30 is 70. You get two different answers.

One way to manage this is to rely on parentheses. Since operations inside parenthesis are always evaluated first, you could create the formula =(40+10)*3 to get 150 or =40+(10*3) to get 70.

Or, you could rely on the operator precedence. In this case, multiplication has higher precedence than addition. Without parentheses, the formula =40+10*3, by rule of precedence, equals 70. Multiplication is done first, then addition. Table 9-2 shows the order of precedence for all operators—the higher in the table, the sooner the operation is performed.

Whenever a precedence level is the same for two operations, the formula is evaluated from left to right. So, if a subtraction is further left than an addition, the subtraction is done first.

()	Parentheses (done first)
%	Percentages
^	Exponentials
+, −	Positive or negative numbers (sign appears before a cell address)
*, /	Multiply, divide
+, −	Add, subtract
&	Concatenate text
=, >, <, >=, <=, <>	All comparisons (done last)

TABLE 9-2   Order of Precedence for Spreadsheet Formulas

TIP *When in doubt, use parentheses. That way you'll be able to decide exactly how a formula is evaluated.*

Add Functions to Your Formulas

You'll soon come up with a reason to do more than just basic mathematics between a few different cells. You've already seen that the SUM function can be used with a range of cells to add them all together and get a total. But what if you need to do something more sophisticated in your formulas?

In that case, it's time to call in a function. Here's how you add one:

1. Select the cell where you want the function to appear.

2. Next to the Entry Box on your spreadsheet document window is the Function (Fx) button. Click it and the Paste Function dialog box appears (see Figure 9-6).

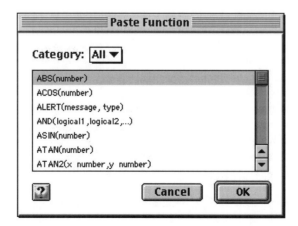

FIGURE 9-6   The Paste Function dialog box helps you enter functions into your spreadsheet.

3. Choose one of those functions and it's added to the Entry Box, where you can edit it.

4. Edit the function to taste (usually, you'll add cell addresses and values) and exit the cell.

AppleWorks offers a number of different types of functions:

- **Numeric**   These functions allow you to work with numbers and ranges of numbers. They include SUM (sum of numbers), RAND (generates a random number), ROUND (rounds a number), and SQRT (returns the square root of the number).

- **Business and Financial**   These are functions like PV (present value), NPV (net present value), RATE (tells you the interest rate of a payment schedule), and PMT (figures the payment required to satisfy a particular type of loan or payment scheme).

- **Date and Time**   These functions allow you to perform various calculations regarding time. The date, day of the week, and time can all be stored as numeric values, allowing you to easily do math using them. That's discussed in more detail later in this section.

- **Information**   These functions are used to send information, as in alert boxes and error tones, to your user.

- **Logical**   These programming-like functions can be used to determine if a number of values are true (AND) or if any values are true (OR), or it can evaluate values and perform other calculations based on whether they're true or not (IF). Other functions determine whether a value is present or if there's an error.

- **Statistical**   These functions take the MEAN, find the MODE, determine standard deviation, and more.

- **Text**   Text operators allow you to find certain words programmatically, change words to upper- or lowercase, get the length of a word, and perform similar functions.

- **Trigonometric**   Here are those crazy functions all about angles. You can figure the cosine, sine, and tangent and convert between radians and degrees, among other things.

Learn About Functions

The functions are too numerous to list here—and it'd be redundant anyway, since you can learn about any of the AppleWorks functions through the AppleWorks Help system. Select Help | AppleWorks Help. The Help window appears. Enter the keyword **Functions**, then look for a link that says "Alphabetical List of Functions." Click it to see every function spelled out for you, alphabetically. Click an individual function's name to get a full explanation of that particular function.

Now, when you go to add a function, you can switch between the Paste Function dialog box and AppleWorks Help to get the answer regarding your particular function.

Some Cool Functions

Okay, I'm well over my allotted pages for this chapter, but I just had to show you some cool functions available for your spreadsheet. I'll try to get through these very quickly so you can get back to your regularly scheduled tutorial.

Total Selection

This is a shortcut from the AppleWorks' button bar. It allows you to quickly generate a total in a spreadsheet of numbers like a budget or financials. I used it for the sample budget in this chapter. Here's how it works:

1. Highlight the column or row of numbers you want to total *plus* an additional cell at the end of the list.

2. Click the Total Selection button.

That's it. The sum automatically appears in that blank cell (see Figure 9-7). Now you can do it again for the next row, or just use the Fill Right command for all the other Total cells in that row of your budget. Since the Total Selection creates a SUM function with relative addresses, the function will copy just fine for the rest of the row.

Other values that work like SUM include AVERAGE, MIN, and MAX, all of which can accept a range of cells such as AVERAGE (B2..B10).

Text to Date, Date to Text

In the spreadsheet, AppleWorks allows you to deal with dates in an interesting way—you can add and subtract them, if you like. How? It turns a typical date into a serial number. That number, by the way, represents how many days the entered date is since January 1, 1904. Pretty weird, huh?

The TEXTTODATE function accepts a text entry of the current date. (The year should be in four digits to avoid those pesky Y2K issues.) In Figure 9-8, enter the date in cell B2 in the format 00/00/0000. In cell B4, enter the formula **=TEXTTODATE (B2)**. Now, you have a serial number.

What can you do with that? You can add or subtract from it. In Figure 9-9, I'll figure out what date is seven days past the date entered by adding 7 to the serial number in cell B5 (**=B4+7**). Now, I'll use the DATETOTEXT function to turn the serial date back into one read by humans. The formula typed into cell B7 is **=DATETOTEXT (B5, 1)**. The 1 represents the date format I want to use—the numbers are explained in AppleWorks Help for the DATETOTEXT function. The result? A readable date that's seven days after the one entered above (see Figure 9-9).

Total Selection button

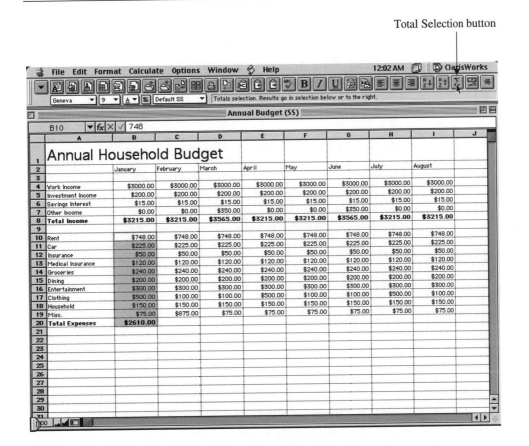

FIGURE 9-7   Quickly create a total of an entire selection of cells.

If you'd like to work with time, too, it works much the same way, except that time's serial number is a decimal—it's the percentage of 24 hours. The time 6:00 p.m. (18:00 hours) is represented as 0.75. You could figure that out with the formula TEXTTOTIME ("18:00") or TEXTTOTIME (B2) if cell B2 contained the text 18:00.

IF Function

Here's a great one for all sorts of analysis. IF accepts a logical expression, followed by what it should do if an expression is true and what it should do if an expression is false.

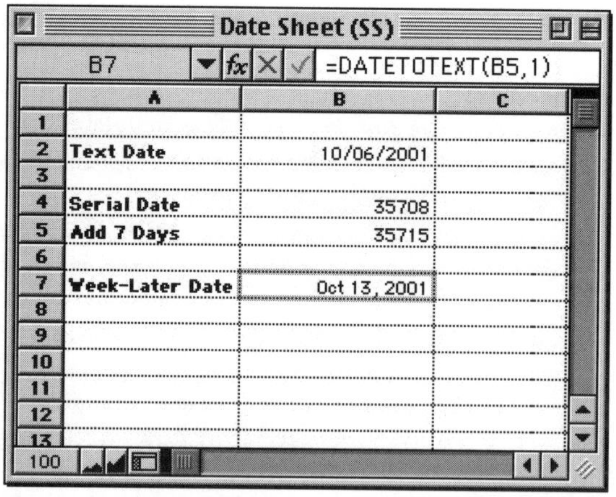

FIGURE 9-8   Use TEXTTODATE and DATETOTEXT to do math with dates.

For instance, let's say that the value of cell B22 in my budget spreadsheet represents my over/under value for the month. If I come out more than $300 ahead on my budget, then I'll put half of it in my retirement account. If I have less than $300, then I'll put 0 in my retirement account.

So, with that in mind, I can create an IF function that checks out my amount over/under balance and decides what to do. It'll look like this: =IF (B22>300, B22/2, 0). That is, if B22 is greater than 300, return B22 divided by 2 as the value. If B22 isn't greater than 300, return 0. Here it is in action:

Household	$150.00	$150.00	$150.00
Misc.	$75.00	$875.00	$75.00
Total Expenses	**$2610.00**	**$3010.00**	**$2210.00**
Over/Under	**$605.00**	**$205.00**	**$1355.00**
Retirement	$302.50	$0.00	$677.50

Chart Your Data

Once you've got the data in your spreadsheet arranged, calculated, and accounted for, you may find the best way to communicate the data is to create a chart. Charts go a long way toward making numbers in rows and columns much more bearable—plus, it's possible to see the relationships between data more clearly when you're looking at a chart. Here are a few suggestions about charts:

- ■ **Make sure your data is "chartable."**   You should have data sets in your spreadsheet that have an obvious relationship that makes a comparison worthwhile. Sales figures among different regions, budget categories, and demographic numbers are all very chartable. (If your rent doesn't change month to month, it won't be very effective in a chart.)

- ■ **Charts should convey one comparison.**   If I take all of my expenses and chart them over six months, the chart will be unreadable. Instead, I should chart either *one* expense over six months or many expenses in one month, but not both.

- ■ **Don't include totals.**   If you chart all of your expenses in one month—including the *total* of all those expenses—you'll throw your chart way off. Make sure you're not accidentally including totals when you're comparing data.

- ■ **Totals look great in graphs.**   If you chart *only* totals, that's another story. In a budget, for instance, you might chart total income over six months. That'll make a great chart—especially if income has been going up.

Create the Chart

Creating a chart is really very easy in AppleWorks—it's really more about choosing the right data than it is about using odd commands. In fact, you may need to replicate your data in another part of the spreadsheet before you can chart it. When necessary, you can always re-create a part of your chart somewhere else on the sheet. You can simply have formulas that point to another cell, like =B20, to allow you to copy the values to a part of your document that you can chart more easily. (See Figure 9-9.)

Here's how it works:

1. Choose a range of data you want to chart.

2. Select Options | Make Chart. The Chart Options dialog box appears (see Figure 9-10).

3. In the Gallery, choose the type of chart you want to use. Use the check boxes at the bottom of the window to add options.

4. Click the Axes button. Here's where you label each axis of the chart. Choose the X-Axis radio button, enter a label in the Axis Label entry box, then make other choices for how you want the axis to appear in the final chart. (If you don't customize the tick marks, min/max values, and step values, they'll be done automatically.) Choose the Y-Axis value and make the same choices.

9

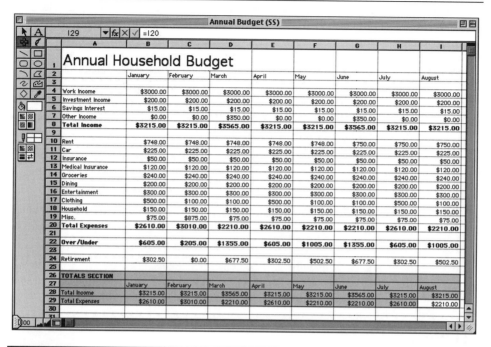

FIGURE 9-9 Creating a section of chartable data in your spreadsheet can make creating the chart more bearable.

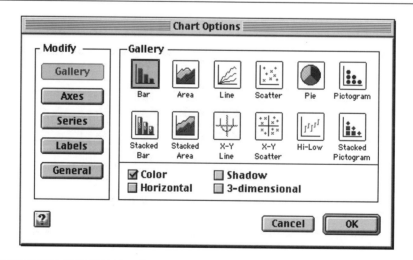

FIGURE 9-10 The Chart Options dialog box is home base for creating your chart.

5. Click the Series button. Most of this you won't need to worry about. You can, however, click the Label Data check box, then place the label, if you'd like each individual part of the chart (each column, pie piece, and so on) to include a label that gives the exact data amount it represents.

6. Click the Labels button. Here you can decide if you're going to have a title (click the Title check box) and what that title will be. You can also decide if you'll have a legend (check or uncheck the Legend check box) and how it will be arranged.

7. Click the General button. Now you get to choose the series that is listed in the legend. You can change this by clicking the Rows or Columns radio button. This is significant—the series you choose is what each colored bar or area will represent. (If your chart comes out backward from what you expected, create another one and change the series you graph.)

8. Click OK. A chart appears in the document window (see Figure 9-11).

Need to move the chart around? It's a graphical object—it's not in a cell or attached to the spreadsheet. If you like, just click somewhere in the chart and hold down the mouse button, then drag the mouse to move the chart to another part of the spreadsheet document window.

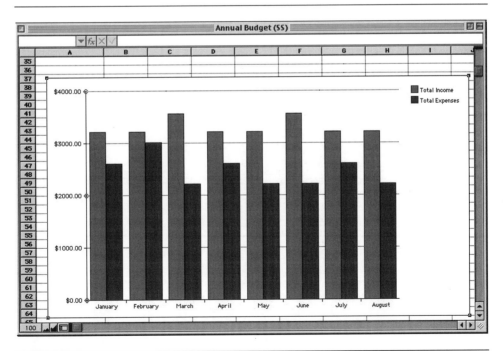

FIGURE 9-11   The final chart—looks pretty spiffy.

If you need to change anything about the chart, you can double-click it to change the Chart Options, then click OK, and the chart will update to reflect the new changes.

So what else can you do with your chart? Actually, you can do quite a few things, thanks to the power of AppleWorks. For one, you can copy and paste it into any other AppleWorks document. Or, you can drag the chart to your iMac desktop, where it becomes a Picture Clipping document. You can rename the chart and file it away, or you can drag it into another document in almost any applications on your iMac.

You can even use the Show Tools command in the Window menu to view the drawing tools, which allow you to change the way the chart looks with new colors, backgrounds, text, and other elements. We'll talk more about using the drawing tools in Chapter 11. And we'll talk more about the Show Tools command in Chapter 12.

Chapter 10

File Information and Ideas with Databases

How to...

- ■ Learn about databases
- ■ Create the fields for your database
- ■ Enter data in Browse mode
- ■ Sort the database
- ■ Create a new layout
- ■ Build a quick report

The database module in AppleWorks is probably the most misunderstood of the components. So many people instantly associate the idea of a database with, well, computer programming or something. It seems like too much work to create a database, too much effort to get that organized.

But the fact is, the database module in AppleWorks is very easy to work with—and there are a lot of things you can track in a database. The basic rule is this: If you have something you need to store, sort, or search through, then it's probably a good idea to consider creating a database.

What's a Database?

A database is a document that stores many different *records,* each of which is composed of several *fields* in which data is stored. Databases and spreadsheets have a lot in common— in fact, you can view databases in rows and columns just like you can spreadsheets (see the following illustration). But databases are really designed to do something quite different from spreadsheets—they're designed to track data and help you create reports based on that data.

The best metaphor for a computer database is probably a card catalog at the local library. Each record is a card; each field is a line item on one of those cards. The author's name is a field, the title of the book is a field, even whether or not someone currently has the book on loan is a field. As you know, electronic databases of books are popular these days in libraries. A well-made library database offers many advantages, including reports on loaned books, searches based on author's names, searches based on titles, and so on.

When Can You Use a Database?

You probably think of databases in terms of business uses—invoice tracking, project management, contact management, phone logs, inventory, or records for a mailing list or customer-tracking database. But there are other things you can do with a database for home, school, or organizations.

Sure, you can track your CDs, movies, books, and recipes. (Those are such old standards that they're built into AppleWorks' Stationery system.) But think of this: You could keep a personal or professional journal in a database, creating a new record for every day, and you'd be able to search the database using keywords. That'd be great for tracking creative ideas or remembering events. Or you could create a photo database of your insured belongings. If you're planning a wedding, party, birthday, or fund-raiser, you might track people in a database (see Figure 10-1).

Same goes for your block association, church group, scout troop, or sports team—anything that needs a little tracking can be stored in a database. Membership dues, training requirements, awards and certificates, ranks and accomplishments, scoring, attendance, and grades can all be tracked in a database.

Then, you can create reports that tell you what still needs to be followed up on—you haven't gotten an RSVP from the Williamses, you haven't gotten a medical release from your goalie, or you don't yet know what Mildred plans to bring to the bake sale. All of these items can be tracked with databases.

How Databases Work

You'll begin by creating a database file and defining the fields that will be used by the database to create each record. Once the fields are defined, you're ready to create your first record. It's shown to you using a default *layout*—the data entry screen. If desired, you can edit this layout, or you can create other layouts for your database.

Different layouts can be composed of different fields, if you desire, allowing you to look at the same record in different ways. Or you can use alternate layouts for different methods of data entry and/or searching.

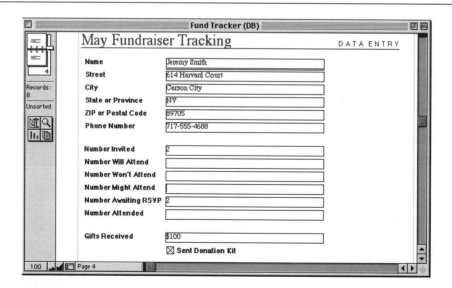

FIGURE 10-1 Databases aren't just for business.

Layouts also allow you to create different reports based on the data, too. For instance, you could create a layout that shows all of the books in your classroom that haven't been returned (and who checked them out) or all of the invoices in your small business that are 30 days past due. Layouts can be very complex, if desired, since you're offered most of the same drawing and formatting tools you'll find in AppleWorks' drawing module (see Chapter 11 to learn about the drawing tools).

And a big part of using a database is generating useful reports. The fact that layouts support the drawing tools also means you can create reports that will look good (and be useful) when printed.

Create Your Database

Creating your database is really pretty simple. In AppleWorks choose File | New, then choose to create a Database document and click OK in the New dialog box. Things get complicated in a hurry, though. Immediately, you're confronted with the need to create fields for your database. And in order to do that, you'll need to think a little about your database.

Plan Your Database

With AppleWorks you'll begin by creating a new database file into which you will eventually store records. After you've launched the new document, you're asked to create fields for that database—each record will be composed of these fields. It's important to know ahead of time what sort of data you'll be tracking, since you need to define your fields before you can begin to use the database.

The key to planning your database is getting a good feel for what information you'd like to store in each record. Begin with what will be unique about each entry—if you had to give each record a title, what would it be? Would it be a customer, student, or contact ID number? Would it be an invoice number? Would it be a recipe name, a CD title, the name of the photographer, or a room in your house? Once you know why each record will be unique, you may have a better idea of what you'll want to store in that record and what fields will be necessary.

For instance, I might have a database that stores information about my students in a particular class I teach. Before the semester begins, I'll want to seriously consider all of the information about each student that I'll want to record over the next four or five months. I'll want names, addresses, phone numbers, and other contact information. I also know I'll be giving five major tests and twenty graded homework assignments. I'll need to have fields available to record all of that information, too.

But what about teacher conferences? Should I include parental contact information and a check box to show that each of the three conferences has been completed? How about a special section for storing notes so I can remember what to discuss with the parents?

Field Types

AppleWorks offers a number of different types of fields you can define for your database. Some are general in purpose—text fields are designed to hold pretty much any combination of text and number characters like addresses or zip codes; number fields are designed to hold numbers you plan to use in calculations. Others do very specific, techie kinds of things like offer you a pull-down menu of options or allow you to click a radio button or check list. Table 10-1 shows you all the different fields.

By the way, the fact that there are a lot of fields doesn't mean that database building is hard. It can be a little intimidating, but usually only in the beginning. Once you have the correct fields set up, you'll definitely like having the database available when you need to find, search, or sort something important.

Most of the fields you create will be text fields—they're the catchall for personal and small business databases. You're more likely to use menus, radio buttons, and check boxes—fields called *controls*—if you're designing a database for someone else to do the data entry. (Controls are a good way of limiting typos by offering multiple choices.) You'll also likely use name and date fields in most any database you create, especially for business, organizational, or social databases.

Other fields that are very interesting are serial fields (important for invoices and inventory), calculation fields, and record info fields. All of these can be used to automate your database in a way that can make it much more valuable to use. Later in the chapter, you'll see how calculations can be used to automate important database functions.

Add Your Fields

Once you know the field types, you can add them to your database. The process for that is simple. If you've already chosen File | New to create a new database document, you're presented with the Define Database Fields dialog box.

Here's the process for creating a new field:

1. In the Field Name entry box, enter a unique name for your field. It should be reasonably short and avoid additional nontext characters, especially if you think you might one day export this database to another database program.

2. In the Field Type menu, choose the type of field you want to create.

Type of Field	What It Can Contain	Examples
Text	Any combination of letters, numbers, and symbols up to 1,000 words	Salutations, personal titles, addresses, notes, phone numbers, product names, product numbers, customer ID codes, zip codes, social security numbers
Number	A negative or positive integer or decimal up to 255 characters	Dollar amounts, student grade percentages, number of children, quantity of purchased items
Date	Date, month, and year (offers different formats)	Current date, shipping date, date order received, date of birth, wedding date, party date
Time	Hours, minutes, and seconds (in 12- or 24-hour formats)	Current time, time of order, time shipped, time of birth
Name	Full, proper names	People's names, company names, organization names
Pop-up menu	A menu of values; use anytime you want a limited response from many options	Compass direction, city names, U.S. states, demographic groups
Radio buttons	Multiple choice; similar to a pop-up menu but designed for fewer choices	People's titles (Mr., Ms.), name suffixes (Jr., III), computing platform (Mac, Windows, Unix), housing payments (rent, own), marital status (single, divorced, married, widowed)
Check box	Yes or no answer	Want further information? U.S. citizen? Self-employed? Product shipped? Checked zip code?
Serial Number	AppleWorks assigns a new, ordered number for each record; good for giving each record a unique value	customer ID, product ID, invoice ID
Value List	Choose from a list of values or enter your own	Local restaurants, election candidates, favorite computer games, magazines you subscribe to
Multimedia	An image or movie file	Photo of employee, photo of household item, movie walkthrough of property for sale
Record Info	Time, date, or name of person who created/modified data	Record creation date, date/time modified, name of entry clerk
Calculation	Result from a formula using other fields	Total of invoice, sales tax, final student grade, days since shipped
Summary	Calculation from fields in this and other records	Total receivables, total of unshipped items, class average, number of items due

10

TABLE 10-1   Database Fields

3. Click the Create button to create the field.

4. If desired, click the Options button to make specific choices about the field's behavior. The Options dialog box allows you to make basic choices about your field, such as setting default values, a range of accepted values, and so on.

5. Done with all your fields? When you're ready to create your first record, click Done in the Define Database Fields dialog box. (Don't worry, you can still add fields later if necessary.) The dialog box disappears and you're presented with the entry screen for your database. Enjoy!

This is a good time to save your database by choosing File | Save and giving the database a name.

Control Fields

Certain control fields—menus, radio buttons, value lists, and record info fields—will require additional information from you before the field is accepted. If the field contains radio buttons, a value list, or a menu, you'll need to enter values for those lists. A dialog box will appear right after you click the Create or Modify button in the Define Database Fields dialog box.

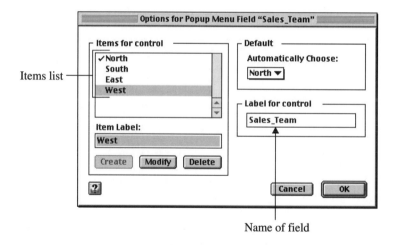

Here's what you can do in this dialog box:

- ■ To enter a value, type a name in the Item Label entry box and click the Create button (or press RETURN).

- ■ To create another value, type a different name and click the Create button.

- ■ To modify an existing value, highlight the value in the Items list, then type a new name for it and click the Modify button.

■ To choose the default value for the control, pull down the menu in the Default section of the dialog box and choose the default value. This is the value that the control will be set to until the user changes it.

Click OK when you're done fixing the control. If you've chosen to create a Record Info field, you'll see a different dialog box.

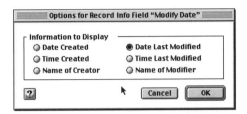

This one is more straightforward—just click the corresponding radio button to create the field you want in your database.

> **NOTE** *How does AppleWorks know the name of the person creating or modifying? It looks up the iMac's Owner in the File Sharing control panel. Sneaky, huh? (See Chapter 28 for more on networking.)*

Calculation Fields

Here's another instance where you won't get away with a quick swipe of the Create or Modify button. A *calculation* field is one that requires you to enter a formula, somewhat akin to a formula in a spreadsheet.

If you're creating a calculation field, you'll be asked to create the calculation before the field is complete. To do that, you'll work with the Enter Formula dialog box, which appears when you first create a calculation field.

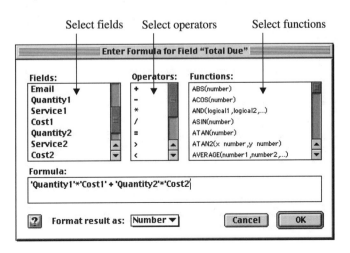

If you read Chapter 9 closely, you might notice something familiar here in the Enter Formula dialog box—the functions. In fact, most of them are exactly the same as those functions found in the spreadsheet module, although some are more limited in the database module. Still, you'll find that many of the same calculations are possible. (Refer to Chapter 9 to learn about some of the special ones.)

In database formulas, you'll find that field names are your variables—they replace the cell names in a spreadsheet when you create mathematical formulas or build functions. Most of the time you'll want to use number fields in your calculations, although you can use the built-in text functions to work with text fields, if necessary, and the date and time functions to deal with date, time, or record info fields.

There are a couple of different ways to create a formula:

■ To create a basic formula, you can click a field name, click an operator, and then click another field name. (Perfect for adding together costs in an invoice, for instance.)

■ If you want to use a function, you'll usually choose the function first, then choose the field name(s) it should operate on.

■ Just type it—if you already know the exact field names, operators, and/or functions you want to use.

At the bottom of the Enter Formula dialog box, choose how the result should be formatted from the Format Result As menu. (Remember, when you're entering data, this field will show the *result* of the calculation in each record, not the calculation. So, you've got to decide what sort of value that's going to be, just as with other fields.)

Then, click OK to save your formula. If AppleWorks thinks you've formatted things correctly, the dialog box goes away and the field appears in your field list. If not, you'll see an alert box telling you something is wrong. Fix the problem and click OK again.

> **TIP** *Since a calculation field only stores the result according to the field type you specify in the Format Result As menu, you can use the field name as a variable in other calculations. For instance, you can have a calculation field called Total, then a calculation field called Sales Tax, and a Final Total calculation field that calculates Total+Sales Tax. Just make sure all the results are formatted as numbers if you're going to be adding and multiplying them together.*

Enter and Find Records

Once you've defined your fields, you're ready to enter your first record. AppleWorks immediately drops you into Browse mode, the mode used to create records and move between them manually (see Figure 10-2). The mode is chosen from the Layout menu in the menu bar.

In Browse mode, you can click near a field name to begin entering data in that record. Press TAB to move to the next field after you've entered data; press SHIFT-TAB if you need to move back up to a previous field. Once you've entered all the data you need to enter, you can quickly choose File I Save or press ⌘-S to Save, then choose Edit I New Record or press ⌘-R to begin entering a new record.

List View

If you prefer, you can also do your data entry in List view, which makes it a little easier to see more than one record at a time. If you have many fields, though, the window will need to scroll quite a bit. To switch to List view, choose Layout I List.

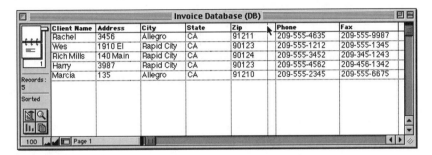

 *You can drag the line that separates columns to make them wider or narrower, just as in the spreadsheet module.*

Find Records

If you only have a few records in your database, it won't be that tough to click around in Browse mode and find a particular one. But if you have quite a few records, or you're interested in looking at only certain ones, then you need to instigate a Find.

SHORTCUT *This is easiest to manage if you select Window I Show Tools to display the spiral-bound note cards in the left margin (shown in Figure 10-2).*

It's actually really easy to find records. Just follow these steps:

1. Choose Layout I Find.

2. You'll see a blank version of the Browse screen. Enter data in one or more of the fields that you'd like to match with your Find.

3. Click the Find button in the left margin.

4. If any records are found, they'll be displayed. The found records are now a subset of the total database. You can scroll back and forth through the records and see only the found records.

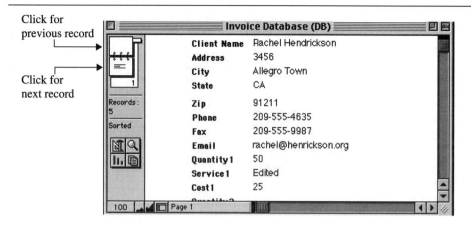

Click for previous record

Click for next record

FIGURE 10-2 Browse mode is where you move through records and enter new data.

Choose Organize | View All Records when you're ready to deal with the entire database again.

By the way, it might be helpful to know that number fields (and calculated fields with number results) can accept basic comparisons. For instance, if you have a field that calculates a testing average, you can enter **<65** to see every record that has an average under 65. The same goes for a number field that's holding a dollar amount—use <, >, <>, <, >=, or = to see which records match up. And it's the same for dates and times. You can enter **<10/10/01** in a date field to find records with dates before October 10, 2001, for instance.

Save Your Search

Want to create a Find that lasts for a while? You can do it with the Search button that appears on the Tools palette in the left margin of the database window. The Search button is the magnifying glass; click the button to see its menu. Choose New Search and you can name the search before you enter criteria in the Find layout view.

Now, when you want to perform that search again, it appears right there on the Search button menu. Just click the button to see all your named searches.

Print Records

If you choose Print while viewing records in your database, the Print command automatically defaults to printing *all* visible records. (This doesn't mean the records you can see with your eye—it means records that are visible within the database after a Find command has been done. If you want to print records numbered 1-5, for instance, perform a Find to find records with record numbers less than 6.)

If you just want to print one record, you'll need to look for an option in the Print dialog box that allows you to Print Current Record. If you can't find this option, look for a pull-down

menu in the Print dialog box that says General; select it and choose AppleWorks. Now you'll
see the Print Current Record option.

Give It a New Layout

Whenever you create a new database, AppleWorks designs a very basic layout, called
Layout 1, which offers only the rudiments of design. Fortunately, you can do something
about that by editing the layout.

Layouts are used for more than just the data entry screen—they're also used for creating
and printing reports. As you'll see, a report is simply a sorted, searched database that uses a
particular layout to make it look good. A layout doesn't even have to include every field in
your database, so you'll often create different layouts to correspond to different reports you
want to build (see Figure 10-3).

Since a database can have more than one layout, you might decide it's best to have
different layouts for data entry and reports. It's up to you, but even if you don't, you can jazz
up your layout so that it looks good for both a report and data entry.

Choose a Layout or Start a New One

To begin, you should figure out which layout you're currently using. Click the Layout
menu to open it and look toward the bottom. Whether or not there is more than one layout
in your database, the current one is the layout with a check mark next to its name. If you
want to use a different layout, choose it in the Layout menu. If you want to create a new
layout, choose Layout I New Layout.

If you choose to create a new layout, you'll see the New Layout dialog box. Give the
layout a meaningful name, then choose whether you want the basic layout (like Layout 1),
a duplicate of an existing layout, or a blank layout. You can also choose a Columnar
Report, which helps you build a simple report layout that will place information about each
record on its own line, as shown in Figure 10-3.

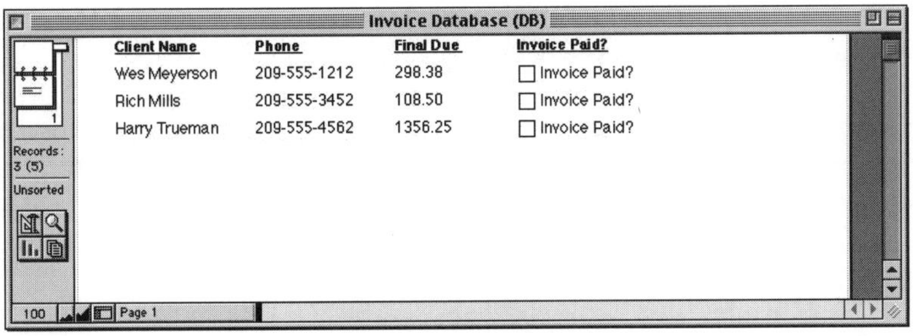

Client Name	Phone	Final Due	Invoice Paid?
Wes Meyerson	209-555-1212	298.38	☐ Invoice Paid?
Rich Mills	209-555-3452	108.50	☐ Invoice Paid?
Harry Trueman	209-555-4562	1356.25	☐ Invoice Paid?

Invoice Database (DB)

Records: 3 (5) Unsorted

FIGURE 10-3   Here's a report layout I've created specifically to show me payments that
haven't come in yet. Notice that it uses very few of the fields in my
inventory database.

Edit the Layout

The fun is just beginning, because you can edit as you please. You edit in Layout mode. To get into Layout mode, pull down the Layout menu and choose the layout to edit. Now, go back to the Layout menu and choose the Layout command.

What can you do? You can move your text and fields around, you can draw boxes around parts of your layout, or you can add graphics and text. For the most part, the drawing and painting tools are the same ones used in the drawing and painting modules, so I'll point you to Chapter 11 to learn things like drawing and moving shapes around. But there are a few things specific to the database layout process you should know:

- Don't forget the SHIFT key. You can click a database field, then click the field's label while holding down SHIFT. Now you can click and drag one field and the other will follow along.

- You can also use the SHIFT key to select all of the field labels at once, then you can use the Format menu to change the font, size, style, or color of the field labels.

- If you want to add something that appears at the top of every record, choose Layout | Insert Part, then choose to add a Header. You can drag the Header line around on the layout to resize it, then add the text or image above the Header line and it'll appear at the top of every page in your layout.

- If you want more than one record on a page, you'll need to edit the layout so that more than one will fit, then drag the Body line up under the abbreviated layout. If you only have a few fields and want each record to appear on one page, do the opposite and drag the Body line down to the bottom of the page.

- To change the appearance of a field, you can select it (or more than one field) and use the text formatting options in the Format menu. For both text and number fields, you can also double-click the field to quickly format it. (This includes things like formatting for currency and setting the precision of decimals.)

- Switch to Browse mode to test things (assuming you have more than a few records in your database). That'll give you a good idea how things look. You can switch back to Layout mode to keep editing.

After a while you'll have a nice, edited layout designed for data entry or for a report, depending on your needs. Figure 10-4 shows the report in Layout mode; Figure 10-5 shows that same report in Browse mode.

Sort and Report

The slash-and-burn report works like this—create the layout that you want to use for the report. Perform a Find and create a subset of matching records you want to report on.

The Header line

Drawing/
painting
tools

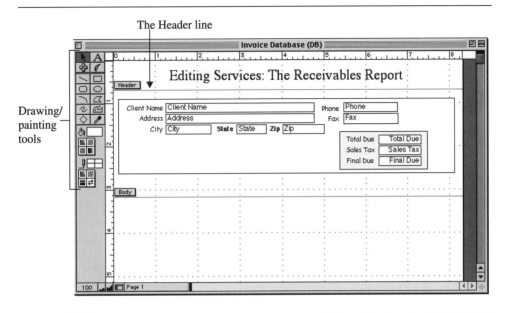

FIGURE 10-4   A new layout, still in Layout mode

10

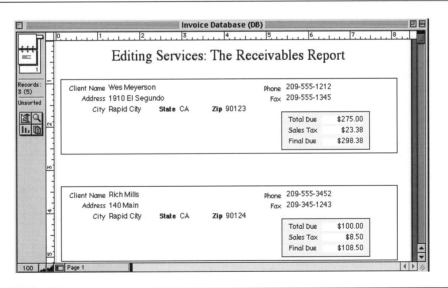

FIGURE 10-5   Here's how the new layout looks in Browse mode.

Switch to the report layout in the Layout menu, then change to Browse mode. If the report looks good, print it.

You can even get more sophisticated. If you're going to be creating the same report over and over again, you can go ahead and save the whole thing—the search, the sort, and so on. You might also want to perform a quick sort before you run the report—that way you can find whose grades in the database are below 65, for example, and you can organize the report alphabetically or based on some other criteria.

Sort

Once you get a number of records in your layout you may find, for many different reasons, that it's useful to have them sorted. This isn't always a priority while you're entering data, but it can be very important when you're ready to generate a report.

Here's how to sort:

1. To begin a sort, choose Organize | Sort Records.

2. In the Sort dialog box, select the Field name you want to sort, then click the Move button.

3. Click the Ascending or Descending button in the bottom-right corner of the dialog box.

4. Next, choose the secondary field you want to sort on. This is the "sort-within-the-sort" field. If your first-level sort is on the State field, for instance, and you have more than one record within a given state, then the records could be secondarily sorted based on, say, the Phone Number field.

5. Continue until you have enough sort fields, then click OK. Your database is now sorted.

So, things are sorted. If you add records and want to sort them again, just choose Organize | Sort Records again. The criteria should still be there in the dialog box and you can just click OK again.

Save a Sort

Want to save a sort for posterity? You might find reason to work with more than one sort. If that's the case, you'll need to head down to the Sort button on the Tools palette in the left margin of the database window. Select the Sort button (it's the one with the three bars) and choose New Sort. You'll get the same dialog box as with a regular Sort, except there's an entry box at the bottom to name the sort. Do so, then set up the sort criteria. Click OK and the sort is created.

Now you can return to the Sort button to perform the sort or edit it. Any new sorts you create show up on the Sort button's menu.

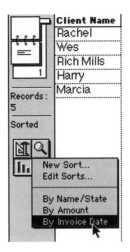

Build a Report

I'm not trying to rhyme the titles of these last two sections, I promise. It's appropriate, though, because the processes are so similar. If you're ready, it's time to head to the Report button and create a new report. The Report button is the one with an image of two sheets of paper on it.

Pull down the Report button menu and choose New Report. The New Report dialog box appears. Here's the crazy part—all you do is give the report a name, then choose a saved Layout, a saved Search, and a saved Sort from the menus. If you want the report automatically printed when you choose the item in the Report button menu, then check the Print The Report check box. Otherwise, you've just built and saved a report. Pretty easy, huh?

Chapter 11

Paint, Draw, and Create Presentations

How to...

- Distinguish between painting and drawing
- Create a painting
- Add text to your painting
- Save the painting
- Create a drawing
- Add AppleWorks elements (charts, paintings, text) to your drawing
- Create a presentation from scratch
- Get serious about presentations with the AppleWorks presentation template

People seem to love to play with the Paint and Draw modules in AppleWorks, which allow you to create some of the great graphics that Macs are known for. If you're quite the artist, especially with a computer mouse, then you'll want to head directly for the Paint module, which puts both your free-form and shape-driven ideas on a virtual canvas.

If you're a little less abstract in your thinking, you'll prefer the drawing tools, which can be used to create diagrams, drawings, signs, labels, and even desktop layouts with precision. Drawing documents are about creating straight lines, curves, boxes, circles, and shapes, and adding text when necessary.

With your graphics and text, then, the logical result is to create presentations. AppleWorks has the built-in ability to take over your iMac's screen and give a slide show presentation, allowing you to manually or automatically move through slides created in almost any one of the AppleWorks modules.

First, you'll need to learn to draw and paint.

Painting vs. Drawing

You may be wondering why AppleWorks offers two different modules for what seem to be very related tasks. The answer is simple: *objects*. The definition of objects, however, will take a little more discussion.

The Draw module in AppleWorks allows you to create objects—shapes, lines, text—that can be moved around, grouped together, and placed relative to one another on the drawing document. This is different from the Paint module, which treats the document window more like an actual artist's canvas. Once you put a shape, line, brushstroke, or text on the canvas, that's it—it can't be moved again as an individual shape. You can select a portion of the painting and move it, but the shape itself is now part of the painting.

You *can* cut and paste portions of a Paint document, and you can erase parts, too, but you can't pick up an individual shape or text object and drag it around—you can only cut, copy, paste, or erase parts of the canvas. The difference is a little like watercolor painting versus collage art. In a collage, you can lay down elements on your canvas, then pick them up and move them around. In watercolor painting, once you paint something onto the canvas, you have to either wipe it off (if you can) or paint over it to change it. But once you've blended colors and shapes together, you can't move them again.

Of course, the AppleWorks painting tools offer a little more freedom than that. After all, you can select square chunks of your Paint document and drag them around. And the Magic Wand tool can be used to grab shapes from within the painting and drag them around. But, if you want to create boxes and lines that can be moved around and organized on the page, you're better off using the Draw module.

Start Your Painting

To create a new Paint document in AppleWorks, select File | New, then choose to start a Paint document. Your untouched document "canvas" appears onscreen along with the tools you'll need to get started. If you'd like to immediately save, choose File | Save As to give this document a name and find a folder to store it in.

Document Size

Depending on your reason for creating this painting, the first thing you might want to do is create a document that's a certain size. If, for example, you're building a newsletter page or a page on the World Wide Web, you may want to create a painting that's less than the standard document size. You can then place it in the larger document, wrap text around it, and create an interesting layout.

NOTE *Layouts are covered in more detail in Chapter 12.*

Choose Format | Document and you can determine exactly how many pixels wide and long you want your document. In the Document dialog box, use the entry boxes under Size to determine the width and height of your painting in *pixels*. (Pixels are *picture elements* or individual dots on the screen.) When you close the Document dialog box, your canvas will change to reflect your sizing.

Document	
Margins	**Page Display**
Top: `1 in`	☑ Show margins ⌘M
Bottom: `1 in`	☑ Show page guides ⌘G
Left: `1 in`	**Size**
Right: `1 in`	Pixels Across: `600`
☐ Mirror Facing Pages	Pixels Down: `400`
Page Numbering	
Start at Page: `1`	
`?`	`Cancel ⌘.` `OK`

NOTE *This is another distinction between Paint and Draw—the painting tools can be used for editing individual pixels if you zoom in close enough. The drawing tools can't be used on individual pixels.*

Use the Tools

With document size set, you're ready to begin work with the painting tools. There are quite a few of them, but they fall into basically four different categories: shapes, pickers, brushes, and color controls. Before you can see any of them, you'll need to make sure that Window | Show Tools has been chosen. (If you see Hide Tools when you choose the Window menu, that means that the tools are currently being shown. See 'em?) Figure 11-1 shows the different tools available for your painting pleasure.

Shape Tools

If you want to create a shape, simply select a Shape tool by clicking it in the toolbar. Then, move the mouse pointer to the window and choose a starting place for your shape. Now, click and hold the mouse button, then drag out to create the shape. When you release the mouse button, the shape is committed to the document canvas.

> **TIP** *Double-click the Rounded Rectangle or Curve tool's icons to change some options that govern how the shapes look.*

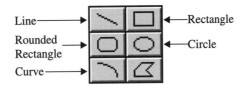

11

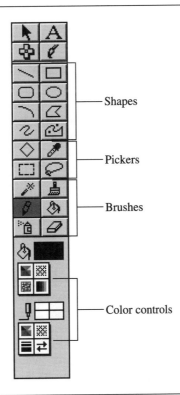

FIGURE 11-1   The different tools in the Paint module

The first five Shape tools, Line, Rectangle, Rounded Rectangle, Circle, and Curve, all work in the same way—just select and drag. The next four Shape tools work a little differently. Each requires a little extra input before you can draw the shapes. Here's how to use each of them:

■ **Polygon**   Choose this tool, then click once in the document to begin your polygon. Move the mouse to the next point in the shape and click again. Continue to click for each point on the shape until the next-to-last one—you can double-click that point to automatically draw a line back to the original point. (The lines of your polygon can be curved, if you like—just hold down the OPTION key while you move the mouse.)

■ **Freehand**   Select this tool, then click and hold down the mouse button in the document window. Drag around the screen to create a curvy, filled shape. When you release the mouse button, a line is drawn straight back to the starting point and the shape is filled in. (If you're trying to create a particular shape, draw it so that you end up as close to the starting point as possible.)

■ **Bezigon**   Choose the tool, click the mouse button in the document window, then move to the next place you want to create a point. Click the mouse button to create the point. To close the shape, double-click the mouse on your last point or click very close to the original point to end the shape.

■ **Regular Polygon**   This one allows you to create a polygon by dragging, just as you do with the Rectangle and Circle tools. The difference is, you get to specify the number of sides. To choose the number, double-click the tool's icon. In the dialog box, enter the number of sides for this polygon. Now, in the document window, click and hold the mouse button and drag the mouse to create the shape. Let go of the mouse button when you've got the shape the size you want it to be.

Selection Tools

The next set of tools are the Selection tools, which allow you to select different parts of your painting in order to copy, paste, clear, or drag the part to some other section of the canvas. Here's how they work:

■ **Eyedropper**   This tool does one thing—picks up the color that's under it when you click the mouse button. Choose the Eyedropper, point at a particular color, and click the mouse button. That color then becomes the Fill color.

■ **Rectangular Selection**   This tool is designed to select a rectangular section of the document. Choose the tool, then click and hold the mouse button in the top-left corner of the part of the document you want to select. Now, drag down toward the bottom-right corner of the portion you want to select. Let go of the mouse button and it's highlighted. (Double-clicking the tool icon selects the entire window.)

- **Lasso**   The Lasso allows you to be a little more cavalier in your selection. Select the Lasso's icon, then click and hold the mouse button in the document window while you draw, freehand, the shape you want to select. Release the mouse button and your selection is highlighted.

- **Magic Wand**   With this tool, you won't need to drag and release—the Magic Wand is designed to "magically" select shapes in the document window. Select the tool, then head over to a shape and click it. All or part of the shape will be highlighted. If you don't get what you want, try a different part of the shape. (You can also hold down the SHIFT key while selecting in order to select more of a shape or more shapes.)

What do you do once something is selected? Hit the DELETE key and everything in the selection box will disappear. Or pull down the Edit menu and choose any of those commands—Cut, Copy, Paste, Duplicate—to perform such functions on the selection.

Brush Tools

With all of the Brush tools, you hold down the mouse button and move around on the document window when you want to draw; release the button when you don't want to draw. Brushes do a couple of specific things:

- **Paint Brush**   Use this tool to paint brushstrokes of color onto your document. You can change the shape and size of the brush by double-clicking the tool's icon. Select a new size and/or shape and click OK. Also, notice the Effects menu, which allows you to change the way the Paint Brush works, offering more sophisticated special effects like blending and tinting.

- **Pencil**   Use this tool to draw thin lines or to fill in a drawing at the pixel level. The pencil can be used at high magnification to fill in individual pixels with color. Double-click the pencil to switch instantly to 800% magnification.

- **Paint Can**   This is the fill tool—choose the Paint Can and click in your document and any shape or form is filled in with color. You can draw a closed shape, then fill it with this tool, or click outside of a closed shape to fill the entire screen with color.

- **Spray Can**   The Spray Can creates a spray-painting effect, making it look as if some paint is scattered. The more you spray on one particular area, the better the coverage of paint in that area. Double-click the Spray Can to change the size of the dots and the amount of coverage the Spray Can shows. You can also test the settings in the testing area in this window.

11

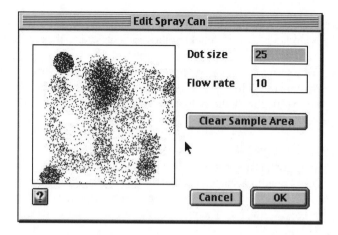

- ■ **Eraser** The last Brush tool is actually an "antibrush" of sorts—the Eraser. It erases all layers of shapes and color on your document, taking it back to the original white background.

Options for most of these Brush tools can be found in the Options menu, where you'll also find options to change the Paint Mode from the standard Opaque to Transparent Pattern, and Tint, which mixes your paint color with any colors you paint over.

Color Tools

The last tools in the toolbar are the Color tools, which offer two different ways to color—Fill and Line. The Fill color is used for the bulk of all shapes you create; it's used whenever you use one of the brushes, and it's used when you select the Fill Paint Can. The Line color is used for drawing lines and for outlining shapes.

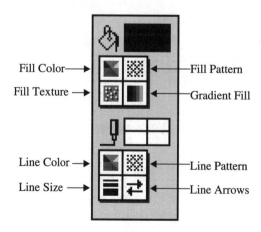

Let's start with the Fill Color tools:

■ **Fill Color**   To change the Fill color, click on the Fill Color button. A palette of colors appears. Select one of the colors; the palette disappears and the Fill color indicator changes to show the new color.

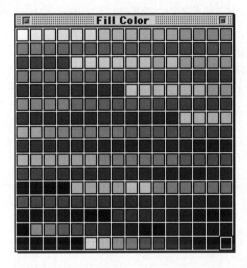

■ **Fill Pattern**   Next to the Fill Color button is the Fill Pattern button. Click it once to see the various patterns you can fill with. Select one and the palette goes away. (Note the first two patterns in the palette. The first one causes no fill to appear; the second is the solid Fill color with no pattern.)

■ **Fill Texture**   Open this palette and choose a texture to fill with instead of a color.

■ **Gradient Fill**   If you'd like to fill shapes and paint with a gradient instead of a Fill color, choose one from this palette. A *gradient* is a pattern that moves from one color to another gradually across the shape or background you fill. You can edit the gradients by choosing Options | Gradients.

Want one of these palettes on the screen all the time? All you have to do is click and hold the particular button that interests you, then drag the mouse pointer along and off the end of the palette. That *tears* the palette off the menu. When you release the mouse button, the menu *floats* above the document, so you can change colors or patterns on a whim.

NOTE   *You can edit the color palettes if you want to. Choose Edit | Preferences. In the Preferences dialog box, choose Palettes from the pull-down menu. Click the option for Editable 256 Color Palette. Now, back in the document window you can tear off the color palette. Then, you can double-click an individual color on that palette to edit the color.*

11

Below the Fill tools you'll find the Line tools. These tools determine the color and pattern used for lines and the outlines of shapes. Each one of these works just like the other palettes—click the icon, then click to select the color or pattern. Here's what each does:

- **Line Color**   Choose the color for the line from the color palette.
- **Line Pattern**   This works the same as Fill Pattern, but it pertains only to line and outline patterns.
- **Line Size**   Choose the size of the line in points. If you want something larger than 8 point, choose Other, then enter the point size desired.
- **Line Arrows**   Choose whether or not you want arrows on the end(s) of your lines.

TIP
Want my limited artistic tips? When painting an object or landscape, remember your light source. Figure out where the light is coming from, then use darker versions of your colors on the farther side and use lighter versions of your colors on the side closer to the light. Also, a nicely placed shadow goes a long way toward making a painting look more realistic, if that's your goal. You can use the Tint and Transparency options to create distance and perspective effects, too.

Add Text

Here's the last thing I'll show you in the Paint module—you're going to have to figure out the artistic part yourself. Hopefully, you've already got a start. If you need to add text to your masterpiece, it can be done. Here's how:

1. At the top of the toolbar, choose the Text tool (the letter "A").
2. Click in the document where you want the text to be. An insertion point appears.
3. Head up to the menus and format the text using the menus just as you would text in the word processing module.
4. Type the text you want. If you need to change formatting, quickly type ⌘-A to invoke the Select All command, then format the text.
5. When you're done entering and editing the text, click somewhere else on the document outside of the text box. You can click the Pointer tool in the top-left corner of the toolbar to switch back from the Text tool and use the painting tools.

Once you've placed the text, it's there for good. It can't be moved (unless you also move the background behind the text) or edited. It has become part of the painting, just like a brushstroke or a shape. (Sometimes, but not always, you can manage to select text with the Magic Wand, especially if you zoom in close, as discussed in Chapter 12.)

Save Your Image

You know that File | Save allows you to save your Paint image in AppleWorks document format. But if you'd like to use the Paint image in other programs—to edit the image in PaintShop or add it to a professional layout or World Wide Web page, for instance—you'll need to save it as a more common file format. To do so, you can choose File | Save As. In the dialog box, give the file a name, then choose the file type from the Save As menu.

If you plan to use the document in an earlier version of AppleWorks or in ClarisWorks for Kids, select one of those options. If you want to use the image in an application other than AppleWorks, save it as one of the remaining four image file types. Click OK to save the file.

NOTE   *Need to know more about image file types? They're described in Chapter 14.*

Draw Objects and Text

The drawing tools can be used much the same way the painting tools are used—for fun, for artistic creation, or for logos and images you'll use elsewhere. The Draw module can be used for more businesslike reasons than the Paint module. As I've said, the drawing tools are a good way to present information graphically. Using these tools, you'll be able to create signs, posters, certificates, and more. In Chapter 12 we'll take a close look at some of the Stationery that's provided for the Draw module and all of the publications you can create with its tools.

Draw in Databases and Spreadsheets

By the way, the drawing tools are also found elsewhere in the AppleWorks suite, including the Database module and the Spreadsheet module when you're dealing with charts. You'll notice that a lot of the object manipulation commands (as well as some of the drawing tools) are found in those parts. If you're trying to create a database layout or improve the appearance of a chart, what you'll learn in this section on the drawing tools will help.

Create Objects

To begin, open a drawing document by choosing File | New, then select Drawing and click OK. A new drawing document appears.

You can place text, graphics, shapes, other multimedia objects, and even spreadsheet objects in your drawing document. When you're in the Draw module, everything is an object, meaning that everything you add to your drawing document remains its own entity. You can pick objects up, move them around, and even stack objects on top of one another (see Figure 11-2).

There are three basic types of objects you'll create in the Draw module: shapes, text, and objects from other modules. That includes spreadsheet objects, charts, painted images,

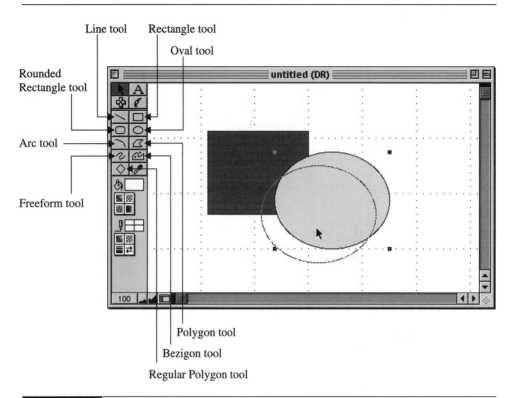

Line tool   Rectangle tool

Oval tool

Rounded
Rectangle tool

Arc tool

Freeform tool

Polygon tool

Bezigon tool

Regular Polygon tool

FIGURE 11-2   In the Draw module, you create objects that can be moved around.

scanned photos, QuickTime movies, and other multimedia objects you can bring in from other applications.

Shape Tools

The shapes you find in the Draw module are a subset of those found in the Paint module, and they work pretty much the same. One important thing to remember is that most objects in the Draw module can easily be reshaped or resized after they've been created, so your dimensions don't have to be as perfect as they do in the Paint module.

Here are the tools you can use to draw different shapes:

■   **Line**   Click the Line tool, then click once in the document window. Move the mouse pointer and click again to create a line between the original point and the final location.

- **Rectangle**   Choose the Rectangle tool, then click and hold the mouse button in the document window. Drag the mouse to create your rectangle, then release the mouse button when the rectangle is the size and shape you want it.

- **Rounded Rectangle**   Choose this tool, then click and drag in the document window to create the oval. Release the mouse button when you've got it the right size. To shape the corners of the rounded rectangle, make sure the tool is selected, then choose Edit | Shape Corners.

- **Oval**   Select the Oval tool in the toolbar, then click and drag to create the oval. Release the mouse button when it's the correct dimensions and circumference.

- **Arc**   Select the Arc tool, then click and drag in the document window until the arc is the correct size. To change the arc's characteristics, make sure the Arc tool is selected, then choose Edit | Arc Info.

- **Polygon**   Select the Polygon tool, then click in the document window to place the first point. Move the mouse pointer and click to place a second point; repeat until all the points for the shape have been laid out, then double-click to draw a line between the last point and the first point, closing the polygon.

- **Freeform**   Select the tool, then click and drag in the document window. Drag out the shape you want to create, ending as close to the starting point as possible. In the Draw module, this shape isn't forced closed—it can just be a squiggly line, if you prefer.

- **Bezigon**   Select this tool, then click in the document to create the first point. Now, move the mouse and click to create additional points for the shape. End as near the first point as possible, then double-click to complete the shape.

- **Regular Polygon**   Select this tool, then click and drag in the document window to create a polygon. To change the number of sides, make sure the tool is selected, then choose Edit | Polygon Sides.

11

> **TIP**   *The SHIFT key can be used to constrain many of these tools. Hold down the SHIFT key while you draw a line (or draw the side of a shape) and the line will be perfectly straight. Hold it while using the Rectangle tool to draw a square. Hold it down while using the Oval tool to draw a circle. Hold it down while drawing an arc to keep the arc symmetrical.*

The Draw module also includes an Eyedropper tool and the same Color tools described in the Paint section. The Color tools work slightly differently, though. You can select a shape that's already been created, then choose a color, texture, or pattern if you like. Same with lines—even if they've already been created, just select them in the document window and choose a new color, pattern, or size, or add arrows. You can always change them back later, if desired.

 *To change the Polygon tool's behavior, choose Edit | Preferences and make sure the Topic menu shows Graphics. Now, click to change the shape-closing behavior in the Polygon Closing section. With the Manual option, you need to click to place the last point pretty much right on top of the first point in a shape.*

Text Tool

To create a text object, click the Text tool in the top of the toolbar. It's the tool that looks like a capital "A"; it allows you to click and drag in the document window to create a text box.

Notice that this is a little different from painting. You've actually created a word processing object within the drawing document here—it's almost like you opened up a little window into the word processing module. Watch carefully and you'll notice that the button bar and menus change when you're editing inside the text box. The insertion point appears and you're ready to type.

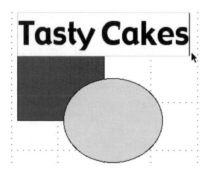

Type your text, then format it using the menus. When you're pleased with your text, click the Pointer tool in the toolbar or click outside the text box to switch back to the drawing tools.

If you want to edit the text again, just double-click it if the Pointer tool is selected, or select the Text tool and single-click the text. The text box appears (it may be a little smaller), the menus change, and you're ready to edit the text.

Other Objects

We'll get into this topic in much more detail in Chapter 12, but I want to touch on it now. You can create spreadsheet and painting objects right here within the Draw module. Just as you can create a text object that switches around your menus and button bars, you can create spreadsheet and paint objects.

For a spreadsheet object, select the Spreadsheet tool (the small cross) at the top of the toolbar, then click and drag in the document window to create the spreadsheet object. A table of cells appears and the insertion point is ready to edit. Start your spreadsheet. You can enter anything you might enter in a typical AppleWorks spreadsheet.

You can even create a chart. Try it. Enter data that works for a chart, then choose Options | Make Chart. (If you don't see that option, double-click the spreadsheet to make sure it's selected for editing.) Now, create a chart as discussed in Chapter 9. When you click OK, the chart appears in your document. Best of all—it's an object, just like everything else (see Figure 11-3).

It's a similar process to create a paint object within your Draw document. Select the Paint Brush, then drag out a paint object in the document window. You'll notice that the tools and menu commands change to those of the Paint module. Paint all you want inside the paint object, then click outside it when you're done.

Manipulate Objects

Once you've got your objects created, you're ready to work with them. The key is to figure out how to select and drag them around—that part's pretty easy. With the Pointer tool selected, point to an object, then click and hold down the mouse button while you drag the object around the screen. Drop the object when you're done moving it by releasing the mouse button.

TIP   *Don't forget Undo! Most of these manipulations can be immediately undone by choosing Edit | Undo right after you perform the change.*

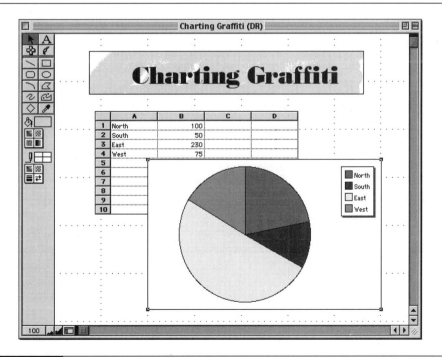

FIGURE 11-3   A chart from spreadsheet data can easily be added to your Draw document.

Select Objects

If you want to change an object's size, just click once on it to select it. You'll see the resizing handles appear. You can click and drag one of the handles to make the object larger. This includes text boxes, spreadsheet objects, and paint objects, all of which can be stretched to offer you more space to work in.

Charting Graffiti

But that's not all you can do. With an object selected, you can hit the DELETE key to delete it from the document, or choose any of the Edit menu commands like Cut, Copy, or Paste. You can paste an object from any AppleWorks module into any other module. (The major exception is the Paint module, which will accept the Paste command, but won't store the object as an object—it just turns it into part of the painting document. That's even true of spreadsheet objects, which can be painted right over in the Paint module.)

Arrange Objects Front and Back

Sometimes you'll find you have one object that's "on top of" another object—it's obscuring part of the second object. This often happens, for instance, if you decide to create the background for a text object after you've created the text object. Drag the background to the text and it'll obscure the text.

If you really want that background in the, well, background, then make sure it's selected and choose Arrange | Move Backward or go for the gold and choose Arrange | Move to Back. In either case, the selected object is moved behind other objects. The Arrange | Move Backward command is designed to move objects back one layer at a time (just in case you have three or four objects stacked on one another). Move to Back immediately moves the selected object to the back of all objects on the screen.

As you might guess, you can bring objects to the foreground just as easily. Select an object, then choose Arrange | Move Forward or Arrange | Move to Front.

Align Objects

There are two different ways to align objects. You can select a particular object and choose Arrange | Align to Grid. This only does something if you've previously selected the Options | Turn Autogrid Off command. Autogrid is what forces objects to "snap" to a particular position on the page whenever you drop them. It keeps you from making precise little movements, but helps you by aligning everything to the grid. If you've turned it off, but you now want an object aligned to the grid again, choose the Align to Grid command.

The Align Objects command is even cooler. Select two or more objects that you want to align relative to one another. Now, choose the Arrange | Align Objects command. You'll see the Align Objects dialog box.

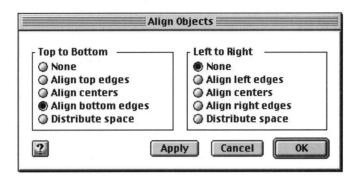

See the options? Decide how you want objects aligned, asking yourself some questions like:

■ If your objects are in a vertical column, do you want them aligned on the right or left edge? Should the vertical distance between the objects be distributed evenly?

■ If it's a horizontal row of objects, should the bottom or top be aligned? Should the horizontal distance between the objects be distributed evenly?

■ In either case, should the centers of the objects be aligned?

Make your choices and click OK.

Reshape Objects

As mentioned, objects in drawing are unique because they can be changed and reworked after they've been created. One way to do that is to change the way the shape is made with the Reshape command. This works with objects created using the Arc, Polygon, Freehand, Bezigon, and Regular Polygon tools. Choose Arrange | Reshape and you'll see resize handles that let you change the shape of the object.

After you've changed the shape, you'll still be in Reshape mode until you select Arrange | Reshape again. So, click another object and reshape again. Or choose the menu command to return to normalcy.

Free Rotate

The Free Rotate command works much the same way that the Reshape command does:

1. Choose Arrange | Free Rotate from the menu and you're in Free Rotate mode.

2. In the document window, select an object to rotate.

3. Now, click and grab one of the image's handles, then move the mouse. You'll see the object rotate along with your mouse movement.

4. Release the mouse button when you have the object where you want it.

Don't forget to choose Arrange | Free Rotate again when you're done rotating to leave Free Rotate mode.

Flip and Rotate

These are more precise controls that allow you to do exactly as much rotation and flipping of an object as you'd like. For these, you'll select the object in the document window first, then choose the command from the Arrange menu. Here are the commands:

- **Flip Horizontally**   Quickly flips an object from left to right.

- **Flip Vertically**   Flips the top and bottom of an object.

- **Rotate**   Brings up a dialog box that allows you to enter how many degrees the object should rotate. Rotation works counterclockwise (entering **90** causes the object to rotate counterclockwise 90 degrees), but you can enter a negative number to rotate clockwise. (Note that **–90** and **270** give the same results, since rotation covers the total (360) degrees in a circle.)

- **Scale by Percent**   Brings up a dialog box that allows you to reduce or enlarge your object vertically or horizontally. Enter a percentage for each to stretch or enlarge the object.

Group and Lock

With the Lock command, you fix an object so that it can't be moved, reshaped, or rotated. Locking is simple—just select the object and select Arrange | Lock (⌘-H) from the menu. The object becomes locked—it can't be moved or shaped. (You can edit text and make changes in spreadsheets and similar objects, though.) To unlock the object, select it and choose Arrange | Unlock (SHIFT- ⌘-H).

The Group command allows you to take two or more objects and cause them to function as a group—move one and you'll move them all. They become, in essence, one object. To group objects, select them all (hold down the SHIFT key as you click additional objects in order to select more than one). Choose Arrange | Group (or ⌘-G) and the different objects become one object. You'll notice that the object handles change so that the entire group can be selected, moved, resized, shaped, or rotated as one object.

To ungroup, select the object and choose Arrange | Ungroup (SHIFT-⌘-G). Once you've created a grouping, you can also group that grouping with other objects (and so on, and so on) although that can get a touch complicated.

Obviously, it's best to group related elements, especially things that always need to be together as one object or together but a certain distance apart. (It can be annoying to get everything set up correctly and then accidentally move one of the related objects. Just group them and that can't happen.) It's also easy and recommended that you group objects temporarily when you want to move them, together, across the screen. Select, group, move, ungroup—you can do it very quickly and it keeps all those objects the same relative distance from one another.

Creating a Slide Show

I've mentioned that the Draw module is a great way to communicate information graphically, and it doesn't end with creating flyers or posters. In fact, many of AppleWorks' parts also have the ability to display documents on the screen in the form of a slide show—the type you might use for a presentation or for a kiosk of some sort.

So, you can create a series of Word Processing, Spreadsheet, Draw, Paint, or Database screens (usually pages within a document or a series of documents) and create a slide show that advances automatically or can be advanced by pressing a key or clicking the mouse button.

> **TIP** *Need more than one page in a drawing or painting document? Choose Format | Document, then enter the number of pages across and down for your document.*

You'll start by creating multiple screens or pages within a document that can be used for the slide show. You'll want the pages or documents to be pretty much the same size, have a similar appearance, and generally work well as a group. Here's how to display them as a slide show:

1. Load the document you want to display as a slide show. Make sure it's frontmost in AppleWorks.

2. Choose Window | Slide Show.

3. Now you'll make some choices. Begin by deciding whether your pages are going to be opaque or transparent. Click on the transparency icon next to each page to change its condition (see Figure 11-4). A transparent page simply builds on the page before it, allowing you to see the content from both pages. This is a clever way to build slides if you want it to appear that text or images are appearing on a slide that already exists (for example, a new bullet point appears on the same slide when you click the mouse button).

> **TIP** *It's okay to create every third or fourth slide as an opaque slide, while the ones in between are transparent. Put each bullet point (or other element) on an individual transparent slide, one right after the other, but in such a way that they don't overlap. Then, each item will appear when you're ready to talk about it. The next opaque slide will be a "new slide" since it will cover up the previous transparent ones. Doing it this way just adds a little drama to the presentation, while keeping your audience focused on each individual point you're trying to make.*

4. In the top-right corner of the dialog box, you can change how the page will appear onscreen, although the defaults are usually good choices. You can also determine whether you'll see the cursor on the screen. The cursor can be used for pointing and emphasis, but probably isn't necessary for an automated kiosk or display.

11

Changes the background colors

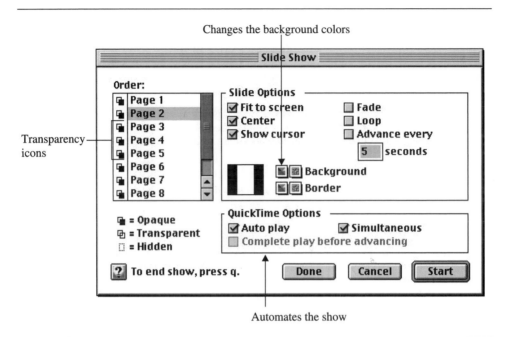

Transparency icons

Automates the show

FIGURE 11-4   The Slide Show setup window

5. Still in the top-right corner of the dialog box, you can also choose to Fade between slides (which provides an attractive transition effect) and to Loop so that when the last document is shown, the first one is repeated and the show goes on. Finally, click the Advance Every option and enter the number of seconds between each slide in the entry box.

6. If you want, you can choose a Background color or pattern for your slides. The background of your document pages (the pages that are being turned into slides) will show up, but if your document doesn't completely fill the screen, the background surrounding your document will be this color or pattern. The Border palettes can simply be used to create a border around the slide window, which you may or may not find attractive.

7. The final option, QuickTime Settings, is only relevant if you have QuickTime sounds or movies stored in your slide show document. If you do, you can choose to have the QuickTime sound or movie auto-play when the slide appears. If you have more than one QuickTime element, you can choose to have them play simultaneously. If you have the slide show set to auto advance, you can choose the final option, Complete Play Before Advancing, to force it to complete the

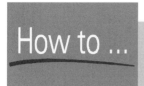

Use the Presentation Template

Having trouble getting things to line up and look good? Or are you creating a class, lecture, or business presentation from scratch? You might consider using Stationery to create a well laid-out presentation. The best one is provided within AppleWorks, although the module where you'll find it might surprise you. It's a Database document.

> **NOTE**   *Actually, there are two different approaches to presentations; there's also a Presentation Assistant that will walk you through creating a presentation in the Draw module. You can find it under the Slide Backgrounds Stationery.*

To create a presentation using Stationery:

1. Choose File | New.

2. Select the Use Assistant or Stationery option.

3. Choose the School Curriculum menu item, then choose the Making a Presentation database Stationery.

4. Click OK and your presentation database is built.

Why does using a database to create a presentation make sense? Because all you have to do is enter a new record to create a new slide. It's really pretty brilliant. Each slide (record) has four major fields that you can use to enter your points. Then, you can present it as a slide show, moving from record to record (or slide to slide) very easily.

The first thing you'll want to do is edit the slide layout—it's not the most gorgeous layout I've seen. Choose Layout | Layout to change how each of your slides will work. In Layout mode, you can use the Layout tools discussed in Chapter 10 to change the way the layout looks. Also, select Window | Show Tools and you'll have some drawing tools you can use to make your slides look that much better.

When you're done designing the slide, switch back to Browse mode and start entering the data for each slide. (To begin with, you'll probably want to change the first four slides, which contain instructions for the Stationery.) Each field is a new line in your discussion. To create a new slide, just create a new record. You can format each individual field for font size, emphasis, or whatever else you'd like.

When you're done creating all your slides (or whenever you want to test the presentation), choose Window | Slide Show, then go through the options and begin the show. It's that easy, and the template makes things look really good. Experiment and have fun—it's a great way to build a quick presentation.

11

QuickTime sound or movie before moving to the next slide. (If this option isn't on, you'll need to click or OPTION-click the movie to get it to start.)

 Consider the possibilities! You could actually record your own voice or some music and have it play when a new slide appears. It's an instant, self-running, narrated slide show.

8. You're ready to begin. Click the Start button to start the slide show. You can stop the show by pressing Q.

While the show is running, you'll have some choices for controlling it:

To go to the next slide	Press SPACEBAR, RIGHT ARROW, DOWN ARROW, or RETURN
To go to the previous slide	Press SHIFT-SPACEBAR, LEFT ARROW, UP ARROW, or SHIFT-RETURN
To go to the beginning of the show	Press HOME
To stop the show	Press Q or ESC

As you might imagine, the size of the pages can affect the way the presentation looks and you might need to play with document sizes—or make sure you're only typing in certain parts of your document. If you can set the pixel size of your documents (like in Paint documents) you should choose 640 × 480, 800 × 600, or a similar multiple that matches typical screen resolutions.

TIP *If you plan to show the images on another Mac, you need to take that Mac's screen resolution into consideration when you set up your Paint documents.*

Chapter 12

Use AppleWorks for Layout

How to...

- Work with page layouts
- Use Assistants for common documents
- Create a layout using drawing tools and text frames
- Add images and wrap text around them
- Draw shapes and create floating text for your layout
- Create layouts quickly using the word processing tools
- Merge data from your databases with your layout documents

Y ou've seen text layout and management in Chapter 8, numbers and calculations in Chapter 9, data management in Chapter 10, and artistic creation and communication in Chapter 11.

Now, what if you could put all this stuff together?

AppleWorks is a special sort of program. Although we've taken a reasonably thorough look at the individual parts and what they can do for you, in this chapter we'll look at AppleWorks as a whole. If you're interested in creating dynamic, professional-looking, and creative documents, you're going to enjoy this chapter.

How Layouts Work

These days, the desktop publishing revolution has made it so that most of the *page layout* process—the steps used to create a newsletter, newspaper, or magazine page—happens on a computer screen. You type and edit your story in a word processor, then you simply cut and paste it (or some close equivalent) into *frames* that are laid down in a special desktop publishing program. With the text laid down in columns, you can change fonts, sizes, spacing, and alignment. Then you can drop digital images right into the document itself and move them around on the page.

Popular programs for this sort of layout include Adobe InDesign and QuarkXPress. They usually cost hundreds of dollars apiece and can take a little training to master.

Or, you can use AppleWorks and get somewhat similar results. The tools aren't all as advanced as those in the layout programs, but AppleWorks does offer you the ability to format documents in columns, create text frames, add images, and even create graphic elements in the Paint and Draw modules. The best part is how all the modules work together.

12

The AppleWorks Frame

You already know that you can create different types of documents—word processing, spreadsheet, Paint documents, and so on—in the different AppleWorks modules. What you may not have realized is that you can use almost any of the tools and commands to create one single document.

You do that by creating frames in a particular document. While you'll have a basic document in the background—say, a Draw document—you can create a word processing frame or a spreadsheet frame and place it on the Draw document, the same way you might lay out a strip of typeset text on a paste-up board to create a newspaper. Figure 12-1 shows an AppleWorks document with multiple frames.

A frame is sort of a window into another part of AppleWorks—when you double-click in the frame, the AppleWorks menus and tools change to the tools that are available in that module. Double-click a spreadsheet frame and you'll see the spreadsheet tools and commands; double-click a text frame and you'll see all the word processing tools. With frames, you can create a sophisticated document that communicates very effectively.

Text frame   Spreadsheet frame

Paint frame

FIGURE 12-1   Using multiple frames in an AppleWorks document makes sophisticated layouts possible.

What Can You Lay Out?

You'll be able to use AppleWorks to lay out many different sorts of documents using all the different frames and tools at your disposal. What sort of things can you create? You can use just a few frames in a document to spice it up, or you can create entire documents out of nothing but frames that work together to create a whole. Here are some ideas:

- Add charts and graphs to your word processing reports.

- Create text frames in spreadsheet documents that explain the spreadsheet or help the novice user enter data in the spreadsheet form. You can similarly use a text frame in a database layout to offer instructions.

- Add Paint or Draw images to your spreadsheet, database, or word processing document.

- Create text frames within text documents in order to create headlines, pull-quotes, or other special elements (like the Tips, Notes, and Shortcuts you see in this book) on the page.

- Create spreadsheet charts within other types of documents, like Draw or word processing documents.

- Create text and image frames within a database to create a presentation, slide show, or flash cards that can be used for teaching or lecturing.

- Create a merge, in which data from a database can be merged into a word processing document or a text frame. This is great for mail merges (personalizing form letters and addressing envelopes) and it works for other things, too.

And there's much more—you can use layouts to create brochures, holiday letters, reports, and newsletters; you'll likely use all the different permutations. Want to create a newsletter that features text, graphics, painted objects, drawn objects, charts, and spreadsheet data? How about a newsletter that does all that, then allows you to print multiple copies and automatically address them from a database of names and addresses?

Don't ever let anyone tell you AppleWorks isn't a powerful program.

Assistants

In fact, AppleWorks is so powerful that you don't even have to create your own layouts—you can start with help from the Assistants. There are five Assistants to help you create different layouts:

- **Business Cards** This Assistant walks you through adding the company name, address, title, and phone number to create a business card, which it then generates as a database document. Using the database tools, you can modify the card in Layout mode, then switch to Browse mode, which automatically fills a page with eight instances of the card. The cards can then be printed to plain paper and taken to your print shop, or printed on card stock and cut at home. You can also get perforated card stock at most office supply stores, which can be used to create business cards.

- **Calendar** Using the spreadsheet tools, this Assistant quickly creates a monthly calendar, automatically placing the dates correctly, based on the month(s) you choose. There's really only one choice—a single month per sheet of paper.

- **Certificate** This Assistant quickly tosses together a certificate, award, diploma, or something similar. The result is a Draw document that can easily be edited.

- **Envelope** This Assistant walks you through the process of setting the alignment and printing path for the envelope. Envelopes can be tough to print—you'll need to read your printer's manual carefully to figure out how to orient and feed the envelope to your printer. Then you can make an informed decision on how to set up this Assistant, which generates a word processing document that's easily edited.

- **Newsletter** This Assistant automates the process of creating a newsletter in the Draw module, providing between 2 and 16 pages worth of columns, headlines, boxes, and so on. I think the final layout can be somewhat lacking (some of the

12

Stationery options for newsletters are better), but it's a decent start for using the techniques you'll learn later in this chapter.

To use an Assistant, choose File | New from the AppleWorks menu. Click the Use Assistant or Stationery option in the Open dialog box, then choose Show All Assistants from the Category pull-down menu. Choose an Assistant and click OK.

Assistants work by asking you a series of questions about your document. You enter information in the Assistant dialog box, then click the Next button to move on to the next series of questions.

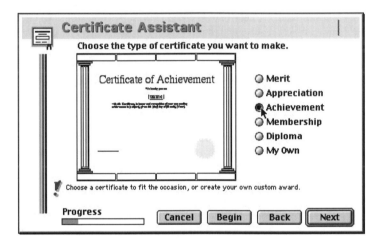

When you get to the end of the Assistant, you'll see a Create button, which causes the Assistant to take all the information you've input and create the document based on that information. You can also click the Cancel button to leave the Assistant, click the Back button to go back to the previous questions, or click the Begin button to return to the beginning of the Assistant.

Now, you're ready to learn how to jazz up that Assistant-created document by moving things around on your layout.

Layout Basics: Text Frames

Let's begin by creating a newsletter that incorporates all the different sorts of frames. We'll create text frames in columns, drop in images, add headlines—it'll be fun. Plus, what you learn in creating a newsletter can be applied to any sort of layout, from creating business cards and brochures to report letterhead and mail merge documents. We'll get to those other things later in this chapter, but right now let's cover the general instructions for dealing with frames on a page.

With a newsletter, there's actually a more fundamental problem to broach before you can start typing and framing things. You need to choose which type of AppleWorks document—word processing or Draw—to use as the foundation for your newsletter. Here's the basic rule—if you're more interested in the text than you are in the layout, then choose the word processing module for creating the basic document. Your newsletter may come out looking a little more like a pamphlet, but you'll have a more structured document with headers, columns, and other tools for automating the layout.

If your primary focus is the appearance of the newsletter—you want it to be visually pleasing, creative, and incorporate a lot of different framed elements—then you'll want to create a Draw document. Draw documents give you the most flexibility, since they're specifically designed for creating and moving objects around in the document window.

Getting Started

Create your Draw document by choosing File | New, selecting Drawing, and clicking OK. The first thing you need to do is make sure you're seeing all the drawing tools (select Window | Show Tools)—they'll be important throughout this process. You'll also probably want to view the rulers in the document window (select Window | Show Rulers), since you'll be lining things up and spacing them evenly.

Next up is a little tool we've ignored until now: magnification. You'll find that changing the magnification is a handy thing to do when you're trying see the whole page at once and get a feel for its overall design. The magnification level allows you to see more of your document (decrease magnification) or to see a smaller portion of your document up close (increase magnification). It's helpful to drop back to 75 or 67 percent sometimes, because then you'll be able to see the whole page. Then, return to 100 percent so you can actually see the text and detail in the images. While you're at it, you can also zoom in up to 800 percent to get a very close look at part of an image, text layout, or other feature of the page.

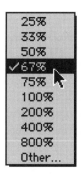

To change the magnification, select the percentage in the bottom-left corner of any AppleWorks document. It's actually a menu—you can simply choose the percentage to change the size of the document.

TIP *You can use multiple "views" to open different windows showing the same document at different magnifications. To create a new view, choose Window | New View. Notice that the title bar of the new view has ":2" in it. It's still the same document—this is just a convenient way to look at the same document in two different magnifications so you can switch quickly between the two.*

12

Next, you'll probably need to set up the document's margins and pages. This works the same as with any other Draw document. Choose Format I Document, then enter numbers for the margins on the page and the number of pages down or across you'd like the document to have. (I prefer to place all my pages horizontally, since that just looks more like a newsletter to me. Your approach is up to you, though.)

NOTE *Most inkjet printers and many laser printers can't print all the way to the edges of a page, so you'll probably want a minimal margin even if you plan to use most of the page for your layout. If you're using a typical letter-sized page, a margin of .25 inches on each side gives you 8 inches for your document's width and 10.5 inches for the height; 0.5 inches for each margin leaves you 7.5 by 10 to work with. Later in the chapter you'll be measuring things pretty closely, so keep these numbers in mind.*

Now you're ready to create the frames that will hold the different parts of your newsletter. If you're serious about creating a newsletter *right now*, remember that you can pre-type your stories in the word processing module to get them nicely spell-checked and formatted, and you might want to have some graphics or images on hand to drop into the layout. (Chapter 14 discusses manipulating digital images, while Chapter 27 discusses scanners and digital cameras.)

You can also type directly into the layout, as you'll see, but sometimes it's easier to have written the story beforehand so it can be checked and edited.

Create Text Frames

Much of your layout will likely be composed of text, so you'll be working with text frames a lot. Fortunately, they're pretty flexible. After all, a text frame is sort of a window into the word processing module of AppleWorks. Draw your text frame on the page and you'll have all the text tools at your disposal.

In drawing projects you'll create a text frame, type text, and then the text will become an object. Unfortunately for our newsletter, AppleWorks, by default, collapses the text frame around the typed text so that only that text becomes the text frame, regardless of the size of the frame you draw.

That won't quite work for us in the newsletter, since we want the column to stay a fixed size. That way we can move text around within the columns and the column won't change sizes just because we don't have enough text to fill it. It can be convenient to have the frame grow around your text in certain cases. But in order to build a newsletter-type document, you'll want to create frames that are a fixed size.

To do that, you must create a *linked* frame (this might be a good time to drop back to 67 percent magnification, by the way).

1. With the Pointer tool selected, choose Options I Frame Links.

2. Now, select the Text tool and drag out a frame on the page.

3. Release the mouse button and the insertion point appears—you can type in the frame if you want.

4. To see the entire linked frame, click once outside of the frame. Its handles appear to show you the entire frame object.

The text frame is an object in the same way that a drawn rectangle or line is an object—it can be rotated, resized, moved, or even sent to back or sent forward (see Figure 12-2).

So why is it called a "linked" frame? Well, it'll take some explaining, which I'll do later in this chapter in the section called "Link Text Frames." For now, suffice it to say that linked frames allow text to flow from one frame to another, like text flows from column to column on a newspaper page.

> **TIP** *The frame borders keep disappearing after you select other objects! To see your frames at all times, select them and choose to surround them with a line (choose Hairline from the Line Width button menu in the Tool Panel at left). Just don't forget to remove the lines before you print the document.*

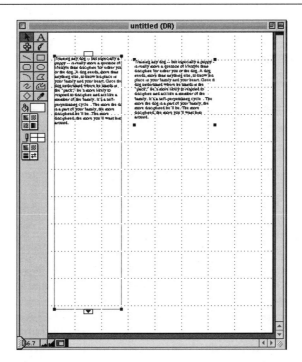

FIGURE 12-2   On the left, a linked text frame; on the right, a typical text frame—it collapses around the text instead of maintaining its shape.

Add Text

There are four basic ways you can add text to a linked frame. The first three start with clicking in the frame to make sure it's selected for input—the insertion point appears and you can type, if desired. In fact, that's the first way to add text:

- **Type**   You'll notice that, when you're in the insertion mode in the text frame, your tools (menus and the button bar) are all the same as they are in the word processing module. That should make it easy to type, format, and even clean up your newsletter story.

- **Cut and Paste**   If you have parts of an existing word processing document that you'd like to drop into this frame, you can open the document, select the text you want in your frame, then use the Edit | Copy and Edit | Paste commands to copy the text from the word processing document into your frame.

- **Insert Command**   A real pro does it this way. (That's a challenge, not an admonition.) You've already created your story in the word processing module, you've edited it, and you're ready to simply drop it into your layout. Select the text frame, then choose File | Insert. Find the word processing document you want to insert, then click OK. If you subsequently want to change the inserted document, you can select all the text by choosing ⌘-A, then insert a different document. (Or you can clear the text first and then insert the document.) Note that changing the text once it's been inserted doesn't affect the original word processing document's text at all.

- **Drag-and-Drop**   If you have good hand-eye coordination, you can select text in a word processing document and drag it into your text frame. Arrange the document windows so that you can see the text frame even if you have the word processing document in front of the Draw document. Select the text in the word processing document, then click and hold the mouse button on the selected text and drag the text to the frame. When the frame becomes outlined in blue, release the mouse button and the text should appear in the frame.

Again, once you have text in the frames you can format it just as if you're working in the word processing module—pull down the Font, Size, and Style menus, for instance, or use the Stylesheet button bar (select Window | Stylesheet) to change the alignment, create lists, and so on.

If you insert text into a frame from another document—or if you simply have a lot to type—then you may run into a little problem, because you may end up with a frame that's too big after it has been resized to fit your text. You can use the frame's handles to move the frame around and try to make things fit, but that probably won't work if you're creating a newsletter, report, or similar document. Instead, you'll probably want to move the additional text to a new frame and have it flow nicely so the story continues onto the next column. Almost as if, say, those frames were *linked*. Hey now!

Link Text Frames

If you've created one text frame that's overflowing with text, you can create another one to link to it so that it takes up the slack. Here's how:

1. Select the first frame to see its frame handles.

2. At the bottom of the frame, locate the continue indicator. Click it once.

3. Now you're ready to draw the linked frame. Drag to draw the frame onto your page. (Don't worry—you can resize it later.)

4. When you release the mouse button, text flows into the frame from the original frame. They're linked. When selected, the new frame will show a linked indicator (a little chain link icon) at the top and, if the story is long enough to overflow the frame, it'll show a continue indicator at the bottom, as shown in Figure 12-3.

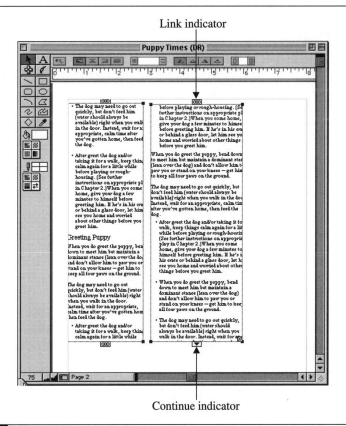

Link indicator

Continue indicator

FIGURE 12-3   Linked frames allow text to flow from one frame to the next.

What's important to realize about linked frames is that they flow just like different pages in a word processing document flow. So, if you go back to the original frame and add or delete text, the linked frame will change to reflect the added or subtracted text. If you simply had two frames into which you'd cut and pasted text, you'd be in for quite an experience if you added text to or subtracted text from either of them, because you'd need to do some crazy cutting and pasting to make the columns look right again.

 If you're used to expensive desktop publishing programs, you'll find these linked frames useful but limited. You can't reorder the links or link to an existing frame. You can only create linked frames by clicking the continue indicator and drawing the frame. Also, cutting or copying the frame breaks the link—a pasted frame can create its own linked frames, but it's no longer linked to the original.

Frames don't have to be the same sizes or shapes to be linked, so you can link a narrow column of text to a large rectangle of text and it will still flow fine. In fact, you can create a linked frame on a new page, if you like.

Resize Frames

Once you've got a couple of text frames on your page you'll probably realize that it's nearly impossible to get them to look like perfect columns on the page—after all, you're drawing and arranging them by hand. This can be frustrating, to say the least.

Fortunately, there are some tools to help you. The first is the Size window, which allows you to make some very precise decisions about how each frame will appear. Choose Options | Object Size and the Size window appears.

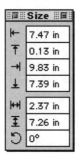

This is a great little window, because it gives you amazing precision in placing and aligning your frames as columns. From top to bottom, the measurements are

- ■ **Left Location**   The point, in inches, where the left side of the frame appears.
- ■ **Top Location**   The point, in inches, where the top of the frame appears.
- ■ **Right Location**   The point, in inches, where the right side of the frame appears.
- ■ **Bottom Location**   The point, in inches, where the bottom of the frame appears.

- **Object Width**   The width, in inches, of the frame.
- **Object Height**   The height, in inches, of the frame.
- **Rotation**   The amount of rotation, in degrees, of the frame.

While you're creating your layout, you should keep in mind how useful these measurements are. For instance, if you want all of your frames to be aligned at their tops, you can choose a measurement and enter it for each. Similarly, you can check all your columns to make sure their bottoms align exactly. This will also help to keep the text aligned across columns so the column layout doesn't look jagged. An example of what you *don't* want is shown here:

The dog may need to go out quickly, but don't feed him (water should always be available) right when you walk in the door. Instead, wait for an appropriate, calm time after you've gotten home

let him see you home and worried about other things before you greet him.
When you do greet the puppy, bend down to meet him but maintain a dominant stance (lean over the dog) and don't allow him to paw you or

Probably the best tools here are column width and height—two measurements that are almost impossible to eyeball. Select one of your columns and check its width—if you've got three columns, it's probably about 2.5 inches or so wide, right? Go ahead and make it a nice, round number. Now, select another column and make it 2.5 inches wide. Do it for the last one, and your columns will all be a uniform width.

Align the bottoms of your frames, then give them all the same height measurement if you want them to align at the tops, too. Columns of different heights simply can't align at both the top and bottom. It goes against the laws of physics.

While you're doing these measurements, you'll probably want to keep in mind a little mathematics. By default, a Draw document shows all 8.5 inches of a standard letter-sized sheet of paper. If you have margins for your document, you probably have 8 or 7.5 inches for your document's width. If you have an 8-inch wide document with three 2.5 inch columns, that will leave you 0.25 inches for the *gutters*—white space—between the columns. (There are two gutters for three frames, remember.) That's a good size. If you only have 7.5 inches to work with, though, you'll need to pare back those column widths a bit to get a decent gutter—say, about 2.333 inches for each column, which would give you back 0.25 inches per gutter.

You can select more than one column (or another frame) at the same time by holding down the SHIFT key as you select them. Then you can apply uniform sizing to them all at once.

12

Align Frames

Keep repeating to yourself that frames are objects and objects can be manipulated, as we saw in Chapter 11. You're using the Draw tools, so all of the same tools for shapes can be used to manipulate frames. That includes the alignment tools.

Here's a neat trick to align frames as columns and get that gutter just perfect:

1. On your layout, place your left- and right-most columns where you want them on the page relative to the edges.

2. Now, select all three frames by holding down the SHIFT key while you click them.

3. Choose Arrange I Align Objects.

4. In the Align Objects dialog box, choose Distribute Space in the Left To Right section.

5. Click Apply.

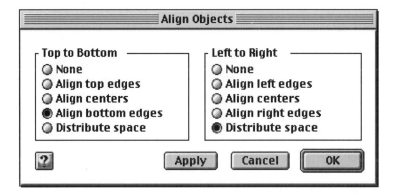

See what happened? Your columns snapped into place, distributing the remaining space equally between the two gutters. Perfect. If you like what you see, click OK to get out of the Align Objects dialog box. Or you can use the other settings—like Align Bottom Edges under the Top To Bottom options—to change other alignment issues regarding your columns.

Lock Frames

When you've finally got your frames in place the way they need to be, go ahead and lock them down. That'll keep you from accidentally moving the columns around once they've been carefully arranged. Select the frames to lock (hold down the SHIFT key as you select more than one frame), then choose Arrange I Lock. You can still select the frames and edit text within them, but you can't move them on the page until you unlock them.

Graphics, Floating Text, and Shapes

Once you have your main column frames created and locked down, you're ready to start adding text and images around the columns in order to create a more vibrant layout. The basic concept is simple—you create frames that can be placed near or even over the existing frames that you've created. Then, using a special command, you can force text to wrap around the floating frames, creating the effect that an image or block of text is diverting the columns around it, drawing attention to the visual element. Fortunately, it's very easy to do.

Add Graphic Frames

Let's begin by adding images to your layout. The graphics can be from a variety of sources, including graphics you create or one of the many images that comes with AppleWorks, which you can find by selecting File | Library. And you can just as easily scan graphics or digital-camera images into your computer and store them as image files. Any of these are easily added to your layout.

There are four basic ways to add graphic images to your layout:

- ■ **Build the Graphic**   Using the tools in the Draw module, a Paint frame, or a spreadsheet frame, you can add images (or spreadsheet cells) you've created in AppleWorks.

- ■ **Insert from a File**   If you don't have a frame selected and you choose File | Insert, you can search your hard disk (or connected network disks) for image files that can be added to your document as their own frames.

12

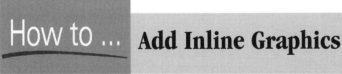

How to ...   **Add Inline Graphics**

You can also add graphics in another way—as inline graphics (or other objects) that become embedded in the text. Instead of floating freely in their own frames, embedded images are placed at a specific point in the text. You accomplish this by inserting, pasting, or choosing an image from a library while you have the Text tool selected and the insertion point placed somewhere in the selected text frame. The image appears as part of the text instead of in its own frame. You can learn more about this in "The Word Processing Layout," later in this chapter.

■ **Insert from a Library** AppleWorks offers libraries of *clip art*—small images, royalty-free, that you can add to your documents—which can be used to augment your layout.

■ **Cut and Paste** In most cases, you can select images or parts of other documents, then copy and paste them into your Draw document using the Edit I Copy and Edit I Paste commands. They'll show up in their own frames that can then be moved, stretched, rotated, and so on.

You already know from Chapter 11 how to create and manipulate AppleWorks graphics, and you know how to cut and paste. Let's look at adding a graphic from a file or library.

To add a graphic from a file, make sure no frames are selected in the document (so that AppleWorks doesn't try to add the graphic into that frame), then choose File I Insert. The Insert dialog box appears. Find the file you want to add and click OK. The graphic appears in your document in its own frame. Note that the file *format* of your graphic is important—you'll need to have it in PICT, TIFF, JPG, GIF, BMP, or a similar format. (You can see them all by pulling down the Show menu in the Insert dialog box.) Graphic file formats are discussed in detail in Chapter 14.

If you're adding from a library, choose File I Library, then select the type of clip art you'd like to look at. (The topics appear in a submenu that pops up when you select the Library menu.) That opens the Library window.

Find the graphic you want to use by selecting the names in the bottom half of the window—the top half will change to show the graphic. Once you find the graphic you like, simply drag it from the Library window to your document (see Figure 12-4). It becomes an object in your layout. If you're done with the Library window, click its Close box.

Notice your floating graphic and your text commingling in an uncomfortable way? We'll cover that in the section "Wrap Text," coming up shortly.

Create Floating Text

You've already seen quite a bit on adding text in frames—this really isn't much different. You may find that creating a linked frame is the best approach here, if only because a linked frame doesn't collapse around the text. You likely won't actually be linking it to anything—you just want the additional control it gives you. Here's how to create floating text:

1. Make sure Frame Links is selected (with a check mark next to it) in the Options menu.

2. Click the Text tool and drag to create a text frame on the page.

3. Enter the text (a pull-quote, headline, and so on) for this floating text frame. Format the text.

4. Click outside the text frame. The text frame should be selected, with handles showing. (If it's not, click it once to select it.)

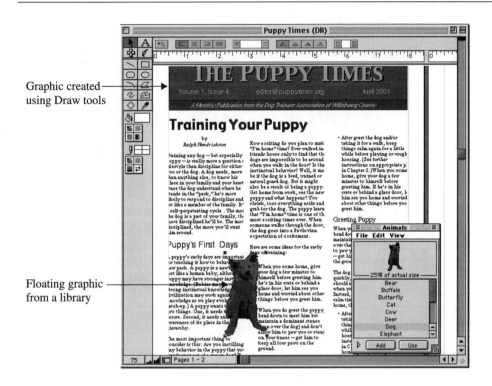

Graphic created using Draw tools

Floating graphic from a library

FIGURE 12-4   Drag the image from the library to your document, where it becomes an object.

5. Click and drag the text frame to its final destination. It's OK if the frame obscures the text beneath it—you'll fix that momentarily. (See Figure 12-5.)

Note that not all of your floating text will necessarily have other text wrapped around it. You can use this same approach to create two-column headlines over three-column stories.

Wrap Text

Whether it's a text frame or a graphic, if you've created a frame that you want to float among the columns of your layout, then you'll want to wrap text around it. This is a great way to add visual appeal and a hint of professionalism to your document. It's also simple to do:

1. Select a graphic or text frame that's currently overlapping text. (It may be a little tough to select—try to make sure the underlying columns aren't also selected. If

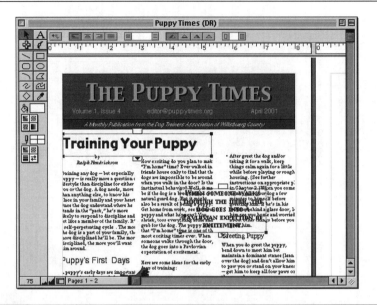

FIGURE 12-5 Floating text may at first obscure the text in column frames, but you can use it to format headlines and other elements more creatively.

they are, SHIFT-clicking one of the selected frames will deselect it while leaving others highlighted.)

2. Choose Options I Text Wrap.

3. In the Text Wrap dialog box, choose the type of wrap you want. Regular wraps text around the frame, while Irregular will wrap the text around the actual image or shape within the frame. No Wrap, of course, eliminates the text wrap if it was there.

4. Enter a number for the gutter, if desired. This determines the number of points to keep between the frame (Regular) or graphic (Irregular) and the wrapped text. The typical text size of typed output is 12 points, so something like 6 points might be good for each side (6 points is 1/12 of an inch).

5. Click OK.

That's it—the text is wrapped either regularly or irregularly, as shown in Figure 12-6. This gives your layout a great look, although you'll still need to look at it carefully to make sure everything is lined up nicely. If things aren't working out, you may need to resize the graphics frame or choose Regular instead of Irregular wrap, for instance.

Regular wrap

Irregular wrap

FIGURE 12-6   Notice the irregular wrap around the dog clip art has resulted in some odd text placement. Regular wrap might be preferable for this particular graphic.

12

Shape and Lines

In Chapter 11, you saw how to create various shapes and add them to a drawing. Your layout is also a drawing, meaning it can just as easily accept lines, shapes, and curves if you'd like to use them. Just draw them right on the document, then arrange them—back to front, text-wrapped, and so on—as you like.

A couple of ideas stand out. First, you can take an odd shape—a curve, oval, jagged shape, or something similar—and group it with an image or text frame, putting the shape behind the text or image.

Now, if you choose to make the border of the shape invisible and wrap text around it, you can create some very interesting text wrap shapes that will give your layout even more artistic flair. Similarly, you can create a shaded or patterned background for your floating images or text, if you like.

You can also use shapes around individual stories in your layouts—surround shorter stories with boxes (or boxes with light-colored backgrounds in them) to separate them from the surrounding text. And, of course, you can combine shapes with text and use other Draw tools to create special elements like a table of contents for your newsletter.

This Issue...

Wagging the Owner	1
On Leashes	2
Visit the Vet	2
Life at Ten	3
Smell and Seek	4
Adoptables	5
Editor Letter	6

Lines are also a great addition to layouts, especially since they no longer require the special "border tape" that was required in the days of yore. (That same tape still decorates the drafting table I have my iMac situated on at this very moment. It was certainly a big part of the journalist's life at one time.)

You know how to draw the lines. My only suggestions are:

- **Remember the different sizes and shapes available.**   If you like, you can pattern lines so that they're dashed, broken, or otherwise more interesting.

- **Arrange your lines To Back.**   Traditionally, gutter lines go behind other elements, including images and shaded background. You can get this effect by selecting the lines, then choosing Arrange | Move to Back.

- **Lock your lines!**   Put the lines in the gutters of your document, then select Arrange | Lock to keep them there. Nothing gets more annoying than replacing your lines every few mouse movements because you've accidentally selected and moved them.

- **Copy and paste.**   Want lines that are the same size, width, and orientation? Copy an existing line, then immediately paste it into the layout. It shows up as an object, ready to be added to the layout.

Figure 12-7 shows some of these line suggestions in action.

Build Layouts Quickly

The Draw tools, as we've seen, are exceptional for creating dramatic layouts. You can use many different elements to design a few pages and create complex newsletters and other documents. But you can also see why people have full-time jobs as graphic designers and layout artists. It can take quite a while to get each page right.

the dog. A dog needs, more ything else, to know his your family and your nce the dog understand e stands in the "pack," he's ely to respond to discipline like a member of the It's a self-perpetuating The more the dog is a part family, the more ned he'll be. The more ned, the more you'll want und.

then you won't mind it in your lap as a grown dog. But if you have a retriever as a puppy, as tempting as that lap looks to both of you, you might consider playing with

WHEN SOMEONE WALKS THROUGH THE DOOR, THE DOG GOES INTO A PAVLOVIAN EXPECTATION OF EXCITEMENT.

your dog a few minutes hims greet If he crate a glas let hi home wom other befor greet

the dog only on the floor and only at certain times.

- When you do greet the bend down to meet hir maintain a dominant st over the dog) and don him to paw you or star your knees -- get him 1 four paws on the grou

Puppy's Days

y's early days ortant for ; it how to in its new . puppy is a n just like a baby, h the puppy ve stronger ...1

How exciting do you plan to make "I'm home" time? Ever walked in a friends house only to find that their dogs are impossible to be around when you walk in the door? Is that instinctual behavior? Well, it may be if the dog is a bred, trained or

The dog may need to go o quickly, but don't feed hir should always be availabl. when you walk in the doo:

This Issue...

FIGURE 12-7 Lines help break up the text, offering a professional flair.

What if, instead, you're trying to create a good-looking layout that takes a little less time to create? There are a number of templates and Assistants in AppleWorks to help you do just that—you can create business cards, brochures, flyers, invitations, signs, birthday cards, posters, and many other publications. If you're creating a more serious report or similar document, you can also get it done more quickly by sticking with the word processing module. You'll get a less graphical, more formal publication, but it can be accomplished much more quickly.

The Word Processing Layout

Say you've already typed a long document as a word processing document and you'd prefer not to format it using drawing tools. And yet, you're interested in adding some graphical elements to the text—in fact, you might even want to format the document as a newsletter. It can be done.

Columns

To begin, you can place the document in columns. This is much easier than creating columns in the Draw module, although it gives you less flexibility. You can create the columns in two ways:

- **Click the More Columns button.** In the ruler bar of the word processing document, click the more (or less) columns button to add (or remove) columns for the document. The columns are added immediately.

■ **Add columns to the section.** Choose Format | Section. In the Section dialog box, enter the number of columns for that section in the Number of Columns entry box.

The Section dialog box also allows you to choose the width of the columns and/or the width of the gutters (choosing one affects the other, by necessity). Note that if you have more than one section defined in your document, you'll need to define columns for each section.

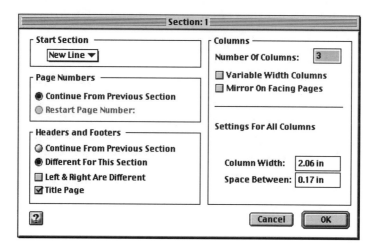

Graphic and Spreadsheet Frames

You can use any of the four previously discussed methods to add graphics or spreadsheet frames to your word processing document: draw them, use the File | Insert command, copy them from a library, or paste them in. (See the section "Add Graphic Frames," earlier in this chapter.) You can also move them around, wrap text, and generally have the same sort of rollicking good time you can have in the Draw module.

If you're inserting or pasting an object into your word processing document, you must have the Pointer tool selected in the word processing document. That allows you to add an item as a frame. If you have the Text tool selected, the pasted, inserted, or library graphic (or other object) will appear *inline*. In this case, the image appears as part of the text, not as a floating object. An inline image is useful for those little graphics people like to put in newspapers and newsletters that show you when a story has ended.

• If he's in his crate or behind a glass door, let him see you home and worried about other things before you greet him. End

NOTE

This book is using the same inline vs. floating concept. The graphic just above is inline—it flows with the text so I can talk about the image and ensure that it's in the same place as the text that discusses it. This book also features "floating" images—they're the ones with Figure numbers.

Draw and Text Frames

You can't create a text frame in the word processing module, supposedly because a word processing document is sort of one big text frame. This can be a little annoying, though, since it's tough to create pull-quotes and multicolumn headlines without using text frames. (You can create paint frames with text in them, but it's not the same since paint frames can't be edited as objects.)

The trick is to create your text frames in a Draw document, then copy and paste them into your word processing document. It's convoluted, but it works:

1. Create (or switch to) a Draw document and create your text frame.

2. Select it and choose Edit I Copy.

3. Switch to the word processing document.

4. Make sure the Pointer tool is selected in the word processing document (you may need to choose Window I Show Tools first) to verify that you're placing the frame as an object and not as inline text.

5. Choose Edit I Paste. The text should show up in a text frame.

12

Training Your Puppy

by

Ralph Hendrickson

Training any dog -- but especially a puppy -- is really

The most important thing to consider is this: Are you instilling any behavior in the puppy that you won't want out of a grown dog? If you have a lap-dog as a puppy, then you

Now you can move the text frame around, use Text Wrap, and generally do the same things that are possible in the Draw module. It's just a little more of a pain. You'll probably want to keep a Draw document open just as a sort of "scratch" document to allow you to create these objects and paste (or drag-and-drop) them into your word processing layout.

This is actually the process used to get any complex drawn object into the document. You can draw basic shapes—rectangles and circles—directly on the word processing document. But if you have a more complex drawn object, then you'll want to create it in a Draw document and transfer it to the word processing document as an object. Then you can manipulate it just like any other frame, making things look good.

At least you saved a lot of time by not having to worry about creating columns!

Stationery

The Stationery options that help you create layouts are too numerous to mention—you'll just have to take a look at them. They range in capabilities from fax cover sheets to memos to letterhead to full-fledged newsletter layouts. And, of course, there is other Stationery available for other types of documents, like spreadsheets, databases, and drawings.

You saw how to use Stationery in Chapter 8—just select Use Assistant or Stationery in the New dialog box, then select the Stationery to use and click OK. The document pops up in AppleWorks, ready for you to save it under its own name and then edit it.

One way to get a sense of what Stationery is available is to choose About Stationery from the Category menu in the New dialog box. (It appears when you've selected Use Assistant or Stationery.) A number of Stationery indexes appear; each index is a document that shows two or more related types of stationery—it's a quick way to get a sense of what's available and how many options you have for quickly creating a new layout or document.

Mail Merge

The ultimate meeting point for automating documents and generating layouts is the concept of mail merge. Mail merge allows you to take data elements that are stored in a database document and automatically create new layouts that fold the information into the document automatically.

It's called a "mail merge" because the most obvious use for this scheme is to take names and addresses out of a database file and drop them into a letter or newsletter so that it can be mailed. You're creating a form letter. While it's possible to create a form letter as a layout in the database module, a mail merge allows you to use all of the sophistication of the word processing part—spell checking, sections, footnotes, and headers—to create more advanced form letters. In fact, any form letter more than a page long is best created in the word processing module.

A mail merge is created in three different steps: setting up the database, altering the document, then generating the merge.

Set Up the Database

First, you need to make sure your data is well arranged for a merge. AppleWorks' Help feature offers this example: If you want to use a salutation in your merged letter that includes a first name, then you're going to need a field in your database that stores that first name. You're also going to need logical address fields—address lines, city, state, zip—if you want to add addresses.

Remember that you can create any sort of merge you want using database fields. If you need to add fields that correspond to invoice numbers, products ordered, hair color, registration number, or whatever you have stored, you can put those fields in your database.

Now, before you create the merge document, find and sort the database as if you were creating a new report. If you only want certain documents in the merge, you should find them now. Similarly, you should sort to put the database in the order in which you want the merged documents generated. After doing this, leave the database open in the background.

Add Field Variables to Your Document

Now you're ready to edit the document. What you're going to do is add *field variables* to your document. The field variables tell the mail merge which field's data should be inserted into the document and where.

Here's how to add field variables to a document:

1. Open the document you're going to merge with your database.

2. Choose File | Mail Merge.

3. In the Open dialog box, find the database you want to use for the merge. Select it and click OK. (You need to perform this step even if the database document is already opened in AppleWorks.)

4. The Mail Merge window appears. Choose the field you want to add as a field variable, then click the Insert Field button.

5. Meanwhile you can still edit the document, adding text around the fields being merged, punctuating them, and so on (see Figure 12-8). You can add the same field variable more than once, if desired.

If you'd like to see the data in the document (instead of the field variable names) put a check mark in the Show Field Data box. You can then scroll through each document of data and see what it'll look like, just by clicking the up and down arrows next to the Record Number box.

TIP   *Creating a mailing label for your newsletter or brochure? You can make a text frame that includes your field variables and use the Arrange | Rotate command to rotate the text 180 degrees, so you can fold the newsletter over and have the address printed correctly. The merge still works, even upside-down!*

12

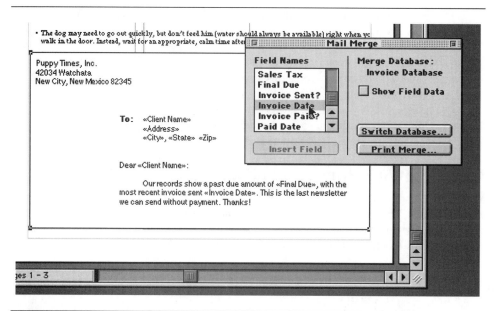

FIGURE 12-8 The field variables fit right in with any sort of text, formatting, or punctuation. If you're building a form letter, for instance, you can even have field variables with paragraphs of text.

Print the Merge

When you're done adding field variables, you're ready to print the merged documents. This part is simple. Click the Print Merge button in the Merge window. Your printer's Print dialog box appears. Click Print and the merge begins. If all goes well, you'll have an entire database of merged documents coming out of your printer.

TIP *Scared? If your large mail merge has typos, you could waste a lot of paper. Click the Print Preview button in the Print dialog box to make sure everything looks OK before you go ahead with the entire printing. You could also consider finding only a few documents in your database to test the merge the first time around; then, if it looks good, give it a go for the whole database.*

Chapter 13

Manage Your Finances with Quicken

How to...

- Install Quicken and get started
- Use the built-in Help system
- Create an account and enter your transactions
- Reconcile your checking, savings, or cash accounts
- Create and manage your budget
- Manage loans and investments
- Generate quick reports and edit them

You've already put a good deal of money into your iMac; maybe it's time to try and recover some of that investment. Fortunately, your iMac comes with the means to do that—Quicken, the money management software from Intuit. In fact, the iMac ships with Quicken Deluxe, the full-featured version of Quicken that allows you to manage all different types of investments, accounts, loans, and other financial operations.

Quicken is a pretty complete tool. In this chapter we'll cover the basics of creating accounts and entering data. I'll also spend some time discussing the budget, report, and analysis capabilities of Quicken. Hopefully, by the end of this chapter you'll be ready to computerize all your personal or small business finances. Who knows—the extra financial management tools might one day generate savings or profits that cover the iMac's price!

What Is Quicken?

At first blush, Quicken is a checkbook management program. It allows you to enter the checks you write, along with other bank activities—deposits, fees, ATM transactions, and debit card purchases. After you enter all of those transactions, you're able to do a number of things with the data—create budgets, reports, graphs, charts, and more.

Quicken does a lot of other things, too, allowing you to manage other accounts—credit cards, cash, debits, investments, loans, and mutual funds. In a sense, it's one-stop financial management.

Here's the trick: You've got to enter the data. That's the only way Quicken can help you work with it. So, you create different accounts within Quicken, then you enter the transactions in those accounts.

NOTE   *The version of Quicken included with many iMacs is Quicken 98; however, a new version, Quicken 2000, has been released at the time of writing. While I cover Quicken 2000 in this chapter, I point out only what's different or changed from Quicken 98, so that you can use this chapter regardless of the version you have.*

13

Install Quicken

Not all iMacs come with Quicken preinstalled, and if you've run the Restore iMac CD, you won't have Quicken. So, you'll need to install it. Fortunately, that's pretty easy to do. Here's how:

1. Locate the Quicken CD-ROM. It should be in the folder of CDs that came with your iMac.

2. Insert the CD-ROM in your CD-ROM or DVD-ROM drive.

3. The CD window should open automatically. Double-click the Quicken installer icon to launch it.

4. Now, move through the installer. Click the Continue button on each screen until you reach the main installation screen. (You should read the license agreement and the Read Me document before you click Agree or Continue.)

5. At the install screen, choose the disk you want to save Quicken to in the bottom-left corner. (It should probably be the Macintosh HD.) Click Install, and Quicken will begin the installation process.

NOTE *If you've used Quicken in the past and you have Quicken data files on your hard drive, you may be asked if you want them moved to the new Quicken folder. You can do that, or you can keep the files stored in another folder on your iMac. If you'd prefer to keep them stored elsewhere, that's fine—you can easily open them in Quicken after it's been installed.*

You'll need to restart your iMac after Quicken has been installed. Once your iMac has restarted, head to your hard disk and look for the Quicken folder. Open the folder and double-click Quicken or Quicken Deluxe 2000 to start it.

The Tutorial and Quicken Help

If you like, Quicken can run you through a quick tutorial to help you learn the application, create a new account, and get started with Quicken. We'll cover some of the same material in this chapter, but you'll find that the tutorial is a good way to get started with the application. To run the tutorial, click the New User button after you've launched Quicken for the first time.

If you work with the tutorial in Quicken, you'll find that it uses the Apple Guide system (described in Chapter 7) to walk you through some of the basics of creating an account and entering data. Just follow the instructions in the Guide window that floats over everything else, click the right-facing arrow to move to the next topic, and watch for Quicken to draw on the screen when it wants you to notice something.

Also, if you have Quicken 98 and the CD-ROM is in your iMac, make sure you have your iMac's volume turned up—the Quicken Help system actually speaks!

TIP *Actually, you may notice that the Quicken 98 Help system offers a lot of movies and audio help. In order for them to work, you'll need to have the Quicken CD-ROM in the CD-ROM drive of your iMac while you work with the program. The CD-ROM isn't required for day-to-day operations, though—just for the multimedia stuff. If necessary for your sanity, pulling the CD-ROM from the CD-ROM drive is also a convenient way to get Quicken to stop talking to you. The Quicken 2000 version seems to have forgone these multimedia intrusions, which is just as well.*

Create Accounts and Enter Data

If you follow the tutorial, you'll create your first account in Quicken. In fact, anytime you create a new Quicken file, you'll be asked to create the first account for that file. A Quicken file can be used for multiple accounts, including all types of banking, investment, and loan accounts. Either you can create accounts in the file that Quicken creates for you (called Quicken Data and stored in the Quicken folder) or you can create a new file, if you'd like.

To create a new file, choose File | New File. (In Quicken 98, you'll see a dialog box that asks if you want to see a video about creating a new file. Click the appropriate button.) After that, you'll see the New File dialog box that asks if you really want to create a new file. Click OK if that's what you want to do.

A dialog box appears allowing you to give the file a new name. You can also choose the categories—personal, business, or both—that you would like to use in this file. Click Save to create the new file.

In Quicken 98, you'll immediately be asked to save a backup of the original Quicken file. Choose a name for the backup and a folder to save it in, then click the Backup button. In Quicken 2000, backups are made automatically.

NOTE   *Quicken 2000 automatically backs up your Quicken data to a special Backup Folder inside the Quicken folder. You can also have Quicken 2000 prompt you to back up after every session; choose Edit | Preferences and select the File Backup icon in the Preferences dialog box. Now, turn on "Remind me to back up my data file when closing" and choose how many times you should be reminded.*

Create a New Account

After creating a new file you're asked to create its first account. Or if you've already created a file, you can create additional accounts by choosing the Registers button menu and choosing the New Account command. Choose the Account Type you'd like to create in the Set Up Account dialog box, then enter a name in the Account Name entry box. Now, you can click the Create button to create the account.

13

SHORTCUT   *In Quicken 2000, choose Add Account to Toolbar if you'd like a small button for this account to appear in the toolbar for quick access.*

The new account will appear in the Accounts window, which appears to the right of the Set Up Account dialog box. You'll also see a Register window appear for this account, which allows you to enter transactions that occur for this account. At this point, you can see that the basic Quicken interface is like a checkbook, making it pretty easy to understand, even if you're new to the program.

If your account is a checking, savings, cash, or credit card account, you'll probably want to enter an opening balance. To do so, click the Deposit or Receive column of the Opening Balance entry (for cash/banking accounts) or the Charge column for a credit card account if you have an outstanding balance. Enter the amount of the balance, then press RETURN to store the transaction. Now you're ready to enter new transactions.

> NOTE
>
> *It's probably best that you begin your credit and banking accounts with your most recent statement (or you can go back and use earlier statements if you want previous months or even years recorded). Enter the beginning balance for that statement as the account's opening balance. Then, enter every transaction since the opening balance. When you get to the end of your data entry, you'll be able to reconcile the account and begin entering transactions that have occurred since that statement.*

Add and Edit Transactions

The heart of using Quicken is adding transactions to your records—you'll want to be pretty vigilant with your data entry, since Quicken needs to be up-to-date if you're going to make effective use of its analysis tools.

To open one of your registers, double-click its listing in the Accounts window or click its entry on the toolbar. You can also click the Registers button in the toolbar and choose the register from the pop-up menu. (In Quicken 98, click the Accounts button and choose the account's name.) The selected register appears in a new window. You're ready for data entry. Here's how it works in most of the different registers:

1. The register creates a blank transaction at the bottom of the window. Click in the date column to change the date for the transaction, then press TAB. (You can also click the mouse in the next column to move on.)

2. The next column is the transaction number or type. If it's a check number or a similar number, you can just enter the number in the space provided. If it's another sort of transaction, you can choose that transaction type from the pull-down menu that appears in the box. Or, you can type the first few letters of the transaction type, and it'll appear automatically. When you've chosen, press TAB.

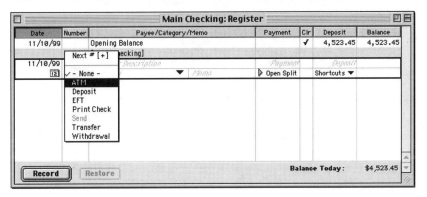

3. Now, type a Payee for the transaction (in your stock portfolio, it'll be the name of a security; in an assets account, it'll be the name of the asset) and press TAB.

4. If you need to enter a payment, charge, or debit, enter it now. (Don't worry about dollar signs—just enter a number with a decimal, if necessary.) Press TAB.

5. If you need to enter a deposit, payment, or credit, enter it in the appropriate column. Press TAB.

6. Now you should find yourself in the categories section. Choose a category for this transaction either from the menu or by typing the category name. If you're typing, you can type the name of a major category, then a colon (:), then the name of the subcategory. If you type the name of a category or subcategory that doesn't exist yet, Quicken will ask you if you want to create it. (Click the Set Up button to create the category or the Select button to select an existing category.) Back in the register, press TAB.

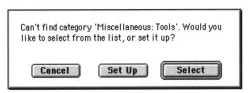

7. Enter a memo for this transaction if you'd like. Then press RETURN.

That's it. The transaction is entered. Continue until you've entered all the transactions that are required. To close an account window, just click its close box.

Quicken has an AutoFill feature that will automatically enter the name of a Payee or Description after you type the first few matching letters. If the autofilled entry is correct, just press TAB. If it's incorrect, continue typing the name.

 *You'll notice that Quicken autofills the whole transaction, including amounts. You can force Quicken to memorize a particular transaction for autofill purposes if you like. Select the transaction, then choose Edit | Memorize. Now, whenever you type the memorized Payee, that particular transaction's values—that exact amount and category—are autofilled.*

If you need to edit an existing transaction, you can. Just click in the portion of the transaction that you want to change, then edit. Press RETURN and the change is made.

Delete or Void a Transaction

If you need to delete a transaction, click it once in the register and choose Edit | Delete Transaction from the menu. You'll be asked if you really want to delete it. Click Yes to delete it or No to return to the register.

You can also void a transaction, which leaves it in the register but zeroes out the payment or deposit number and inserts the word VOID in the payee/description section. To void a transaction, select it in the register, then choose Edit | Void Transaction.

Create a Recurring Transaction

If you're fairly sure a transaction will recur every so often, you can go ahead and have it automatically enter itself into the register. For instance, you may know for a fact that your bank will autopay your car payment on the first of the month or that your paycheck will always come in on the fifteenth. If that's the case, set up a recurring transaction:

1. Enter the transaction as usual. When you've finished, choose Schedule This Transaction from the Shortcuts menu. (It's underneath the Deposit or Receive entry box for this transaction.)

2. In the Schedule Future Transaction dialog box, pull down the Frequency menu and choose how often the transaction should occur.

Frequency: | Twice a month ▼ |

3. Once you've made that choice, you'll get a few others. You can decide if there are a finite number of these transactions (enter the number in the Stop After entry box) or an unlimited number.

4. From the Future Transactions menu, choose whether you want to be reminded about the transaction or if it should be entered automatically. If you want to be reminded, enter the number of days in advance you want the reminder to appear.

5. Click Record.

The future transaction is recorded. Notice back in the register that only payments within the range of the current date will appear in the register.

> TIP *Select Lists | Scheduled Transactions to show all transactions that recur automatically.*

Create and Edit Categories

If you followed along in the previous section, you saw that it's easy to assign a category to your transactions. Categories are simply labels for types of expenses and income that you may have. Having your transactions categorized makes it easier to create meaningful budgets and reports, since you can tell, for instance, what expenses are going toward "Auto" or what income derives from "Salary" versus "Investments," or something similar. Quicken offers dozens of preset categories.

You may find you'd prefer to create or edit categories to suit your own needs, before you enter more transactions. That's easy enough to do.

Here's how to create new categories:

1. Choose Lists | Categories and Transfers.

2. In the Categories and Transfers window, click the New button.

3. In the New Category dialog box, enter a name for the category and a description, if desired.

4. Choose the type of category (whether it's an income or expense item) and whether it's tax-related.

5. Click Create.

The category is created. Notice that you can also highlight a category and click the Edit button to edit it or the Delete button to get rid of it if you're pretty sure you won't need it.

13

Here's another reason categories are important: When you create a credit card or loan account, the category tells Quicken to deduct payments from the balances owed in those accounts if you choose it correctly in your checkbook register. If you're making a payment to your VISA card, make sure you choose the name of the account—probably something like [Visa]—as the category for that payment.

Reconcile Bank Accounts

Quicken provides some tools to make it easy to reconcile your account with your monthly bank statement or some other mechanism (like your bank-by-phone service or a banking Web site that generates statements). You'll want to have the statement in front of you, because you'll need to know the beginning and ending date of the statement period, the beginning and ending balances, banking fees, and any interest earned by the account.

NOTE *Quicken has a very cool feature if you've activated online banking. (I don't have room to discuss that in this chapter, but the first time you choose Online | Getting Started with Online banking, you'll see a Help topic to guide you through the process.) When you're ready to reconcile, choose Online | Download Transactions, and your bank will automatically send all cleared items into Quicken, which automatically "checks" each transaction as cleared. If a transaction doesn't match up, then Quicken will ask you about it. That's it—when you get through the process, you're reconciled, nearly automatically.*

The Reconciliation

Now you're ready to reconcile the account:

1. Press the Reconcile button on the toolbar or choose Activities | Reconcile.

2. In the Reconcile Startup dialog box, enter all the beginning and ending statement dates and balances. For the fees and interest earned you can choose the appropriate category from the pull-down menu.

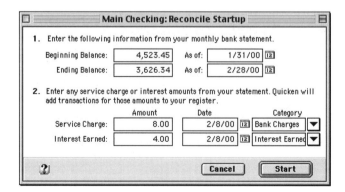

3. Now you'll see the Reconcile dialog box. The left side of the box shows payments and checks, the right side shows deposits. Compare each to your statement, and click once on each transaction that matches your statement. You'll see the transaction change color and a checkmark appear to indicate that the transaction is cleared.

4. If you find a transaction that doesn't match your statement exactly, you can double-click it in the Reconcile box to bring up the register and alter the transaction. (Or you can call your bank and yell at them.) If you find a transaction on your statement that you haven't entered in Quicken, click the New Transaction button to create the transaction.

5. Once you've created, edited, or cleared all transactions on your statement against those in the Reconcile window, you should see a $0.00 difference in the bottom-right corner. If you don't, you'll need to figure out what went wrong—either you have a value wrong in your Quicken entries, you've cleared a transaction that isn't on your statement, or you've not cleared a transaction that is on your statement. If none of these is the case, then perhaps your bank has made an error. It wouldn't be the first time.

6. If you have a $0.00 balance, click Finish. You can also click Cancel to back out of the reconciliation process if you'd prefer to return to the register for a while before reconciling. If you click Finish and all goes well, Quicken will report that you've reconciled and will commit the reconciliation to memory.

> **NOTE** *If you click Finish and you don't have a $0.00 difference, Quicken will ask if you want it to automatically adjust the account. This isn't often wise, since it means your account didn't actually reconcile. Quicken will enter an adjustment that will make it seem the register is balanced, even though you haven't found the error. If you still think it's worthwhile, though, click the Adjust Register button. Otherwise, click the Return To Reconcile button to return to the Reconcile dialog box and find the problem.*

Now, the next time you go to reconcile the account, the ending balance from this reconciliation period will be the beginning balance for the next one.

Re-reconcile

Need to un-reconcile and/or re-reconcile? It's tough to do but not impossible. What you do is throw the reconciled balance for a loop—Quicken checks against the previous reconciled balance before allowing you to go forward with a new reconciliation. If you mess up the original balance, it'll try to help you resolve the problem.

> **NOTE** *You may need to do this if you've accidentally deleted or altered a transaction that was previously reconciled. The procedure is the same, starting with step 2 in each Quicken version.*

Here's how to re-reconcile an account in Quicken 2000 if you need to make changes for some reason:

1. Begin by selecting one of the transactions that was reconciled and removing its "cleared" checkmark. To do this, OPTION-click its check box in the register. Click the Remove Checkmark button in the dialog box that appears. Now, press Return to record the transaction. In the dialog box, click Save.

2. You'll see a dialog box that notes a discrepancy for a prior statement. Click Reconcile Again. You'll be back in the Reconcile Startup window, ready to reconcile that statement once more.

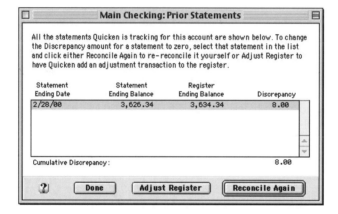

In Quicken 98, you have to be even more devious:

1. Begin by selecting one of the transactions that was reconciled and removing its "cleared" checkmark. To do this, OPTION-click its check box in the register.

2. Press Return to record the transaction and click Save when asked if you want to save the transaction.

3. Select the Reconcile button in the toolbar. The result is a dialog box that lets you know there's a discrepancy and asks if you want to resolve it. Click Resolve.

4. Select the statement where your error was introduced, then click Reconcile Again.

5. That brings up the Reconcile Startup dialog box. Enter the amounts for the beginning and ending balances and click Start.

6. Now you're back to the Reconcile dialog box. Do what you need to do to reconcile the account and click Finish when it's all worked out.

Budget Your Money

It's good to get your accounts entered and up-to-date in Quicken, especially if they always reconcile nicely and, even more to the point, if they always have a lot of money in them. But that's only part of what Quicken can do for you. Its real power comes in the way you can manage and report the management of your money. It's with these tools that you'll really get a sense of whether you're doing a good job with your money and what, if anything, needs to improve.

Using the categories feature in your checkbook register, Quicken can track your spending against your desired, budgeted spending. Not only is it easy to do, but it provides you with information in a quick glance and, best of all, it automatically updates as you routinely enter transactions for your account registers.

NOTE   *Quicken 2000's new Insights feature (click the Insights button on the toolbar) is an interesting way to get a glance at many items related to your financials, including a quick look at your budget. To change the way Insights displays items, choose Customize from within its window.*

Create a Budget

One way to get quickly to the budgeting tools is to click the Planning tab in the toolbar at the top of the Quicken window. (In Quicken 98, the Planning button is in the button bar that extends down the left side of the Quicken window.) Clicking this tab or button changes the toolbar at the top of the window, showing you the planning tools that include the budgeting tools. From here, you can create a budget:

1. To begin your budget, click the Budget button.

2. The Create Budget dialog box appears. Give the budget a name, then choose if you want to budget all categories or selected categories. If you choose selected categories, they'll appear in the Select Categories window. Click to remove the checkmark next to any category you don't want to include in your budget. When you're through choosing, click OK.

3. Back in the Create Budget dialog box, choose the starting amounts for your budget entries. If you choose zeros, each budget category will begin with a zero amount (jump to step 5).

4. If you choose QuickBudget, Quicken will enter budget numbers based on your actual past dollar amounts. It begins that process by popping up the QuickBudget dialog box. In the dialog box, you'll choose the timeframe for your budget from the Date menu, or you can choose the dates individually in the From and Through

13

entries. Then, choose whether the values should be calculated as averages or taken directly from the register in the selected timeframe. (You could average the numbers over the past six months to get budget figures, for instance, or you could just take last month's payments and budget based on them.) Finally, you can choose to round values to the nearest whole dollar amount and/or you can choose to inflate your budget categories by some percentage. When you've made all those choices, click OK.

5. Click the Create button to create the budget.

6. The Budget Setup window appears, as shown in Figure 13-1, allowing you to create your budget.

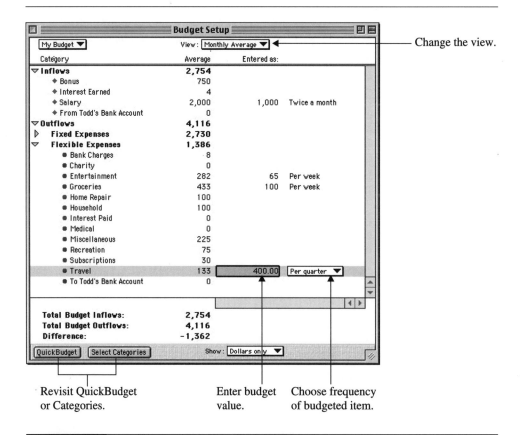

FIGURE 13-1   The Budget Setup window offers you controls for creating a budget.

The Budget Setup window gives you a number of different options for arranging your budget. By default, you're encouraged to enter a monthly average for each budget item. Click once on the item, enter an amount in the Entered As column, then choose how often that amount will recur in your budget in the pop-up menu next to the amount you just typed. If you've chosen QuickBudget, you'll already have a guide to the amounts based on previous transactions.

There are a couple of other things you can do in the Budget Setup window:

- **Use QuickBudget**   Click the QuickBudget button and you can revisit the QuickBudget dialog box to choose a different stretch of time to use for average budget numbers or other criteria.

- **Select Categories**   Click the Categories button to bring up the Categories dialog box, where you can place checkmarks next to the categories you want to use in your budget.

- **Choose Lists | Categories and Transfers**   If you need to add or change categories to more accurately reflect your budgeting needs, select Lists | Categories and Transfers. Now you can edit categories as described in the section "Create and Edit Categories," earlier in this chapter.

- **Change the Budget View**   At the top of the window, the View menu allows you to change the range of time used to calculate budget data. You can view things as a monthly, quarterly, or annual average. You can also choose to view the data for each month, allowing you to enter different numbers for each individual month in your budget.

- **Name Your Budgets**   In the top-left corner there's a small menu that allows you to choose between budgets if you have created more than one. You can also choose New Budget to create a new budget, Rename to rename the current budget, or Delete to delete the current budget.

Monitor the Budget

In Quicken, a budget that you create is filled with budget numbers only, not *actual* numbers. (You can use QuickBudget to create budget numbers *based* on last month's or last year's recorded checks and deposits, but that's not the same as seeing the current numbers.) If you want to compare the actual situation against your budget, you're ready to monitor the budget.

Here's how it works:

1. Select Activities | Budgeting | Budget Monitoring from the Quicken menu.

2. The Budget Monitoring window appears. In the top-left corner of the window, choose the budget you'd like to monitor from the pop-up menu.

13

3. Now, in the top-right corner, check the timeframe you'd like to monitor (see Figure 13-2).

You're now seeing the budget compared to actual numbers. Quicken's monitor works the way a stoplight works—red means you're in trouble, yellow means caution, green means you're well within your budget. The length of the line will also fill up each category's bar to show you when you've gone over budget.

If you want to see the actual sum within a particular category, point the mouse at that category and hold down the mouse button to see the exact amount.

You can monitor different categories within the budget if you like. To do that, click the Set Up Monitoring button in the lower-left corner. Now you can place a checkmark next to any of the categories you want to monitor; click a checked category to deselect it so that it no longer shows up in the monitoring window.

Manage Loans and Investments

Aside from your cash and checking accounts, you can also manage your stocks, bonds, loans, and assets through Quicken. And, in most cases, it's pretty much the same as

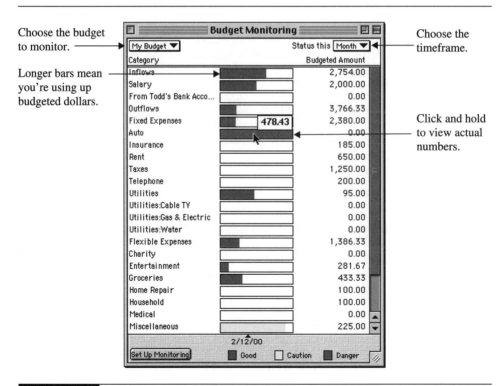

Choose the budget to monitor.

Longer bars mean you're using up budgeted dollars.

Choose the timeframe.

Click and hold to view actual numbers.

FIGURE 13-2   The closer you are to your budget numbers, the longer the bar in the middle. Red means you're over budget.

managing your cash/checking accounts. You'll use a similar register for most all of these transactions. You'll also be able to integrate these accounts with your existing accounts to get a full picture of your financial status.

Create a Loan

If you've just taken out a loan for a house, car, business, or similar purchase, you'll want to track it in Quicken. You can track loans that already exist, too, so that you can schedule the payments and the interest paid. Creating a loan does two things: it allows you to schedule payments, and it allows you to track your principal to see what's still owed. In fact, you can play a little what-if game to see how quickly you can recover the balance and pay off the loan.

To create a new loan, select the Assets & Debts tab at the top of the Quicken toolbar (or choose the Assets/Debt button in the left toolbar in Quicken 98). Now, in the toolbar, click the Loans button. (You can also choose Lists | Loans to bring up the Loans window.) Here's how to create a new loan:

  This process will probably go smoother if you have the information regarding your loan in front of you while you're creating the loan in Quicken. You'll need to know dates, the number of payments, principal amounts, and so on.

1. In the Loans window, click the New button.

2. The Loan Interview dialog box appears. Answer each question and click OK. If you're setting up a loan for a product you've bought, the default values are likely to be pretty close.

3. Now you'll see the Set Up Loan window. Enter data relevant to your loan. Begin by entering the name of the lender (or borrower if you're the lender) at the top of the window.

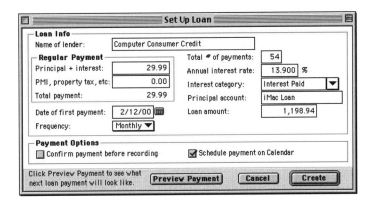

4. In the Regular Payment section, enter the principal plus interest payment you're making on this loan. (That should be obvious from your loan materials.) If you're

also paying taxes, insurance, or other amounts that don't pay down the loan, enter them on the next line.

5. Enter the date of the first payment—you can choose it from a calendar by clicking the small calendar button next to the date box. If you started paying this loan a while ago, you can enter that date, and it will be taken into account.

6. Choose how often you make a payment from the Frequency menu.

7. In the top-right corner, enter the number of payments that are supposed to be made.

8. Next, enter the interest rate you're paying (or charging) on this loan.

9. The Interest Category is the category you want the interest portion of the payment to be filed under. You can choose it from the pop-up menu by clicking the triangle next to the entry box.

10. The Principal Account is the account where the principal for this loan will be tracked. You'll be able the view the account at any time to see where the loan stands. Enter a name for the account—if you enter the name of an account that doesn't exist, you'll be asked if you want to create that account.

11. Enter the Loan Amount. You'll notice that the loan amount has been estimated—if the estimate is very far from the amount you plan to enter, your calculations might be off (you might be over- or underpaying, or your interest rate or the number of payments might be wrong).

12. Finally, in Payment Options, choose whether you want to be notified before this payment is deducted from the principal account. This is probably only necessary if you plan to vary the payments at all, for instance if you'll sometimes be paying more against the principal. You can also choose to schedule the payment so that it automatically deducts from your checking account at the appropriate time.

13. Click Create to create the loan.

Now the loan is created. If you've chosen to schedule payments on the calendar, then the Schedule Future Transaction window appears. Check to make sure the payment is coming out of the correct account in the menu at the top of the window. Also, choose from the Future Transactions menu whether you'll be reminded or if the transaction will simply be entered at the appropriate time. If you want to be reminded, enter the number of days before the transaction is due that you want to see the reminder. If everything else looks good, click Record.

If the Calendar is open, click its close box. Now, in the Loan window, you'll see your new loan. Want to check the payment schedule? Select the loan and click the Payment Schedule button. That opens the Payment Schedule window, which shows you when payments are due, how much interest each payment covers, and how long it will take you to pay off the loan. As you pay it off, the amount paid will continue to change in the Loan window.

Plus, you now have a loan account and a new transfer category that corresponds to the name of the loan. That means you can watch the balance being affected by payments simple by opening the loan account. You can also enter payments in your checkbook register that directly affects the loan account.

For instance, when you enter a payment in your check register, you'll enter the name of the lender in the Payee slot. When you do so, up pops a dialog box that allows you to enter either the typical amount or the loan amount plus a prepayment.

Computer Consumer Credit Payment	
Current balance:	1,182.84
Annual interest rate:	13.900 %
Regular Payment:	29.99
Additional prepayment:	0.00
Other regular charges:	0.00

Cancel   OK

TIP *Want to play "what if" with your loans? The Loan Calculator (Activities | Planning Calculators | Loan) can really help. You enter the loan amount and current interest, but you can experiment with prepayments and the number of overall payments to see the best way to manage the loan. You may find that you can pay a loan off more quickly by simply adding a few dollars in prepayment to each payment.*

13

Create a Portfolio

Here's another fun way to use Quicken to its fullest—track your stock, bond, or other portfolio of investments. It's easy to do, plus you can link it to your checking or other accounts and, eventually, report on your success as an investor.

To create an investment portfolio:

1. Create a new account. You can click New in the Accounts window or choose Edit | New Account. In Quicken 98, you can also select New Account from the Registers button in most toolbars.

2. In the Set Up Account dialog box, choose Portfolio. Give the account a name and click Create.

3. Now you'll see the portfolio register. Adding an investment transaction is a lot like entering a payment or deposit in a checking register. To begin, enter a date.

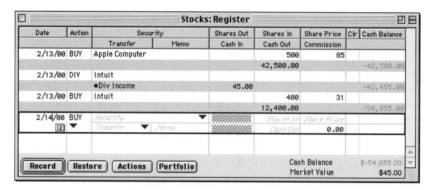

4. Now, choose the type of transaction from the Action menu (the arrow below the word BUY in the Action column)—if you're buying shares, leave it as Buy; choose Sell if you're selling shares; or choose one of the other options from the menu.

5. Now enter the name of the security. If it's a new security, you'll be asked if you want to set up the security. Click Set Up Now to set up the security.

6. In the Set Up Security dialog box, enter information about this particular security. When you're done, click Create.

7. Now, back in the register, move to the appropriate field by pressing TAB. Depending on the type of transaction, only the parts of the transaction window that are appropriate will be active. (For instance, a Dividend transaction just allows you to add a cash amount in the Cash In field, while a Buy transaction will allow you to enter the number of shares you that you've acquired in the Shares In field.)

8. If the money involved in a transaction is going to or from another of your accounts, you should note it by choosing that account from the Transfer menu which appears in the Category section in the checking register (just below the security's name).

9. Finally, press RETURN when you're done with the transaction.

That's it. The register now knows which securities you own and can help you track the amount of money you're spending on investments. It can also help you see how the portfolio is performing for you. To do so, click the Portfolio button on the toolbar or in the portfolio register window, or choose Activities | Investment Portfolio. You'll see the Portfolio window:

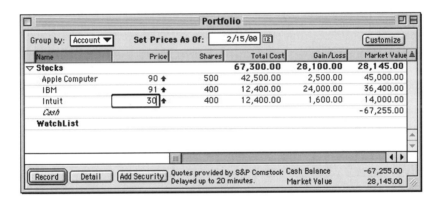

To check up on your securities, enter the current price in the Price box. The window will change to reflect the performance of the security. You can also select the security and click the Detail button, which shows you a number of things about the security, including the information you entered when you set up the security earlier. (You can change some of the numbers if you like—just click the Edit button.) You can also click the tabs to see other information about the security, including past transactions, prices, and more.

13

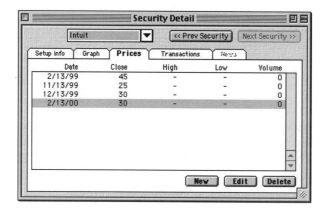

 You can look up the current value of your stocks online. Just select Online | Quicken Quotes, and Quicken will connect to the Quicken quote service over your Internet connection. (In Quicken 98, Quicken quotes defaults to a CompuServe-based service. If you want to get quotes over the Internet, choose Edit | Preferences and select the Quotes icon. Now, choose the Use Internet option and click OK to close the Preferences dialog box. Now, when you access Online | Quicken Quotes, you'll get quotes over the Internet.)

Generate Reports

You already know that you can generate the sophisticated budgets you saw in the previous section. You're also able to create some amazing reports—you won't believe the range of things you can report.

Ultimately, a report in Quicken is designed to be printed. The idea is to take the raw data you've entered in your iMac and spit it back out on a page that allows you to make sense of some aspect of your spending, saving, or budgeting. Of course, you don't *have* to print the budget—you can peruse your data onscreen in different ways.

Click the Reporting tab at the top of the toolbar (or click the Reporting button on the left toolbar in Quicken 98) and you'll see the top toolbar change to the reporting tools.

 *This section covers only creating a quick report. For more involved reports, choose the Reports button in the toolbar and walk through the EasyAnswer interview. Or select one of the tabs (Standard, Business, Investment) to create a more sophisticated report.*

QuickReport: Search the Registers

QuickReport allows you to simply toss some information from your accounts onto the page. It works a lot like a search in Sherlock—you'll be searching your account registers for certain transactions that meet particular criteria, then those transactions will be reported. (More advanced reports are beyond the scope of this book, but you can create them by clicking the Report button or choosing Activities | Reports and Graphs | Reports.) Here's how:

1. Click the QuickRep button or choose Activities | QuickReport.

2. In the Create QuickReport dialog box, choose the part of the transaction you want to search from the first menu. (Options include Payee and Description, Category, Class, Memo, and so on.) The rest of the dialog box changes depending on what you select in this menu.

3. In the entry box, type the keyword or value on which you want to base your search. If you're searching Payees, for instance, you might type **Joe's Cartopia** or **Internal Revenue Service** to report payments to those particular payees. If you've chosen Category, you might type **Auto**, **Insurance**, or **Utilities: Water**.

4. In the Date menu, choose the range of transactions you want to search. Possibilities include All Transactions, Year-to-Date, Current Month, and so on.

5. Click OK to create the report.

SHORTCUT   *As you type your keyword, the AutoFill feature will help you enter something if it's previously been typed into one of your account registers.*

```
┌──────────────────── Create QuickReport ────────────────────┐
│                                                             │
│  Show transactions in all accounts where                    │
│                                                             │
│    [ Category ▼ ]   contains    [ Auto              ]       │
│                                                             │
│  Date : [ All Transactions ▼ ]                              │
│                                                             │
│                  [ Cancel ]    [   OK   ]                   │
└─────────────────────────────────────────────────────────────┘
```

13

The result is a report document that includes the results of your search laid out in a nice, printable document. You can choose to print the report (File | Print), or you can alter its appearance before printing. We'll discuss that in detail next.

Edit and Print the Report

Once you've created QuickReport (or a regular report), Quicken pops up the Report window, allowing you to make any number of changes to the way the report will be printed, what information is shown, and more mundane things like the font and page breaks. As I mentioned, the point with most reports is to get them printed. This window helps you do just that (see Figure 13-3).

Print Preview the printout onscreen.

Add a page break.

Collapse the report's header.

Change the columns.

Customize the report.

Font controls

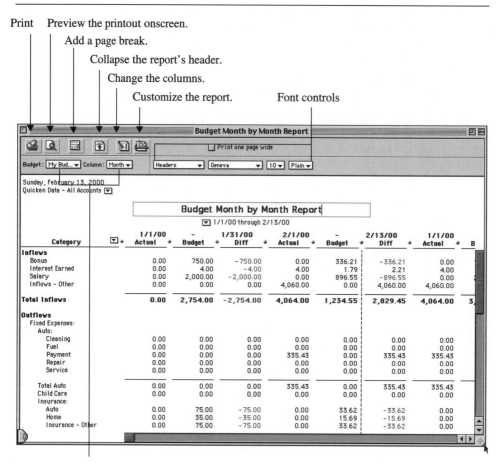

Change the nature of the report (varies).

FIGURE 13-3 The Report window shows you the report and allows you to make changes before printing it.

Here's a quick breakdown of what everything does:

■ **Font Controls** At the top of the Report window, you can change the fonts and font sizes used to display the report. The first menu (it defaults to "Headers") allows you to choose which part of the report you'd like to alter. Once you've done so, you can change the font, font size, and font style for that particular section of the report.

■ **Print One Page Wide**   Also in the top of the window, click the Print One Page Wide option to cause the report to be formatted only as wide as a single sheet of paper.

■ **Page Break**   In the top-left of the window you'll find a button that allows you to create a page break. For instance, you might want to begin a new section of the report on a new page if you're getting close to the bottom and the natural page break would make the report look awkward.

■ **Collapse Headers**   This button allows you to collapse the headers in the report, so that you hide the title area while it's onscreen. (The headers still show up in the printed report.)

■ **Change Columns**   Click the Columns button and you're shown a list of the columns currently displayed in the report. If you want to change them, click to place or remove the checkmark next to each column. If it doesn't have a checkmark, then the column disappears from the report.

■ **Customize Report**   The Customize button can be used to revisit the Customize Report dialog box to change the way the report works.

Below these buttons, you'll find a few menus that allow you to choose the actual data that's acted on, the subtotals to show in the report, how the report is sorted, and certain timeframes—these menus change depending on the report you're building. Experiment with them to see how you like to view the report.

Once you're done changing the report, you can choose the Print Preview button to see what the report will look like on your printer. (You can click the close button to do away with the Print Preview window.) If you're ready to print, click the Print button (or click Print in the Print Preview window), and you'll get the Print dialog box. Make your choices as you would for any printed document, then click Print.

13

Chapter 14

Work with Movies, Sounds, and Images

How to...

- View a movie
- Work with images
- View and edit images
- Edit a QuickTime movie
- Play an audio CD
- Watch a DVD movie

Macs are known for their *multimedia* capabilities—their ability to integrate sound, video, and images. The technology behind a lot of the multimedia capabilities of any Mac, including the iMac, is something called QuickTime.

So what can you do with QuickTime? With both QuickTime and other technologies, you can play digital movies and movie clips, create and edit digital sounds, and work with images to incorporate them more easily into your documents.

QuickTime Movies

Just as your iMac requires underlying technologies to allow it to print—you may have noticed that nearly every application offers almost identical Print dialog boxes—it also benefits from underlying technology to play digital movies and digital sound. That technology, developed by Apple, is QuickTime.

What QuickTime Is to You

QuickTime is a rather advanced digital technology that, in a way, mimics an animation flipbook. It stores images in the form of ones and zeros, then displays them in rapid order, usually between 10 and 30 frames per second. (For comparison, a film is generally shown at 24 frames per second, while television is displayed at about 30 frames per second. Any more than about 10 frames per second gives a reasonable sensation of movement to the viewer.)

QuickTime is also capable of recording audio and layering it in with the video so that it can be synchronized with the video or complementary to it. Audio can also stand alone within a QuickTime "movie" file, then be played back at any time using the QuickTime Player application or many others that support QuickTime technology.

NOTE *QuickTime is also a translation technology—built into it is the ability to translate between different audio, video, and image file formats. Different applications and computer platforms (like those from Microsoft, Sun Microsystems, Silicon Graphics, and other computing companies) save files in different formats. QuickTime, and applications that take advantage of QuickTime, offer the capability to translate to and from Macintosh file formats. In that way, it's easy to play or display nearly any movie, sound, or image file you find on the Internet or elsewhere.*

14

Want QuickTime to do more? It can. QuickTime VR is a special technology that allows certain special QuickTime movies to behave more like the "virtual reality" scenes you may have seen in movies. QuickTime VR isn't quite that sophisticated, but it does allow you to explore 3-D panoramas by dragging the mouse around to change perspectives and clicking on objects or "hot spots" that take you elsewhere in the virtual tour.

QuickTime Streaming is a technology that makes it possible to view QuickTime movies as they are transferred over a network connection—generally, this is done over the Internet. With streaming, it's possible to view a movie as it arrives, instantaneously, over long distances. This has many applications, not the least of which is the possibility that you can watch live events via *Webcasts* or "narrowcasts." This can be a very interesting technology, especially if the event wouldn't otherwise be broadcast for television.

Finally, QuickTime is multimedia. You've probably heard that catchphrase before and wondered why it's significant. *Multimedia* is defined as the bringing together of many different media—audio, video, still imagery, text, virtual reality—to communicate ideas, educate, or entertain. Obviously, QuickTime fits the bill quite nicely.

The QuickTime Software

The manifestation of QuickTime on your iMac comes in the form of Mac OS Extension files that are stored in the System Folder on your iMac's hard drive. These files include QuickTime, QuickTime MPEG Extension, QuickTime Musical Instruments, QuickTime Powerplug, and QuickTime VR.

There's also a QuickTime Settings control panel stored in the Control Panels folder in the System Folder. If these extensions aren't in the Extensions folder in the System Folder, then some or all of your QuickTime movies won't play correctly. They're most likely there, but you can have trouble with QuickTime if you start your iMac with extensions disabled (by holding down the SHIFT key while the iMac starts up), or if you move the extensions for some reason.

NOTE   *Dealing with extensions and control panels is covered in Chapter 30.*

Although they're not integral parts of the QuickTime technology, a big part of the QuickTime experience for us humans is the QuickTime Player and PictureViewer applications. Both of these can be found in the Apple Extras folder on your main hard drive. You also probably have an alias to the QuickTime Player on your iMac's desktop if you haven't deleted it (it's installed there automatically). You can just double-click that alias anytime you want to launch the QuickTime Player.

At the time of writing, the latest version of QuickTime is QuickTime 4. If you have an iMac made before the summer of 1999, however, it may include an earlier version of QuickTime. I recommend that you upgrade to QuickTime 4 (or later) for two reasons— first, it's much better than earlier versions and, second, it's what I'm discussing in this chapter. QuickTime 4 is a free download from **http://www.apple.com/quicktime/** or you can get it by upgrading your iMac to Mac OS 9.

NOTE *Plan to work a lot with movies and multimedia? Then I recommend you upgrade to QuickTime Pro. To get QuickTime Pro, you must register with Apple and pay a small fee (about $30 at the time of this writing). In exchange, you'll get a registration code that upgrades the capabilities of the QuickTime Player, PictureViewer, and Web browser plug-in. To register, visit Apple's QuickTime Web site—**http://www.apple.com/quicktime/**—and select the button or hyperlink to upgrade to QuickTime Pro. (I'll point out through this chapter when I'm talking about a Pro-level feature as opposed to a basic QuickTime feature.)*

The QuickTime Player Application

If you have a QuickTime movie that you've downloaded over the Internet or copied from a CD-ROM, you can double-click it to launch the movie file. When you do, most likely the QuickTime Player application will launch (see Figure 14-1).

The QuickTime Player offers controls that look a lot like a cassette recorder's or a VCR's controls. When you have a digital movie file loaded, you'll find Play, Stop, and Fast Forward buttons. You'll also find a slider bar that shows the progress of the movie as it's playing. Grab the slider and drag it back, and you can play part or all of your movie again. You'll also find you have control over the volume by dragging the little volume wheel up and down with the mouse.

Select the Movie menu (from the menu bar) and you can choose the size at which your movie will display. Movies generally open at their optimum size for quality viewing. If you'd like to see the movie a little larger, you can choose Movie | Double Size. The quality of the video won't be as good (it'll most likely appear more "pixelated" or jagged) but it'll be larger. The further back you sit from your monitor, the better it will look.

You can also get some information about the movie—click the Info button to see the Info window. Here, you can find out about the different audio and video tracks in the movie and view other relevant information.

NOTE *There are three kinds of tracks that a QuickTime movie can have: video, audio, and text. Each track is a separate line of data in the movie document that is synchronized with the others. The digital data stored in the video and audio tracks is compressed because video and audio, without compression, require huge amounts of storage. These compression schemes are called codecs, which stands for "compressor/decompressor." The better the codecs, the better the quality of a QuickTime movie file and the smaller and more transportable the movie will be.*

By default, you may not be seeing all of the controls in the QuickTime Player window. That's because some of them—that reverse and forward panel, step (frame-by-frame) controls, and sound controls—are hidden when you open the QuickTime window. Toward

14

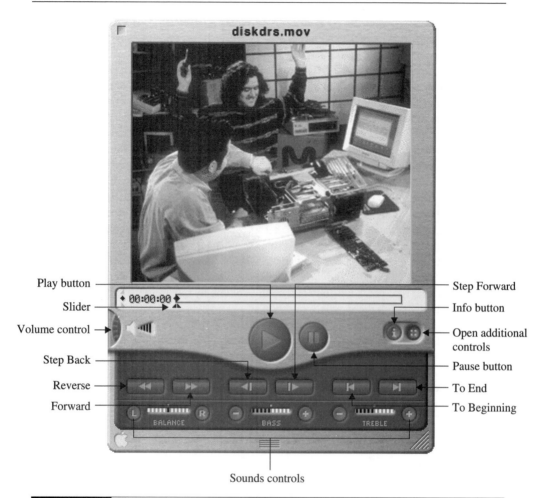

Play button — Step Forward
Slider — Info button
Volume control — Open additional controls
Step Back — Pause button
Reverse — To End
Forward — To Beginning

Sounds controls

FIGURE 14-1   The QuickTime Player interface is a little like a VCR, but with a bunch of other little features.

the bottom-right corner of the display window is a small button with four little dots on it—that's the button you use to reveal the additional controls. Click it to get access to more options. (See Figure 14-1 to figure out those buttons.)

QuickTime Player Favorites

Down at the bottom of the QuickTime Player is a little "drawer" of sorts—you can click on the four little lines in the middle of the drawer, then drag down to open it up. There you'll find your QuickTime Player Favorites—movies or Internet locations you can access to view QuickTime over the Web. With the push toward QuickTime "streaming" technology, Apple has made it possible to view things like newscasts, music videos, and live events over the Internet, just using the QuickTime Player.

With the Favorites drawer open, you can single-click one of the Favorites to load it into the QuickTime Player. If it's an Internet site (as most of the presaved Favorites are) then you'll probably need to have your Internet connection active (or set to automatically connect) before the movie can be played in the viewer. Eventually, depending on the speed of your connection, you'll see a new movie appear in the window. It may be a streaming video, or it may be a special screen that incorporates Macromedia Flash technology. In this case, you can actually click in the movie window to view different types of content.

You can save your own movies as Favorites, if you like. Usually, you open movies using the File | Open command or by double-clicking a movie in the Finder. If you'd like to open a movie from the Favorites drawer, you'll need to add it first. With the movie open in QuickTime Player, choose Favorites | Add Favorite. Now, a small icon appears in the Favorites drawer that represents your newly added movie file. When you return to QuickTime Player, you can open the drawer and click that movie again to add it.

> **TIP** *You can do this with streaming movies over the Internet, too. If you find one you like, just add it to the Favorites. Now you can single-click it in the Favorites drawer anytime you get the urge. You'll be connected to that Internet site and the movie will play—if it's still out there.*

To edit your Favorites, choose Favorites | Organize Favorites from the menu. Now you'll see a dialog box that lets you scroll through and select the Favorites you've saved (along with those that were presaved by Apple). Select a Favorite, then click Delete to remove it from the drawer or click Rename to give it a new name. Click Done when you're finished with your editing.

14

 *You can also drag Favorites from the Favorites drawer to the Finder's Trash icon to delete them. Likewise, you can drag movie icons from the Finder to an open slot in the Favorites drawer to add them as Favorites.*

View a Streaming Movie

You've actually already seen one way to view a streaming movie—by selecting one of the brand-name Favorites in the Favorites drawer, you'll often be connected over your Internet connection to a streaming movie site, and the movie will appear in your QuickTime Player window.

NOTE *Again, don't forget that a streaming movie doesn't necessarily have video. You can listen to National Public Radio (NPR), for instance, using one of the QuickTime Player's Favorites. The live broadcast is sent as a streaming "movie" (since that's what all QuickTime media is called) but it only has an audio component. You'll just hear it—you won't see any video in the Player.*

There are other ways to viewing streaming movies, though. The most common way is to locate a streaming QuickTime *feed* somewhere on the Web using your Web browser application. You'll click a link or a button on a Web page that begins the streaming movie. When you do that, your Web browser is often automatically launched (or switched to if it's already running) and the streaming movie appears. You might see indications of the streaming process before the movie actually starts—QuickTime Player gives you messages to show what's happening, like "Connecting," "Negotiating," and "Buffering." Those are all indications that your streaming movie is being loaded over the Internet and preparing to play.

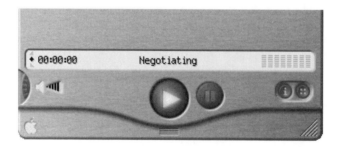

Your streaming movie experience may be a little different than playing a movie. First, you'll probably notice that your streaming movie is lower quality than a typical QuickTime movie you play from your hard disk or a CD-ROM. Why is that? Because the data has to be sent in real time over the Internet. *Real time* means it's played almost as it arrives, to give you a seamless viewing experience. Good-quality QuickTime movies need a lot of data to flash up a pretty picture 15-30 times per second, and many Internet connections can't handle that sort of demand. So, picture size and quality are compromised in order to allow you to see *something* in your QuickTime Player. The slower your Internet connection (and the slower the Internet server computer that's sending the movie data) the worse the picture quality. That's one good reason to get a cable modem or special DSL access! (See Chapter 23 for more on high-speed access.)

The second thing that's a little weird about streaming video is the way fast forward and rewind work. Usually, a QuickTime movie played from a regular hard disk, CD-ROM, or DVD-ROM allows you to flip through each frame or use the Fast Forward/Rewind buttons to shuttle through the movie just like a VCR does. With a streaming movie, though, things don't work that way. You can often go to a different section of the movie, but you generally do this by moving the slider bar in the QuickTime Player. Then, the connection has to be renegotiated (you'll see those messages again) before the movie can begin playing in its new spot.

If the streaming movie you're watching is a *live event* or *live broadcast* then you obviously can't fast forward or move to a later part of the movie, since it hasn't happened yet! With live broadcasts you also generally can't pause the movie and return to the same spot—when you click Play again, you'll see the connection negotiated and you'll start at the current spot in the live broadcast. In other streaming movies, you can pause and play again at the same spot.

View a QuickTime VR Movie

QuickTime VR movies—often called *panoramas*—have slightly different controls since you're supposed to "look around" and "move through" a QuickTime VR movie (see Figure 14-2).

You don't "play" a QuickTime VR movie—you manipulate it. Point the mouse at the video image. The cursor you see will tell you what to do next. If you see a little circle that looks sort of like a dartboard, hold down the mouse button, then move in any direction to explore the 360 degrees of the panorama. (In most QuickTime VR movies you can spin all the way around, but can only tilt up or down about 10–20 degrees.) While you're holding down the mouse button, the cursor changes to an arrow that points in the direction you're scrolling the panorama. The closer to the edge of the image you get, the faster you scroll.

If you move the mouse around (without holding down the mouse button) and your cursor changes to a hand pointing at a globe, that's a *hot spot*. Click there once and release the mouse button and another node of the VR movie loads—you move to another part of the image where you'll have another 360-degree panorama to enjoy.

The controls at the bottom of a VR movie screen really just allow you to magnify or widen your view of the panorama. You can also accomplish this with the keyboard. Hold down the SHIFT key to magnify; hold down CTRL to pull back and see more of the panorama.

QuickTime Web Browser Plug-in

Along with the QuickTime Player comes the QuickTime plug-in, an addition to Web browsers that allows them to display QuickTime movies directly within the Web browser's document window. You'll notice that the controls are pretty much the same whether you're

14

Move back — |—Move around in the scene

Magnification — |— Move to next panorama

FIGURE 14-2   QuickTime VR works a little like a video game, allowing you to "move around" within the movie.

viewing a movie with QuickTime Player (playing from your hard disk) or with a Web browser (playing across the Internet).

QuickTime movies must be embedded in the Web page for them to appear in the browser—otherwise they're downloaded to your iMac first, and you view them in the QuickTime Player. If they're embedded in the page with special HTML codes, the movie, QuickTime VR, or QuickTime audio movie plays from within the browser screen itself. This works great for streaming QuickTime, which allows you to watch a movie *while* it is being transmitted over the Internet.

NOTE   *If QuickTime movies aren't displaying correctly, the QuickTime plug-in may not be in the right place. It should be stored in the Plug-ins subfolder found in your Web browser's folder. If it's not there, do a quick Sherlock search for QuickTime Plug-in, then copy a version of the file to the Plug-ins folder.*

If you've upgraded to QuickTime Pro, you'll be given a few other options with the plug-in, including the ability to save movies directly from Web pages. Click and hold the mouse button on an embedded QuickTime movie (or CONTROL-click the movie) and a pop-up menu appears. Choose Save As QuickTime Movie to save the movie to your iMac's hard drive. Then you're free to view it in the QuickTime Player.

PictureViewer and Images

The PictureViewer is a small utility program that uses QuickTime's ability to work with various digital image file formats. Like movies, sounds, and other document types, there are many different types of digital images floating around in the computing world. They've been created in different programs, on different types of computers, and follow differing standards. So how can you possibly work with all of them?

Well, there's a lot of translation that needs to happen. At its most basic, the PictureViewer simply displays images onscreen and allows you to view them. You can do some very basic manipulation, but you can't save the images unless you have QuickTime Pro, so there isn't much point. In its basic form, PictureViewer is a convenient tool for examining images.

View Images

To load an image into the PictureViewer, you can usually either double-click the image file, drag-and-drop the image document on the PictureViewer icon, or choose File | Open from within PictureViewer.

If the image isn't immediately opened in PictureViewer or in another application or utility, the Mac OS may not know which application to use. You can pick PictureViewer from the list and it will most often load the image.

Once you have the image open in PictureViewer, you can change the size at which the image is displayed by selecting one of these commands: Image | Half Size, Image | Normal Size, Image | Double Size, or Image | Fill Screen. You can also rotate the image by choosing Image | Rotate Left or Image | Rotate Right, or you can flip the image by choosing Image | Flip Horizontal or Image | Flip Vertical. These commands help you when viewing an image—if you happen to get your hands on an image that's been scanned, downloaded, or saved "sideways," then you can flip it accordingly to see the full image.

You can also make some changes using the mouse and modifier keys:

- Drag the bottom-right corner to resize the image.

- Click SHIFT and drag to resize the image with different proportions.

- Click SHIFT-OPTION and drag to resize the image in increments of 12.5%, 25%, 50%, and 75%. You can also hold down SHIFT-OPTION and drag all the way out to return the image to its original size.

Image Format

If you're working with an image from a digital camera, one that's been scanned into a computer, or one that's been created in a high-end graphics application, the big question is: What format is it saved in? There is no single standard for digital images, although there are a handful of common ones.

In order for different types of both applications and computers to be able to read and display these image files, we need some standard formats. QuickTime's PictureViewer, for instance, can read many popular formats, as shown in the following table.

Format	Extension	Description
BMP	.bmp	The Microsoft Windows "bitmap" graphics format, the native format for Windows-based computers.
GIF	.gif	Graphics Interchange Format, originally developed by CompuServe. This format is popular for nonphotographic images (like buttons, arrows, and stylized text) that are created for the World Wide Web.
JPEG	.jpg	Joint Photographic Experts Group format, developed by the group of the same name. This one is used on the World Wide Web for photographic images because it offers high-quality images with lots of color information, and it compresses into small files that don't take up a lot of storage space on hard drives.
PICT	.pic, .pict	Macintosh Picture file, the native format for Mac OS. When you take a screenshot (⌘-SHIFT-3), or copy and paste images, this is the format that results. Many graphics programs can save files to PICT format and exchange them.
PNG	.png	Portable Network Graphic, a file format designed to replace the GIF format for Web development because GIF relies on patented technology. PNG is gaining some popularity, but GIF remains very popular.
QuickTime Image	.qif	QuickTime image format, best used for editing frames within QuickTime movies.
TIFF	.tiff, .tif	Tagged Interchange File Format, used extensively in publishing. This high-quality format creates very large files that take quite a bit of storage space but maintain clean scanned and edited images.

One way to identify the different sorts of images is to look at the filename's extension, especially if you've downloaded the images from the Internet or otherwise transferred them from non-Macintosh computers. Unix and Windows both deal heavily in these filename conventions that help each program figure out what format a particular file is using.

Save Images

If you've upgraded to QuickTime Pro, then PictureViewer Pro is capable of saving files to a number of different formats, effectively working as a file format translator. Once you have an image loaded in PictureViewer in any of the listed formats, you can save it as a BMP, PICT, PCX, QuickTime image, or Photoshop image file. Here's how:

1. Choose File | Export.

2. In the Save As dialog box, choose the file format from the Type menu.

3. Click OK and your image is saved.

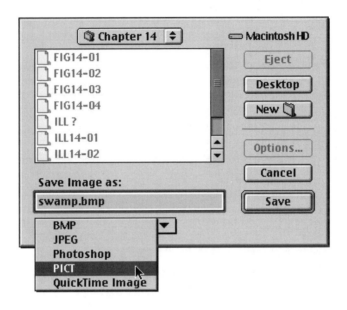

Notice that PictureViewer will automatically append a filename extension to the file's name, making it easier to transfer this file between computing types (from Macs to Unix or Windows, for instance).

QuickTime Player Pro

If you've upgraded to QuickTime Pro, you also have QuickTime Player Pro capabilities at your disposal. QuickTime Player Pro is a mini-recording studio of sorts, allowing you to edit movies, make changes to the compression schemes, layer in new audio tracks, and much more.

Like the PictureViewer, the QuickTime Player can read and play a number of different file types. Likewise, QuickTime Player Pro can save movies in a number of different formats, effectively serving as a translator between different movie file formats.

Movie Types

The first thing you might want to do is translate to and from the QuickTime movie format. Again, there are a number of popular formats used by different types of computers and different applications that deal with digital movies. Here are a few that QuickTime can translate and that QuickTime Player can read directly:

Format	Extension	Description
AVI	.avi	Audio/Video Interleave, the Microsoft Windows standard. Popular on the Internet and some CDs, especially those designed more exclusively for Windows users.
DV	.dv	A standard for storing and transmitting digital video between DV camcorders and computers. QuickTime can work directly with these files, both inputting and outputting in DV so that QuickTime Player and other QuickTime applications are able to edit DV video easily.
MPEG	.mpg, .mpeg	Motion Picture Experts Group, a standard in digital video editing that rivals QuickTime for popularity. It's used in a variety of situations including multimedia CD-ROMs and on the Web.

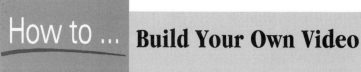

How to ... Build Your Own Video

Are you an artist or cartoonist? You can create a QuickTime movie from a series of images you've created in another program:

1. If you have a series of images, give them the same name with a number appended to the end like, image1, image2, image3.

2. In QuickTime Player, choose File | Open Image Sequence.

3. In the Open dialog box, choose one of the numbered images.

4. The Image Sequence Settings dialog box appears. Choose the number of seconds per frame from the menu to determine how long each image should stay onscreen. Then click OK.

The images appear in the form of a QuickTime movie.

Sound File Formats

QuickTime Player can also import and work with sound files as well, whether it's to store the sound as its own audio-only QuickTime movie or to integrate the sound into an existing QuickTime movie as an audio track. To open a sound file, just choose File | Open, then look for the file. Select it in the Open dialog box and the Open button changes to Convert if it's a sound format that QuickTime recognizes. Click Convert and the sound file appears in the QuickTime Player.

Since sound files don't have a video component, nothing shows up but the controls and slider bar.

Which sound files does QuickTime deal with? There are a number of sound files out there on the Internet and elsewhere, including some that can be translated using special utilities available for the Mac. QuickTime handles the following sound file formats:

Format	Extension	Description
AIFF	.aiff	Apple's Audio Interchange File Format is an older standard that offers decent sound, but isn't as compressible or as high quality as more recent standards.
AU	.au	Also know as the μlaw format. This popular format was originally used by Sun and Next Computer systems. It's a common, low-quality format used often on the Web.
MPEG	.mpeg	Both the MPEG audio and video formats set the standards in multimedia, especially in consumer applications like DVD video and high-quality audio. MPEG Level II is a popular standard for recording sounds to your own hard drive; MPEG Level III offers FM-radio-to-CD quality audio that can be downloaded over the Internet.
WAV	.wav	This format is native to Microsoft Windows and very popular among PCs and on the Internet. It offers decent quality and can be compressed with many of QuickTime's codecs.

If you plan to save audio that you're creating yourself, you'll probably want to choose either AIFF or MPEG, although you can also save audio tracks as QuickTime movies if you like. If you plan to send your sounds to a Windows user, then WAV is the best way to go.

Edit Video

Although QuickTime Player doesn't really offer the highest forms of editing, programs exist—like Apple's Final Cut, iMovie (shipped with the iMac DV models), or Macromedia's Director—that give you amazing control over the fades, wipes, effects, sound synchronization, and similar components of a good movie.

With QuickTime Player, it's more like cut and paste. You can still create some interesting effects, though, and have fun doing it.

14

Say you've got two movies and you want to add part of one movie into the middle of another movie. That's easily done:

1. In QuickTime Player, select portions of a movie by moving the small selection triangles at the bottom of the movie window (right below the slider). If you want to select the entire movie, choose Edit | Select All.

2. For minor corrections to your selection, click one of the selection triangles, then tap the left or right arrow keys.

3. Now, select Edit | Cut or Edit | Copy (if you don't want to cut the selection from the original movie).

4. To paste the selection into the other movie, choose the point on the slider bar (by moving the diamond selector or clicking the slider bar once) where you want the selection to enter the first movie. Then, choose Edit | Paste. The selected part of the first movie is now part of the second movie. You might notice that this works best, by the way, when the movies have the same-sized video image.

If you'd like to trim a movie down a bit, you can do that, too. Use the slider and the SHIFT key (or just drag the little selection triangles) to select the section of the movie that you want to *keep*—it should be the part that's highlighted. Now, hold down the OPTION key as you select the Edit menu. You'll see a new command, called Trim. Select that and the highlighted segment becomes the whole movie.

Saving the Movie

When you're ready to save an altered movie, you may have to make some choices first. If you want to simply update the movie you've made changes to, choose File | Save. If you want to change the name and create a new movie with your changes (a good idea so that you don't overwrite the original), choose File | Save As. In the Save As dialog box, you'll need to find a folder to store the movie in and give it a new name. You'll also choose from one of two options:

- **Save Normally** Creates a dependency to the original movie, which means the original movie needs to be on the same hard drive as this version of the movie in order for it to work correctly.

- **Make Movie Self-Contained** Saves the movie as a completely new movie file, allowing you to move it to another computer and use it. This makes for a much larger file (since it includes all of the movie data needed to play the movie), but this way you don't have to remember to copy the other movie file upon which this movie is dependent.

When you've made your choice, click Save to save the file.

Export Video or Sound

Once you have a movie open in QuickTime Player Pro, you can export the video, audio, or both to other file formats. This is actually one of the more common uses for QuickTime Player at the hobbyist level of audio and video production. QuickTime Player allows you to deal with many different types of audio and video, as do other applications based on QuickTime. Then you can feed these exported files into other applications that deal with them on a more sophisticated level.

To do this, choose File | Export. The Export dialog box appears. Here you'll name the file, find a place to store it, then choose how you'd like it saved. You have three basic choices:

- **Export to Image File**   This allows you to export the frame of the movie currently being shown in QuickTime Player as an image. Your choices are Movie To BMP, Movie To Image Sequence, or Movie To Picture (PICT).

- **Export to Movie File**   This exports the entire movie to another movie format, including Movie To AVI (Microsoft Windows' primary format), Movie To DV Stream (for sending to digital cameras), Movie To FLC (to save as a FLI/FLC animation), Movie To Hinted Movie (to create a movie suitable for QuickTime streaming) or Movie To QuickTime Movie.

- **Export to a Sound File**   This takes the audio track of the movie and stores it in the sound format of your choice. The sound choices include Sound To AIFF, Sound To System 7 Sound, Sound To Wave, and Sound To μLaw.

After you've chosen the type of export you plan to perform, you can choose some options from the Use menu. These options generally determine how the file is going to be compressed, making it smaller (for one) and suitable for a variety of different purposes.

The Use menu changes according to the type of file you're exporting to. Here are some of the options you'll find, based on the type of export you're trying to accomplish:

- **Movie To AVI**   Choose the type of compressor to use depending on where the AVI movie is going to be run from by your user. In most cases, 2x CD-ROM should be fine.

- **Movie To BMP**   The compressor is BMP, but you can choose the number of colors and the quality of image. The fewer colors and the lower the quality, the smaller the resulting file will be.

- **Movie To DV Stream**   In this one, you just pick your local TV format, PAL or NTSC, and the MHz level. NTSC is standard in the U.S. and Japan; PAL is used for cameras in Europe.

- **Movie To FLC**   For animations, you select the type of colors and the frames per second of the animation.

14

■ **Movie To Image Sequence**   Choose the type of movie images you want to create and the frames per second that should be exported.

■ **Movie To Picture**   Photo JPEG is appropriate if you want the image compressed, or choose Uncompressed for the best quality. Choose PNG to use the Portable Network Graphic format for Web graphics.

All of the sound exporting options also allow you to choose 8-bit or 16-bit sound (8-bit is lower quality but takes up less storage space), and mono or stereo (mono takes up less storage space). An 8-bit mono sound is somewhere around the quality of AM radio, while a 16-bit stereo sound file can approach CD quality, depending on the file format and compressor used.

You can also use the Options button to set more advanced options for each of your Export file types. Choose the type from the Export menu, then click the Options button to choose a particular compressor and set other options. This gets a bit complicated, but you can learn more about the various options by selecting Help | On-line QuickTime Player Help. This loads Apple's latest QuickTime Help files in your Web browser (you'll need an active Internet connection).

Play Audio CDs

Your iMac comes with a special AppleCD Audio Player application that allows you to play audio CDs using the CD-ROM or DVD-ROM drive that's built-in. The AppleCD Audio Player works a lot like a home CD player, allowing you to access individual tracks of an audio CD, name the tracks, program it to play songs out of order, and so on. If you're into CD music at all, you'll enjoy this program.

Launch AppleCD Audio Player

To launch the AppleCD Audio Player, choose it from the Apple menu. (If you have Mac OS 9 installed on your iMac, you may find the AppleCD Audio Player in the Applications folder on your hard disk.) You'll see the player's interface appear on your iMac's screen. Now, pop an audio CD in the CD-ROM or DVD-ROM drive if you don't already have one in there. Figure 14-3 shows the AppleCD Audio Player.

You'll note that many of the controls are already familiar to a CD hound like yourself—you have all the usual suspects like Play/Pause (the same button), Stop, Eject, Forward, Backward, and so on. (The volume slider on the edge just changes the volume on the CD, not the system volume, which you can change from the Sound control panel or the control strip's Sound module.)

The player also has some familiar program buttons, like Shuffle, which randomly switches between tracks on the CD. Prog can be used to program the playlist—you'll see that in a minute.

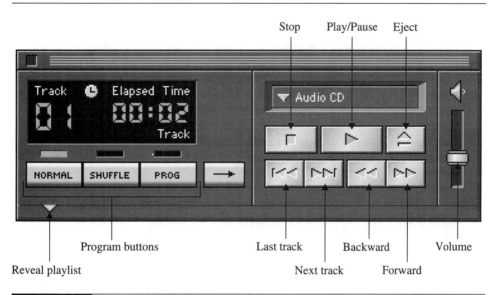

FIGURE 14-3   The AppleCD Audio Player lets you control audio CDs in your iMac's CD-ROM or DVD-ROM drive.

Customize Tracks and the Playlist

To see details on each track, click the little arrow to reveal more information about the disc. Here you can do some interesting things. For one, you can actually double-click on the name of the CD (currently "Audio CD") and give it a name. Click outside the name to save your editing. You can do the same thing for each individual track—double-click its name, then start editing (see Figure 14-4).

You may have already guessed that you can't actually save data to a CD, since it's not designed to store computer data (and it's read-only, anyway, like all CDs in your iMac's CD drive). Good call. But what you may not know is that it doesn't matter, since these changes are actually stored in your iMac's System Folder, in the Preference folder. The iMac can tell which CD you pop in, and will automatically load the name and tracks correctly the next time you go to listen to it.

But wait, there's more! If you'd like to customize the way your CD is played, you can do that, too. Select the Prog button and a new panel—the Playlist—appears. You can drag tracks from the left side (the correct order of the CD) to the Playlist side to customize how the CD is played. Want to play the same track three times in a row? Just drag it to three of the slots. Drag others around on the Playlist, too—there's a little arrow that appears next to the Playlist to show you where a song will be placed. Release the mouse button and it's put there in order.

Now, click the Play button and listen to your newly customized CD!

FIGURE 14-4 You can edit the name of your CD and each audio track.

 *There's an option in the Options menu called AutoPlay that allows your audio CDs to play automatically when you pop them in the drawer. If you like that idea, make sure there's a checkmark next to AutoPlay. The next time you insert an audio CD, it will begin playing, even if the AppleCD Audio Player isn't active.*

Play a DVD Movie

If you have an iMac DV or later model, you have the special ability to play DVD movies using the DVD-ROM drive and some special software included with your iMac. All you have to do is insert a DVD movie title in your iMac's DVD-ROM drive and launch the Apple DVD Player application, which you'll find in the Applications folder on your iMac's hard disk.

Once you've got the player up and running, you'll see the Viewer window and the DVD controller, a small, sleek disc that offers some controls that should be familiar if you've ever used a VCR or even a tape recorder.

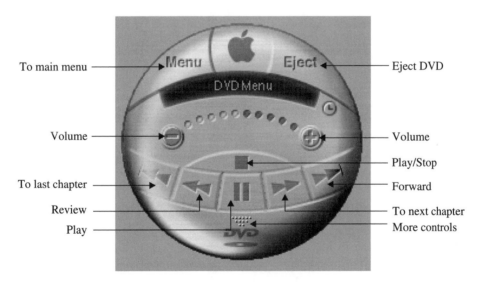

To begin playing the DVD movie, click the Play button. You should see the movie's opening sequence and then, in most cases, you'll see the movie's main menu. You can then use the mouse to click in the Viewer window itself to select what you'd like to do next— view the movie, see additional features, and so on.

While you're viewing the movie, you can use the different controls to move forward or back within the film. Most DVD movies are divided into chapters, so you can use the Previous Chapter and Next Chapter buttons to move back and forth between different chunks of the movie. And, at any time, you can click the Menu button on the Controller to

14

return to the DVD's main menu. The volume buttons are marked with + and – signs that allow you to click to raise or lower the volume, respectively.

You can change the size of the movie fairly easily. Choose the Video menu and choose the size you'd like, or choose Present Video on Screen if you'd like to watch the movie without seeing window controls or the menu bar. To bring the menu bar back, simply move the mouse up to the top of the Mac's screen and the menu reappears.

> **TIP** *While you're watching the movie you may also want to get that controller out of the way. You can do that by selecting Window | Hide Controller. To get the controller back, choose Window | Show Controller.*

Many DVD movies include significant additional features, including more than one sound track (often in different languages), the ability to display subtitles, and even wackier features like the ability to change the camera angle while you're viewing a movie. To access these controls, click the DVD logo at the bottom of the controller. This causes the bottom part of the controller to "open up," revealing more controls. (Once revealed, there is a small control at the bottom-center of the controller that you can click to close the DVD controller back up.)

Point the mouse at one of these buttons and leave it there for a moment—you'll see a small label appear, showing you what the purpose of the button is. Click the button to activate that option—you'll likely see a response in the small indicator in the Controller.

When you click the Stop button, your place in the movie is saved; you can click Play again to resume from that point. If you're done with the movie, you can click Eject to eject the DVD from your iMac.

Chapter 15

Edit Your Own Movies

How to...

- Get your movie into your iMac
- Edit the clips
- Add transitions, sounds, and titles
- Lay in your soundtrack
- View, save, and export the movie

I t's happening again. We've talked about *killer apps* in other chapters in this book. Killer apps are those applications that introduce an entirely new capability to computing, drawing in new people, creating new careers, and altering the technological landscape. In the past, killer apps have included spreadsheet computing, desktop publishing, and Web publishing, all of which are covered in this book, because the iMac is capable of all those killer apps.

If you have an iMac DV model, then you're ready for the next killer app for personal computers: desktop video. Using a digital camcorder, the Firewire port on your iMac DV, and a wonderful little program called iMovie, you can turn your iMac into the most inexpensive nonlinear video editing bay that the world has yet seen. The funny part is that iMovie is incredibly easy to use and gives really good results.

Digital Video Explained

Personal camcorder technology is in something of a transition right now, with many more new *digital* than *analog* models being introduced. Digital video (DV) camcorders have also hit a magical price point, now coming in well under $1,000 for a consumer model. That's made them very popular among the folks who like to buy camcorders. But they're becoming even more popular for the folks who like the idea of *editing* videos, not just shooting them.

But what is a digital camcorder? Instead of laying down analog information (electronic signal information) to a VHS or Betamax tape, digital camcorders work sort of like computer scanners with a lens. They immediately translate what you see in the viewfinder into digital data—ones and zeros. Most of them then store that data on magnetic tape, just as some computers write backup computer files to magnetic tape.

The advantage of this is two-fold. First, the image can be corrected digitally as it's brought into the camera. If you shop for them, you'll notice that digital cameras have a lot of interesting features—built-in effects, image stabilizers, digital zoom—that aren't available on most analog cameras.

Second, digital data doesn't lose quality from copy to copy (in the biz, they say "from generation to generation"). This *generational* loss is more than evident whenever you copy from one VHS video to another; the copy is always worse than the original. With digital data, there's nothing to degrade over multiple copies (unless the tape starts falling apart). Just like a word processing document or a PICT image file, the quality of a digital video recording doesn't fade as you copy it.

In fact, a digital camera is basically just creating a computer file that's stored on that digital tape. And, since it's already a computer file, that means it'll be easier to work with on your iMac, right?

Yup. Since the iMac DV has Firewire ports—and nearly all digital camcorders have Firewire ports—you can connect your camera to your iMac DV. Now, with the right software, you can copy video directly from the camera to your computer. The easiest way to do that is with iMovie, which can actually control your camera (at least, many models) from within the software.

15

Then, since the video is already a computer file, it's a simple matter to cut, paste, add in transitions, lay down a soundtrack—a lot of that stuff that we discussed in Chapter 14 regarding QuickTime. That same technology can be used with a DV movie to edit it, enhance it, and make it that much more interesting to watch.

Then, you can save the digital video as a QuickTime movie and put it on the Web, send it in e-mail (if you have a nice, fast connection), or save it on your hard disk. Or you can copy the video back to your camcorder, then use your camcorder as a VCR to play the movie on your TV (or transfer it to typical VHS tape).

The bottom line? With a DV camcorder and an iMac DV, you've got a video editing studio. And depending on the quality of your camcorder, the images pretty much rival those that the professionals are putting together for the six o'clock news.

You can see why desktop video is a killer app—all of a sudden it's gotten much cheaper and easier to edit high-quality video.

Get Video into Your iMac

Before you can edit your movie, you'll need to connect your camcorder to your iMac and launch iMovie. Then you'll copy the video *clips* into the program so you can edit them.

 *If you don't have a DV camcorder, iMovie includes a sample project that you can use to practice your editing. In fact, iMovie has an Apple Help–based tutorial that's pretty good for learning the basics of iMovie.*

Hook Up Your Camera

You can hook up your camera at any point—Firewire is hot-pluggable and iMovie will recognize the camera once the camera is plugged in. So, I'd recommend launching iMovie first, just so you can see the status of things. (iMovie is in the Applications folder on your iMac's hard disk.)

 If iMovie has been used before, it may open to the most recent project. In this case, use File | New Project to create and name a new project. It may also ask you if it can change your screen resolution; iMovie prefers to run at 1,024 × 768.

Now, use a Firewire connector to connect your DV camcorder to one of the Firewire ports on the side of your iMac. Both of the connectors are designed to fit only in the correct direction. The longer, flatter connector plugs into the Firewire port on your iMac; the smaller, square connector connects to the camera.

Once you've got the camera connected, turn it on. If all goes well, iMovie will recognize the camera, as shown in Figure 15-1.

Depending on the camera, you may need to be in Playback or VCR mode in order for iMovie to control the camera. Then, click the small camera icon to put iMovie in Camera

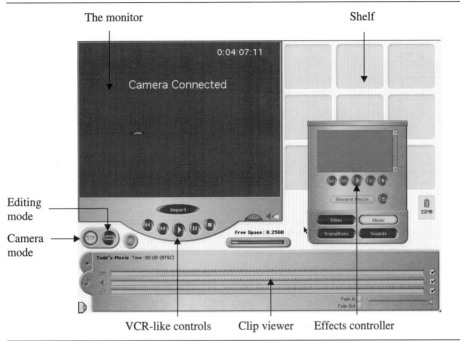

The monitor   Shelf

Editing mode

Camera mode

VCR-like controls   Clip viewer   Effects controller

FIGURE 15-1   iMovie has recognized my camera and is ready to import video clips.

mode so it can control the camera. If the camera is in its recording mode, then you may see the image play through the iMovie viewer (called the *monitor* window) in real-time.

 Apple maintains a list of compatible cameras and manufacturers at ***http://www.apple.com/imovie*** *on the Web.*

Import the Clips

Once you have iMovie connected to your camcorder, you're ready to import clips. Click the Import button on the iMovie interface and iMovie will fire up your camcorder and start importing clips from the camera.

 If you want every clip on your camcorder, make sure you've rewound the tape. You can do so using iMovie, if you like, by clicking the rewind button in the monitor window while you're in Camera mode.

iMovie moves through the tape and finds clips to import, then it places them on the "shelf" on the upper-right side of the iMovie screen. Each clip is a distinct segment of

15

video; once you're in iMovie, you'll be able to drag-and-drop movie clips to change the order of the segments in your video.

TIP

iMovie ends the current clip whenever it encounters a point on the tape where you pressed Stop. If you use the Pause button on your camera while filming, iMovie doesn't recognize that as a new clip. So, it's best to hit Stop while you're shooting video whenever you think you'll be creating a new clip, and Pause when you want to stop filming for a moment but you don't want to end the current clip.

Let iMovie continue to import clips until you've got all the clips you need. At that point, you can click the Import button again to stop the process. Note that you can also use the VCR-like controls (when Import is not selected) to move around on the tape if you need to find the clips you want.

You should be aware that digital video clips take up *tons* of hard disk space. In the iMovie window, you can see a Free Space indicator that shows you how much hard disk space is left on your iMac. You'll have to watch this carefully. In raw DV format, a video takes about 1MB per second of video being created. That means every 15 minutes of video takes up about 1GB of hard disk space.

NOTE

If you're planning to save the video in QuickTime format, it will be compressed and take up much less space.

Preview Your Clips

Once your clips are imported, you can preview them if you like. Click a clip on the shelf and it appears in the monitor. Now, click Play to see that clip, or use the other VCR-like controls to fast forward, rewind, stop, or pause. There's also a volume control in the monitor window if you need to change the volume.

Toss a Clip

Do you have a clip on the shelf that you don't want? You can toss those clips into iMovie's special Trash receptacle. Just drag the clip from the shelf to the small Trash icon. (This is not the same as the iMac's Trash can.) You can empty the Trash by selecting File | Empty Trash.

NOTE

Parts of clips that get cropped or otherwise trimmed are put in this Trash as well. And emptying the Trash will reset the Undo function, so you won't be able to undo anything you've done prior to emptying the Trash. So, make sure you're happy with all the edits you've made recently before emptying.

Edit Your Video

Once you have your clips imported into iMovie, you're ready to start editing. You'll do this in two steps. First, you'll clean up your imported clips, if necessary. Then, you'll lay the clips down on your timeline and arrange them to please.

Crop Your Clips

Although you're free to edit your clips once you've placed them in the *clip viewer* (the timeline at the bottom of the screen), I think it's best to clean them up while they're still on the shelf. Then you can organize the clips a little more easily.

Select a clip on the shelf by clicking it once. It will appear in the monitor window. Now, you can do some basic cropping to the clip to get it to the rough length you want it to be. To crop a clip, you'll need to get to know the monitor's controls a little more intimately.

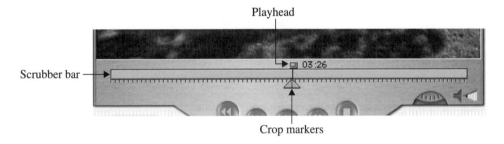

The scrubber bar is a bar that shows you the length of the clip. As the clip plays, you'll see the playhead move along the scrubber bar to show you where you are in the clip. You can drag the playhead to any point in the clip to start at that point. Once you have the playhead in about the right place, you can use the arrow keys on the keyboard to get it to exactly the timecode you need.

The crop markers appear when you click the mouse just below the scrubber bar. These markers can be used to select the area of a movie that you'd like to crop. Just drag the crop markers to the beginning and end of the section of the clip that you'd like to keep, then choose Edit | Crop from the menu. Only the part of the clip between the two markers is kept.

15

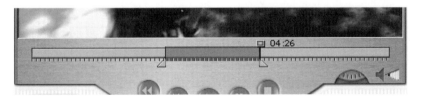

If you'd like to undo the cropping, you can do that. In fact, iMovie is capable of multiple Undo commands, so you can undo a series of edits or changes if you're not pleased with them. Just select Edit | Undo to undo a change.

Split Your Clips

If you need to split a single clip into two different clips, you can do that, too. Use the playhead to choose the exact point where you'd like to split the clip into two, then choose Edit | Split Clip at Playhead to split the clip. The clip now becomes two clips on the shelf.

Rename Clips

If Clip 1 and Clip 2 aren't creative enough for you, you can give your clips new names. Click the mouse button on the name of a clip that's in the shelf. Wait a second and the name becomes highlighted, just as if you were renaming an icon in the Finder. Now you can edit the name of the clip; press RETURN when you're finished.

Arrange the Clips

With your clips cropped down to the parts you want, you're ready to drag them from the shelf to the clip viewer. Make sure the clip viewer tab (the one with the eye on it) is selected, then drag clips down to the viewer. You can drag them in any order—in fact, you're using the clip viewer to create the order for your video.

Once you have clips on the clip viewer you can still move them around all you want. Just drag-and-drop a clip to its new location. And once you've got everything arranged on the clip viewer, you can play the whole movie through if you'd like. Make sure you don't have any of the clips selected (you can use the Edit | Select None command to make doubly sure), then click the Play button in the monitor window. You'll see the video from start to finish.

You can also select one, two, or more clips in the clip viewer and play them back in the monitor window. To select more than one clip, hold down the SHIFT key while you select them. Then, click Play in the monitor window to view the series of clips you've selected.

To remove a clip, drag it back to the shelf. If you're sure you don't need it any more, you can drag it to iMovie's Trash icon or you can select the clip and press DELETE.

Transitions, Sounds, and Titles

If you've been reading along so far, you're probably impressed with how easy this is. You've already got an edited video! Well, it's not going to get any harder. Instead, you're just going to easily lay in some transitions and sounds, and add titles to your movie using a little more drag-and-drop.

Transition Between Clips

Transitions are just the fades and wipes between clips in your video. You don't have to use transitions; often, a clean cut between two clips looks fine. But you'll find that transitions are useful in many cases, either to suggest the passage of time, to help the viewer change thoughts along with you, or just to make things a little smoother in your video. Plus, adding a transition is a great way to make your video look a little more professional.

Before you can add a transition, you'll need two clips between which you can create a transition. Or you can create a transition at the beginning or the end of your video. In either case, you need to consider where the transition will look good.

Once you've got that location locked in your head, click the Transitions button in the effects controller. The transition list pops up, along with the preview screen that shows you how your transition will look. Select the transition you'd like to use from the list. Whenever you click a transition, you'll see a small preview in the preview window. Likewise, you can click the Preview button to see the transition previewed in the monitor window.

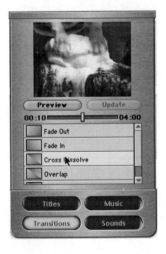

TIP   *If I'm planning a transition between two clips, I like to select the two clips in the clip viewer (hold down the SHIFT key while you're selecting the second clip), then I select transitions from the list. The preview shows a sample of the transition between the two selected clips.*

Once you've found the transition you like, drag it from the transition list down between the two clips (or in front of the first clip or behind the last clip) where the transition should take place. A small box appears, representing the transition. You'll also see a small red line as the transition is rendered. (You'll need to wait for this to complete before you can view the video in the monitor. You can do some other dragging and dropping if you like, though.)

Add Titles to the Video

Another pro-level touch is to add titles to your video. You can add titles anywhere in your movie if you'd like to introduce the video, roll some credits, or just have a little fun with written commentary on the screen.

To superimpose titles on a particular clip, select the clip in the clip viewer and click the Titles button. The effects controller shows you a list of title styles and some options for those titles.

To get started, select one of the title styles, then enter text for the title. You can also choose the font for the titles and a color for the text from the pop-up menus, if desired. (For now, leave the Over Black option turned off.) You'll see what your title looks like in the small preview window, or you can click the Preview button to see the titling in the big monitor window.

There are a number of different types of titles. As you click through them, you'll notice that they offer different ways you can type information, too. For instance, some titling schemes will support scrolling or centered credits, and they offer you multiple lines for those credits. Other options will enable you to create just a single title line. Still others allow for an entire block of text, which can be scrolled, centered, and so on. Experiment with the different types depending on the titling you're trying to do.

Also, notice the slider bar in the effects controller. This slider allows you to determine how long the titling clip will last. This may be important if you'd like the titles to fill the clip that they're overlaying—you'll need to use the slider to make the length of the titling sequence the same as the length of the clip it's overlaying. If it's longer, the titling will overlap two clips. (You'll notice that the shortest amount of time the title sequence can span is dictated by the effects that are being performed. After all, the title can only scroll so fast, for instance.)

NOTE   *If your titling sequence is shorter than the clip it overlays, then a split is created when you drag in the title style. The titled clip is followed by the rest of the original clip in the clip viewer.*

Once you've got the length of the title the way you want it (again, you can test by clicking Preview), you can drag the title style from the style list down to the clip viewer. Place the title style in front of the clip that the title should overlay. The titled clip appears in the clip viewer. The titling needs to be rendered, so you'll see a small red progress indicator on the clip. You can't play the clip until it's done rendering.

Once the titled clip is rendered, you can view the movie again to see how it fits into the scheme of things.

TIP   *You can have a transition into a titled clip, but you need to render the titled clip first, then render the transition. For instance, if you want to fade into a titled clip, create the titled clip first, then place the Fade In transition before it.*

Drop in Sound Effects

You can create an entire soundtrack for your movie, but, before you do that, you might want to add some simple sound effects. Click the Sounds button in the effects controller and you'll see some sample sounds you can add to your video.

15

How to ... Add Credits

If you'd like to create credits on a standard black background, you can do that easily. In the titling window, select a title style that's designed for credits (Rolling Credits, Rolling Centered Credits, and Centered Multiple are good choices), then turn on the Over Black option. Choose White as the text color. In the text area, you'll likely find a number of text boxes for typing your credits; you can click the Add button to add more. (Click the Preview button to see how the credits line up—you may need to type different parts of each credit line in different text areas to make the credits looks right.)

When you're done building your credits, just drag the title style to the clip viewer and drop it where you want the credits. (You'll probably place that title clip at the end of all your other clips.) The black-screen credits are rendered and, once they're ready, you can play your video to see them.

> **TIP** *You can add more sounds by dragging them to the Sound Effects folder inside the Resources folder in the iMovie folder on your hard disk. Sound clips need to be AIFF files.*

To view the sound portions of your movie, click the sound viewer tab (the one beneath the clip viewer tab that looks like a musical note). Now you'll see three different tracks, each looking like a bar graph. This is the *audio viewer*. The top track is the video track—you'll see bars that represent the video clips you've added to the movie. The second track is the sound effects track; you can add the sound effects by dragging them to this track. The third track is the music track, where you can add underlying music if you'd like it in your movie.

iMovie Tutorial Time: 01:12 (NTSC)   Audio Selection: Crowd Applause 02 Time: 06:11 Start: 41:29 Stop: 48:10

41:29

Fade In
Fade Out

To add sounds, simply drag them from the sound list in the effects controller to the audio viewer. Place them on the sound effects track where you'd like them to occur relative to the video clips. You can then play the video to see how the sounds are matched up with the video. If the sound isn't in the right place, just drag-and-drop it to a new location in the sound effects track.

To remove a sound from the sound effects track, select it with the mouse and press DELETE.

Lay in Some Music

The last editing step is to lay in your background music. With iMovie, you'll need to have either an AIFF file or a CD handy for adding music.

Here's how to add music from an AIFF file:

1. Place the playhead where you'd like the music to begin. (It's probably easiest if you've got the audio viewer showing.)

2. Select File I Import File.

3. In the Open dialog box, find the AIFF file you want to import. Click Import.

That's it. The audio is imported into the program and placed on the music track. When you play back the movie, you'll hear the music in the background.

To add music from a CD, do the following:

1. Place the playhead where you'd like the music to begin. (Again, it's probably easiest if the audio viewer is active.)

2. Click the Music button in the effects controller.

3. Insert an audio CD in the DVD-ROM drive. (If there's already a CD in the drive, click the Eject button in the effects controller or switch to the Finder and eject the CD.)

4. You'll see the tracks for the CD appear in the effects controller. Select a track. If you want to record music from that track, click the Record Music button.

5. Now, as the music records, you'll see the video in the monitor window. When you get to the point where you'd like the music to stop, click the Stop button.

TIP   *If you record at least a few extra seconds of music after your video ends, you can have it fade out nicely.*

15

Once you have your music clip on the music track, you can drag the music clip around to place it perfectly. You can also drag the end of the music clip toward the beginning of it to shorten the clip. The additional recorded music isn't actually lost—you can drag the clip back out again to recover it.

You can delete the music track by selecting it and pressing DELETE. It's placed in iMovie's Trash.

NOTE *At the bottom of the audio viewer you'll see controls that let you set the volume for the background music or select the fade options. Turn on Fade In if you want the music to fade in as it begins; turn on Fade Out if you want the music to fade out as it ends.*

View and Export Your Movie

If you've gotten this far, hopefully you've pulled through the editing phase and you're ready to do something with your masterpiece. You can view it full screen to make sure everything looks good, then you can export the movie either back to your camcorder or as a QuickTime movie.

View the Movie

There's a special button that enables you to preview the movie full screen. It's just to the right of the Edit Mode and Camera Mode buttons, just below the monitor window and the VCR-like controls. I wish I could describe it, but hopefully the picture helps. (I guess it's supposed to be an iMac's monitor, but it looks sort of like a mailbox to me.)

To stop viewing the movie while it's full screen, simply click the mouse button or press any key.

TIP *If you choose Edit | Preferences and click the Playback tab, you can choose whether the movie playback in iMovie is Smoother Motion or Better Image quality. If the former, you'll see a more pixelated image on screen, but you'll see more frames of video per second. If you choose Better Quality, the images will look good, but the video may appear to jump a bit. This only affects playback onscreen. Once you get the movie back out to your digital camera, it should be smooth and as high quality as your camera is capable of producing.*

Export to Your Camera

If you plan to view the video on your television or transfer the video to videotape, your best plan is to export it to your camcorder (unless you have a DV video deck, in which case I envy you). Your camcorder is designed to hook up to all that analog equipment quite nicely, so it's the perfect place to put your finished video.

 Don't forget the length of the cassette in your camcorder may limit the length of the movie it can store from your iMac. (Your iMac has the potential to edit a one-to two-hour movie, depending on hard disk space, and some mini-DV cassettes have only a 30-minute capacity.)

Here's how to export to your camera:

1. Make sure the camera is connected via Firewire and, if necessary, put the camera in VCR or Playback mode.

2. Choose File | Export.

3. In the Export dialog box, choose Camera from the pop-up menu.

4. Enter the number of seconds of black before the movie and the number of seconds iMovie should wait while the camera gets ready to record. (This is often at least five seconds.)

5. Click Export.

A progress slider will appear onscreen and you'll see the video in the background. You'll also likely see the video on your camera's viewfinder or LCD display.

That's it. iMovie will stop your camera when the video is done recording. Now you can hook up to the TV and show the in-laws (or your producers and the studio hawks to see if you can get funding for that 35mm print).

Export to QuickTime

Want to distribute your masterpiece via the Internet or place it on removable media to hand out? You'll need to export it to QuickTime.

15

Before distributing any videos you create publicly, you should take pains to make sure you aren't violating copyright laws. If you used copyrighted music or images in your video, for instance, it may not be a good idea to distribute your video publicly over the Internet.

This process can be time-consuming, because the QuickTime movie needs to be compressed well beyond the minor compression that happens for the DV format. This compression is sophisticated and processor-intensive. Its end result is a much smaller QuickTime movie that can play back with good quality. To create that compressed movie file, though, takes time.

Here's how to export to QuickTime:

1. Choose File | Export from the menu.

2. In the Export Movie dialog box, choose QuickTime from the Export To menu.

3. Now, select the type of video you want to create in the Formats menu. You can choose from different recommended compression schemes based on the type of movie you're creating. (The CD-ROM settings are equally applicable if you plan to simply store the movie on your hard disk or place the movies on removable media disks.)

If you know a little something about compression schemes (translation: if you know more than I do), you might want to select Export from the Formats menu. You'll then be presented with a dialog box that enables you to specify the compression settings for your QuickTime movie.

4. In the Export QuickTime Movie dialog box, select the location to save the movie, give the movie a name, and click Save.

Now, give yourself a pedicure, go for a bike ride, or hit the phones and see if you can find some friends who'll go bowling with you. You'll be waiting a while, depending on the length of your video and the compression scheme you chose. In the meantime, you can't really use your iMac for much of anything—the whole processor is given over to the complex task of rendering the movie. (You will, however, see the video's progress in the monitor window, so at least you can check in every once in a while and see how things are going.)

When it's done, you'll have a new QuickTime movie that you can view in the QuickTime Player or distribute to your heart's content.

Chapter 16

Play Games with iMac

How to...

- Play Nanosaur
- Play Bugdom
- Check out your iMac's 3-D capabilities
- Adjust the InputSprocket for game controllers
- Access the World Book Encyclopedia

S ince its strong showing in the consumer market with the original iMac computer, Apple has been pushing for more and more gaming titles on the Mac platform. That push has paid off with new and exciting titles being released for Mac OS computers. The iMac continues to be improved to the point that the latest iMac and iMac DV models offer very impressive capabilities for gaming. That means the three-dimensional graphics-acceleration requirements of almost any Mac OS game are easily handled by the iMac.

Just to get you started, your iMac comes with a few different games. In this chapter we'll take a specific look at some of the games that come with the iMac, and you'll learn how to install, optimize, and use other games. Plus, we'll take a quick look at the World Book Encyclopedia that's included with many iMac models.

Play Nanosaur

Nanosaur, shown in Figure 16-1, has developed something of a cult following since the release of the iMac. After being included on every iMac made, more than two million copies of Nanosaur have been distributed with the machines, leading to quite a bit of Nanosaur fever. It's pretty well deserved, since the game's theme makes it appropriate for reasonably young kids, even if it is what's called a "first-person shooter" (meaning that you follow just behind your character and shoot at the enemies).

NOTE   *Nanosaur is not installed by default on some iMacs. Instead, you'll find its installer on the iMac Software Install CD in the Nanosaur folder inside the Applications folder.*

In this game, you're a Nanosaur—a type of genetically altered dinosaur brought back to life by humans in the future. Unfortunately, the humans die out, but the Nanosaurs thrive and create a technological civilization. You've been elected to head back in time, to recover the eggs of different species of dinosaurs from preextinction days. That'll give the Nanosaurs more genetic material to work with to ensure their survival.

The point is to run around the screen and find the colorful eggs. You then go back to a certain place where you toss the eggs into a time portal and they are sent back to the future. You only have a limited amount of time before a meteor crashes into the Earth and drives the dinosaurs to extinction. (Too bad you didn't set that time machine further back a few months.)

The eggs of different species are different colors—the first egg is worth 20,000 points and subsequent eggs of that same color are worth 5,000 points. The ultimate goal is to find the eggs of all five species and send them through the time portal so that life can be wonderful back in the future. (You also get a bonus of 150,000 for accomplishing such a feat.)

16

FIGURE 16-1   Nanosaur is a first-person "shooter" where you play the dinosaur.

Get Started

Once Nanosaur is installed on your iMac, open the Applications menu and look for the Nanosaur folder. Open the Nanosaur folder and you'll see the game; double-click the Nanosaur icon to start the game. You'll see the Nanosaur opening screen—press the SPACEBAR. You'll see the opening animation; when you see the dinosaur running, you're ready to access the game's controls—press the SPACEBAR again.

You move between the game's control commands by pressing the LEFT and RIGHT ARROW keys—you'll see that the ring rotates and a new picture will be in your view. To select that particular option, press the SPACEBAR.

Here's what each command does:

- **The Dinosaur**   This allows you to start playing the game.
- **The Check Box**   Press the SPACEBAR to see some options you can change. The fewer options selected, the faster the game can be played.
- **The Question Mark**   This is the Help screen—it shows you the keys used for commands during the game.
- **The Exit Sign**   This allows you to quit the game.
- **The Medal**   This shows you the high scores and scorers.

When you're ready to play the game, put the dinosaur to the front, and press the SPACEBAR. The game begins.

Play the Game

As the game starts, your Nanosaur is dropped to the ground, ready to begin running around the screen. You move with the ARROW keys, which allow you to run in all four directions. Immediately, you'll see a *power-up*—gamers' lingo for something that you're supposed to run directly into and which gives you extra powers or some other goodies. In this case, the power-ups you initially see give you more ammunition for your laser gun, which is the weapon you have at the start of the game.

Move and Jump

There are a number of different controls you'll want to master right away. These commands enable you to move the dinosaur and play the game:

Press This	To Do This
ARROW keys	Move the dinosaur
SPACEBAR	Fire weapon
⌘	Jump
OPTION	Pick up (egg)
SHIFT	Change to next weapon
A, Z	Move up and down with the jetpack

You'll move using the ARROW keys, then press the SPACEBAR to fire at any hostile dinosaurs. Your typical *T rex* takes about two shots before he disappears—other dinosaurs can take more or less.

Jumping can be very useful—in fact, you should get used to both jumping and double-jumping. If you press the ⌘ key once, you'll jump; press it twice in succession (or anytime while the Nanosaur is still in the air) and you'll jump again, doing a flip in the process.

Gather Eggs

When you find an egg, move up close to it and stand still, then press the OPTION key. The Nanosaur bends down and attempts to pick up the egg in its mouth. If you've got it, it's time to return to a time portal, since you can only carry one egg at a time. Check the temporal compass and head off in that direction.

Once you arrive at the time portal, you need to toss the egg into its time stream. Press the OPTION key again. You'll see the egg leave the Nanosaur's mouth and fly straight forward—hopefully it encounters the time stream before it hits anything else or lands on the ground. Try not to hit OPTION accidentally while you're running with an egg, since you

16

could accidentally toss the egg into water, lava, a crevice, or under a dinosaur you don't feel like getting close to. (Fortunately, those sturdy dinosaur eggs don't break.)

Change the Camera and Options

Aside from the commands for controlling your Nanosaur, other keyboard commands enable you to change the gaming environment.

Press This	To Do This
< > (brackets)	Spin the camera around
1 2	Zoom the camera in and out
CTRL-M	Toggle music on and off
CTRL-B	Toggle sounds on and off
+/-	Raise or lower volume
F8	Show the current frame rate (performance of the game)
ESC	Pause the game
TAB	Change the camera mode (look from behind the Nanosaur or look through the Nanosaur's eyes)
G	Toggle the GPS map on and off (which gives you an overview of your current position and the surroundings)

The Quit command is the same in Nanosaur as in other applications—press ⌘-Q to quit the game. There are no Save and Load commands—you simply have to play a new game straight through or quit.

Get More Help and Update Nanosaur

You've learned enough here to start playing quickly, but you'll want to consult the Nanosaur manual, an Adobe PDF document to learn more about weapons, power-ups, and the creatures you'll encounter. You'll find the manual in the Nanosaur folder in a file called Nanosaur Instructions.

You should also check **http://www.pangeasoft.net/** for updates and information about Nanosaur.

NOTE   *Free updates can take Nanosaur to version 1.1.6 or beyond for bug fixes and better performance. You can download the Nanosaur update, then unstuff it to see the new application, which you can simply drag into your Nanosaur folder— no need to download the entire thing. If you have an original iMac (in Bondi Blue) then you many need a special updater that supports that iMac's 2MB of video RAM.*

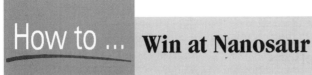

How to ... Win at Nanosaur

Here are some hints for playing the game:

- **Move quickly.**   If you want to win the game, you've got to get eggs back through time, fast.

- **Don't gather all eggs.**   You get 5,000 points for each egg gathered, but each species of egg (that is, each different color) is located on a different "section" of the map. For instance, the first egg color is found in the marshes where you begin the game; the next egg color is found in the lava flow portion of the world. Keep moving along. There are five different-colored eggs you need to gather.

- **Learn to use the jetpack.**   You can fill the jetpack by standing over a gas vent that's shooting up out of the ground. Then use the jetpack, but spend as little time in the air as possible—it uses up fuel fast.

- **Pick your weapons.**   The SHIFT key lets you toggle between weapons. Some weapons—like the "nuke"—are only appropriate when you need to hit many enemies at far range. Make sure you've selected the best weapon for the job.

- **Try new things.**   There are a few different "tricks" that will help you get more points or additional bonuses. For instance, you can jump on the backs of pterosaurs (the flying ones) if you do a double-jump at the right moment. That'll result in some interesting bonuses.

Play Bugdom

Bugdom, by the same Pangea folks who brought you Nanosaur, is a painfully cute game. Ideal for kids but addicting for adults (at least this one), this is a nice game to have included on your iMac.

 *Bugdom is a recent addition to the iMac bundle, only being included with iMacs made in fall of 1999 or later. If your iMac doesn't include Bugdom, you can download a demo version from **http://www.pageasoft.net/** on the Web.*

The story is simple: After years of benevolent rule by the Rollie Pollies and the Lady Bugs, Bugdom has been swarmed by hostile forces—the Fire Ants and the bugs they've recruited to perform their evil. The kingdom is now ruled by King Thorax, who holes up

16

in the anthill. You, Rollie McFly, have to get to the anthill, defeat Thorax, and crown yourself king, hopefully returning the kingdom to the peaceful paradise it once was.

As Rollie, your basic job is to walk through Bugdom kicking things. (This seems to be Rollie's forte. I guess when you have that many legs, you develop certain skills.) A number of things can be kicked, including the power nuts (walnuts scattered around that include power-ups), enemies, and the cages that hold Lady Bugs hostage. The point of the game is to kick walnuts to get power-ups, keys, and other special powers, like buddy bugs. (You can use buddy bugs, who follow you around, to dive-bomb your enemies.) You also seek out Lady Bugs who are trapped in cages and kick their cages to free them. As you proceed through gates and tunnel between levels, your ultimate goal is to come up against King Thorax and defeat him.

Get Started

When you first launch Bugdom you'll see the main menu, which allows you to view the high scores, change settings, load saved games, read the credits, or begin the game.

Here are some things you can do from the main menu:

- To load a saved game, double-click the Saved Games icon. You'll see an Open dialog box that allows you to locate a saved game.

- Double-click the High Scores icon to see who has done the best at the game.

- Double-click the "?" walnut to see the credits for the game.

- Double-click the Start icon to begin the game.

To change settings, double-click the Settings icon. This brings up a dialog box where you can choose a few different settings for the game:

- **Easy Mode** Select this option if you'd like Rollie to sustain less damage when attacked.

- **Configure InputSprocket** Click this button to bring up the InputSprocket dialog box, where you can alter settings for your input device (joystick, gamepad) if you have one that supports the InputSprocket. (See "Configure InputSprocket" later in this chapter.)

- **Keyboard Controls Are Player-Relative** Select this option if you'd like controls to be player-relative instead of camera-relative. (This is discussed in the "Control Rollie" section.)

- **Rage II Mode** This option allows you to downgrade the quality of graphics for the original iMac or other early Power Macintosh G3 computers. It's not necessary on recent iMac and iMac DV models, but should be turned on for Bondi Blue iMacs.

■ **Clear High Scores**   Clear out the names and scores when you're sick of seeing your sibling's or children's embarrassingly superior scores.

Once you're done setting options, click OK to return to the main menu.

Play the Game

As the game begins, Rollie appears on the ground, ready to start running around the screen. You move with the ARROW keys, which allow you to run in all four directions. Immediately, you'll see a walnut that likely contains a power-up. Go and kick it by pressing the OPTION key. In this case, the early power-ups you kick to reveal are likely to be clovers, which add bonus points to your score.

Control Rollie

Rollie has two basic modes—bug mode and ball mode. (Remember, he's a Rollie Pollie.) Press the SPACEBAR to switch between modes. While he's a bug, Rollie can jump, kick, and walk. While he's a ball, he can either roll or roll *faster*. As a ball, he can also roll into enemies, walnuts, and Lady Bug cages instead of kicking them.

There are a couple of different ways you can control Rollie:

■ **Mouse**   You can use the mouse to move Rollie in any direction, and click its button to kick. If he's in ball mode, clicking the button gives him a turbo boost while rolling.

■ **Mouse and Keyboard**   Using the mouse while holding down the SHIFT key, you can control Rollie's direction while he walks forward. This is the recommended mode of play, if you have enough dexterity for it.

■ **Keyboard**   Using only the keyboard, you can use arrow keys to get Rollie to move just as you would with the trackpad. In this case, the OPTION key is used to kick or boost speed, depending on Rollie's mode.

> *TIP* *You can switch to what Pangea calls player-relative controls, which allow you to use the UP ARROW to move Rollie forward, the DOWN ARROW to move him backward, and the LEFT and RIGHT ARROWS to turn him without moving him. Used in concert, the arrow keys give you more controls, but they can also be tough to get used to.*

You can also use the keyboard to accomplish a few other things including jumping, changing modes, or launching a buddy bug. Table 16-1 shows the controls.

> *TIP* *You can also freeze the screen (and the game) in a special pause mode that allows you to take a screenshot. Press F12, then press ⌘-SHIFT-3 to take a picture of the entire screen.*

Key	What It Does
OPTION	Kick in bug mode, turbo boost in ball mode
SPACEBAR	Switch between bug and ball mode
⌘	Jump (in bug mode only)
TAB	Launch your buddy bug at an enemy
+/-	Raise or lower the volume
⌘-Q	Quit the game
ESC	Pause the game
M	Toggle music on and off
1/2	Zoom in/Zoom out
</>	Swivel camera

TABLE 16-1 Controlling Rollie and Setting Options in Bugdom

Scoring Points and Tracking Health

You score points in two ways, by gathering clovers (within walnuts that you kick open) or rescuing Lady Bugs. Each is registered in the status bar at the top of the screen.

At the far left of the status bar you'll see the number of lives Rollie has left. Next to it, you'll see the two types of clover you'll encounter—each new clover you discover in a walnut and walk over to pick up is added to its respective four-leaf clover in the status bar. In the middle, you'll see Rollie holding up any special items he's found, like keys or money. Next, you'll see the Lady Bug gauge. If the image of the Lady Bug has wings, then you've freed all Lady Bugs on this level. If not, you still have work to do. On the far right you'll see a tally of how many Lady Bugs you've freed.

There are two indicators near the picture of Rollie in the middle of the status bar. The green curved indicator tells you how much more "ball time" you have—Rollie can only stay in ball mode for so long. If you've depleted your ball time, you'll have to find a power-up that gives you more. The red straight line is a health indicator. Run out of health and you'll lose a life.

A third indicator appears whenever you're fighting a level "boss" (a meaner bug that you have to defeat to end some levels). That indicator, which appears on the bottom of the screen, tells you how much health the boss has left.

Whenever you see a large candy cane–colored pipe with a bubble of water coming out of it, you've reached a checkpoint. Jump up to pop the bubble and register at the checkpoint. Now, if you lose a life while playing, you'll return to this checkpoint instead of the beginning of the level.

Fight Bad Bugs

One of Rollie's strengths seems to be running away, and since you don't score additional points for beating up an enemy, you can run away with impunity. That said, sometimes you've got to stop, clinch your feet into fists, and take on the bad bugs.

Some bugs can't be beat, like the snails. Instead, avoid those. Others have to be kicked (or rolled into) more than once before they're knocked out. It's easier to roll into bad bugs than kick them, especially if they have weapons. Remember that you only have a certain amount of ball time before you have to stand up and take it like a, uh, bug.

You've got another trick up your sleeve—the buddy bug. If you've got a small bug following you around that you can't get rid of (after kicking a walnut where he was hiding) it might be because he's your buddy. While you're in a fight, press the TAB key to launch the buddy bug at an enemy. He can knock most of them silly with one punch.

Get More Help and Update Bugdom

As with Nanosaur, Bugdom has a manual that can help you learn more about it. The Bugdom manual is an Adobe PDF document (discussed in Chapter 6) that can help you learn more about the power-ups, levels, and creatures you'll encounter. You'll find the manual in the Bugdom folder in a file called Bugdom Instructions.

You should also check **http://www.pangeasoft.net/** for updates and information about Bugdom.

Check Your 3-D Specifications

Your iMac features an ATI graphics chip that's designed to accelerate the drawing of 3-D images. With the correct ATI drivers installed, your iMac should take advantage of the 3-D acceleration code built into popular games, especially those that support QuickDraw RAVE or ATI Rage acceleration. You should look for this sort of support when you're buying a game—check the side of the box.

Similarly, games may require a minimum processor speed. Your iMac has at least a 233MHz PowerPC G3 processor and at least 32MB of system RAM, just in case the game asks. The original iMac also has a 4GB hard disk. This table shows the gaming-related specifications for different iMac models:

Mac Model	Processor Speed	RAM (base)	Hard Disk	Video Card	Video RAM
Rev. A (Bondi)	233 MHz	32MB	4GB	ATI II	2MB
Rev. B (Bondi)	233 MHz	32MB	4GB	ATI II	6MB
iMac 266 (Colors)	266 MHz	32MB	6GB	ATI Pro	6MB
iMac 333	333 MHz	32MB	6GB	ATI Pro	6MB
iMac (slot-loading)	350 MHz	64MB	6GB	ATI Rage 128 VR	8MB
iMac DV	400 MHz	64MB (128MB SE model only)	10GB (13GB SE model only)	ATI Rage 128 VR	8MB

 These are just specifications for gaming reference. To learn more about screen resolutions, see Chapter 24. To learn more about upgrading RAM, see Chapter 27.

Add Game Controllers

One other variable when you're playing games on your iMac is the controller. In many cases, you'll play the game using the keyboard—a lot of games are designed to allow you to do that. Others will specifically encourage the use of a joystick or gamepad. (Joysticks work like flight sticks in fighter planes; a gamepad is usually similar to the controllers that come with Nintendo or Sony Playstation game boxes.)

On the iMac, joysticks require driver software to allow them to operate correctly. That driver software can come in three forms:

- It can be a generic driver that allows the controller to be a substitute for the mouse with a particular game.

- It can be a specific driver that works with certain games.

- It can use the InputSprocket driver software created and installed by Apple for easy gaming.

The easiest way for this to work is with the InputSprocket driver software, but then the game must specifically support Game Sprockets, a special technology that Apple has created to make gaming easier. Unfortunately, not all games use this, so sometimes you have to get creative.

Configure InputSprocket

If your game and controller are both compatible with the InputSprocket, then configuration is simple. The controller should say on the box that it's compatible with InputSprocket or Game Sprockets, and it should include a CD that allows you to install drivers for its particular characteristics. (In other cases, it might not require a special driver and will work with the InputSprocket drivers that are already installed on your iMac.) You'll install a driver for your particular controller (in some cases), then you'll install a compatible game. Once support for both has been established, you're ready to set things up.

In the game itself, look for an option to change controller preferences. That will cause a special dialog box to appear—the InputSprocket configuration dialog box (see Figure 16-2). In this dialog box, you'll be able to choose what each button on your controller will do. Click a particular button to see a list of different options available for your particular controller. Each game has its own control mappings, so look carefully at each. For instance, in the game "Future Cop" (the Ariston Hermes example shown in Figure 16-2) there are three different weapons at your disposal—each needs to be mapped to a particular button on the gamepad.

Since this dialog box is designed as part of Apple's InputSprocket software, you'll find it's similar for nearly every device you use and every game you play that supports InputSprocket.

Other Drivers

If your input device supports other sorts of drivers, you'll be able to do one of two things. First, you may simply be able to use your input device as a substitute for an external mouse. If that's the case, use the preferences in the game to select a mouse as one (or the only) input device. You can use the joystick instead, although the game will believe you're using a mouse.

Second, you may be able to use your joystick specifically with a particular game. Some games offer built-in support for certain joystick brands with specific features—for instance, many controllers from Thrustmaster and Microsoft are specifically supported by particular games. Likewise, your controller may offer a special driver that makes it act like popular controllers that are supported by individual games.

NOTE   *At the time of this writing, a shareware driver for some USB devices was making it possible to use USB gaming controllers with non-InputSprocket games. Basically, the driver, called USB Overdrive, maps USB buttons to keys on the keyboard. You'll need to figure it out on your own, but if you're an advanced iMac gamer and you'd like to experiment with the driver, check out **http://www.montalcini.com/**.*

Select buttons

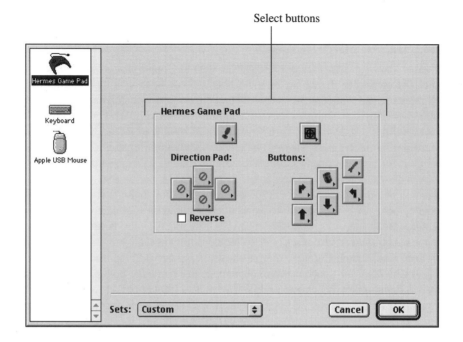

FIGURE 16-2   Configuring a joystick using InputSprocket

The World Book Encyclopedia

Your iMac comes with the World Book Encyclopedia, the electronic version of the venerable encyclopedia set. With the CD version, the World Book Encyclopedia offers more than articles and pictures on every sort of topic—you also get multimedia features like QuickTime video and audio.

 The World Book Encyclopedia does not come with the Bondi Blue Rev. A or Rev. B iMacs, which feature Compton's Encyclopedia instead.

Get Started with World Book

Before you can use the World Book Encyclopedia, you'll need to get it installed on your iMac. The World Book Encyclopedia includes two CDs that are bundled with your iMac. Insert the CD labeled Disc 1 and launch the installer program. Read the license agreement and click Agree, then enter the CD key (registration code) that's printed on the disc sleeve that Disc 1 came in. (Note that the CD key is case-sensitive—it needs to be entered exactly as it appears.)

Next, click Install and locate a place on your hard disk for the World Book folder, which requires about 45MB of space on your hard disk. When the installer is finished, you're ready to begin working with the encyclopedia.

Using the Encyclopedia

To use the World Book Encyclopedia, place Disc 1 in the CD-ROM or DVD-ROM drive of your iMac and double-click the World Book icon in your World Book folder. After a moment, you'll see the main menu for the World Book Encyclopedia. Beyond this main menu, most of the World Book's information is presented in a format designed to mirror a Web browser (in fact, it can actually be used in conjunction with an Internet connection to access updated articles on the World Book Web site, as discussed later). This Weblike interface makes using the encyclopedia fairly familiar. You'll find that you can click hyperlinks—either underlined text or small graphics—to move to new articles, hear multimedia clips, or otherwise move around and make things happen.

Likewise, the interface includes a button bar of items that appear across the top of the encyclopedia browser window. These buttons allow you to move quickly among the different types of items you can access within the encyclopedia. You can use the familiar Back and Forward buttons to move back and forth between articles or items you're viewing. To return to the main menu, click the Home button.

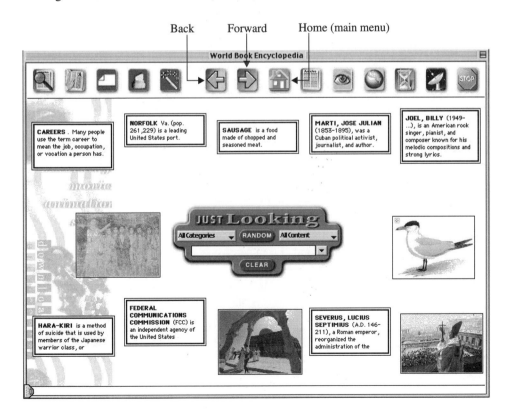

16

Many of the articles will have a special Article Media browser that looks a little like a roll of 35mm film. Click the down arrow next to the roll to see any available multimedia items, or click the up arrow to roll the film back up. You can then single-click a media item to see its reference in the article or double-click it to view it, listen to it, or see a larger version, as appropriate.

Browse the Encyclopedia

You can begin your quest through the World Book in one of two ways—you can browse or you can search. Browsing is a great way to dive into the encyclopedia and see what sort of interesting tidbits you can learn. To browse, click on the World Book, Media, or Monthly Spotlight icons. Here's what each does:

- **World Book**   Allows you to use the "Just Looking" interface to find random topics that may be of interest. Click the Random button to see a listing of different articles.

- **Media**   Leads you to the Browse Media page that lets you view or listen to different media clips.

- **Monthly Spotlight**   Brings up a special article that offers interesting information pertaining to the current month. From here you can click to browse the articles or media mentioned.

Search for Articles

Often you'll consult the encyclopedia because you have something specific you want to research. If you know what you're looking for, click the Articles button under the Search topic in the main menu. This brings up the Search by Topic window in the World Book

Encyclopedia interface. In the Search by Topic window, enter keywords in the entry box and click the Go button.

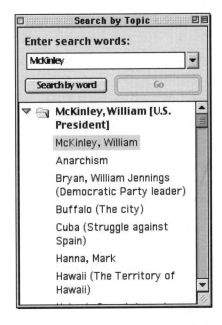

You'll see a list of results and the interface will switch to show the first related article. You can double-click article titles in the results list to see those articles displayed.

If the results don't net the article you're looking for, you might have better luck using the Search by Word scheme. This will actually find articles that include the word in the text of the article. You can also search videos, maps, multimedia clips, and other items in the encyclopedia for matches.

To use the Search by Word tools, click the Search by Word button in the Search by Topic window. Now the window changes to the Search by Word window. Here's how to use the window (see Figure 16-3):

1. At the top of the window, place a checkmark next to the items you'd like to search. You can leave the checkmark next to All to search all of the items in the encyclopedia.

2. Enter a search word in the entry box.

3. If you'd like to enter two or more search words, enter them in the subsequent entry boxes below the first entry box. Then, use the pop-up menu to determine whether you're searching using And, Or, or Not between the search keywords.

16

NOTE

This type of a search is called a Boolean search, and it allows you to limit the search in very specific ways. Note that the keywords "Steve And Jobs" will limit your search, while the keywords "Steve Or Jobs" will broaden the search. The keywords "Steve Not Jobs" will cause more specific results to appear (that is, those that include the word "Steve" but do not include the word "Jobs").

4. Next, you choose how close together the words should appear. They can appear in the same sentence, in the same paragraph, in a subhead's text, or within an entire article. You choose those from the pop-up menu, or select the radio button and enter a maximum number of words that the keywords can be separated by.

5. Finally, click Go to begin the search. You'll see results appear in the bottom portion of the window. Double-click an article to view it.

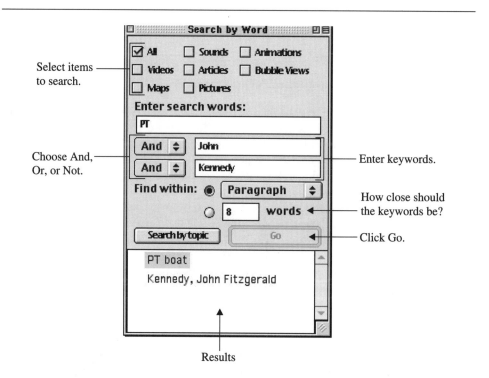

FIGURE 16-3   The Search by Word window lets you create a more detailed search.

Other Special Features

Back in the main menu, you'll find even more specialized search items under the Search heading. All of them use the basic concepts of the browser and search windows to help you approach the articles in the encyclopedia in different ways:

- ■ **Maps**   Click the Maps button to focus on regional articles and articles that have to do with particular countries. As you view each map, you'll see the cursor change so that you can either zoom in on part of the map or click part of it to bring up a linked article.

- ■ **Dictionary**   The Dictionary button brings up a Dictionary search window that allows you to enter a word to be defined. (Enter it as a keyword, then click Go.) You can also use the dictionary while you're reading articles in the encyclopedia. When you see a word that needs to be defined, make sure the dictionary window is active (there's a button in the encyclopedia browser window that can open it as well) and double-click a word in the article window. This will cause the word to be looked up automatically in the Dictionary window.

- ■ **Time Frame**   Click this button and you can look up articles by time frame. The New Time Frame window allows you to set the year, decade, century, millennium, or era that you'd like to research. You can then view a timeline of articles within the time frame you've specified. To set a particular time frame, click the button that relates to the time frame you'd like to see. Then, enter a date that helps to set the time frame. For instance, if you'd like to read about the 1960s, click the Decade button and enter a year between 1960 and 1969. If you'd like to view an entire century, click the Century button and enter a date that occurs in that century. You can also choose a category from the Categories menu, then click Go to see the time frame. Once you've viewed a time frame, click the New Time Frame button to reopen the window and search again.

- ■ **What's Online**   This link allows you to explore some of the World Book's online options.

Consult a Wizard

Aside from the features discussed, the World Book includes a few extras that are of particular help to students. These are the wizards, which allow you to perform some specialized tasks using the articles and multimedia available from within the World Book. To use a wizard, click the Homework Wizards button on the main menu, or click the Wizard button in the World Book Encyclopedia browser window. You'll see a window that allows you to choose a wizard.

The wizards are very involved, step-by-step tutorials that work like the Mac OS Internet Assistant or similar wizards in AppleWorks. Just follow the onscreen instructions. When you're done with a particular set of instructions, you'll usually click the Next button to move forward or the Back button to go back.

Update the World Book

It's important to update the World Book occasionally, and it's easy to do, but it can take quite a while if you've never updated before (or if you wait many months between updates.) So, it's probably best to allow an evening or some other time when you can tie up your Internet connection for a while in order to complete the update.

To update, make sure your Internet connection is active, if relevant (especially if you use a modem to connect). Then, click the Update Now button on the main menu. (You can also find the Update Now button on the What's Online page.)

Now, the encyclopedia's browser connects to the World Book Web site and downloads updated articles to your iMac. These articles are stored in the World Book folder on your hard disk, but they're accessed seamlessly while you're browsing and searching the World Book. While the update takes place you can't really do anything else within the World Book software itself. You can, if desired, switch to another application and continue working while the updates take place in the background. When the update is finished, you'll see a dialog box that tells you so.

Chapter 17

Tracking Your Schedule and Contacts

How to...

- Schedule appointments on your calendar
- Deal with your To Do's
- Jot down quick reminders
- Track your contacts
- Sync your iMac with a Palm OS handheld computer
- Install Palm applications

The iMac ships with the Palm Desktop, an application from 3Com that allows a Palm Pilot or Palm OS handheld computer to synchronize data with a Macintosh computer. Of course, the iMac doesn't come with a Palm Pilot (don't I wish), but the Palm Desktop is perfectly functional with or without a Palm Pilot. On its own, the Palm Desktop is a fairly complete calendar and contact manager, allowing you to track appointments, To Do lists, notes, and information about people you know in your work or personal life.

> NOTE *A Palm Pilot is a popular handheld computer made by 3Com, Inc.'s Palm Computing division. (Other companies also make handheld computers that run the Palm OS, including IBM's Workpad and the Mindspring Visor. The Palm Desktop software works with those handheld computers, too.)*

In fact, Palm Desktop is a good program precisely because Apple wrote it—at least, initially. When it was clear that the Palm handheld computer was going to be popular with Mac users, 3Com bought Claris Organizer, a datebook and contact manager program, from Apple. (Claris was a subsidiary company of Apple before it was folded back into Apple in early 1998. The Claris people are the same folks who wrote AppleWorks, which was once called ClarisWorks.) Using Claris Organizer as a basis, the Palm Computing/3Com folks wrote the new Palm Desktop software that not only tracks appointments and contacts, but also syncs up nicely with a Palm handheld computer. Then, even cooler, they released the software for free and allowed Apple to bundle it on the iMac.

> NOTE *Only iMac models shipped in the Fall of 1999 and later include the Palm Desktop software as part of their software bundle. However, you can still download the software for free from Palm Computing (**http://www.palm.com/**). You can also get the Palm Desktop software when you purchase a Palm OS handheld computer or a Palm connection kit.*

Get Started with Palm Desktop

Palm Desktop isn't installed initially on your iMac, although the software is already there on your hard disk. In the Applications folder, open the Palm Desktop folder and double-click the Palm Desktop Installer. This will step you through the installation process. At the end of the installation, you'll enter a name to associate with Palm Desktop's original data file when it first launches. Enter a name and click Continue.

After you enter a name, you can choose whether or not to set up HotSync. If you click Setup Now, you'll be asked to choose the type of connection for your Palm OS handheld's connection—with the iMac, you're likely to use a USB connection for your Palm OS handheld. (You'll need a special USB connection kit, which is a separate purchase for your Palm device.) To set up HotSync later (or to not set it up at all if you don't have a Palm OS device), click Setup Later.

The Palm Desktop adds some extensions and control panels, so you'll need to restart your iMac after it's installed.

17

The Instant Palm Desktop Menu

Once Palm Desktop is installed (and your iMac has been restarted after the installation), you'll see something different about your iMac's desktop. It will likely have a small icon up in the corner of the menu bar, next to the clock. This is the Instant Palm Desktop menu, a special menu that allows you to quickly access the Palm Desktop software and the HotSync capabilities for getting your iMac to talk to a Palm Pilot.

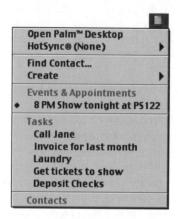

The menu also has a Create menu, which allows you to select individual items you'd like to create within Palm Desktop. And, if you have anything that's currently scheduled or due, you can see those things quickly by looking at the menu instead of opening up or switching to the Palm Desktop software.

If you need to launch Palm Desktop, switch to it if it's already open, or just quickly check your current tasks and appointments, pull down this menu. It's a lot easier than finding the Palm Desktop icon and launching the program.

If you'd like more information about a particular task or appointment that's listed, select it in the menu. A dialog box will appear for that particular item, with the complete text of the item, the date, times, and whether or not an alarm is set. You can change things in the dialog box or just click OK to dismiss it.

The Palm Desktop Interface

Once you've gotten the Palm Desktop launched or switched to, you'll see a more complete application ready for just about any data you'd like to organize. The nerve center of the Palm Desktop software is its toolbar, which gives you quick access to just about every major command available in the software.

NOTE   *You can use the mouse to point at a button in the toolbar if you don't know what it does. Its name will appear just below the button. If you don't see the name, click the disclosure triangle at the far-left end of the toolbar so that it's pointing down. Now you'll be able to see the names of buttons.*

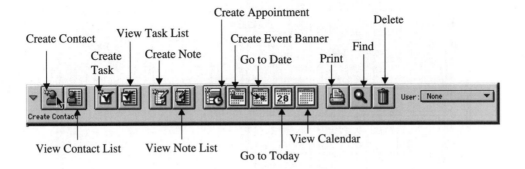

As you can see, the toolbar allows you to accomplish quite a lot without ever touching a menu. Just point your mouse at a button and click it to execute that command.

By default, you'll also see the Calendar window, and you'll likely keep it up most of the time, since it can be tucked behind other windows (like the Task List, Note List, and Contact List), always hanging out there in the background.

To quit the Palm Desktop, choose File | Quit. Even though the Palm Desktop quits, the Instant Palm Desktop menu will always stay on the menu bar—it's actually a Mac OS system extension.

Manage Appointments, Events, and Tasks

Since the Calendar is what you'll see first in the Palm Desktop interface, let's go ahead and talk about it first. The Calendar allows you to manage three different things—appointments, event banners, and tasks. You can also manage these things from three different views—Daily, Weekly, and Monthly. Each gives you a different overview of the items you've scheduled. Figure 17-1 shows the Daily calendar; Figure 17-2 shows the Weekly calendar; Figure 17-3 shows the Monthly calendar.

To change the view, click the tab on the far-right side of the Calendar window. This immediately switches you between different views. If you're currently viewing a Weekly or Monthly view, you can switch to a Daily view by double-clicking a date (the actual number) in the calendar.

As you can see, the different views are useful for different reasons. The Daily view lets you jump into today (or some day in the future) and get an exact idea of all the appointments you have and the tasks that need to happen. The Weekly view gives you a sense of what's going on over a five-day period, especially when it comes to appointments. The Monthly view is simply useful for knowing roughly what's going on at some point in the month and just generally what a busy person you are.

NOTE   *The toolbar has buttons for Go To Date and Go To Today, if you'd like to quickly get to a particular date on the calendar.*

17

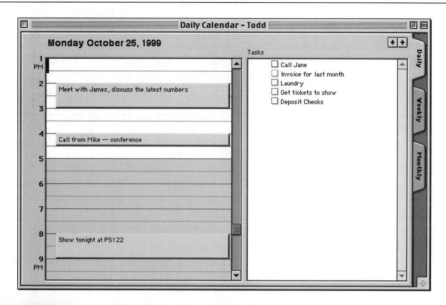

FIGURE 17-1 The Daily calendar gives you a look at the day's appointments and tasks.

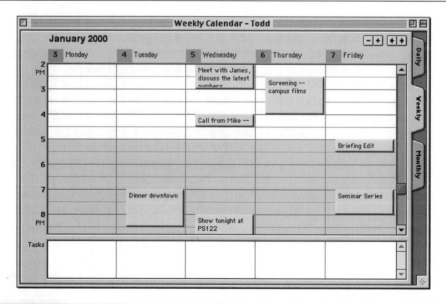

FIGURE 17-2 The Weekly calendar is good for getting a handle on your immediate tasks.

The following is a representation of the Monthly Calendar screen:

```
┌──────────────────────── Monthly Calendar – Todd ─────────────────────────┐
│ January 2000                                                      [◄][►]  │
│ Sunday    Monday    Tuesday    Wednesday  Thursday   Friday    Saturday   │
│ 26        27        28         29         30         31        1          │
│                                                                           │
│ 2         3         4          5          6          7         8          │
│                     7 PM Dinner 2PM Meet with 2:30 PM  5PM Briefing Edit 3PM Rental car — │
│                     downtown   James, discuss the Screening -- 7 PM Seminar Drive locations │
│                                4 PM Call from         Series              │
│ 9         10        11         12         13         14        15         │
│           Trip to Colorado                                                │
│ 16        17        18         19         20         21        22         │
│                     2 PM Edit Session      4 PM Class                     │
│                                            Discussion                     │
│ 23        24        25         26         27         28        29         │
│                     ● Irfon's Birthday                ● Pamela's          │
│                     (Due: Jan 30)                     Birthday (Due:      │
│ 30        31        1          2          3          4         5          │
│ [▼] Irfon's Bir...                [▼] Pamela's...                         │
│ ● Irfon's Birthday                ● Pamela's                             │
│                                   Birthday                               │
└───────────────────────────────────────────────────────────────────────────┘
```

FIGURE 17-3   The Monthly calendar shows you an entire month at a glance.

The Calendar views can be handy not just for getting a sense of what you need to do, but also for creating events and moving things around. For instance, most items on your calendar will respond to drag-and-drop—just point at an item and hold down the mouse button. The mouse pointer should turn into a fist. Now, drag the item to the time or date where you'd prefer to see it and release the mouse button. It's moved.

> **TIP**   *If you'd like to see just the appointments or just the tasks in a particular view, select View | Calendar, then choose either Show Appointments or Show Tasks. The Show command that you select will have its checkmark (in the menu) removed and those items will no longer be shown. To see them again, return to the command and select it to replace its checkmark. The items reappear in the calendar.*

Before you can move events around, though, you'll probably need to create some.

Create an Appointment

To create an appointment, you can do a number of different things, depending on where you are in the Calendar view (or even if you're not looking at the calendar):

■   From anywhere, pull down the Instant Palm Desktop menu and choose Appointment from the Create menu.

17

■ From within the Palm Desktop software, click the Create Appointment button in the toolbar.

■ In a Monthly view, double-click the box that represents the day on which you'd like to set the appointment. In the dialog box, select Appointment and click OK.

■ In a Weekly or Daily view, point at the start time within the day's schedule area and hold down the mouse button while dragging to create the new appointment. If you aim well, you can create the appointment for the correct start and end time. You can then begin typing the text for your appointment. When you're done, click elsewhere on the calendar.

In all but the last case, you'll see the Appointment dialog box, where you can enter the text for your appointment, set the date and time, set an alarm, and choose categories for the appointment.

NOTE *In Weekly or Daily view you can double-click any appointment to see its dialog box, which you'll need to do if you want to set an alarm or the categories for the appointment.*

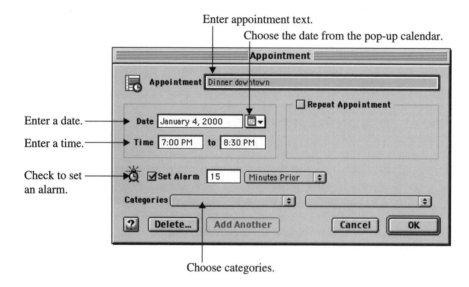

Enter appointment text.

Choose the date from the pop-up calendar.

Enter a date.

Enter a time.

Check to set an alarm.

Choose categories.

To move between each element in the Appointment dialog box, press the TAB key. Here's how each part of the dialog box works:

■ **Appointment** In the Appointment entry box, enter the text that describes the appointment. It can be reasonably long, if you like, but if you have extensive notes that relate to the appointment, those are best stored as a separate note, which I'll describe a little later in this chapter.

■ **Date**   Either enter a date in the Date entry box or choose one from the Calendar pop-up menu. Select the menu and you'll see a small calendar. You can use the arrows to move between the months, then click the particular date on which you'd like to set this appointment.

■ **Time**   Enter the beginning time and the ending time in the entry boxes. Note that when you enter a beginning time and press TAB, the ending time is switched to one hour after the beginning time automatically. This may not be what you want, but it's helpful when it's right.

■ **Set Alarm**   Check this box if you want to be reminded (by a tone and an alert box) of this appointment. Once checked, you can enter a number and then choose from the pop-up menu whether the number represents the number of minutes or hours before the appointment that the alarm should appear.

■ **Categories**   You can choose a category for this appointment from the pop-up menu. If you like, in fact, you can choose two categories.

When you're done creating the appointment you can click the OK button to dismiss the dialog box or click the Add Another button to add another appointment without getting rid of the dialog box. This clears it out and let's you create a new appointment without going to the hassle of invoking another command.

Create a Banner Event

Do you have an event that isn't quite an appointment and doesn't exactly fit the bill of a task? Then it's probably a banner event. Banner events can span one day, many days, or many weeks, if desired, and they aren't tied to a particular time. As a result, you can set an alarm for a banner event, and they don't show up in lists like tasks do.

I use banner events in two ways. The more obvious way is for vacations, trade shows, or anything that will take me a couple of days, or for events that take one day but are special. With a banner event, you'll see immediately when you have a trip scheduled or a birthday or anniversary coming up, especially in Weekly and Monthly views.

The other way I use them is to track project deadlines. Since I'm a writer (by trade if not by calling), a lot of what I deal with are chapters. I'll create banner events for each chapter and place them on the dates when they're due or when I plan to get them done. Then, when I need to reschedule (as my editors well know, this happens more often than

17

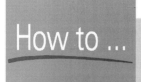 **Set a Repeating Appointment**

If you have an appointment that needs to repeat on a regular basis, you can set that in the Appointment dialog box. (If you're not currently viewing the particular appointment's dialog box, double-click the appointment in the calendar.) To set a repeating appointment, place a checkmark next to Repeat Appointment in the Appointment dialog box. (So far, it ain't brain surgery.)

Next, you'll see a pop-up menu appear. Select from that pop-up menu how often you'd like the appointment to repeat. If you don't see the right time frame in the menu, you can select More Choices to set the frequency yourself. In the More Choices dialog box, use the radio buttons, pop-up windows, and check boxes to determine exactly how often this appointment should occur. When you're done, click OK.

```
┌──────────────────── More Choices ────────────────────┐
│                                   S  M  T  W  Th  F  S │
│  ● Every  [Week          ◆]      □  □  ☑  □  ☑   □  □  │
│  ○ Every  [1]  [Days        ◆]                         │
│                                                        │
│                        [  Cancel  ]  [    OK    ]      │
└────────────────────────────────────────────────────────┘
```

Back in the Appointment dialog box, you'll see an entry box labeled Until. Enter the date when this repeating appointment should stop repeating or choose it from the Calendar pop-up menu. Now, your repeating appointment is scheduled and added to your calendar.

not) I can simply drag the banner event to a new day. If things are getting tight, I can drag two or more banners to a particular day and virtually see the work starting to pile up.

In any case, creating a banner event is easy. Here are the different ways to do it:

- ■ From the Instant Palm Desktop menu, choose Create | Banner Event.

- ■ With the Palm Desktop software active, click the Create Banner Event button in the toolbar.

- ■ From the Palm Desktop software, choose the Create menu, then choose Banner Event.

- In a Monthly view, double-click a day's box and choose Event Banner from the dialog box, then click OK.

- In a Weekly or Daily view, double-click just above the appointment area, just below the date and day of the week.

After choosing one of these fabulous options, you'll see the Event Banner dialog box. Don't worry—this one is easy.

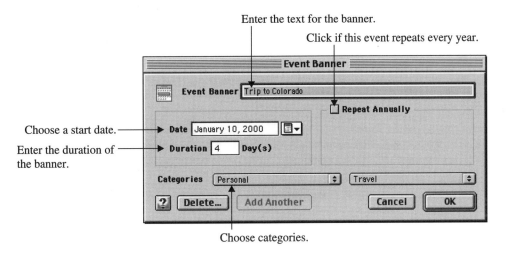

Enter the text for the banner.

Click if this event repeats every year.

Choose a start date.

Enter the duration of the banner.

Choose categories.

In the Event Banner entry box, type the text for your banner. Then, enter a start date in the Date entry box (or choose it from the Calendar pop-up menu) for the banner. Next, enter the duration of the banner if you want it to last more than one day. Choose categories for the event banner from the Categories menus, if desired.

If this is an event that repeats annually, click the Repeat Annually check box. Once selected, you can choose to be reminded of the event a number of days before it happens—perfect for birthdays and anniversaries.

When you're done, click the OK button to dismiss the dialog box, or click Add Another if you'd like to create another Event Banner. When you're done, you'll see your event banner back in the Calendar window. The banner will span the relevant dates in the Monthly view, or you'll see it at the top of the window in the Weekly view or the Daily view.

Add Your Tasks

Aside from appointments and banner events, you can use the Palm Desktop to manage your tasks, or To Do's. By default, your tasks appear in the calendar on the day for which

17

the task is scheduled. Plus, tasks will be held over and shown on subsequent days if you haven't checked off the task once it's completed. If you often use Daily or Weekly views in the calendar, then you'll be able to conveniently view both your appointments and tasks from those views.

You can also manage your tasks in a special list. The list makes it easy to see all pending tasks, including those scheduled for the future. And it's a simple matter to add and delete tasks from the Task List. I'll cover both ways in the following sections.

Create a Task

First, you need to create a task. You can do that in a number of ways:

■ From the Instant Palm Desktop menu, choose Create | Task.

■ With the Palm Desktop software active, select the Create Task button in the toolbar.

■ From the Palm Desktop software, choose the Create menu, then choose Task.

■ In a Monthly view, double-click a day's box and choose Task from the dialog box, then click OK.

■ In a Weekly or Daily view, double-click in the Tasks area of the windows. (In the Weekly view, this is at the bottom of the window. In the Daily view, tasks are on the right-hand side.)

Once you've chosen to create a task, you'll see the Task dialog box. Here you'll enter the information for this particular task.

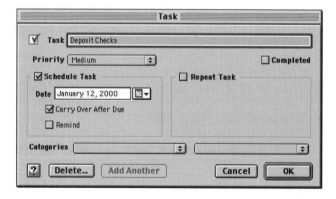

Here are the different items you can enter or set for your task:

■ **Task**   Enter the text that describes the task.

■ **Priority**   Choose a priority level. In the various task areas and the Task List, you can sort by priority so that the most important tasks appear at the top of the list.

■ **Schedule Task**   If selected, the task will have a due date. If you check the box to deselect it, then the task will simply appear in your Task List on the current day.

■ **Date**   Enter the due date or choose it from the pop-up calendar.

■ **Carry Over After Due**   If you'd like this task to continue to appear in your task areas or the Task List after its due date, select this box. Now it won't ever leave until you purposefully mark the task as done.

■ **Remind**   If selected, this option will allow you to enter the number of days before the due date that the software will remind you of the task (via an alert box).

■ **Categories**   If you'd like to associate particular categories with this task, select the categories from the pop-up menus.

When you're done entering the information for your task, you can click the OK button to store the task, or click the Add Another button if you'd like to continue adding tasks without dismissing the Task dialog box.

Manage Tasks in the Calendar

Once you've entered some tasks, you'll see them in your Calendar window. They're easier to see in the Weekly and Daily views, since those calendars have special areas for tasks. In the Monthly view, tasks appear in the same listing as appointments, below the appointments in a date box. (They have a bullet point before the task description instead of a time.)

In the Weekly and Monthly views, you can select a task and drag it to another day. This changes the start date of the task, not the due date. If you drag a task past its original due date, the due date will disappear.

NOTE   *Tasks without due dates will have the date the task was created in parentheses after the task description. Tasks with due dates will have "due:" plus a date in those parentheses.*

In the Daily view, you can't drag a task to a different day, because there aren't other days to choose from. Instead, you can drag a task to a different location in the task area if you'd like to see your tasks in a different order.

To edit a task, double-click it in any view. This brings up the Task dialog box.

In the Daily and Weekly views, you can do one other thing to a task—you can mark it as complete. When you've completed a particular task, click the small check box that precedes it in the task area. You'll see a checkmark, marking that task as complete. Now it won't show up in the task area in future days' listings. (To do this in the Monthly view, double-click the task and place a check in the Completed box.)

SHORTCUT   *Don't forget that your current tasks also show up in the Instant Palm Desktop menu, so you don't even have to open the Palm Desktop software in order to see what you need to accomplish for the day.*

17

Manage Tasks in the Task List

Want to see all your tasks in one place? Just click the View Task List button in the Palm Desktop toolbar or choose View | Task list from the menu. Now you'll see the Task List (see Figure 17-4).

The Task List can make it easier to view and manage your tasks all at once. It allows you to view quite a bit of information about the tasks, including the description, priority, date, and any categories.

Here are some management tasks you can accomplish in the Task List:

- To check off a completed task, click the check box at the far left of the item's row. If you check an item you haven't completed, you can click the check box again to remove your checkmark.

- To edit a task, double-click it in the Task List. You'll see the Task dialog box, where you can change the description, priority, schedule, or categories for the task.

- From the View menu in the top-left corner of the Task List, you can choose to view all tasks, this week's uncompleted tasks, or today's uncompleted tasks. You can also create your own views by selecting View | Memorize View. You'll then see a dialog box that lets you give the view a name and decide what, exactly, is memorized. Once you've created a memorized view, you can select it at any time from the View menu. (You'll want to change things around elsewhere in the Task List, as described in the next bullet points.)

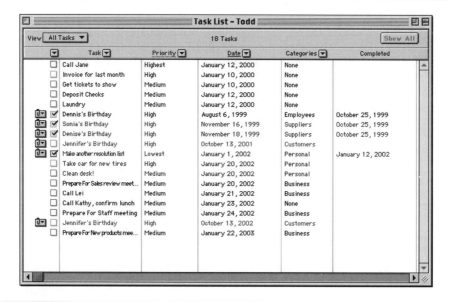

FIGURE 17-4   The Task List lets you manage tasks without flipping through the calendar.

■ You can sort the list by any of the columns listed. For instance, if you want to sort by date, click the heading Date in the Task List. Your list is sorted by date.

TIP *Want to move the columns around? Click and drag the column name to a new location in the Task List and it'll appear when you release the mouse button.*

■ You can also use filters to help you see exactly what you need to see in the Task List. To do this, select the small triangle next to one of the column headings. In the pop-up menu, you can choose one of the filters. For instance, if you choose the Priority column's pop-up menu, you can see only tasks with the Highest priority by selecting that filter. With the Date column's pop-up menu, you can view tasks dated for the next week or for today and tomorrow, for instance. To return to the unfiltered view, choose the pop-up menu again and select No Filter.

SHORTCUT *If you've filtered like mad and you want to quickly get back to the entire list of tasks, choose the Show All button up in the top-right corner of the Task List. This will immediately do away with all filters and show you the complete list.*

■ You can create your own filters if you don't see one that meets your needs. From a column heading's pop-up menu, choose Custom Filter. You'll then see a dialog box that allows you to create a filter that will work for that column head—each dialog box is different since each column offers a different type of information.

SHORTCUT *The checked column has its own filter menu, too. You can choose that pop-up menu and select Unchecked if you'd like to see only the tasks that haven't yet been checked as completed.*

To close the Task List, just click its close box. You can get back to it at any time through its toolbar button or the View | Task List command.

Manage Your Contacts

Aside from serving duty as your taskmaster and date book, the Palm Desktop can also replace that dog-eared address book you have floating around your desk...somewhere. You can create and manage individual contact records for everyone you know, then view them all at once and edit at will. If you've got a Palm OS handheld computer, you can then synchronize your Contact List with the handheld so you can carry your address book with you.

Plus, contacts can be attached to calendar items in the Palm Desktop software. If you've got an appointment with John Doe or Jill Buck, you can attach that contact to the appointment and access that person's information quickly from within the calendar.

Create a New Contact

Before you can manage your contacts, you'll need to create some. These can be colleagues, family members, or friends.

17

If you need to create colleagues or friends, you might consider getting a job; developing a profession; or joining a sports team, hobby group, or a fraternity or sorority. Creating family members is something I'll leave up to you.

Once you have these sorts of people at your disposal, you can create a contact record within the Palm Desktop software to track them. There are, of course, a number of ways to create a contact record:

- From the Instant Palm Desktop menu, choose Create | Contact.

- From within the Palm Desktop software, click the New Contact button in the toolbar.

- In the Palm Desktop software, choose the menu command Create | Contact.

Now you're ready to enter information about your contact in the Contact dialog box.

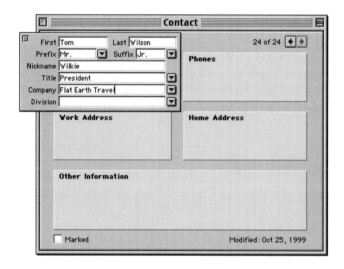

To enter information, just begin typing. The first entry box by default is the First name—type this person's first name, then press the TAB key. Keep entering information in each entry box. If you get to an entry box that you don't have information for or you otherwise want to skip, just press the TAB key again.

Each item has a small triangle pop-up menu next to it. After you've entered a few contacts, you'll notice that these arrows will include the entries you've made previously. And, you'll notice a little "auto-fill" going on: As you type the first few letters of items in many fields, they will be automatically filled in with previous entries. If those entries aren't correct, just keep typing. If the auto-fill entry is correct, you just press TAB to move to the next field. This is a great way to quickly enter data that you've typed before.

The Contact dialog box is divided into different sections, each of which includes different entry elements that help you enter information about this person. When you reach the end of one section (like the Name section), pressing the TAB key takes you to the first entry box in the next section. If you'd like to go directly to another section, select it with the mouse pointer and click once.

You'll also find that some of the entry options include pop-up menus. For instance, in the Phones section you can choose the type of phone number you're entering from the pop-up menu next to each entry. Options include Fax, Home, Main, Cellular, Work, and others.

TIP

You can create your own entries for these menus. Choose Other to enter a one-time name for this menu, like "Upstate" or "Vacation home." When you choose the Other command, you'll see a dialog box that lets you enter this one-time name. If you'd like to permanently add an item to the menu, choose Edit Menu from the pop-up menu. Now you'll see the Edit Menu dialog box that lets you delete, edit, or add items to the menu.

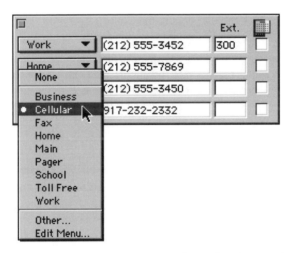

Now, just move through each section and add information that you have about this person. You'll find that in some of the boxes you can choose the type of information you're entering from a pop-up menu—for instance, you can choose the type of address you want to enter from a pop-up menu in one of the address sections. You don't have to enter a Work Address and Home Address (the defaults). You can choose School or Business or you can customize the menu to reflect a different type of address (like billing, shipping, vacation, or whatever you'd like to enter).

In the Other Information section, you'll see a number of Custom entry boxes. To change the name of a Custom entry box, double-click the existing name. In the dialog box, you can customize a number of features, including the name, whether or not items in the entry box are capitalized automatically, whether or not the entries typed are saved to the triangle pull-down menu, and whether or not the entry will include a button icon that runs an AppleScript when clicked. You'll notice, in the Script File menu, there are a few AppleScripts that have already been set up for you.

17

Know something about AppleScript? If you do, you can create more scripts to associate with buttons in the Contact dialog box. Place those scripts in the Scripts folder inside the Palm folder on your hard disk and the scripts will appear in the Script File menu.

Done with all that data entry? Click the Contact dialog box's close box and the entry is saved.

View the Contact List

Once you've gotten a few contacts entered, you're ready to manage them from the Contact List. To open the Contact List, choose the View Contact List button in the toolbar or choose View | Contact List from the menu. You'll see the Contact List in all its shimmering glory, as shown in Figure 17-5.

Once you've got the Contact List open, there are plenty of management tasks you can perform:

- To edit a contact, double-click it in the Contact List. You'll see the Contact dialog box, where you can change the information for this contact.

- If you have a contact who has information that's similar to another contact you'd like to create, select that contact and choose Edit | Duplicate Contact. Now you can change what's different about your new contact, but leave the other information intact.

FIGURE 17-5 The Contact List shows you contacts and selected information about them.

- You can sort the list by any of the columns listed. For instance, if you want to sort by company, click the heading Company in the Contact List. Your list is sorted by company.

Want to move the columns around? Click and drag the column name to a new location in the Contact List and it'll appear when you release the mouse button.

- You can also use filters to help you see exactly what you need to see in the Contact List. To do this, select the small triangle next to one of the column headings. In the pop-up menu, you can choose one of the filters. For instance, if you choose the Categories column's pop-up menu, you can see only contacts within your Personal category by selecting that filter. With the Company column's pop-up menu, you can view contacts who work for a particular company by selecting the company name. To return to the unfiltered view, choose the pop-up menu again and select No Filter.

If you've been filtering a bit and you want to quickly get back to the entire list of contacts, choose the Show All button in the top-right corner of the Contact List. This will immediately do away with all filters and show you the complete list.

- You can create your own filters if you don't see one that meets your needs. From a column heading's pop-up menu, choose Custom Filter. You'll then see a dialog box that allows you to create a filter that will work for that column head—each dialog box is different since each column offers a different type of information.

- From the View menu you can choose All Contacts if you've been filtering and sorting. If you've created a series of filters and sorts that really tickle your fancy, you can store that view of the Contact List by selecting View | Memorize View. You'll then see a dialog box that lets you give the view a name and decide what, exactly, is memorized. Once you've created a memorized view, you can select it at any time from the View menu.

You can view different columns of information, if you'd like to. To select the columns to view, choose View | Columns. In the Columns dialog box, click an item to place or remove the checkmark that denotes whether or not the item will appear in the Contact List. You can then drag items to new locations to change the order in which the columns will appear. A small number next to the checkmark indicates its order (from left to right) in the Contact List.

Attach Contacts to Items

One of the really powerful features in Palm Desktop is the ability to attach a contact to appointments, events, or tasks on your calendar. This makes it easy to associate data between the different parts of your calendar in many different ways. For instance, you can associate a contact with a particular task that involves that person, like a task you create that reminds you to Call Pamela. If you attach Pamela's contact info to the task, you won't have to go digging for her number.

Attach from the Contact List

One way to attach a contact to a particular item is from within the Contact List. With the Contact List open, select the Attach menu for the contact in question (it's the file folder icon with a paperclip on it). In the menu, choose the item you'd like to attach this contact to from the Attach To menu. If you choose Existing Item from the Attach To menu, a small window opens up at the bottom of the screen.

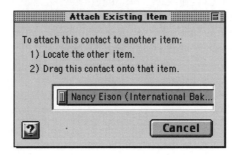

You'll notice that this window is holding a little draggable version of the contact you've chosen. Now, switch to the Calendar or Task List and find the item to which you'd like to attach this contact. Once you've found it, drag the contact from its Attach Existing Item window to the event. When you drop the contact on the event, they become attached.

Now, when you encounter that event, you can select the attached icon to bring up a menu that allows you to view the attached contact, detach the contact, or attach it to another item.

 *If you have both the Contact List and the Task List or Calendar open, you can drag a contact straight from the Contact List to the item to which you'd like to attach the contact. This attaches the contact instantly.*

Auto-Attach

If you don't feel like opening the Contact List, you can attach contacts from within the Calendar or while you're creating an item. If you create an item that has part of a contact's name (or more than one contact's names) in the entry, you'll see the Auto-Attachments dialog box after you've created the item. For instance, creating an appointment called "Lunch with Bob" will bring up the Auto-Attachments dialog box, complete with listings of contacts that may fit the description.

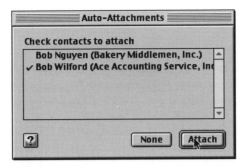

If one of the contacts matches, you can click that contact to place a checkmark, then click the Attach button in the dialog box. That attaches the contact to the item you've created.

If you want to attach a contact to an existing item that includes part of the contact's name, click the item, then choose Create | Attach To | Instant Attach. That will cause Palm Desktop to analyze the event and see if any contacts might match.

Create and Manage Notes

If you synchronize the Palm Desktop software with your Palm OS handheld computer, you'll probably see the immediate value of creating notes in the Palm Desktop program. After all, it can be nice to have extensive notes and reminders on your handheld computer, but it can put a cramp in your style to have to write all of those notes on the handheld's little screen. Well, what if you could type them up (or copy and paste them from your iMac's applications) first, then get them on the handheld computer with a quick menu command?

Even if you don't have a handheld, the Notes feature in Palm Desktop is worth using. It's a great place to put thoughts, ideas, lists, or anything else you'd like to keep track of. Plus, you can attach notes to events, appointments, and tasks in your calendar, making it easy to add extra text to a calendar event. If you've got directions to a meeting, for instance, you can store them in a note, then attach them to an appointment (or to a task or contact). That way the note is safely stored away, and it can be attached to a future item if necessary.

Create the Note

If you've been reading along in this chapter so far, you know there are multiple ways to create items with Palm Desktop. Creating a note is no exception. Here's how:

- From the Instant Palm Desktop menu, choose Create | Note.
- From within the Palm Desktop software, click the New Note button in the toolbar.
- In the Palm Desktop software, choose the menu command Create | Note.

17

All of these result in a new Note window appearing in Palm Desktop, as shown in Figure 17-6.

To create your note, just enter a title in the Title entry box, then press TAB to move on to the Date. Today's date and time are entered automatically, but you can edit them if desired. (Usually, the date is used to reflect when the note was created.) Next, you can select a category or categories for the note. Then, you're ready to edit. Type your note in the text area of the note.

> **TIP** *Want to insert the current date and time without typing them? Click the small clock icon on the left side of the window, just above the text area. That automatically inserts the current date and time at the insertion point. You can do this at different times if you like to keep a running journal or add to an existing note.*

Notes are pretty much plain text—you can't format with fonts, boldface, italics, and other styles. One of the reasons for this is simple—most Palm OS handheld computers can't handle too much styled text, so anything you do in the Note window wouldn't translate well anyway.

Once you're done creating the note, you can click the Close box in the Note window. Your note is done.

> **NOTE** *The Note window is also used for reading notes that you've written previously. In the top-right corner you'll find two arrow keys that can be used to move back and forth between the notes that you've saved. This makes it easier to read notes quickly.*

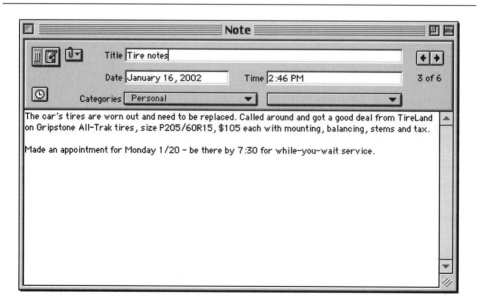

	Note	
Title	Tire notes	← →
Date	January 16, 2002	Time 2:46 PM	3 of 6
Categories	Personal	

The car's tires are worn out and need to be replaced. Called around and got a good deal from TireLand on Gripstone All-Trak tires, size P205/60R15, $105 each with mounting, balancing, stems and tax.

Made an appointment for Monday 1/20 - be there by 7:30 for while-you-wait service.

FIGURE 17-6 The Note window allows you to title, categorize, and edit your note.

View the Note List

Like contacts and tasks, you can view all of your notes using the Note List. To open the Note List, click the View Note List button in the toolbar or choose View | Note List.

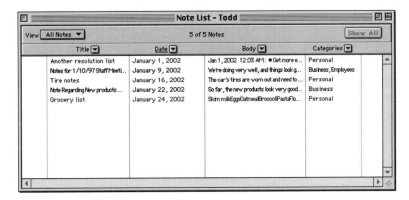

And, as with the Contact List and the Task List, there are a number of management tasks that you can accomplish in the Note List:

- To edit a note, double-click it in the Note List. You'll see the Note window, where you can retitle, edit, or add to your note.

- You can sort the Note List by any of the columns listed. For instance, if you want to sort by title, click the heading Title in the Note List. Your list is sorted alphabetically by title.

TIP *Want to move the columns around? Click and drag the column name to a new location in the Note List and it'll appear when you release the mouse button.*

- You can also use filters to help you see exactly what you need to see in the Note List. To do this, select the small triangle next to one of the column headings. In the pop-up menu, you can choose one of the filters. For instance, if you choose the Categories column's pop-up menu, you can see only notes in your Personal category by selecting that filter. To return to the unfiltered view, choose the pop-up menu again and select No Filter.

SHORTCUT *If you've been filtering a bit and you want to quickly get back to the entire list of notes, choose the Show All button in the top-right corner of the Note List. This will immediately do away with all filters and show you the complete list.*

- You can create your own filters if you don't see one that meets your needs. From a column heading's pop-up menu, choose Custom Filter. You'll then see a dialog box that allows you to create a filter that will work for that column head—each dialog box is different since each column offers a different type of information.

17

■ From the View menu you can choose All Notes if you've been filtering and sorting. If you've created a series of filters and sorts that really tickle your fancy, you can store that view of the Note List by selecting View | Memorize View. You'll then see a dialog box that lets you give the view a name and decide what, exactly, is memorized. Once you've created a memorized view, you can select it at any time from the View menu.

Attach Notes

Like contacts (and most other events, for that matter) you can attach notes to other events in Palm Desktop. This is great for situations where you'd like to store extensive notes about something—say, a log of phone conversations or written directions to a meeting site—and then associate them with a contact, appointment, or other event. Plus, you can associate one note to any number of events, making it easy to cross-reference an important document while you're viewing an event or contact.

Attaching a note works pretty much the same as attaching any other event. There are two basic ways to accomplish it:

■ From the Note window, open the Attach menu (the small menu that looks like a folder and paperclip). Select Attach To, then choose the type of item. If you choose Existing Item, an icon for the note appears in a floating window. Locate the existing item and drag the note icon from the floating window to that item.

■ From the Note List, drag a note to an item in the Calendar, Contact List, or Task List.

Synchronizing with a Palm Device

Although Palm Desktop is a powerful organizer program in its own right, ultimately its goal is to synchronize calendar and note-taking data with a Palm OS handheld computer. If you have one of those, and you have a USB-based PalmConnect kit (which allows a Palm cradle to connect to an iMac, iBook, or similar computer via USB), then you can synchronize your calendar, contacts, and notes with the handheld computer easily.

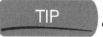 *You don't have to have a PalmConnect USB connection kit, although that's certainly the easiest way. Some USB adapter manufacturers make USB-to-serial connection kits that allow you to connect a serial PalmConnect cable to a USB port on your iMac. See Chapter 23 for details on adapters.*

Set Up HotSync

Once you have your Palm's cradle connected to your iMac, you'll want to make sure you've got HotSync configured correctly. From within Palm Desktop, choose HotSync | Setup. Now, in the HotSync Software Setup window, check to make sure that HotSync is enabled. You may also wish to make sure that the Enable HotSync Software At System

Startup option is checked, so that you can sync data by pushing the cradle's HotSync button instead of using a menu command.

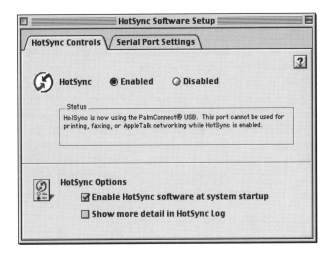

Click the Serial Port Settings tab to set up the connection for your Palm's cradle. With these settings, you can choose whether you'll be synchronizing over a local connection (most likely the USB cable), a modem connection (if your Palm OS handheld has a modem), or both if you'd like the option of switching between the two. Then, set up the speed and port for each relevant setup. (For the local setup, you'll likely choose As Fast As Possible and PalmConnect USB from the pop-up menus.)

Set Conduit Settings

Your next step is to determine what, exactly, you'd like to have synchronized when you perform a HotSync between the Palm OS handheld and your iMac. To do that, choose HotSync | Conduit Settings.

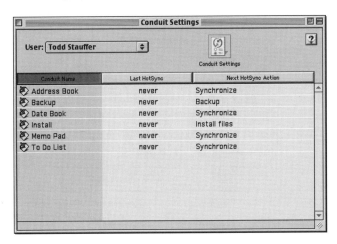

17

The Conduit Settings window shows you the currently installed applications that include a *conduit*. For the Palm software, a conduit is a mechanism by which a Mac OS application and a Palm OS application can share data. For instance, all of the standard applications on a Palm OS computer (To Do, Memo Pad, Address Book, and Date Book) have conduits that allow them to share data with their counterparts in the Palm Desktop software. Likewise, if you install other applications that can share data via a conduit, that conduit will appear in the Conduit Settings window.

To alter a particular conduit, double-click it in the window. Now you'll see a Settings dialog box that gives you the options for that particular conduit. (While the bundled conduits are similar, you'll find that third-party conduits vary more greatly.) Change whatever settings you think are necessary, or leave things as they are, and click the OK button when you're done.

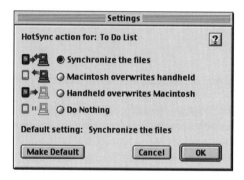

Note that for the bundled applications, the conduit settings allow you to change the way a HotSync works. By default, a HotSync causes all data to be synchronized between the two devices—that is, any event or item that appears on one computer but not the other will now appear on both computers. That's useful, but it may not be how you always want things handled. If you'd prefer to have one of the two computers be the dominant partner— for instance, so that all data on the handheld is overwritten with the data that's in the Palm Desktop software—you can choose that from the Settings menu for certain conduits.

Synchronizing Data

Once you've got your settings in place, synchronizing between the Palm OS handheld and the Palm Desktop software is simple. Simply place the handheld in its cradle and press the HotSync button. You'll see the HotSync alert box appear and a status bar will indicate that your Palm OS handheld is being located. Once located, your data will begin synchronizing.

If you don't see the HotSync alert dialog, check the connection between the Palm's cradle and your iMac. You should also ensure that HotSync is enabled on the HotSync Enabled dialog box and that your local connection settings are correct on the Serial Port Settings tab.

Install Palm Applications

You can also use the Palm Desktop software to install applications on your Palm OS handheld. To do that, choose HotSync | Install Applications from the menu. In the Install Handheld Files dialog box, drag Palm OS applications to the Applications list. (Palm applications have the three-letter extension ".prc" as part of their filenames.) Figure 17-7 shows files being dragged to the Install Handheld Files window.

Now, the next time you perform a HotSync, these files will be installed on the Palm OS device. To perform the HotSync immediately, place the Palm OS handheld in its cradle and press the HotSync button.

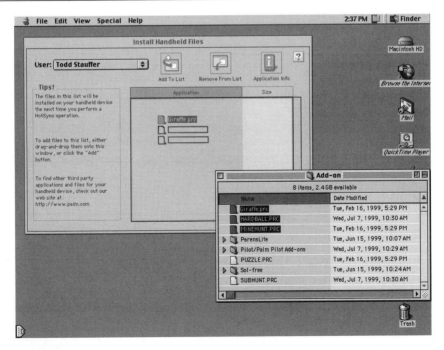

FIGURE 17-7   Installing files on your Palm OS handheld

Part III

Get Online

Chapter 18

Manage Your E-mail

How to...

- Set up your e-mail account
- Check your mail
- Read messages and respond
- Create new e-mail messages
- Send and receive e-mail attachments
- Create mail rules to automate your mail
- Add more than one account or more than one user

Y ou may have bought your iMac for the express purpose of getting e-mail—a lot of people do. Even if it wasn't your primary goal, you probably think e-mail is a big part of the computing experience. Electronic mail (e-mail) gives you the opportunity to communicate inexpensively and rather quickly in a written format. What were once letters between family, friends, and business associates have become electronic messages. What used to take days now arrives in seconds.

In this chapter I'll focus on Outlook Express, Microsoft's full-featured e-mail program that's included with the iMac. If you want to experiment, though, you'll find a number of demos and shareware versions of e-mail client applications online—check out the sites mentioned in Chapter 20 that allow you to download and install shareware applications. Popular e-mail programs include Eudora Pro and Eudora Lite (**http://www.eudora.com/**), Mailsmith (**http://www.barebones.com/**), and the Messenger components of Netscape's full Communicator suite of Internet tools, which is also included with your iMac (**http://www.netscape.com/**).

*The latest version of Outlook Express, version 5.0, became available during this writing and is covered in this chapter. Many iMacs, however, shipped with Outlook Express 4.0 or 4.5. I'll try to point out the differences between the versions in this chapter, but if you have an earlier version, you can upgrade by visiting **http://www.microsoft.com/oe/** on the Web.*

Is Your Account Set Up?

The first thing you'll need before you can send and receive e-mail is an e-mail account. Most likely you already have one—after all, an e-mail account is created for you when you sign up for Internet access. And the best part is, with most ISPs you'll have an e-mail account that corresponds to your Internet account name. If you were given the user name toddstauffer when you created the account, for instance, then your e-mail address is probably toddstauffer@earthlink.net (assuming, of course, that you're using the Earthlink service).

Plus, if you've walked through the Internet Setup Assistant in Chapter 1 and taken a quick look at getting your e-mail in Chapter 2, then you've already tested to see if your e-mail account is properly set up. If everything works and you can receive e-mail, move on to the section "Get, Read, and Reply to E-mail," later in this chapter. If you're having trouble, though, you may need to set up the account manually, which is covered in this section.

How E-mail Addresses Work

In order to receive e-mail, you have to tell others your e-mail address. You may also need to enter the e-mail address when you set up your e-mail program. (Or if you ever change e-mail programs, you may need to enter it again.)

The e-mail address can be broken up into three or more different parts. These are

- **Account Name**   The name that identifies you or your e-mail account (if more than one person is using it) is unique among the accounts on your ISP's mail server computer. That's the "toddstauffer" part of toddstauffer@earthlink.net.

- **Server Computer**   Some, but not all, mail servers will include the actual name of the mail server computer in the address. An example might be todd@mail.mac-upgrade.com where "mail" is the actual mail server computer.

- **Domain Name**   The domain name is a name given to a group of computers at a particular organization. If you work for Apple, for instance, your address might be todd@apple.com. The "apple" part suggests the domain for that company.

- **Domain Name Extension**   Sometimes considered part of the domain name, the domain name extension suggests the type of organization you're dealing with. A commercial entity (like Apple) gets a .com, while an ISP (like Earthlink) generally gets a .net extension, as in earthlink.net. Other extensions include .edu (educational), .mil (military), .org (organization), and country codes for organizations and companies outside the United States like .uk (United Kingdom), .fr (France), and .au (Australia).

It's not terribly important to remember what each part of an e-mail address is intended to signify. What's more important is remembering that whenever you enter an e-mail address, you need to enter the entire address as you've been given it, so that it can reach its destination account. Otherwise, you may not be entering enough information to deliver the e-mail. I still have that problem with people who don't put the suite number in my office address. I can't get the package if it's not properly coded, just as with e-mail.

The Internet Control Panel

Using the Internet control panel, it's possible to quickly and easily customize your e-mail account setup. You've likely already used the Internet Setup Assistant, so the basics are already entered regarding your e-mail account. If you dig into the Internet control panel, though, you can change some options, too.

NOTE   *If your iMac is currently running Mac OS 8.1, it doesn't have an Internet control panel. Instead, there's a utility called Internet Config, located in the Internet Utilities folder inside your Internet folder. You can use that utility to change settings discussed in this section.*

The Internet control panel serves as a repository of information about your Internet account(s) and preferences. This is good because it means you can change e-mail or Web applications and still have all of your arcane Internet addresses stored within the Mac OS itself. That way you don't have to repeat the setup process if you decide to use a different application (see Figure 18-1).

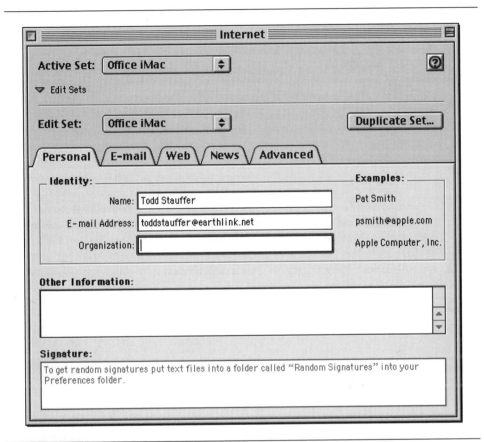

FIGURE 18-1   The Internet control panel is a convenient repository of Internet addresses for e-mail, Web browsing, discussion group preferences, and more.

The Personal tab is where you enter information that recipients of your e-mail messages will see. This is an important distinction; technically, you can enter anything you want and it won't affect the way that your e-mail program logs into your ISP's mail server computer—that stuff is on the E-mail tab. These entries are still important, though, because they tell your recipients who you are and how to respond to you. Here are some things you can customize on the Personal tab:

■ **Name**   This is your full name as you'd like it to appear in e-mail messages. The "From" section of messages would include a portion with your full name, like "toddstauffer@earthlink.com (Todd Stauffer)" if you enter your name here.

18

■ **E-mail Address**   You can create a special "reply to" address. This may or may not be different from your e-mail account. For instance, I have a domain name set up for my Mac-Upgrade Web site—mac-upgrade.com. I like people to send e-mail to todd@mac-upgrade.com. It's easy to remember and I can change it easily if I change ISPs. The actual e-mail *account*, though, is "todds@isp.net" because I have an ISP that manages that mac-upgrade.com account. Since the ISP manages it, I actually log into the todds@isp.net account on that ISP's mail server, not into the todd@mac-upgrade.com account. The *e-mail account* is entered on the E-mail tab. The one you're entering here is the e-mail address where people can reach you.

NOTE   *There isn't always a difference between an e-mail address and e-mail account. For instance, if you have a regular Earthlink account, you probably don't have a separate e-mail address and e-mail account. They're probably both you@earthlink.net. There can also be subtle differences, like an e-mail address of tstauffer@tamu.edu and an e-mail account of tstauffer@science.tamu.edu.*

■ **Organization**   Enter the name of your organization, if it's relevant. It'll show up in the *headers,* the information at the top of your e-mail message.

■ **Signature**   This is a block of text sent at the bottom of your messages to identify you, offer related Web sites, and so forth. People usually put three or four lines of text saying who they are, give a phone number, list accomplishments, share a favorite quote or a joke. Etiquette dictates that this be kept to six lines or less and not overwhelmed with dashes, asterisks, and so on—just tasteful and interesting.

```
----------------
Todd A. Stauffer
<TStauffer@aol.com> <http://shutup101.com/todd/> for Book Updates

It's Here!! Mac Upgrade and Repair Bible <http://www.mac-upgrade.com/>
Disk Doctors -- Knowledge TV, 8:30 PM (EST) Thursdays
    <http://www.jec.edu/ktv/index3.html> for local channel info
```

Now, click the E-mail tab and you're ready to enter the information your e-mail program will need to access the ISP's mail server computer and get your mail. Most of these entries have already been completed for you by the Internet Setup Assistant. You can change them if desired or necessary—sometimes you'll get a new password or a mail server address from your system administrator. You'll enter those here on the E-mail tab. (You can also rerun the Internet Setup Assistant, which is located in the Internet folder on your main hard disk.)

There are two elements I want to point out for customizing purposes:

■ **E-mail Notification**   In e-mail programs that fully recognize the Internet control panel, you can determine how they'll tell you about new messages by placing a checkmark next to every option you want active.

■ **Default E-mail Application**   Choose the application that gets loaded whenever you double-click the Mail icon or otherwise click an e-mail link in an Internet-savvy application.

Get, Read, and Reply to E-mail

The checking part is easy—in fact, we've already gone over it in Chapter 2:

1. If you have modem access to the Internet, fire up your Internet connection via either the PPP control panel, the Remote Access control panel, or the Control Strip's Remote Access button. (If you've set up PPP or Remote Access to dial automatically, you can skip this step. If you have an Ethernet or wireless connection to the Internet, you don't need to do anything special.)

NOTE   *You can set your Remote Access connection to dial your ISP automatically whenever you use an Internet application. See Chapter 23 for details.*

2. Once the Internet connection is active, click the Send and Receive button on Outlook Express's window. (If you don't see it, select Window | Outlook Express.) You can also use the keyboard shortcut ⌘-M to send and receive all mail.

NOTE   *If you have Outlook Express 5.0, you can use the Send & Receive button in the toolbar as a menu, where you can choose to download e-mail from individual e-mail accounts if you have more than one.*

3. If you have mail, you'll see the Progress window appear, complete with an indicator that shows you how many messages you have and how many are left to come in. The progress bar indicates that Outlook Express is communicating with the mail server. If you don't see the Progress window, you can view it by selecting Window | Progress.

Once all of your mail has been downloaded, it'll appear in the Inbox window pane of Outlook Express. If you don't see it, you may not have the Inbox selected. Click the Inbox icon on the left side of the Outlook window and the Inbox will appear. (You may also need to scroll up or down in the Inbox to see your mail if you already have lots of messages.)

18

Read Your Mail

Unread mail appears in the Inbox's message list in bold type, so that it's clear you haven't read it yet. To read it, just click once on the topic of the message—the message text appears in the bottom window (the *preview pane*, as Microsoft calls it), where you can scroll to read the message. If you prefer, you can also double-click a message subject, which causes a new window to appear, containing that message.

Once a message has been read, it stays in the Inbox message list but its subject and other information switch to plain text, so that any other unread messages stand out with bold type.

Change the View

Want to switch the view around a bit? Each message in the Inbox message list takes up a full row—the columns represent the subject, sender, date, and other information. You might notice that these columns work a little like the columns in Finder windows. You can click the column heading in each case to change the organization of the Inbox (see Figure 18-2).

The Folder List

Click the heading to organize by that column.

Click again to change the order.

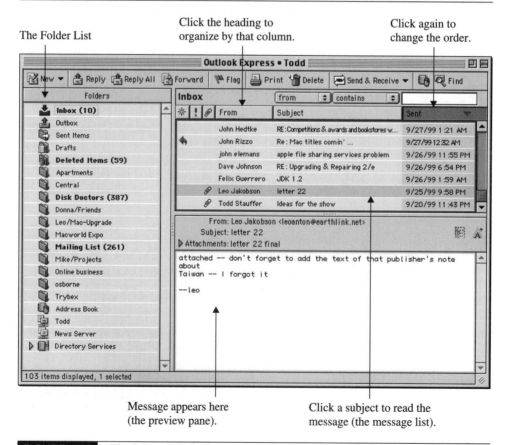

Message appears here (the preview pane).

Click a subject to read the message (the message list).

FIGURE 18-2 The Inbox interface

Once you have the message list arranged according to one of the column headings, you'll notice that it's in a particular order, either ascending or descending. You can change that order by clicking the heading again. You'll notice that the little triangle flips sides to indicate that you've switched from ascending to descending order or vice versa.

You can choose the columns that are shown in the Inbox. Choose View | Columns, then choose the column you want to display or hide. A displayed column has a check next to it. Also, you can organize the Inbox by read/unread status. Just click the column at the far left. Click it again to change the sort order.

Filter the Mail

If you have a whole lot of messages in your message list, you can filter the view—that is, you can show only messages that match a certain string of characters or a particular word.

In Outlook Express 5.0 you have two menus – the first menu allows you to choose what portion of the message to filter (from, to, subject) and the second menu allows you to choose how to filter (starts with, contains). Then you enter the letters or keyword you want to use for the filter. The result will be many fewer e-mail messages listed, since only those that meet your criterion will appear.

In Outlook Express 4.0 and 4.5 there is only one menu. Choose what to display from the small menu just above the subject headings, then enter a few letters or a keyword that indicates what you're trying to find.

Inbox			subject ⬍	contains ⬍	let
❋	!	🖉	From	Subject	Sent ▼
		🖉	Leo Jakobson	the mega letter	10/23/99 3:36 PM
			Leo Jakobson	updating letter bin.txt on site	10/23/99 1:47 AM
		🖉	Leo Jakobson	letter 23	10/3/99 8:01 PM
		🖉	Leo Jakobson	letter 22	9/25/99 9:58 PM

Reply to a Message

If a message deserves a reply, then click the Reply button while you're viewing that message and a new window appears, ready for your reply.

You should see that the original message has already been "quoted" for you—that just means that the original message has been included in your reply so that the person you're replying to can have his or her memory jogged about what, exactly, you're replying to. Now you can just begin typing, creating a message that probably looks something like:

```
Mike:
I'm glad to come. You know me...I'll bring my queso dip!
- Todd
----------
>From: Mike L. Lawrence <mike@earthlink.net>
>To: <toddstauffer@earthlink.net>
>Subject: Party
>Date: Feb 14, 2001, 9:50 AM

>I was hoping you could come to the party.
>So far, people are just signing up to say what they'll bring.
>
>ml
```

Notice that the quoted part appears at the bottom of the message with the new reply (the part I wrote) at the top of the message. This is Outlook Express's default treatment of quotes. You can tell the quoted text, by the way, from the greater than sign (>) that comes in front of every line.

Another common method is to go through the message itself and reply after a particular quoted spot. That makes it looks something like:

```
>>I was hoping you could come to the party.
I'm glad to come!
>>So far, people are just signing up to say what they'll bring.
You know me...I'll bring my queso dip!

- Todd
```

This is the more common Internet tradition for quoting. First, it gives a solid sense of a back-and-forth conversation. It also takes up less space, since Internet etiquette dictates that you edit the message so that only the relevant parts are quoted. Third, in many e-mail programs (including Outlook Express) the quoted text is a different color than the reply text when you receive a message with quotes in it. That makes it really easy to quickly read the new message.

Of course, the Outlook Express default method doesn't force your readers to page through the message to see the new parts—everything new is right up top. If the readers need their memories jogged, they can scroll down. So, the final decision about quoting is really up to you, as long as you remember to keep your quoted sections as short as possible.

You can change the way OE handles quoting by default. In Outlook Express 5.0, choose Edit | Preferences, then click the Compose tab and select "Place insertion point after default test." In Outlook Express 4.0 and 4.5, choose Edit | Preferences, then click Message Composition. Put a checkmark next to the Use Internet Style Replies option. Your cursor appears at the bottom of the quoted text (ready for you to edit the message) instead of at the top.

When you're done with the reply, you're ready to click buttons in the Reply window:

- **Send (or Send Now)**   This one sends the message immediately if you're still online. If you're not connected, and you don't have your connection set up to connect automatically, Outlook Express will store the message in the Outbox and wait until you next click the Send and Receive button.

- **Send Later**   In Outlook Express 4.5 and above, you have the option of clicking the Send Later button. This places the message in the Outbox even if you're currently online. The message is sent the next time you select the Send and Receive command.

- **Save (or Save as Draft)**   This saves the message in the Drafts folder. It won't be sent until you open it and click the Send button. Drafts are just that—rough versions of e-mail messages you don't yet want to send.

Don't forget your drafts. The Drafts folder label becomes boldface when it contains mail that hasn't been sent. When you see that boldface label, check every once in a while so you don't forget about a message you still need to edit and send. (I do it all the time.)

- **Add Attachments**   Click this button to send an attachment. I'll discuss sending and receiving attachments later in this chapter.

- **Signature**   Click this button to add your signature to the bottom of the message. This will only work if you've actually added a signature in the Internet control panel or in the Outlook Express preferences.

- **Contact**   This allows you to open the Contact Manager so you can find and add other recipients if you need to do so. (This menu does not appear in Outlook Express 5.0.)

- **Options**   In Outlook Express 5.0, you can use the Options button menu to choose from a few different options, including whether or not the message is formatted in HTML, what priority is assigned to the message, what character set to use, and whether or not the sent message should be stored in a folder after it's sent successfully.

- **Rewrap**   In Outlook Express 5.0, you can click the Rewrap button to clean up the display of the text if it's not wrapping correctly in the text window.

18

How to ... Reply to All Senders

This is a special case—if you're reading a message that was sent to more people than just you, you can send your reply to all recipients. If Mindy sends a message to you, Jack, and Tina, the question is whether or not you want to send a reply just to Mindy, or if you want everyone to see the reply. If you want to send it just to the original sender, click Reply; if you want to send it to all recipients to keep the group conversation alive, click Reply All.

Otherwise, things work the same. Edit the message, then click Send to send it or Save to save it as a draft.

Create a New Message

If you're interested in sending a new message, it's even a little easier to do than replying. The only difference is that you need to know the e-mail address of the person you want to send the message to and to write a subject for the message.

Here's how to send it:

1. Click the New button in the toolbar or select File | New | Mail Message.

> **NOTE** *If you have more than one account set up in Outlook Express, you should choose the account from which you want to send the message in the Account menu.*

2. In the window, enter an e-mail address for the To box. In Outlook Express 5.0, press TAB to enter another To recipient.

> **NOTE** *In Outlook Express 4.0 or 4.5, you can type a comma (,) between each e-mail address if you're entering more than one. You can also press TAB to move between entry boxes in these versions of Outlook Express.*

3. Now, select the CC tab to type an e-mail address if you'd like to send a "courtesy copy" to anyone. Press TAB.

4. Next, you can select the BCC tab and type an e-mail address in the BCC box (blind courtesy copy). If you do so, this person's e-mail address won't appear to any other recipients. Only you and the BCC recipient will know that you sent a copy to that person. You can have more than one recipient on this line, too—type a comma between e-mail addresses.

5. Now you'll enter a subject for your message. With any e-mail message your subject should be informative without being terribly long. Press TAB.

6. Type the message in the body of the message window, then press the Signature button if you're set up to add a signature to your messages.

From here it's pretty much like a reply—press Send or Save, or add attachments as I'll discuss later in this chapter.

 *You can set up Outlook Express to check the spelling of all outgoing messages by choosing Edit | Preferences, then clicking the Spelling button. Put a checkmark next to the options you want active. Choose Always Check Spelling Before Sending, for instance, to have the spell checker look over a message after you've pressed the Send button. This only works if you have Microsoft Office installed, since Outlook Express uses the dictionary capabilities of Microsoft Office to provide spell checking.*

Delete a Message

You can highlight a message in the message window and click the Delete button to delete it from the message list. It's not gone forever, though; it's simply moved to the Deleted Items folder, where it stays until a prescribed time, such as the next time you quit Outlook Express. Open the Deleted Items folder to get a message back, if you like. You can also drag messages from the message list to the Deleted Items folder to delete them without going through the process of clicking the Delete button.

Empty the Deleted Items folder by selecting it in the folder list and choosing Tools | Run Schedules | Empty Deleted Items Folder.

You can set Outlook Express 5.0 to empty the Deleted Items folder when you quit the program. To make this setting, choose Tools | Schedules and double-click the Empty Deleted Items Folder entry. In the When section of the Define Schedule window, pull down the menu marked Manually and choose On Quit. Now click OK in the window.

 In Outlook Express 4.0 and 4.5, you switch to the Deleted Messages folder and choose Edit | Empty Deleted Messages. You can also set Outlook Express to automatically empty the Deleted Messages folder by selecting Edit | Preferences and choosing Startup & Quit. Under the Quit Settings, place a checkmark next to Empty Deleted Messages Folder.

Format Your Message

You may have been wondering why I haven't mentioned those text tools—font size, bold, italics, and so on—there in the message editing window. (If you don't see the tools, open a new message and choose Format | HTML from the menu. In Outlook Express 4.0 and 4.5, the command is Format | Rich Text.) These tools use the HyperText Markup Language—the same language used to create Web pages—in order to format the document. That makes it look pretty and adds practical value, like giving you the freedom to create bullet lists and align your text.

There's a reason I haven't mentioned those tools: HTML e-mail can be annoying. Not everyone has the capability to read HTML e-mail, so, instead of seeing a formatted document, they see something that looks more like Figure 18-3.

If you plan to use HTML controls, you'll want to do so only when you're reasonably sure that your recipients are also using an HTML-aware mail program. If they are, though, go ahead and format. You'll find that most of the tools work the same way that they do in a word processor or similar program. Here are the basics:

- **Text** You can either select a text size or style before typing, or highlight the selection and format its size or appearance (bold, italic, underlined) after typing it in. You can also press ⌘-B for bold text, ⌘-I for italics, and ⌘-U for underlining while typing.

- **Lists** You should type each list item, pressing RETURN between each. Then, highlight the entire list and choose either the Bullet List button or the Numbered List button.

- **Indent** Again, you're probably best off typing the paragraph first, then choosing to indent it. This is actually called a "blockquote" in HTML parlance—the entire paragraph is indented as if it were a long quote in an academic paper or book.

- **Alignment** Choose alignment before or after typing. There is no justified setting—just left, center, and right.

- **Color** Specify the text color before or after typing (highlight the text, then choose the color). Click on the triangle next to the Text color button (the letter A with a color under it) to choose the text color. You can also click on the triangle next to the the background color button (the paint can) in the formatting toolbar to choose a background color from the list.

Send and Get Attachments

Outlook Express can help you send a file—a document, application, or compressed archive of different sorts of files—to recipients through Internet e-mail. In fact, you can even send attachments to recipients using Intel-compatible PCs. The only major limitation is that it can take a while to upload and download attachments. While most e-mail messages are about 5-10 kilobytes in size, the typical graphical image document—a photo, for instance—begins at 50,000 kilobytes and spirals upward from there.

There are two rules about sending attachments to someone. First, etiquette dictates that the person should be expecting the attachment or otherwise not likely to balk at receiving it (for instance, they're employees or colleagues and they need the file). It's important to remember that a lot of people pay for their time online and their e-mail service—a very large download could cost them time or money.

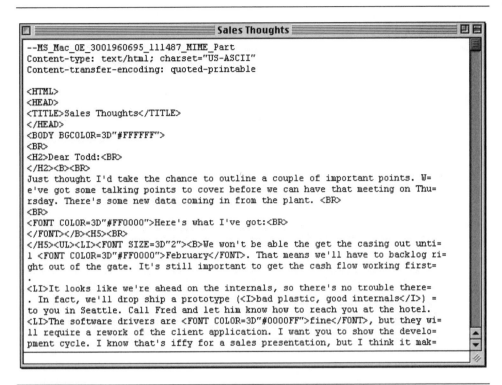

```
──────────────────────────── Sales Thoughts ────────────────────────
--MS_Mac_OE_3001960695_111487_MIME_Part
Content-type: text/html; charset="US-ASCII"
Content-transfer-encoding: quoted-printable

<HTML>
<HEAD>
<TITLE>Sales Thoughts</TITLE>
</HEAD>
<BODY BGCOLOR=3D"#FFFFFF">
<BR>
<H2>Dear Todd:<BR>
</H2><B><BR>
Just thought I'd take the chance to outline a couple of important points. W=
e've got some talking points to cover before we can have that meeting on Thu=
rsday. There's some new data coming in from the plant. <BR>
<BR>
<FONT COLOR=3D"#FF0000">Here's what I've got:<BR>
</FONT></B><H5><BR>
</H5><UL><LI><FONT SIZE=3D"2"><B>We won't be able the get the casing out unti=
l <FONT COLOR=3D"#FF0000">February</FONT>. That means we'll have to backlog ri=
ght out of the gate. It's still important to get the cash flow working first=
.
<LI>It looks like we're ahead on the internals, so there's no trouble there=
. In fact, we'll drop ship a prototype (<I>bad plastic, good internals</I>) =
to you in Seattle. Call Fred and let him know how to reach you at the hotel.
<LI>The software drivers are <FONT COLOR=3D"#0000FF">fine</FONT>, but they wi=
ll require a rework of the client application. I want you to show the develo=
pment cycle. I know that's iffy for a sales presentation, but I think it mak=
```

FIGURE 18-3   An HTML-formatted e-mail in a non-HTML mail program.

Second, make sure that the attachment arrives in the correct format for them to use. For that to be the case, know what sort of computer and e-mail program they're using. That way you'll know how to *compress* and *encode* your attachment.

Encode the Attachment

By definition, Internet e-mail programs are designed to send text, not computer files like documents, programs, or system code. Because of this limitation, it's historically been up to other Internet protocols, like the File Transfer Protocol, to focus on sending files from one place to another.

There is a way to get around this limitation, though, and it's exactly what Outlook Express and many other mail programs do to send an attached file—it's called *encoding*. Through the process of encoding, a file made up of binary data (ones and zeros) is literally translated into a transmittable format following a particular encoding method. Once the file arrives on the other side of the Internet transmission, it's decoded back to its original form. In the meantime, even after you've sent or received the file, it's useless until it's translated back to a usable format.

18

There are four basic methods for encoding supported by Outlook Express:

- **uuencode**　Also called "Unix-to-Unix encode," this one is most popular when sending to Unix machines. These days, despite the name, most versions of Netscape and many Windows-based e-mail programs recognize the format.

- **BinHex**　This is probably the most popular Mac format, especially useful when sending from a Mac to a Mac and if you're transmitting Mac-specific documents and/or applications. Some, but not all, Unix- and PC-based e-mail programs recognize BinHex.

- **Base64/MIME**　This is arguably the most popular encoding/decoding format for Microsoft Windows. This one is a safe bet if you know you're sending to a Windows PC.

- **AppleDouble**　This is probably the best to choose if you regularly send files to both Windows and Mac users. It maintains the special elements of a Mac file (if you're sending to another Mac) while being compatible with most Windows e-mail programs, too.

In Outlook Express, you can't individually encode an attachment. In Outlook Express 5.0, open the Preferences (Edit | Preferences) and choose the Compose tab, then click the button marked "Click here for attachment options." (In Outlook Express 4.0 or 4.5, set the encoding preference by selecting Edit | Preferences and clicking Message Composition. You'll see a pull-down menu for the encoding process.)

> **TIP**　*It's probably best to choose AppleDouble (which is safest for most circumstances), then come back and change to uuencode if you plan to send specifically to a Unix user or to Base64 if you're having trouble with AppleDouble sending to Windows users.*

Compress the Attachment

Files can be compressed (as described in Chapter 20) so that they're easier to transmit over the Internet. You can perform the compression two different ways. The first method allows you to compress from within Outlook Express. Choose Edit | Preferences and click the Compose tab. Now, click the button "Click here for attachment options." Turn on the option Macintosh (StuffIt) under the Compression heading. Now, attachments are compressed using the StuffIt format. The problem with this, though, is that the StuffIt/DropStuff standard is not as prevalent on the Windows platform as it is on the Mac platform. (Aladdin Expander for Windows is available, but it's not as universally available as it is on Macs, iMacs, and iBooks, where StuffIt Expander and DropStuff are actually installed with many applications.)

In Outlook Express 4.0 and 4.5 you can turn StuffIt compression on and off by choosing Message | Compress Attachments. This activates the option so that any subsequent attachments are compressed.

So, the second method is to compress the file beforehand using another program such as PKZip, discussed in more detail in Chapter 20. That way, you can simply attach the file after it's been compressed and send it on its way.

Most of these compression utilities do it automatically, but if you're sending compressed files, especially to Windows users, you'll want to make sure the filename has its three-letter extension like .zip or .sit (this is the standard extension for StuffIt archives).

Add the Attachment

In Outlook Express, add an attachment to an outgoing message by dragging it from the Finder into the message window or selecting Message | Add Attachments. To remove attachments that you decide not to send, select Message | Remove Attachments. Now, send your e-mail as usual and the attachment goes right along for the ride. Remember, it may take a while to transmit over the Internet, especially if the attachment is an image, application, or large document.

Get an Attachment

E-mail messages that include attachments appear in your Inbox list with a small paperclip icon. There are a number of different ways you can receive an attachment from an e-mail message if one has been sent to you:

1. Highlight a message with an attachment in the Inbox list (or another folder's list) and choose Message | Save All Attachments. This displays a dialog box that allows you to choose a folder on your iMac where the attachments will be saved.

2. In Outlook Express 5.0, click the disclosure triangle labeled Attachments in the preview pane or message window. You'll see icons for the attachments. You can highlight attachment(s) and click Open to open them in their associated application or Save to save them to your iMac's hard disk.

3. In Outlook Express 4.0 or 4.5, you'll see attachments in the paperclip menu that appears in the preview pane when you view a message that has attachments. From that paperclip menu, choose All to save the files to your iMac's disk or choose the attachment's name to open it in its associated application.

4. In Outlook Express 4.0 or 4.5, you can view the full message window and drag the icons for attachments from the bottom of the window to the desktop.

18

Opening attachments to e-mail messages is one known way to contract a computer virus. You should only open or use attachments from known senders and only when the attachment is expected from that user. It's possible for some viruses to automatically send virus-infected attachments automatically from a user's e-mail program, making it look like the user sent the message to you. If you're not expecting an attachment, don't open it until you've talked to the sender and confirmed that he or she meant to send you the attachment.

Use More Than One Account

Do you have more than one e-mail account? You'll be happy to know that Outlook Express can handle mail from more than one e-mail account, allowing you to download it all at one time, manage it all in one Inbox, and, as we've already seen, send your e-mail from the account of your choice.

TIP *One way to get additional accounts is to sign onto a Web-based e-mail service like HotMail (**http://www.hotmail.com/**) or USA.Net (**http://www.usa.net/**). Look for one that offers "POP" (Post Office Protocol, the standard e-mail server protocol) access so you can download your mail to Outlook Express. Or, if you have Outlook Express 5.0, it specifically supports downloading e-mail from your HotMail account.*

Creating a new account is pretty much the same as creating the original account except that you don't get to use Internet Setup Assistant or the Internet control panel. You'll have to dig into Outlook Express's preferences.

Here's how to add an account to Outlook Express:

1. In Outlook Express 5.0, choose Tools | Accounts. In Outlook Express 4.0 or 4.5, choose Edit | Preferences (or click the Preferences button on the Outlook Express window) and click the E-mail button.

2. In Outlook Express 5.0, choose Mail from the New button menu. In Outlook Express 4.0 or 4.5, click the New Account button near the top of the dialog box.

3. In Outlook Express 5.0, the Account Setup Assistant takes over from here. You can use the Assistant to set up an existing or new e-mail account. You can also create a free HotMail account from within the Assistant. If you're using Outlook Express 4.0 or 4.5, enter a name for the account and choose POP. Click OK.

4. Now, in Outlook Express 4.0 or 4.5, enter all of the information for this account. Notice that Account ID just requires your e-mail account name, not the full e-mail account address. The e-mail address up top, though, should be your full reply-to address.

5. If you want this to be your default account (the one that you've automatically set up to send e-mail from, unless you change it), then choose Make Default. When you're done entering information, click OK.

The account is created. Now, whenever you create a new message you have the choice of using the new account instead of your original one. Similarly, when you select Send and Receive, both (or all) of your e-mail accounts will be accessed and the new e-mail will show up in the Inbox. (Notice that each message has a column entry that tells you what account it was sent to.)

You can also check this account individually. In Outlook Express 5.0, choose the account name from the Send and Receive button menu. Or, in all versions, choose Tools | Send and Receive, then select the name of the account that you want to check.

TIP *Want this account to not get checked when you check others? In Outlook Express 5.0, open the Accounts window (Tools | Accounts) and double-click the account name. Now, you can use the option "Include this account in my 'Send and Receive All' schedule" to determine whether or not it is checked when you check others. In earlier Outlook Express versions, head back to Edit | Preferences, click E-mail, and choose the account from the menu at the top of the dialog box. Now, click Advanced. Among other options, you'll find Do Not Include This Server With Send & Receive All. Select that and you'll only be able to check the e-mail individually.*

Note that this is how you manage multiple accounts that the *same* person uses. If you have more than one person using Outlook Express, check out the section "Add a New User," later in this chapter.

Organize Your E-mail

Once you start to get some messages you'll probably become interested in managing those messages, putting them into folders, and storing them away. Outlook Express makes that easy enough to do, allowing you to create folders and subfolders for filing your e-mail. But Outlook Express does more than that to help you organize your e-mail.

Create and Delete Folders

The most basic organizational step is adding folders to the folder pane that runs down the side of the Outlook Express interface. You may have already experimented with these folders—if you click them once, the contents appear in the right-side pane. You can also double-click a folder to open it in its own window.

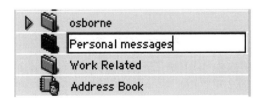

18

Creating a new folder is simple—just choose File I New I Folder. The folder appears in the Folder List, with the name highlighted and ready to edit. Type the name for your folder and press RETURN when you're done. If you need to reedit the folder name, click once on the name and wait a few seconds, just as though you're editing a folder name in the Finder.

To move messages to the folder, select them in the message list, then drag-and-drop items from there to the folder. You can also CTRL-click on a particular message, choose Move To from the pop-up menu, then choose the folder to which you want to move the message.

To delete a folder, select it in the Folder List, then choose Edit I Delete Folder.

Create a Subfolder

You may find it useful to place subfolders within main folders in the Folder List. That makes it easier to stay organized and see the entire list at once without forcing too much scrolling. To create a subfolder, select the folder that will be its parent in the Folder List, then choose File I New I Subfolder. The subfolder appears, ready to have its name edited.

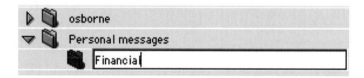

You can also take an existing folder and drag-and-drop it on another folder to cause the dragged folder to become a subfolder. The parent folder now has a triangle. When it's pointed down, you see the subfolder; when it's pointed to the right, you don't.

With the subfolder created, you may think it's harder to drag-and-drop messages from the message list to a subfolder, but that's not true. There are two ways to do it. The obvious one is to click on the triangle to reveal the subfolders, then select your messages in the message list and drag them to one of the revealed subfolders.

There's also another way. Select and drag your message(s) from the message list to the "closed" triangle. Point directly at the triangle, and it should pop "open." Now the subfolders are revealed and you can drag the message(s) to the subfolder of your choice.

 *Folders in the Folder List are alphabetized, so the rules for organizing the Apple menu apply to the Folder List—a space in front of the name moves folders to the top of the list and a bullet (OPTION-8) can move items toward the bottom of the list.*

Automate Using Rules

Need to automate your e-mail? Outlook Express allows you to build filters (called *rules*) that look at incoming mail and compare the messages against certain criteria. You create a rule for what happens to a particular e-mail message. If the mail matches a rule, then a

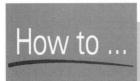

Compact Folders in Outlook Express 4.0 and 4.5

After working with folders for a while in Outlook Express 4.0 or 4.5, you'll find that it's a good idea to *compact* your folders, a process that cleans up the database entries and recovers the storage space that had been used for deleted files. You can compact your folders either manually or automatically. To do it manually, select Tools | Compact and then select the folder you want to compact or All Local Folders. You can see the potential savings by pulling down this menu. Entries like "Inbox (+25k)" tell you that you can save 25 kilobytes of space by compacting that folder.

The option to automatically compact folders is in the Preferences dialog box under the Startup & Quit settings. There you can check the Automatically Compact Folders option and type in the entry box how much space will be saved before the automatic compacting takes place. (You can wait until 50 or 100 kilobytes will be saved, for instance, before the compacting process is begun automatically.)

certain action is taken—the message is deleted, moved to a particular folder, or automatically replied to, for instance.

Rules in Outlook Express 4.0 or 4.5

Here's how to create a rule in Outlook Express 4.0 or 4.5:

1. Select Tools | Mail Rules.

2. The Mail Rules window appears. Click New Rule to create a new filter.

3. The Define Mail Rule window appears (see Figure 18-4). This one looks a little intimidating, but it makes sense. Begin by giving the rule a number in the Rule Name entry box. You can leave the Apply To Incoming option checked if that's the sort of rule you're planning. (You can also apply rules to outgoing messages, but you'll probably find less reason to do that.)

4. In the Criteria section, build your "rule" using the menus and entry boxes. Pull down each menu to build a statement against which each piece of mail will be compared. This can require a little thought, since you need to consider why you're filtering and what it is the messages will have in common.

5. If you want more than one criterion statement, place a checkmark next to the second entry and build another rule.

18

Click to add more
criteria to the rule.

Choose whether one or
all criteria must be met.

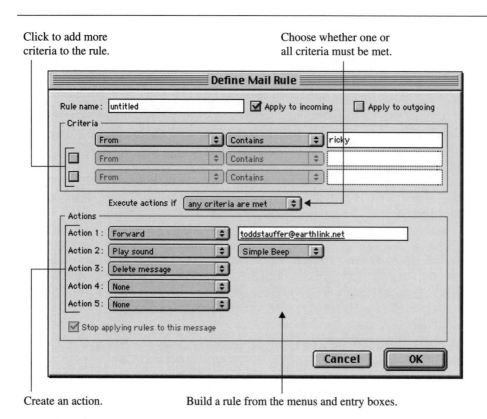

FIGURE 18-4　Creating mail rules to automatically filter incoming mail

Create an action.

Build a rule from the menus and entry boxes.

6. In the Execute Actions If menu, choose whether one or all of the criteria need to be met.

7. Now, select an action. You'll usually only have one, but you may have more than one. Notice that most of the actions will need a little more information in order to be complete, so they'll create another menu or entry box depending on which action it is.

8. The last thing to decide is whether to leave the Stop Applying Rules To This Message check box active. If it's active, then a message caught in this rule won't be compared to any other rules. That's probably what you want (once this rule finds a valid message, you'll perform the actions and be done with it), but you may occasionally want such a message to go through the rest of the rules, too.

9. Click OK.

Rules in Outlook Express 5.0

If you have Outlook Express 5.0, the tools for creating mail rules are a little different—you have more options while, at the same time, the dialog box has been simplified a bit. Here's how to create your rule:

1. Choose Tools | Rules.

2. In the Mail Rules dialog box, select the tab for the type of mail or news account for which you'd like to create a rule. If the rule is for a standard POP e-mail account, choose Mail (POP).

3. Click the New button, or choose the type of rule you'd like to create from the New button's menu.

4. In the Define Mail Rule window, give the rule a name in the Rule name box (see Figure 18-5).

5. In the If section, build your rule using the menus and entry boxes. Pull down the menu that says "All Messages" and choose the beginning of a statement against which each piece of mail will be compared. (You might choose From, for instance, to create a statement that will compare the From portion of every incoming e-mail message against your criterion statement.) This can require a little thought, since you need to consider why you're filtering and what it is the messages will have in common.

6. If you want more than one criterion statement, click the Add Criterion button.

7. In the Execute Actions menu, choose whether the action is performed "if any criteria are met" or "if all criteria are met."

8. Now, in the Then section, select an action. You'll usually only have one, but you may have more than one. Notice that most of the actions will need a little more information in order to be complete, so they'll create another menu or entry box depending on which action it is.

9. The last thing to decide is whether to leave the Stop Applying Rules To This Message check box active. If it's active, then a message caught in this rule won't be compared to any other rules. That's probably what you want (once this rule finds a valid message, you'll perform the actions and be done with it), but you may occasionally want such a message to go through the rest of the rules, too.

The Logic of Rules

Building rules can be tough—in a sense, it approaches the logic you need to create an AppleScript or a similar computer program. It's a basic "IF…THEN" statement—in order to use mail rules, you'll have to think that way.

18

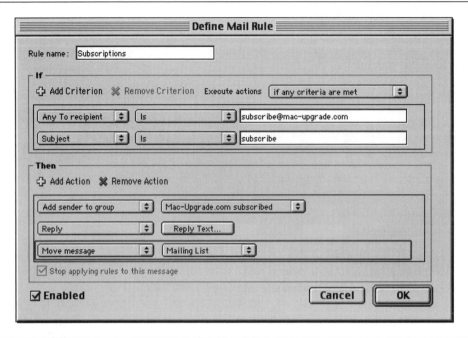

FIGURE 18-5 The Outlook Express 5.0 Define Mail Rule window

Once you get your mind set to the problem, you'll find solutions. Let me tell you about a couple of rules I use. I have an e-mail newsletter I send out once a week to subscribers. People subscribe by sending an e-mail to a particular e-mail address (subscribe@mac-upgrade.com). The e-mail is automatically forwarded to my main mac-upgrade account. So, the first criterion is: Was the message sent to subscribe@mac-upgrade.com?

```
To Is subscribe@mac-upgrade.com
```

Next, the user can enter either **subscribe** or **unsubscribe**, depending on what they want to do. So, the second criterion is this: Does the subject say "subscribe"? (If it says something else, it'll need to be caught by another mail rule, for instance, that's designed to notice that the message is sent to subscribe@mac-upgrade.com but with the subject "unsubscribe.")

```
Subject is subscribe
```

Now, if those two criteria are met (I'll choose All Criteria Are Met from the Execute Actions If menu), the rule will go through a series of actions. The rule adds the sender's name to a mailing list I've created in the Contacts window of Outlook Express. Then it'll automatically reply to the sender to say that he or she was successfully added. Finally, it'll file the sender's message in a special folder I've created that allows me to quickly check the number of subscribers and access the subscription e-mail messages if there's a problem. So, the actions are:

```
Action 1: Add Sender to mailing list
Action 2: Reply
Action 3: Move message
```

NOTE   *In Outlook Express 5.0, the first action would be "Add Sender to group."*

Because all criteria have to be met in order to invoke this rule, it's OK to keep the Stop Applying Rules To This Message check box checked, since only messages that met all the criteria have been affected. Other messages have already met a "try again" command in Outlook Express and have moved on to the next rule.

Add a New User

We've already seen that you can add a second or third e-mail account and integrate it into Outlook Express. But what if you want to share Outlook Express between two users? Having two people's mail come into the same Inbox can be confusing at best, unworkable at worst. Fortunately, there's a solution—creating a new user. Here's how:

1. In Outlook Express 5.0, choose File | Switch Identity. (In Outlook Express 4.0 or 4.5, choose File | Change Current User.) You'll go through a short process of closing down Outlook as if you were quitting the program. Then the Select a User window appears.

2. Click the New or New User button.

3. In the New User dialog box, enter a name for this user profile and select the existing user or default upon which Outlook should base this new user's initial settings. Click OK to create the new user. (In Outlook Express 4.0 or 4.5, click Save.)

4. In Outlook Express 5.0, you'll now see the Outlook Express Setup Assistant, which walks you through the process of creating a user. In Outlook Express 4.0 or 4.5, the program opens up as if it were the first time anyone had used the program. You add an e-mail account, create folders, organize mail, and build rules all without affecting any other user's setup.

18

Whenever you need to switch back and forth between users, just choose File | Switch Identity or File | Change Current User. After shutting down the current user, Outlook Express will offer up the Select An Identity window and allow you to choose who's using Outlook Express now. Highlight the user name and click OK.

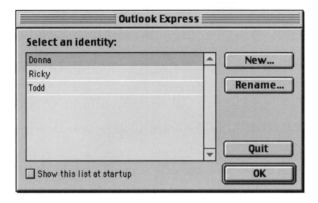

Chapter 19

Surf with Internet Explorer and Netscape

How to...

- Surf the Web with a browser
- Work with Internet addresses
- Get on the Web and surf the hyperlinks
- Choose a home page and set it up
- Manage your browser history, your favorite sites, and your Bookmarks
- Fill in forms and check for secure connections
- Add plug-ins and work with Java applets

Throughout this book I've mentioned Web sites that you might enjoy visiting, so hopefully you've already had some experience with your Web browser. Even if you haven't been out on the Web, in this chapter we'll take a look at how you can get online with your Web browser and use the basic tools, then we'll move on to the more advanced features to become a power surfer.

Web Browser Basics

The World Wide Web is really a *protocol*—a set of computer-coded rules for transmitting information—more than it is a place or program. While it may seem that you're connecting to a central computer or some mechanism that broadcasts information like a TV network, the fact is that Web server computers are distributed all over the Internet and, therefore, all over the world. Since each individual server has its own address and each one speaks the same HyperText Transport Protocol (HTTP), it's possible for you to connect to and read documents from computers all over the globe.

Consequently, you don't really "log onto" the Web. Instead, you connect to the Internet through your ISP (Internet Service Provider), then you use your Web browser to visit particular server computers and view their Web documents.

The Web Browser

You may be surprised to learn that the Web browser is a fairly simple program. It's designed to read Web documents and format them to fit on your screen. The documents have instructions—things like "make this text bold" and "place an image document here on the page" that the Web browser interprets. Those instructions are in the HyperText Markup Language (HTML), which is actually fairly simple to learn.

These Web pages can include instructions to the browser to load all sorts of different documents and files, which is why the Web seems more complicated than it really is. For instance, a Web page can include a special instruction that says "load a Java program" or "display a QuickTime video." When this happens, part of your Web browser screen is given over to the video or Web program. But the Web page itself really isn't terribly complicated.

Instead, your Web browser's features are more about helping you organize, search, and approach the Web in a structured way. The browser includes Bookmarks or Favorites to help you save pages you like, a History file that helps you track the pages you've seen, and other features that make it easy to send e-mail, download files to your iMac, and view or save images. The Internet Explorer (IE) and Netscape Navigator or Communicator versions included with your iMac also feature advanced security and encryption to help you make online payments and transactions safer.

NOTE   *This chapter focuses on Netscape Communicator, the version included with many iMac and iMac DV models made in 1999 and beyond. If your iMac has Netscape Navigator, you'll find that the Web browsing component is very similar to Communicator's. In most cases, you can simply substitute the word "Navigator" wherever you see "Communicator" in this chapter.*

19

The Internet Address

The basis of surfing the Web is the Uniform Resource Locator (URL), which serves as the primary mechanism for addresses on the Web. The idea of the URL is simple—every Web document has its own address on the Internet. That way, if you want to view a particular document on a particular computer in a particular country, you simply enter the address.

Some URLs are simple, such as:

```
http://www.apple.com/
```

This URL points to the *index* page of Apple's Web site. In fact, the full address above is **http://www.apple.com/index.html**, although you don't have to type that entire address since it's assumed that if you don't enter a particular page name, you want to view the index page.

Another address might be:

```
http://www.mac-upgrade.com/imac_book/index.html
```

This URL allows you to load the index page of the site that's dedicated to this book. In fact, it's pointed directly at that page—this is a unique address for a particular document on the Internet.

URLs are made up of three basic components—the protocol, the Web server address, and the path to the document. In the above example, *http://* is the protocol, *www.mac-upgrade.com* is the Web server computer's address, and */imac_book/index.html* is the path on the Web server computer to that file.

Here's what each component does and how they work:

- **Protocol** The protocol tells the browser what sort of Internet server you're trying to access. Enter **http://** for Web servers, **https://** for Web servers that have security enabled, and **ftp://** if you're accessing a File Transfer Protocol (FTP) server (FTP allows you to download files).

NOTE   *Actually, there are protocols for any kind of Internet service, although they vary a bit. For instance, mailto: is a protocol for sending e-mail from a Web browser—mailto: tstauffer@aol.com results in a new e-mail message addressed to me opening in your e-mail application. Other protocols include gopher://, news:, and telnet:.*

- **Server Computer Address** Often this starts with *www*. It's simply the address of a particular computer or group of computers running a Web server application. That can even be an individual Mac, since modern Macs (and all iMacs) include Web Sharing server software. For individual Macs, the server computer address will likely be a numbered address like *206.100.129.49* instead of a named address like *www.csindy.com*. (In fact, as far as the Internet is concerned, all computer addresses are numbers, not names. The names are just for human convenience.)

- **Path Statement**   A path statement tells the server computer what folder a particular document is stored in. Something like */imac_book/index.html* tells the server computer to "look in the *imac_book* folder and get me the *index.html* file." The server computer complies and sends a copy of that document, which is then displayed in your Web browser.

In order to load a page (or access some other Internet service) in your browser, enter an URL. There are a few different ways you can do that, as described in the next section.

*The browsers included with your iMac (Internet Explorer and Netscape Communicator) both allow you to enter Web addresses without the full URL. If you prefer, type **www.apple.com** or **206.100.129.49** without the protocol. It's a little quicker.*

Start Up and Open an Address

Once you understand the concept behind an URL, you're ready to load that URL in your Web browser. It's actually quite simple.

Before you can enter an URL, you need to connect to the Internet and start up your browser. To begin, open your Internet connection using the Control Strip or the Remote Access control panel.

You can set your iMac to autodial your Internet provider whenever you launch an Internet application. See Chapter 23 for more on this setting. And, if you don't use a modem for your Internet connection, you probably don't need to do anything special before you launch your browser.

When you're connected to the Internet, do one of the following:

- Double-click the Browse the Internet icon on your desktop.

- Choose Internet Access I Browse the Internet from the Apple menu. (You may not see this option if your Mac is running Mac OS 9 or higher.)

- In the Finder, double-click the icon for Netscape or Internet Explorer.

You'll see the browser start up and the default page—called your *home page*—will appear in the browser window. Now you can enter an URL in the Address entry box in the browser window.

Address: ▼ http://www.apple.com/

19

Actually, there's another way to open your Web browser and enter an URL all at once. From the Apple menu, choose Internet Access | Connect To. (You may not have this option if your iMac shipped with Mac OS 9 preinstalled.) This doesn't immediately open your browser—it opens a dialog box that asks you to enter an URL. Enter it, then click Connect or press RETURN. Your Web browser starts up and the page associated with that URL will be loaded.

If you don't like your default browser, you can change it. Open the Internet control panel, click the Web tab, and change the default browser. (Chapter 23 discusses the Internet control panel in more detail.)

Surf the Web

It's called "surfing" because, just like riding waves in the ocean, you never know exactly how you're going to get somewhere or how far down the beach you'll end up. In a Web browser, though, you surf by clicking a *hyperlink*.

Once you've loaded your first page (or when you're looking at the home page) you'll probably see hyperlinked text. A hyperlink is text or an image that can be clicked in the Web browser window. When you click the hyperlink, a new URL is automatically entered into the Address entry box and you're taken to a new page. That's the point of a hyperlink—it loads a new page.

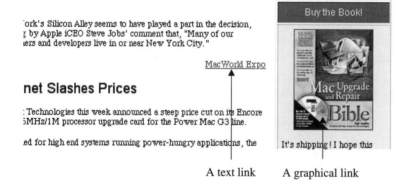

A text link   A graphical link

Sometimes people have to adjust to single-clicking hyperlinks—they only need to be clicked *once*, not twice. This can be counterintuitive for many users, since we're used to double-clicking items that we want to open up. But that's not true in a Web browser; you'd tire quickly by continually double-clicking links.

> *Don't forget about those Back and Forward buttons we discussed in Chapter 2.*
> *They're a convenient way to maneuver while surfing.*

TIP

When you pass over a hyperlink using Internet Explorer or Netscape Communicator, your pointer icon will turn into a hand with an index finger sticking up—that means the pointer is over a hyperlink that can be clicked. To select it, just click the mouse once.

> *Don't be surprised if some links open a new Web document in your window.*
> *There's a special code Web authors use to make a link open a new window. It's*
> *harmless enough, but if you don't like it, click the close box in the new window.*

NOTE

Click a Multimedia Link

Actually, a hyperlink can be used to load other things, such as images or multimedia, or you might even click a link that allows you to download a file. Other than loading a new Web page, there are three different things that can happen when you click a link:

- ■ **A Helper Program Is Invoked**   Your Web browser recognizes many types of files and passes them on to the appropriate application. For instance, if you click a link to a RealAudio file—a document that sends audio over the Internet—it will be passed on to the RealPlayer application, assuming it's installed on your iMac. Similarly, clicking a hyperlink that leads to a mailto: URL activates your e-mail application.

- ■ **A Plug-In Is Activated**   The most common plug-in is QuickTime, which allows you to watch movies in your Web browser. There are also others, including plug-ins for Macromedia Flash documents, virtual reality documents, audio and video formats, Java applets, and more.

> *Plug-ins and helper applications are discussed in more depth later in*
> *this chapter.*

NOTE

- ■ **A File Is Downloaded**   If a link points to a file using an FTP protocol URL, the file will be downloaded to your iMac's hard disk. You can view it with another application, decompress it with StuffIt Expander (which is often done automatically), or perform a similar task.

Sometimes you'll click a hyperlink to a particular file and the Web browser won't recognize it. In that case, you can usually choose to download the file, ignore it, or search for the correct application to view it, as instructed by the dialog box.

Work with Frames

With some Web sites you'll encounter an *HTML frames* interface. This is a special sort of page that actually breaks a single Web browser window into different window panes (hence "frames") that are used to display different pages. In most cases, the idea is to click a link in one of the frames, then have the page change in another frame. Frames allow you to view many pages' worth of information without refreshing the entire window every time (see Figure 19-1).

If necessary, you can choose commands to allow you to go Back, Forward, and so on within that particular frame. Click and hold the mouse button within a frame to see a

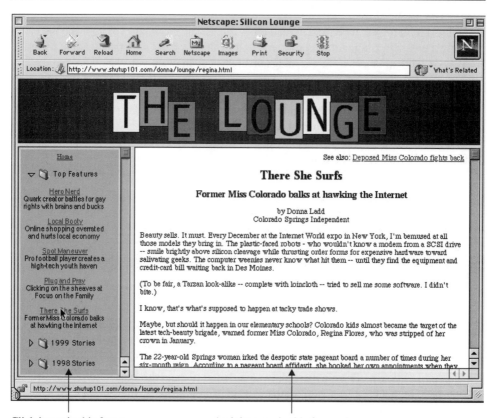

Click items in this frame...   ...And the page in this frame changes.

FIGURE 19-1   A Web page that uses an HTML frames interface

pop-up menu. You can then choose Back, Forward (if applicable), and other commands that will affect only that frame.

Choose a Home Page

If you plan to spend a lot of time online, you'll want to get organized. The best starting place I know for getting organized is a good home page. In Internet Explorer or Netscape Communicator, it's easy to decide on a particular home page where you'd like to start your Internet adventure every time you sign on. (In fact, the home page is usually loaded every time you open a new browser window.) You can link to your company page, a page you particularly enjoy reading, a professional *portal* page (a home page with news, sports, and other topical headlines) from one of the big Internet companies, or even to a page you create yourself.

Change Your Home Page

If you use Internet Explorer for your Web surfing, your home page is already set for you—it's the Excite Live home page. If you don't need or want to change from these defaults, skip down to the section "Edit the Home Page." You can change the home page, though, if you find one you like more or if you just want to experiment.

Popular sites that allow you to customize your own home page include:

My Excite	**http://www.excite.com/**
Apple Excite (offers Apple news)	**http://apple.excite.com/**
My Netscape	**http://www.netscape.com/**
Microsoft Network	**http://www.msn.com/**
My Snap	**http://my.snap.com/**
Go Network	**http://www.go.com/**
My Yahoo	**http://my.yahoo.com/**
Earthlink Personal Start Page	**http://start.earthlink.net/**

You don't have to go with one of the big names. Equally useful may be a smaller site that you enjoy visiting—one associated with a hobby or interest of yours. Of course, it should also be the sort of page that changes often—making a home page out of a page that's never updated is a little dull, unless it's filled with interesting hyperlinks.

Making any page into your home page is pretty simple, although you have a decision to make. Do you want to set this as your home page for all Web browsers you might open, or just for the current browser?

19

All Browsers

If you want to set your home page for all of your browsers, do the following:

1. Open your potential home page in your browser.

2. Highlight the URL and choose Edit | Copy or press ⌘-C.

3. Select the Apple menu and choose Control Panels | Internet.

4. Select the Web tab in the Internet control panel.

5. In the Home Page entry box, highlight the contents of the box and delete the address that's currently there.

6. Select Edit | Paste or press ⌘-V to paste your home page URL into the Home Page entry box.

7. Press TAB or click the close box in the control panel. When you do, you'll be asked if you want to save the new settings. Choose Save.

Now, the Home Page button in your Web browser should lead you to the new home page whenever you click it. Similarly, you'll see the home page every time you open a new browser window while you're connected to the Internet.

Specific Browser

If you want to set the page just for one particular browser, you'll follow different directions depending on whether you're using Internet Explorer or Netscape:

- **Internet Explorer** Open the page you want to use as a home page, highlight the URL, and choose Edit | Copy. Now, choose Edit | Preferences and click the Home/Search button. Paste the URL into the Address entry box under Home Page.

- **Netscape Communicator** Open the page you want to use as a home page. Choose Edit | Preferences and click the Navigator entry. Under Home Page, click the Use Current button.

Edit the Home Page

If you're using one of the major services for your home page, you should realize that you'll probably be able to edit it, if desired. Look for a link that says "Personalize This Page" or something similar. Click that link and you'll likely find yourself with tools that allow you to change what you view on the home page and the order in which you view it.

In most cases, you'll place a checkmark next to items you want on the page. You'll then enter a number next to each item to choose how you want it prioritized—whether you want it to appear at the top or bottom of the page, for instance. You should be able to choose from a variety of topics, financials, types of news, entertainment, and so on.

You'll also likely be asked for some demographic information, as well as your zip code and perhaps your birthday (especially for horoscopes). If you're worried about the information getting out, look for a link to the company's privacy statement; also, look for an option you can check telling them they can't sell or use your information for advertising purposes.

Manage Bookmarks, Favorites, and History

Eventually you'll come across a site that's worth remembering, and at that point you'll want to create a Bookmark (Netscape) or a Favorite (Internet Explorer). These browser features each do the same thing—save an URL for future reference. It's pretty easy to do.

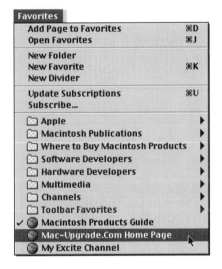

To set a Bookmark or Favorite, open the page in the browser window. Now, in Netscape, choose the Bookmark menu (in some versions it's actually a little Bookmark icon) and select Add Bookmark. In Internet Explorer, choose Favorites | Add Page to Favorites. When you do this, the browser stores the URL to the open page and places the title of that page on the Bookmarks/Favorites menu.

Now, whenever you want to return to that page, simply choose the Favorites or Bookmarks menu in your Web browser, then select the site. Your Web browser will find that page again and display it.

Each Web browser also provides tools for editing the Favorites/Bookmarks once you've created them.

Edit Favorites

In Internet Explorer you can edit your Favorites list by choosing Favorites | Open Favorites. In the Favorites window, you can drag-and-drop Favorites to move them into folders or to change their order. When you're dragging a Favorite around, notice that a thin black line moves along the window with you to show you where it will appear when you drop it.

You can rename a Favorite the same way you rename a file or folder in the Finder—click once on the name and wait a few seconds. When the name becomes highlighted, type the new name.

You can also create folders and dividing lines by choosing Favorites | New Folder or Favorites | New Divider. If you want to create a Favorite from scratch, choose Favorites | New Favorite. You'll then need to manually enter a name and URL for this Favorite.

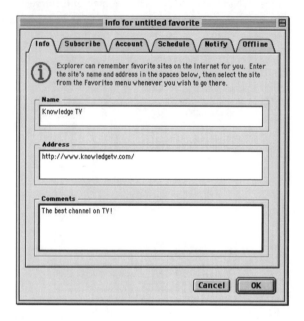

To delete a Favorite, select it in the Favorites window and choose Edit | Clear, or drag the Favorite from the Favorites window to the Trash can in the Finder. (You can also press ⌘-DELETE.)

 *In Internet Explorer you can edit the Toolbar Favorites to change the favorite items that appear on the toolbar just below the Address entry box.*

Edit Bookmarks

To edit your Netscape Bookmarks, choose Bookmarks from the Bookmarks menu (in Netscape Communicator 4.5 or higher.) In the Bookmarks window, you can move folders and individual Bookmarks around by dragging and dropping. A black line moves with you to show you where the Bookmark (or folder) will appear in the list when you drop the item.

If you have Netscape Navigator, choose Bookmarks from the menu that looks like a ship's wheel—the Netscape Navigator logo.

To edit the name or URL of a Bookmark, select the Bookmark and choose Edit I Get Info. The Info window appears where you edit the name or URL and/or enter a description. Click OK.

![Apple Computer info dialog box showing Name: Apple Computer, Location (URL): http://www.apple.com/, Description: The home page for Apple Computer, Inc., Last Visited: Less than one hour ago, Added on: Oct 14 16:23:41 1999, There are no aliases to this bookmark, with Cancel and OK buttons.]

To add folders or separator lines, choose File I New Folder or File I New Separator. You can also manually create a Bookmark by choosing File I New Bookmark. This allows you to enter a new title and URL for the Bookmark using the same Get Info window.

Close the Bookmarks window; the Bookmarks menu has been changed with your edits.

Follow Your History

Both Netscape Communicator and Internet Explorer maintain a *history* of the sites you visit using two completely different methods. The history is simply a list of recently visited URLs that you can revisit from the Go menu in both browsers. Netscape Navigator maintains a history of each window individually and only for the life of that window.

 In both browsers you can open a new window by selecting File I New Window. In fact, you can browse simultaneously in two, three, or more windows. In Communicator each window has its own history tracking that is deleted once you close the window. Explorer tracks them all and remembers visited sites despite closing windows.

In IE's history, visited sites are tracked and saved regardless of the windows you use. What's more, IE also tracks history for many days, limited only by a Preference setting on the Advanced button in the IE preferences.

You can also edit the history in IE if you'd like to delete items or if, perhaps, you'd like to drag-and-drop between the History window and the Favorites window. Choose Go I

19

Open History to open your history, where you can drag the links from the History window to the Favorites window, the browser window (to view that Favorite), or the Trash (to delete that link from the History).

 *In Internet Explorer you can access both your History and your Favorites by clicking the tabs located at the left side of the browser window. This opens up the tabs to reveal a panel where links (either History Links or Favorites) are listed. Click a link and the main window will show that page.*

Fill in a Form and Buy Things Online

Web browsers are capable of displaying Web pages that include form elements. Interface items that you might find in a dialog box within the Mac OS can be added to a Web page so that you can send information back to the Web server computer. These elements include familiar items like entry boxes, menus, check boxes, radio buttons, and regular buttons. All of these form elements are used pretty much like they are within the Mac OS.

The difference is, you're usually filling in personal information that you plan to send to the Web server computer so that it can be processed in some way. Perhaps you're buying computer software or subscribing to an online newsletter—or maybe you're setting up a home page, as discussed earlier in this chapter.

Fill in the Form

Usually filling in a form is pretty easy—you just enter the necessary information by typing in entry boxes and choosing items in lists or menus (see Figure 19-2).

FIGURE 19-2   Web pages can allow you to fill in information and send it across the Internet.

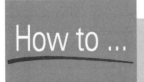

Use AutoFill in Internet Explorer

In Internet Explorer 4.5 or higher, you may see the Forms AutoFill dialog box that asks you if you want to use the form to set up AutoFill. AutoFill is a feature that allows you to enter common form data (your name, address, phone number, and so on) once in Internet Explorer, then you can click the AutoFill button on the toolbar whenever you encounter a new form. Click Yes in the dialog box to view and edit your AutoFill profile. Or, at any time you can click the AutoFill button to manually enter your AutoFill profile.

In the Preferences dialog box, you'll see entries for common items about yourself that forms will request. Edit those to taste, then click OK in the Preferences dialog box. Now, whenever you visit a site requesting your information, just click the AutoFill button in the toolbar and Internet Explorer will fill in with as much information as it can.

Other elements are also familiar. Press TAB to move between most of the parts of the form (you'll probably have to use the mouse to choose items from pull-down menus).

Once you have the form filled in, you'll need to look for a way to *submit* that form. Your data needs to be sent to the Web server computer, but it can't go until you say it can. In most cases you'll see a Send or Submit button that you click with the mouse. You may also see a Clear button that will clear the form of everything you've just entered. Don't click that button unless you're sure you want to clear the form.

Click Submit (or Send, or Search, and so on) and your data is sent over the Internet to the Web server computer where it's processed. In most cases clicking the Submit button also loads a new page into your Web browser that includes either results from your data or a page telling you that your submission has been received.

Did I say your data is sent over the Internet? But what if it's private data like credit card numbers, salary figures, or e-mail addresses? Are you sure you want them floating around?

Check for a Secure Connection

In most cases where a Web site wants you to send financial or private information, they'll do so over what's called a *secure* server. What this means is simple—the Web site and your browser establish a connection over which data is encrypted. It's coded like a military transmission. The code can only be broken once your data gets to the server computer.

Each browser reports a secure connection in its own way. In Netscape, you'll see a small padlock icon in the bottom-left corner—it's locked and glowing when connected to a secure page. In Internet Explorer the window is highlighted in blue

19

and you'll see a message at the bottom of the screen attesting to the page's security. (In Internet Explorer 4.5 and higher you'll also see a padlock icon.)

Browse Offline and Automatically

Internet Explorer has a few different features that help you automate the use of Internet Explorer, and you can even browse the Web without actually being connected to the Internet.

Subscribe to Sites

Subscribe to a Web site and have Internet Explorer automatically update the site on a regular basis. This does two things for you. Periodically, while you're connected to the Internet, a site that you've subscribed to can be checked automatically. When the site is found to have changed, the Favorite will appear with a checkmark next to it in the Favorites folder. If the Favorite happens to be a Toolbar Favorite, you'll see the icon next to it change to a sort of starburst, suggesting the site has new changes since the last subscription check.

> **NOTE** *You don't need permission and the site itself doesn't need to be specially set up in order for you to subscribe to it—IE is simply automatically checking the site for you to see if there have been changes.*

Here's how to turn a Favorite into a subscribed Favorite:

1. Open the Favorites list for editing by selecting Favorites I Open Favorites.

2. Select the Favorite which you'd like to subscribe to and choose File I Get Info.

3. In the Info window, choose the Subscribe tab.

4. Place a check next to Check This Site For Changes. This causes the site to be subscribed; it will be checked according to the Subscription preferences.

If you'd like the subscription checked at some different interval, select the Schedule tab in the Info window for that particular Favorite. Place a check next to Use A Custom Schedule For This Site. Then, change the options in the window to reflect how you'd like the site updated.

Java and Plug-ins

You've already seen that your Web browser is capable of displaying and arranging images and text in the browser window. But Web browsers are also capable of giving over part of the browser window to other mini-applications that allow you to interact with an online program of some sort. These are called *embedded* programs—in the case of Java, they're often called *applets*. That just means that they're small programs that allow you to perform a simple task. Let's take a look at each.

Embedded Plug-in Files

Using plug-in technology, the Web browser can actually give control of part of the browser window to another little program which can be responsible for dealing with user input and displaying things on the screen. In most cases, these plug-ins add more multimedia, perhaps offering animated graphics, a unique interface to the Web site, and so on. One very popular plug-in technology is Macromedia's Flash technology, which allows you to view animated graphics within the browser window (see Figure 19-3).

Flash (**http://www.macromedia.com/software/flash/**), a very popular plug-in, can be used for audio and video—most often for presentations, although you'll find comic books, advertisements, games, and other multimedia experiences authored in Macromedia's multimedia software applications.

Other plug-ins let you view a variety of embedded multimedia documents, like Real Networks RealPlayer (**http://www.realnetworks.com/**). With RealPlayer you can view streaming audio and video (audio and video that are played as they arrive across the Internet in a data stream so you don't have to wait a long time for the data to download). Other popular plug-ins offer 3-D vistas, Virtual Reality Modeling Language (VRML) controllers, and so on. A great place to find many of the plug-ins available today for Web browsers is at Netscape's Browser Plug-in Web pages (**http://home.netscape.com/plugins/index.html**).

news ○
product info ○
gallery ○
try it ●
file format ○
support ○
contact us ○

search ○
buy ○

FIGURE 19-3 Plug-in technology adds interactivity (and visual effects) to Web pages.

19

Of course, one of the most important plug-ins is the QuickTime plug-in, which is installed automatically. See Chapter 14 for more on using the QuickTime plug-in. Likewise, Macromedia Flash plug-ins are preloaded on your iMac.

Add Plug-ins

Plug-in programs need to be placed in a particular folder—the Plug-ins folder—that's located within your Internet Explorer or Netscape Communicator folder. Most of the time you'll simply download the plug-in installer application, which will automatically place the plug-ins in the correct subfolder within your Web browser's folder.

But if you need to install a plug-in manually, begin by quitting the browser. Then, drag the plug-in program to the Plug-ins folder located within your Internet Explorer or Netscape Communicator folder. Drop the plug-in program in that folder.

Now, when you restart your Web browser, it will automatically search for and detect new plug-ins. Their functionality will be noted and the next time you encounter an embedded multimedia document, the correct plug-in will be loaded and used.

Work with Java

Aside from being an incredibly popular buzzword in the computing world, Java is two things. First, it's a programming language invented in the past few years, offering advanced programming language constructs that many programmers really like. It's a lot like the C++ language, which is popular among computer scientists.

Second, Java is a *virtual platform* or *virtual machine*. What that means is simply this: The Java virtual machine allows a Java language program to run, unaltered, on just about any sort of computer made. It does this by emulating a less sophisticated virtual "Java" computer.

With most applications, you have to specifically buy a Mac OS application or a Microsoft Windows application. And, as you know, one type of application won't run on another type of computer. Java changes that by allowing a Java program to run on the virtual machine without forcing it to notice which computer it's actually being run on. The Java virtual machine is written specifically for the particular OS—Apple writes the MRJ (Macintosh Runtime for Java), for instance, that makes it possible for you to run Java applications on your iMac.

*Read about MRJ and download updates at **http://www.apple.com/ java/**. This is a good idea because Apple often updates MRJ (even between Mac OS updates) to make it much faster and cooler. To figure out what version you currently have, open the Apple Extras folder, open the Mac OS Runtime for Java folder, and see what Read Me file is in there (About MRJ 2.1.4, for instance). If the Web site offers a newer version, download and install it. If you have Mac OS 9, you can use the Software Update control panel to check for new versions of MRJ, too. The Software Update control panel is discussed in Chapter 24.*

In most cases, Java works seamlessly on your iMac—there's nothing in particular you need to do. In fact, if you download and install a Java applet on your iMac, it'll work just like any other iMac program.

Often, though, Java applets are loaded over the Internet and displayed in your Web browser. To use Java applets, if it requires any user interaction, simply point and click the mouse like you would with any Mac application (see Figure 19-4).

Troubleshoot Java Applets

If you're encountering trouble with Java, you can change the virtual machine in Internet Explorer. (As of this writing, Netscape Communicator 4.7 and lower uses its own Java

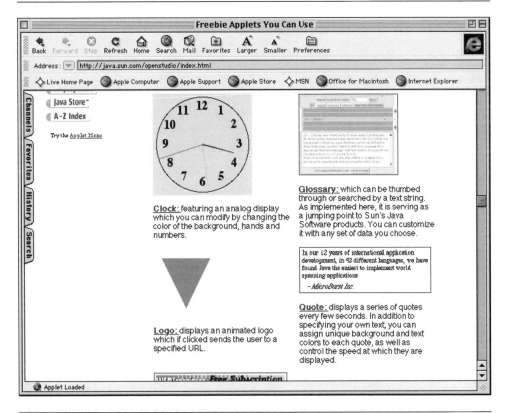

| FIGURE 19-4 | Java allows small applications to appear within the Web browser window. |

virtual machine, which can't be changed.) In IE, here's how to choose the Java virtual machine:

1. Choose Edit | Preferences in IE.

2. Click the Java button.

3. At the top of the preferences window, make sure Enable Java is checked.

4. In the Java Virtual Machine menu, choose MRJ. (Or choose Microsoft Virtual Machine, if desired.)

5. Click OK.

If you've changed the Java machine you're using, you'll need to restart Internet Explorer. If you continue to have trouble, you may need to increase the amount of memory that's allocated to Internet Explorer (or run IE with fewer applications in the background). See Chapter 24 for more on allocating memory to your applications.

Chapter 20

Download, Back Up, and Transfer Online

How to...

- Back up files from your iMac to the Web
- Use the File Transfer Protocol to upload and download
- Compress and decompress files
- Create and use floppy disk images
- Find and use shareware and freeware applications

The iMac is designed to live on the Internet, more so than most computers. It's built to transfer files online, back up files online, and get most of its updates, new installations, and new tools online.

In this chapter, let's take a look at how you upload to and download from the Internet. (*Upload* means to send files from your iMac to a distant computer, while *download* means to bring files from a distant computer across the Internet to your iMac.) You'll also see how to back up your iMac files using the Internet and learn some ways to get new applications and application updates into your iMac over the Internet.

Transfer Files over the Internet

There are several different ways you can transfer files over the Internet. We've already discussed one of them in Chapter 18: You can attach files to e-mail messages in order to transport them from one computer to another. This is one way that some iMac users move documents from work to home, for instance—if you have different e-mail accounts for each location, then you can just mail an attachment to yourself.

You can also send files via the File Transfer Protocol (FTP) using special applications for the task. You'll need to download the applications, but it's really very convenient after that. We'll discuss that method in a moment.

First, though, let's use the familiar Web browser to access an online storage method that has gained in popularity since the iMac was first introduced.

The Virtual Floppy

One great way to transfer files is to take advantage of a number of Web sites that offer a service called the *virtual floppy*. In essence, a virtual floppy is a few megabytes of storage space available via Web browsers, allowing you to transfer a file up to the Web site using one computer, then get it again from another computer. These services are usually provided free of charge because they sell advertising.

All of these sites can have slightly different interfaces, so you'll need to read the instructions posted at the site. Let's look at one example—a site called iMacFloppy.com.

 You need a membership in order to create your virtual floppy the first time. Head to the site and choose the New User button (or Sign Up Here!) to create a membership. There's some optional demographic information when you sign up, but all that's required is a name and e-mail address.

Here's how to transfer files using the iMacFloppy.com service:

1. Connect to the Internet and use your Web browser to go to **http://www. imacfloppy.com**.

2. Now, log in with your member name and password. Your download space is password-protected so nobody else can access it.

3. When you get to the main screen, you'll see two boxes—one represents your online space, while another represents your iMac (or the computer that you're currently on). Now you can copy a file from your computer to the virtual floppy. To do that, click the Browse button on the "my computer" side.

4. Now, in the Open dialog box, find the file you want to upload to the virtual floppy. Select the file and click Open.

5. The filename appears in the window next to the Browse button. Click the arrow (>>) button to send the file on its way.

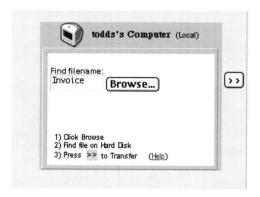

6. After the upload takes place, you'll see a dialog box letting you know the transfer was successful. Click OK and you'll see the new file appear in the file list on the right.

7. If you're done transferring, log out. Down at the bottom of the Web page you'll find a link that allows you to log out from the site. Click this link to leave the site.

The file has now been uploaded and is being stored on your iMacFloppy. Now you can go to another computer where you want the file to ultimately arrive (at work, at the beach house, at grandma's house) and download it. Here's how you download files:

1. Log into iMacFloppy.com again as you did before.

2. When you see the main transfer screen, find the file on the iMacFloppy side that you'd like to download. Click that file's radio button.

3. Now, click the left arrow (<<) button to send the file from the iMacFloppy down to your computer. (I'd say "your iMac" instead of "your computer" but remember, you can do this from any computer, as long as the file that you're uploading and downloading is compatible with both computers.) You'll see the Download Manager (in Internet Explorer) or a download window (in Netscape Navigator). The file will be downloaded to your computer.

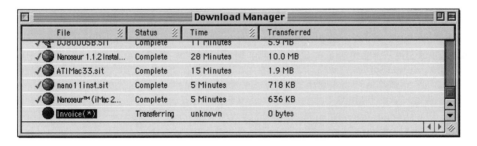

4. Finally, you should see the file on the desktop or wherever the default folder is for downloaded files on your computer. (The default folder is set in the Internet control panel, under the Web tab.)

Now you'll want to manage your files at iMacFloppy. First, you can view files within your iMacFloppy, assuming they happen to be files that can be easily viewed by a Web browser (that includes text files, HTML documents, GIF and JPEG documents). Click the radio button next to the file you want to view and click the View button in that window. The document will appear in a new window, assuming the browser can display it. You can close the Viewer window by clicking its Close button.

You can also delete files from the iMacFloppy. Click the radio button next to the file you want to delete, then click the Trash icon. This will immediately delete the file (there's no "Are you sure?" dialog box).

20

File Transfer Protocol

You should get to know how FTP works, especially if you have large files, many files, or if you'd simply prefer knowing that your files are privately stored and not located on a commercial server. (Even though it's unlikely anyone will bother with your files, you might sometimes feel like being extra careful.)

The process is simple—you download a particular type of application designed to allow you to transfer files over the Internet. These programs make file transfer simple—in most cases, it's a drag-and-drop procedure.

> **NOTE** *You can also use a Web browser to download files from FTP sites, but using an FTP program offers you more options and control, especially for uploading files.*

Once you have the application, you'll also need some FTP storage space, most likely through your ISP. (If you have AOL, you'll see how to do this in Chapter 21.) If your ISP offers Web storage space, then you can use that; otherwise, you might ask them if they make storage space available to users. It's rare, but they may for an extra charge. In most cases, standard Internet accounts have at least some storage space available.

The FTP Address

FTP servers have an address, just as Web servers do. The difference is, some FTP servers will require you to log in as a registered user of that server, then you'll get access to certain or all files on that server. You'll be able to use the FTP program to upload and download files that are stored in your Internet space. So, the burning question you need to ask your ISP is, "What is the address I use to access my Internet space?" In most cases it'll be an address like ftp.*mac-upgrade.com* or, perhaps, www.*companyname.net*, depending on the type of server computer.

> **NOTE** *Some FTP servers, called "anonymous" servers, allow you to log in and download files without specifically having an account on the system. Anonymous FTP access is discussed later in this chapter. For servers where you'll be uploading files, you'll generally need to be a registered user.*

Please Login to a Server	
Address:	ftp-www.earthlink.net
Username:	toddstauffer
Password:	••••••••••••••••
Directory:	
	Connect

You may also need an account on that computer—presumably, you have one if you're using the free space provided by your ISP. If that's so, then you'll just need to know your user name and password in order to access the FTP server computer. (That's where you'll be storing your files.) Most likely they're the same as your user name and password for the dial-up connection, but they may be different. Ask your ISP.

The FTP Application

So what should you use for an FTP application? It's up to you, although any of them need to be downloaded from the Internet before you can use them. My personal favorite is a relatively new FTP application called Transmit, shown in Figure 20-1. I like the way it looks, for one, and I like the way it makes it easy to see what's on your computer vs. what's on the Internet computer. In a sense, it's a little like the iMacFloppy.

Transmit is written by Panic Software and can be downloaded from **http://www. panic.com**. It costs $24.95 to license the software if you like it. (It's shareware, which is discussed later in this chapter.)

Other popular FTP programs include Fetch (**http://www.dartmouth.edu/pages/softdev/fetch.html**) and Anarchie Pro (**http://www.stairways.com/**), both of which are great programs with a long history on the Mac platform. They work slightly differently from Transmit, but the concepts are the same.

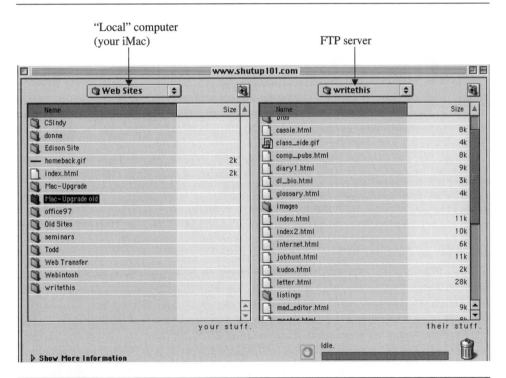

FIGURE 20-1 Transmit makes it easy to transfer files via FTP—just drag-and-drop.

Upload and Download

Once you have your FTP program installed and you've made sure that your Internet connection is active, you're ready to transfer files to the distant site. In FTP parlance, uploading a file uses the Put command and downloading a file requires the Get command. If you're using Transmit, you won't see these commands by default, but Anarchie Pro and Fetch both use them.

1. Start up the FTP application and enter an FTP server computer address. You should also enter user name and password information, if relevant. Click the button that allows you to log on.

2. Once you've successfully logged on, you'll see a file list. Create a folder that you can use for uploading and downloading files. (In Transmit, use File | New Folder.) I like to call my folder "Transfer" since that's what I tend to use it for.

NOTE   *If the free FTP space offered by your ISP is for a Web site, then you may be shown, by default, a folder that is available to everyone on the Web. Instead, you need to create a private folder. Ask your ISP how to do that. If your FTP space has a folder called Webpage, then it's possible that the parent of that folder is where you can create a private subfolder.*

3. Double-click that folder.

4. Now, if you're using Transmit, you can select the files you want to upload in the My Stuff window, then click and drag the files to the Their Stuff window. If you're using Fetch or Anarchie Pro, you can drag files from the Finder to the open folder in that application. (You can also use the Put command in Fetch or Anarchie Pro.)

That's it—you should see the files now available in that folder. To retrieve or download a file, the process is reversed—you can drag-and-drop a file from the Web server folder to the desktop or a folder in the Finder. Or you can select the file and drag it to the My Stuff window (in Transmit), click the Get button (in Fetch), or choose the Get command (in Anarchie Pro). The file is downloaded and saved on your hard disk.

Encode as MacBinary

Before you get too busy uploading and downloading, there is one basic issue we need to touch on—encoding. As you may recall from Chapter 18, it's often necessary to encode files before you can send them as attachments through e-mail. That's not quite the case with FTP, which has built into it the ability to save and store files in a binary state.

That said, uploaded files are often not stored in a Mac-native state. That is, the unique elements of a file that make it a Mac file—things like the icon, the document association that allows a document to launch its parent application, and so on—can be lost when you upload to another computer, especially a Windows or Unix server. So, you have a choice to make.

If the file is cross-platform anyway—a Microsoft Word document, a GIF or JPEG graphic, or a text file like an HTML document—then it's fine to store it as a regular FTP binary file. But if the file or document is Mac-specific—or if you'd simply prefer to maintain all the Mac-like qualities of your uploaded files—then you should save them as MacBinary as you upload them. You can usually accomplish this by choosing to save them as MacBinary either from the preferences of your FTP program or as you're uploading them.

In Transmit you can encode a file as MacBinary before you upload it—select the file in the My Stuff window and choose File | Encode as MacBinary. Notice that the letters ".bin" are appended to the document's name. Now you can upload the file without worrying about its saved state. When you download the file back to another computer, you can decode the MacBinary and use the file.

NOTE   *If you plan to download a file for use on a Windows or Unix computer, then store it as a typical FTP upload instead of encoding it first. If you need to transfer a file from your iMac to a Windows/Unix computer and then, finally, to another Mac, encode it in the MacBinary format. The Windows/Unix computer can transmit such files, it just can't use MacBinary files as documents.*

Compress Files and Decompress Files

Since large files take a long time to transmit over the Internet, it's sometimes preferable to *compress* them. This is another encoding process—using sophisticated algorithms, the compression software is able to reduce redundant information in a document or program and make the file more compact. The catch is that the file is completely useless until it's expanded using the reverse of the compression scheme.

The other thing you can often do with most compression schemes is create a compressed archive of more than one file, so that a number of files or an entire folder can be stored and sent within a single archive file, almost as if it were a shipping envelope. Once the file arrives at its destination, the decompression program is used to separate the files and bring them back to full size.

To do all this, you need to pick a compression scheme. There are three major schemes used for compressing files on the Internet. They are:

- **StuffIt Expander**   This format (with the filename extension .sit) is used almost exclusively by Macs, although there is a Windows version of StuffIt Expander available. Windows users who have Expander for Windows can expand "stuffed" archives created on a Mac.

- **PKZip**   This format is used almost exclusively in the Windows world. A number of utilities are available on the Mac to create PKZip (or just .zip) files, and StuffIt Expander can expand .zip files if the Expander Enhancer is installed.

20

■ **Gzip and Unix Compress** These formats are generally used by Unix machines (the files have .gz and .Z extensions). StuffIt Expander can decompress these files if the Expander Enhancer is installed.

StuffIt and DropStuff

For decompressing files that you download, StuffIt Expander will work with any files created on a Mac, even older formats like Compact Pro. If you need to decompress archives created on Windows or Unix machines, you must make sure you have DropStuff with Expander Enhancer installed.

DropStuff is shareware; you'll pay $25 if you find it useful. In the meantime, install it to add the ability for StuffIt Expander to decompress .zip, .gz, and .Z archives along with its built-in ability to decompress .sit archives. Just drag the files to StuffIt Expander once DropStuff has been installed.

NOTE *There may be a more recent version of StuffIt and DropStuff available since you purchased your iMac. Check **http://www.aladdinsys.com** to find a new version.*

The procedure for *decompressing* most archives is to simply drag-and-drop the archive onto the StuffIt Expander icon. (It's a good idea to create an alias to StuffIt Expander and place it on the desktop if you download files often.) When you drop an archive on StuffIt Expander, it will expand the archive if it possibly can. And StuffIt knows quite a bit about expanding archives.

SHORTCUT *You can usually decompress .sit files easily by double-clicking them. Also, many Web browser and e-mail applications, including those bundled with your iMac, will automatically decompress .sit files when you access them.*

How about *compressing* files? If you're sending a file to a Macintosh, compress it as a StuffIt file. To do that, simply drag-and-drop the file, folder, or group of files (and folders) to the DropStuff icon. When you release the mouse button, DropStuff goes into action, stuffing the files into an archive.

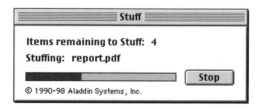

NOTE *You don't always have to compress a file yourself before sending it. Outlook Express, for instance, can be set to automatically compress a file before you send it as an attachment. See Chapter 18 for details.*

If you're only stuffing one document, then the archive file is named for that document with a .sit filename extension. If you're stuffing more than one document, you'll get a file named archive.sit. You can rename the file just as you can rename any other file. One suggestion, however: Keep the .sit part so that your receiving party (assuming you're sending this to someone else) knows to drag it to StuffIt Expander.

If you encounter a file with the extension .sea, it's a self-extracting archive. It doesn't require StuffIt Expander in order to decompress—just double-click it and it will decompress itself. It has a tiny version of Expander built into it.

Compress Using PC/Unix Formats

If you're sending a file to a Microsoft Windows machine, use PKZip. And if you're sending to a Unix machine, you should probably skip compressing the file. (After all, it's unlikely that you're sending a binary document or application to a Unix machine.) If you really need to compress the file, there are utilities available. Here are the main ones:

Utility	Description	URL
ZipIt	Creates and decompresses Windows PKZip archives	**http://www.awa.com/softlock/zipit/**
AsiZip PKZIP for Mac	Creates and decompresses Windows PKZip archives	**http://www.asizip.com/products/pkzipmac.htm**
MacGzip	Creates and decompresses Unix Gzip archives	**http://persephone.cps.unizar.es/~spd/gzip/**

Back Up Online

Since an iMac has no floppy drive (or other built-in removable disk for storage) one important option to consider is backing up online, especially if you haven't bought an add-on external disk drive or if your iMac doesn't connect to a local network where you can back up your files. It's vital that you back up your files—even your personal documents—so that if something happens to your iMac, you still have your data. If you use your iMac for business or for school, or even if you just use it for your personal financial tracking in AppleWorks, you should definitely back up regularly.

One way to back up your files is to use an application to transmit your backup data to a storage area on the Internet. This storage space can be a little pricey—starting at $15-30 a month—and the backup can take a long time to transmit if you have a lot of documents. Still, if you're considering backing up a limited amount of data and you'd like it done without purchasing a removable drive or over a local network, then Internet backup is the way to go.

Using a removable drive for backup is discussed in Chapter 27.

By far the best software for backup is Retrospect Express, a lower-cost version of the most popular Mac backup utility, Retrospect. Retrospect Express can be purchased at local computer stores and popular online software stores. You can also find information about it and purchase it directly from Dantz at **http://www.dantz.com/**.

You'll also need an online backup service. You can use FTP space that you lease from your ISP or other company, and it may be inexpensive. (The data files generated by Retrospect Express can be compressed and encrypted, so your ISP won't really have access to your files.) The only issue then becomes, how much do you trust your ISP to guarantee the *integrity* of your data? You might ask them if they're backing up and if they recommend you use their FTP servers for online backup.

Some services exist specifically to help you with online backup. They generally guarantee a certain level of security, privacy, and redundancy—some go so far as to have redundant servers in secure buildings in different parts of the world. Here are some backup services recommended by Dantz:

Recover-iT!	**http://www.recover-it.com/**
MacBackup	**http://www.macbackup.com/**
Portland Communications (UK)	**http://www.portland.co.uk/retrospect.html**

Work with Floppy Images

Now we're going to deal with floppy disks—even though the iMac has no disk drive. Instead, we'll talk about floppy *disk images*.

Floppy disk images are files that act just like floppy disks (or similar removables). Once you double-click a floppy disk image, the floppy disk is mounted.

Once the floppy disk is mounted, it acts just like any other disk. You can drag files to its icon, for instance, to copy files onto the disk. Similarly, you can double-click the floppy disk to open its window and copy files from (and sometimes to) that window. But it's not a disk at all—it's just a special kind of file.

Types of Floppy Images

There are two different kinds of floppy disk images—self-mounting images (.smi) and regular disk images (.img). A self-mounting image can be used on any Macintosh, since it mounts itself. This is how most update and other software is distributed by Apple these days, making it easy to download the images and double-click to mount them. Then you can install from them as if they were regular disks.

To use regular image files, you'll need the Disk Copy software, which can be downloaded from the Apple Software Updates site (**http://asu.info.apple.com/**) or copied

from the Mac OS CD-ROM and installed in the Utilities folder on your hard disk. Once
you have the Disk Copy software downloaded and installed, you can mount regular image
files just as if they, too, were regular disks. Just double-click them.

Create an Image File

You can create your own image files as well. This can be useful in two ways. First, you
can take any folder or group of documents and mount it onto a disk image. You can then
transfer that image to other Macs so that they can use the folder of files. Plus, the disk
images are compressed, just like StuffIt files. So, the files are compressed, convenient,
and very cool—and these disk images are easy to understand and use.

Second, you can use a Mac *other than* an iMac to create a floppy image of a particular
floppy disk that you need to use. Once the disk image is created, the disk image file can be
transmitted to your iMac and used as if it were a diskette. That makes it that much easier to
move old documents or backups you may have stored on floppies to your iMac.

*A good use of floppy images is to store them on CDs. Check with your local
Macintosh retailer, Apple Specialist, or Mac User Group to see if they offer a
floppy-to-CD service. It's a valuable service to have your floppy disks copied onto
a CD that you can use with your iMac. With over 600MB of capacity on a CD,
that's more than 425 floppy disks!*

Here's how you create an image file:

1. Start up Disk Copy (discussed in the previous section).

2. When the Disk Copy window appears, drag-and-drop the folder or the floppy disk
icon you want to create an image of. (Remember, if you're on a Macintosh that has
a floppy drive, you can create the image from an actual floppy disk icon that has
been mounted on your desktop.)

3. The Save Disk Image As dialog box appears. Give the disk image a name and
choose a folder in which it should be stored. (You may want it saved on the
desktop.) You can also choose various options, including whether the image will
be Read Only or Read and Write (if it's Read and Write then you'll be able to save

files to it when it's mounted) and whether the image should be mounted once it's created. You can also choose the size of the image, from a fixed size like 1.4MB or 500MB, or you can choose the Data Size option, where the size varies with the data you're creating an image of. Once you've made your choices, click Save.

4. Disk Copy goes to work and creates an image of the disk or folder and places it on the desktop.

NOTE

Remember, even if your disk image is in a folder, the mounted disk icon will always appear on the desktop, just like any other disk.

Find and Use Shareware and Freeware Programs

One of the main reasons to learn the nuances of uploading and downloading programs is so that you can start to work with shareware and freeware programs. These are computer programs available on the Internet (or online services) for downloading and using immediately on your iMac.

If the software is shareware, you'll find yourself with a grace period during which you can use the program—often 30 days. If you go past the 30 days, a number of things might happen. You may not be able to save documents anymore. You may not have access to all the features. Or, you may be able to use the program as before, but you'll see "nag" screens—screens that pop up reminding you to pay for the program—more frequently.

NOTE

"Demo" versions of commercial software often work like shareware, at least in some respects. Usually, you'll have a demonstration period where you can use all or most of the software's features. After the demo period expires, you generally have to pay for the software to continue using all of its features.

With freeware, the program is simply free, although there may be other licensing restrictions. (It may be free in certain settings, like education and nonprofit, but not free for corporate use, for instance.) As you can tell, much of freeware and shareware is sold on the "honor system," and this is done for two reasons. First, it's easier for smaller companies and individuals to distribute software this way on the Internet because they don't have to pay for boxes, books, and shipping to major retail stores. Second, these applications and utilities are often meant for a more focused audience—people who need a specific solution to a problem, not a general application or utility.

Don't for a moment think that shareware and freeware aren't good programs just because they aren't sold at electronics stores. (By way of comparison, shrink-wrapped, packaged programs are called *commercial* software.) There is a lot of great shareware and freeware available for downloading—programs that do amazing things and have wonderful interfaces. In fact, you've already learned Transmit, Fetch, and Aladdin's StuffIt products, all of which are distributed as shareware. (And StuffIt Expander is freeware!)

If there's an application or utility (or even a game) that you currently desire, it's a great idea to pop online and search for such a solution in an online library of shareware solutions. You might find exactly what you're looking for, and shareware is often cheaper than a trip to the computer store.

Find Good Shareware

Fortunately, you're not on your own when it comes to finding decent shareware. There are a number of ways to use your browser for shareware, including great services that help you search for exactly what you're seeking. You can usually search by keywords, or you can take a look at the most popular downloads, most recent additions, and so on.

SHORTCUT *These days, some of the Macintosh magazines—MacAddict (**http://www.macaddict.com**), Mac Home (**http://www.machome.com/**), Inside Mac Games (**http://www.imgmagazine.com/**)—and many of the large Macintosh user groups, like Arizona Mac Users Group (AMUG, **http://www.amug.org/**), offer CD subscriptions. Subscribe and you'll regularly receive a CD-ROM in the mail, allowing you to sample the latest shareware and freeware as sampled by the editors of that magazine or CD service.*

You can begin by heading out to a Web download site using your browser. There, you'll be able to search using keywords and locate shareware and freeware that can solve the problem or fill the gap that you want filled. Many of them even feature weekly updates, stories that suggest new programs, and ways to figure out what would be best for you.

Here are a few of my favorite places to find shareware on the Web:

CNet's Download.com	Repository of all sorts of downloadables, including shareware, demos, patches, and updates	**http://www.download.com**
CNet's Shareware.com	Great search engine for shareware and freeware	**http://www.shareware.com**
ZD's MacDownload.com	Mac focus with ratings from the Ziff-Davis Mac magazine staffs (*Macworld, MacWeek*)	**http://www.macdownload.com**
Version Tracker	Tracks new programs and new versions, both commercial and shareware, available on the Internet	**http://www.versiontracker.com**
SoftWatcher	Tracks new programs and updates; offers a Mac-specific section	**http://www.softwatcher.com/mac/**

20

Chapter 21

Get on America Online

How to...

- Distinguish between AOL and the Internet
- Sign onto AOL
- Customize your screen name, including Parental Controls for kids' accounts
- Get your e-mail and send some of your own
- Visit the different channels on the service
- Check out the chat rooms
- Post in message areas
- Get on the Internet with AOL's tools

There's often confusion over what, exactly, the America Online service is. AOL is an online service that uses its own special application software for accessing the information, e-mail, chat groups, and message areas that are run by AOL staff. Ultimately, your iMac uses the AOL application to dial into server computers in AOL's headquarters in Virginia, which send requested information (news, stocks, e-mail) back to your iMac.

AOL is not the Internet, although you can use AOL as your Internet Service Provider and you can access Internet services through AOL. Instead, the AOL service is its own distinct place, complete with news, sports, magazines, interest groups, chats, and more. With more than 17 million users, it's a very popular place to be.

But AOL *can* be your only connection to the Internet if you so desire. In fact, the AOL software can work just like the Remote Access software in the Mac OS. All you do is sign onto the service, then start up Internet Explorer, Netscape Navigator, or an FTP program and start surfing.

AOL is easy to use, it's accessible from most anyplace in the United States (and most places around the world), and it offers a lot of unique content. If you don't want to mess with other ISPs, then sign onto AOL and enjoy yourself.

Sign Up and Dial In

For the America Online service, you'll need an account name and password—if you don't have those things, you can sign up directly via the service. If you already have an AOL account, then you can skip a few steps. For any connection, though, you'll need to start up AOL by double-clicking its icon in the AOL subfolder of the Internet folder, or you can choose America Online from the Apple menu.

Before starting this process, check the sound volume on your iMac and turn it down a bit. When AOL goes to dial the modem the first time, it can be very loud and obnoxious and you can't change the volume until it's done dialing.

Dial In the First Time

Here's what happens the first time you start up AOL:

1. You'll see the AOL Setup screen. Choose Begin Automatic Setup. AOL will try to find your iMac's modem, which it should do with no problem. Wait until this process is complete.

2. Next you'll see the Confirm Your Connection screen, where you're asked to confirm that you want to use the iMac's internal modem. If you want to do this, just click Next. You may also want to use a TCP/IP or LAN connection. (This would be true if you prefer to connect to AOL over the Internet using either the Remote Access control panel or an Ethernet connection.) Select that option and click Next. AOL will attempt to sign on over your TCP/IP connection. If it does, move ahead to the next section, "Create an Account."

3. Now you'll need to make some dialing choices (assuming you're still on the modem path). If you have a touch-tone phone, you're fine. If you have special dialing needs, select the appropriate check boxes and make whatever changes are necessary for your particular phone system. (A comma, entered in any situation where numbers will be dialed, tells the AOL software to pause for a few seconds at that comma.) Click Next.

4. Now, choose the country you're dialing from and, if appropriate, the area code where you are currently located. Click Next.

5. AOL is about to dial its special toll-free number. Make sure the phone line is clear and click Next.

6. The dialing takes place. Hopefully, everything is successful and you'll move on to the Search for AOL Access Numbers screen.

7. Now choose a local phone number for AOL to access (assuming one is listed). Highlight that number on the left and click the Add button. Your iMac is most compatible with V.90/Flex connections, but it should work fine with any of the other V.90 connections, as well as 33.6, 14.4, and so on. The smaller the number, the slower the connection, with V.90 being the fastest. Each time you click Add, you'll see a screen that asks you to set up the number exactly as it should be dialed.

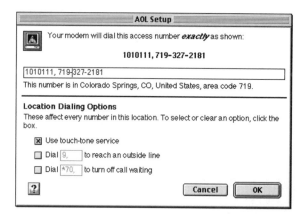

8. After you've selected all the phone numbers you want to use, click Next.

9. Now AOL will hang up and dial in to the first local access number you've selected. It will attempt to connect to the service (you'll hear the modem screeching). If successful, you'll see the Create an Account screen. At this point, things diverge slightly.

Create an Account

If you plan to create a new account, follow these instructions. If you already have an account, head to this chapter's next section, called "Use Your Existing Account."

Here's how to create a new account:

1. Select You Want To Create A New Account in the Create Your America Online dialog box. Click Next.

2. Now, enter a bunch of information about yourself, pressing TAB to move to each entry box. Click Next when you're done.

3. Now, read all about the exciting new membership that awaits you, then click Next.

4. Choose the credit card you want to use for your billing, or explore other options by clicking the Other Billing Options button. If you click that button, other credit cards and a checking account option are shown. Select one and click Next.

5. You'll then pass through various screens that ask you to enter credit card information, verify it, and so on.

6. After entering your credit card or banking information, you'll read and accept the member agreement. To read it, click the Read Now radio button, then click Next. If you've read it and you agree, click the I Do button and click Next.

7. Once all that is out of the way, you can choose your screen name. Enter the name you'd like to use for your main AOL account. Enter something that sounds good and click Next.

8. AOL may report that it's able to set up your screen name, but probably not. Instead, AOL will offer a contraction of what you entered, probably with some randomly generated numbers. If you like that one, click Next. Otherwise, choose the radio button next to I'd Like This Screen Name Instead. When you select the button, another text box appears and you can enter a different name. Click Next when you've typed it. You may have to go through this a few times, but, eventually, you'll either break down and accept that awful name, or you'll hit on something that works.

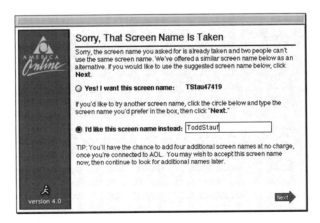

9. Next, you confirm your screen name and click Next.

10. Now you'll enter a password. Your password should be at least six characters long and can include both letters and numbers. The best passwords have nothing to do with your life—but those can be tough to remember. So, a combination of remembrances—something like your childhood house number plus that funny name your college roommate used to have for his one green sock—can mix into something no hacker could ever guess. After you've entered the password twice (to verify that you're trying the same thing both times), click Next.

11. Now you may be asked dumb demographic question(s). Click to answer them.

That's it. You're online. You'll be "welcomed" and told that "you've got mail." Don't get too excited, though—it's just a canned message from Steve Case, chairman of AOL. If you like, you can click Yes, Let's Get Started in the QuickStart dialog box and take a tour of AOL. (Notice you can click Don't Show Me This Again if you don't want and don't need a tour of AOL, thanks very much!)

OK, now skip the next section in this chapter (lucky you!) and jump ahead to see how you'll generally go about signing on and off AOL.

Use Your Existing Account

If you already have an AOL account and you just want to set up your iMac to use that account, you can do that, too. Here's how:

1. On the Create Your America Online page, choose You Already Have An AOL Account You'd Like To Use.

2. Two entry boxes appear where you can enter your name and password. Do so, then click Next.

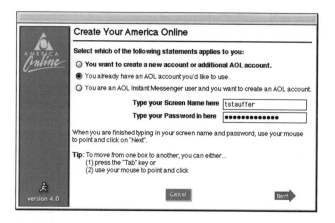

Easy enough, right? As long as you've entered a valid user name and password, you're set. Now you can learn about signing on and off in the next section.

Sign On and Off

Generally, you'll start your AOL session at the Welcome screen, where you'll see your screen name (and any others you've created) along with space for your password. Here's how to sign on:

1. Make sure your modem and phone line aren't currently in use. (You can't sign on while someone is talking on the phone or while your iMac is busy accepting a fax.)

2. Choose a screen name you'd like to use to sign on from the Select Screen Name menu.

3. Enter the password for the chosen screen name.

4. Choose the location you're dialing from, if appropriate, in the Select Location box.

5. Click Sign On.

Now the modem will dial (if your connection uses the modem) and the familiar connection screen appears. Watch the messages to see how things are going. Once you've gotten through the log-on process, you'll see the regular screen and you'll be welcomed, then told "you've got mail" if, in fact, you have some.

Once you're signed on, there are really three ways to sign off. First, you can sign off and allow someone else to access AOL or otherwise leave AOL active so it can be used again. (It won't be using the modem; it'll simply be open and waiting at the Welcome screen.) To do this, choose Sign Off | Sign Off. You can also choose Sign Off | Change Screen Name if you'd like to change to a new user without being forced to redial the modem.

You can also quit AOL, which will sign off and quit the program all in one swift motion. Just choose File | Quit.

Create a New Screen Name

One of the first things you might want to do is add a second screen name to your account. In fact, you can give each member of your family a unique screen name up to AOL's limit of five total screen names. Each screen name gets its own individual e-mail, its own storage folders, and even its own 2MB of storage space for Web pages. You can also change the Parental Controls for a particular screen name, limiting what can be done on AOL while that screen name is signed on. And the best part is, only the original screen name is the administrative account, so as long as you keep that screen name's password to yourself, you have total control over the other screen names.

To create a new screen name:

1. Sign on to the service under your original screen name (that's the administrative account) and wait until you've been fully connected. Once you've seen the main screens, you can select My AOL | Screen Names. (Pop-up menus appear when you select many of the buttons in AOL.)

21

2. In the dialog box that appears, double-click the Create A Screen Name entry.

3. Now you'll see another dialog box that allows you to enter a screen name that you'd like to add to this account. This is the same process you went through when you were trying to create your main screen name—you may or may not get your first choice.

4. If you don't get your choice, then AOL will respond with an alternate name. If you like it, choose Create A Screen Name. If you don't, enter another name and then click Create A Screen Name. You'll go through the process until you get a name you like.

5. Once you've hit on an acceptable name, you're ready to enter a password for this account. Enter that same password in each box, then click OK.

6. Now you're able to set up the age group for this account. Basically, this screen allows you to invoke the Parental Controls that are built into AOL. Choose the age group you feel appropriate for this user—the younger the group, the less access the user will have to parts of the service that may offer more adult content. Click OK when you've chosen.

 You can read more about Parental Controls by selecting Help | Parental Controls.

7. Now you'll see the New Screen Name confirmation, which will include information about the particular Parental Control you've chosen (if you've chosen one). Click OK to head back to the service, or click Custom Controls to move on to customizing the Parental Controls for each screen name in your account.

Parental Controls

AOL really gives you a lot of control over how your account and screen names can be set up. Parental Controls allow you to choose what parts of the service a particular screen name can use, which allows you to decide, for instance, that a particular screen name can't accept e-mail with attachments or can't chat in chat rooms.

Beyond that, you can move on to the Custom Controls, which allow you to fine-tune the Parental Controls to the levels that you feel are appropriate for a given screen name. So if you don't like the AOL defaults, you can change them.

To set Parental Controls:

1. Choose My AOL | Parental Controls.

2. Now, in the dialog box that appears, choose the Set Parental Controls Now button.

3. In the dialog box, you'll see a menu at the top of the screen that allows you to choose each screen name you've created. Choose one from the menu, then click the button next to the type of Custom Control you want to change (E-mail control, Chat control, IM control, Web control, and so on).

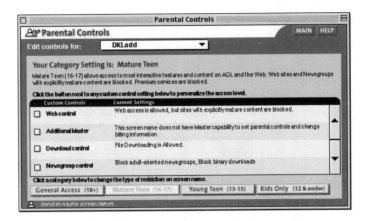

4. You can also click the category at the bottom on the screen to choose a general restriction setting from the options: General Access, Mature Teen, Young Teen, and Kids Only.

5. Once you've chosen a Custom Control, you'll see a dialog box that gives you various options to set regarding that particular control. In the Newsgroup control, for instance, you can choose to have all newsgroups blocked, you can block newsgroup downloads, or you can block a list of newsgroups or newsgroups that have certain keywords in them like "binary" (which usually means pictures, often adult-related) or "games" if you feel games are a waste of time for this particular user. Click Save in the Custom Control settings dialog box and you're returned to the Parental Controls where you can do more management.

Delete a Screen Name

To delete a screen name you need to be signed on with the original account name (or a Master Screen Name). Here's how you do it:

1. Select My AOL | Screen Names.

2. In the dialog box that appears, click Delete A Screen Name.

3. Click Continue in the Are You Sure dialog box.

4. Now, choose the screen name to delete from the menu, then click Delete. The screen name is deleted.

Restore a Screen Name

Just because it's gone doesn't mean a screen name is gone forever—at least, not if it's been less than six months since you deleted it. To recover a screen name:

1. Select My AOL | Screen Names.

2. In the dialog box that appears, click Restore A Screen Name.

3. Now you'll see a dialog box that includes recoverable screen names. Select one, then click Recover.

Click OK in the dialog box that confirms recovery, and you're ready to roll with the screen name, now back from the dead!

Get Your E-mail

If you're like most AOL users, you're itching for that e-mail. Well, reading your e-mail is easy, assuming you have some. You'll usually know—if the volume control is allowing any sound to get through your iMac's speakers, you'll hear "you've got mail" when you sign onto the service if you've been sent some. To read that mail, just click the You Have Mail icon that appears in the corner of the Welcome screen.

You'll see the Mailbox with a list of messages you've received.

Switch between unread, read, and sent mail.

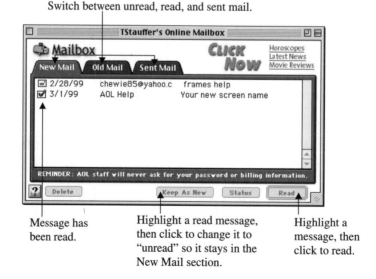

Message has been read.

Highlight a read message, then click to change it to "unread" so it stays in the New Mail section.

Highlight a message, then click to read.

If a particular message looks interesting, double-click it (or select it and click Read) to open it up in its own window (see Figure 21-1). This window allows you to read the message using the scroll bars down the right side of the message window. But it also allows you to do a lot more than that. You can reply, forward the message, delete it, or just move on to another message.

Here's what each of the controls does:

- **Arrows**   If you choose the right arrow, you can move to the next message without returning to the Mailbox. The left arrow gives you the previous message in the list.

- **# of # Box**   This is actually a button, which shows the current message you're reading of a certain total number of messages. Clicking the button returns you immediately to the Mailbox.

- **Delete**   Choosing the Delete button causes the message to immediately leave the Mailbox. A deleted message is not kept in the Old Mail folder (part of the

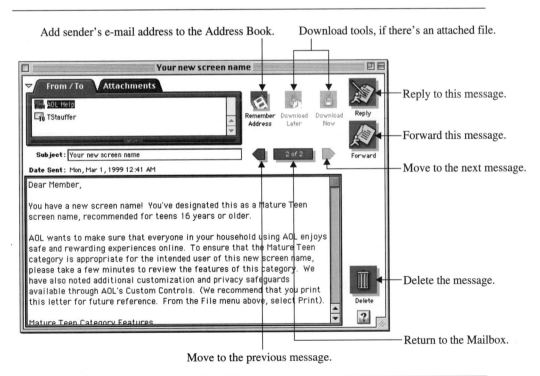

Add sender's e-mail address to the Address Book.   Download tools, if there's an attached file.

Reply to this message.

Forward this message.

Move to the next message.

Delete the message.

Return to the Mailbox.

Move to the previous message.

FIGURE 21-1   The Read E-mail window gives you a number of choices for dealing with your incoming messages.

21

Mailbox); messages that are read but not deleted are left in the Old Mail folder for a few days or weeks (depending on your volume of mail) before they're deleted.

- ■ **Remember Address** This adds the sender's e-mail address to the Address Book, which can be accessed from the Mail Center button menu in the AOL toolbar.

- ■ **Reply** Highlight the text you'd like to *quote*—text that you'd like to appear in your message reply that reminds the recipient what he or she originally said in the e-mail to you. Then, click the Reply button to create a new message that includes the sender's e-mail address as the recipient of the reply. Now type your message and click the Send Now or Send Later button to send the reply.

- ■ **Forward** Click Forward, then enter an e-mail address in the Address section of the new message to whom you want this message forwarded. Click Send Now or Send Later once you have the forward addressed properly. (You can also type a few lines, if you like.)

- ■ **Download Later** If you have an attachment with this message, you can choose to add it to your Download Manager—a part of AOL where different download files can be specified. Then, at a given time, you can choose to download them all at once, instead of waiting for each to download. This allows you to get up and move around, since the Download Manager can even sign off automatically.

- ■ **Download Now** Select this button to download any attached files to your iMac immediately. You'll get a Save dialog box so you can choose where you'd like the attached file saved.

And, as always, you can simply close the message you're reading by clicking its Close box. A check now appears next to its name in the Mailbox. The next time you open the Mailbox, the read message will have been moved to the Old Mail tab.

 *Just FYI—AOL staff members will never ask you for your account password, nor will they direct you to a Web site that asks you to enter such information. Never, ever, ever. Any e-mail you get that suggests that you need to enter your password (usually in exchange for something free) is a hoax. That's just evil users trying to get your password so they can create some mischief. Little devils.*

Create a New Message

If you'd like to create a new message from scratch, the beginning part is simple—just click the Write button in the AOL toolbar. That causes a new message window to appear (see Figure 21-2).

By the way—you don't have to be connected to start a message. You can write messages without being signed on to AOL, then choose Send Later (after writing

Choose the type of recipient from the menu.   Get an address from the Address Book.

Enter a recipient.   Attach files.

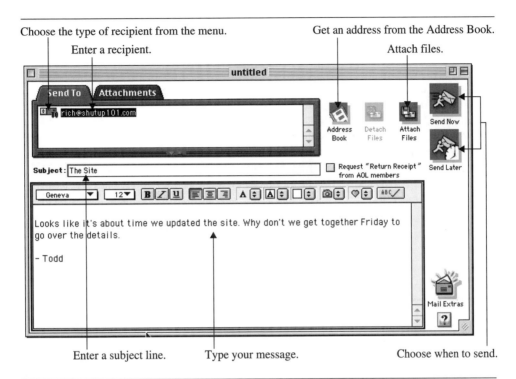

Enter a subject line.   Type your message.   Choose when to send.

FIGURE 21-2   The new message window offers many options for formatting
your e-mail.

the message) to send it once you've signed on. You'll see how to do that at the end of
this section.

> NOTE   *Many of the issues discussed in Chapter 18 are relevant to e-mail in this chapter
> too—things like the memo-style headers, formatting your e-mail, and so forth. If
> you haven't already, check out Chapter 18 to learn more about how e-mail works
> and some of the etiquette involved.*

Once you've got the new message window open, you're ready to address the message.
To do that, either type an e-mail address that you happen to know for your recipient, or
select the Address Book button, then choose a name from the Address Book window.
Highlight a name, then click the appropriate button—Send To, Copy To, or Blind
Copy—depending on how you want to send the message. When you're done with the
Address Book, click its Close box. (To get rid of a recipient, select the name in the To
window and press the DELETE key.)

21

If you need to add an attachment, click the Attach Files button. An Open dialog box appears, where you can find an attachment. Select it, then click the Attach button. If you choose to compress the attachment, click the Compress Attachments check box. (The attachments are compressed with the StuffIt format, which is not recommended for sending to Microsoft Windows or Unix users.) The files are now attached—you can see them by clicking the Attachments tab. You can remove them by highlighting the filename and clicking the Detach Files button.

Now you can click in the body of the message and type your message. Remember that you only need to press RETURN at the end of a paragraph, just as when you're typing in a word processor. At this point you might want to make formatting decisions about your e-mail—again the tools for bold, italic, or underlining are like those in a word processor.

AOL also offers some other formatting tools for your messages, which allow you to do more e-mail-specific things.

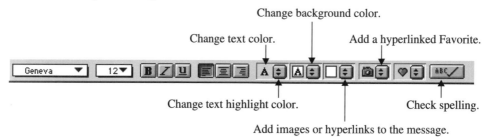

AOL offers many options that you can learn more about from the Mail Extras button down in the bottom-right corner of the message. Most of them allow you to add Web page–like tools—such as hyperlinks and graphics—to your e-mail documents.

NOTE   *As discussed in Chapter 18, it's not always advisable to send messages as HTML documents instead of as plain text e-mail. To avoid problems, simply refrain from formatting your messages with bold, hyperlinks, and so on. If you know your e-mail recipients can handle HTML documents (for instance, they use Outlook Express or Netscape Communicator), then go nuts.*

When you've completed the message, you might want to click the Check Spelling button, then you can click Send Now to send the message immediately. If you're not currently connected to AOL you can click Send Later and it'll be sent when you sign on.

Send Waiting Mail

If you've elected to Send Later, you can send your mail all at once. You do that by opening the Mail Waiting to Be Sent window from the Mail Center button menu. You'll see the window, which allows you to click Send All or select individual messages and click Send to send them over the Internet.

This is great if you want to compose your messages offline, then sign onto AOL and send them quickly. It keeps you from tying up the phone lines, spending money on long distance, or eating into your connect time if you have a limited-time plan for your AOL access.

Move Around the Service

There's a lot to do on AOL besides get your e-mail. In fact, figuring out where to go can be tough, so there are different ways to search and be guided around AOL to get a full sense of how it works.

In most cases, moving around AOL is simple. You click buttons to move to another section—sometimes there will be hyperlinks, too, which take you to a new topic. If you want to get rid of a window, click its Close box.

Welcome

Aside from access to your Mailbox, the Welcome screen usually offers the latest and most exciting news on the service. You can click any link to jump into a news or entertainment story. You can also click the AOL logo to find a special section, What's New on AOL. Once you become a seasoned AOL surfer you'll probably spend some time with this service, since it tells you what's changed most recently on the service.

Channels

The place to start is probably the Channels, which you can access through the Channels window (which appears when you sign onto the service) or through the Channels button on the AOL toolbar. The Channels allow you to quickly explore different topic areas on AOL such as Travel, Finance, Education, Sports, and Kids Only. Choose a channel and you'll see its main page. From there, click the latest links to see what's going on in that particular topic area.

People Connection

I'll discuss this section in more depth in the section "Chat and Read Message Boards." The People Connection is an area where you'll learn about AOL chatting, find out what's available online that day (what celebrities and notable folks are chatting today), and discover how to go about all this chat business. Plus, there's plenty of advice on meeting people and getting to know one another better, virtually. You can get to the People Connection from the Channels screen or by choosing People | People Connection.

Find by Keyword

Keywords are quite a commodity on AOL—if you happen to know the keyword for a particular area, you can get there immediately by typing the keyword into the entry bar at the top of the screen and clicking Go or pressing ENTER. Keywords often make sense.

Use AOL Favorites

If you find a place you like on AOL, you can turn it into a Favorite. That way, it's easily accessible from within the Favorites button menu. This works a lot like a Favorite in Internet Explorer or a bookmark in Netscape Navigator or Communicator. (In fact, you can use the Favorites feature from within AOL's Web browsing tool.)

To use a Favorite, click the Favorites button in the toolbar, then select the Favorite from the menu that appears.

To create a Favorite, all you need to do is locate the small heart in the top-right corner of the window—it should show up in any window that can be designated a Favorite. Click that heart. Now you'll see a dialog box that allows you to choose what to do with this particular page. In this case, you want to add it to the Favorites menu.

The keyword **writer** opens the Writers Club, the keyword **dog** opens the Pets Interest page, the keyword **finance** takes you to the Personal Finance area, and the keyword **movies** takes you to the reviews pages.

Keywords and searches can work on the World Wide Web, too—enter the keyword **Time**, for instance, and AOL takes you to *Time Magazine*'s Web site.

You can figure out a site's keyword pretty easily once you've visited it. Just check the lower-right corner, where you'll see the keyword.

Chat and Read Message Boards

Another major reason to fire up America Online and spend some time connected is to get to know people through special interest groups, informal chats, or online forums. First, of course, you've got to find that stuff.

Chat: The People Connection

Using the People Connection, you can find chats on all sorts of topics, ranging from romance to fan chats to particular, and serious, topics regarding current events, the news, or regional discussions. Here's how:

1. Open the People Connection by selecting People | People Connection.

2. In the People Connection window, click Find a Chat.

3. Now, highlight a category, then click View Chats. You'll see the Chat Groups change on the right side of the window.

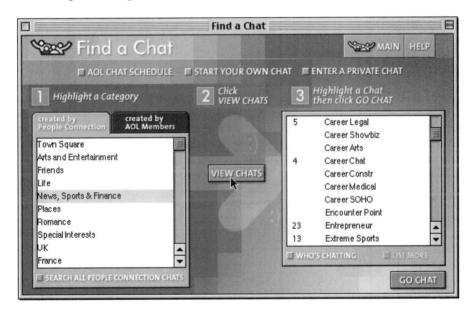

4. When you see a chat that interests you, highlight it and click the Go Chat button. Now you'll enter the chat room.

You'll also find chat rooms elsewhere on the AOL service, including in special interest and hobbyist areas. Instead of searching for those, just double-click an icon to enter the chat room.

Chat window   Double-click a person to see options.

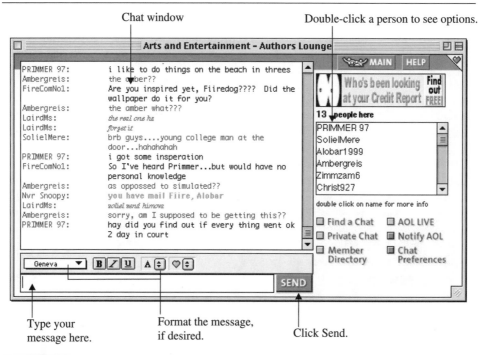

Type your   Format the message,
message here.   if desired.   Click Send.

FIGURE 21-3 The AOL chat room interface

NOTE *Sometimes a chat room is full. If that's the case, AOL will ask you if you'd like to be automatically routed to a similar chat topic.*

Once you're in a chat room, the interface is pretty much the same from room to room (see Figure 21-3). You'll see the people who are chatting on the right side of the window, while the actual chat lines scroll down the left side. (These are lines that have been typed by other folks who are participating in the chat.)

Chatting is actually pretty easy. You just type a line of text in the entry box, then click the Send button or press RETURN. You can also format your entry, if you like, just to add some color and style. Once you click Send, your message (sometimes after a brief delay) will appear in the Chat window.

The real options come when you're dealing with individual users. In the User window, you can double-click a particular user name to bring up a dialog box about that user. Here's what you can do:

- Click Ignore Member if this person is annoying, obnoxious, or bothersome. You now will no longer see that person's comments in the Chat window.

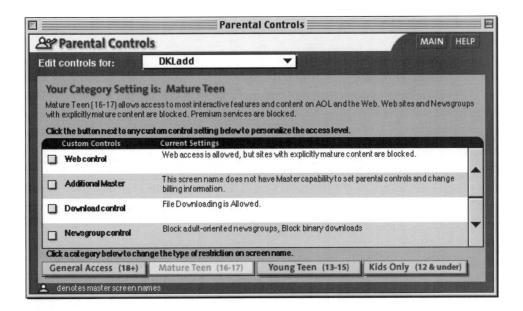

NOTE *You can also use Ignore Member in a more positive way—if you're chatting in a large room with many people in it, you might choose to ignore members that aren't currently participating in your conversation. That will make your discussion easier to follow.*

■ Click Send Message to send an Instant Message to this user. Instant Messages are special one-on-one chats between AOL users (or Internet users with the special AOL Instant Message software installed).

■ Click Get Profile to see if this person has a Member Profile on file.

TIP *You can create your own Member Profile by choosing My AOL | My Member Profile.*

Read and Write in Message Boards

You'll find message boards more in the interest areas on AOL. While you're wandering around AOL, anything that says "read what others have to say" or "exchange messages with like-minded folks" is probably a message board. Message boards are areas that work almost exactly like Usenet newsgroups—you read the messages, post your replies, mark things as read, and so forth.

If you're looking at a typical AOL list, the message boards stand out because of their card and thumbtack icon. (This suggests a "bulletin board" where you can post your bulletin for others to see and reply to.)

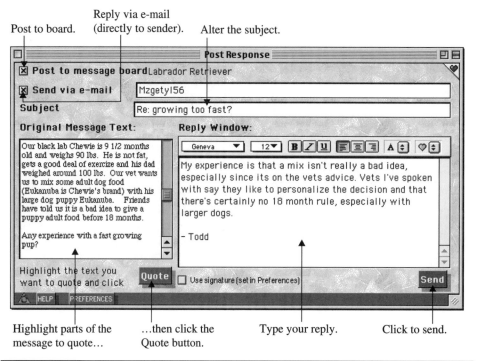

Post to board.

Reply via e-mail
(directly to sender).

Alter the subject.

FIGURE 21-4 The Post Response message window

Highlight parts of the
message to quote...

...then click the
Quote button.

Type your reply.

Click to send.

Double-click such an entry and you'll see the message board interface—it's remarkably similar to the Usenet newsgroups interface. Double-click a topic to see its listing window, then double-click a subject to read the posts. Posts are simply a series of replies to a particular topic of discussion. Once you get down to the post level, you're seeing each individual message.

To read the next post in this same subject, click the Next Post button; to read the next subject, click the Next Subject button. To reply to the subject (that is, to add your own post to the ongoing discussion), click Reply. You'll see the Reply window, which offers some features of its own (see Figure 21-4).

Notice that your reply can be sent two different ways—you can post it to the message board or you can send it as an e-mail directly to the person who is shown in the message when you click Reply. You can also do both, or you can enter a different screen name if you'd like to send this message to someone else (perhaps to alert them to an interesting topic).

It's important to note that if you decide to post the message, it doesn't actually have to be a reply to the original poster. You don't even have to quote their message—you can simply go off on some other topic and post the message at the end of the particular subject. Or, you can highlight text, click Quote, then reply specifically to a particular person's comments. It's up to you.

When you're done entering your post, click Send.

 Your post is available for all to see, including AOL. Make sure your post doesn't violate AOL's terms of service and that you're really saying what you want to say to people—not just something angry in the heat of the moment. You should also double-check the entries to make sure you're doing what you want with the reply. If you're trying to send an e-mail, for instance, you'll want to make sure that you've checked only the Send Via E-mail option.

Use AOL Link and Get on the Internet

You may already have noticed that AOL is tightly integrated with the Internet. As you move from topic area to topic area, you'll find that Internet links are mixed in with the regular links—after all, AOL 4.0 has an integrated Web browser that is actually a version of Internet Explorer. (With America Online's acquisition of Netscape Corporation, this may change in future versions.) The browser tool is certainly capable, and assuming you have a reasonably fast connection, it's pretty painless to surf the Internet from within America Online.

But you can also, as mentioned, use AOL as your Internet Service Provider and run other Internet applications, using AOL as your connection to the Internet. All you have to do, in most cases, is fire up the Internet application and start working. AOL takes care of the rest.

AOL's Internet Tools

You've already seen that you can load AOL's internal Web browser tool simply by clicking on a Web link of some sort. You can also choose a Favorite that happens to point to a Web site. If you do, then the browser tool opens and you'll view that site.

If you'd like to enter a URL directly, you can do that, too. In the Find entry box in the toolbar, enter the URL directly. Press RETURN and AOL will attempt to load that page. You'll notice in this illustration that the AOL toolbar actually turns into a sort of browser toolbar, complete with Back, Forward, Refresh, and Home buttons as well as the location entry box.

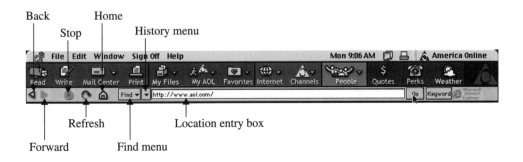

21

You can access the History menu (the arrow just to the left of the location box) to revisit pages you've been to recently. You can also pull down the Find menu (in the toolbar) and choose Find on the Internet to open up a search page and begin searching the Internet.

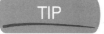

Want to set your own home page? Choose My AOL | Preferences. In the Preferences dialog box, click WWW. Now you can enter a new home page, and many other preferences regarding Web browsing. Click OK when you're done.

Other Tools

AOL offers support for FTP as well. (FTP, short for File Transfer Protocol, is a common way to transfer files to and from other computers over the Internet.) You can use keyword: **FTP** to get to the special FTP tools, or enter an FTP URL in the location box and use the browser tools to download files.

And AOL has tools built in for accessing Usenet newsgroups. You can get there by entering the keyword: **Newsgroups**. The controls are similar to AOL's Message Board interface discussed in this chapter.

Basic Usenet usage and terminology is discussed in Chapter 18. FTP is discussed in Chapter 20.

AOL Link and Internet Applications

AOL uses the AOL Link technology to allow America Online to serve as an ISP connection for some of your other Internet software. If you're connected through a dial-in connection to AOL, you could go to Control Panels in the Apple menu and choose TCP/IP. You'll see that the current profile is an AOL profile. That means that instead of using the AOL software, you can use other TCP/IP software—Web browsers and FTP programs like Transmit or Fetch. That way, you can use faster or more full-featured Internet programs if you like.

Occasionally, you'll notice AOL asking you to switch to AOL Link as you're starting up. AOL does this if the TCP/IP control panel is set to use some other connection (like Ethernet or Remote Access) and if you're trying to use AOL to dial your modem, instead of using AOL over an existing Internet connection. If that's the case, AOL will switch to AOL Link in the TCP/IP control panel to run its Web tool and other Internet programs.

So, with AOL up and running over a modem connection, just choose Browse the Internet or launch your FTP tool to get started. Note that e-mail programs will work, too, but only for accessing e-mail in ISP-based accounts. You'll still have to use AOL to retrieve your AOL e-mail. (Claris Emailer, an e-mail application that's sold by Apple, can also access AOL e-mail.)

AOL's Web Storage Space

Every AOL screen name gets access to 2MB of storage space that can be used for Web pages. The pages can be accessed by anyone with a Web browser and an Internet connection by entering the URL **http://members.aol.com/*username*/** where the *username* is one of your screen names. Upload pages through the My Place interface, which works almost exactly like the FTP controls discussed in the earlier section, "AOL's Internet Tools." In order to upload your Web files, you'll access keyword: **My Place**, then upload your documents to the My Place directory. Those files will then be available to anyone who has Web access.

Chapter 22

Create Your Own Web Pages

How to...

- Get started with PageMill
- Create your Web page
- Style your text
- Add images and links
- Put your page on the Web

Ah, the siren song of the World Wide Web. Your chance to publish whatever you desire for all the world to see. It's quite an opportunity and iMac, being the little Internet devil that it is, has made it easy once again. It's even easier if you bought one of the iMacs that includes PageMill in the bargain.

Even if you didn't get PageMill, you can download the demo and get started creating Web pages. Web pages are fairly easy once you know the code—you'll be creating attractive, meaningful Web publications in no time.

 *Actually, you'll find that there are many, many applications designed to help you with Web pages. This chapter covers PageMill because it comes with many iMacs. Even if you prefer another application, you'll find that a lot of this chapter still applies.*

The Web Page Revealed

There are a couple of important facts about Web pages that we should get right out into the open. First of all, Web pages are not quite the same as AppleWorks or Word documents. In particular, Web pages are not self-contained documents, where images and styled text exist in one big file. A Web page is really just a plain text document—often called an ASCII document.

That might shock you, since you're used to seeing Web pages with menus, entry boxes, images, moving parts, and so on. But a Web page is nothing more than a text document that includes HyperText Markup Language (HTML) commands.

It's the HTML that has you fooled. HTML is a language that "marks up" regular text and turns it into something more interesting. Those markings are read as instructions by an application—say, a Web browser program—that then styles the text, arranges the page, and drops in image files, QuickTime, or whatever else the HTML instructs the browser to add.

```
<H2>Terry</H2>

<DL>
    <DD>This two-year-old <A HREF="http://www.huskies.co.net/">Siberian</A>
    Husky mix might be named that because she's a terror. She needs
    a good, fenced yard and enough loving attention -- best spent
    throwing a tennis ball over and over again until Terry tires
    out. If you let her snuggle with you, though, you'll find that
    there's no dog sweeter.
    <DT> 
    <DT> 
```

So, in order to create these wonderful HTML documents, you need to know the codes that make up the HyperText Markup Language, right? You need to know which commands make text bold, which commands add images, which commands create horizontal lines, right? Well, you can start by taking a look at Table 22-1.

Format	Code
Bold	<B> </B>
Italic	<I></I>
Teletype (monospace)	<TT> </TT>
Paragraph	<P> </P>
Line return	
Horizontal rule (line)	<HR>
Image	<IMG SRC="*filename.ext*">
Largest heading	<H1></H1>
Smallest heading	<H6> </H6>

TABLE 22-1   Commonly Used HTML Codes

Actually, knowing the codes really isn't all that important. It helps to know how the codes work, but actually knowing the codes themselves is secondary when you have a program like PageMill at your disposal. PageMill is a graphical Web editor that allows you to place text, headings, and other elements on the page. PageMill then writes the HTML codes for you.

The thing to remember is this—HTML *marks up* regular text documents. The images, QuickTime movies, and other things you see on the page are not really embedded in the HTML file; they're separate document files that the HTML document instructs the Web browser to place somewhere in its window. That means when you go to upload the HTML files to a Web server, you'll need to upload the image files, too.

It also means that you're going to have to get used to naming files with logical names and filename extensions (like .html and .jpg) because those are important in the Web jungle.

Create Your Page

To begin a Web page, you'll want to fire up PageMill. If you have a colorful iMac (including a slot-loading model) then you probably have PageMill in the Applications folder on your hard drive. (If it's not yet installed, you'll find it on a CD in your iMac's CD packet.)

If you didn't receive PageMill with your iMac, you can follow along with this chapter for 30 days using Adobe's time-limited demo of PageMill. You can get the demo from Adobe's Web site at **http://www.adobe.com/products/pagemill/**. The idea is to get you just hooked enough on the program that you decide to go ahead and buy it. It's not a bad investment—PageMill is a pretty decent program.

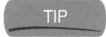 *Check out the Web Pages folder on your iMac—you'll find some home page templates that will help you design pages. After you've gotten to know PageMill, you can get even more creative with the templates.*

Begin the Page

Launch PageMill and you'll get a blank document window to begin creating your page. The first thing you should do is save your page. This is important so that the images and hyperlinks you add to the page know where they are relative to your page. (That'll make more sense when you're adding images.) Choose File | Save Page As and find a place on your hard disk to save the page. It's also a good idea to create a new folder for your page, just in case you get a little out of control and end up creating a Web site.

It's also a good idea to name the page index.html if this is the first page of the site that you're creating. It's customary for the first page of a site to be called "index.html," since Web server applications recognize it as the initial page of a Web site.

 In some cases, a Web server will require that the file be named with the three-letter file extension .htm, as in index.htm, instead of the four-letter .html. Check with your Web administrator.

With the page saved, you can perform a little housekeeping. To begin, you can edit the title for your page. Click on the portion toward the top of the page (under the toolbar) that says Untitled Document. Now, edit that to the title of the page you're creating.

```
Title: This Week's Adoptable Dogs
```

With that out of the way, you can begin typing. You're already in paragraph mode (you can probably see Paragraph in the Format menu in the toolbar). Just type away. When you reach the end of a paragraph, press RETURN.

 Before you can edit a page, PageMill needs to be in edit mode. It's in that mode by default when you start a new page, but not when you load an existing page. If you do that, you'll need to click the little globe icon in the top-right corner, which takes PageMill out of preview mode and puts it into edit mode. At the same time, the icon changes to a pen and scroll to represent the fact that you're in edit mode.

Style Your Text

If you want bold text, press ⌘-B and type. Press ⌘-B again to turn off bold. You can do the same with italic (⌘-I) or underlined (⌘-U) text. You can also select text with the mouse after you've typed it and use the toolbar buttons, shown here, to change the text style.

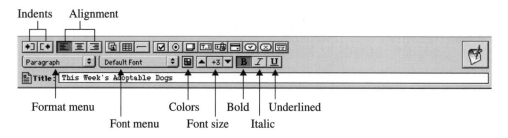

Beyond simple appearance styles, you can also invoke more functional styles. Remember that HTML was first invented by scholarly university types. These folks were more interested in the organization of the document than in the way it looked, as long as it was presentable. So, they created a number of different commands that allow HTML to organize a document.

You've already been typing in paragraphs. If you have text that would be suitable for a heading, go ahead and select it, then select a heading size (H1 is largest, H6 is smallest) from the Format menu. You can also select a paragraph and choose Blockquote from the Format menu to indent the paragraph at both margins. Formatting something as preformatted text means it will use a monospaced font. That's perfect for manually lining up columns of text.

You can also select entire paragraphs or sections of your document and click the alignment buttons—left, center, right—just as you can in a word processing document. The same goes for the indent buttons in the toolbar, which allow you to indent entire paragraphs of text.

PageMill also allows you to change the font and text size within the document. It's not a good idea to pick obscure fonts, since the user will need to have a particular font on his or her computer in order to see the special styling. You can highlight text and choose a new font from the Font menu. I'd recommend sticking to some basics: Times New Roman, Helvetica, Arial, Courier New. Use other fonts and they probably won't show up correctly in a user's browser.

NOTE   *Let me emphasize that you can skip picking a font and the user's browser will use its default. That's probably best, since many browsers simply won't be able to see any special fonts you choose.*

If you want to change the size of text, select the text and click the Up and Down buttons that appear next to the font size number. Notice that the text size can be either a positive or negative number—it doesn't represent a particular point size, just the difference in size from the default point size.

Create a List

HTML offers many different kinds of lists. To create a list, type a series of items, pressing RETURN after each. Select the list and choose Bullet or Numbered from the Format menu.

The definition lists are another story. They're actually designed to work with two formats together—you alternate between a Term and a Definition, creating an attractive list.

> Terry
>
> This two-year-old Siberian Husky mix might be named that because she's a terror. She needs a good, fenced yard and enough loving attention -- best spent throwing a tennis ball over and over again until Terry tires out. If you let her snuggle with you, though, you'll find that there's no dog sweeter.
>
> George
>
> George is a black Lab/German Shepherd mix that's known for being quite friendly and making the rounds. If you live in a friendly neighborhood, George will make sure everyone gets to know you really well. Around the holidays, just tie cards to his collar and set him loose. He'll get them delivered for you. George needs plenty of exercise, but he doesn't mind sauntering. And just be ready to cross the street with him if he sees a chance to meet a new person.|

You can also type an entire series, and then select either Term or Definition, if you like. That gives a certain listlike effect without a bullet or a number.

Add Images

A Web page isn't complete without images. You can add either JPEG or GIF images to your Web page; most browsers recognize both types of image. JPEG is best for photographic images, while GIFs work well for images you create yourself in a drawing program. You can also use the PNG (Portable Network Graphic) format that is gaining popularity.

TIP *It's best to use a program like Adobe PhotoDeluxe or the shareware GraphicConverter to do everything you can to make the image file take up less storage space—the smaller the file size, the faster the image will load across the Internet. For starters, you can use fewer colors (256 colors is a good choice) and crop the image to make it smaller.*

To add an image, place the insertion point where you would like the image to appear on the page. Now, click the Insert Object button (it's just to the right of the alignment buttons—it looks like a little picture) or select Insert | Object | Image. That brings up the Insert Object dialog box. Find the image you're looking for, then click Insert.

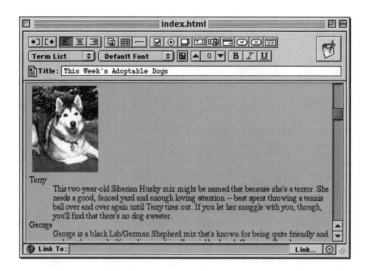

Now you can make some choices about the image. Probably the most important choice is this: Do you want text to wrap around the image, or do you want the image to be part of the text, flowing along with the text, anchored to a particular gap between words?

Click the image to select it and you'll see some tools appear in the toolbar. They show you how you can align the image relative to the text. Click the button that suggests the way you'd like the image to behave.

You should also give the image an "alternative" label. You do that over in the Inspector window (the floating window that appears when you're editing a page) when the image is selected. Just type a label that describes the image in the Alternative Label entry box. Now, visitors who don't load the images in their browser window (or those that don't have a graphical browser) can get some sense of what your image represents.

Copy your images to your Web site folder or, better yet, to a subfolder within it called Images. That way, PageMill doesn't end up creating bizarre paths to the image files all over your hard drive. If you need to manually upload your Web site at a later date, you'll appreciate having all your images in one place relative to the index page.

Add Links

Adding links to other pages either within your Web site or on the World Wide Web is easy. To begin your link, highlight the text on your page that you'd like to turn into "clickable" text.

With the text highlighted, click on the Link To entry box at the bottom of the document window. Now, enter the *filename* of the page (including the subdirectory path, if the page document is stored in a subdirectory of your Web site directory) or enter a URL to another site. Examples might be:

```
products.html
http://www.apple.com/help/questions.html
http://www.mac-upgrade.com/upgrade_guy/index.html
```

When you're done entering the URL, press RETURN. The URL is registered and the highlighted text becomes a hypertext link.

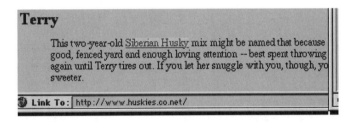

You can change the hypertext just as easily—highlight the hyperlinked text and change the URL in the Link To entry box. To get rid of the hyperlink completely, select the hyperlinked text and choose Edit | Remove Link from the menu. You can even choose just part of the hyperlinked text and remove the link from that text, allowing you to pick and choose the words that are linked within the document.

You can also turn images into links. To do so, select an image and enter a URL in the Link To entry box. Press RETURN and the image becomes a link. If you'd like the image to be outlined in blue (indicating that it's a link), put a number other than zero in the Border entry box that appears in the Inspector window when you select the image.

You might also enjoy experimenting with target links. With the hyperlinked text still highlighted (right after you've entered a URL), click and hold the mouse on the small bull's-eye target in the bottom-right corner of the browser window. You'll see a pop-up menu that allows you, for instance, to load the link in a new window automatically.

How to ...   Put It Online

Once you have your page developed, you're ready to upload it to your Web directory. Most likely your ISP has offered you some free Web space that you can use for your site. You just need to figure out how to upload it. You can do that within PageMill— you just need the FTP address, account information, and a password. You should be able to get this information from your ISP or system administrator.

Here's a tip: If you signed up with the Earthlink service you have 6MB of free Web space. You'll need to sign up at **http://www.earthlink.net/benefits/** to use the space.

Now, in order to upload your site, you can do one of two things. First, you can use an FTP program like Transmit or Fetch to copy your Web files from your iMac to the distant server. If you do this, make sure you're selecting all the HTML and image files that are used in your site. If you created a new folder for your Web site, you probably don't want to upload the folder—just the contents of the folder, along with any subfolders.

Built into PageMill is the ability to upload your page to a Web server computer via FTP. When you're ready to upload your page, you just select File | Upload | Page. Then, you'll need to choose some basic options to get it online. Here's what you do:

1. You'll be asked if you want to create Site settings. Click Yes.

2. Give the site a name and make sure the correct folder has been chosen for the site. Click the Create button.

3. Now, in the Edit Web Project Settings dialog box, enter the FTP information for your Web server—server name, user name, password, and a directory. When you're done, click OK.

If you're currently connected to the Internet, PageMill will connect to the server and attempt to upload your site. If you have trouble, check your name, password, and other server settings, especially the folder you're trying to upload to. PageMill won't create a folder that doesn't already exist, so you'll need to manage your folder creation in Fetch or Transmit.

To get to the server settings in PageMill again, select Site | Show Settings, select the site you want to look at, and click Edit.

Chapter 23

Customize the Internet and Go Faster

How to...

- ■ Customize your Internet connection
- ■ Get higher-speed Internet access for your iMac

The iMac is usually simple to get up and running with an Internet Service Provider (ISP)—that's part of the reason I've left the gritty details to this chapter, instead of explaining the Internet-related settings and control panels earlier in the book. After all, there's the Internet Setup Assistant and the setup procedures in the Internet applications that make them pretty easy to use.

So, if you're happily signing on and off with your Internet connection, and you're not particularly intrigued by how it works, then there probably isn't much reason to read this chapter.

But if you're having trouble with your connection, if you're interested in customizing your setup, or if you'd like to explore new, faster Internet connection technologies, you've come to the right chapter.

Configure TCP/IP, Modem, and Remote Access

In order to have an Internet connection you need two things. First, you need a method for connecting to the Internet: an Ethernet cable, a telephone line (connected to your iMac's modem), or a wireless connection if your iMac has an AirPort add-on card installed. Then, you need to configure the software for your connection. For a modem, that means configuring the Remote Access and TCP/IP control panels. For Ethernet, you'll just configure TCP/IP. For a wireless connection, you'll configure the AirPort application, AirPort Base Station, and TCP/IP.

The Internet Assistant, encountered when you first turn on your iMac, manages most of these options for you. If you've already used it and had great success, there's no reason for you to bother with this chapter.

The TCP/IP Control Panel

This control panel is used to set up the basics of your Internet connection, whether or not you're using a modem. In the control panel you can choose the type of connection that will be used and enter a bunch of different Internet addresses that tell the computer where it's located and how to access the Internet (see Figure 23-1).

The best way to get these numbers (the IP address, subnet mask, router address, and name server addresses) is to ask your ISP or system administrator what they should be. If you're connecting via Point-to-Point Protocol (PPP), you won't need to know the exact IP address, subnet mask, or router address, since those will be assigned to your iMac when you dial into your ISP. You will need to know your name server addresses and what sort of configuration scheme you'll use for PPP.

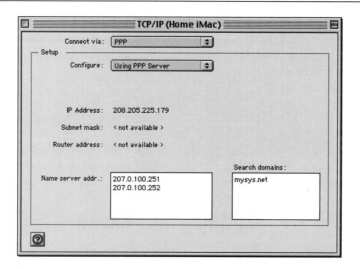

FIGURE 23-1 The TCP/IP control panel

> **NOTE** *A fixed IP address simply means that your Internet address never changes. This is usually true of Ethernet-based connections—they're often fixed. (In larger organizations they may not be, especially if your TCP/IP control panel is set for DHCP—Dynamic Host Configuration Protocol—connections.) PPP connections, though, are often dynamically assigned. You usually have to pay extra if you want a fixed IP address over a modem connection. If you do, though, then you'll know your address, which can be useful when Web surfing and using FTP.*

Here's how the TCP/IP control panel works:

- **Connect Via** Use this menu to choose how you'll connect to a TCP/IP network. If you're using a modem, choose PPP; if you're using an Ethernet connection (such as with a university or company), choose Ethernet. If you've installed America Online, then you might also find the option in here to choose AOL Link, which allows you to use AOL's special protocol for a PPP-like connection to the Internet. (AOL Link is discussed in Chapter 19.)

- **Configure** This option determines the configuration scheme used to log into your ISP's server. If you're configuring an Ethernet connection, choose Manually or DHCP, most of the time; if it's a PPP connection, choose PPP connection. (The other configuration schemes will be specified by your ISP or system administrator if they're needed.)

In Mac OS 8.6 and later you can choose a DHCP server if you are connected to other computers over an Ethernet and you'd like to network using TCP/IP. If the iMac can't find a DHCP server (like on a small network in your house), it will assign a random IP number, allowing you to use TCP/IP. You can then use Web Sharing to share files between TCP/IP-running computers using Web browsers or FTP programs.

- **IP Address**   This is your iMac's address on the Internet.

- **Subnet Mask**   This is the numbering scheme required to help your iMac find its way around your local network or ISP.

- **Router Address**   This is the IP address of your Internet router or gateway.

- **Name Server Addr.**   These are addresses for server computers that can translate between Internet names (like **mac1.mac-upgrade.com**) and numbered addresses (207.0.129.169).

- **Search Domains**   This is usually left blank. If you enter a domain (like **mycompany.com** or **mysys.net**), it will search those domains for particular computers, in some cases.

The Remote Access Control Panel

If you're configuring a PPP connection, you'll need to do that in the Remote Access control panel. In this control panel you're basically setting up the dialing part of your connection—the phone number, user name, password, and other things your iMac needs to know to get you signed onto your ISP's computers. Figure 23-2 shows the Remote Access control panel.

The Remote Access menu in the Remote Access control panel can be used to switch between related control panels, including TCP/IP, Modem, AppleTalk, and DialAssist.

This control panel is a little less intimidating than the TCP/IP control panel. Here's how it works:

- **User Buttons**   Choose whether you're going to connect as a Registered User or as a Guest. In most cases, you'll choose Registered User for a PPP connection.

- **Name**   Enter the account name your ISP has assigned to you. This may or may not be the same as your e-mail name. (For instance, my e-mail name is **todds** as in todds@shutup101.com and my account name is also **todds**. With a different account, though, my e-mail name is **publisher** as in publisher@mac-upgrade.com, but my account name is **todd**. So, in the second case, I need to make sure I enter the account name in the Remote Access control panel.)

- **Password**   Enter the password for your ISP account.

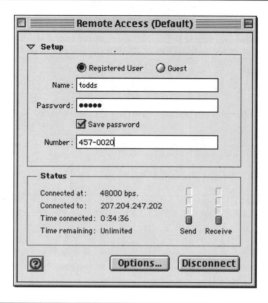

FIGURE 23-2 The Remote Access control panel

- ■ **Save Password**   Check this box if don't want to enter the password in the future. Remember, this will allow anyone with access to your computer to use your Internet account.

- ■ **Number**   Enter the phone number that the Remote Access control panel will use to dial the modem and reach your ISP. Usually this will be a seven-digit number (in the U.S.) unless your area uses ten-digit dialing for local numbers.

- ■ **Status**   Once you're connected to the Internet, you'll see the status of that connection at the bottom of the window. If you're not connected, it'll just say "Idle." Otherwise, it lets you know the current connection rate and whether or not data is being received.

The Remote Access control panel also offers a Connect/Disconnect button that you're probably already familiar with if you've connected successfully. And there are some options behind that Options button. When you click the Options button, you can access the Options dialog box, which offers three different tabs: Redial, Connection, and Protocol. Here's what you can do from each:

- ■ **Redial**   Select this tab and you'll see the Redial menu. Pull it down and choose an option. You can choose to not redial the connect number, to redial the connect number a certain number of times, or to redial the connect number and alternate number(s). In each case, the text boxes you need in order to fill in the options will appear.

■ **Connection** In this section you can choose how the log file of connections is kept. (You can view the log by choosing Remote Access I Access Log while you're viewing the Remote Access control panel.) You can also make some other setting decisions, including whether Remote Access automatically logs off and how it alerts you when it's still active.

NOTE *Verbose logging is only necessary if you're trying to troubleshoot a problem with your connection, probably with the help of a tech support person. Otherwise, leave it off—it creates a large log file that isn't necessary if you're not having a problem.*

■ **Protocol** From the menu you can choose the protocol that Remote Access should attempt to use. By default it attempts to connect using both PPP and AppleTalk (ARAP) protocols. If you're reasonably sure you won't be using Remote Access's AppleTalk features, then choose to only use the PPP protocol from the menu— doing so may speed up connection time slightly. You can also make some other choices, including TCP header compression and allowing error correction—both should work fine with an iMac's modem. Note one interesting choice: Remote Access can start up automatically whenever a TCP/IP application is started. When Outlook Express tries to check the mail or Netscape Navigator tries to find a Web page, for instance, you could have your iMac automatically dial the ISP and connect on its own.

TIP *There's another feature available under Protocol—you can enter a script for signing onto a command line host. There are few such hosts these days, but if you ever need to enter a "dialing script" or "connection script" using a particular ISP, this is where you'll do it.*

The Modem Control Panel

The Modem control panel is very straightforward—just pick the driver for the iMac's modem and make some basic settings. Open the Modem control panel by choosing it from the Control Panels menu in the Apple menu or from the Remote Access menu in the Remote Access control panel.

Now, pull down the Modem menu and select iMac Internal 56k (or Apple Internal 56k) if it's not already chosen. Then decide whether the modem's sound will be on (if you'll hear the dialing and screeching); you can also tell the modem whether to dial over your phone line using tones or pulses. Finally, place a check in the Ignore Dial Tone check box—this is a good idea if you have stutter-tone message notification or some other line conditions that can confuse the modem.

 *If you're having trouble getting your iMac's modem to connect, switch the Modem entry to Apple Internal 56k (v.34) or iMac Internal v.34. This will cause the modem's connection to be a bit slower, but often more reliable.*

DialAssist

If your dialing requirements are more complicated than what Remote Access can handle—one line that offers seven- to ten-digit dialing or so—then use DialAssist to help you set up. Open the control panel and you'll see many different options for choosing how your modem is dialed.

Enter your own stats up top—area code and country. Then, choose your special dialing requirements—Prefix, Long Distance Access code, and/or Suffix. If you don't see an option that suits your needs, click the associated button in the bottom of the control panel window. The resulting dialog box will allow you to create new dialing combinations to fit your circumstances. In those dialog boxes (each button has its own dialog box), click the Add button to add numbers to dial.

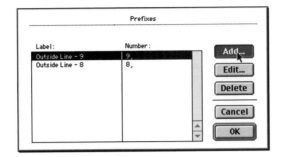

Configure a New Account

If you're adding an entirely new account, you'll need to head to the TCP/IP and Remote
Access control panels (assuming both use PPP). Before you begin changing settings,
though, choose File | Configurations in either TCP/IP or Remote Access. This allows you
to create a new, named configuration for your new account. This way, old settings can be
accessed quickly—just change back to the previous configuration.

To create a new configuration, select one of the existing configurations and click the
Duplicate button. Now, you'll be asked to give the configuration a name. Type a name and
click OK.

To edit the configuration, choose it in the Configurations dialog box and click Make
Active. The TCP/IP control panel switches to reflect that new configuration. Now you can
edit away. When you close the TCP/IP control panel, you'll be asked if you want to save
the changes. Choose Save. To choose another configuration, select File | Configurations
again, select the configuration you want to work with, and choose Make Active.

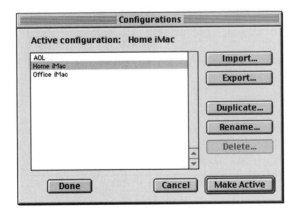

Remote Access allows you to do the same thing—store different phone numbers,
names, passwords, and so on, in separate Remote Access configurations. That way each

member of your family can dial in individually to his or her account, or you can easily switch between two different dial-up accounts.

I strongly recommend using different configurations if you're changing your setup after moving your iMac or getting a new connection type (like ADSL or a new LAN connection). That way you'll be able to revert to the old settings using a simple Make Active command.

Get High-Speed Internet Access

Just emerging on the market are a few technologies that may change the way many households get on the Internet. And most of these new methods use Ethernet or an AirPort connection, which just so happens to be built into your iMac. (In fact, it's high-speed 100Mbps Ethernet.) Here are some of those high-speed technologies:

- **DSL** Digital Subscriber Line technology connects via your regular phone line, using high-frequency signals to transmit data even when you're talking on the phone. The connection uses a special DSL modem, which can connect directly to the Ethernet port on your iMac. You can also use a special DSL router, which would allow you to add a DSL connection to a network of iMacs (or other computers on a network). DSL can range in speed from about 128KB per second (twice the iMac's modem speed) to 1.5MB per second, or about the speed of most corporate LAN connections. (Some DSL implementations are even faster, but they aren't likely to be used with your iMac.)

- **Cable Modem** A cable modem usually splits off from your cable TV line, giving you an Ethernet-based Internet connection using the wiring that's already in your home. Cable modems can be very fast—up to 10MB per second—although those speeds usually aren't guaranteed because a cable modem feed may be shared by an entire neighborhood. In peak times, then, speeds may slow down, but they're not likely to dip below modem speeds and should usually be well above the speed of your modem.

- **Satellite Connections** You may find that the local satellite TV provider (for the 18-inch dishes) in your area offers Internet access. In this case, you'll usually connect via Ethernet, but make sure they offer Mac compatibility and support. The speeds from the satellite can be four to ten times faster than a modem, though you'll probably need a modem connection and an available phone line to send data back to the ISP, since you can't send data back to a satellite or transmitter.

In any of these cases, all you'll need to do is order the service—a technician will install the service and set up the Internet settings. (If he or she isn't terribly Mac-savvy, you might point out the Configurations option discussed earlier so your existing settings aren't messed up.)

If you need to tell the technician anything, it might be your Ethernet ID number. Fortunately, it's located on a sticker on the bottom of your iMac. Just pop open that door and show the technician when he or she comes to install the equipment.

 **Use an Internet Software Router**

What do you do if you have one modem-based Internet connection but more than one computer that you'd like to give access to the Internet? One solution is to use an Internet software router. You'll set up the software on one of your computers, which will act as a router for the other computers to which you want to give Internet access.

Two popular third-party Internet routers are IPNetRouter by Sustainable Softworks (**http://www.sustworks.com/**) and SurfDoubler from Vicomsoft (**http://www.vicomsoft.com**). Both are commercial products, although you can download demonstration versions that work for a few weeks before you have to pay.

You install the router on a Mac that has both a modem connection (or other Internet connection) and a network connection to your other Macs. With the router application running on the one Mac, other Macs access that Mac for their Internet connection, either using fixed IP addresses or a DHCP addressing scheme. Whenever a TCP/IP request is made by an Internet application on one of your computers, that request is processed by the software router and the Internet data is retrieved via the single Internet connection.

Part IV

Customize Your iMac

Chapter 24

Change iMac's Appearance and Attitude

How to...

- Change the resolution and color depth of your iMac's screen
- Change the dimensions of your iMac's display
- Calibrate the screen's colors
- Set basic preferences for how your iMac looks and acts
- Set the time and date
- Customize how your iMac uses memory
- Save energy and automate startup, shutdown, and sleep
- Set up your keychain in Mac OS 9
- Listen and talk to your iMac

In this chapter I discuss the atmospheric, behavioral settings for your iMac—what it looks like and how it operates. You can change these settings using certain control panels. Other control panels are discussed in other chapters—those that govern networking, the Internet, and your modem, for instance. In this chapter, we'll focus on the control panels built into the Mac OS that handle appearance, the monitor, sound, memory, and other basic settings.

Adjust Your iMac's Monitor

Instead of using knobs and buttons on the outside of the monitor, you can control the horizontal and vertical display directly from the Monitors control panel (in Mac OS 9 and some versions of Mac OS 8.6).

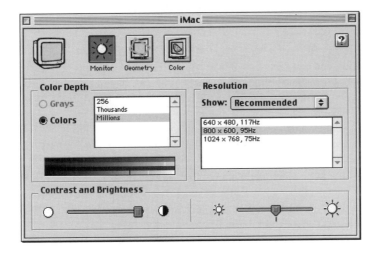

NOTE   *If your iMac has an earlier version of the Mac OS, you'll find these same controls in the Monitors and Sound control panel.*

There are three different parts of the Monitors control panel that concern your monitor—the Monitor, Geometry, and Color settings. Each will affect how your iMac's screen looks, and each has its own area of responsibility.

Monitor Settings

Click the Monitor button (these buttons work like tabs in a typical tabbed dialog box) and the controls change to show you the monitor settings. There are three sections you'll look at here: Color Depth, Resolution, and Contrast and Brightness.

Color Depth

Your iMac can display a range of colors from 256 to thousands to millions. This represents the color *palette* available to your iMac—the number of distinct colors that could potentially be shown on the screen. The more colors that appear on screen, the more photo-realistic the images on your screen. A JPEG photo file displayed at 256 colors will offer less detail than one rendered at millions of colors.

In most cases, leaving this setting at Thousands or Millions of colors is fine. You can change the color depth, though, if you find that you have images that don't look right—they seem less than sharp in places, have too much gray or black in the image, appear too light or dark, or simply seem jagged. To change the color depth, simply click one of the options.

Resolution

The iMac supports three different screen resolutions: 640 × 480, 800 × 600, and 1,024 × 768. So what does resolution mean? Technically, it means the number of pixels that appear on the screen, expressed in terms of a grid. For instance, 800 × 600 resolution divides the screen into 800 pixel columns and 600 pixel rows. Multiply it all together and you'd get 480,000 pixels on the screen.

The significance of resolution is two-fold. First, the more pixels on the screen, the more information you can see—at 1,024 × 768, you can see a lot more of a given word processing page, for instance, than at 640 × 480. Second, the more pixels on the screen, the smaller the pixel. In order to see more of the page on your iMac's screen, the elements on the screen will have to get smaller, since the size of your monitor stays the same. Figure 24-1 shows a screen at 640 × 480 and the same screen at 800 × 600.

It's most important to pick a resolution that balances how much information you want on the screen with how comfortable you are looking at it for long periods of time. That likely means 800 × 600, which is recommended for two other reasons, too. At 800 × 600, your iMac's screen is closest to WYSIWYG (a silly computer acronym, pronounced "wizzy-wig," which means What You See Is What You Get) resolution. What's on the screen will be a close approximation of the printed document. The second consideration is that many documents—especially Web sites—are designed to work optimally at 800 × 600, since that's the prevailing resolution among Macs and PCs on the Internet. You'll find that 640 × 480 resolution will often make Web pages look a little cramped.

Contrast and Brightness

These options are relatively self-explanatory. You can use the sliders to change the brightness and contrast shown on your screen. There are two considerations. First, you should never set any computer monitor to its highest brightness setting, since that can wear out the monitor more quickly, causing it to dim prematurely. If you're having trouble where you need the monitor very bright, make sure you've tried different contrast settings before setting brightness all the way up.

Second, changing brightness and contrast may affect how the screen looks compared to printed documents, especially color documents. You'll calibrate the monitor to correct for lighting conditions and to create optimum color output later in this section. You might want to calibrate before going nuts with the brightness and contrast.

24

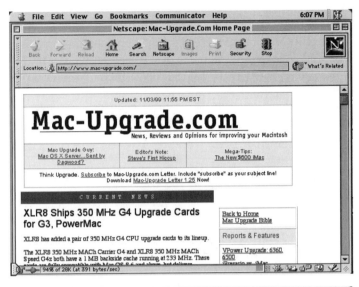

| FIGURE 24-1 | 640 × 480 (top) offers less information on the screen than 800 × 600 (bottom). |

Change the Geometry

The iMac's software settings include the ability to fine-tune the screen characteristics so that you get a perfectly square image with all the right proportions—assuming that's your desire. For most people, Murphy's Law of Vertical Hold takes effect—the more you mess with any of these controls, whatever your intent, ability, or skill level, the worse the picture looks. Maybe you'll have better luck.

You get to these controls by clicking the Geometry button in the Monitors control panel.

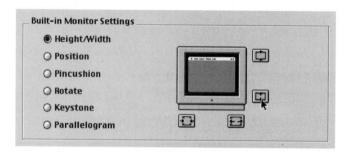

Now, you can go about changing many, many different settings regarding the size and dimensions of your monitor's picture. Here's what each does:

- **Height/Width** This setting allows you to change the size of the screen's image. You may notice that your screen, by default, doesn't fill the available space. That may be a good thing, since the very edges of a monitor tend to distort the picture somewhat. But you might also be able to tweak out a slightly larger picture using these controls.

- **Position** With this setting, you can change the vertical and horizontal placement of the screen image so that it's centered as much as possible.

- **Pincushion** If your screen appears to bow in or out at the middle or edges (giving it a pear or an hourglass shape) then you can use Pincushion controls to take it back to a rectangular shape.

- **Rotate** The screen may appear slightly higher in one top corner than the other. If that's the case, you can rotate the image to bring it level again.

- **Keystone** If the top or bottom of the screen is bowed in or out, you can change that with the Keystone setting.

- **Parallelogram** If the screen rectangle slants in one direction or the other, you can shift it back with this control.

To change a setting, just click the radio button next to the setting you want to alter and the controls on the right side of the window will change to reflect that. Click the little control buttons that appear around the image of an iMac screen to make your changes. You should see the screen react immediately.

If you mess it up beyond recognition, click the Factory Settings button. This will reset the picture to the way it was calibrated back at the Apple assembly line.

Calibrate the Monitor

Apple has created a technology, called ColorSync, that makes it possible for you to fine-tune the color, brightness, and other characteristics of your iMac's monitor. This is useful for two reasons—first, it allows you to calibrate the display for different lighting conditions. Second, ColorSync allows you to create a color profile for your monitor, so that printing to a color printer looks as true as it can. The more accurate the color on your display, the closer it will be to the final, printed product if you have a color printer that also supports ColorSync.

To begin calibrating, choose the Color button in the Monitors or Monitors and Sound control panel (whichever you have). You can calibrate in one of two ways. The easy way is to simply make sure that iMac Display is chosen in the ColorSync Profile list. This will give you a decent approximation that should cause your display screen to look fine in average indoor lighting conditions. It should also match color reasonably well between your display and your color printer.

The second method takes a little more work. Begin by selecting the iMac Display entry, then click the Calibrate button. Now the Monitor Calibration Assistant appears to guide you through the calibration process.

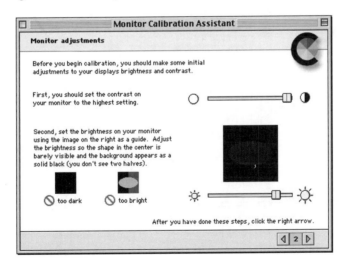

You may have trouble with the Assistant if you have red-green or similar color vision impairments.

When you're done with the Assistant, you'll have a newly calibrated display, and perhaps even a more richly colored screen. In the last step of the Assistant you'll give it a unique name—that name is added to the ColorSync Profile list. For instance, you might name the color settings Bright Day and Night. Now, whenever you want to change calibrations, you can quickly select different profiles from the ColorSync Profile list.

Sound and Alert Settings

In the Sound control panel (or the Monitors and Sound control panel, if you have Mac OS 8.6 or earlier) you can make some sound adjustments. You're able to adjust the volume, change the input device for recording, and enable 3-D sound. You can also change your system alert and, if desired, record some alerts of your own.

 Slot-loading iMacs that came preinstalled with Mac OS 8.6 also have the separate Sound control panel.

Sound Settings in Mac OS 9

If you have Mac OS 9 or higher installed on your iMac, you'll use the Sound control panel to make your sound settings. On the left side of the Sound control panel, you'll see entries for the different types of settings. Click one of those and the right side of the control panel changes to show your options.

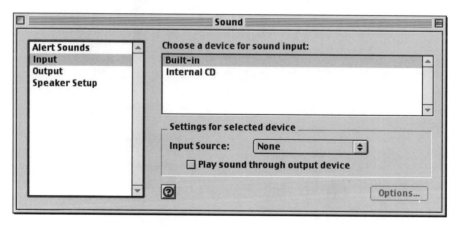

The Sound control panel lets you choose the input device and output device for sound on your iMac, plus it lets you manage the speakers, volume, and other basics. Most of the time you won't need to play with these too much. By default, the settings will allow you to record from the iMac's microphone, play audio CDs, and so on. If you need to get serious about recording audio or outputting audio to different equipment, that's when you'll dive into the Sound control panel. Here's what you can do in each section of the control panel.

Input

Click the Input entry and you'll be able to choose a device for sound input in the top of the control panel. In most cases you'll be choosing between the Built-in option and the Internal CD player. Once you've chosen, you'll have new options in the Settings for Selected Device section. Choose the Input Source from the pop-up menu, then, if appropriate, you can place a check next to Play Sound Through Output Device if you'd like to hear the sound from this input source on the output device. (For instance, sound from an internal CD to your speakers should play through—that makes sense. If you're using the microphone to record your voice, however, you may not want it to play through, since that could cause feedback.)

Output

In the output section you'll choose the device that the iMac should use for sound sent out of applications. If you don't have any external speakers or receivers attached to your iMac, you'll see Built-in as the only option. You can set the volume for output sound using the slider in this window. If you have other output devices attached, you'll select them here.

Speaker Setup

In the Speaker Setup section you can test the arrangement and volume of your speakers. Click the Start Test button and you'll hear a static tone that helps you set the balance of your speakers using the small volume sliders under each speaker. When you're done, click the Stop Test button.

Sound Settings in Monitors and Sound

Click the Sound button in the Monitors and Sound control panel (if your Mac OS version includes it) and you'll see controls for the sound settings. It's here that you can change the way things sound through your iMac's speakers, through additional speakers you've attached to the speaker port on the side of your iMac, or through headphones that are plugged into the front of your iMac.

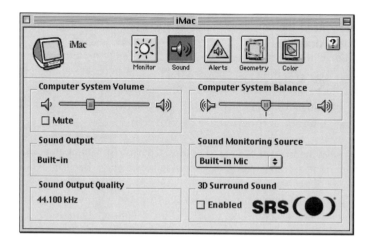

Here's what you can accomplish in this window:

■ Change the volume and balance settings with the Computer System Volume section.

■ Sound Output is set at Built-in unless you've installed some external speakers, at which point you can select between the two.

■ The Sound Monitoring Source dictates what the iMac will record from if you set it to record something (using a shareware sound manager, a sound-editing application, or even the Alerts portion of the Monitors and Sound control panel). Use the menu to change what your iMac is "listening" to.

■ Set the Surround Sound quality. It sounds better through the iMac's speakers or through third-party speakers. If you're using headphones to listen to a music CD, I recommend turning off Surround Sound, although some games benefit from it, whether or not you're using headphones.

Alerts

Click the Alert Sounds item in the Sound control panel (or, in earlier Mac OS versions, the Alerts button in the Monitors and Sound control panel) and choose an Alert sound for the Mac OS to let you know that there's a problem, a question, or something else going on. Just select the alert you want to use and adjust the volume using the slider control.

You can also record your own alerts. Click Add and you'll see a recording interface that resembles the controls for a cassette recorder.

Click the Record button to record up to ten seconds of sound based on whatever the Input Source is set to back in the Input controls. If it's the internal microphone—the tiny hole above your iMac's display—start speaking, singing, or doing whatever you want to record. When you're done, click the Stop button. You can click Play to hear the sound or click Save to save the sound to your list of Alerts. Name the sound and click OK. Now you can select it in the Alerts list.

Time and Date Settings

Two of the basic settings for your iMac are the time and date. You probably set these when you first plugged in, turned on your iMac, and ran the Setup Assistant. But you may have some reason to revisit them, including a move to another time zone or perhaps recognition that something is set incorrectly. To change the time and date, head to the Apple menu, then choose Control Panels I Date & Time.

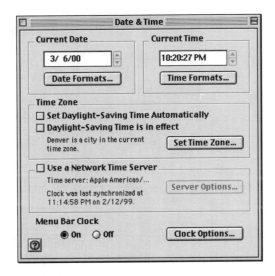

There are a number of things you can do in this control panel:

- **Edit Date and Time**   In the Current Date section, click in the Date entry box and either type or use the arrows to change the date. You can do the same thing for setting Time in the Current Time section.

- **Format Date and Time**   Under each setting, click the Formats button to change the date and time formats. Each section provides several options for the time or date display.

- **Set the Time Zone**   Click the Set Time Zone button to choose your locale. You can also click the check boxes if you want to automatically track daylight savings or to let the iMac know that daylight savings is currently in effect.

- **Use a Time Server**   When you're connected to the Internet, the Time Server option can synchronize your iMac's clock to an Internet Time Server clock.

(Internet Server Time is based on official atomic clocks, making them very accurate.) There's also a Server Options button that checks the clock against the server closest to you.

■ **Turn Menu Bar Clock On or Off** Want a clock on your iMac's menu bar? Click the On radio button. You can set other options (fonts and colors) by clicking the Clock Options button.

General Controls

Once, General Controls was the main control panel for specifying the look of an iMac. These days, it's relegated to a smaller, but still important role. It has basic controls over how the Finder and menus work. Select Apple | Control Panels | General Controls.

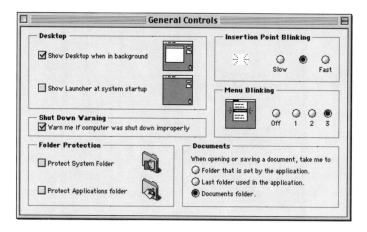

Here's what everything does:

■ **Desktop/Launcher** These are controls for whether or not the Desktop or the Launcher should appear in the background when you're using other applications. (The Launcher is a special window that quickly launches applications. Drop aliases in the Launcher subfolder of the System Folder to access them through the Launcher.)

■ **Shut Down Warning** If your iMac is shut down incorrectly (due to a freeze-up, crash, or power failure), you'll get a warning and Disk First Aid will check your iMac's hard drive. If you don't want this option, remove the check from the check box.

■ **Protect System Folder/Protect Applications Folder** If either of these is checked, then files or folders can't be moved or deleted from the folders. This is useful for avoiding accidentally deleting important files.

■ **Blinking**   Change the speed and number of times the insertion point and menus blink.

■ **Documents**   Choose what folder the Open and Save dialog boxes will display by default.

Memory Settings

The Memory control panel offers an opportunity to manage the RAM in your iMac and, perhaps, get a little more performance out of your system. Some of the settings are automatic, but you can make changes. Choose Apple | Control Panels | Memory.

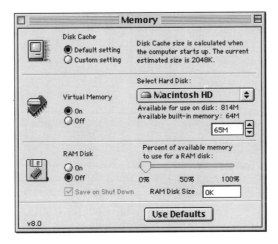

Here's what each setting does:

■ **Disk Cache**   This setting determines how much system RAM is set aside for a disk cache. A *disk cache* is a special portion of memory where "look-ahead" data is stored to be accessed more quickly than if the Mac OS was forced to load the data straight from the disk. Usually, this is set automatically, but if you'd like to enter your own number, click Custom Setting and enter an amount, in kilobytes, for the cache.

■ **Virtual Memory**   Virtual memory allows your iMac to use part of the hard disk to store items that should be in memory, but can temporarily be placed on the hard disk. This makes it possible to run more programs at once. Click the On and Off radio buttons to turn Virtual Memory on and off. (You should always have Virtual Memory turned on unless you have an application or utility that specifically suggests you turn it off.) Choose an amount in the entry box or use the arrows. How much? Add between 1 and 10MB to the current built-in memory.

NOTE *If you only have 32MB of RAM installed in your iMac and you're running Mac OS 9 or higher, you must leave virtual memory on and set higher than the recommendation—between 40 and 64MB. Otherwise, there simply isn't enough RAM for typical operations. If you find that your iMac runs a little slowly, you should quit some open applications and try, in general, to work with fewer applications open. You should also consider upgrading to at least 64MB (or more) of RAM, as discussed in Chapter 27.*

■ **RAM Disk** A RAM disk allows you to create a sort of "virtual" disk that's actually stored in RAM. The advantage of this is that RAM is much faster than a hard disk, so placing data or applications on the RAM disk can make your iMac run a little faster. The disadvantage is that a RAM disk is just as volatile as regular RAM. Don't store important data on a RAM disk since one system freeze or power surge could wipe away all the data. To create a RAM disk, click the On button and choose a size. To get rid of the RAM disk, go to the Finder and delete everything from the RAM disk, then click Off in the Memory control panel.

RAM Disk

NOTE *File Sharing needs to be turned off in order to get rid of a RAM disk.*

I don't recommend using more than half of the built-in RAM in your system for a RAM disk, although the more RAM you have, the more you can devote to a RAM disk. If you have 32MB of RAM, then you really can't spare any for a RAM disk—your iMac is using all of that RAM just to function. If you have 64MB of RAM, I'd recommend keeping your RAM disk under 10-15MB or so. With 96 or 128MB of RAM (or more) you're free to have a much larger RAM disk, if you find one useful. Remember, a RAM disk subtracts from the amount of RAM used for running applications. Check Save On Shut Down to make sure data on the RAM disk is saved when you shut down your iMac. The contents saved on a RAM disk can survive a restart, but not a shutdown, unless you choose to save the data.

Don't like the Memory control panel settings you specified? Click the Use Defaults button to return to the original settings.

TIP *What do you put on a RAM disk? Here are a few good options: Place your Web browser's cache storage here by using the Preferences control panel in your Web browser to change the location of stored cache files. Also, store QuickTime movies here so they'll run smoother and be easier to edit. Otherwise, it's best to store nondocuments such as applications and games—you'll speed things up and save energy.*

Save Energy by Automating Startup and Shutdown

The Energy Saver control panel allows you to do some interesting things—you can actually automate the startup and shutdown of your iMac. You can also cause it to dim the monitor and even go to sleep after a period of inactivity. When your iMac sleeps, the processor, hard disk, and monitor all consume much less energy, but the power stays on and applications and documents stay open. Tap a key on the keyboard and the iMac will spring back to life. Choose Apple | Control Panels | Energy Saver.

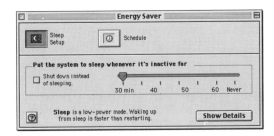

Sleep Timer

To set how quickly your system goes to sleep during periods of inactivity, choose the Sleep Setup button, then move the slider to the amount of time you want the iMac to wait before it puts itself to sleep. You can also check the Shut Down Instead Of Sleeping check box to force iMac to shut down after that amount of time.

If you'd like to turn off the display and hard disk sleep options or change the default settings, click the Show Details button. You'll see separate entries for the display and hard disk. If you want to set those times, click the check box next to each entry, then move its slider bar.

Startup and Shutdown

You can also schedule your iMac to automatically start up and shut down, if you'd like. To do that, click the Schedule button or the Scheduled Startup & Shutdown button, depending on your version of the Mac OS. Now, place a checkmark next to the option you'd like to automate, then from the menu choose the days of the week that this should take place. Finally, choose a time when the startup or shutdown should take place.

To schedule startup and shutdown in Mac OS 9, you'll need to turn on the Schedule shutdown instead of Schedule sleep option. Otherwise, the available options let you automate putting the iMac to sleep and waking it up at certain times.

That's it—close the Energy Saver control panel and the system is armed.

Change the Appearance

Our final major control panel is the Appearance control panel. This allows you to choose how the Mac's interface looks—the colors, the textures, the behaviors—as well as how the arrows work on the scrollbars and what sort of sounds are made as you're working. To manage all that, it has to have a lot of tabs. Choose Apple | Control Panels | Appearance.

NOTE *This section covers the Appearance control panel in Mac OS 8.5 and above, including Mac OS 9.*

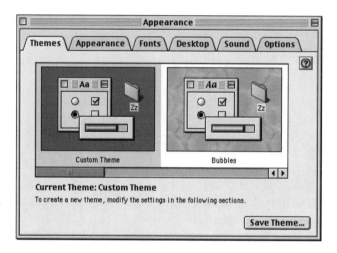

Here's what happens on each tab:

- **Themes** Themes are, overall, cohesive collections of all the other settings tabs—appearance, color of the desktop, sounds, and so on. Each theme offers a different overall experience. To use a theme, select it from the scrolling list. Close the Appearance control panel and work with that theme, or you can alter it. If you alter it (by visiting the other tabs), return to the Themes tab to name and save your altered creation using the Save Theme button.

- **Appearance** Your iMac ships with a default appearance, but theme files (offered by third-party companies) can be stored in the System Folder within the Appearance subfolder. This changes the whole look of the windows, icons, and everything. You can also change the highlight color (the color used when you select text or an icon) and the variation color (used for the highlight bar in menus and for the scroll boxes in windows).

- **Fonts** With the Fonts tab, change the font face used for different parts of the Mac OS. Feel free to experiment. You can also experiment with font *smoothing*—this technology causes fonts larger than a certain point size (which you can change with the arrows and Size entry box) to be smoothed or *anti-aliased* onscreen. This makes some fonts look better onscreen, although the overall look varies depending on the fonts used. Text smaller than 14 point can sometimes be too blurry to read when smoothed, so it's probably best to leave this option on for 14 point or higher text.

■ **Desktop**   This tab allows you to place a pattern or picture on the desktop to give your iMac some personality. To place a pattern, use the Patterns list. To place a picture, click the Place Picture button and find the picture in the Open dialog box (the Sample Desktop Pictures folder in the Apple Extras folder has some sample desktop images), then click Choose. Back in the Appearance control panel, position the image using the Position menu. You can choose Tile On Screen (several copies pasted together to fill the screen), Center On Screen, Scale To Fit (filling the screen while maintaining the correct ratio), or Fill The Screen (regardless of dimensions). You can also leave it at the default, Position Automatically, especially if the image is already the same resolution as your desktop. When you've made your choices, click Set Desktop. To remove the picture, click Remove Picture and click Set Desktop again.

TIP

It's a good idea to match your desktop image's resolution to your screen's resolution—if you're running at 800 × 600, then the desktop picture can also be 800 × 600. Also, you can use any PICT, JPG, or GIF image, and it can be stored anywhere on your hard disk.

■ **Sound**   Choose a soundtrack for your theme. The soundtrack offers preset sounds for many different things you can do in the Mac OS, including selecting from menus, moving icons, scrolling windows, and so on. Choose a soundtrack from the menu, then, by checking or unchecking the different sound effects, choose the sounds you'd like to hear.

■ **Options**   This last tab offers you two check boxes. First, should your scroll arrows appear at just one end of the scrollbar? And, second, should you be able to double-click a title bar in order to invoke the Windowshade command? Make your choices.

If you've changed the settings extensively, don't forget to return to the Themes tab and give your new theme a name. Otherwise, you're done—click the close box to exit the Appearance control panel. Your new appearance is now in effect.

Keychain Access

In Mac OS 9, you can use your personal *keychain* to store user names and passwords for servers, encrypted files, and, in some cases, Internet sites. Many items that you access on your iMac using a password can be stored on your keychain, just like you can store the keys for your car, house, office, and safe-deposit box on a real keychain.

With your Mac OS keychain, you only need to remember one password. The keychain stores the passwords for many other resources, all of which are locked behind a single password that you memorize. Now, instead of looking up passwords on that hidden sheet of paper taped to the bottom of a desk drawer, you can unlock your Mac OS keychain and access passwords automatically.

How does it work? In certain applications, you'll find an Add to Keychain option, which allows you to add a user name and password to the keychain automatically. Now, the next time you try to access that user name and password, the application will attempt to retrieve it from your keychain. If your keychain is unlocked, then that password-protected connection (or item) will be opened automatically—you won't have to enter a password! If your keychain is locked, though, you'll have to enter your keychain password before the application can continue. So, as long as you're diligent about locking your keychain, others won't be able to access it and get into your password-protected items.

NOTE *In most cases, applications need to support the keychain in order for it to work. So, it'll take an upgrade in some applications—like Web browsers—before they'll support the keychain. In Mac OS 9, the Network Browser supports the keychain, so you can automatically store your network logins using keychain technology. Likewise, the Apple File Security application supports the keychain, so you can encrypt files on your iMac for safe storage and store the password in your keychain.*

Create Your Keychain

Before you can do any of this, you'll need to create your keychain. To do that, head to the Keychain Access control panel. If you've already created a keychain (or if one has been created for you, which may have happened if you're using the Multiple Users feature) then you'll probably see a dialog box asking you for your keychain password. (See the next section, "View Your Keychain.")

If you haven't created a keychain before, you can create one. Here's how:

1. Open the Keychain Access control panel.

2. You'll see a dialog box asking if you'd like to create a keychain. Click the Create button.

3. In the Create Keychain dialog box, enter a name for the keychain (for instance, your name) and a password. (You can press TAB to move between entry boxes.) You'll enter the password twice—once in the Password box and once in the Confirm box—to ensure that you type it the same way each time. Click Create.

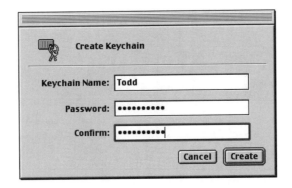

NOTE   *The password you use should be at least six characters long and ideally include a mix of letters and numbers. If you create a password that the Keychain Access control panel determines isn't very secure, you may be asked to reconsider your password. (Click No and change your password.) Also, don't forget your password! There's no way to get into your keychain if you do.*

View Your Keychain

Once you've created a keychain, you'll be able to access the keychain in the future by opening the Keychain Access control panel. If the keychain is locked, you'll see the Unlock Keychain dialog box. Choose your keychain from the Unlock Keychain pop-up menu, then enter your password for the keychain. Click the Unlock button and your keychain will be unlocked.

Once your keychain is unlocked (or if your keychain was already unlocked) Keychain Access opens the keychain's window. Now you can see the items that are stored on your keychain.

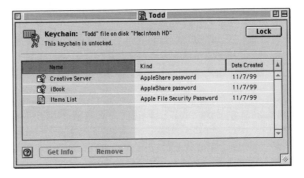

Use the Keychain (and Encrypt Files)

You don't really add items to your keychain using the Keychain Access control panel, although in some cases you can drag items (like Internet location files) to the Keychain Access control panel. At this point in the implementation of the keychain technology, however, that doesn't often do much good. (At some point in the future drag-and-drop may work well when many different applications support the keychain.) In the meantime, you'll generally add keychain items using applications. One that supports the keychain is the Network Browser, discussed in Chapter 28.

Another application that supports the keychain is Apple File Security, another new addition in Mac OS 9 that *encrypts* files in the Finder. Encryption is a process that turns the document into a jumble of nonsense, as far as any snooping eyes are concerned. Like an encrypted transmission between nations at war, it'll take a passphrase to get into this file. Without it, you won't be able to open this file.

Drag-and-drop a document or program onto the Apple File Security icon, located in the Applications folder on your iMac. (You can also CONTROL-click an item in the Finder and select Encrypt from the pop-up menu.) You'll see a dialog box asking you for a *passphrase*, which is the same thing as a password. Enter a password twice (press TAB between entries) and make sure the Add to Keychain option is selected.

```
┌─────────────────────────────────────────────┐
│             Apple File Security             │
├─────────────────────────────────────────────┤
│        Enter a passphrase to encrypt        │
│   🔶   "Invoice":                            │
│        ┌─────────────────────────────────┐  │
│        │ ●●●●●●●●●●●                      │  │
│        └─────────────────────────────────┘  │
│        Confirm your passphrase:             │
│        ┌─────────────────────────────────┐  │
│        │ ●●●●●●●●●●●                      │  │
│        └─────────────────────────────────┘  │
│  ☑ Add to Keychain      [Cancel] [[Encrypt]]│
└─────────────────────────────────────────────┘
```

When you click the Encrypt button, the file is encrypted. At the same time, the password for this item is stored on the keychain. Now, if you double-click the encrypted item in the Finder, you'll be asked for your keychain password if it's locked. Then, once unlocked, the password for this encrypted file is accessed automatically and the file is decrypted!

To learn more about an item, select it in the window and click the Get Info button. If you want to remove an item, select it and click Remove. If you'd like to lock your keychain, just click the Lock button. This immediately locks the keychain. The next time an application attempts to access it, the keychain will ask you for your password to ensure that you want the application to have access to your keychain.

You can also set some important preferences for your keychain using the Keychain Access control panel. Select Edit | *Name* Settings (where *Name* is the name you've given to your keychain). You'll be asked to enter your keychain password. Now, in the Change Settings dialog box, you can enter (and confirm) a new password for your keychain. You can also turn on some options:

- **Allow Access Without Warning**   If this is turned on, applications will be able to immediately access your keychain if it's unlocked. If the option is turned off, you'll often see a dialog box that confirms that you want a particular application to have access to your keychain.

- **Lock After Minutes Of Inactivity**   Turn on this option and enter an amount of minutes of system idle time the control panel should wait before automatically locking your keychain. I'd recommend turning on this option, especially in an office or organizational environment. If you forget to lock your password and you leave your workstation, then the keychain will be locked automatically after the idle time has passed.

- **Lock When The System Sleeps**   Select this option if you'd like your keychain to lock itself whenever the system sleeps. That way you can simply put your iMac to sleep for increased security when you need to step away from it for a few minutes.

Click the Save button to save your changes in the Change Settings dialog box.

Speech Technologies

Most iMacs are capable of working with Apple's Text-to-Speech and Speech Recognition technologies, although only Text-to-Speech is turned on by default. Let's look at both quickly in this section.

Text-to-Speech

Text-to-Speech is the technology that allows your Mac to read text out loud. It's as simple as that. You may not have encountered it much unless you have Talking Alerts turned on in the Speech control panel. In that case, you may already be familiar with the clipped female voice that occasionally reads the contents of dialog boxes to you after they've sat on the screen for a while.

Talking Alerts is one basic implementation of Text-to-Speech—you can turn it on or off by opening the Speech control panel and selecting Talking Alerts from the Options pop-up menu. Now, in the Speech control panel, turn off the Speak The Alert Text option and you'll no longer hear items in alert dialog boxes. You can also turn on or off the Speak The Phrase option, which is just a cute way for the iMac to add a little character to its reading—it can say "Alert," "Rats," "Shoot," and many other phrases before it speaks the alert text, if you like. You can also use the slider to determine how long Talking Alerts should wait before it reads the text in alert dialog boxes.

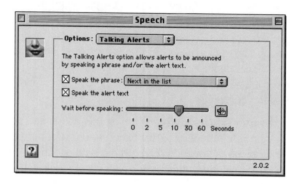

You can also use the Speech control panel to change the voice used for speech. Select Voice from the Options menu and you can choose a different voice (from the Voice pop-up menu) and a rate of speech using the slider bar. To test the voice, click the small speaker icon. You'll hear a sample of speech at the current settings.

Another way you can use Text-to-Speech is within applications that support it. One such application is SimpleText. In the Sound menu within SimpleText, you can choose the command Speak All to have SimpleText read you the open document, or Speak Selection to speak only text that's been highlighted in the document window. Other applications can speak text or selections, including some that are designed specifically for the task.

Speakable Items

The other side of Apple's speech technology is Speech Recognition, also known as *Speakable Items*. This technology allows your iMac to recognize words that you speak into its microphone, then perform commands based on what you say.

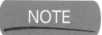 *If you have an early iMac with Mac OS 8.1 or 8.5, you need to update Speech Recognition to version 1.5.4 for it to work correctly with your iMac. It's available in Mac OS 8.6 or 9 or consult **http://asu.info.apple.com/** on the Web.*

Chapter 25

Set Up Your iMac for Multiple Users

How to...

- ■ Turn on the Multiple Users feature
- ■ Set up individual users
- ■ Set the global options
- ■ Log in and out of the iMac
- ■ Create your Voice Verification voiceprint

Mac OS 9 offers an interesting new capability to its bag of tricks—support for multiple users on one iMac. While any iMac can be shared by family members and friends, Multiple Users technology in Mac OS 9 goes one better. You assign a password and user name to each user, and each user logs into the iMac (using a new Login window that appears when you start up the iMac) when he or she is ready to get something done. That user, once logged in, has his or her own files, applications, and appearance settings—just about everything is customized.

What that means for the typical iMac owner is pretty simple—your files are private and your settings are secure. If you're using your iMac at home, then you'll appreciate the ability to secure your documents, the control you have over who gets to use certain applications, and the fact that your desktop picture won't mysteriously change every other day.

In a professional or academic setting, user accounts mean each user can store his or her own files without concern that others will see, move, or otherwise mess with them. And, again, the owner (or administrator) of the iMac can determine what applications are available to different users, perhaps even increasing productivity in the office or Mac lab a bit.

How Multiple Users Works

When you first set up Multiple Users, it creates an account called the Owner account. There is only one owner, who is responsible for creating and managing accounts for other users on the iMac.

Multiple Users works by allowing the owner to create user accounts that each have a user name and password. Information about those accounts is stored in a folder called Users that only the owner can access. When a user logs in using his or her user name and password, that user's information is "mirrored" from the appropriate folder in the Users folder to the System Folder. For instance, all of that user's preferences are mirrored onto the Preferences folder in the System Folder, so that applications that access the System Folder actually access that user's preferences.

What this means is that each user can work with an iMac that's set up specifically for that user. Appearance, application, document, folder, desktop, and many other settings and preferences will change for each different user. If I elect to have a staid, boring desktop, but if someone else in the office decides to have something a little crazier, it doesn't really matter—once she's logged out, I'm free to log in and see my own desktop again.

As the owner, you can set up a number of different options, including different types of interfaces for your users. For many users, you'll offer full Finder access—they'll have control of just about everything that a user typically can control on an iMac, except some control panel settings that are reserved only for the owner. For the most part, they can do whatever they want, especially since it won't harm your settings.

For other users, though, you can offer a Limited Finder interface or even the special Panels interface (see Figure 25-1). This does two things. First, it makes it easier for your user to find his or her files, especially if the user is younger or simply isn't very computer-savvy. Second, limited accounts can do less than normal user accounts, meaning that you can control

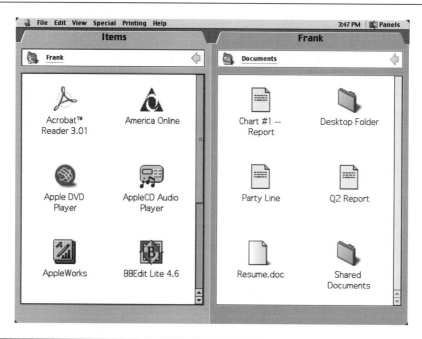

FIGURE 25-1   The Panels interface gives the user a limited but useful way to launch applications and save documents.

the applications these users have access to. If you'd like to cut down on the gaming in your college Mac lab, for instance, limited accounts would be one way to do it.

Turn On and Create Users

The Multiple Users feature manifests itself as a control panel in Mac OS 9. In this control panel you'll turn on Multiple Users (so that it's active), you'll create accounts, and you'll set some global options for your users.

The first time you open the Multiple Users control panel, you may get an error message if you don't have an owner name entered in the File Sharing control panel. Multiple Users uses the owner name to assign an owner account in the Multiple Users control panel.

Turn on Multiple Users

To turn on Multiple Users, open the control panel and click the On button next to Multiple User Accounts at the bottom of the window. Now Multiple Users is active. Even if you do nothing else but close the Multiple Users control panel, you'll find that there's a new Logout command in the Special menu. You'll use this command to leave your owner account and return to the Login screen. The Login screen will now also appear whenever you start up (or restart) the iMac, as long as Multiple Users is active.

Now, even with one account, there's a measure of security for your iMac. If you log out of the iMac using the Special | Logout command, only someone who knows your password can log into your iMac. (The password is the same as the owner's password in the File Sharing control panel. You can change that password, as detailed in the section "Change Your Password," later in this chapter.)

But, of course, there's a lot more you can do with Multiple Users.

Create User Accounts

Once you've turned on Multiple Users you'll want to create user accounts for everyone to whom you want to give access to your iMac. You do that by clicking the New User button in the Multiple Users control panel. Now you'll see the Edit "New User" window.

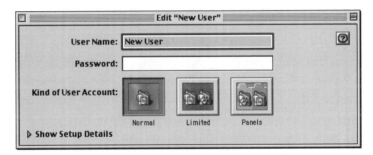

Begin by entering a name for this user in the User Name entry box. Then, press TAB and enter a password for this user in the Password entry box. (Users can change their own passwords as they're logging in, if they like, so you can set up passwords now and they can change them later if they want.)

Now, click the button for the type of account you'd like to give this user. There are three choices:

■ **Normal**   This type of account gives the user access to all but a handful of control panels that are off-limits to all users but the owner. Otherwise, the user is free to save files anywhere on the iMac's disk, work with any applications on the disk, and even install applications. You also can't limit this user's access to CD-ROMs or DVDs. You can, however, give this user the ability to manage other Multiple User accounts.

■ **Limited**   A Limited account uses the regular Finder for the user's interface but allows you (the owner) to choose which applications the user has access to. The user can only save documents to his or her own personal folder and can only access system resources (like the control panels, removable media, Apple Menu items, the Chooser, or Network Browser) that you decide he or she can access.

■ **Panels**   This gives you the same control over what the user can access as the Limited account does, but Panels uses a different interface, shown back in Figure 25-1. In fact, the Finder doesn't even load for these users—they only use the limited Panels interface to interact with the iMac.

Once you've chosen the type of account you're going to give the user, you have some other choices to make in the Edit "New User" window. Each set of choices is found on the tabs at the bottom half of the window.

User Info

Choose the User Info tab to set some basic information about the user. You can choose the picture for the user's icon by clicking the small arrows next to the User Picture image.

You can also set the following options:

■ **User Can Change Password**   If this option is turned on, the user can click the Change Password button in the Login window to enter a new password.

■ **Can Log In**   If you turn this option off, you can temporarily deny access for a particular user without deleting all of that user's information, documents, and settings.

■ **Can Manage User Accounts**   This option is only active for Normal users. If the option is turned on, this user can change settings for other users through the Multiple Users control panel. This user cannot, however, change settings for the owner or turn off Multiple Users.

■ **Access By Others To User's Documents**   Turn on this option if you want to allow other users to access this user's documents. If you do, you can choose how those users will have access from the pop-up menu: Read Only, Read & Write, or Write Only. In many cases you'll want to leave this turned off, but you may have a case where other users should be able to view this user's documents (for instance, you may want other users in your household to be able to view the files of a young child).

Applications

For Limited and Panels accounts you can select the Applications tab to decide which applications the user will be able to launch and use. Selecting applications is simple—just scroll through the list and place a checkmark next to any application that the user should be able to access.

The User Applications list can be a bit daunting. At the bottom of the window you'll find a Show pop-up window that may make it easier for you to view the applications list by showing all applications but AppleScripts or by showing only selected applications.

If you don't see an application on the list that you want this user to be able to access, click the Add Other button. You can then use the Open dialog box to find the application you want the user to be able to access.

You can also use the Select All or Select None button as a convenient way to select every item on the list or clear the list out, respectively.

Privileges

For Limited and Panels users you can select the Privileges tab to determine what Mac OS components and resources each user will be able to access.

Here's a list of the items you can select; each item you turn on becomes an item that the user can access:

- ■ **CD/DVD-ROM**   Turn this option on to allow the user to use CD-ROM and DVD-ROM titles. If turned on, you can choose to let the user access any title or only the titles on an approved list. (You create the list later in the section "Global Multiple User Options.")

- ■ **Other Removable Media**   Turn this option on if you want users to be able to access Zip disks, SuperDisks, or other removable media attached to this iMac.

- ■ **Shared Folder**   Multiple Users creates a special folder that is used as a shared folder for all users that have access to it. (Once a user is logged in, he or she will find the shared folder inside his or her personal folder. The owner can find the shared folder by opening the Users folder on the iMac's disk.) Turn this option on if this particular user should be given access to the shared folder.

- ■ **Chooser and Network Browser**   Turn this option on if you want the account to have access to these items so that the user can log in to network disks.

- ■ **Control Panels**   Turn this option on to allow this account access to the control panels.

- ■ **Other Apple Menu Items**   Turn this option on to allow the account access to the Apple menu items like the Calculator, Key Caps, Apple System Profiler, and others.

The last option on the Privileges tab allows you to determine whether or not this user can print. If turned on, you can select the allowed printer from the Allowed Printer pop-up menu, or you can select All Printers to let the user choose the printer from multiple desktop printers or from the Chooser.

Alternate Password

This tab is only active if you've enabled alternate password usage in the Global Multiple User Options dialog box. (If you'd like to turn this option on, click the Options button in the Multiple Users control panel. Then, on the Login tab in the Multiple User Options dialog box, turn on the Allow Alternate Password option.)

On the Alternate Password tab turn on the This User Will Use The Alternate Password option if you wish to allow the user to use the alternate password scheme that's been chosen in the Global Multiple User Options dialog box.

> NOTE
>
> *Although Voice Verification is the only Alternate Password scheme that comes with Mac OS 9, it's not the only scheme possible. That's why this tab is Alternate Password instead of Voice Verification—third-party companies can create alternate schemes that Multiple Users can use to allow access to your iMac.*

If you've chosen Voice Verification as your Alternate Password scheme in the Global Multiple User Options dialog box, then you'll see Voice Verification settings here on the Alternate Password tab.

To create a voiceprint, you'll need the user handy (so he or she can speak to create the voiceprint). Then, click the Create Voiceprint button and follow the instructions later in this chapter in the section "How To…Create a Voiceprint Password."

If the user isn't handy, just make sure the Allow This User To Change His Or Her Voiceprint option is turned on. The user will be able to create his or her voiceprint when logging in the next time.

Save and Edit Users

Once you've finished setting the user's information, applications, and privileges, you can save that user's settings by click the close box in the Edit window. Now the user will appear in the Multiple Users control panel.

To edit that user account again, double-click the account's icon in the Multiple Users control panel or select it and click Open. If you'd like to create a similar user, you can select that user and click Duplicate. Now you'll be able to rename the user and create a similar account.

Delete a User

You can delete a Multiple User account by selecting the user name in the Multiple Users control panel and clicking the Delete button. You'll see an alert asking if you want to delete the user; click Delete again. Now, you'll be asked if you want to delete the user's folder. If you click Delete, that user's settings and documents are deleted. (It'd be a good idea to have a backup of that user's folder before deleting it.) You can also click Keep, which will leave the user's folder on the iMac. Now, if you ever create another user with this same name, you can use the same folder, settings, and documents, if desired.

Global Multiple User Options

The Multiple Users control panel offers some global options that you can set affecting all of your users. These options are accessed by clicking the Options button in the Multiple Users control panel. That brings up the Global Multiple User Options dialog box. In the dialog box you'll see three different tabs where you'll make settings: the Login tab, the CD/DVD-ROM Access tab, and the Other tab. Click a tab to see that tab's options. When you're done setting options, click the Save button in the dialog box to save your settings.

Login Settings

On the Login tab you'll find some general settings that let you determine what users see on the Login screen and how they go about logging in.

Here are the options:

- **Welcome Message**   In the Welcome Message text area you can enter a short message that appears at the top of the Login window. This is a good place for quick notes to your users, perhaps to tell them when the lab closes, inform them when the staff meeting is scheduled, or warn them to finish homework before playing games.

- **Allow Alternate Password**   Turn on this option if you want to allow users to use a system other than typed passwords to log in. By default, your only option for this setting is Voice Verification, which you select from the pop-up menu. If you have other password verification schemes (perhaps installed by a third-party utility), then you can select them in the pop-up menu.

> NOTE   *The Allow Alternate Password option must be turned on in order for you to configure the Alternate Password scheme when editing a user, as discussed earlier in the section "Create User Accounts."*

- **Users May Speak Their Names**   If you turn this option on, users can speak their names instead of selecting them from the Login window. For this to work, you must have Speech Recognition installed and Speakable Items turned on in the Speech control panel.

- **If the User Is Idle For**   Turn on this option, then enter a number of idle minutes that Login should wait before taking action. Then, you choose what happens—either the user is logged out of his or her account (Log Out User option) or the screen is locked (Lock The Screen option). In either case, the user will need to reenter his or her password in order to gain access to the iMac again.

CD/DVD-ROM Access

When you set up Limited and Panels users, one of the options is to restrict those users' access to CD-ROM and DVD-ROM titles. If you do restrict them (as discussed in the section "Create User Accounts") then you have two options—you can restrict a user from all CD/DVD-ROMs or restrict them to a list of CD/DVD-ROMs. It's on the CD/DVD-ROM Access tab of the Global Multiple Users Options window (see Figure 25-2) that you'll build this list of authorized CD/DVD-ROMs.

This can be a bit tedious. What you need to do is insert each CD/DVD-ROM title in your CD or DVD drive so that it's mounted on the desktop. Once inserted, the disk appears in the Inserted pop-up menu (if you have more than one CD/DVD drive you can choose the inserted disc from this menu). Now, to add the CD to the list of authorized titles, click the Add to List button. The title appears in the List for Restricted Users.

Now, you can get even more controlling, if you like. In the Restrict Content To pane of the window, you can turn on and off individual items on that CD/DVD title so that the user can only access parts of the authorized disc. If there are only certain folders or items you want restricted users to access, place checkmarks next to those items.

Repeat for all other discs to which you want to grant your restricted users access. When you're done, you'll have a list of titles that are the only CD/DVD-ROM titles those users can access. If they insert others, the discs will be ejected and they'll see a message saying they don't have enough access privileges to use the disc.

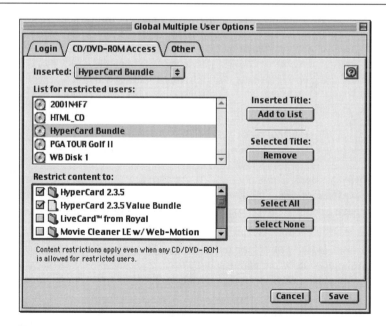

FIGURE 25-2   The CD/DVD-ROM Access tab helps you build a list of discs that your restricted users can access.

25

NOTE *You can't create different lists for different users—they are either restricted to this list, restricted from all discs, or able to use any disc. Also, note that a restricted user can't play audio CDs, because they can't be added to the list of authorized discs. You can, however, add DVD video discs. In order to play audio CDs, the user must have unrestricted access to the CD/DVD drive.*

Other Options

On the Other tab in the Global Multiple User Options dialog box you'll find a listing of miscellaneous options you can use to affect the way Multiple Users works. Here's what each does:

- ■ **Allow A Guest User Account** If you turn this option on, you can create a guest account that allows users who don't have a user name and password to log onto the iMac.

CAUTION *The Guest User account is given Normal access by default, which is quite a bit of control for a guest. You might want to immediately edit the account so that it has a Limited or Panels interface.*

- ■ **Notify When New Applications Have Been Installed** If you turn on this option, you (the owner account) will see a dialog box after you or a Normal account user has installed a new application on the iMac. In the dialog box, you will be able to decide what users will have access to the new application. The dialog box only appears when you're logging *out* of your account after an application has been installed. For instance, Sally (a Normal user) installs an application while working on the iMac, then logs out. Then, you, as owner, log into your account and do some work. When you log out of your account, you'll see the dialog box.

- ■ **When Logging In** This option offers two radio button selections: Users Choose Their Names From A List or Users Type Their Names. The first is easier for the users, because they don't have to remember their user names (they'll see them in the list along with their colorful icons). The second is more secure, since users must remember their login names.

■ **User Account Will Be From** In most cases this should be Multiple User Accounts (Local). If you happen to have a Macintosh Manager account server on your network, you can select Macintosh Manager Account (On Network). (Macintosh Manager is software used by Mac OS X Server and AppleShare IP professional server packages.)

Login and Passwords

Once Multiple Users is configured, you're ready to put it to use. In this section I'll describe the user experience when using Multiple Users, then you'll see how users change their passwords or create a Voice Verification password.

Log In to Your Account

The Login window (see Figure 25-3) appears whenever the iMac is started up, restarted, or after a user has logged out of his or her account. By default, you'll see a list of user account names and icons that go along with them. To log in, you simply double-click a user account name, or click it once and then click the Log In button.

FIGURE 25-3   The Login window is shown before the iMac is completely started up.

Once you've selected your user name, you'll see the Enter Password dialog box (unless an alternate password has been specified). Enter your password and press RETURN or click the OK button. If the password is correct, your user account will be loaded and the Finder (or Panels) interface will begin to load.

If an alternate password is activated, then you'll see the alternate password's dialog box. If this is a Voiceprint Verification password, you'll see the Voiceprint Verification dialog box. As the line scrolls along the dialog box, speak your voiceprint phrase. If your voice matches, then the dialog disappears and the Finder or Panels interface will begin to load.

TIP   *You can click Cancel in the Voiceprint Verification dialog box if you'd prefer to enter your typed password.*

It's important to note that two other things happen at this point. First, any items in your personal Startup Items folder are launched—each user in a Multiple Users setup has his or her own Startup Items folder in the System Folder. (Technically, it's *mirrored* onto the System Folder, but when you're logged into your account you can access the Startup Items folder in the System Folder if you have enough privileges to do so.) That means you can place items in your Startup Items folder if you'd like them launched when you log in.

TIP   *You can hold down the SHIFT key to bypass your startup items immediately after you've entered your password.*

Second, your keychain is automatically unlocked if you haven't changed your keychain password. (In some cases, your keychain will not be opened automatically if you're the owner, especially if you created and used your keychain before you enabled Multiple Users for the first time.) By default, creating a Multiple Users account also creates a keychain whose password is the same as the Multiple Users account password. If you don't want your keychain opened automatically when you log in, change the keychain password (see Chapter 24 for details).

Once the Finder or Panels interface appears, you're free to go about your business. You may occasionally find that an alert box appears telling you that you don't have enough privileges to access something. If you feel that's an error, consult the owner to change your account type and/or privileges.

You'll also notice (unless you're the owner, who can store documents anywhere) that you have either a special folder or a special panel that's got your user name on it. This is your personal folder on the system. Store your documents in this folder and others can't access them (unless the owner has allowed access to your files). You can also install applications in this folder, if you have enough privileges. Likewise, Limited and Panels users will have an Items folder (or panel) where aliases to authorized applications are stored.

To log out, choose Special | Logout from the Finder or Panels menu. You'll see an alert box asking if you really want to log out. If you don't, click No. If you do, click Yes or wait 90 seconds and you'll be logged out automatically.

Before you're completely logged out, any items in your Shutdown Items folder will be executed.

Change Your Password

If you'd like to change your password, you can do that as you log into your account. Select your user name from the Login window, then click the Change Password button.

In the Change Password dialog box, enter your current password in the Current Password entry box. Then, with the Change Password option turned on, you enter your new password twice: once in the New Password entry box and again in the Verify New Password dialog box. Now, click OK and your new password is set.

If your keychain and your account password were the same before you changed the account password, you'll see another dialog box. Enter your old account password and click View. (This button name is a glitch in Mac OS 9 that may be fixed in future releases.) Now, your keychain password is automatically changed to your new account name password, so that both may be opened whenever you log in.

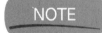 *If you elect not to enter your keychain password (clicking Cancel instead of View) then the keychain will no longer unlock automatically when you log in. You'll need to unlock it manually, using the old password.*

The Change Password dialog box offers another option that I skipped over—Reset Alternate Password. If you turn this option on and click OK, you'll be taken to the Voiceprint Setup dialog box, where you'll create your voiceprint. (See the following section "How To…Create a Voiceprint Password" for details.)

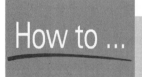 *If a different alternate password scheme has been set up, you'll be taken to that scheme's configuration, not Voiceprint Setup. Also, this option will be inaccessible if the owner hasn't turned on Allow Alternate Password in the Global Multiple User Options dialog box.*

How to … Create a Voiceprint Password

There are two ways to get into Voiceprint Setup if your Multiple Users control panel is configured for an alternate password. The first way is to click the Voiceprint Setup button on the Alternate Password tab of a user's Edit User window. The other way is to choose Reset Alternate Password in the Change Password dialog box as you are logging into your iMac. Both bring up the Voiceprint Setup dialog box.

```
┌─────────────────────────────────────────────────────┐
│ ▓▓▓▓▓▓▓▓▓▓▓▓▓▓▓ Voiceprint Setup for Donna ▓▓▓▓▓▓▓▓▓▓ │
├─────────────────────────────────────────────────────┤
│  To create a voiceprint, you need to record yourself  │
│  speaking your phrase four times.                      │
│                                                        │
│  ┌ Your current phrase is: ─────────────────────────┐ │
│  │   "My voice is my password."                      │ │
│  └───────────────────────────────────────────────────┘ │
│                                                        │
│  [ Change Phrase... ]           [ Cancel ] [ Continue ] │
└─────────────────────────────────────────────────────┘
```

From here, you can change your phrase if you like. Click the Change Phrase button and enter a new phrase. Note that the phrase itself isn't important—the Voiceprint system doesn't recognize the words that you speak, it recognizes *how* you speak them. Make your phrase about five to seven words long and one sentence. If you make it two sentences, it will be harder for the Voiceprint system to match your voiceprint, because you're likely to vary the pause between the sentences.

When your phrase is set, click the Continue button in the Voiceprint Setup dialog box. Now you'll see another dialog box that shows you a listing of recordings. You'll record yourself saying your voiceprint phrase four times. To begin recording, click the Record First button.

Now you'll see the Recording dialog box. Select the microphone you want to use from the Select Microphone pop-up menu (it will likely be the Built-In Mic unless you have another installed) and click the Record button. Speak your phrase as you normally would. (Don't speak slower or faster or try to enunciate more than usual. Remember, it's just recording your voice, not trying to recognize the words.) When you're done, click Stop. If you want to hear yourself, click the Play button; otherwise, click Done.

Now you'll go through the process three more times. After you've recorded all your voiceprints, you'll see a button marked Try It. (You may see a dialog box first asking you to re-record if your four voiceprints vary too much.) Click the Try It button and speak your voiceprint password one more time. If all goes well, you'll see a dialog box telling you your voiceprint has been recognized. (If it fails more than once or twice, you may need to re-record the voiceprint.)

Chapter 26

Print Your Documents, Manage Fonts, and Send Faxes

How to...

- Decide what type of printer to use with your iMac
- Connect the printer to your iMac (or to your network)
- Use Page Setup and Print dialog boxes to print your documents
- Manage documents with the PrintMonitor or Desktop Printer
- Change the fonts that are installed on your iMac
- Send and receive faxes from your iMac

You probably want to print stuff. Whether you already have an iMac-compatible printer, you're wondering if you can make your current printer iMac-compatible, or you're still in the shopping phase, let's take a look at your needs and figure out how to get you up and printing. It's actually pretty easy with an iMac, especially if you're able to buy a USB printer.

To begin, let's talk about the different types of printers you can get and what the advantages are of each. Then, we'll take a look at how you set up a printer and print to it. Finally, we'll end with a discussion of fonts and how to manage them on your iMac.

Choose a Printer

There are two major types of printers that are used in the home, home office, or most businesses and organizations: laser and inkjet. There are also different technologies for setting up the printers. And the different types of printers can even use different font technologies. So, let's take a closer look at the printers you might be able to buy or use with your iMac.

Laser vs. Inkjet

Inkjet printers tend to be less expensive, more home-oriented machines with fewer bells and whistles. These days, most inkjets can print in color and they print pretty quickly, although higher-quality printing is much slower than it is with a laser printer. Inkjets can be slightly easier to set up, but they rely strongly on their own software drivers, whereas most laser printers use a driver written by Apple that integrates well with the Mac OS.

Laser printers are faster and usually quieter, and offer better print quality. Most inexpensive lasers don't print in color, though, and laser printers are more expensive at the outset. Most laser printers will connect to an iMac using the Ethernet port, making it easy to share the printer with a number of different iMacs or other computers. Laser printers tend to have more professional-level options—paper trays and envelope feeders, for instance. And laser printers that use the PostScript printer language tend to print better-quality graphics than inkjet printers that don't use PostScript.

If you're trying to decide between the two, probably the most important considerations are your volume of printing, the need for color, and the desired quality of black-and-white printing. If you expect to print a lot—or if you'll be in situations where you need to quickly print 20- to 100-page documents and send them somewhere—then you'll want a laser printer. You'll also want a laser printer for a lower cost-per-page over the long term. And you'll want a laser if you print many important documents that are mostly text and require no color.

Inkjet technology has improved remarkably and you can get a good color printer for less than $200 in some cases. These are great if you run a small business and plan to print brochures, signs, menus, thank you notes, invitations, overhead slides, and so forth. While not always workhorses for hundreds of pages per month, an inkjet printer provides flexible printing with a variety of options. Look for an inkjet that accepts a number of different types of paper and transparencies, especially if you plan to make full use of color on business cards, overhead slides, and handbills.

If you want to share one printer between two or more computers, your best choice is a laser printer connected to the Ethernet port. At the time of writing, most printers connected to the USB port can't be shared over a network, although this may change if Apple and/or printer manufacturers write new "printer share" drivers. (For instance, there's a shareware driver for popular Epson USB inkjet printers that allows them to be shared over a network.)

Connection Technologies

Printers also offer a variety of ways that they can be connected to your iMac. There are two ways to directly connect to an iMac—USB and by a network (either Ethernet or wireless). In the case of USB, you'll often find that inkjet printers offer a special cable or adapter for the printer that can be added to give it USB connectivity. The cable can be $50 or more, so factor that in when you're shopping for an inkjet. Other inkjet printers offer USB right from the box, without special add-on cables.

Laser printers will often connect via Ethernet, although how you're connecting dictates the type of Ethernet cable you need. If you're just connecting the laser printer to your iMac, you'll need an Ethernet *crossover* cable, which is designed to allow two Ethernet devices to talk to one other. This is different from a typical Ethernet *patch* cable, which is used to connect a device to an Ethernet hub.

You'll also need an Ethernet hub if you plan to use the laser printer with more than one computer. You can do that easily with all the devices plugged into the hub; all the computers (especially if they're Macs and compatible with the printer) will recognize the printer when you set them up.

There's a third type of connection—a LocalTalk connection. LocalTalk is an earlier style of Mac networking that allowed older Macs to network to one another without using Ethernet cabling. It's a slow technology that's not as popular anymore, but some printers, especially older Apple laser printers, newer Apple-branded inkjets, and many popular HP inkjet and laser printers for Mac, use LocalTalk for their connection. The problem is, the iMac doesn't have a LocalTalk port. (This is the "printer" port on old Macs, if you're familiar with them.)

The solution is a LocalTalk adapter. With one of these adapters, you're able to hook your iMac to a LocalTalk printer through the Ethernet port. The connection is usually seamless—your printer driver is able to find the printer once it's connected, even though you're using an adapter.

The fourth type of connection, a serial connection, is similar. Older Apple StyleWriter inkjets, inkjets from Canon, HP DeskWriters, and some popular Apple Personal LaserWriter printers use serial connections. They don't use LocalTalk, but they do connect to the "printer port" (or the "modem port" in some cases) on older-style Macs. In this case, you need another adapter—a serial adapter. Different companies make different types of adapters—USB-to-serial or serial-to-Ethernet. Which you use is up to you, with one caveat—if you plan to do much networking, I'd go ahead and leave the Ethernet port free and use one of the USB adapters. If you'll just be using your iMac at home with no other computers in the mix and no major plans for DSL Internet or a cable modem, then a serial-to-Ethernet adapter is fine.

See Table 26-1 for a list of LocalTalk and serial adapter manufacturers.

Printer Languages

Printers can use different languages for describing a page. If your printer uses the PostScript language, then it's generally capable of more graphically complex pages. Professional publishers tend to use PostScript-language printers for their high-end printing needs. A PostScript-language printer includes a special processor, its own RAM, and some PostScript Type 1 fonts built into the printer itself. In this case, a program that wants to print to the printer simply sends a series of PostScript commands to tell the printer how the document should be printed. Then, the printer does all the work using its own processor to create the printed page.

Many inkjet printers use a different language, the Printer Control Language (PCL), a standard originated by Hewlett-Packard Corporation. In this case, the printer requires a special driver so that your iMac can speak the PCL language, create the page, and send it to the printer in the proper format. iMac does all of the processing, which is why inkjet printing can be slower than laser printing; it's also why most inkjet printers are cheaper, since they don't have their own processor, RAM, and so on—they rely on the iMac for all that.

This situation is also why inkjet printers need to have special driver software written for them, while PostScript-language printers, even if they aren't specifically designed to be Mac-compatible, often work just fine using the LaserWriter 8 driver discussed later in this chapter.

NOTE	*Earlier non-PostScript printers were made specifically for Macs using the QuickDraw printer language. For instance, HP's DeskWriter series, although nearly identical to the DeskJet series, used QuickDraw instead of PCL for the Mac version. These days that's much less common, especially for USB-based printers.*

Manufacturer	Adapter(s)	Web Site
Ariston	USB-to-serial	**http://www.ariston.com**
Entrega	USB-to-serial	**http://www.entrega.com**
Farallon	Ethernet-to-Localtalk Ethernet-to-serial	**http://www.farallon.com**
Keyspan	USB-to-serial	**http://www.keyspan.com**
Momentum	USB-to-serial	**http://www.momentuminc.com**

TABLE 26-1   Printer Adapter Manufacturers and Their Web Sites

26

Using PC Printers

Some of the newer PC printers can be used with either Windows-based PCs or Macs, depending on the software driver you use, since both use USB.

With a product called Infowave's PowerPrint USB (**http://www.infowave.com/**), it's possible to connect a parallel-port PC printer—either an inkjet or a non-PostScript laser printer—to your iMac, using the USB-to-PC parallel port adapter and special driver software.

PowerPrint works with Canon, Epson, Lexmark, and NEC printers as well as HP's LaserJet and DeskJet series. During the installation process choose the type of printer drivers you want to install, or a generic set of drivers, if appropriate.

> **NOTE** *Both HP and Epson have USB-to-parallel kits that also work with their own brands of printers. The Infowave kit is specifically designed for older printers that don't have iMac-specific driver software.*

After the installation is complete, simply access the printer's driver in the Chooser as discussed later in this chapter. The printer is treated the same as if it were a regular Mac-compatible printer.

Set Up Your Printer and iMac

You've seen a number of different ways to attach an iMac and a printer, including special adapters and cables. In most of those cases, you'll have a particular adapter cable that plugs directly between the printer and iMac.

It so happens that the type of cabling you use generally dictates the type of software driver you'll use, too. All printer drivers are selected in the Chooser, which you open from the Apple menu. The Chooser allows you to select printers and determine certain characteristics about how that printer will conduct itself, including how it's connected. If you have a USB or serial-adapted printer, you'll use an individual printer driver from the manufacturer. If you have a laser printer that's connected via Ethernet, you'll likely use the LaserWriter driver.

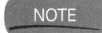 *If your laser printer offers a special driver written for Macintosh, you should use that driver. If the driver comes on a floppy diskette, contact the company to see if they have a downloadable or CD-ROM version; you might also examine the discussion of creating disk images in Chapter 20.*

Choose a USB or Serial-Adapted Printer

If your printer is an inkjet or a laser printer that's been adapted to your iMac via a serial-to-USB or serial-to-Ethernet adapter, then choose the individual printer driver for that device. The driver will say DeskJet 880, USB LaserJet, Epson 740, or something similar. If your particular printer's driver doesn't appear in the Chooser, then you may not have installed it.

Check the CD that came with the printer for a Mac driver installer program. If you don't find Mac drivers, try the manufacturer's support Web site or contact customer support to get the drivers. The easiest way to get the driver software is to download it from the manufacturer's Web site.

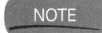 *Printer drivers are installed right in the Extensions folder in your System Folder, just in case you want to look for them. Your printer may also require some other support files in the Extensions or Control Panels folder.*

Once you've installed the printer drivers, select the printer from the Chooser. Hopefully, the connection will be found (by your iMac) on the right side, where you'll see the USB symbol and the printer's name. (It's also possible you'll see a Printer Port symbol if you're using an adapter.) When you've selected the connection, choose the Setup button (if one appears) to set basic printer preferences. Otherwise, just click the Close box and your printer is set. In some instances, a desktop printer icon will appear.

Choose an Ethernet Printer

If your printer is connected via Ethernet, either using a crossover cable or plugged directly into an Ethernet hub, setting up the printer is usually very simple.

In the Chooser, select the LaserWriter 8 printer driver (or the driver you specially installed for your laser printer). Now, on the right side of the Chooser window, select the printer you want to use. In cases where your iMac resides on a large network, you may see more than one choice.

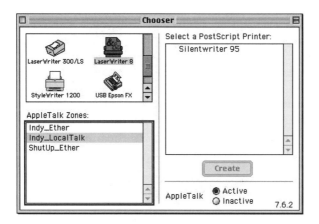

NOTE *Not all networks will have the AppleTalk zones pictured here. If yours doesn't, you'll simply see all available PostScript printers when you click the LaserWriter 8 driver. If your network does have zones, you may need to select the appropriate zone for the printer you want to print to. Ask your system administrator for details.*

Select the PostScript printer and click the Create button. This allows you to create (or use) a PostScript Printer Description (PPD) file that can be used to control this printer.

If you believe you have a PPD installed for this printer (PPD files are stored in the Extensions folder inside the System Folder), then you can choose Select PPD and search for it. If not, then you're best off choosing Auto Setup where the LaserWriter driver will help you decide what the printer is capable of. You can get information about the printer by clicking the Get Info button. If you have your printer manual around and you want to set some options for your particular printer, click the Configure button. Otherwise, click OK.

Now, close the Chooser. When you do, your desktop printer icon for this printer will appear.

NOTE *If you don't see your printer when you select the LaserWriter 8 driver in the Chooser on an AirPort-enabled iMac, the printer may not be configured correctly. Ethernet printers that use IP (instead of AppleTalk) can be used by AirPort-enabled iMacs and Macs. If you have such a printer, you may need to use the Desktop Printer Utility (located in the Apple Extras folder in the Apple LaserWriter Software folder) to configure a desktop printer. Consult your AirPort documentation or system administrator for details.*

Print Stuff and Manage Print Jobs

Once you have your printer set up, you're ready to print. If you've changed printers recently, you may have been asked to open the Page Setup item in your applications.

Or you may want to explore the options in Page Setup before printing, so that you know everything is set up correctly.

After you've invoked the Print command and sent the print job to the printer, it's passed to either the print spooler or the desktop printer. In the case of a spooler, you'll simply see its entry in the Application menu—you can switch to it if desired to see your progress. If your print driver uses a desktop printer, you can manage the print job from there.

Page Setup

When you've created a document and you're ready to print it, begin by choosing File | Page Setup. That brings up the Page Setup dialog box.

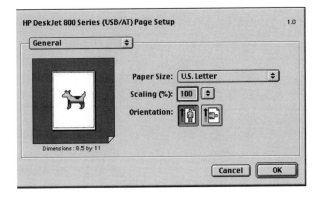

Actually, you don't need to visit this dialog box every time you plan to print—only when you need to change a major option for your printer or when you've recently changed printers (while the application was open) and you need the application to recognize the new printer. The Page Setup dialog box is most significant because it introduces you to Clarus the DogCow, one of Apple's official mascots. But it's also where you set some important options:

- **Paper Size**   Choose what size paper the application should plan on printing to. (The default is 8.5 × 11-inch paper.)

- **Scaling (%)**   Enter a percentage if you'd like the document to be printed at anything other than 100 percent.

- **Orientation**   Choose whether the document should be printed in Portrait mode (regular orientation on the page) or in Landscape mode (lengthwise, as with ledger sheets).

- **Options**   The Options button provides options unique to your particular printer model.

Changes in the Page Setup dialog box are noted with Clarus. Change the paper size and you'll see the page change relative to Clarus; change the orientation and you'll see the image change to reflect that, too. When you're done setting up the page, click OK.

NOTE *Clarus, a DogCow, says "Moof," according to Apple's technical information library.*

The PrintMonitor

Once the print job is sent, you'll probably hear the printer come to life and prepare to feed paper and print. You may also see a new entry in the Applications menu called the PrintMonitor (or something similar, like Epson Monitor). The PrintMonitor works in the background to allow your iMac to print while you continue to work on other things. You can also use the PrintMonitor to manage your print jobs.

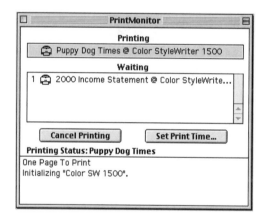

Using the PrintMonitor, you can view the print jobs that have been sent to the printer; if you've sent more than one document to the printer, each appears in the PrintMonitor queue, with the current job at the top. Select a print job and click Cancel Printing to clear the job from the print queue, or click Set Print Time to schedule the print job to print sometime in the future.

While the PrintMonitor is open you can also select File | Stop Printing to suspend printing for the moment. If you'd like to continue printing, select File | Resume Printing.

The Desktop Printer

Many Mac-compatible inkjet printers and Ethernet laser printers will create a desktop printer icon that you can use to manage your print jobs. It works a lot like the PrintMonitor, but is a little friendlier and a little more powerful.

Once you've sent a print job to the printer, you should see your desktop printer icon change to reflect the fact that it has a document that's ready to be printed.

If you need to, you can manage that print job by double-clicking the desktop icon to open the print queue window, where you can see the scheduled print jobs.

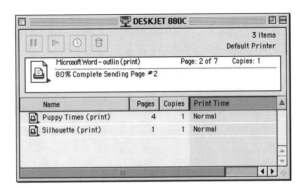

Select a print job in this window, then use the controls at the top of the window to control it—you can pause a job, start it again, give it higher priority, schedule the print job, or delete it.

TIP   *Dragging a print job from the queue list to the current print job window will change its priority to urgent, moving it to the top of the queue.*

You'll also notice that while the desktop printer queue is open, there's another command menu in the Finder's menu bar—the Printing menu. Pull it down and select Stop Print Queue to halt all printing; choose Start Print Queue to continue printing. Click the close box to close the queue window and the printer will continue printing in the background.

SHORTCUT   *If you have more than one desktop printer, then you don't have to return to the Chooser to switch between them. A small printer icon appears on the menu bar, very near the Application menu in the top-right corner. Click that icon and you'll get a menu where you can change the active printer.*

Understand and Add Fonts to Your iMac

A *font* is a collection of letters, numbers, and punctuation marks with a particular typeface, weight (bold or not bold), and size in plain or italic. However, the word "font" is also frequently used to mean a typeface with a particular design, such as Courier or Arial. I'll use the term "font" loosely.

When you select a font the application passes that information to the Mac OS, which helps the application render that font. Fonts are stored in a subfolder of your System Folder called the Fonts folder. The font files serve two purposes. First, font files tell your printer how printed text should appear. Second, they tell your iMac how to display text on the screen.

Add Fonts

You can buy both TrueType and PostScript Type 1 fonts from computer stores or online computer sales outlets—any such fonts should work fine with your iMac. To add a font for your iMac's applications, just drag-and-drop the font file onto the System Folder icon. A dialog box will appear telling you that this file will automatically be added to the Fonts folder. Click OK.

If you're using PostScript Type 1 fonts, you should have Adobe Type Manager (ATM) installed and working on your iMac. ATM is a control panel that's installed along with Adobe Acrobat Reader, so by default your iMac should have it active. If you have Mac OS 9 installed on your iMac, you'll need ATM 5.4.2 or higher; older versions are incompatible.

Fonts can be stored loose in the Fonts folder, or they can be saved in a special kind of folder called a *suitcase.* Because there's a limit of 128 items in the Font folder, a suitcase can be used to get around that minimum by, for instance, grouping all the Times New Roman fonts (TrueType and bitmap versions) in the same suitcase.

You can also use suitcases for organization—drag as many fonts as you want into a suitcase and name it "Special Design Fonts" or something similar. Now, drag this suitcase into the Fonts folder before you launch QuarkXPress, GraphicConverter, or another application that you use with these fonts. At other times when you're working in regular applications, you can store the font suitcase in a different folder on your iMac, so that those fonts aren't used. The fewer fonts you have active, the faster your applications will run. If you open the Fonts folder, you'll see that many of the fonts are already stored in suitcases.

Double-click a suitcase and you can drag-and-drop fonts in and out of the suitcase. The best way to create your own suitcase is to create a duplicate of an existing suitcase and rename it. (You'll also want to delete the fonts in your duplicate suitcase by dragging them to the Trash.)

Arial Black

If you'll deal with fonts a lot, you might clean out a duplicate suitcase and save it as your "master" suitcase. You can duplicate your master suitcase whenever you need a new suitcase. This way, you won't have to clean out the fonts every time.

The renamed suitcase can now store font files. Just drag all fonts for that suitcase—both bitmap and TrueType fonts, if you've got them—onto the suitcase icon.

Delete Fonts

To delete a font, just open the Fonts folder and drag the font (or suitcase) to the Trash.

It's a good idea to think carefully before deleting a font file, because you can't always anticipate when an application or document might need that particular font. If you want to simply deactivate a font, drag it to a folder outside of the System Folder. (Create a "Disabled Fonts" folder on your hard disk, for instance.) Now that font won't appear in the Font menu of any of your applications. If you get error messages requiring the use of a disabled font, you can still drag the font back into the Fonts folder if it's needed.

Remember, too, that many of the files in the Fonts folder are actually suitcases that have more than one font inside of them (usually, but not always, in the same typeface family). If you don't want to delete the entire suitcase, you can double-click the suitcase to open it, then drag the font files to the Trash individually.

Fax with Your iMac

Your iMac comes bundled with a program called FaxSTF that makes it possible—perhaps even easy—to send and receive faxes. All you have to do is have your modem plugged into the telephone line and make some basic preference settings. The rest of it should be set up and ready to use.

Send a Fax

Obviously, your iMac, right out of the box, doesn't offer the full functionality of a fax machine, since it doesn't have a mechanism for getting pages to fax into your iMac so you can send them along. If you have a scanner (see Chapter 27), you can replace your fax machine. Without one, you're relegated to sending documents that you create—in AppleWorks, Microsoft Word, QuarkXPress, Adobe PhotoDeluxe, or other programs—to distant fax machines. In that sense, faxing is just a substitute for printing.

In fact, that's how it works on your iMac. While you're viewing a document you want to fax, hold down the ⌘-OPTION keys while selecting the File menu. If your fax software is working, you won't find a Print command on the menu. Instead, you'll see a Fax command. Select it and you'll see the FaxPrint dialog box.

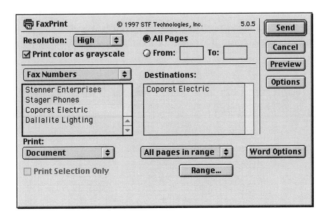

In the dialog box, choose the resolution of the fax, which pages to send, and so on. (A low-resolution fax will send a bit quicker but look worse at the other end.) Then, select your recipient from the list of names and drag it to the Destinations window. If your recipient isn't listed, add him or her through the FaxSTF browser (discussed in the next section). You can add a temporary fax number by selecting Temporary Address from the Fax Numbers pull-down menu. Then, fill out the dialog box and click ENTER.

With your addressee chosen, click Send. (You can click Preview, first, if you'd like to see what your fax will look like.) After you click Send, your modem will dial the number for the distant fax machine and transmit the fax. You'll see the Fax Status window, apprising you of the success or failure of the connection.

Receive a Fax

FaxSTF, unfortunately, doesn't have an option that allows you to manually accept a fax. In order to have your iMac receive a fax, you'll need to configure the FaxSTF Browser application to listen for the phone ringing. Here's how:

1. First, launch the FaxSTF Browser, which is located in the FaxSTF folder inside the Applications folder.

2. With the browser open, select Edit | Preferences.

3. Select the Fax Modem icon on the left side of the dialog box.

4. On the right side of the dialog box, pull down the Answer On menu and choose the number of rings the fax software should wait before it picks up the phone line.

5. Click OK.

Now the iMac will answer after the designated number of rings and attempt to receive a fax, if one is incoming. When the iMac detects a call on the line, you'll see the Fax Status window appear to tell you if a fax has connected and is being transmitted. The Fax Status window includes a Stop button, which will allow you to stop an attempted connection, just in case you decide it's a person on the line that you need to speak with.

Read the Fax

Received faxes appear in the FaxSTF Browser window. First, launch the FaxSTF Browser, which is located in the FaxSTF folder inside the Applications folder. On the left side of the window, select the Fax In folder and a list of received faxes will appear on the right side of the window.

To view a fax, double-click it. It'll appear in its own window. From there, you can print the fax using the File | Print command. You can also use the Action menu to alter the fax somewhat, making it look better, print faster, or align correctly.

26

Chapter 27

Upgrade Your iMac

How to...

- Add USB and Firewire peripherals to your iMac
- Add a removable drive
- Add a CD-R or CD-RW drive
- Add speakers or a USB microphone
- Upgrade the RAM in your iMac
- Install the AirPort card in your slot-loading iMac

The Universal Serial Bus has done wonders for Apple's entire line of computers in terms of ease of use and convenience. USB is very easy to use—it offers hot-swappable technology, it's a snap to set up, and in most cases it simply works when you plug something in.

USB is convenient because the iMac relies on it for upgrading nearly all peripherals from keyboards and mice to printers and removable drives. That means all the peripherals for the iMac are reasonably new, fast, and easy to configure. This is an important distinction between most of Apple's current computer models and nearly every other computer made—since they primarily use only new connection technologies like USB, the iMac and other Macs are only compatible with the latest and most modern peripherals.

If you have an iMac DV model, you've also got another option for upgrading— Firewire. Firewire ports offer high-speed access with the same convenience as USB, making Firewire perfect for digital cameras, high-speed external disks, and removable storage drives.

If you absolutely must connect older peripherals, that's possible, too. You simply need the right adapter for the job. We'll take a look at all those options in this chapter.

 *This chapter doesn't cover printers, although many of them use a USB port on your iMac. See Chapter 26 for information on installing and configuring a printer.*

Upgrade with USB and Firewire

All iMacs include USB ports for upgrading. USB is a technology designed to allow other technologies that have traditionally been connected to Macs via "serial" ports to connect to a faster, more modern equivalent. The connector, the speeds, and the methods of connection have all been updated.

iMac DV models also include Firewire ports, another technology that enables you to easily and quickly hook up peripherals. Firewire is much faster than USB, meaning it's better suited for devices that transfer a lot of data to and from your iMac. Those devices include hard disks, removable drives, scanners, and similar devices.

Why USB?

There are three major improvements that USB offers over the serial ports that have been used in both Windows-based PCs and older Macintosh computers for nearly two decades:

- **Speed**   Each USB bus on an iMac can transfer data up to 12 megabits per second, or over 12,000 kilobits per second. In fact, this speed makes it possible to connect devices—like removable drives and scanners—that have traditionally relied on an external SCSI connector. While USB isn't as fast as SCSI (and Firewire is faster), USB is fast enough for these peripherals, and it offers some other advantages over SCSI, like easier configuration.

27

NOTE *On slot-loading iMac models, there are two USB buses in the iMac, so that each port can transfer 12 megabits per second independently. On earlier iMacs, that 12 megabits per second is shared by the two ports, meaning a device on one port can slow down a device on the other port if they're both in use at the same time.*

- **Ease of Use** Aside from being *hot-swappable* (meaning you can plug and unplug devices without damaging them or your iMac) USB ports can also provide power to some peripherals, meaning fewer of them require their own power cords and adapters.

- **Device Support** Old serial ports offered one peripheral per port; USB can support up to 127 devices per bus, as long as those devices don't mind sharing the connection. That means you'll easily be able to hook up a scanner, joystick, printer, Zip drive, digital camera, mouse, keyboard, and most anything else without much trouble.

NOTE *On slot-loading iMacs, each USB bus can support 127 devices, and there are two buses. So, just in case you need to hook up 254 devices, you're set.*

With these improvements you can see why USB is a boon for the iMac—not only is it quick and extensible, but it's also simple to use.

Why Firewire?

If you have a slot-loading iMac, you have Firewire ports available for connecting devices to your iMac. These are also a boon, particularly because Firewire is very fast compared to most other external port technologies. Firewire can transfer data at up to 400 megabits per second, which is quite a bit more than USB, older serial ports, or even external SCSI ports. That makes Firewire ideal not only for connecting external DV camcorders, but also for high-speed devices like external hard disks and removable disk drives.

Firewire is just as easy to hook up as USB, with up to 63 devices supported between the two ports. Even better, Firewire devices don't require a hub—you can actually *daisy-chain* them together by plugging one device into the iMac, the next device into the first device, and so on. USB, by contrast, requires a hub.

NOTE *While Firewire hubs are available, hubs aren't necessary for Firewire devices; they're simply convenient. A Firewire hub allows you to connect and disconnect Firewire devices without affecting other devices. If you have devices arranged in a daisy chain, disconnecting one of them may interrupt others on the chain until you get the whole thing plugged back in again.*

The real advantage, though, is choice. With an iMac DV model, you can choose to buy higher-speed peripheral devices that use Firewire for best performance. Then, you'll also have USB ports available for Zip drives, input devices, and other lower-performance external devices. You've got the best of both worlds!

USB Ports and Hubs

Your iMac has two USB ports. One of those ports probably has your iMac's keyboard plugged into it, with a mouse plugged into the keyboard.

That leaves one port open on the keyboard and one port open on the side of the iMac. After a rough count, that's two ports available for devices. Hardly comes close to 127 (or 254, for slot-loading iMacs), does it?

In order to use more than two devices, you'll need to get a device called a *USB hub*. This device will probably have its own AC adapter so it can provide power to the USB ports. It'll also have four, eight, or more USB ports that you can use for additional devices (see Figure 27-1).

Hubs are reasonably inexpensive, but you won't even need one until you have more than two additional devices for your iMac—one can plug into the keyboard, which is a passive hub in its own right (it doesn't supply power), and the other can plug directly into the iMac. If all you have is a printer and a joystick, for instance, you might plug the joystick into your keyboard and the printer into your iMac's side. Once you get more than two devices, though, it's hub time.

27

FIGURE 27-1   With USB, hubs are necessary to connect more than one device to a single USB port.

A number of vendors sell hubs. Here's a partial list of the vendors and their Web sites:

Ariston Technologies	**http://www.ariston.com/**
Belkin Components	**http://www.belkin.com/**
Entrega Corporation	**http://www.entrega.com/**
Interex	**http://www.interex.com/**
MacAlly	**http://www.macally.com/**
Newer Technology	**http://www.newertech.com/**

Install a USB or Firewire Device

Some USB and Firewire devices require drivers that are placed in the Extensions folder and used whenever the device is connected and recognized by the Mac OS. These drivers vary from specific for a particular device to more generic that use Game Sprockets technology, for instance. (Game Sprockets drivers are included with your iMac.) Keyboards and mice don't necessarily require drivers (plug them in and they should work) although they will require special drivers in some cases—for example, to program more than one mouse button or to remap the Windows key to the ⌘ key. All of these require special driver software.

The normal game plan is to install the driver software, then connect your device to the iMac. If all goes well, your device will be recognized and the driver will be properly loaded and used with the device. (This can sometimes appear to freeze the iMac while the driver gets situated. You should always wait a few seconds after you've plugged in a device before you panic.) In other cases, you may need to restart your iMac in order for the device to be recognized. If the device is a game controller that uses Game Sprockets drivers, you won't be able to use the device until you're playing a game that supports Game Sprockets. (See Chapter 16.)

NOTE   *In order to use many USB and Firewire products reliably, your older iMac needs the latest software, Mac OS, and iMac Firmware updates. (This is especially true if you have an older iMac, although Apple regularly updates both USB and Firewire support.) See Chapter 30 for more on updating your iMac.*

Add a Mouse, Keyboard, or Controller

All controllers and input devices use USB for their connection, since Firewire is overkill for a mouse, keyboard, or controller. Mice and keyboards are generally the easiest devices to add—in many cases, they don't even require special drivers. Apple's USB software has built into it some generic drivers that can recognize nearly any USB mouse or keyboard that's been plugged into an available USB port and use it easily.

In other cases, though, you will need a driver. This will usually come in the form of an extension or control panel, which you drag to the System Folder to install. After you've restarted your iMac, you'll have access to the device. If the driver is a control panel, you can open that control panel to set preferences for the device.

Keyboards usually require even less customization, unless the keyboard has special features like a built-in pointing device. Some keyboards originally designed for Windows require a special driver that allows the Windows keys and other keys to be used as Mac OS equivalents. Although the keyboards are basically the same, the Mac OS recognizes the ⌘ and POWER keys, which are unique compared to many Windows-oriented keyboards.

A number of companies offer unique pointing devices and keyboards for the iMac. Here are a few of those companies and what they offer:

Ariston Technologies	**http://www.ariston.com/**	Mouse
Belkin	**http://www.belkin.com/**	Mouse, keyboard
CompuCable	**http://www.compucable.com/**	Mouse
Contour Design	**http://www.contourdesign.com/**	Mouse
iMaccessories	**http://www.imaccessories.com/**	Mouse, keyboard, trackball
Interex	**http://www.interex.com/**	Mouse
Kensington	**http://www.kensington.com/**	Mouse, trackball
MacAlly	**http://www.macally.com/**	Mouse, keyboard, trackball, joystick
Microsoft	**http://www.microsoft.com/**	Mouse
Wacom	**http://www.wacom.com/**	Pen tablet

What's a pen tablet? It's a flat surface that allows you to use a pen for moving the mouse pointer—great for drawing, touch-ups, or just for a familiar interface for moving the mouse pointer.

A lot of iMac users are less than pleased by the iMac's round mouse—well, there's one unique product designed to deal with that without requiring a new mouse. It's called the iCatch from Macsense Connectivity (**http://www.macsensetech.com/**) and it's a snap-on addition to the iMac's mouse that gives it a more traditional shape. It's easy to use and does seem to make the mouse a little more comfortable.

Game controllers are covered in Chapter 16.

Add an External Drive

A removable drive can be an important addition, since the iMac lacks a floppy drive and many users aren't connected to local area networks. Online backup and file transfer is certainly one option, especially if you have a higher-speed connection. (Online backup is discussed in Chapter 20.) But if you'd like to be able to back up on physical disks, then a removable drive is a good idea.

 *External drives come in both USB and Firewire varieties. In most cases, Firewire is preferable if you have an iMac DV model, since Firewire is much faster for copying data to and from the drive.*

There are two basic approaches to removable media—removable disks and writeable CD technology. Removable disks include Iomega's Zip drive, Imation's SuperDisk, and the Castlewood Orb drive. All of these are designed to use compact floppy-like disks that can store between 100MB and 2.2GB, depending on the drive used. Here's a look at each:

- **Iomega Zip (http://www.iomega.com/)**   The Zip drive is a popular choice for removable storage, offering from 100-250MB of storage space. (For 250MB, you'll need the special Zip250 drive.) It's reasonably quick and Zip disks are very popular with Mac and PC users alike. If you plan to share media among different computers, this may be the best solution.

- **Imation SuperDisk (http://www.superdisk.com/)**   The SuperDisk offers the unique ability to read traditional 1.4MB floppy disks as well as the special 120MB LS120 disks. The SuperDisk is a touch slow compared to other removables, but very flexible. This is a good solution if you need to read floppy disks but also want extra capacity.

- **Castlewood Orb (http://www.castlewood.com/)**   The Castlewood Orb drive offers 2.2GB of storage on reasonably inexpensive media, making it easy to back up nearly your entire iMac to a single disk. If you plan to rotate your media, a single Orb disk should suffice for each backup session, even if you have a lot of files.

You'll also find some external drives on the market that don't quite fit the "removable" mold but are popular ways to extend your iMac nonetheless. A few companies make floppy drives for iMacs, allowing you to use a typical 1.4MB floppy diskette. Other companies make actual external hard disks in gigabyte capacities.

If your iMac doesn't support Firewire, then you may opt for a USB-based hard disk. Be warned that USB is a little slow for use with a hard disk; the external disk will never be as fast as your iMac's internal disk. That doesn't mean it won't be useful, though, since having such a large capacity for backup—along with the option of unplugging the drive and using it with another computer—is a convenient touch. Here are some manufacturers of floppy and hard disks for iMacs:

iDrive	**http://www.idrives.com/**	Floppy drive, hard disk
LaCie	**http://www.lacie.com/**	Hard disk
Newer Technology	**http://www.newertech.com/**	Floppy drive
VST Technologies	**http://www.vsttech.com/**	Floppy drive

If you have an iMac DV model that does support Firewire, you'll find external Firewire hard disks that are fully as fast and useful as your iMac's internal disk. In fact, Firewire hard disks are a great addition to your iMac, since you can easily back up to the disk, transport the disk, and move the disk between iMacs and other Macs that support Firewire. VST Technologies, LaCie, MacTell (**http://www.mactell.com/**), and other manufacturers make Firewire hard disks as well as other Firewire-based external removable drives.

Install an External Drive

External drives often require special software for installation on an iMac, since each may have its own unique USB or Firewire driver. Once the driver is installed, hooking up the drive should be simple. Just plug the USB or Firewire cable into the drive, then into either the port on your iMac's keyboard (for USB), the port on the side of the iMac, or an available port on your USB hub. (Firewire devices can usually be plugged into an available port on the side of your iMac or the back of another Firewire device.) Right after you plug in the drive, either you'll have success or you'll see a message that suggests you haven't correctly installed the drive's software.

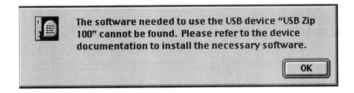

The software needed to use the USB device "USB Zip 100" cannot be found. Please refer to the device documentation to install the necessary software.

OK

CAUTION   *If you're connecting multiple Firewire devices in a daisy chain, make sure that none of the connections loop back on any of the already connected devices. Device 1 should be connected to the iMac's Firewire port, device 2 to device 1, device 3 to device 2, and so on.*

You'll want to be careful with your removable drives, because some of them don't react well in certain configurations. In some situations, you also need to consider *where* you put your removable drive on the USB bus. Some removable drives work better with older iMacs if they have access to their own port. With slot-loading iMacs, each USB port is its own 12Mbps bus. In this case, you'll probably get better performance if you place the removable drive on a different port from your other demanding peripherals, like scanners or printers. While you're not likely to encounter errors, placing your demanding peripherals on separate ports may help you get the best performance.

NOTE   *If you have an iMac DV, you can see that it's better to get Firewire storage devices instead of USB, whenever possible, to avoid these slowdowns.*

If you can't dedicate a whole USB port to the removable drive, it's best to connect and use your drive while other peripherals on the same connection are inactive. That is, you'll see worse performance if a scanner, removable drive, keyboard, mouse, and gaming device are all being used on the same bus at the same time. It's not a huge problem, although there's a chance it could result in data loss.

 *Another consideration—Iomega's documentation for the Zip drive suggests you not plug or unplug other devices on the USB while the drive is being used (written to or read from). This also translates to other types of removable drives, since it could be a problem to have the iMac looking for a USB driver while it's supposed to be paying attention to the drive. This shouldn't be a problem on newer slot-loading iMacs, especially if you're plugging and unplugging devices that are connected to the other USB port or to a Firewire port.*

Once you have the drive connected up with the drivers correctly installed, pop in a disk. It should appear on the desktop, like any other disk.

With older iMacs, it isn't possible to boot from USB-based disks and drives, even if the disk has a System Folder on it. With slot-loading iMacs, it is possible to boot from external USB peripherals, thanks to the dual-channel nature of the USB implementation. (It still isn't possible to boot from Firewire devices, at least, not at the time of writing.) If you'd like to boot from a removable drive, insert a disk that includes a valid System Folder, then open the Startup Disk control panel. Select the removable disk and close the control panel. Now, when you restart, your iMac will start up from the removable disk.

With any iMac, you can still boot from a CD in the internal CD-ROM or DVD-ROM drive. Place a CD with a valid System Folder in the drive and restart your iMac. Immediately after you hear the startup tone, hold down the C key until the Welcome to Macintosh message appears.

Back Up to the Removable

The Iomega Zip drive comes with special software to help you manage backing up to the drive—other removable drives may include the same. Whether or not you use that same software or a backup application like Retrospect or Retrospect Express, you can use the removable drive to automatically back up your important files to the removable disk.

You've already seen (in Chapter 20) that online backup can be automated in this way, and with great success. When you're dealing with disks, though, there are some things to consider:

- **Rotate Media** If you can, rotate backups between three or more different disks. If you need to back up often, you can back up Mondays, Wednesdays, and Fridays. Then, the next week, you can use your software to do an incremental backup, which simply adds files that have changed since the last backup. If you don't want to back up that often, back up once a week and rotate new media in each week for three or four weeks, then start over.

- **Archive** This is important: Every so often (say, once a week in a business situation, once a month at home) archive one of your removable disks—that is, drop it out of the rotation and store it somewhere safe. This does two things. It gives you a reasonably up-to-date emergency copy of your data. It also gives you a copy of your data that's fixed in time. If your iMac subsequently gets infected with a virus, or if you accidentally delete or change a file, you still have the older copy to return to.

NOTE *If you're serious about archiving disks, you should consider a CD-R or CD-RW drive. CDs are much better for long-term storage than many removable disks. CDs are also cheaper than most removable disks, making it less expensive to back up to CDs over the long haul.*

■ **Test** Especially in a business situation (or even with your thesis, business plan, novel, or personal investment portfolio), test the backup media occasionally to make sure they're working OK.

Once you get into the swing of things, you should find it's easy to automate the backup process. In many cases, it's just a question of telling the backup software when to schedule the backup, then leaving the right disk in the drive when it's time for the backup (see Figure 27-2).

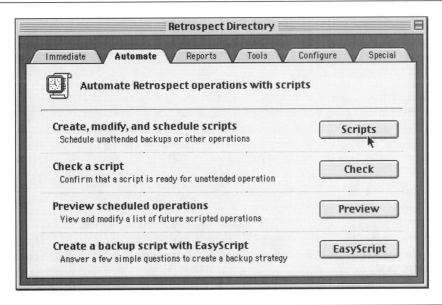

FIGURE 27-2   Retrospect or a similar product can be used to automatically schedule a backup to your removable drive.

CD-R and CD-RW Drives

You might also want to consider a CD-R (CD-Recordable) or CD-RW (CD-Rewriteable) drive for your iMac. These drives work a lot like other removable drives, although they tend to be a little slower for saving data and a little pricier for the drive itself. The discs, on the other hand, can often be cheaper.

A CD-R drive can write once to a CD-R disc, which can then be read by nearly any CD-ROM drive. This is a convenient way to transfer files or send files great distances, since CD-R discs are cheap, they can hold up to 650MB of data, and they're pretty resilient. CD-R discs are also a great media for archiving important documents from your hard disk since the CD-R discs store well, don't take up a lot of space, and can be popped into any Mac if there's trouble with your iMac.

CD-RW discs are slightly more expensive, but allow you to erase information on the disc and write to it again. In this way a CD-RW drive is very much like a Zip or similar removable drive. CD-RW drives tend to be capable of writing to CD-R media, too, so you can have the best of both worlds. Companies making CD-R and CD-RW drives for the iMac (via USB and/or Firewire) include:

Fantom Drives	**http://www.fantomdrives.com/**
Freecom	**http://www.freecom.de/**
LaCie	**http://www.lacie.com/**
QPS, Inc.	**http://www.qps-inc.com/**
Sony	**http://www.sony.com/**
WinStation	**http://www.winstation.com/**

CD-R technologies sometimes require special software, the most popular being Adaptec Toast, a program that allows you to "burn" an entire CD at once. You can also write to CDs in "sessions," meaning you can write to the disc at different times, storing data sequentially on the disc. This process usually necessitates two things. You have to set up the software to copy over a number of different files, then you have to leave it to its task, since CD-R works more slowly than other removables, which are often closer to hard disk speeds. Toast also lets you create audio CDs and CDs designed to use the file format that Windows computers generally read.

If Toast doesn't sound right to you, another popular Adaptec software tool is DirectCD, which allows you to mount the CD on your desktop and copy files to it just as if it were simply another disk attached to your iMac. That means you can drag-and-drop files onto your CD-R disc or save directly from applications to the disc instead of taking the time to set up all your files and burn them to the CD-R.

Scanners and Digital Cameras

Scanners and digital cameras are also being designed to support USB and Firewire these days, offering an easy way to get digital images into your iMac for use in newsletters, reports, and Web sites. Scanners allow you to place an image or document flat on the glass bed of the scanner's top—like a copy machine—and digitize the image or document so that it can be used on your iMac's screen. In fact, some scanners include special Optical Character Recognition (OCR) software that allows a scanned document to be turned into a regular word processing document, enabling you to edit and store the document in an application like AppleWorks.

Add a Scanner

Scanners for the iMac tend to be inexpensive and they include decent bells and whistles. If you're comparison-shopping, look for high-end color support (32-bit color or better), high *true* resolution (600 × 600 or better), and extras like Photoshop plug-ins and OCR software. Here are some scanner manufacturers with iMac-compatible products:

AGFA	http://www.agfa.com/
Artec	http://www.artecusa.com/
Microtek	http://www.microtek.com/
Umax	http://www.umax.com/

Generally, you'll simply install the scanner's software, plug in the scanner, and start scanning. Some models offer buttons on the scanner that can be used to activate the scanner and start up its software; other models are software-driven only, using either a special program or a Photoshop plug-in to acquire images from the scanner. Most scanners include a copy of Adobe PhotoDeluxe, for instance, that supports the plug-in and allows you to scan images directly from the scanner into PhotoDeluxe so you can then manipulate the images.

 Many scanners are TWAIN-compatible, allowing you to scan images directly from applications that offer a TWAIN acquisition command.

Add a Digital Camera

There are two different types of iMac-compatible digital cameras. One is a *still camera*, designed to be carried around and used just like a typical 35mm point-and-shoot camera. The difference with a digital camera is that, instead of taking pictures on film, it takes pictures that are stored in a computer-compatible format, often JPEG. These images can be downloaded from the camera and used immediately in a photo-editing program, in a desktop layout, or for Web pages.

The other type of digital camera is a video camera. These come in two varieties—DV camcorders and low-end video capture cameras. Nearly all DV camcorders support Firewire, making it simple to transfer digital movies from the camcorder to your iMac DV model. If you plan to make home movies, corporate videos, or other high-quality video, a DV camcorder that supports Firewire is the best choice.

 Attaching a Firewire-based DV camcorder to your iMac DV is covered in Chapter 15.

If you have an older iMac or you don't want to invest in a DV camcorder, you can get small cameras that are attached via USB and create video of you and your immediate surroundings. These cameras offer lower resolution and picture quality than your typical video camcorder, but they're useful for Internet conferencing and similar applications.

These cameras have their own software and drivers that must be installed. In the case of a digital still camera, you'll acquire images much the same way as you do from a scanner—using PhotoDeluxe, Photoshop, or the camera's own software to download images from the camera to your iMac.

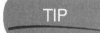 These days you can also purchase video capture devices that enable you to hook up a VHS camcorder and digitize video via the USB port. You'll generally do this if you want to create QuickTime movies from videos you've filmed using a traditional camcorder.

Here's a list of current digital camera manufacturers. Note that many digital still cameras are being announced that support USB as an interface. If you buy one of these cameras, make sure it includes Macintosh driver software. Here's some of what's available at the time of this writing:

Ariston Technologies	http://www.ariston.com/	Video cameras, video capture device
Belkin Components	http://www.belkin.com/	Video capture device
Epson	http://www.epson.com/	Still cameras
Logitech	http://www.logitech.com/	Video cameras
Kensington	http://www.kensington.com/	Video cameras
Kodak	http://www.kodak.com/	Still cameras
Newer Technologies	http://www.newertech.com/	Video capture device
Ricoh	http://www.ricoh.com/	Still cameras
XLR8	http://www.xlr8.com/	Video capture device

Digital cameras, like removable drives, can be demanding on the USB bus, so it's recommended that you use digital video cameras and similar devices on a different USB port from removable disks and/or while the removable disk isn't operating. You'll get better performance that way.

Special USB and Firewire Adapters

Because USB and Firewire are newer technologies, not all devices designed to work with Macs in the past will work with an iMac or iMac DV. In a sense, that's a good thing, since it means only the latest technology works with an iMac and that technology is more likely to be fast enough and advanced enough to integrate well with the iMac. At the same time, though, it means you can't hook up older peripherals that you may already own.

Fortunately, there are a number of companies making adapters for the USB ports on the iMac (and the Firewire port on iMac DV models) to allow you to connect other sorts of devices that don't natively support USB or Firewire. We already saw some adapters for hooking up printers in Chapter 26. Here's a list of some adapter manufacturers and the types of adapter products they offer:

Ariston Technologies	**http://www.ariston.com/**	USB-to-serial, USB-to-SCSI
Belkin	**http://www.belkin.com/**	USB-to-serial, USB-to-parallel, USB-to-SCSI
Compucable	**http://www.compucable.com/**	USB-to-serial, USB-to-parallel, USB-to-ADB
Entrega	**http://www.entrega.com/**	USB-to-serial
Griffin Technologies	**http://www.griffintechnology.com/**	USB-to-ADB, USB-to-serial
iMaccessories	**http://www.imaccessories.com/**	USB-to-parallel
Keyspan	**http://www.keyspan.com/**	USB-to-serial
Microtech	**http://www.microtechint.com/**	USB-to-SCSI
MidiMan	**http://www.midiman.net/**	USB-to-MIDI
Newer Technologies	**http://www.newertech.com/**	USB-to-SCSI
Opcode	**http://www.opcode.com/**	USB-to-MIDI
Orange Micro	**http://www.orangemicro.com/**	Firewire-to-SCSI
Second Wave	**http://www.2ndwave.com/**	USB-to-SCSI

What are all these technologies? Here's a quick look:

- **Serial** Pre-iMac Macs use serial ports for many connections, including external modems, some digital cameras, PDA synchronize cables, and non-Postscript printers.

- **ADB** Apple Desktop Bus is used to connect keyboard, mice, and other pointing devices for pre-iMac Mac computers.

- **SCSI** Used by Macs and PCs to connect external drives and scanners to the computer, SCSI is a faster technology than USB, so a USB-to-SCSI connector isn't recommended for daily use (although a Firewire-to-SCSI adapter should work well). USB-to-SCSI is a great way to hook up an existing scanner or hard disk occasionally, if only to get a few files or images transferred to your iMac.

- **Parallel** Parallel adapters are used on Intel-compatible PCs to connect to many printers (and some other devices). These adapters can be used to connect PC printers to your iMac, as long as you have a driver that allows your iMac to print to that printer.

- **MIDI** The Musical Instrument Digital Interface allows you to connect MIDI keyboard synthesizers and other devices to your iMac to edit music and play back songs.

Add Microphones and Speakers

Although not reliant on USB or Firewire, your iMac can support some external speakers and an external microphone through the sound in and sound out ports on the side of the iMac. The only caveats are this: For speakers, choose powered, computer-shielded speakers, preferably those designed to be used with the iMac. This is important because speakers not designed specifically for a computer can affect the monitor picture and other aspects of the computing experience.

The output for speakers is actually a line-level output, which means you can plug your iMac directly into a stereo amplifier, if you like and if you have the right audio cable adapter, and listen to iMac sounds through your stereo system. To connect, you'll need an adapter from the iMac's 1/8" RCA stereo mini-plug connector to the inputs on your stereo system.

The microphone port is also a line-level device, meaning you'll need either a special Apple PlainTalk microphone (available in Mac-friendly computer stores) or a signal from a powered microphone or from a line-level device, like an external receiver or even an external device like a CD player. Typical karaoke-style microphones won't work. If you want to use an inexpensive microphone, Griffin Technology (**http://www.griffintechnology.com/**) offers a special adapter for connecting such microphones to your iMac.

Install RAM or the AirPort Card

The slot-loading iMac makes it easy to install RAM or install the AirPort card, a special wireless networking card designed to be installed inside your iMac. You'll need to get inside your iMac to make these upgrades, but it's not tough to do.

 *Whenever you access the insides of a computer, you need to guard against static electricity discharge, which can damage computer components. The best way to do this is to buy and wear a wrist strap, which grounds you and discharges static. You can get a wrist strap from most computer and electronics stores.*

Unfortunately, you can't get into the original iMac as easily to install RAM or other upgrades. (There are a few other upgrades, especially for iMac 233 revision A and B models, which featured an undocumented internal slot.) Because installing RAM in the original iMac requires removing many screws and connectors and carefully sliding the iMac's main circuit board and CD-ROM drive out of the iMac, I'm not covering it in this book. If you feel adept at such upgrades, you'll find instructions in Apple's Tech Info Library at **http://til.info.apple.com/techinfo.nsf/ artnum/n43012** on the Web. I have, however, noted which RAM you'll want to use to upgrade your iMac, in the next section.

RAM Types and Installation

The type of RAM your iMac requires depends on the model. All Macs prior to the slot-loading models support one type of RAM, while slot-loading models require a different type. All iMacs have two memory slots, one of which is filled with the base memory that shipped with the iMac. It's possible to remove the base memory and install a larger memory module, if necessary, to bring the iMac to the maximum allowable amount of RAM.

If you have an iMac 233, iMac 266, or iMac 333, your iMac uses 3.3 volt SO-DIMM SDRAM. Specifications are: unbuffered, 64-bit wide, 144-pin. Speeds should be 100MHz and 10ns or faster (which would mean a number lower than 10).

Officially (according to Apple), the revision A iMac 233 supports 64MB modules in each slot; the iMac 266 and iMac 333 support up to 128MB modules in each slot. However, it is possible to get larger memory modules and install them successfully. Note, however, that if you plan to install memory in the "lower" slot on these iMacs (which is where the base memory is installed) you'll need a specially designed smaller module to fit that slot (consult Apple dealers for details).

The slot-loading iMacs support standard PC-100 DIMMs that are 64-bit wide, 168-pin modules. There should be a maximum of 16 memory devices (chips) on the DIMM and it needs to be unbuffered with a maximum height of 2.0 inches. Most Mac vendors will precertify RAM for compliance with these specifications, but you should look carefully if you're buying standard PC-100 DIMMs from a different source, like a PC-centric vendor.

On slot-loading iMacs, you'll find two DIMM slots accessible from the bottom of the computer. (As far as I can tell, all models already have one of the slots filled.) You can release the upgrade panel simply by turning its screw with a coin. You then have access to the DIMM slots.

> NOTE
>
> *The handbook that comes with your iMac includes step-by-step instructions and drawings to help you install RAM. Make sure you place the iMac face-down on a soft surface (like a lint-free towel) and touch the metal cage that surrounds the slot in order to discharge static electricity. Also, make sure you press the DIMM all the way in so that the small plastic guards snap up snug to the DIMM. Don't force it—the DIMM is only designed to go in one way (look to make sure the notches in the DIMM match up with the DIMM slot).*

The maximum DIMM size for each slot is 256MB. With the two slots full, the maximum RAM is 512MB plus the base amount of RAM that's been installed for your iMac. If you have a regular slot-loading iMac or an iMac DV, that base amount is 64MB; if you have an iMac DV SE, the base amount is 128MB.

The AirPort Card

Slot-loading iMacs also support an AirPort card for wireless networking. If your iMac didn't come with the card preinstalled, you can buy an AirPort card separately and install the card yourself. You'll need to install both the card and its software. (If you already have the card installed, you can use this section to help you configure the software.)

Install the Card

You install the AirPort card using the same opening that you use to access the memory DIMMs. Here's how to install the card:

 The handbook that comes with your iMac (and with the AirPort card) includes drawings that show this process in some detail.

1. Shut down the iMac and unplug all cables except the power cable. (This electrically grounds the iMac.) Place the iMac screen-down on a soft surface or cloth.

2. Using a coin, open the access door.

3. Touch the metal shield inside the port door (just behind the plastic). This will discharge static electricity.

4. Detach the antenna from the plastic guard on the left side. You pull the plastic antenna cap away from the guard, then you pull the antenna out of the plastic cap.

5. Attach the antenna to your AirPort card and insert the card into the slot until it's locked in. (Don't press too hard, but you should feel when it locks into place.)

6. Close the access door, plug everything back in, and fire up your iMac.

Configure the Software

Once you've installed your AirPort card, you'll need to install the AirPort software. Here's how:

1. Insert the AirPort CD in your CD-ROM or DVD-ROM player.

2. Double-click the Installer icon.

3. In the installer, choose a disk for installation, read the Read Me file, and agree to the license agreement (click Continue between each screen).

4. On the Install/Remove Software screen, click Start. This installs the software. Once installed, your iMac will need to restart. (Click the Restart button.)

5. When you restart the iMac, you'll see the AirPort Setup Assistant appear. The AirPort Setup Assistant helps you set up your iMac to access an existing wireless network or set up an AirPort Base Station. Walk through the Assistant, clicking the right arrow to move to the next screen.

Once the software is installed, you can use the AirPort control strip or the AirPort application (in the Apple menu) to turn the AirPort card on and off or to change your network connection (for instance, to connect computer-to-computer instead of using a Base Station). See Chapters 23 and 28 for details on networking with AirPort.

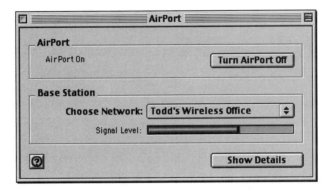

27

NOTE   *By the time you read this, Apple may have made the AirPort Software Base Station available (it wasn't ready at the time of writing). This software will allow you to use your iMac (or any AirPort-compatible Mac) as a base station, allowing you to offer Internet and LAN access to other AirPort-capable Macs, iMacs, and iBooks.*

Chapter 28

Network iMac and Transfer Files

How to...

- Set up an Ethernet network
- Enable AppleTalk, TCP/IP, AirPort, and file sharing
- Set up users, groups, and permissions
- Connect to your network
- Create a server

Ohne of the nice things about Macs in general is their ability to easily network with one another. They can share files and resources like printers without special software, without much special hardware, and, usually, without you needing a master's degree in information systems.

Networking an iMac is actually simpler, if that's possible. The iMac has two basic ways to network—through the Ethernet port or without wires at all, using AirPort technology (on certain iMac models). From there it takes just a few control panel settings to get you up and running with connected machines.

NOTE *Only the "slot-loading" iMac and iMac DV models support AirPort technology as of this writing. You'll need to install and configure the card, as discussed in Chapter 27.*

Let's take a look at what's required to get on an existing Mac network—the type you'd find at school, work, or perhaps in your dorm. Then, you'll see how your iMac can be a server on the network. We'll also discuss remote networking—signing onto a network from across modem lines or the Internet.

Get Connected to a Network

A *network* is two or more computers connected by special cabling (or, these days, wirelessly) for the purpose of sharing files and resources like printers. With a file sharing network, you can place files on other computers that are attached to yours. Likewise, other computers can access your computer, if you think that's a good idea.

The Internet is a network by this definition—it just happens to be a very large one. Using either your modem, AirPort connection, or Ethernet cabling, you're able to connect to the Internet. Then you can *log on* to different computers on the Internet and download data. If you set your computer up for Web sharing, then others can access files on your iMac, too.

For a regular network, there's a similar control panel called File Sharing that allows you to turn your iMac into a file server, allowing others to sign onto your iMac and access certain files. This sort of a network is called a *peer-to-peer* network.

The other type of network is a *client-server* network, where one central computer acts as the server and all the other computers—the clients—log in to the central server. This is the type of system you'd use in a larger organization or campus where it would be chaotic to have many machines all accessing files on one another.

Ethernet Connections

In either a peer-to-peer or client-server network, your iMac gets connected the same way. First, you need to wire up your Ethernet connection so that it connects your iMac to the other machine(s) in your network. If you're connecting the iMac to one other machine, you can use a *10baseT crossover* cable. If you're connecting to more than one machine, you'll use a regular Ethernet *patch* cable to connect your iMac to an Ethernet hub, which then allows you to connect to many other machines (see Figure 28-1). Once you have the Ethernet all wired up, you'll configure the networking protocol.

You'll notice that the connector on the end of an Ethernet cable looks a lot like a phone cable connector, only it's larger. When you're connecting it to your iMac, make sure you've chosen the Ethernet port, not the modem port. (The connector won't fit in the modem port, but you could create trouble by trying to squeeze it in.)

To remove the Ethernet connector, press the small tab on the connector in toward the connector, then pull the cable out. This works just like removing a phone cable connector from a wall jack.

Choose Your Protocol

Once you have the network set up between your iMac and other Macs (or other computers) on a network, you need to choose the protocol you're going to use to pass data between them. There are two major protocols in use today by Macs: AppleTalk and TCP/IP. AppleTalk is the traditional favorite of Mac users—it tends to be easier to configure on smaller networks and can allow newer Macs to network with much older (10 years or more) Macs.

TCP/IP, the protocol used over the Internet, is quickly becoming a popular option, however. In Mac OS 9, it's now possible to set up a small network that includes file sharing over TCP/IP. Likewise, larger Mac networks can also use TCP/IP to share files. And you can use TCP/IP as the basis for a connection to Unix, Microsoft Windows, and other computers over a network.

FIGURE 28-1   An Ethernet hub allows many computers to connect to one another using Ethernet cables.

Which do you use? Your protocol choice is dictated somewhat by circumstances. If you're connecting to a lab of Macs in an educational or organizational setting, you'll need to be configured to use the protocol that the system administrator has chosen. That may be AppleTalk or TCP/IP. If you're setting up your own LAN, you can choose either, keeping in mind that AppleTalk is best for communicating with older Macs and peripherals, while TCP/IP is faster and may be necessary for tasks like multiplayer gaming.

You can only have one TCP/IP configuration at a time, so if you decide to use it for creating a LAN, you may not be able to simultaneously use your iMac's modem for Internet access. If you don't have a special *router* (either hardware or software) or some sort of Internet gateway for accessing the Internet over your LAN, then you'll probably want to use AppleTalk to connect your Macs and TCP/IP, as discussed in Chapter 20, for your Internet access.

The AppleTalk Control Panel

28

In the AppleTalk control panel, you choose the connection you're going to use for your network. If you choose Ethernet or AirPort, you might also see another menu, the Zones menu. This menu allows you to determine which AppleTalk zone your iMac will appear in. (You'll only see this if you're connected to a large network.)

NOTE *Zones are designations that network administrators use to artificially separate Macs from one another. For instance, you can separate Accounting computers and Human Resources computers in different zones so that users are less likely to access a hard disk or printer that isn't in their AppleTalk zone. If you're at home setting up your own network, you won't see zones, because they require hardware—either a router or a server computer that acts as a router.*

The AppleTalk control panel has another feature you may find handy—Configurations. Choose File | Configurations to save different AppleTalk configurations, giving each its own name. This can be useful if you move your iMac back and forth between different places where you have a network and you'd like to quickly set different AppleTalk settings.

To create a new configuration:

1. Select an existing configuration and click Duplicate.

2. Give the duplicate configuration a name in the dialog box and click OK.

3. Select the new configuration's name and click Make Active.

Now you can use the AppleTalk control panel to change the settings for this configuration. The original configuration keeps its original settings, and you can switch back to it by opening the Configurations dialog box again, selecting the original configuration, and choosing Make Active.

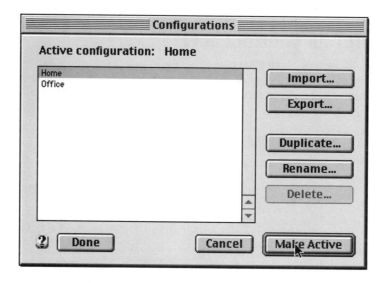

The TCP/IP Control Panel

In some cases you'll want to use TCP/IP as your networking protocol instead of AppleTalk. TCP/IP configuration is discussed in detail in Chapter 20, and configuring for a local network instead of the Internet isn't really all that different.

For most local networks, you'll set the TCP/IP control panel's Connect Via pop-up menu to Ethernet (or AirPort). Now, in the Configure menu, you'll choose either Manually or DHCP. Which you choose, again, depends on circumstances and your network administrator. If you have a fixed IP address on your network (which can be used for both Internet and LAN access, for instance), then you'll enter that IP address, a subnet mask, router address, and name server, if appropriate. In most cases, you'll need to consult your network administrator to learn the correct numbers for this entry.

How to ...   **Connect to a Windows Network**

You may find your iMac is better off using a different protocol if you're not connecting primarily to other Macs. For instance, MacIPX is a control panel that adds Novell Netware to your iMac so you can log into a Netware server. This is a likely scenario only if your office uses Netware to network its PCs or if you're using the IPX protocol specifically for multiplayer games. If your office or organization uses Windows NT Server as a server operating system, you'll likely still sign in using AppleTalk, since Windows NT can allow you to share files and access printers over AppleTalk.

If you're simply trying to connect your iMac to a Windows 95/98 peer-to-peer network, you can use a program called Dave from Thursby Software (**http://www.thursby.com/**). Dave allows your iMac to log into a network of Windows machines running the basic Windows file sharing protocols.

Still another solution is TCP/IP. If you enable TCP/IP on both your iMac and on Windows machines, you can share files using the Web Sharing control panel, as described later in this chapter. This is a convenient way to quickly share files between computers that use two different operating systems.

If you're setting up a LAN for your home or organization, and Internet access isn't a factor, you can set your TCP/IP control panel to DHCP and forget about it. Now, in Mac OS 9, file sharing and Web sharing servers will appear in your Network Browser as discussed in the next section.

NOTE   *If your iMac has Mac OS 8.6 or earlier, you can use it to connect to TCP/IP file servers but not to create one yourself. (You do this by clicking the Server IP Address button in the Chooser and entering the IP address for the TCP/IP file server.) Mac OS 9 is the first Mac OS version to support file sharing over TCP/IP. You can, however, set up Web sharing over TCP/IP, as discussed later in this chapter.*

If you want to simultaneously use TCP/IP for both LAN networking and an Internet connection, then you'll likely need to set up an Internet router or some sort of Internet gateway. If you have an Internet gateway, then you can probably set all of your networked Macs to use either fixed *private IP addresses* or the DHCP protocol. (Consult your system administrator.) Internet software routers are discussed in Chapter 23.

The AirPort Application

If you have an AirPort wireless networking card installed in your iMac, you can use it to access a wireless network. You'll need either an AirPort Base Station or an AirPort Software Base Station, properly configured. Once your wireless network is set up, you use the AirPort application to connect to it. You launch the AirPort application by selecting it in the Apple menu.

In the AirPort application window, you turn the AirPort card on and off if desired. When on, you can select the Base Station to use for your network from the Choose Network menu. If you want to connect to another AirPort-enabled computer, select Computer to Computer from the Choose Network menu. Otherwise, choose the name of the network (this is generally the name given to a particular AirPort Base Station) from the Choose Network menu.

That's it. Close the AirPort application; you can now use AirPort for your AppleTalk and/or TCP/IP connections.

 *You'll also find an AirPort control strip module in the Control Strip, where you can quickly access different Base Stations or turn the AirPort card on and off.*

Browse the Network

Once you've got your network set up and AppleTalk or TCP/IP configured for Ethernet or AirPort, you're ready to log into any Appleshare-compatible server computers on the network with your user name and password. Open the Network Browser located in the Apple menu. With the Network Browser active, you'll see all the different *network neighborhoods* that your iMac can access.

NOTE   *If your iMac has Mac OS 8.6 or earlier, you won't see network neighborhoods— either you'll see the computer names or you'll see AppleTalk zones if your network has zones active. Then you can double-click a particular zone to find the computer you want to access.*

Network neighborhoods represent the different types of servers you'll find on your network. There are a few basic neighborhoods you may encounter. If you're using AppleTalk for your networking, you'll see an AppleTalk neighborhood. You can click the disclosure triangle next to the AppleTalk neighborhood to see the computers that are accessible via AppleTalk. (If your LAN has AppleTalk zones active, you'll see the zones inside the neighborhood, which you can then open to reveal the computers associated with each zone.)

You may also see a Local Services neighborhood, which represents your own iMac's Web server if you have Web Sharing turned on. In addition, if your network has an assigned domain name, you may also see that name in the Network Browser as a neighborhood (like my domain, "mac-upgrade.com").

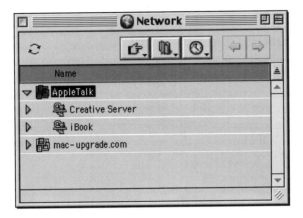

When you find the computer that you want to log into, double-click it in the Network Browser to bring up the login screen. If you don't see the TCP/IP computer that you want to log into, click the Shortcuts button (the hand with a pointing finger icon) and choose Connect to Server. This allows you to enter an IP address for the TCP/IP server.

Now, enter your name and your password, then click Connect to connect to the server. Note that the password is case-sensitive, so don't use uppercase if your original password used lowercase.

 *If you want to change your password, click the Change Password button. Enter your old password, your new password, then click OK.*

If you've entered your user name and password correctly, you're shown the different disks or folders available to you from the server computer. Pick a disk and double-click it to mount it on your desktop. That's it: you've logged in and you're able to access files on the network drive as if they were on your own iMac. The disk is mounted on your desktop, just like a removable disk or a floppy disk image.

SHORTCUT *You can create aliases to server volumes by dragging them out of the Network Browser to the Finder. This makes it easy to sign on again quickly. Just double-click the alias and, if you're connected to the network and the server is available, you'll see the login screen.*

When you're done with a disk, either drag it to the Trash can or select it and choose File | Put Away. That will unmount the disk. Once you've put away all disks and files that you've logged into for a particular server, you'll be logged out of the server computer automatically.

 *The Network Browser offers the same menus for shortcuts, favorites, and recent servers available in the newer Navigation Services Open dialog box that appears in updated applications. Those menus are discussed in Chapter 5.*

Use the Chooser

You can also use the Chooser to log in to servers. Open the Chooser and click the AppleShare button. If you have AppleTalk zones, click the zone you want to access in the AppleTalk Zones menu. In the "Select a file server" area, double-click the server you want to log on to.

If you're going to connect to a TCP/IP-based server, you'll click the button Server IP Address, then enter the IP address for that remote computer. Click Connect, and the Chooser will attempt to access the server.

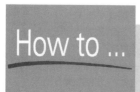 **Store Connections on Your Keychain**

In Mac OS 9, there's a new feature called the keychain, which allows you to store often-used login names and password in one central place, so that you don't have to remember all your user names and passwords for different servers. Connecting to servers using the Network Browser is one place where this comes in handy.

If you'd like to use the keychain, you should first set it up, as described in Chapter 24. Then, you can add a login to the keychain using the Network Browser. Here's how:

1. Locate the computer you want to log into and double-click it as you'd normally do.

2. Now, in the Connect dialog box, enter your user name and password, then click the check box to turn on the option Add To Keychain. Click Connect.

3. If your keychain is locked, you'll see a dialog box that asks you to enter your keychain password. If your keychain is unlocked, then your user name and password are added to the keychain automatically.

Now, whenever you log into the server using the Network Browser, you won't see the Connect dialog box. Instead, your keychain will be consulted, and if it's unlocked, the password will be given automatically. If your keychain is locked, you'll be asked to enter your keychain password, then you may see a dialog box asking whether your want to give the Network Browser access to the keychain. Once you've set it up, you'll never have to remember your server password again!

From here, in either case, it's the same as using the Network Browser—enter a name and password, then double-click the disk you want to mount. To log out, put away all open disks.

Set Up Your Own Network

Once you have your network connections in place and AppleTalk and/or TCP/IP up and running, you're ready to set up file sharing and share folders from your iMac on the network.

Set Up File Sharing

When you set up file sharing, you're actually turning your iMac into a server computer. Other users attached to your network will be able to sign onto your iMac, access any folders that you make available to them, and copy files to and from your iMac. If that's what you want to do, then you can enable file sharing in the File Sharing control panel.

The File Sharing control panel requires that you enter an Owner Name, Owner Password, and Computer Name in the top of the control panel. If you've completed the Mac OS Setup Assistant (after you turned on your iMac for the first time or after you've installed or upgraded the Mac OS), then you should already have entries here. You can change them, if you like. To start up file sharing, click the Start button under the File Sharing Off heading. This begins the process of file sharing. If you have AppleTalk configured and your Ethernet cables properly connected, you're in business—your iMac becomes a server.

In Mac OS 9, you have the additional option of turning on file sharing over TCP/IP. If you'd like to share your files over your TCP/IP network (and you've configured the TCP/IP control panel as discussed earlier in this chapter), you can click the check box next to the option "Enable File Sharing clients to connect over TCP/IP." This allows anyone who knows your iMac's IP address to connect to your iMac and share files.

For file sharing over TCP/IP to be useful, you'll probably want to have a static IP address—one that doesn't change, which you enter manually. If you have a LAN of Macs running Mac OS 9 or later, you can also set iMac to use DHCP, and your file server should appear in those Macs' Network Browser.

Create Users and Groups

Of course, before you can get serious about file sharing, you have to decide who can access your computer and what they can access. By default, you can already access your iMac from another computer, using the Owner name and password. (This gives you special access, by the way, allowing you to see every folder and file on the iMac, regardless of what other security measures you've put in place.)

For other users, you need to create user accounts for individuals accessing your iMac over a network. Do that by selecting the Users & Groups tab in the File Sharing control panel. (If you're running Mac OS 8.6 or earlier, you'll use the separate Users & Groups control panel.)

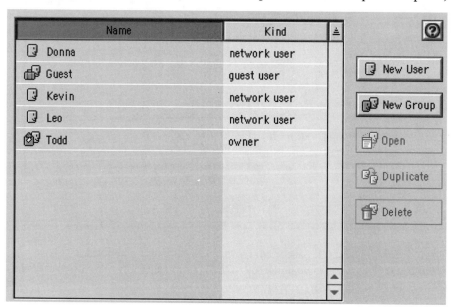

Actually, you don't have to create users if you give Guests and/or Everyone privileges to your Macs. (See "Set Sharing Privileges," later in this chapter.) It's good to go through the motions of creating users, though, so that you can specify privileges and make sure that no one snoops around your network while you're connected to the Internet or connected via Remote Access. Too much security is better than too little.

If you're using file sharing over IP, you should be especially vigilant about your guest access. Since people can potentially access your iMac over the Internet (depending on your configuration), you should only allow users with a user name and password to sign on.

To create a new user in Users & Groups:

1. Click the New User button.

2. You'll see a dialog box that allows you to enter a name and an initial password for this person. If you want the user to be able to change his or her own password, leave the check in the Allow User To Change Password check box.

3. Click the close box to add the person to your list of users.

If you have more than one user (aside from yourself and the Guest account), you'll need to create a new group. A group accepts some or all of your users, so you can set file sharing privileges for the entire group. For instance, if you want people to have access to a folder you've created on your disk called Accounting Files, then create a group that has everyone in it who should be able to access that folder. Alternatively, if you have a special folder called Assistant Files that only your assistant, Rick, is allowed to access, you can set up Rick individually for that particular folder.

Here's how to create a group:

1. Click the New Group button.

2. Give the group a name.

3. Drag names from the Users & Groups window to the window for that group.

4. Click the close box when you're finished.

Now, with your users and groups created, you can set the privileges for those users. Do that by accessing the Sharing settings for each individual folder.

28

Set Sharing Privileges

Select a folder that you'd like to share with a particular user or group and choose File | Get Info. In the Get Info window, choose Sharing from the Show menu. Now you're ready to set privileges for this particular folder.

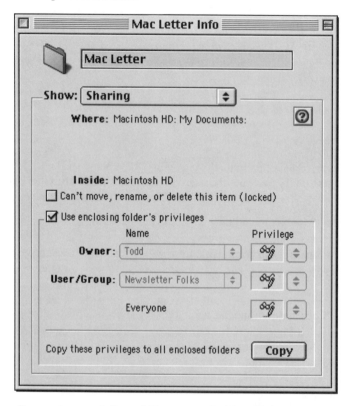

What does it mean to set privileges? You get to decide which user or group can access this particular folder and what he, she, or they can do with it. Here's what the settings do:

- **Can't Move, Rename, Or Delete This Item (Locked)**   Click this box to deny users permission to alter the folder itself. This locks the folder.

- **Use Enclosing Folder's Privileges**   If clicked, the folder should use the same sharing settings as its parent folder. If the Mac Letter folder is in the Documents folder, then checking the check box means the sharing privileges for Mac Letter will be the same as those for the Documents folder. If you uncheck this box, you can set the privileges separately.

■ **Owner**   Choose which user is the owner of this folder. That's usually you.

■ **User/Group**   Choose which user or group has access to this folder. If you want more than one user to have access, you'll need to place those users in a group. If you want more than one group to have access, you'll need to place users from all those groups in one larger group.

■ **Everyone**   If you want to give all users—regardless of their user and group status—certain privileges for the folder, choose from this menu.

CAUTION   *Consider granting access only to the Owner and a particular user or group, not to Everyone. That will help you manage the security of your files.*

Next to the Owner, User/Group, and Everyone entries, a little icon appears showing the privileges assigned to each.

You can assign to a particular user or group one of four access levels:

■ **Read and Write Access**   The user or group can both save files and access existing files.

■ **Read Access**   The user or group can read (open or duplicate) files from a folder but can't save files to that folder.

■ **Write Access**   The user or group can save files but can't access other files in that folder.

■ **None**   The user or group has no access to the files in that folder.

Finally, click the Copy button if you'd like these privileges copied to all subfolders.

Set Up Web Sharing

You've already seen that setting up TCP/IP allows you to transmit files between various types of computers—Macs, Unix machines, Windows computers—without adding special software. But we've used that TCP/IP network so far only for file sharing over TCP/IP. If you don't have Mac OS 9, then you can't turn on this option. Likewise, if your goal is to allow other computers (like Windows, Unix, and so on) to connect to your iMac, those computers probably don't have an Apple File Services client, which would be necessary for them to log into your iMac.

Using the Web sharing capability built into the Mac OS, you can share files with other computers using just TCP/IP. Web sharing works a little like file sharing, but it allows you to share a specific folder with users who don't have Macs (or Mac users to whom you don't want to grant full file sharing access). Open the Web Sharing control panel, select a folder to share, and click Start.

Select the folder you'd like to share.

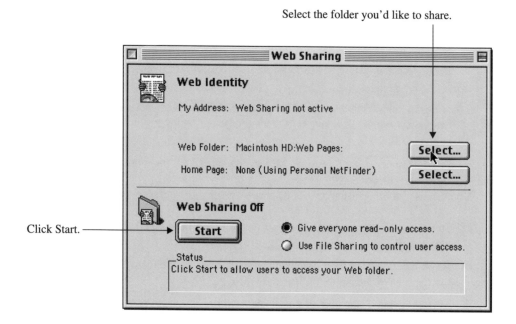

Click Start.

If you select the Use File Sharing To Control User Access option, you can force users to enter a user name and password to access the folder (see the section "Create Users and Groups," earlier in this chapter). Now, using a Web browser or FTP program, any sort of computer can log into your iMac and transfer files. (See Chapter 20 for more on FTP.)

CAUTION   *If your iMac is connected to the Internet and you have Web sharing active, anyone who knows your IP address can access your Web sharing folder. The additional security of turning on Use File Sharing To Control User Access will help mitigate this threat, especially if you disallow guest access and make sure you have set sharing privileges for the folder you've selected as the Web sharing folder. Otherwise, the most secure way to handle this is to not turn on Web sharing while you're otherwise connected to the Internet.*

Network Two Macs Together

If you have one Mac that you'd like to connect to your iMac, you can use an Ethernet crossover cable to connect them without an Ethernet hub. Then set up AppleTalk and the File Sharing control panel and you're ready to sign on.

> **NOTE**   *You can also connect these two machines using TCP/IP and File Sharing over IP if you have Mac OS 9 on at least one of them. You won't be able to simultaneously use the modem on those machines to access the Internet, however, unless you have a software Internet router, as described in Chapter 23. If you're creating a quick little network to swap files, I recommend using AppleTalk.*

Here's the procedure:

1. Connect the two computers' Ethernet ports using an Ethernet crossover cable—a special cable that needs to be bought specifically for this purpose. (Ask for an Ethernet crossover cable from the salesperson at a computer shop. This is assuming, of course, that you can actually find a salesperson in a computer shop, especially if it's a "megastore.")

2. On each computer, open the AppleTalk control panel. If AppleTalk warns you that it's not currently turned on, click Yes to make sure AppleTalk will be turned on after you set up the control panel.

3. In the AppleTalk control panel, choose Ethernet built-in from the Connect Via menu. Do this for both computers. (You'll likely choose the same setting for your other computer, unless it has an Ethernet card instead of Ethernet built in. In that case, it'll say Ethernet Slot A1 or something like that.)

4. Close the AppleTalk control panel on both computers. Choose Save when asked if you want to save the settings. This will set AppleTalk. (You may receive an error if the Ethernet crossover cable is incorrectly installed or if you're not using a crossover cable.)

5. Make sure your Sharing privileges settings are the way you want them for the particular user who's going to sign in. (If it's just you, then you'll want to log into the other computer as Owner so you can get the most privileges available.)

6. On one of the computers, open the File Sharing control panel. Turn on File Sharing.

7. Once file sharing has started up, use the Chooser or the Network Browser to access the server and see if it's available.

8. When you find the server, double-click it to log on. Enter your name and password and click Connect.

9. Finally, choose the disk you want to mount—double-click it and it'll appear on your desktop.

To log out of the server, choose all the disks you've mounted and drag them to the Trash, or select them and choose File | Put Away from the Finder menu.

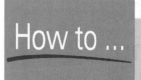 **Connect Two Macs Wirelessly**

If you have an AirPort card installed in your iMac, you can use that card to connect directly to another AirPort-enabled Mac without a base station. To do so, open the AirPort application on each Mac and select Computer to Computer from the Choose Network pop-up menu. Close the Airport application. Now, you can set each Mac's AppleTalk or TCP/IP control panel to AirPort, and share files as discussed in the section "Network Two Macs Together."

Chapter 29

Work with DOS and Windows Files and Programs

How to...

- Read DOS and Windows disks with your iMac
- Exchange files and documents with Microsoft Windows users
- Use the File Exchange control panel to launch Windows documents
- Run Windows and DOS programs with emulation software

The Mac OS has built into it the ability to deal with a wide range of files, including files that were originally created for Microsoft Windows. Part of that capability comes thanks to the File Exchange control panel, which, along with other system extensions, allows the iMac to read disks that were originally created in the Windows (or the predecessor to Windows, DOS) native format.

There are three different types of Windows compatibility that we're concerned with. Out of the box, the iMac can handle two of them; the third requires an extra application purchase. They are:

- **Disks**   Your iMac can mount, display, and manipulate files on many different types of disks, even if they weren't originally designed for the Mac OS. This is true of CD-ROMs as well as removable disk drives—Zip, LS120, floppy disks—that you might connect to via USB or Firewire.

- **Documents**   Your iMac can also store and work with Windows documents on two different levels. First, you can easily store Windows documents in folders using the Finder or move them around as e-mail attachments, via FTP, and so on. Second, you can translate many document types using nothing more than AppleWorks and its included translators.

- **Applications**   Running actual Windows programs on your iMac is a little tougher—it can't be done right out of the box. It is possible to run Windows programs if you've installed either SoftWindows or Virtual PC, both of which are Mac applications designed to emulate Windows. They're not perfect, but they'll get the job done in a pinch.

Mount and Use PC Disks

A disk originally created for a PC usually won't pose a problem, as long as you have a removable drive that can read the disk attached to your iMac. A CD-ROM is a great example. A CD designed exclusively for PCs can still be read by an iMac—just pop it in the drive and take a look. It should appear right on the desktop.

Once it's mounted, you can treat a PC disk like any other—you can move files from it into the Finder. If the disk is a removable disk like a PC-formatted Zip disk, you can copy files to it from the Finder, too. Copy a PC file onto your hard disk or the desktop, and you're also able to rename the file, duplicate it, create an alias, and so on.

 *It isn't always a good idea to rename a Windows file, especially a document. The three-letter code at the end of the original name is important for both the iMac and most Windows computers. Your computer identifies the document with this code—.doc indicates a Microsoft Word document, while .bmp indicates a Windows bitmap graphic, for example. If you don't leave the names intact, the documents can become harder to use.*

You can get rid of the disk the same way you would any other. Drag it to the Trash or select the disk and choose File | Put Away.

Load and Save PC Documents

Certain documents created on your iMac can be read by applications in Windows. For instance, Microsoft Word 2000 for Windows (and other Word versions) can read Microsoft Word 98 documents that have been created on a Mac. ClarisWorks for Windows can read a file created in AppleWorks (if you save it in ClarisWorks 4.0 format).

And there are certain types of files that are universal. Many of the graphics file formats can be read on any platform—GIF, JPEG, and TIFF. Text files (TXT) and Rich Text Format (RTF) documents (which can include some formatting) can be read by nearly any word processor, and Adobe PDF documents can be created on nearly any computer and sent to another type of computer to be viewed.

Translate a Document

With some documents that started life on a Windows machine, it's possible to simply double-click the icon and launch an associated application on your iMac. It usually works better, however, if you open the application first and use the File | Open command to open the document. That makes it easier for the application to recognize that it needs to translate the document before using it.

 If you're working with graphics files, see Chapter 14 for a discussion of translating graphic file formats.

Use AppleWorks

If the document is the sort that could conceivably be edited in AppleWorks (for instance, if it's a word processing document or a spreadsheet), then fire up AppleWorks and choose File | Open from the menu. In the Open dialog box, find the file you'd like to open.

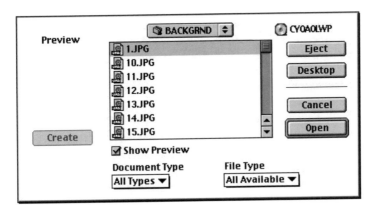

Now, here's the trick: Pull down the File Type menu in the Open dialog box and take a look at the options—these are all of the files that can be translated into AppleWorks format.

Actually, in many cases, files that can be translated will simply appear in the window—this may be tougher with files that don't have the correct filename extension or that have been transmitted over the Internet. In any case, if the file can be translated by AppleWorks, you'll likely be able to select it in the window and choose the Open command. The file will be translated and it'll appear in AppleWorks. You should then be able to edit it.

> **TIP** *The best results always come from using the same program. If you're dealing with a Word for Windows document, Word for Macintosh is the best way to open and edit the file. You don't lose formatting, which can happen when you translate between formats.*

Communicate the Format Type

One of the most important ways to exchange Windows documents is to discuss the document format with the person who is sending you the file. Usually, if they save the file in the most compatible way possible, you'll have better luck translating it into AppleWorks.

For instance, AppleWorks works well with Microsoft Word 6.0 (Word 95 for Windows) documents, as long as they don't have special header and footer formatting. And things like annotation commands or colorful text may not show up at all. Rich Text Format is even better, although the formatting tends to be rudimentary. Translation generally won't work for very complex documents, like those created in QuarkXPress or Adobe InDesign, especially if you're trying to translate into AppleWorks. (You'll have better luck translating directly between the two high-end applications, if you own one of them, but even that doesn't always work well.)

If you find that your work dictates that you use a particular file format and you can't find a happy translation medium, then your best bet may be to break down and buy the same application that's being used on the PC side. Often these applications are file-format compatible, so you can use the Mac version of WordPerfect, for instance, to read WordPerfect for Windows documents.

How to ... Import a File

If you're dealing with a file that isn't a common file format like a word processing document or an image file—or if you simply want to use a different application that you've added to your iMac—then you should look around for an Import command, probably in the File menu of that application. Often you'll be able to import some common file formats into different applications.

For instance, I have FileMaker Pro, the high-end version of the AppleWorks database module, on my iMac. FileMaker Pro can import a number of different types of documents—from dBase database documents to text files that use a comma or a tab between each field entry—directly into a FileMaker Pro database. To do that, I simply choose the Import/Export command in FileMaker Pro.

Actually, AppleWorks can import some of these same types of files into the database module. Choose File | Open to load a DBF or comma-separated text file into a database. Remember to choose Database from the Document Type menu so that the file is imported into the database module. (Otherwise, it'll appear as a word processing document.)

Save a File for Use on a PC

If you're working with a document that you'd like to send to a PC user, you should ask the person which applications he or she uses that might work for the translation. If it's a word processing document, most applications can read Word 6.0, or, if not, they can almost certainly read RTF documents. If you're sending a spreadsheet, it's probably best translated into Excel, then sent on its way.

To do this, choose File | Save As, then find a place to save the file. When you're ready to translate, choose the type of file you want to create from the Save As menu. Then, click Save to save the file.

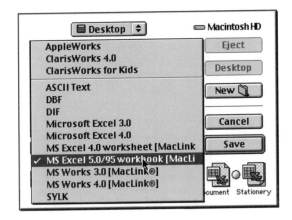

You may want to note that the translators in AppleWorks don't actually append a filename extension to a file as it's being saved. It's a good idea to name the file with the correct extension before sending the file. (In fact, the most compatible filenames are up to eight characters long with a three-letter extension and no spaces, like *filename.doc*.) Here's a quick look at common filename extensions for DOS and Windows computers:

Microsoft Word	.doc
Microsoft Excel	.xls
WordPerfect	.wp
Rich Text Format	.rtf
Plain text, ASCII text (no formatting)	.txt
HTML	.htm
dBase (standard PC database format)	.dbf

Note that ASCII text and "Plain" text mean the same thing—it's the very common text format that allows you to send text characters in a document without *any* formatting (no bold, italics, and so on). In a worst-case scenario, if you're having trouble exchanging word processing documents with a Windows (or Unix) user and you want to send just the bare-bones text, you can do it with a document saved in ASCII text format.

The File Exchange Settings

The filename extension system is pretty important to PCs, since it's really the only way that Windows can tell one type of file from another. The Mac OS works differently—documents created in Mac OS applications have a special creator code built into them that makes it clear to the Mac OS which application created the document even if the name has been changed completely. That's why it's usually so easy to double-click a document and launch the associated application.

PC Exchange Settings

With the File Exchange control panel, some of this functionality is translated to Windows documents that you open on your iMac. File Exchange sits in the background and takes a look at any DOS documents that you copy to your iMac. When it sees a filename extension it recognizes, it gives that document a creator code, so you can double-click to launch the document.

> **TIP** *If File Exchange doesn't seem to be recognizing files that it should, open the File Exchange control panel and make sure the option "Open unmapped files on any disk using mappings below" has a checkmark next to it. If it doesn't, click it to activate the option.*

You might find it useful to edit the way File Exchange manages filename extensions. To do so, open File Exchange and click the PC Exchange tab. Now, notice that you're seeing the Windows filename extensions and their relationships to Mac OS applications.

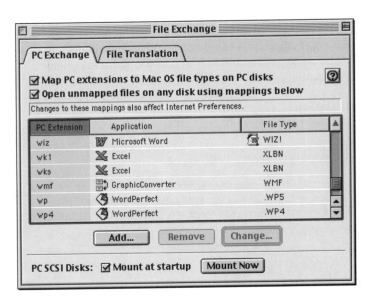

You can select a particular entry and click Change to edit that entry. You'll see a dialog box that allows you to choose which Mac application should be associated with a particular filename extension. (If you don't see the application you want associated with a file type, click the Select button to search for the application's icon on your hard disk.) Scroll to find the application you want associated with the file, then choose the exact type of file it is from the list of types that application recognizes. Then click the Change button to make your alterations.

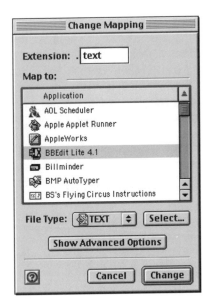

If you're encountering a filename extension that isn't already entered in the File Exchange control panel, click the Add button. You'll see a dialog box that helps you enter the new filename extension and associate it with a Mac application.

File Translation

Usually, if you double-click a Windows document that isn't directly associated with a Mac application, you'll get a dialog box that allows you to choose which application you'd like to use to open the document.

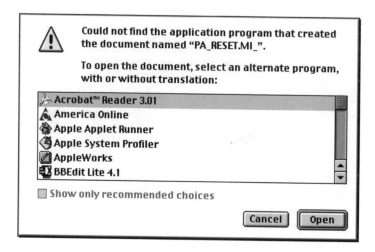

This doesn't necessarily translate the document; if the application can't read the document, you'll probably get an error message. If you'd like to translate that document before it's opened by the application, look for an option in the dialog like "Open in SimpleText using QuickTime translation" or "Open in AppleWorks using MacLinksPro translation." These options will allow you to translate a document, then open it up to edit it.

If you'd like to automatically translate certain files from a Windows format into the format of one of your Mac applications, you can click the File Translation tab in the File Exchange control panel to control translation behavior. To create a new translation scheme, click the Add button. You'll then search (in a typical Open dialog box) for the type of document you'd like to translate. Once you've found it, click Open. You'll then page through a list of applications and choose the one that you want associated with this sort of file.

This works, by the way, with regular Mac documents and applications, too, making it easy to change an association even if you're not working with Windows documents.

Run DOS and Windows Programs

Want to actually run DOS and Windows programs on your Macintosh? You'll need an emulation application—a Macintosh application that simulates the Windows operating system or a Pentium computer environment. These are very sophisticated applications that allow you to recreate a whole computer environment within your iMac—you're literally running Windows and DOS applications within an application that, in turn, runs within the Mac OS.

The sophistication of these applications reaches out to the printer, your hard disk, and even your modem. In most cases, it's easy to use all of these things within the Windows environment, even though the peripherals may actually be designed for a Macintosh.

There are two major emulation packages available for the iMac. Both emulators actually emulate a Pentium MMX computer, but SoftWindows from FWB Software (**http://www.fwb.com/**) uses special drivers to communicate between the Windows environment and your iMac. Performance tends to be optimized for Windows applications and is a great choice if you're running business or productivity applications in the Windows environment. Windows games work well, too.

Connectix Virtual PC (**http://www.connectix.com/**) is the other emulator. As shown in Figure 29-1, it emulates a Pentium MMX computer, but it also emulates other popular PC hardware, making it possible to use standard PC drivers. This offers a little more flexibility—you can run other PC operating systems like Windows NT and Linux, and it is upgradable to new versions of Windows. While more flexible, Virtual PC runs a little slower than SoftWindows because it has to emulate all that other hardware, too.

Both SoftWindows and Virtual PC can generally be purchased for between $100 and $200, depending on rebates, bundling deals, and similar promotions. Both work well with an iMac, but they can require a lot of RAM; if you don't have at least 64MB of RAM in your iMac, you may experience these emulators at slower speeds than you would with more RAM.

FIGURE 29-1   Connectix Virtual PC allows you to run PC applications on your iMac.

TIP   *Both FWB and Connectix offer a less expensive version of their emulators that doesn't include Microsoft Windows as part of the standard package. This can be useful if you already own Microsoft Windows or if you simply plan to play DOS games, which is the target market for these products. Prices are about $50-75 on RealPC from FWB and Virtual PC with DOS from Connectix.*

Chapter 30

Troubleshoot, Update, and Maintain Your iMac

How to...

- Find technical support resources
- Troubleshoot your iMac's hardware
- Troubleshoot software
- Deal with errors
- Fix freezes and hangs
- Reinstall, restore, or update your iMac's software
- Maintain your iMac for long life

I t's never good when your iMac starts giving you serious trouble. Hopefully, you won't encounter this much, although the likelihood is that, eventually, you'll have to troubleshoot something. The nature of today's computing is that it isn't all flawless.

Not that it has to be an intolerable experience, either. One of the tricks is adhering to a good maintenance schedule. If you do that, you'll probably have fewer instances of trouble. Better yet, if you do have trouble, a solid backup routine will help you minimize that trouble, allowing you to get back to work as quickly as possible.

So, let's take a look at the three different aspects of keeping your iMac healthy and happy: troubleshooting, updating, and maintenance. Using these three different steps, you can keep your iMac running well, or get it up and running again after you've had some trouble.

Find Tech Support Online

Since this is the Internet-savvy iMac we're talking about, I recommend that you get to know online resources for troubleshooting your iMac right at the outset. Apple's iMac-specific support pages are very useful and provide some welcome features, including online message areas for iMac users. These sites offer a great way to learn more about your iMac, identify potential problems, and do what is probably the most important step in keeping your iMac tuned—stay up on the latest news and information.

Enter **http://www.apple.com/support/** in a browser, then look around for the link to iMac Support. (There's currently an iMac graphic that you click. Apple likes to change the design of their pages every once in a while, though.) Once you select iMac Support, you'll be taken directly to Apple's special support Web site for the iMac. It's here that you'll find all sorts of information about the iMac, including the latest news, articles on different technologies related to the iMac, and pointers to any software updates that have been released for the iMac.

I won't harp specifically on certain parts of the iMac Support site because the site is likely to change. You'll probably always find a link to the Tech Exchange or a similar message area that allows you to exchange messages with other iMac users and Apple Tech Support specialists. You'll probably also find links to the latest updates, including updates to the iMac's firmware, to the Mac OS, to the applications that came with your iMac, and to the modem's firmware, among others. (*Firmware* is a type of software/hardware driver combination that can be installed to update your iMac. The firmware updates usually fix bugs or add new features and capabilities to hardware like your iMac's modem or the iMac itself.)

While you're online, you might also want to check out some of the popular Mac-oriented sites, where you'll find news and help on various issues affecting your iMac as well as the entire Macintosh industry. Here's a sampling of them:

Mac News Network	**http://www.macnn.com/**
Macworld	**http://www.macworld.com/**
MacCentral	**http://www.maccentral.com/**
MacAddict	**http://www.macaddict.com/**
iMacToday	**http://www.imactoday.com/**
Macintouch	**http://www.macintouch.com/**
MacFixIt	**http://www.macfixit.com/**
Mac-Upgrade.com (my site)	**http://www.mac-upgrade.com/**

All of these sites can help you find new peripherals, follow the news regarding Apple, discuss Mac and iMac troubleshooting issues, and so on. Many of them also have user forums, where you can post questions and read archives of questions and responses between Mac users.

Troubleshoot Your iMac

Your first sign of trouble will probably be that something goes wrong onscreen. The key, as with actual health problems, is to observe the symptoms and look for anything that might be related. To begin, then, let's take a look at the symptoms of iMac trauma and see what should be done as a first aid measure.

There are two basic types of problems you can have with your iMac—hardware and software. With an iMac, most hardware problems are going to require a look from a service technician, since there aren't many moving parts and the iMac can be difficult to get into and service yourself.

You can try troubleshooting software problems, but those problems are more varied and can sometimes be tough to track down. You'll often find solutions, though, and it's not impossible to get your iMac back up and running in fine order.

Hardware Symptoms

There are a couple telltale signs that something has gone wrong with your iMac. Here's what they are, what might cause them, and a few things to try before sending your iMac off to the repair shop.

TIP *The Emergency Handbook that comes with your iMac is also a great source of troubleshooting information. Use it if you don't see the answer in this text. Apple's iMac Support Web pages are equally valuable, especially for getting the most up-to-date information.*

Blank Screen or Tones

If you've just tried to turn on your iMac and gotten no response, you're seeing a blank screen, and/or you're hearing tones, it's possible there's something wrong with the internals of your iMac, like a RAM module that's not properly installed or something that has come loose. Before you open it up or send it to the shop, though, test a few things:

- Make sure the iMac is plugged in properly and the surge protector (if you're using one) is turned on.

- Check for signs that your surge protector is working correctly and that it hasn't absorbed a power surge, which might cause a fuse to blow on the power strip.

- Restart the iMac by pressing CONTROL-⌘-POWER (on the keyboard).

- Some iMacs can be shut down by holding in the POWER button on the front of the iMac for five seconds or more. Then, to restart, press the POWER button again.

- If that doesn't work, restart the iMac with a paperclip as discussed in Chapter 1. (Newer slot-loading iMacs have a raised reset button that can be used for the same purpose.)

- Unplug all USB (and Firewire, on later iMac models) peripherals other than the mouse and keyboard. Try restarting.

If none of that works, you may need to take your iMac in for service. Or, if you've recently installed RAM (or another upgrade, like an AirPort card) inside your iMac, you may need to open the iMac up again and make sure the upgrade was firmly seated and otherwise properly installed. (See Chapter 27 for details on internal upgrades.)

Blinking Question Mark

If a question mark is blinking in the middle of your screen, it's a sign that the iMac can't find a disk with a working System Folder on it. Here's what you can do:

- Wait a minute or so. It may resolve itself. (If this happens, check your Startup Disk control panel and make sure it's set to start up from the iMac's internal disk.)

- Restart with CONTROL-⌘-POWER.

- Reset the iMac using the POWER key or its reset button (shown in Chapter 1).

- Unplug the iMac, wait a minute, then plug it back in and press the POWER key.

30

■ If none of the previous steps does away with the blinking question mark, consider performing a step called "zapping the PRAM" to see if that gets your iMac to notice the drive and boot from it. Do that by restarting the iMac. After the startup tone, hold down ⌘-OPTION-P-R until you hear the startup chime two more times. Then, release the keys. That may cause your iMac to find the internal hard disk and start up normally.

If these things don't work, start from the iMac Software Install CD or iMac Software Restore CD and run Disk First Aid. Here's how:

■ Restart. (You can use CONTROL-⌘-POWER, the paperclip method described in Chapter 1, or you can restart by pressing the POWER button or RESET button, on slot-loading iMac models.)

■ As the iMac starts, place the iMac Software Install CD or Software Restore CD in the drive tray (or the drive slot, on new iMacs). The iMac should start up from the CD. (If it doesn't, you should restart the iMac, this time holding down the C key right after the iMac plays its startup tones.)

■ Once the iMac has started, double-click the Disk First Aid icon, located in the Utilities folder on the CD.

■ Run Disk First Aid as instructed later in this chapter in the section "Disk Doctors."

■ If Disk First Aid finds a problem and can fix it, then the iMac should start up. If not, you may need to run a third-party utility, such as Norton Disk Doctor or MicroMat TechTool Pro.

Your last resort (other than stopping at this point and having a technician look at your iMac) is to reinstall the entire Mac OS, since it's possible that your System file or parts of the Mac OS are corrupted. Reinstalling the Mac OS is covered later, in the section "Reinstall, Restore, and Update."

What Is PRAM?

Parameter RAM (PRAM) is a small portion of RAM that the iMac uses for special settings in control panels, as well as some other internal settings. This RAM always has a little power trickling to it, thanks to a battery inside your iMac. PRAM can also become corrupted, which requires a reset. A reset is usually a last line of defense, but you can try zapping PRAM using the above method or using MicroMat TechTool (discussed later in the chapter).

The battery that powers PRAM eventually runs out, usually after three to five years. When that happens, your AppleTalk, Date & Time, screen resolution, and other settings will sometimes seem to change randomly. That's a sure sign it's time to replace the battery, which any Apple authorized service center can do for you.

Peripheral Doesn't Work

If a USB or Firewire device isn't working, check to make sure it's installed correctly. If the nonworking device is connected to a hub, turn the hub on and off to reset it.

If everything is plugged in correctly, reset the device by turning it on and off. Also, unplug and replug a device's connector (which will often reset its driver) and follow the manual's instructions for resetting the device. Both Firewire and USB devices are *hot-pluggable*, meaning they can be plugged and unplugged while the iMac is on and working.

If a USB or Firewire device requires power from the bus, try plugging it directly into the appropriate port on the side of your iMac. It's possible that your hub isn't powered or isn't working correctly. If the device works, investigate your hub for problems.

If you're having trouble with your USB printer, check to make sure it's selected (highlighted) in the Chooser. Turn it on and off again, or check the printer's manual for a command that allows you to restart the printer.

If none of these troubleshooting steps works, unplug the device and restart your iMac. Now, with the Finder completely started up, plug the device back into the USB or Firewire port. Hopefully it will be detected and begin working again.

> TIP
> *Keeping up with Mac OS and QuickTime updates will keep your Firewire system software updated, too. Updates in the Mac OS improve USB, as well. If you have Mac OS 9, the Software Update control panel will help keep everything up-to-date.*

30

Software Problems

There are three basic causes of software problems. Let's define those quickly, then we'll take a look at the symptoms your iMac may be experiencing. Here are the problems that software can encounter on your iMac:

- **Bugs**   Bugs are the result of mistakes or oversights by programmers who created applications or the Mac OS. Usually, the only fix is to stop using the program (or the problematic feature in that program) and update it.

- **Conflicts**   Conflicts occur when two pieces of software—two applications, an application and a Mac OS extension, or two extensions—don't get along. Conflicts cause crashes and freezes and are usually solved by finding the culprits and updating or disabling them. Extension conflicts (the type between Mac OS extensions that load as the iMac starts up) are discussed later, in "Troubleshoot the System Folder."

> TIP
> *Read the Read Me file that accompanies any application causing you trouble. The Read Me file might tell you that the software is known to conflict with other software on your iMac.*

■ **Corruption**   Corruption occurs when data is overwritten with either bad or nonsensical information. This can cause all sorts of trouble but typically causes crashes and freezes. This is solved by deleting the file, replacing it with a noncorrupt copy from a backup disk or the installation CD, or finding the corrupt data file and fixing it with a disk doctor program.

Software Symptoms

These are the common symptoms and the First Aid you should perform for the problem:

Error   This is an error message in the form of an alert dialog box (outlined in red) that includes an OK button. It tells you the last command you attempted could not be executed because something went wrong.

First Aid: Click OK and save your work. If the error sounds data-threatening—you're out of memory or disk space, a disk couldn't be found, or you're given an error number—it's a good idea to quit the program and restart your iMac.

Crash   In this case, you get an error message and the application shuts down. Sometimes the application itself tells you about the problem; sometimes the Finder tells you there was an "Unexpected Quit."

First Aid: Save data in other open applications and restart your iMac.

Freeze   Sometimes you'll get an error message, but typically the mouse pointer won't move, the clock isn't ticking, and nothing seems to be happening.

First Aid: Wait. See if anything happens. Check the mouse and keyboard connectors— you may have worked the external keyboard loose. Check for any activity (CD-ROM spinning, clicking sounds from the hard disk). Move to the section "Freezes and Hangs."

Hang   Similar to a freeze, but the mouse pointer still moves and you might see the clock change or the application menu blink (if it was blinking before). In other words, there's activity.

First Aid: Wait. Note if any activity in the frontmost application occurs. If your data is important (and not recently saved), you should wait at least ten minutes before forcing the application to quit, as described in "Freezes and Hangs."

Once you've gotten past the immediate first aid, you can move on to diagnose the cause of the problem and attempt a long-term solution.

Error Messages

These are the best sorts of errors to encounter, since they give you some indication of what's going on. If the error didn't crash the application, you'll likely already have some idea what's wrong. A printing error means you should check out your printer or the Chooser; an error loading a Web site or getting your e-mail might have something to do with your Internet connection (Remote Access, PPP, or TCP/IP control panels).

Most of the time, the error message is your guide. Read it, then consult the rest of this section or check out the part of this book where that application or issue is discussed—something may be wrong with your iMac's settings or hardware configuration.

Some of the errors aren't as specific—let's take a quick look at those.

Out of Memory Error

Many times, an error message will tell you that you don't have enough memory or "not enough memory to complete task." This can happen for a variety of reasons.

If the error occurs in the Finder, quit some of the open applications that you have running. If the problem continues, quit all applications and attempt to restart your iMac. If that doesn't work (or if it freezes your iMac), see the section "Freezes and Hangs."

If the Out of Memory error occurs in the application you're using, do the following:

30

■ Save your data.

■ Switch to the Finder and choose About this Computer from the Apple menu.

■ Look to see how much of the application's memory allocation is being used (does it fill the entire allotted space?) and how much is left in the "Largest Unused Block." If the memory's allocation is filled or nearly filled, you'll want to quit the application and assign it more RAM through its Get Info dialog box.

■ If the Largest Unused Block is less than 2MB or so, you might need to quit some of your other applications. You should also check the Memory control panel and make sure Virtual Memory is turned on. If Virtual Memory is turned off, turn it on and restart. Your applications will each require less system memory with Virtual Memory on. (See Chapter 24 for more on the Memory control panel.)

If the problem is with the application's memory allocation, make these changes:

1. Quit the application.

2. Find the application's original icon. Select the icon and choose File | Get Info.

3. In the Get Info box, select Memory from the pull-down menu.

4. You'll see entries for the Minimum Size and Preferred Size of the application. This is the amount of memory, in kilobytes, that the Mac OS allocates for the program. You might add about 512KB to the minimum and about 2000KB (or more) to the preferred.

5. Click the Get Info's Close box to close the window and register the change.

Now you should quit all applications, restart, and see if the error recurs. (You don't have to restart, but it's best to do so since restarting clears out memory and starts over fresh.)

If you get memory errors even though you've increased the allocation and you've shut down some applications, it's possible that memory has become *fragmented.* This is a temporary condition where system memory has only small chunks of RAM available because applications have been launched and quit repeatedly. Memory can also be affected by *memory leaks*, where unattached bits of data are left by applications that don't clear out RAM properly as they quit. (It's sort of like application litter.) If memory gets too cluttered by fragmentation or memory leaks, you need to restart the iMac to get it working properly again.

TIP   *If Out of Memory errors happen often, consider upgrading the RAM in your iMac. Many iMacs shipped with 32MB of RAM, which is a little skimpy, especially if you're running Mac OS 9 and trying to work with graphics applications and games. Consult Chapter 27 for more on upgrading RAM.*

Disk Is Full Error

If your hard disk gets full or close to full, you'll start to see all sorts of errors, including "Disk is Full." Most applications, Internet programs, and games write temporary files, preferences files, and other sorts of data to your hard disk, even when you're not actively saving a document. If your hard disk gets full, it will cause applications and the Mac OS to have trouble it doesn't expect to encounter.

If it happens to you, the best plan is to delete any old documents (especially if you've backed them up to a removable disk) and uninstall any applications or games that you don't immediately need. (You'll find that most application installers also have a Remove or Uninstall choice in their Custom Install menu.)

You should also consider getting rid of image files and QuickTime movies—they are culprits that can take up a lot of disk space, as can games and educational software.

Crashes

There are a couple different kinds of crashes you'll encounter. Often they'll include an error message or an alert, but sometimes they just happen. Here's a look at what could occur:

- **Error Message or Code**   When an error message appears within the application itself, it means the application *noticed* the error. Many error messages are impossible to decipher, but some may lead you to the source of the problem. It may be a bug in the application or corruption of the document.

- **Unexpected Quitting**   The program disappears, followed by a message in the Finder. This sort of crash often happens because there's a bug in the program or the program encountered a corrupt data file. This type of crash can also be due to a conflict, but corruption is the most likely culprit.

- **No Message**   In this case, the program just quits or disappears. You might notice more error messages in the Finder regarding memory. This could be corruption, but it's likely a conflict.

Test for Crashing

So what can you do about a crash? The most important thing is to get data saved in your applications and restart your iMac. After that, your priority is isolating the crash—figuring out when the crash occurs and any factors that contribute to it. Here are some questions to consider when it comes to crashes:

- **Has your iMac been on for quite a while without restarting, or have you been running many different programs?**   If so, it might just be that your iMac needs to be restarted because memory has become fragmented. That happens.

- **Have you added anything recently?**   If you've recently installed a new application or utility program, it's possible it installed a new extension that's causing trouble. You can always try disabling any new extensions (see the section "Troubleshoot the System Folder," later in this chapter, for information on how to do this).

30

■ **Is the crashing consistent?** If your iMac crashes every time you do something in particular—load a QuickTime movie, check your e-mail, load a particular game—then you may be closer to a solution.

If you can reproduce the error fairly consistently, then there are a few things you can test to isolate the error further. Here's what to try:

■ **Test different documents.** It's possible that a particular document is corrupt, especially if the crash occurs as you're opening a document, as you're saving a document, as you're printing, or when you move to a particular page in a document. Find a similar document or two and test the application with them to see if the same crash occurs. If it doesn't, you can try running a disk doctor utility (or a special file fixer utility) or just avoid using that document.

■ **Remove the preferences file.** Most applications have a preferences file that's stored in the Preferences subfolder of the System Folder. Quit the application, move the preferences file to the desktop or another folder, and restart the application. Some of its default behavior may change and the crashing may also stop. If it does, throw away the preferences file and reset your preferences within the application.

■ **Restart without extensions.** As your iMac starts up, hold down the SHIFT key until you see the message "Extensions Off" in the Welcome to Mac OS window. This starts your iMac without extensions. Now, run the application and see if the error recurs. If it doesn't, there might be an extension conflict. See "Troubleshoot the System Folder," later in this chapter.

Fix Internet Crashing

Did the crash happen while you were browsing the Web? There may be a corrupt preferences file or a file in your browser's cache. You can delete the cache in Internet Explorer by choosing Edit | Preference, then choosing Advanced. Click the Empty Cache Now button to empty the cache. In Netscape Communicator, choose Edit | Preferences. In the Preferences window, select the Cache category, then click the button Clear Disk Cache Now. Click OK to close the Preferences dialog box.

There is a special Internet Preferences file that's created by the Internet control panel. That Internet Preferences file gets changed and saved often by different applications, which can lead to corruption after a while. If you are crashing in many different Internet applications, try opening the Preferences folder and dragging the Internet Preferences file onto the desktop. Restart your iMac, reset your Internet Preferences in the Internet control panel, and try out your applications. If the crashing has gotten better, toss the old Internet Preferences file in the Trash. After doing so, you may have to reconfigure the Internet control panel and your Internet applications.

Freezes and Hangs

A freeze will bring the mouse pointer to a halt and nothing else will happen on the screen. A hang is a little different—the mouse pointer moves, even though things otherwise seem frozen. Why the difference? A hang results when an application has gone into an endless loop of some sort and can't break out to give control back to the Mac OS. A freeze occurs when an application goes bad and causes the Mac OS itself to seize up.

Freezes are odd problems, because they can be attributed to all the types of software issues we've discussed: bugs, conflicts, or corruption. Freezes can also be caused by other applications that are running in the background, or even by trouble with printing or networking.

If it's really a freeze, you probably can't recover from it—the best you can do is restart. But that doesn't mean you shouldn't try some stuff. After all, it's important to know if your iMac has actually frozen, or if it's just a hang. Here's what to do:

1. Make sure the mouse and keyboard haven't been unplugged accidentally. Try unplugging and replugging them to see if there is a USB problem.

2. Check the screen carefully for any activity.

3. Wait. Get up and grab a cup of coffee or check to see if the mail has come. Five minutes or more might be a good idea.

4. Press ⌘-. (period) to see if you can interrupt the program. Press ESC. If that doesn't work, try ⌘-Q to quit. If none of those keyboard combinations are working, you can try a Force Quit—press ⌘-SHIFT-ESC. If the Force Quit dialog box appears, click the Force Quit button. The application may quit forcefully and return to the Finder without saving data.

5. As a last resort, press ⌘-POWER (the POWER key on the keyboard). If a dialog box appears, type **G F** (include the space) and press RETURN. Either you'll quit the program, you'll really completely freeze up, or you'll get a crash requiring an immediate restart.

> **NOTE**   *Depending on whom you ask, "G F" may or may not stand for "Go Finder." In any case, that's what the command usually does: it's a low-level programmer's command for forcing the errant application to quit and attempt to recover to the Finder.*

If none of those work, the iMac has frozen. Try to restart using CONTROL-⌘-POWER to force the iMac to restart, or hold down the POWER button on the front of the iMac. If that doesn't work, you'll need to use the paperclip to restart the iMac. (See Chapter 1, which details the location of the reset hole.)

30

If the Force Quit does work, save work in other applications and restart immediately. After a force quit, your iMac is likely to crash or freeze again pretty soon.

Now you should test to see if the freezing recurs. Here are some possibilities:

- If the freeze recurs after you've restarted and launched the application again, check the application's Read Me file for known conflicts with other applications or Mac OS extensions.

- Try removing the application's preferences file from the Preferences folder in the System Folder and launch the application again to see if the freeze recurs.

- Start with extensions off (hold down the SHIFT key through the startup process) and see if the freeze recurs.

- Check with the software publisher's Web site to see if there are any bug fixes or other suggestions. Contact the publisher's technical support folks to see if they have any suggestions.

Fix Problems with Icons and Aliases

If your iMac begins to lose its unique icons—for instance, AppleWorks document icons become just plain white pieces of paper—or aliases begin to fail, that's a sign that the desktop database is corrupt. The desktop database is comprised of some special, hidden files that track the data you store using the Finder.

Other symptoms of desktop database problems include the Finder slowing way down, your iMac taking a long time to start up, and applications taking a long time to load and save documents.

The solution is to rebuild your desktop. You can do that with TechTool (described in the "Disk Doctors" section, later in this chapter), or you can do it the old-fashioned way that's built into the Mac OS. Hold down the ⌘-OPTION keys as the iMac starts up and keep holding them until you see the Rebuilding the Desktop File alert box.

If you haven't run Disk First Aid in a while, it's probably a good idea to do that, just in case other parts of your disk have encountered trouble. (You can run it from the Utilities folder on your iMac.) You could even run a disk doctor tool like Norton Utilities if you have one handy.

Troubleshoot the System Folder

Occasionally, your problems will arise from within the System Folder, usually in the shape of an extension conflict. The extensions, stored in the Extensions folder, are small bits of computer code designed to *patch* or add themselves to the Mac OS as it starts up. For instance, Apple ships extensions that add QuickTime capability—the ability, at the Mac OS level, to identify and work with digital movie data. If you started up your iMac with extensions off, you'd find that it's unable to play QuickTime movies because the proper extensions haven't been loaded.

In most cases, an application that's designed to work with the Mac OS has been tested fairly thoroughly and shouldn't experience a conflict. (This isn't always the case, and many applications have to be updated slightly when a new Mac OS update is created by Apple since small inconsistencies can affect programs.) But application authors, no matter how diligent, can't test their application with every conceivable extension available for the Mac OS—there are thousands of them. So, you'll sometimes experience a conflict or similar problem, thanks to an extension.

One of the solutions that some folks follow is to simply try not to install too many extensions. If you're the type who wants zero trouble from your iMac, I'd recommend that you avoid most utilities, shareware, and other add-ons (except for a disk doctor and a virus scanning program). You should certainly only buy software that specifically mentions the iMac or that has clearly been tested to work well with your version of the Mac OS, Mac OS 8.1–9.0 or later.

The best way to troubleshoot an extension problem is to hope someone has already figured it out and all you have to do is read about the conflict. If that doesn't work, though, then it's up to you to root out the conflict using the Extensions Manager. Let's take a look.

30

> TIP   *Want to know if something has been added to your Extensions folder? Go open it right now. Select every file in the folder—just click somewhere in the folder and press ⌘-A. Now, choose File | Label and give the files a label. Now, when a new extension is added, it won't have a label and the original extensions will. You can check every time you install a new application.*

Is the Conflict a "Known Issue"?

The Read Me file for the application that seems to be suffering a conflict, as well as any other Read Me files you can come across (especially those for applications or utilities you've recently installed), is the first place you should look when you suspect a conflict. If you've recently installed extensions or control panels, you should look into them, as well. It's possible that the conflict is actually a known issue, and that the software publisher recommends you not use the program in combination with certain extensions or particular applications.

You should also check the technical support Web site for the troubled application and call the application publisher's customer support number. If there really is a conflict, you're probably not the first person to ever encounter it, and tech support might be able to point you in the right direction.

Don't forget about the Mac OS Read Me files, which can help you determine conflicts and known problems.

Extensions Manager: Test for Conflicts

When a conflict occurs between an extension and an application—or an extension and another extension—it's tough to diagnose on your own. But if you can't find information from any of the software publishers that seem to be involved, then you have to do your own testing.

You won't enjoy it, though. Set aside a few hours one afternoon and grab a book or magazine, because it can take a while. You'll want to use the Extensions Manager, a control panel that allows you to selectively activate and deactivate extensions and other control panels that are installed on your iMac.

*Conflict Catcher from Casady and Greene (**http://www.casadyg.com/**) does a nice job of automating this process, making it a bit more bearable. Casady and Greene also has a time-limited demo that you can download to test for trouble.*

Here's how conflict troubleshooting works:

1. Select Control Panels | Extensions Manager from the Apple menu to open the Extensions Manager.

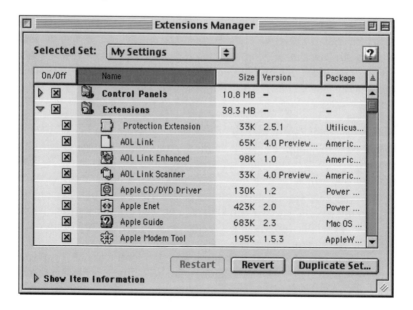

2. In the Extensions Manager, pull down the Selected Set menu and choose Mac OS 8.1 All, Mac OS 8.5 All, Mac OS 8.6 All, or Mac OS 9 All, depending on your Mac OS version. This selects only the extensions that Apple originally designed to work with the iMac.

3. Click the Restart button. After your iMac restarts, launch the application that was giving you trouble and see if the same error persists. If it does, then your application may have a conflict with the Mac OS itself. Contact the application publisher.

4. If you get a different error after restarting, it's possible that you disabled an extension required by the application—if the application gives you some indication of which extension it is, go into the Extensions Manager and reenable that extension. (Click to place a checkmark next to any extension that you want to have installed.) Now restart and test again.

5. If you're not having trouble anymore, that's a sign that you're having a bona fide extension conflict. Open the Extensions Manager again, and choose View | As Folders. This allows you to see everything that's in the Extensions folder at one time.

6. Make sure you're viewing extensions—the Extensions folder is revealed and a list of extensions appears below it. Now, place a checkmark next to three or four extensions at the top of the list. (The first time you do this, you'll be asked to create a new extensions set. Click Duplicate Set, then enter a name like "Test Set" and click Duplicate.) Once you've added three to five extensions in alphabetical order, click the Restart button.

7. Test again for the conflict. If things seem to be working OK, go back to step 6 and keep adding extensions.

8. If the conflict does recur, stop what you're doing, go back and redisable the last batch of extensions you enabled. (It's not a bad idea to write down the extensions you're adding each time.) Now, enable the *first* of those extensions and restart.

9. After the restart, open your application and test for the conflict. If the conflict doesn't occur, go back, enable the next extension, and restart again. Repeat until the conflict does occur. When it does, you've figured out which extension is causing the conflict! Actually, you only know one of the extensions causing a conflict. You still need to do a little more testing.

10. In the Extensions Manager again, pull down the Selected Set menu and choose the Mac OS All entry again. Now, find the extension you've identified as a problem and place a checkmark next to it. (When you do, you'll be asked to create another extension set. Call this one "Test 2 Set" or something similar and save it.) Click the Restart button.

30

11. Test to see if the conflict problem recurs. If it does, then you can pop down to the next section called "Resolve the Conflict." If the conflict *doesn't* recur, then you'll need to start the conflict test again—it looks like your conflict may involve two extensions.

12. Add three or more extensions to the Test 2 Set and restart. Test for the problem. Add more extensions if it doesn't recur. If you do encounter the problem, then disable the last set of added extensions and add them back in one at a time, restarting and testing each time. Finally, when you identify the second extension that's causing trouble, you're getting very close.

13. From the Selected Sets menu, choose Mac OS All once more. Place a checkmark next to the two extensions you've identified as the problem. (You'll be asked to create a third set—call it "Test 3 Set.") Now, with just the Mac OS extensions and the two potential problem extensions enabled, restart.

14. Test again. If you get the conflict, you've found your problem. If you don't get the conflict, you may be in the absolutely rare situation of a three-way conflict. Pop some popcorn and keep testing.

Resolve the Conflict

Now that you know what's causing the problem, the best way to resolve the conflict is to visit the makers of the conflicting software and see if any of them have a work-around, an admission of guilt, or an upgrade posted that deals with this problem. You might also want to call their customer support line and see if you can get any help that way.

If those things don't work out, you might want to select one of the extensions and leave it disabled if it's not absolutely vital to your daily iMac experience. At least then you won't have to deal with the conflict.

You can try one other thing, too. Sometimes extensions conflict because of the order in which they're being loaded. Extensions load alphabetically, so you can change the order by opening the Extension folder in the System Folder and editing the name. Put a space in front of the name to move it to the top of the alphabetical list. If you want the extension to load at the bottom of the extensions list, place a bullet point (OPTION-8) in front of the name. Now, restart with your edited extension names and see if the conflict recurs.

Reinstall, Restore, and Update

Eventually, you may get to the point that you need to reinstall your applications, reinstall the Mac OS, or even update the iMac or Mac OS. As far as reinstalling and restoring go, you can do those things easily using the software CDs that came with your iMac. You can also update your iMac using the updates posted by Apple on the iMac Support Web site.

Uninstall and Reinstall Applications

If you want to get rid of an application, usually the best way to do it is to launch the applications installer program and choose Uninstall or Remove from the Custom Install menu. That's the best way because, in most cases, it removes any special extensions or control panels the application added to your iMac.

If you need to manually uninstall an application, that shouldn't be too much harder. Just drag the application's folder to the Trash. Now, open the System Folder, then open the Preferences folder and drag the application's preferences file to the Trash, too. (Note that this won't uninstall any extensions, fonts, or other system-level components that the application originally installed. You may be able to check the applications documentation to find out if it installed any extensions. Many applications, multimedia programs, and games do not.)

Before doing this, it's a good idea to check the application folder and make sure you didn't store any important documents in that folder—you can reinstall the application, if necessary, but you can't recover the documents you delete accidentally. You should also stop to consider whether you have another application that can read documents created in the uninstalled application. If you don't have one and you think you may need to read those documents at some point, then you might want to translate them to another document format before tossing the application for good.

If you've uninstalled an application in this way, then it's usually pretty simple to reinstall the application—just run the installation program. Before reinstalling, you should probably make sure that the old preferences file has been deleted, and that there isn't another version of the application already on your hard disk. (Two versions of the same application could cause trouble, and they will definitely cause confusion.) Other than that, reinstalling is pretty easy to do.

30

Software Restore

If you ever get in real trouble with your iMac, you have an out that can save you, get things up and running again, and hopefully go a long way to solving your problems. It's called the Software Restore, and it allows you to reinstall the Mac OS and your applications to the state they were when you first pulled your iMac out of the box and set it up.

Even if that sounds enticing, realize that this is a last resort. Doing this can wipe out any changes you've made to the Mac OS, settings you made in various control panels, updates you've made to your applications, and so on. It's important that you not perform a Software Restore lightly, since you're in for some extra work—reconfiguring and reinstalling extras—once you've performed the Restore. Still, it's there if you need it.

To perform the Software Restore, you'll be restarting your iMac and booting off the Software Restore CD. Here's how the Software Restore works:

1. If your iMac is on, insert the Software Restore CD in your iMac's CD-ROM or DVD-ROM drive and restart the iMac. If your iMac is off, start it up, then quickly press the CD-ROM drive's button to open it. Place the Software Restore CD in the drive and close it back up. (On slot-loading iMacs, simply insert the CD after you hear the startup chime.)

2. If your iMac doesn't automatically start up from the CD, restart the iMac and hold down the C key after you hear the startup chime.

3. Once the iMac has started up from the CD, double-click the Apple Software Restore icon on the CD.

4. Now choose between the two basic ways to perform a Software Restore. Click the Restore In Place check box if you'd like the iMac to restore the Mac OS and applications to their original state. Choose Erase Mac HD Before Restoring if you'd like the hard disk to be erased before the restoration takes place. (On newer iMac's you may have a third choice. If you choose Restore, Saving Original Items, then the existing contents of your hard disk will be moved to a folder called Original Items, and your applications and Mac OS will be restored.)

NOTE   *Choosing Restore In Place won't erase your Documents folder or most of the other folders on your hard disk. It will, however, change settings in the Mac OS and erase anything other than the original iMac bundle. Choosing Erase Mac HD Before Restoring will wipe out everything on the disk, including documents, games, and so on. If you've installed a newer version of the Mac OS or any of its components, you'll need to reinstall it after the Software Restore.*

5. If you've chosen Erase Mac HD Before Restoring, you can also choose how you want your hard disk formatted—with Standard or Extended Mac OS format. The Extended Mac OS format gives you more efficient use of the hard disk so that you can pack more files onto the drive. (Extended is the best choice, but you might have some reason to choose Standard that you're not willing to share with the rest of the class.) Make your choice from the menu.

6. Once you've made all your decisions, click Restore to begin the process.

Your iMac starts the process of formatting your hard disk (if you chose that option) and restoring the original Mac OS and applications to your hard disk. After this process is over, your iMac is restarted and, hopefully, starts up from its internal hard disk again in all its splendid, restored glory.

Now it's up to you to go through the process of configuring the iMac again, and copying over documents from your backups. You may also need to reinstall applications, reapply updates, and basically spend an afternoon getting everything back into shape.

Update Your iMac's System Software

Early in this chapter we discussed the fact that you can update the firmware in your iMac. You can also update applications and, occasionally, the Mac OS. In most cases, those software updates use an interface that's exactly like the typical software installer—you choose the installation and tell the installer which drive you want to install on. They aren't tough to use. Check Apple's iMac Support Web site for details on the various updates available for iMac software and the Mac OS.

If you have Mac OS 9, you may be able to skip all this searching if you use the Software Update control panel, which is discussed in the sidebar "How to… Use Software Update" later in this section.

A firmware update is a different type of updater. You'll also find firmware updates on the Apple Support site, but they're installed slightly differently. First, you'll want to download the update from the Web. Then, once the update has been processed by StuffIt Expander, it appears as a disk image. Double-click it to mount the disk. Once the disk appears on the desktop, double-click the Firmware Updater icon.

It's also possible that you'll find updaters for other firmware inside your iMac, like the modem's firmware. In these cases, the instructions may be slightly different. See the Read Me file that comes with those firmware updates for instructions.

Here's how the firmware update process goes:

1. If your firmware is up-to-date already, you'll immediately see a dialog box letting you know that. If it's not, all applications are quit in the background and the update continues.

2. You'll see a dialog box explaining the process. When you click Update, your iMac restarts.

3. Now, after the iMac has restarted, you'll see a small indicator bar that tells you that the update is progressing.

4. When the update is finished, PRAM is automatically zapped (you'll hear a series of startup tones), then the iMac starts up.

5. When you get to the desktop, the iMac should tell you that the firmware was updated successfully.

If all doesn't go well, you may need to go through the process again. Apple also warns of a situation where you may be asked by the updater to shut down your iMac and press the programmer's button using a paperclip. (The programmer's button is the one near the reset button. It's shown in Chapter 1.) To do this, click Shut Down in the dialog box.

Once the iMac is shut down, insert a paperclip into the recessed slot of the programmer's button and press the button. (If you have a slot-loading iMac, you don't need a paperclip; you have a raised programmer's button.) Hold the paperclip in and press the POWER key on the front of the iMac. Now the iMac will start up, and the updater will be able to update the firmware. (You'll see the progress bar.)

*Apple maintains a technical document that should help you determine whether or not your iMac requires a firmware update. Visit the Tech Info Library (**http://til.info.apple.com/**) and search for article n58174. The article is called "iMac: When to Install Available Updaters."*

How to ... Use Software Update

Mac OS 9 comes with a new utility that's specially designed to help you maintain your iMac. The Software Update control panel, new in this version, uses the Internet and a special database maintained by Apple to help ensure that your system software is as up-to-date as possible. It's also very easy to use. Choose Software Update from the control panels and you'll see the Software Update control panel appear.

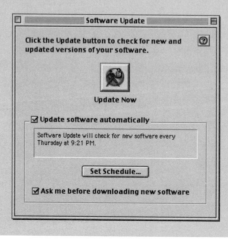

Now, to update immediately, click the Update Now button. If your iMac is set up to connect automatically to the Internet—or if you have an Ethernet or wireless Internet connection—Software Update will jump on the Internet, check Apple's servers, and see if anything important has been updated. (Note: If you use Remote Access to connect, you may need to have your connection running before Software Update can work its magic.)

If Software Update finds anything, it will notify you with a dialog box, asking if you're interested in downloading the update. If it doesn't find anything, you'll see a dialog box to that effect, too.

If you'd like, you can schedule Software Update to check on its own for updates to the Mac OS. Here's how:

1. Turn on the option Update Software Automatically.

2. Click the Set Schedule button.

3. In the Set Schedule dialog box, you can choose the time of day and which days of the week you want Software Update to check for updates. Click OK.

4. Back in the Software Update dialog box, turn on the option Ask Me Before Downloading New Software if you don't want Software Update to automatically download any updates in the background.

30

Maintain Your iMac

One of the best ways I know to help you get the most out of your iMac is a maintenance schedule. It's important to the health of any iMac that some basic steps take place every week, every few weeks, or once every couple of months.

Here, then, are some of the things you do in the course of iMac maintenance. Let's begin with a schedule for the maintenance, then we'll take a close look at what each schedule item entails.

The iMac Maintenance Schedule

A lot of the problems that occur with your iMac's hard disk, Mac OS system files, and other arcana occur slowly—a little file corruption starts to sneak in, causing more problems. Pretty soon things cascade.

What should you do? There are two lists: the daily stuff and the time-based issues. Daily, you should do the following when you're working with your iMac:

■ **Turn your iMac on and off no more than once a day.**   Turning your iMac on and off many times a day could, potentially, shorten its life. If you want to shut it down every evening and turn it on in the morning, that's fine. Otherwise, the settings in the Energy Saver control panel will conserve energy (it's the iMac's monitor that consumes most of the power) and also allow you to power up and down or sleep automatically. You can also choose Special | Sleep when you walk away from your iMac.

■ **When shutting down or restarting the iMac, use the Special commands in the Finder.** You can also use the power key on your iMac's keyboard to shut down or restart. My point is, you shouldn't just turn off your surge protector or throw a light switch to turn off your iMac. If it doesn't shut down in an orderly way, then system files and configuration files can be left open, data can be discarded, and problems can ensue.

■ **Restart occasionally.** After starting and quitting many programs, your iMac's memory can become fragmented, which leads to errors. If you restart (using the Special menu) after lunch or before a major Internet surfing session, you'll get better performance with fewer errors.

■ **Check your hard disk space regularly.** If your hard disk ever fills up or comes close to it, you'll start to see errors in your applications. Make a point of throwing away documents that you're done with and basically keeping things tidy. That way you won't fill up your drive, plus you won't have to commit to major purging sessions every few months to regain disk space. Check disk space by opening your Macintosh HD icon and looking at the top of the window to see how much space is available. You can also select your hard disk icon in the Finder and choose File | Get Info. Check the Available entry.

That's just the stuff you should do constantly while working on your iMac. Here, then, are some issues you should look into on a regular basis:

- *Once or a few times a week:* Back up your hard disk to an online site or to a removable disk. Online backup is discussed in Chapter 20; removable disks and backups are discussed in Chapter 27.

- *Every week:* Since your iMac is designed to live on the Internet, chances are that you're downloading and working with many different files from different sources. This is a great way to catch a computer virus, as discussed later in this chapter. Every week you should run a virus-checking program.

- *Every month:* Rebuild the desktop file and run Disk First Aid. Do this by holding down the ⌘ and option keys and restarting your iMac. Hold down the keys all the way through the startup sequence, until you see the Rebuilding the Desktop dialog box. Disk First Aid can be found in the Utilities folder on your iMac's hard disk.

- *Every one to three months:* Head out to the Apple iMac Support site (**http://www.apple.com/support/**), the SoftWatcher Mac site (**http://www.softwatcher.com/mac/**), and the Version Tracker site (**http://www.versiontracker.com/**) to see if there are updates to your iMac's system software or applications. These updates will often fix bugs and sometimes include new features that you'll want to add. You should also check to see if Apple has posted a new version of the iMac's hard disk driver or an update to the Mac OS that you should consider installing.

NOTE

If your iMac has Mac OS 9 or later installed, you can use the Software Update control panel to update your Mac's system software automatically. See the previous sidebar on Software Update for more info.

- *Every three months:* With a program like Norton Utilities, MicroMat's TechTool Pro, or Alsoft's DiskExpress Pro, you should check your hard disk for problems with corrupt directories or files. You can also, at this point, run a defragmentation utility to determine if your disk has become fragmented and in need of repair. See the section "Disk Doctors," later in this chapter.

That checklist should keep your iMac out of trouble, most of the time. If you follow this sort of schedule, then it's much less likely that problems will fester on your iMac. You'll experience less trouble and more carefree computing.

Check for Viruses

A computer virus is a program that attaches itself to other programs and attempts to replicate itself as much as it can, preferably by being transferred via disks, network connections, and the Internet. Not all viruses are designed to cause harm, although they

30

can, anyway, by accident. Others really are designed to infect your files, rendering them useless or sometimes deleting or destroying them.

In one sense, viruses on computers work the same way that physical viruses work. The more you're exposed to high-risk situations—using the Internet, swapping Zip disks, and using a large computer network—the more likely you are to be infected. And with your iMac, you're probably spending enough time online to be high-risk.

NOTE *In case you're curious, viruses are computer programs written by people. Virus authors are usually interested in causing consternation and fear around the world. Sometimes that's enough—other times, it's important to the virus author that they also cause trouble and loss.*

Viral Symptoms

By definition, viruses are hidden. There are sometimes some symptoms that can tell you when a virus has struck or is present. While these symptoms might be caused by other problems, too, it's a good idea to run your virus-checking program when you encounter issues like these:

- Long, unexpected disk activity, especially when no applications are running.
- The system unexpectedly restarts after running or downloading a program or mounting a removable media disk.
- Apparently automatic behavior that can't be attributed to a program or AppleScript—such as files moving on their own, the mouse pointer doing odd things, or dialog boxes appearing.
- A launched application doesn't appear or appears after a long delay.
- Files and folders disappear or suddenly can't be opened.
- File details, the amount of space on a drive, or similar statistics change on their own.

There are also viruses that work within particular applications instead of within the Mac OS. Viruses appear especially frequently in Microsoft Word, where documents can be automatically turned into templates, making it impossible to access parts of the document or to save the document as a regular Word file. If you notice odd behavior in a Microsoft Office application, that might be time to look for a Word (or Excel) Macro virus.

Detect and Clean Viruses

If you're online a lot with your iMac, consider getting yourself a virus-protection program. These programs generally run in the background, checking files as they appear on your hard disk or from a removable disk. You can also schedule them to check while you're not using your iMac—late at night or on the weekends, for instance.

There are two major virus packages for the Mac OS—Norton AntiVirus (**http://www.norton.com/**) and Dr. Solomon's Virex (**http://www.drsolomon.com/**). Both of these are available from online Mac stores as well as in computer stores and superstores that carry Mac OS products.

Most of the time the scans take place in the background. When the virus program detects a file that it thinks may be infected, it'll let you know. Sometimes the detector will automatically move infected files to a particular folder. Other times, it may be able to clean the virus from the file after it's been isolated.

I wouldn't even try to clean a file unless you absolutely need access to its data and you don't have a good backup. (Remember, the backup might be corrupted as well—you should check). If the infected file is a document that you need, you can try to clean the virus from it.

Both of the major virus protection utilities give you the choice of scheduling scans, scanning files as they're added to your iMac (from the Internet or from removable media), or scanning only when you actively ask the program to scan. For maximum protection you should leave the scanner on all the time to check programs as they're downloaded. If you find this is annoying, then I'd recommend scheduling regular scans for when you're away from the computer.

One thing you should definitely do is update your virus definitions. The virus-protection publishers come out with updates, usually every month, that allow the software to detect more viruses, fight them better, and protect against new types of infections. You should surf to the publisher's site or to **http://www.download.com/**, **http://www.macdownload.com/**, or **http://www.versiontracker.com/** to see what new virus definitions have been uploaded for your checker.

The QuickTime AutoStart Virus

One particularly vicious strain of virus has cropped up in the past few years. It's called the AutoStart virus, and it infects Macs and iMacs through a loophole in QuickTime. When QuickTime CD-ROM AutoPlay is enabled, it allows a CD to be automatically started when it's inserted in the CD-ROM drive. Unfortunately, that same feature allows this virus to be launched, copying itself to your System Folder and potentially causing damage throughout your files.

One way to avoid the virus is to open the QuickTime control panel and choose AutoPlay from the pull-down menu. Now make sure that neither of the AutoPlay options is selected. That will keep the virus from copying itself on your hard disk.

The major virus programs can detect most strains of the AutoStart virus, so run the checker regularly.

30

When a Virus Isn't a Virus

Viruses are a popular topic for e-mail hoaxes—e-mail messages distributed in chain-letter form, telling you to "pass it on" and "spread the word." These messages offer spurious information about some dire problem. The e-mail warnings generally show up in the form of a virus alert that's been released by "the U.S. government," "Microsoft," "a university lab," or some other organization that seems credible. A dead giveaway is misspellings or grammatical errors in the message.

Most of them also claim that reading a particular e-mail message or loading a particular Web page causes a virus to spread to your iMac. This really isn't the case—a virus can't be spread through the text of a message, so simply reading an e-mail message will not give your iMac a virus. If you *execute an attached document or program*, then it's possible to get a virus, so don't use attachments from people you don't know.

For the official word on viruses (and many virus hoaxes), the best place to turn is the Symantec Anti-Virus Research center at **http://www.symantec.com/avcenter/index.html** on the Web.

Disk Doctors

Part of your maintenance routine will require the use of special utility programs designed to help you find corruption, fix disks, and so on. A few of those utilities are free, but others will cost some money. Let's take a look at both.

Disk First Aid

Disk First Aid (see Figure 30-1) is included with your iMac and is designed to find problems with the directory structure of your iMac. Run it every month or so, since it'll allow you to find directory problems before they crop up. To run Disk First Aid, find it in the Utilities folder and double-click its icon.

In the top window, select the disk you want to verify—most likely it's the Macintosh HD volume. You can now click Verify to simply have Disk First Aid take a look at the drive and see how everything is doing. If you want to repair the disk while it's being verified, click Repair. This accomplishes two steps in one click.

Now Disk First Aid runs through the disk looking for corruption in the directory structure. If it finds a problem, it'll alert you, asking if you want to fix the problem. (This is true in some cases; in others, it just goes ahead and fixes things.) Otherwise, you'll get through your session and, hopefully, receive a clean bill of health.

MicroMat TechTool

MicroMat makes two versions of TechTool. The first is a freeware version you can download from their Web site at **http://www.micromat.com/**. TechTool Freeware

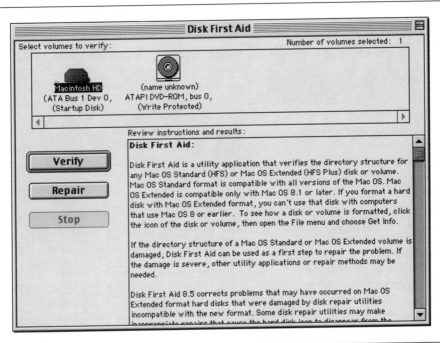

FIGURE 30-1 Disk First Aid can solve many basic problems with your iMac's disk.

(see Figure 30-2) is a program that makes it easy to do two things—rebuild your desktop and zap PRAM. Zapping PRAM is a technique used when you're troubleshooting a Mac. Rebuilding your desktop is something you should do regularly, and TechTool Freeware makes it easier and does it more thoroughly than the OPTION-⌘ method.

TechTool can also be used to save the PRAM or Desktop Database before they're zapped and rebuilt, respectively, just in case any trouble arises. And it can be used to analyze your system for some basic troubles, as well as offering information about your iMac (just click the buttons in the lower-right portion of the window).

Along with TechTool Freeware, MicroMat also makes a version called TechTool Pro, which is commercial software. It adds the ability to analyze your iMac in depth and fix disk problems and file issues, including accidentally deleted files. It's very useful to have around.

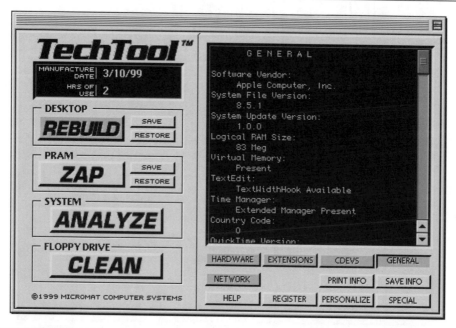

FIGURE 30-2 TechTool Freeware can perform a few basic tasks like rebuilding the desktop and zapping PRAM.

Norton Utilities

MicroMat's major competitor is Symantec Corporation, maker of Norton Utilities (**http://www.norton.com/**). Norton Utilities offers a number of different programs that help you keep your iMac running smoothly, including:

- **Norton Disk Doctor** Analyzes and fixes all sorts of trouble with your hard disk.
- **Volume Recover and FileSaver** Allows you to track and save data from files or entire disks, including removable disks.
- **Speed Disk** Defragments and optimizes your hard disk for better performance.
- **CrashGuard** Recovers from some errors in your applications before they freeze or crash your iMac.
- **UnErase** Tracks and retrieves files you've deleted accidentally.

Norton is a great way to keep your iMac in good shape and guard against trouble, and if you make an occasional mistake, it'll try to bail you out.

Appendix A

Upgrade the Mac OS

How to...

- Update to Mac OS 8.6
- Upgrade to Mac OS 9

If your iMac didn't come with Mac OS 9 (or later) preinstalled, you might want to consider the upgrade. While it's certainly not mandatory that you rush out and upgrade any time a new Mac OS is released, there are some great features in newer Mac OS versions that you may be missing out on. This book, for instance, covers a number of items that are new in Mac OS 9, like Multiple Users, Keychain Access, Apple File Security, and others. Plus, in some ways, Mac OS 9 is a better performer, speeding up parts of your iMac.

At the same time, though, Mac OS 9 costs money, and you may need to upgrade your iMac to run it, especially if you have only 32MB of RAM installed. If that's the case, and your iMac came with Mac OS 8.5, then you should consider the free update to Mac OS 8.6. The update is available on Apple's Web site, and it doesn't cost anything but the time it takes to download the update. (Which can be a significant amount of time, since the updater is a large file.)

Update to Mac OS 8.6

If you have Mac OS 8.5 on your iMac, you can use the free updater on Apple's Web site to update that iMac to Mac OS 8.6. Mac OS 8.6 is an incremental update to Mac OS 8.5, offering few new features. Instead, it's more a release for stability and bug fixing, hopefully resulting in better performance and reliability than Mac OS 8.5.

To download Mac OS 8.6, head to **http://www.apple.com/swupdates/** on the Web and look for a link to Mac OS 8.6 (you may also be able to access the document directly at **http://asu.info.apple.com/swupdates.nsf/artnum/n11386**). Click the link to download Mac OS 8.6, then choose either to download the entire file (which is about 36MB in size) or to download the file in segments.

Once the updater is completely downloaded, you can double-click the file in the Finder. That mounts the Mac OS 8.6 disk image. Double-click the disk image to view its contents, then double-click the Mac OS 8.6 installer.

Here are the rest of the steps:

1. After you've read the introductory screen, click the Continue button.

2. You'll see another screen in the Installer that tells you whether you have enough disk space for the installation. Select the disk that currently has Mac OS 8.5 installed.

3. Now you'll see the Before You Install document, which is simply a Read Me file that tells you last-minute information about Mac OS 8.6 and its known issues and conflicts. Click Continue when you're done reading.

4. Now you'll read the Software License Agreement. After reading it, click Continue. In the box that pops up, click Agree if you agree with the license. If you click Disagree, the Installer reverts to the Welcome screen.

5. Otherwise, you're at the Installation screen. To begin the Mac OS update, click the Start button.

A

Upgrade to Mac OS 9

If your iMac came with Mac OS 8.1, 8.5, or 8.6, you may wish to upgrade to Mac OS 9, which is available as a commercial package in stores, or, if you qualify, through the low-cost Mac OS Up-to-Date program (**http://www.apple.com/macos/uptodate/**). Mac OS 9 adds quite a few different features to your iMac, a number of which are discussed throughout this book.

> **NOTE** *Although Mac OS 9 will technically run on an iMac with 32MB of RAM, I don't recommend you try it unless you upgrade the RAM in your iMac to at least 64MB first. With 32MB of RAM and Mac OS 9, your iMac will run noticeably slower.*

Installing the Mac OS is fairly simple—run the installation program and read the instructions onscreen. To begin, insert the Mac OS 9 CD-ROM in your CD-ROM or DVD-ROM drive.

Here's how it goes:

1. Double-click the Mac OS Install icon. This launches the Installer.

2. After you've read the introductory screen, click the Continue button.

3. You'll see another screen in the Installer that tells you whether you have enough disk space for the installation. (If you have more than one disk connected to your iMac, you can select the disk where you'll install the Mac OS from the Destination Disk pop-up menu.) If you don't have enough disk space, you should switch back to the Finder and delete files you don't need. If you have enough disk space, you can consider performing a Clean Install by selecting the Options button and selecting Perform Clean Installation. Then, click Select.

> **NOTE** *A Clean Install creates a new System Folder on your iMac's hard disk and installs Mac OS 9 into that System Folder. It then makes it the active System Folder, turning your current System Folder into a folder called "Previous System Folder." This has the advantage of starting you off with a clean, perfect new installation of Mac OS 9. It has the disadvantage of not including your preferences files, any new extensions you've installed, or anything else that's changed in the System Folder. If you have a good backup of your current System Folder and you're not having any trouble with it, you can perform a regular installation that installs over the existing System Folder. It should work fine and it's a lot easier than a Clean Install.*

4. Now you'll see the Before You Install document, which is simply a Read Me file that tells you last-minute information about Mac OS 9 and its known issues and conflicts. Click Continue when you're done reading.

5. Next, you'll read the Software License Agreement. After dissecting it and running it by your attorney for approval, click Continue. In the box that pops up, click Agree if you agree with the license. If you click Disagree, the Installer reverts to the Welcome screen.

6. Otherwise, you're at the Installation screen. Here you can do two things. To begin a standard installation of the Mac OS, click the Start button. To customize your installation, click the Customize button. This brings up a list of components to be installed by the Mac OS installer. Place a checkmark next to items you want to install and click to remove the checkmark next to items you don't want to install. Then, click the Start button to begin the installation.

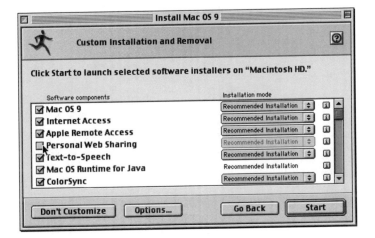

NOTE *You can customize even further, if you like. If you want to customize what each component installs, select the pop-up menu next to that component in the Installation Mode column. Choose Customized Installation from the menu; you'll see more options for customizing what, exactly, the component installs. Click OK once you've customized the component, then click Start to begin the overall installation.*

The installer checks your hard disk for errors, installs a new hard disk driver if one is needed, then begins installing the Mac OS. When it's done, you'll see a dialog box that asks you to restart your iMac. Click the Restart button. When the Mac OS starts back up, it should be Mac OS 9!

Index

References to figures and illustrations are in italics.

A

About box, 103-104
About This Computer command, 21-22
Adobe Acrobat Reader, 136
Adobe PhotoDeluxe, 465, 550
ADSL connection, 478
AIFF files, 318, 319
AirPort, 471, 478, 554, 555
    configuring the software, 556-557
    installing card, 556
    wireless networking, 566
alerts, 40, 492-493
aliases 37
    advantages, 63
    on the Apple menu, 79, 82, 86-88
    creating, 63
    finding the original, 64
    fixing, 64
    troubleshooting, 602
    using to organize documents, 68
America Online. *See* AOL
Anarchie Pro, 425, 426
    See also FTP
AOL, 20, 21, 437-457
    AOL Link, 456, 472
    channels, 449
    chatting, 449, 451-453
    creating an account, 438-440
    creating new messages, 446
    creating new screen names, 441-442
    deleting screen names, 443
    Favorites, 450
    as ISP, 455-457
    keywords, 449-450
    message boards, 453-455
    parental controls, 442-443
    People Connection, 449, 451-453
    restoring screen names, 443
    retrieving e-mail, 444-446
    sending waiting mail, 448-449
    signing on and off, 441
    starting up, 437-438
    using existing account, 440
    Web storage space, 457
    Welcome screen, 449
appearance settings, 498-499

Apple CD Audio Player, 79-80
Apple CD Player, 43, 302-305
    customizing tracks and playlists, 303-305
    launching, 302
Apple Desktop Bus (ADB), 553
Apple DVD Player, 43
Apple Guide, 130-132
    help by topic, 131
    invoking through Apple Help, 131
    looking in index, 131-132
    searching with keywords, 132
Apple Help, 127, 128-130
    browsing, 128-129
    Help Center, 130
    Help Viewer, *128*
    searching, 129-130
Apple menu, 75-88
    aliases, 79, 82, 86-87
    control panels, 78-79, 82
    defined, 77-78
    desk accessories, 78, 79-82
    divider lines in, 88
    Favorites, 84-86
    help, 127
    menus, 79
    recent menus, 83-84
    re-ordering items on, 87-88
Apple System Profiler, 79
Apple Web site
    Mac OS updates, 621, 622
AppleScript
    placing items on Apple menu, 86-87
AppleTalk
    control panel, 473, 563-564
    protocol, 475
AppleWorks, 144
    frames, 235-236
    Help, 133-135
    translating documents, 580-582
Application menu, 104
    floating, 92
applications
    About box, 103-104
    basic commands, 97-102
    check boxes, 103
    copying, 99-100
    creating new documents, 92-93
    cutting, 99-100
    defined, 91

hiding, 105
multitasking, 104-105
opening documents, 93-95
pasting, 199-100
preferences, 102
printing, 97-98
quitting, 101-102
radio buttons, 103
saving documents, 95-97
selecting, 98-99
showing, 105
sliders, 103
starting up, 91-92
start-up trouble, 92
switching between, 104-105
toolbars, 103
undoing, 100-101
uninstalling and reinstalling, 607
using the Application menu, 104
ASCII document, Web page as, 461
Assistants, 18-21
Business Cards, 237
Calendar, 237
Certificate, 237
Envelope, 237
Internet Setup, 20-21
for layouts, 237-238
Mac OS Setup, 18, 19-20
Newsletter, 237

B

backing up
defined, 66-67
to an external drive, 548-549
online, 429-430
backup services, 430
Balloon Help, 132-133
Bugdom, 329-333

C

cable modem, 478
Calendar, 347-357
cameras
adding, 550-552
exporting video to, 321
hooking up, 310-311
CD-R drives, 550
CD-ROM, 40
audio, 302-305
ejecting, 42, 44
icons, 42-44
loading, 42

slot-loading, 10, 13, 25
tray-loading, 10
See also Apple CD Audio Player
CD-RW drives, 550
charts, 188-192
check boxes, 103
Chooser, 80, 568-569
cleaning the case, 6
close box, 38
compressing/decompressing files, 427-429
configuring
high-speed Internet access, 478-479
a new Internet account, 477-478
TCP/IP, 471-473
Connectix Virtual PC, 8, 587-588
contacts, 357-363
contextual menus, 35
control panels
on the Apple menu, 78-79, 82
Control Strip
changing settings, 45-46
moving, 46
turning on, 45-46
controller, adding, 544-545
copying, 99-100
creating documents, 92-93
creating Web pages, 459-468
customizing the Internet, 469-479
cutting, 99-100

D

databases, 193-209
adding fields, 198-200
browse mode, 202-203, *204*
building reports, 209
calculation fields, 201-202
control fields, 200-201
creating formulas, 202
defined, 195
field types, 197-198, 199
finding records, 203-204
how they work, 196-197
layouts, 205-206
List view, 203
planning, 197
printing records, 204-205
saving searches, 204
saving sorts, 208-209
sorting, 208
uses for, 195-196
date and time settings, 493-494
desk accessories, 78, 79-82
desktop, 29-31

DHCP, 472, 479
    server, 473
DialAssist, 473, 476-477
dialog boxes, 39-40
    alerts, 40
digital cameras. *See* cameras
Digital Subscriber Line technology. *See* DSL
digital video. *See* video
Disk Copy software, 430-432
Disk First Aid, 616, *617*
disks
    using PC, 579-580
downloading files
    defined, 421
    with FTP, 426
    with iMacFloppy.com, 423
drag-and-drop, 33
drawing, 221-228
    aligning objects, 226-227
    arranging objects front and back, 226
    creating objects, 221-222, 224-225
    in databases and spreadsheets, 221
    flip and rotate, 228
    free rotate, 227-228
    grouping, 228
    locking, 228
    Pointer tool, 225
    reshaping objects, 227
    selecting objects, 226
    Shape tools, 222-224
    Spreadsheet tool, 224
    Text tool, 224
    vs. painting, 213
driver software, 9
DropStuff, 428-429
DSL, 478
duplicating files, 62-63
DV. *See* video
DVD-ROM, 40, 305-306
    ejecting, 44
    icons, 42-44
    loading, 42
    playing movies, 305-306
Dynamic Host Configuration Protocol. *See* DHCP

E

Earthlink, 20, 468
Eject command, 44
e-mail
    Internet control panel, 376-379

    parts of e-mail address, 376
    retrieving, 50-51, 379-381
    See also AOL; Outlook Express
emulation software, 8, 587-588
encryption
    with keychains, 502
Energy Saver control panel, 497
ergonomics, 16-17
error messages, 597
Ethernet, 471, 478
    network connections 561-562
    ports, 8-9
exporting video
    to camera, 321
    to QuickTime, 321-322
Extensions Manager, 604-606
external drives, 545-550
    backing up to, 548-549
    CD-R and CD-RW drives, 550
    installing, 547-548
    types of, 546
    See also Firewire ports; USB ports

F

Favorites, 84-86, 95
    AOL, 450
    creating, 86
    Internet Explorer, 409-410
    preprogrammed, 49
    in QuickTime, 290-292
    using, 86
faxing, 535-537
    reading, 537
    receiving, 536
    sending, 535-536
FaxSTF, 535-537
Fetch, 425, 426, 468
    See also FTP
file exchange settings, 584-587
    File Translation tab, 586-587
    PC Exchange tab, 584-586
file sharing, 569-574
    creating users and groups, 570-571
    setting up, 569-570
    sharing privileges, 572-573
    Web sharing, 573-574
File Transfer Protocol. *See* FTP
filename extensions, 583
files
    formats, 580-582

importing, 582
saving for use on PCs, 583-584
translating, 580-582, 586-587
financial management. *See* Quicken
Finder
changing how folders are displayed in, 70-73
creating aliases, 63
creating duplicates, 62-63
creating folders, 61-62
deleting icons, 64-66
dragging and dropping icons, 56-58
finding an alias' original, 64
fixing an alias, 64
Get Info command, 66
getting information, 60, *61*
opening icons and folders, 33
opening parent folders, 56
opening Windows to find things, 55-56
organizing files, 66-73
pop-up windows, 57-58
selecting items in, 58-60
spring-loaded folders
Firewire ports, 8, 9, 309
adapters, 552-553
advantages, 542
connecting a camera to the iMac, 310
installing a Firewire device, 544
installing an external drive, 547-548
upgrading with, 541-542, 544
floppy disk images, 430-432
creating, 431-432
types of, 430-431
folders
creating in the Finder, 61-62
parent, 56
spring-loaded, 57
fonts, 146-148, 533-535
adding, 534
defined, 533
deleting, 534-535
formatting documents, 149-162
alignment, 152
formatting sections, 159-161
formatting the whole document, 157-159
indenting, 150
line spacing, 150
lists, 151
multiple paragraphs, 152-153
paragraphs, 149-154
tabs, 161-162
using the ruler, 153-154, 161-162

freeware, 432-433
FTP, 424-427
addresses, 424-425
anonymous servers, 424
applications, 425
encoding as MacBinary, 426-427
uploading a Web site, 468
uploading and downloading, 426

G

games, 323-342
adding game controllers, 334-336
configuring InputSprocket, 335
Bugdom, 329-333
Nanosaur, 325-329
3-D specifications, 333-334
using other drivers, 335
General Controls, 494-495
Get Info command, 66
GIF images, 465
glare, reducing, 15-16
GraphicConverter, 465
Gzip, 428

H

hard disk, 40
icon, 41
Help, 125-138
Apple Guide, 130-132
Apple Help, 127-130
Apple menu, 127
AppleWorks Help, 133-135
Balloon Help, 132-133
Help key, 127
PDF files, 136, *137*
pressing keys for, 127
QuickHelp, 133-135
Read Me files, 136, 138
types of, 127, 133-138
on the Web, 137-138
hiding applications, 105
high-speed Internet access. *See* cable modem; DSL;
satellite connections
hot-pluggable technology, 35
HTML, 461-462
hyperlinks
in Apple Help, 128
defined, 48
HyperText Markup Language. *See* HTML

I

icons, 29-30
 CDs and DVDs, 42-44
 deleting, 64-66
 hard disk, 41
 printer, 44, *45*
 removable disks, 44
 renaming, 37
 Trash, 42
 troubleshooting, 602
 types of, 36-37
iMac
 features, 5-9
 models, 10
iMacFloppy.com, 421-423
iMovie, 310
 audio viewer, 318, 319, 320
 clip viewer, 313
 crop markers, 313
 playhead, 313
 scrubber bar, 313
 See also video
importing a file, 582
indexing a drive, 118-119
InputSprocket, 335
insertion point, 33-34
Internet
 adding plug-ins, 416
 address box, 49
 addresses, 402-403
 Back and Forward buttons, 48
 backing up, 429-430
 Bookmarks, 409-411
 browsing, 48-50
 connecting to, 47-48
 control panel, 381-384
 crashes, 600
 defined, 7
 embedded plug-ins, 415-416
 Favorites, 49, 409-410
 file compression, 427-429
 filling in forms, 412-413
 frames, 406-407
 FTP, 424-427
 getting mail, 50-52
 history, 411-412
 home pages, 403, 407-409
 hyperlinks, 48, 405
 Java applets, 416-418
 searching with Sherlock, 120-124
 secure connections, 413-414
 Setup Assistant, 20-21, 471
 shareware and freeware, 432-433
 signing off, 52
 software routers, 479
 starting up, 403-404
 subscribing to sites, 414
 surfing, 404-405
 tech support on the, 591-592
 transferring files, 421-429
 URLs, 402-403
 Web browsers, 401
 See also Internet Explorer; Netscape
  Communicator
Internet Explorer
 AutoFill, 413
 Favorites, 409-410
 quitting, 50
IP address, 473
 fixed, 472, 479
IPNetRouter, 479
ISPs, 20-21
 signing off, 52
 signing on, 47-48

J

Java applets, 416-418
JPEG images, 465

K

Key Caps, 80
key combinations, 34-35
keyboard
 adding, 544-545
 as USB hub, 35
keychains, 499-503, 568
 creating, 500-501
 using with encryption, 502
 viewing, 501-503
killer apps, 171, 309

L

labels
 using in the Finder, 69
LAN connection, 478
layouts
 adding graphics, 247-248, 254
 adding text, 242
 aligning frames, 246
 Assistants, 237-238
 building quickly, 252-256
 columns, 253-254
 creating shapes and lines, 251-252
 creating text frames, 240-241
 floating text, 248-249
 frames, 235-236

inline graphics, 247
linking frames, 240-241, 243-244
locking frames, 246
resizing frames, 244-245
spreadsheet frames, 254
starting, 239-240
stationery, 256
text frames, 238-246, 255
wrapping text, 249-251
links, adding to Web pages, 467
List view
customizing, 70-71, *72*
dropping items in, 72

M

Mac OS
determining which version you have, 21
Setup Assistant, 19-20
Up-to-Date program, 622
Mac OS 8.1
Find File, 110
Internet Config, 381
PPP, 47
Mac OS 8.5
reading alert text out loud, 40
Mac OS 8.6
upgrading to, 621
Mac OS 9
desk accessories on the Apple menu, 79
floating alerts, 40
scheduling startup and shutdown, 497
Sherlock 2, 110
sound settings, 490-491
upgrading to, 621-623
See also multiple users
MacBinary encoding, 426-427
mail merge, 256-258
adding field variables, 257-258
printing, 258
setup, 256-257
maintenance, 611-618
Disk First Aid, 616, *617*
MicroMat TechTool, 616-618
Norton Utilities, 618
schedule, 611-613
virus checking, 613-616
memory settings, 495-496
See also PRAM; RAM
menus, 30-31
on the Apple menu, 79
contextual, 35
recent, 79, 83-84
MicroMat TechTool, 616-618
microphones, adding, 554

MIDI, 553
modeless dialog boxes, 43
models, 10
modems
configuring, 475-476
control panel, 473
monitor, 485-490
calibrating, 489-490
color depth, 485-486
contrast and brightness, 486
geometry settings, 488-489
resolution, 486, *487*
mouse, 31-34
adding, 544-545
clicking, 32-34
orienting, 31-32
pointer, 33
snap-on adapters, 17
movies. *See* DVD-ROM; QuickTime; video
multiple users, 507-521
allowing guest user accounts, 517
alternate passwords, 514, 515, 519
applications, 512-513
CD/DVD-ROM access, 516-517
changing passwords, 520
creating user accounts, 511-514
deleting users, 514-515
editing users, 514
global options, 515-518
how it works, 509-510
logging in, 518-520
login settings, 515
privileges, 513
saving users, 514
turning on, 510-511
types of user accounts, 511-512
user info, 512
voiceprint passwords, 520-521
multimedia, 288
multitasking, 104-105

N

name server address, 473
Nanosaur, 325-329
Netscape Communicator
Bookmarks, 410-411
See also Internet
Network Browser, 81, 568
networking, 21, 559-576
AirPort application, 566
AppleTalk control panel, 563-564
browsing the network, 566-568
client-server, 561
connecting to a Windows network, 565

creating users and groups, 570-571
Ethernet, 561-562
file sharing, 569-574
keychains, 568
network neighborhoods, 566-567
peer-to-peer, 561
protocols, 562-563
setting sharing privileges, 572-573
TCP/IP control panel, 564-565
two Macs together, 574-575
using the Chooser to log in, 568-569
Web sharing, 573-574
wireless, 566, 576
Norton Utilities, 65, 618
Note Pad, 81
notes, 363-366

O

opening documents, 93-95
opening items, 33
organizing files, 66-73
using aliases, 68
using labels, 69
Outlook Express
adding users, 397-398
attachments, 386-390
changing the view, 380-381
compressing attachments, 388-389
creating a new message, 384-385
deleting messages, 385
encoding attachments, 387-388
filtering, 381
folders, 391-392, 393
formatting messages, 385-386
multiple accounts, 390-391
replying, 381-384
retrieving mail, 50-51, 379-381
rules, 392-397
See also e-mail

P

PageMill, 461-468
demo, 462
edit mode, 463
preview mode, 463
painting, 213-221
adding text, 220
beginning a painting, 213-214
Brush tools, 217-218
Color tools, 218-220
document size, 214
saving, 221
Selection tools, 216-217

Shape tools, 215-216
tools, 214-220
vs. drawing, 213
Palm Desktop, 345-369
attaching contacts to items, 361-363
attaching notes, 366
Calendar, 347-357
contacts, 357-363
creating appointments, 349-351
creating banner events, 351-353
creating contacts, 357-360
creating notes, 363-364
HotSync, 366-369
installing Palm applications, 369
Instant Palm Desktop menu, 346
interface, 346-347
notes, 363-366
repeating appointments, 352
starting, 345
synchronizing with a Palm device, 366-369
tasks, 353-357
viewing Contact List, 360-361
viewing Note List, 365-366
parallel ports, 553
parent folders
opening, 56
passwords
alternate, 514, 515, 519
changing, 520
voiceprint, 520-521
pasting, 99-100
PC compatibility, 577-588
disks, 579-580
documents, 580-584
file exchange settings, 584-587
file formats, 580-582
importing files, 582
running DOS and Windows programs,
586-587
saving files for use on PCs, 583-584
translating documents, 580-582, 586-587
PDF files, 136, *137*
pen tablet, 545
PictureViewer, 295-297
image format, 296
saving images, 296-297
viewing images, 295
See also QuickTime
PKZip, 427, 429
PlainTalk, 40
plug-ins
QuickTime Web browser, 293-295
for Sherlock, 123-124
PNG (Portable Network Graphics) images, 465